AUTHORIZING...

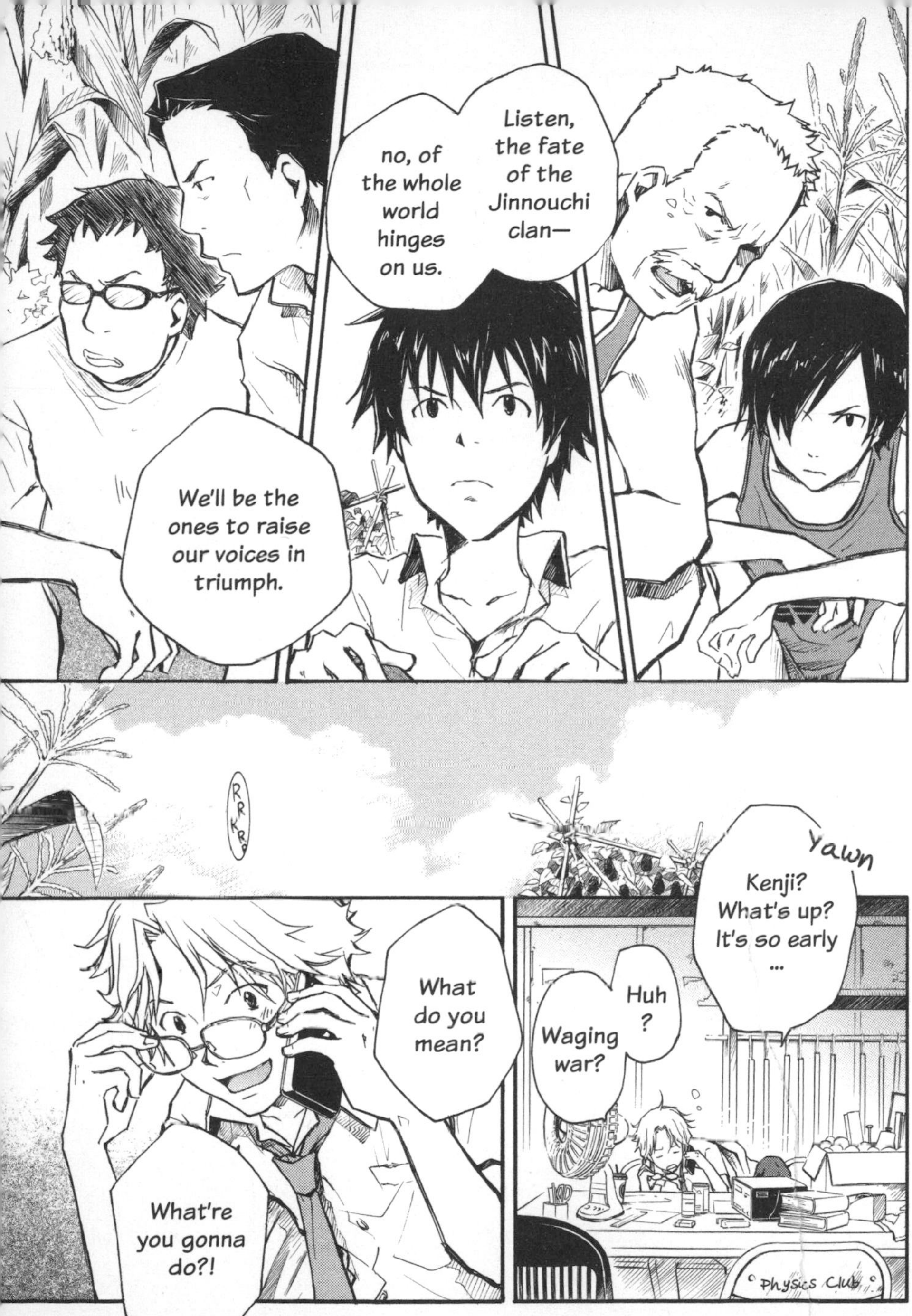
Listen, the fate of the Jinnouchi clan—
no, of the whole world hinges on us.
We'll be the ones to raise our voices in triumph.
RRKR
Yawn
Kenji? What's up? It's so early ...
Huh ?
Waging war?
Physics Club
What do you mean?
What're you gonna do?!

Act Seven Standby OK?

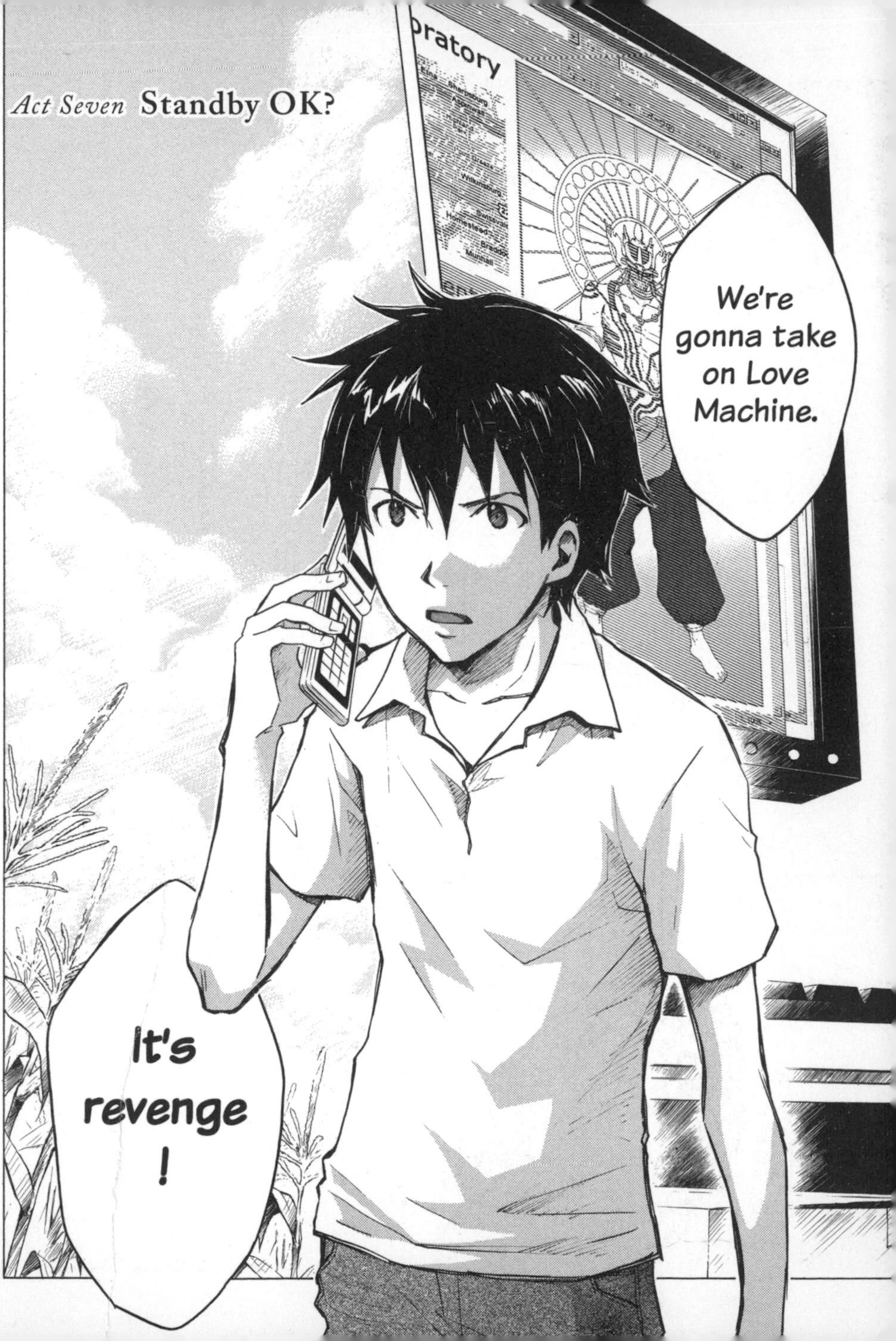

We're gonna take on Love Machine.
It's revenge!

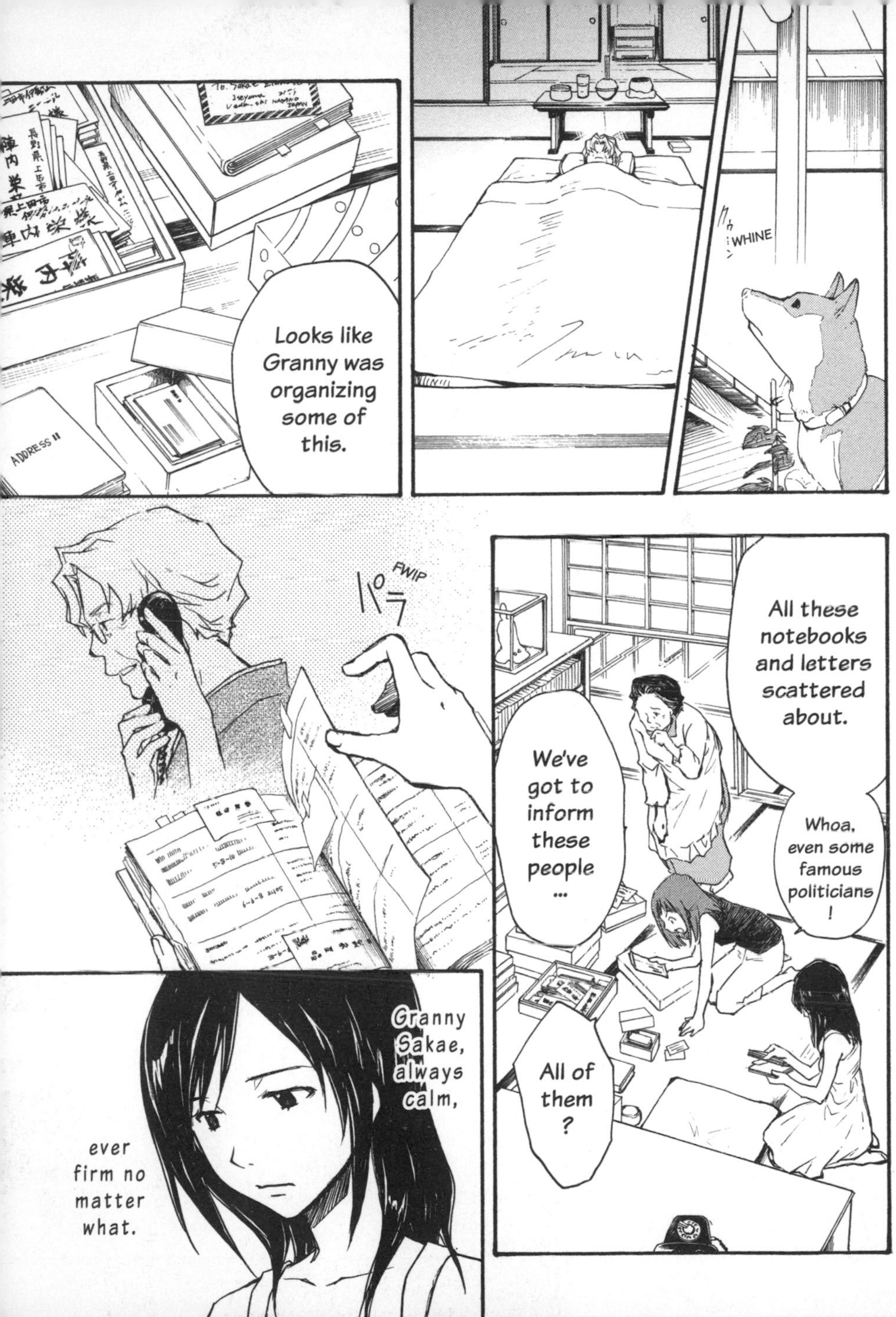
WHINE
Looks like Granny was organizing some of this.
ADDRESS II
All these notebooks and letters scattered about.
Whoa, even some famous politicians!
We've got to inform these people...
All of them?
パラ
FWIP
Granny Sakae, always calm,
ever firm no matter what.

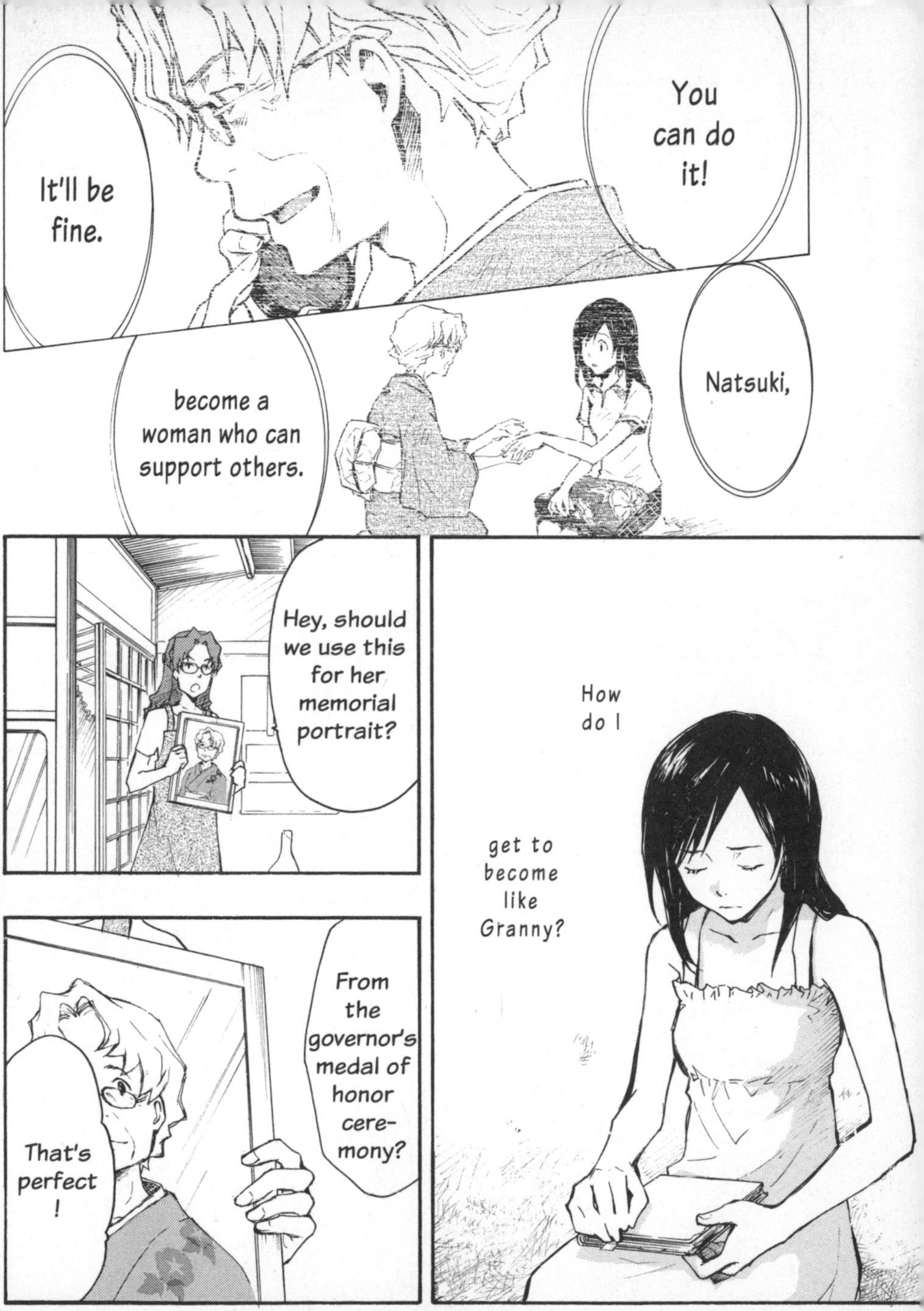

You can do it!
It'll be fine.
Natsuki,
become a woman who can support others.
How do I
get to become like Granny?
Hey, should we use this for her memorial portrait?
From the governor's medal of honor ceremony?
That's perfect!

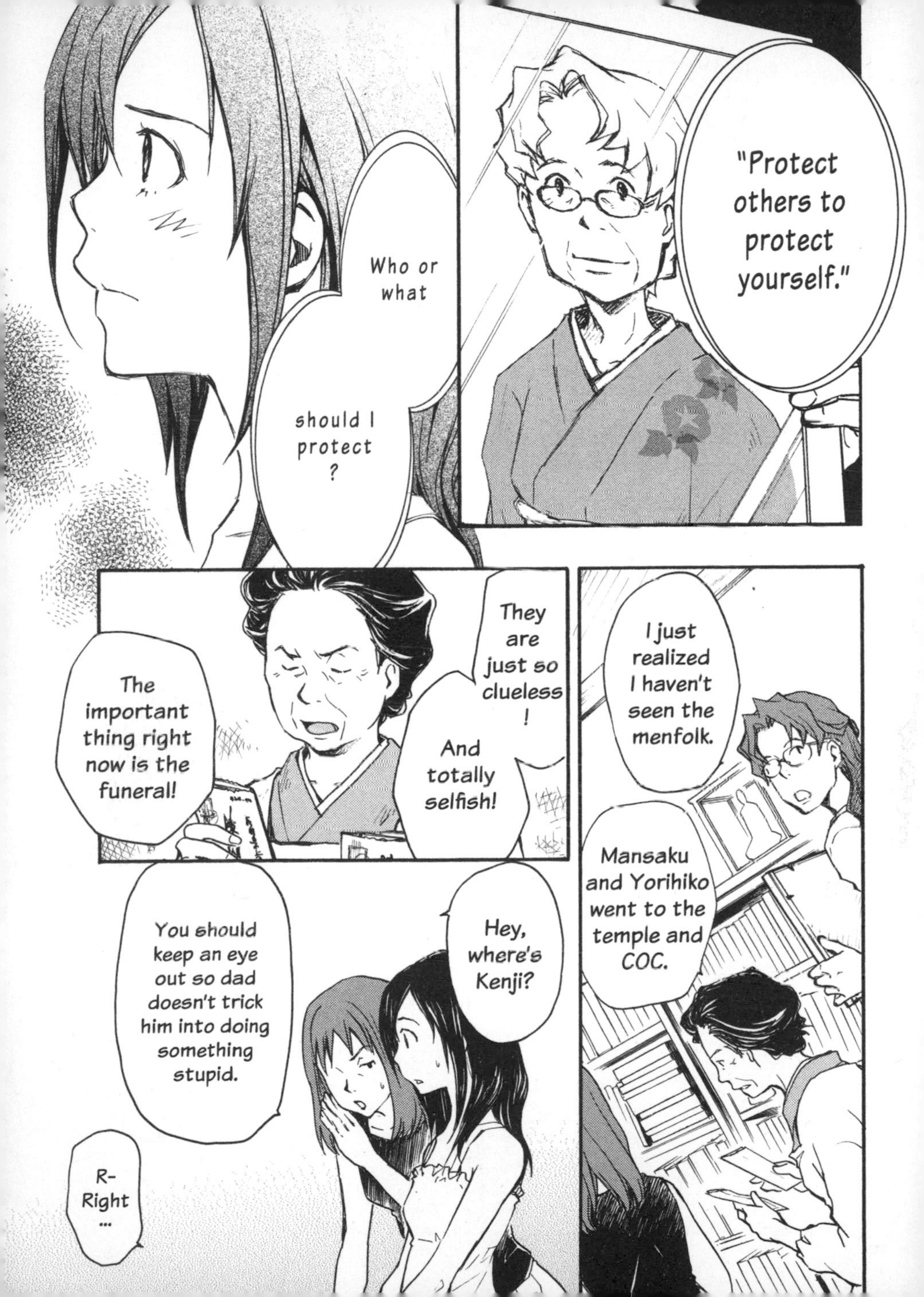
"Protect others to protect yourself."
Who or what should I protect?
I just realized I haven't seen the menfolk.
Mansaku and Yorihiko went to the temple and COC.
They are just so clueless!
And totally selfish!
The important thing right now is the funeral!
Hey, where's Kenji?
You should keep an eye out so dad doesn't trick him into doing something stupid.
R-Right...

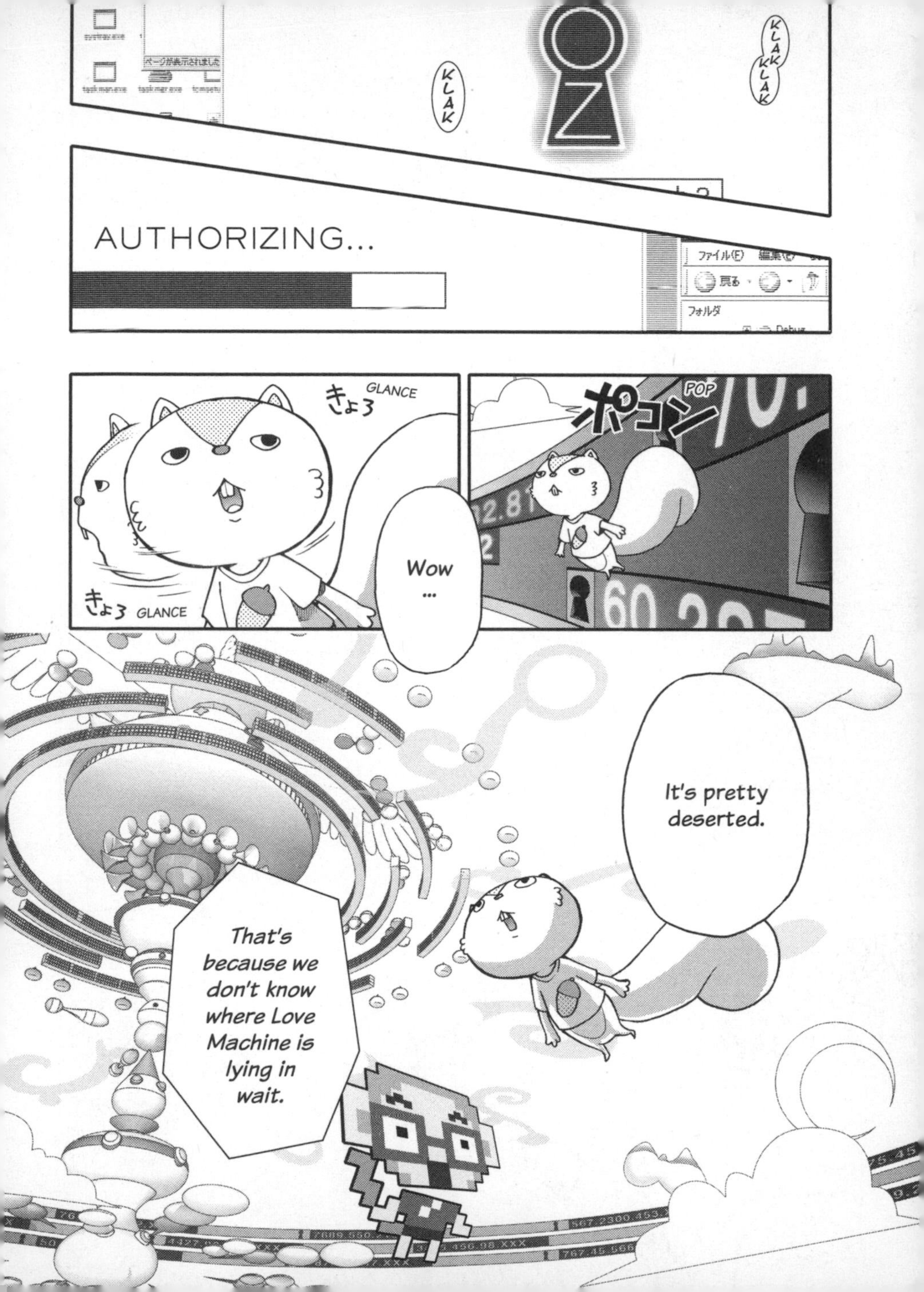

KLAK KLAK
KLAK
OZ
AUTHORIZING...
ファイル(F) 編集(E)
戻る
フォルダ
ポコン POP
きょろ GLANCE
きょろ GLANCE
Wow ...
It's pretty deserted.
That's because we don't know where Love Machine is lying in wait.

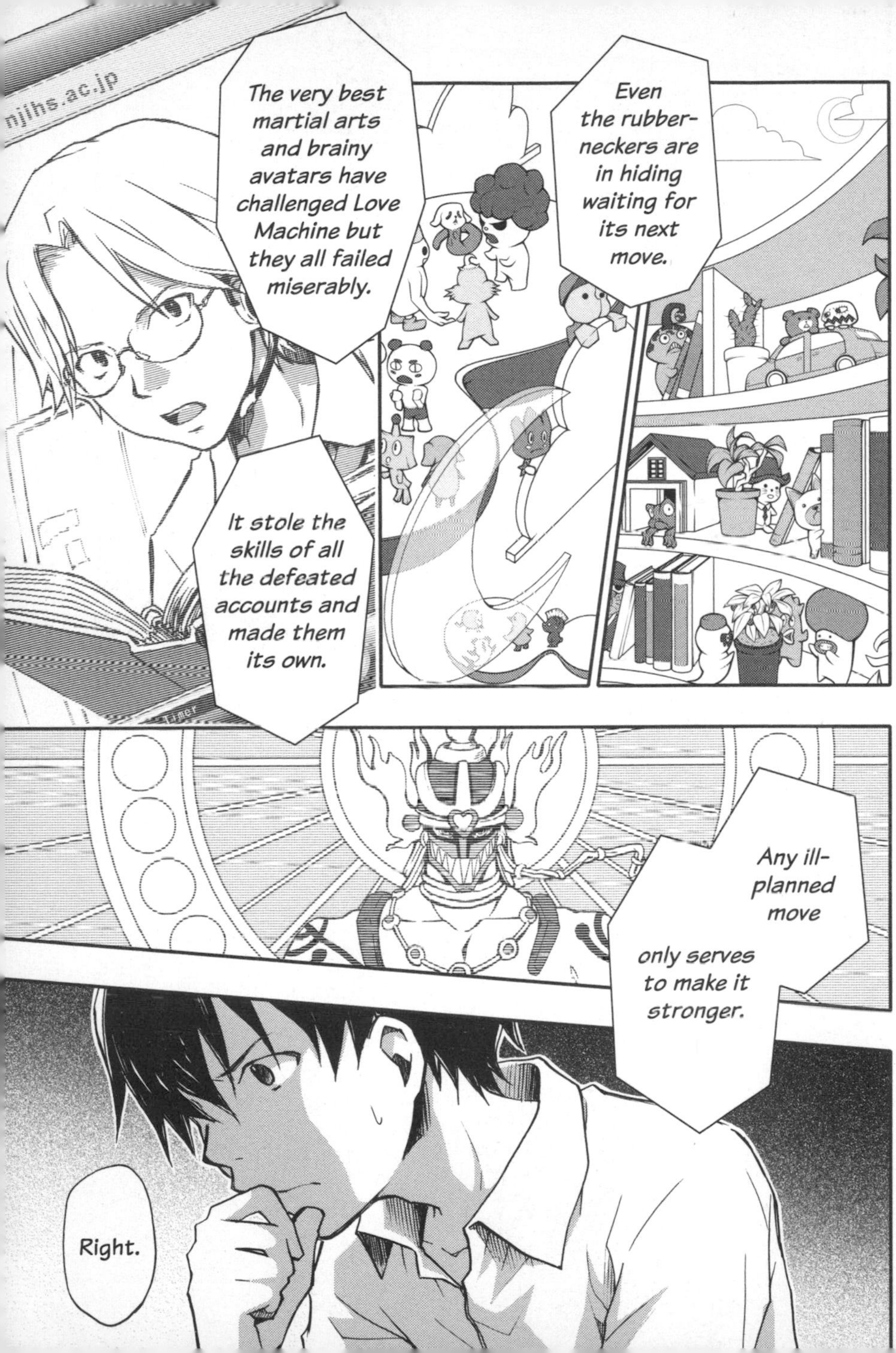
njihs.ac.jp
Even the rubber-neckers are in hiding waiting for its next move.
The very best martial arts and brainy avatars have challenged Love Machine but they all failed miserably.
It stole the skills of all the defeated accounts and made them its own.
Any ill-planned move
only serves to make it stronger.
Right.

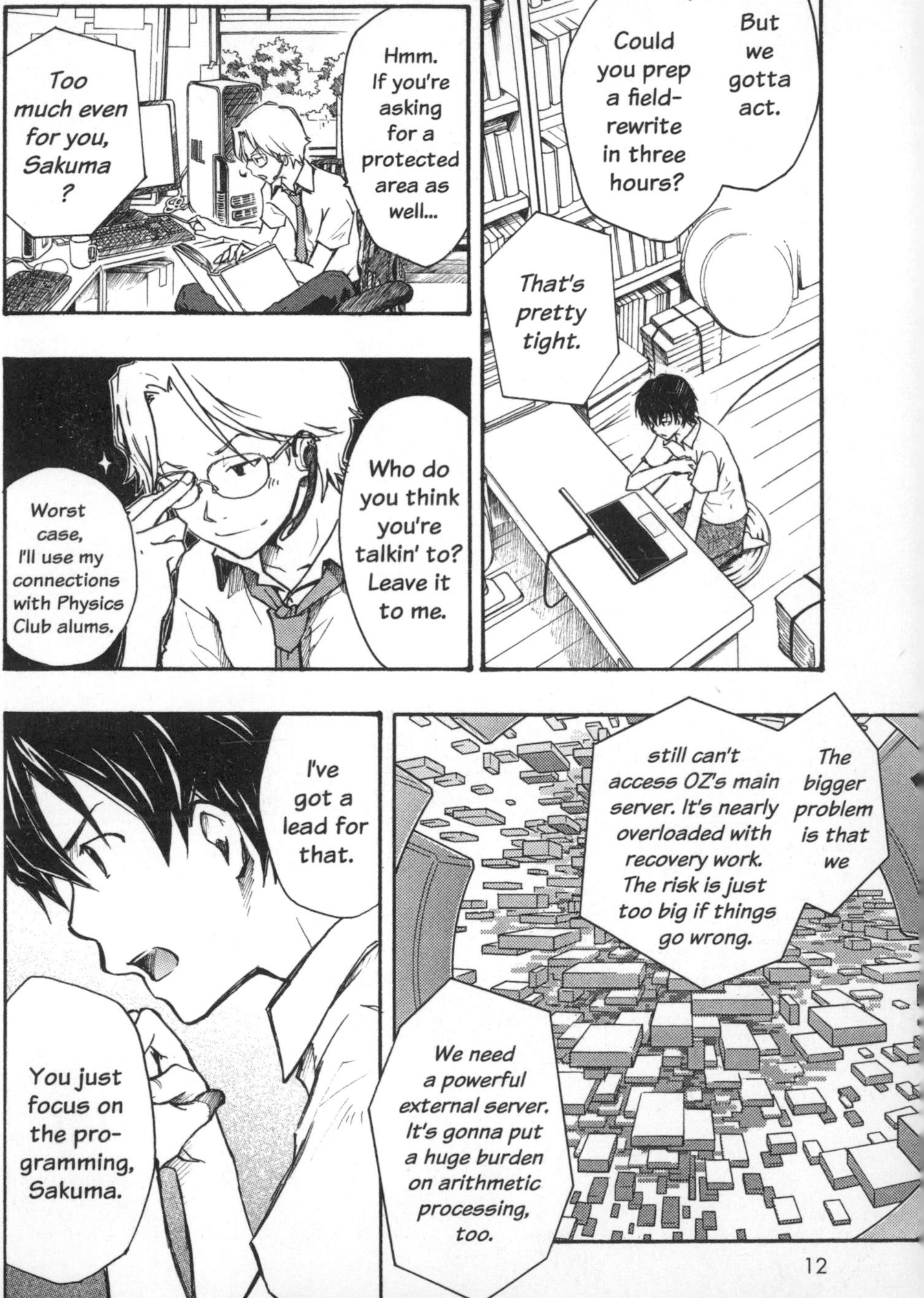
But we gotta act.
Could you prep a field-rewrite in three hours?
That's pretty tight.
Hmm. If you're asking for a protected area as well...
Too much even for you, Sakuma?
Who do you think you're talkin' to? Leave it to me.
Worst case, I'll use my connections with Physics Club alums.
The bigger problem is that we
still can't access OZ's main server. It's nearly overloaded with recovery work. The risk is just too big if things go wrong.
We need a powerful external server. It's gonna put a huge burden on arithmetic processing, too.
I've got a lead for that.
You just focus on the programming, Sakuma.

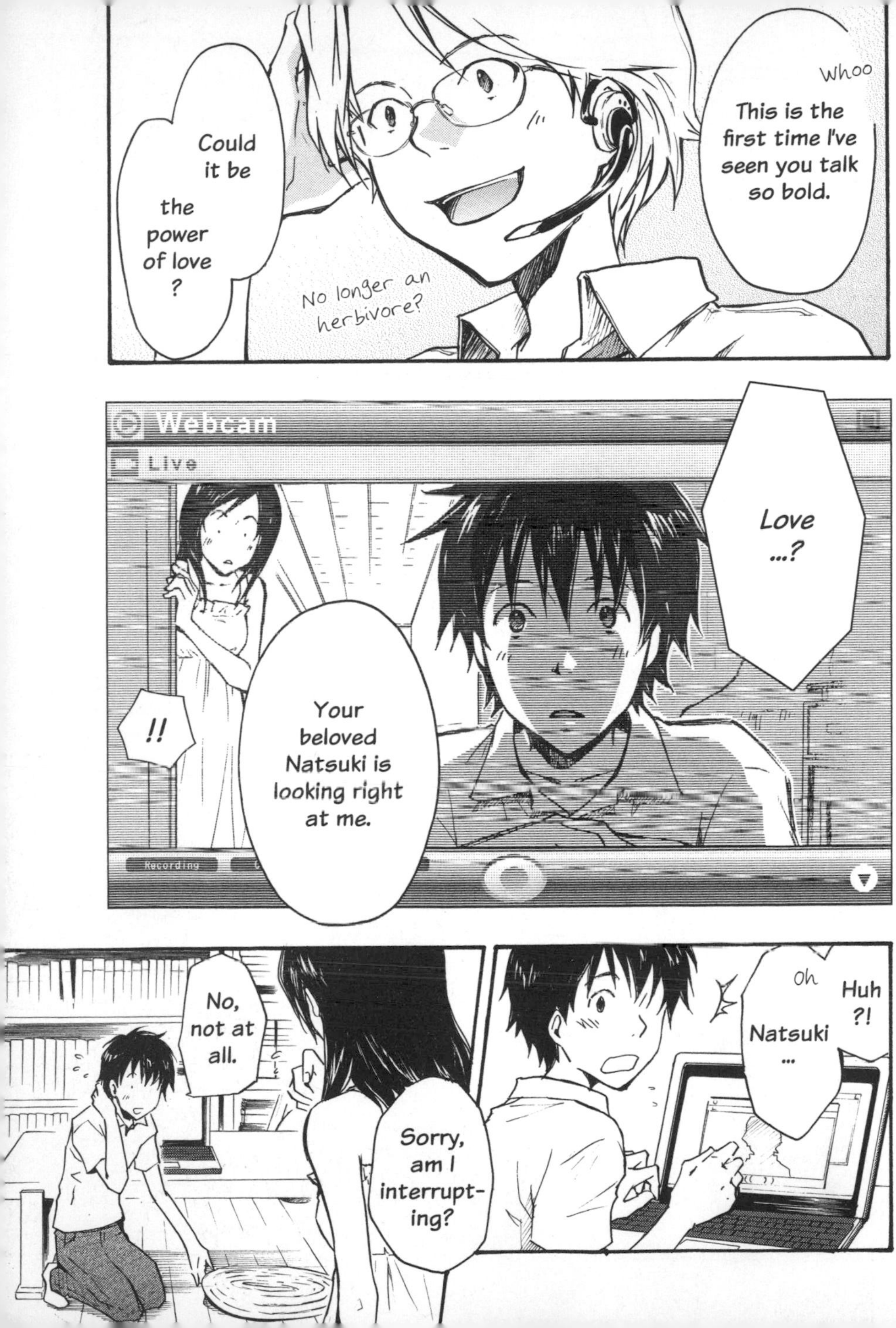
Whoo
This is the first time I've seen you talk so bold.
Could it be the power of love ?
No longer an herbivore?
Webcam
Live
Love ...?
Your beloved Natsuki is looking right at me.
!!
Recording
Huh ?!
Oh
Natsuki ...
Sorry, am I interrupt-ing?
No, not at all.

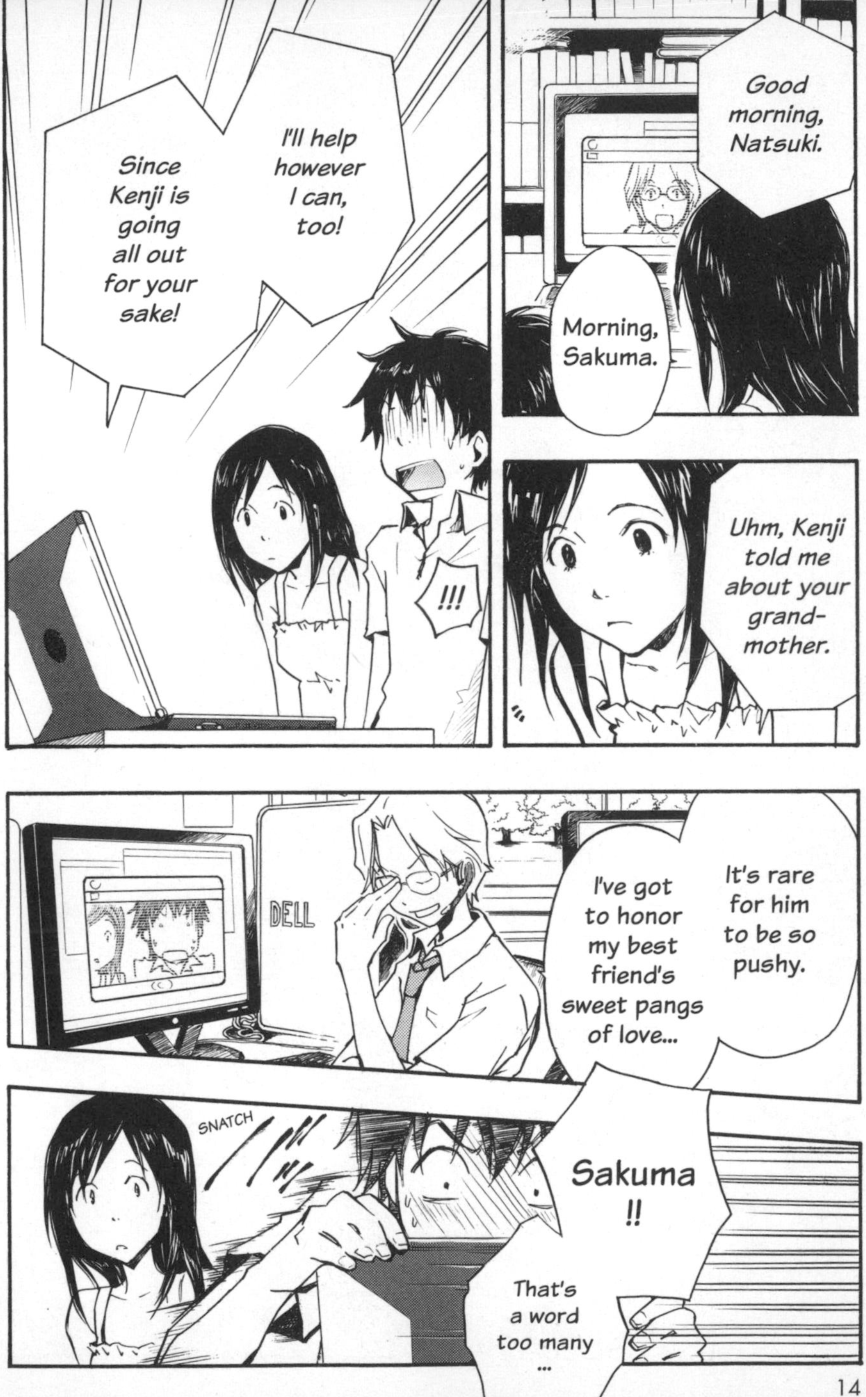
Good morning, Natsuki.
Morning, Sakuma.
Uhm, Kenji told me about your grand-mother.
I'll help however I can, too!
Since Kenji is going all out for your sake!
!!!
It's rare for him to be so pushy.
I've got to honor my best friend's sweet pangs of love...
DELL
Sakuma !!
SNATCH
That's a word too many ...

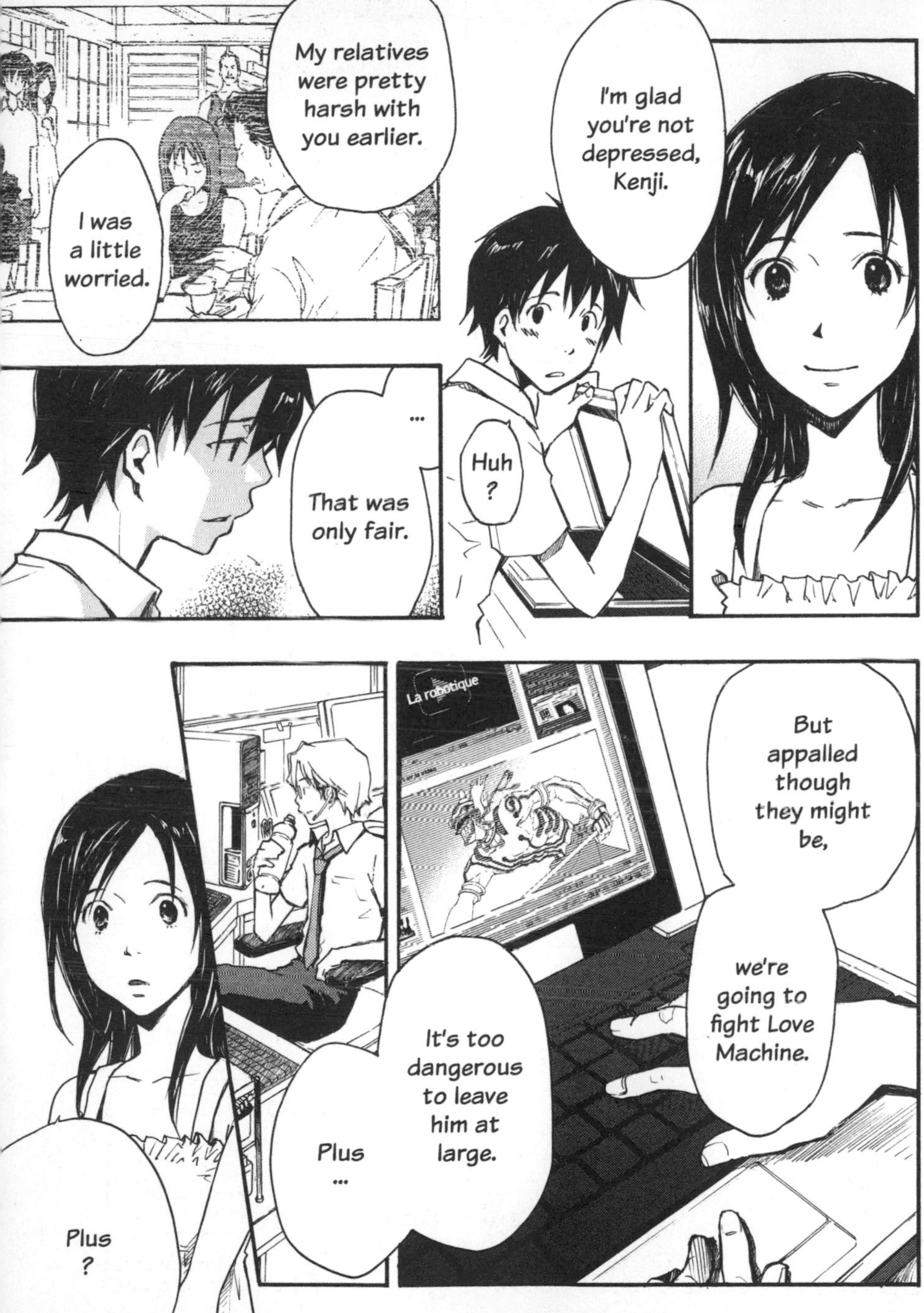
I'm glad you're not depressed, Kenji.
Huh ?
My relatives were pretty harsh with you earlier.
I was a little worried.
...
That was only fair.
La robotique
But appalled though they might be,
we're going to fight Love Machine.
It's too dangerous to leave him at large.
Plus ...
Plus ?

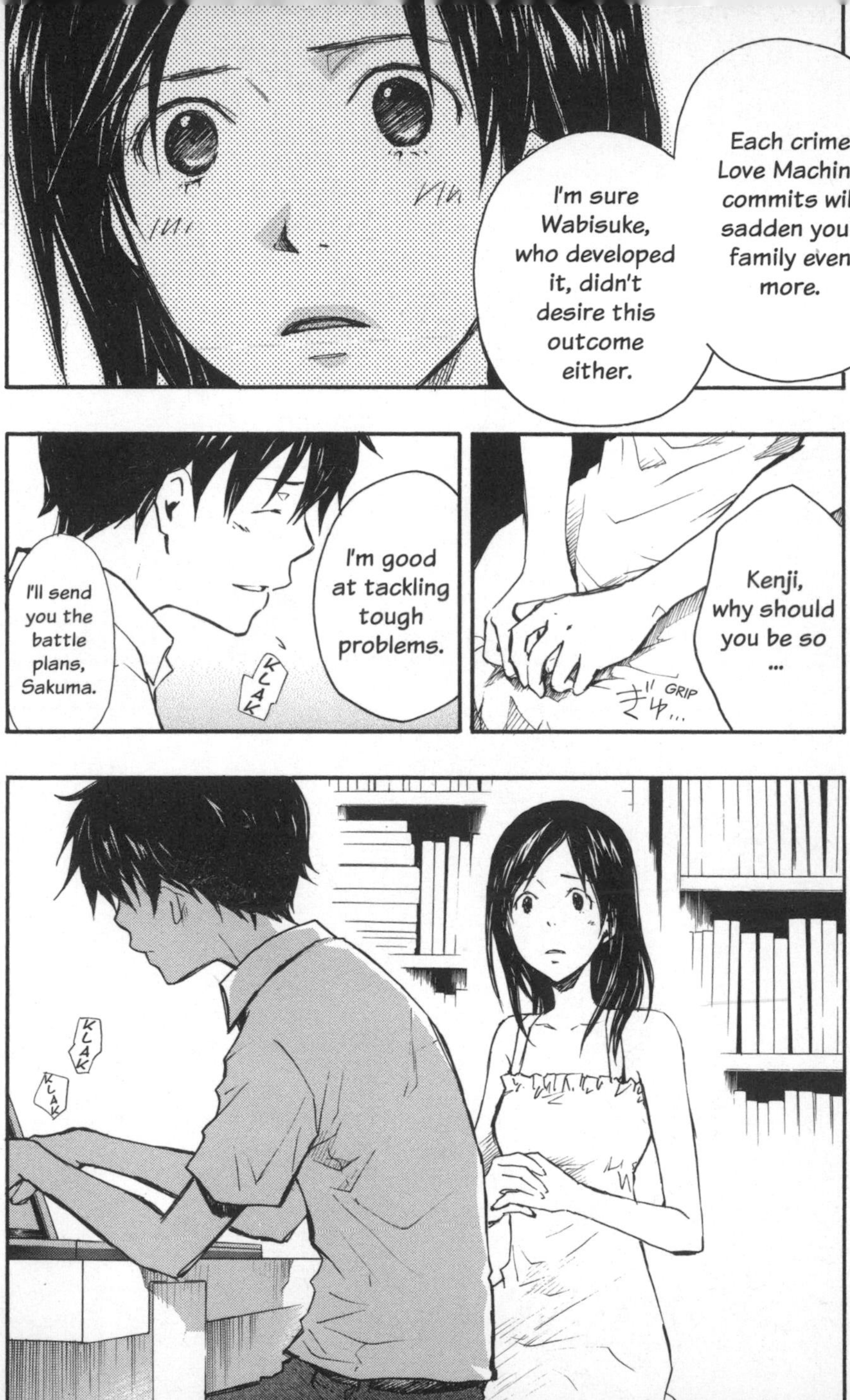
Each crime Love Machine commits will sadden your family even more.
I'm sure Wabisuke, who developed it, didn't desire this outcome either.
Kenji, why should you be so ...
GRIP
ぎゅ...
I'm good at tackling tough problems.
KLAK
I'll send you the battle plans, Sakuma.
KLAK
KLAK

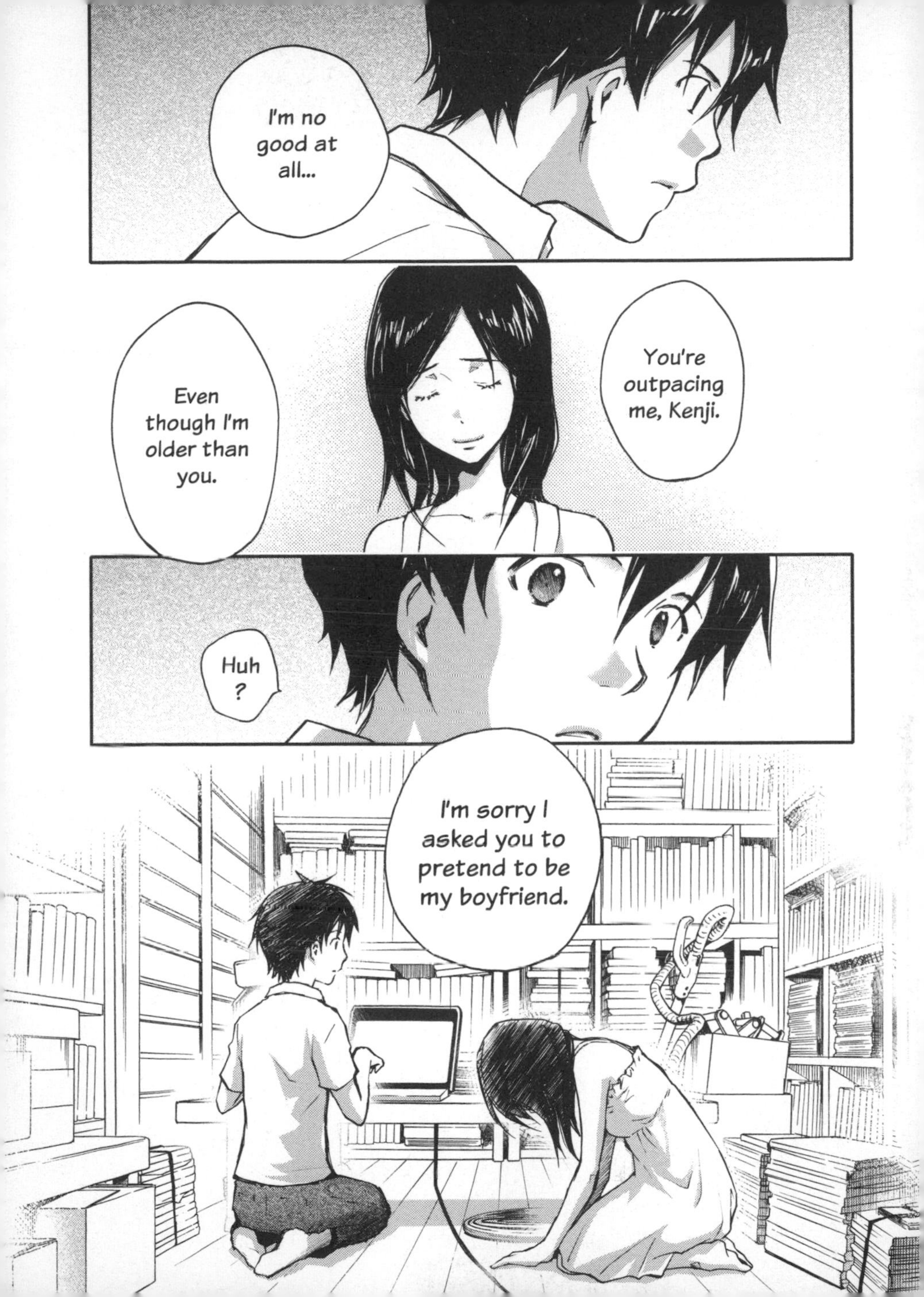
I'm no good at all...
You're outpacing me, Kenji.
Even though I'm older than you.
Huh?
I'm sorry I asked you to pretend to be my boyfriend.

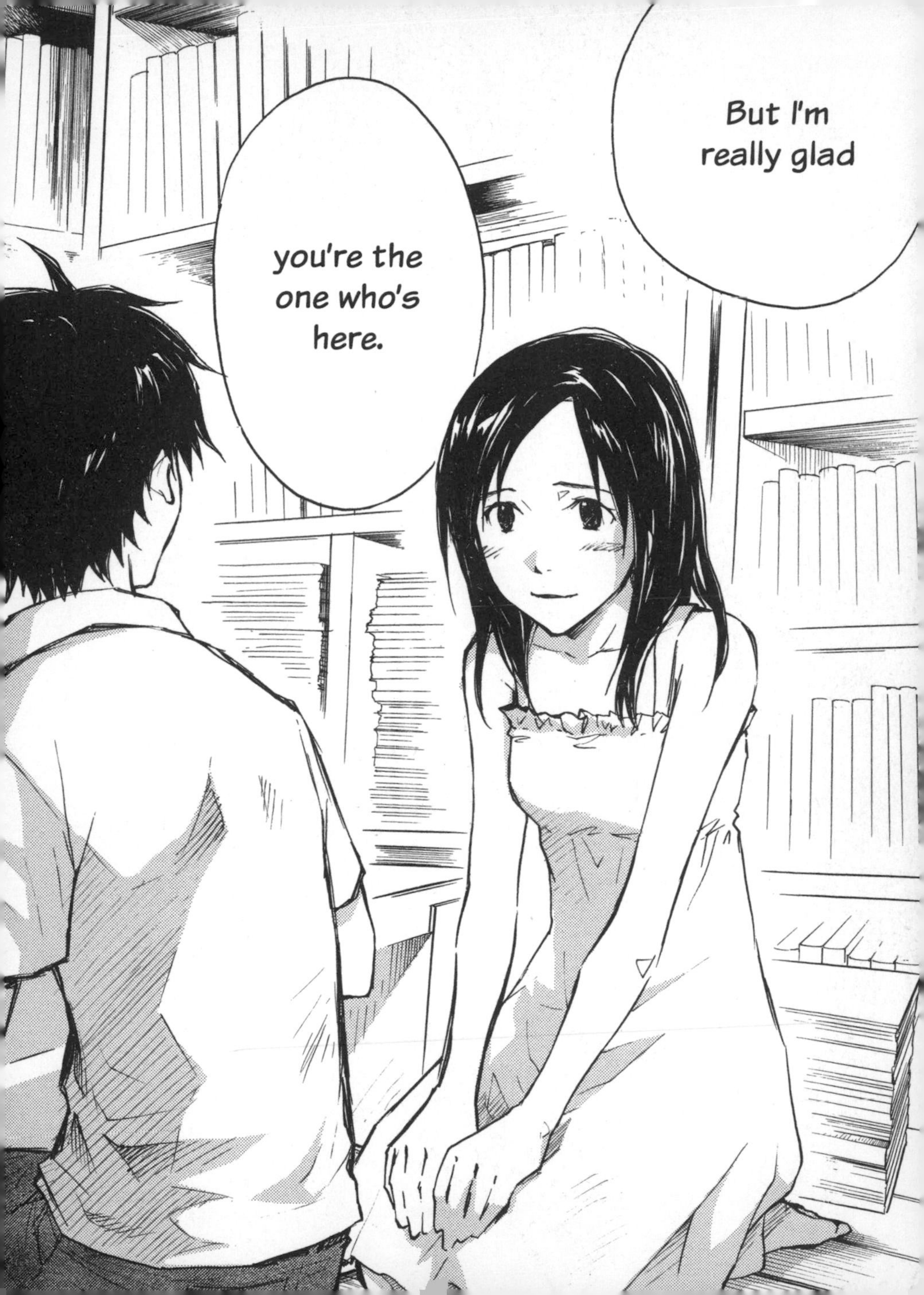
But I'm really glad
you're the one who's here.

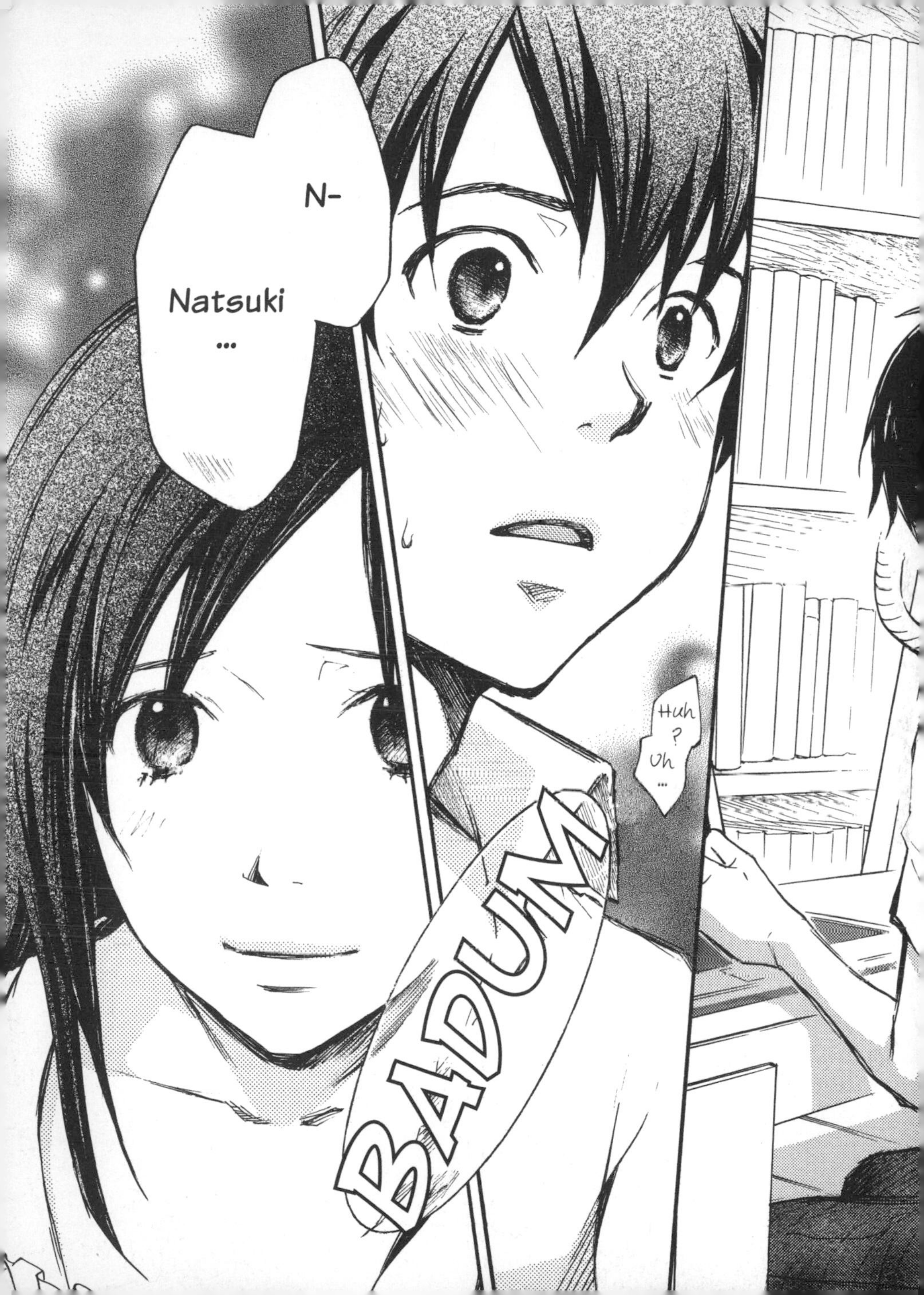
N- Natsuki ...
Huh? Uh ...
BADUM

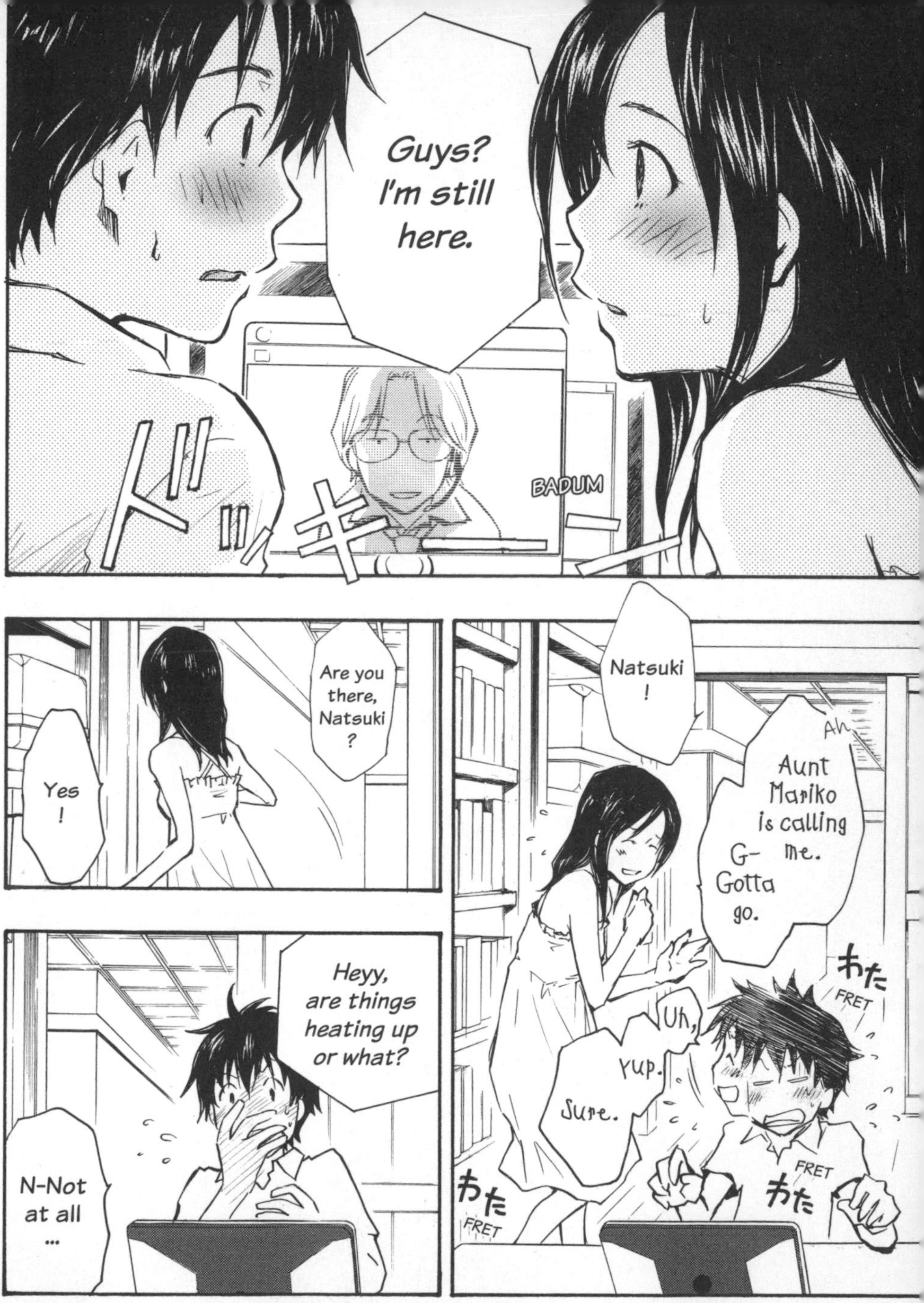
Guys? I'm still here.
BADUM
Natsuki!
Ah,
Aunt Mariko is calling me.
G-Gotta go.
Uh,
yup.
Sure.
わた
FRET
FRET
わた
わた
FRET
Are you there, Natsuki?
Yes!
Heyy, are things heating up or what?
N-Not at all ...

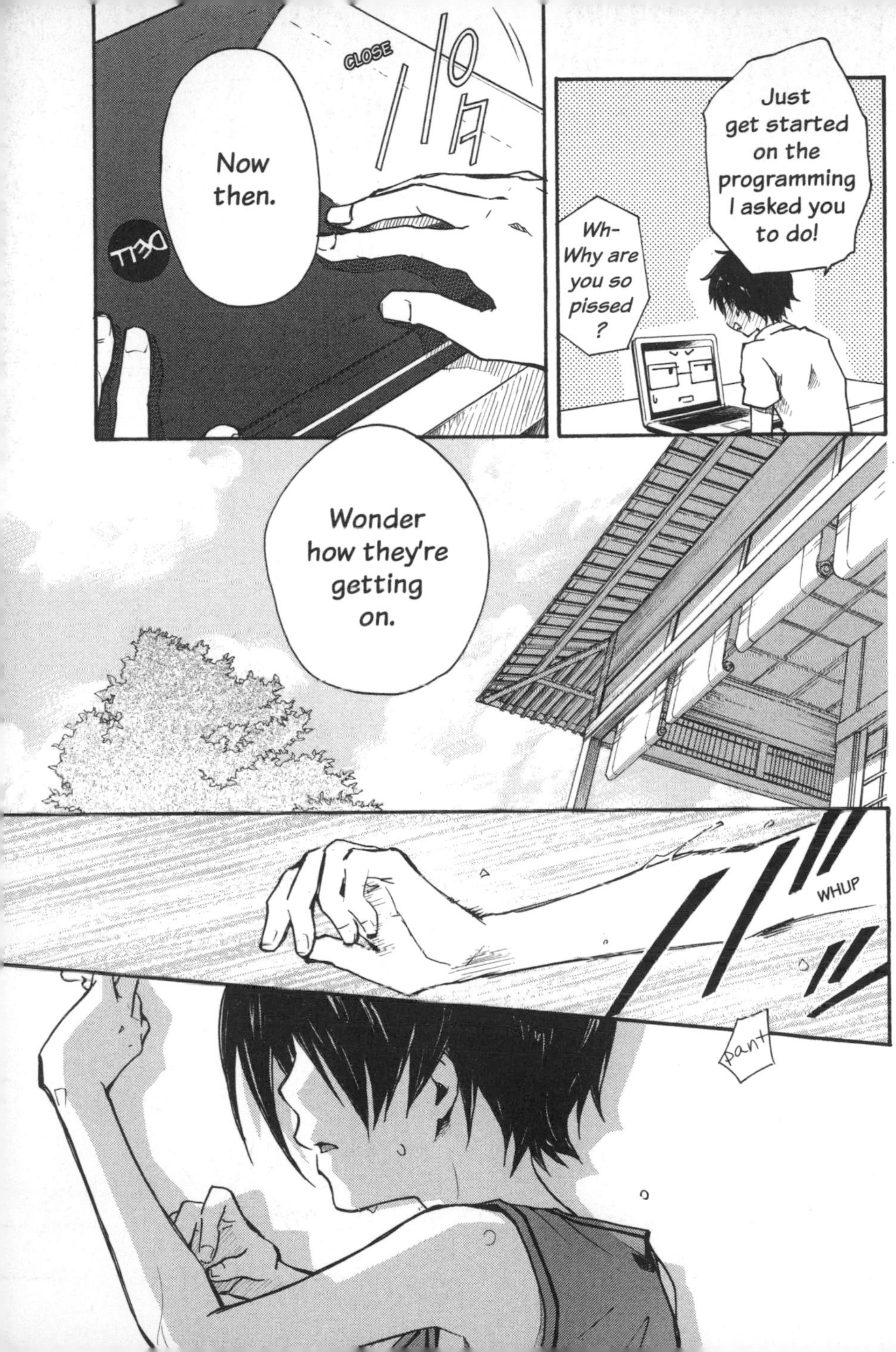
Just get started on the programming I asked you to do!
Wh- Why are you so pissed?
CLOSE
Now then.
Wonder how they're getting on.
WHUP
pant

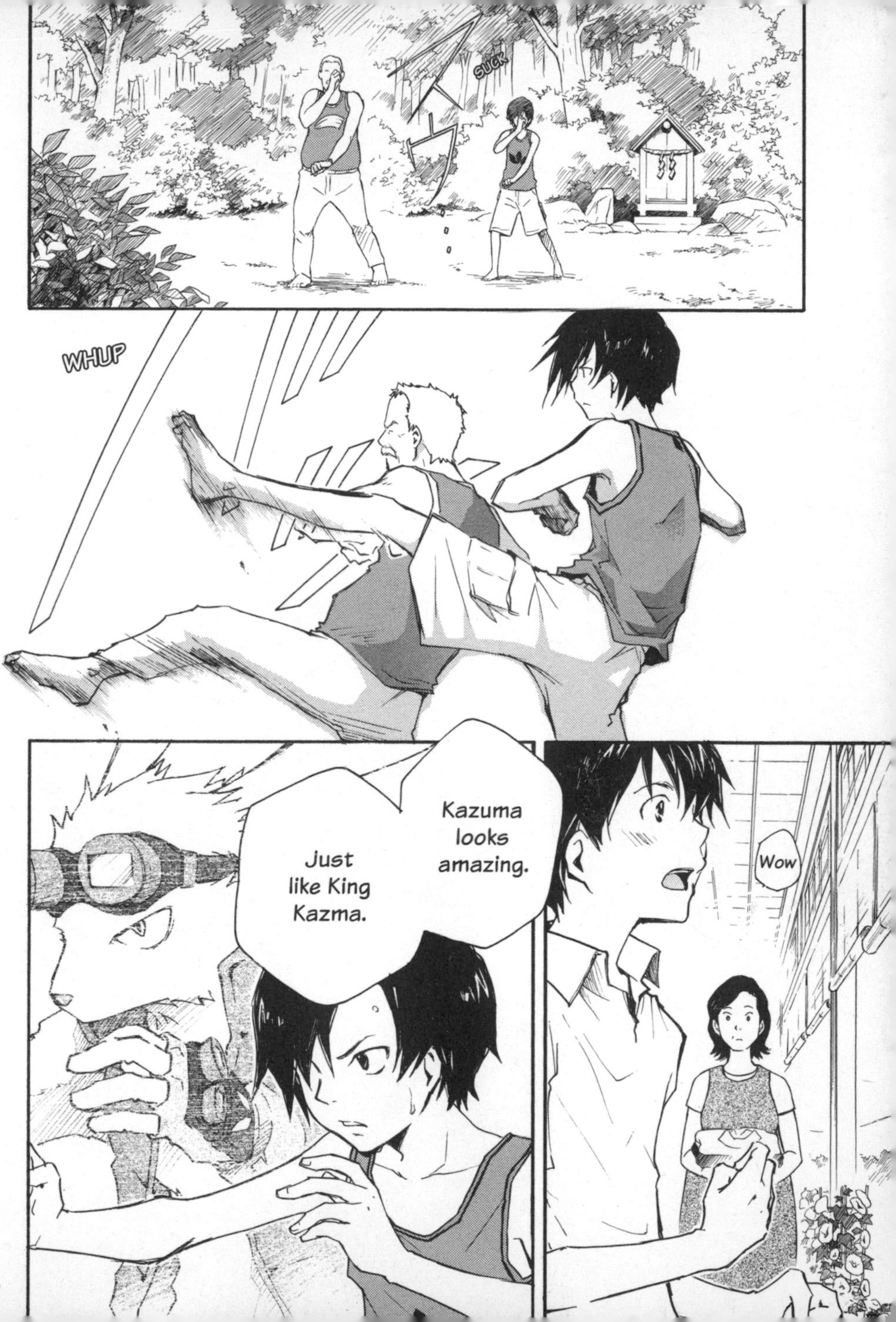
SUCK
WHUP
Wow
Kazuma looks amazing.
Just like King Kazma.

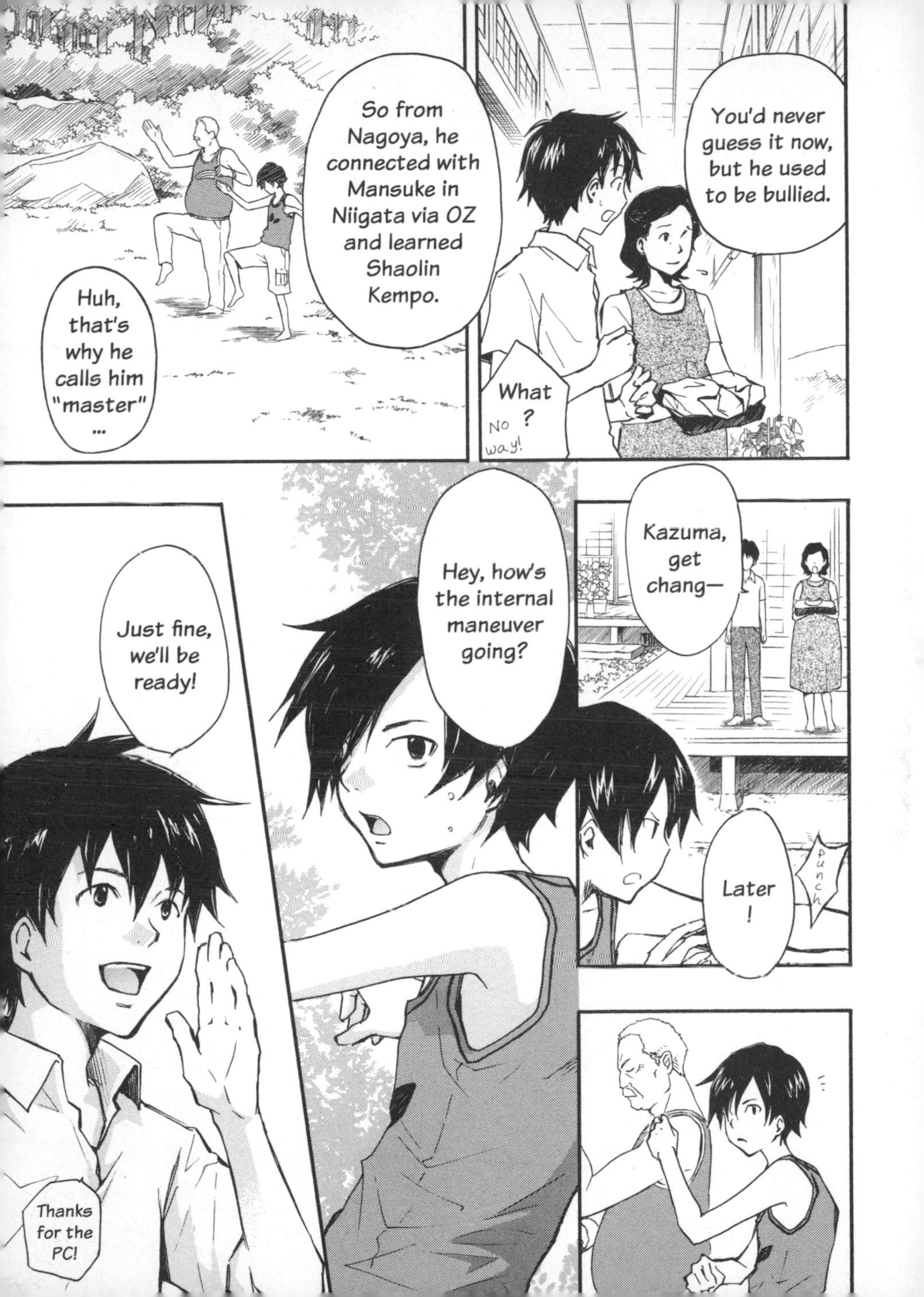
You'd never guess it now, but he used to be bullied.
What?
No way!
So from Nagoya, he connected with Mansuke in Niigata via OZ and learned Shaolin Kempo.
Huh, that's why he calls him "master"...
Kazuma, get chang—
Later!
Punch
Hey, how's the internal maneuver going?
Just fine, we'll be ready!
Thanks for the PC!

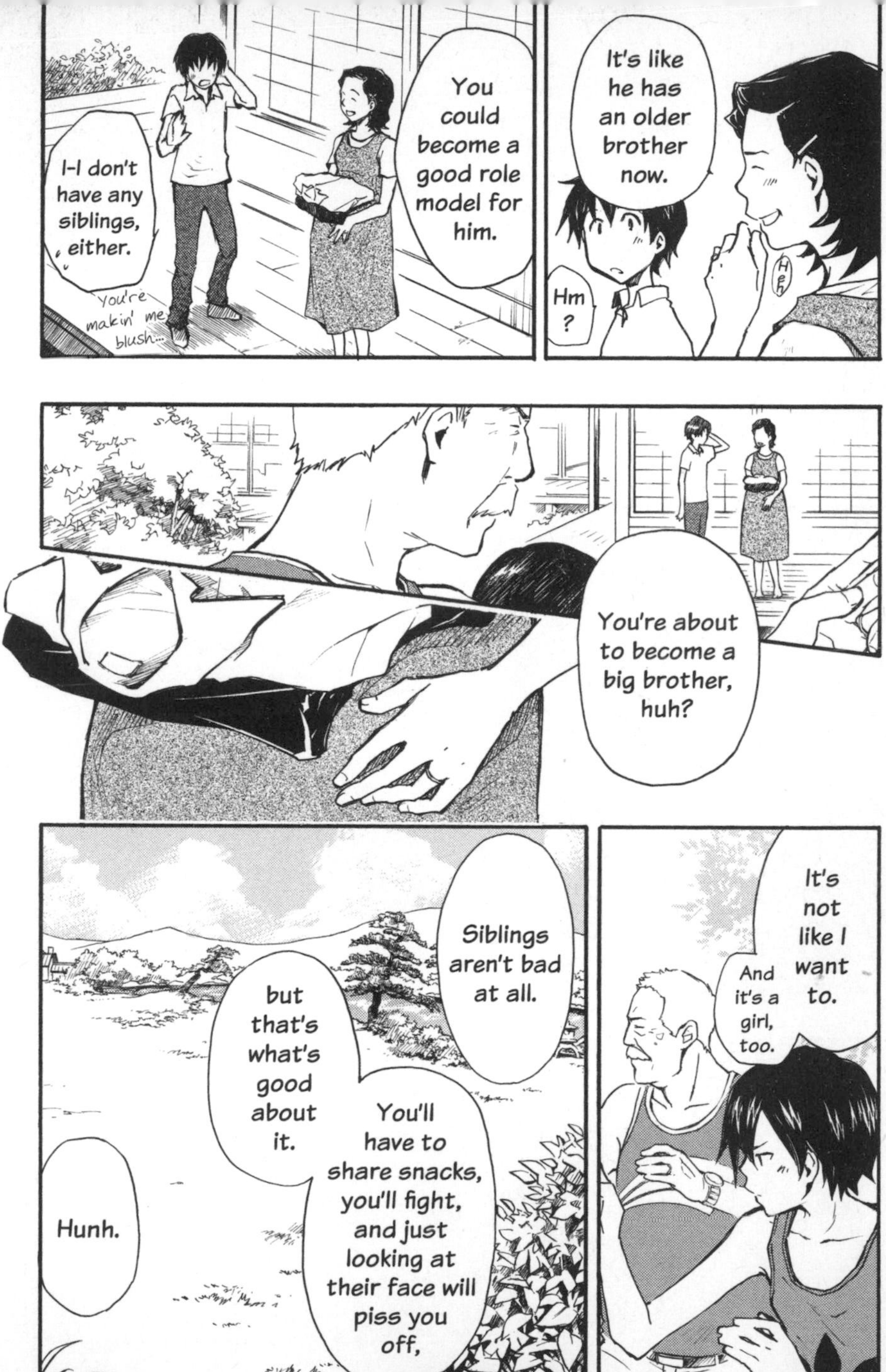
It's like he has an older brother now.
Heh
Hm?
You could become a good role model for him.
I-I don't have any siblings, either.
You're makin' me blush...
You're about to become a big brother, huh?
It's not like I want to.
And it's a girl, too.
Siblings aren't bad at all.
You'll have to share snacks, you'll fight, and just looking at their face will piss you off,
but that's what's good about it.
Hunh.

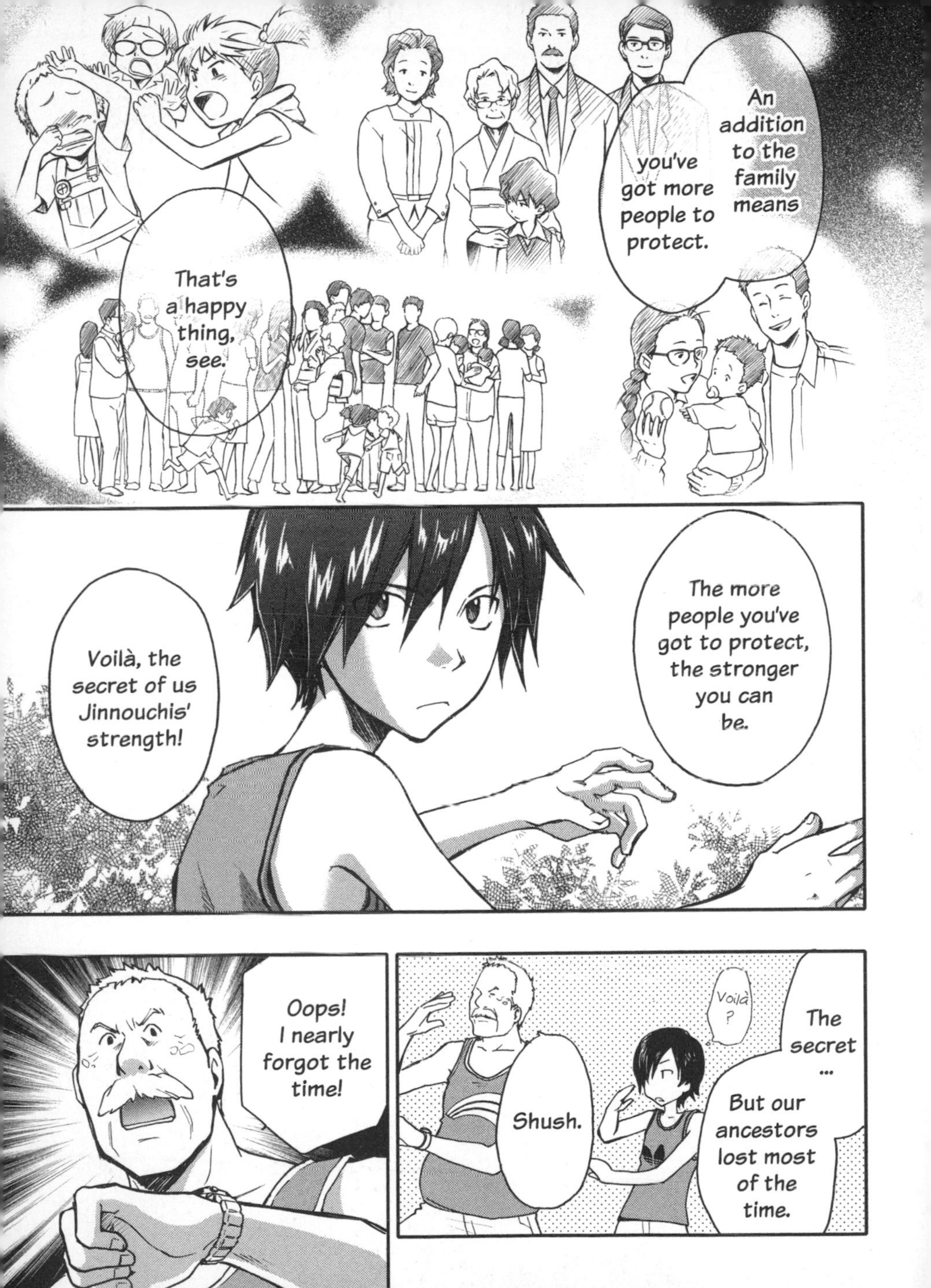
An addition to the family means you've got more people to protect.
That's a happy thing, see.
The more people you've got to protect, the stronger you can be.
Voilà, the secret of us Jinnouchis' strength!
The secret ...
Voilà ?
But our ancestors lost most of the time.
Shush.
Oops! I nearly forgot the time!

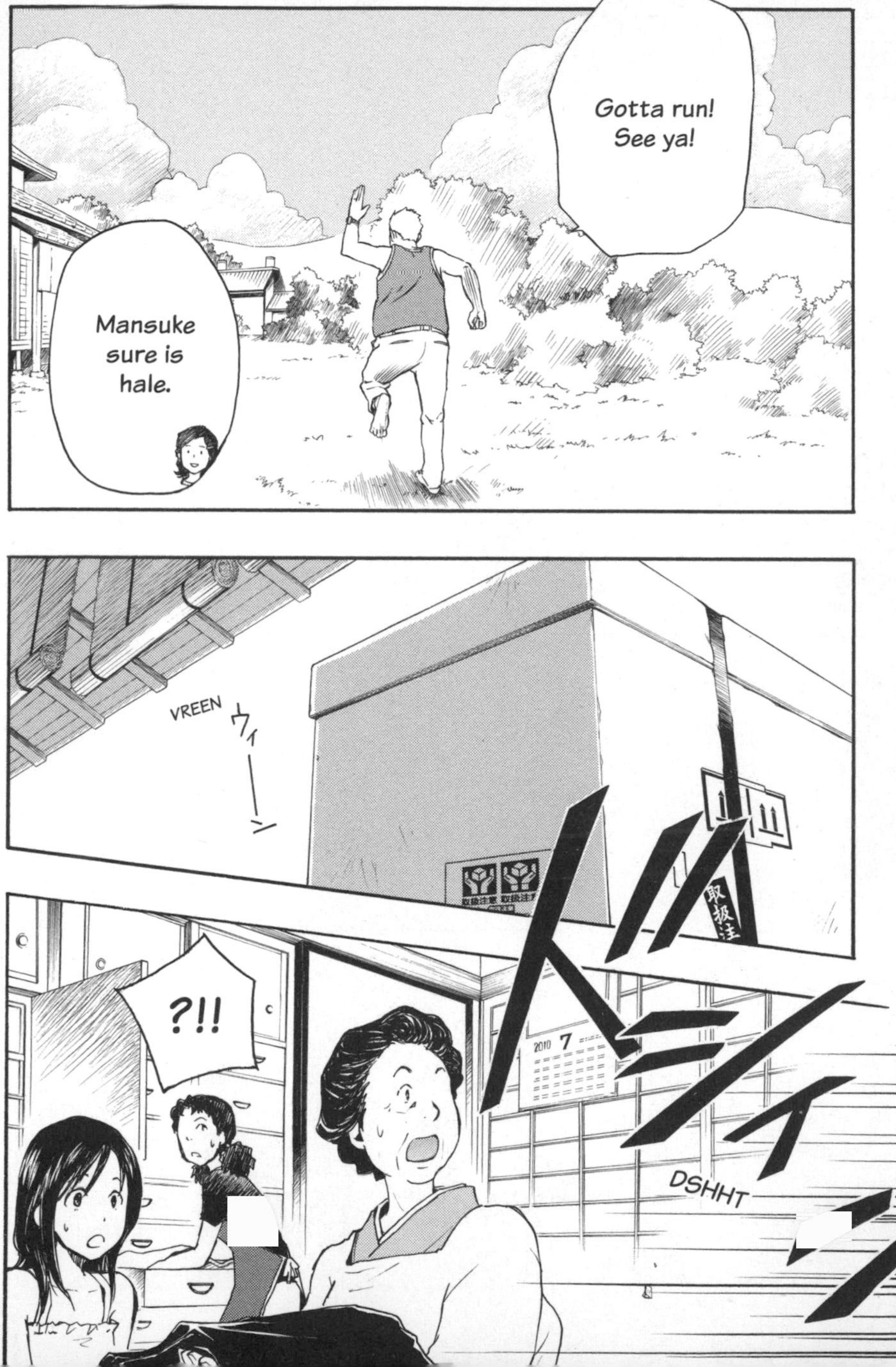
Gotta run! See ya!
Mansuke sure is hale.
VREEN
ウィーーン
?!!
DSHHT
取扱注

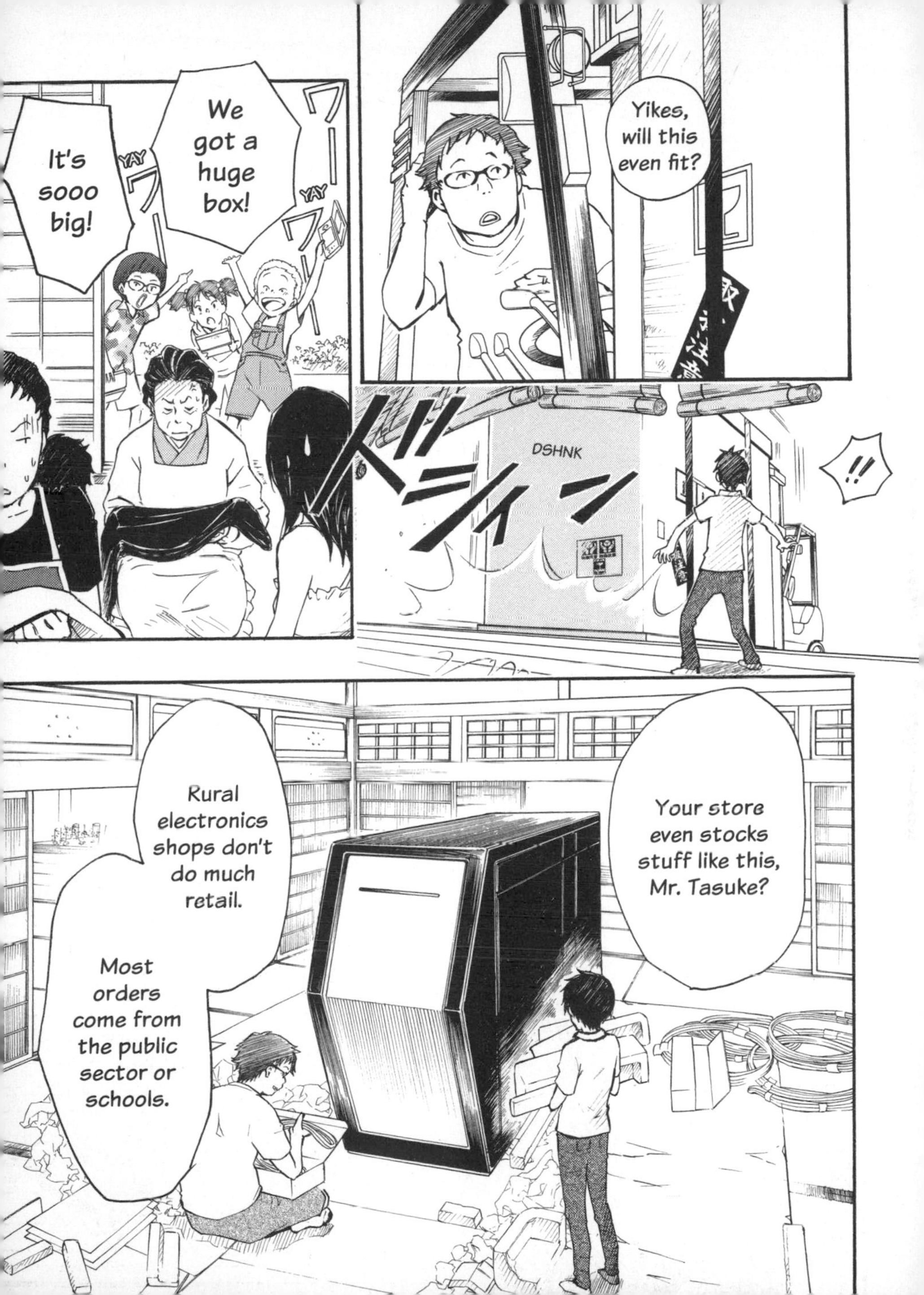

Yikes, will this even fit?
DSHNK
!!
YAY
We got a huge box!
YAY
It's sooo big!
Your store even stocks stuff like this, Mr. Tasuke?
Rural electronics shops don't do much retail.
Most orders come from the public sector or schools.

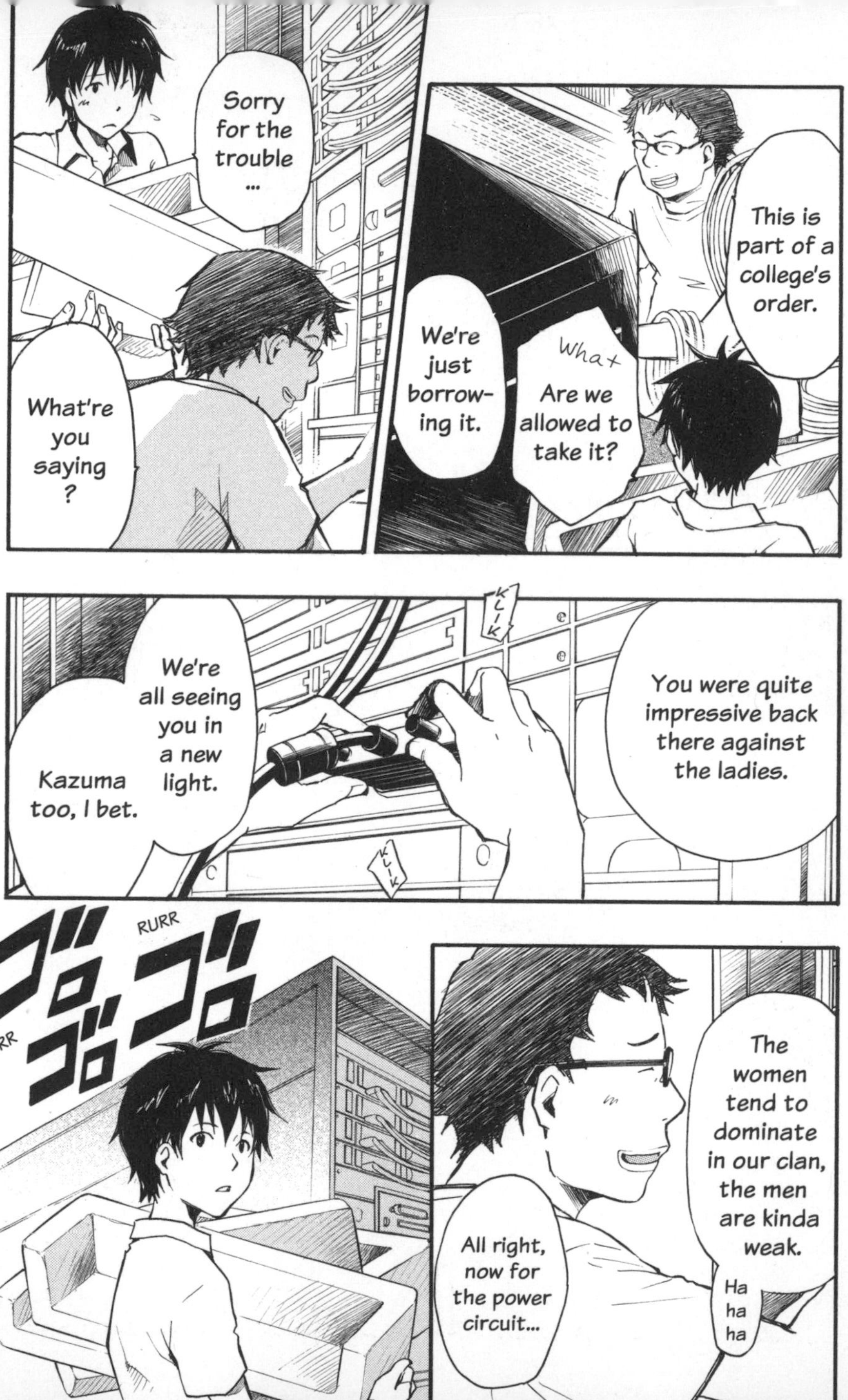
This is part of a college's order.
What
Are we allowed to take it?
We're just borrowing it.
Sorry for the trouble ...
What're you saying ?
KLIK
You were quite impressive back there against the ladies.
We're all seeing you in a new light.
Kazuma too, I bet.
KLIK
The women tend to dominate in our clan, the men are kinda weak.
Ha ha ha
All right, now for the power circuit...
ゴロゴロ RURR
ゴロゴロ RURR

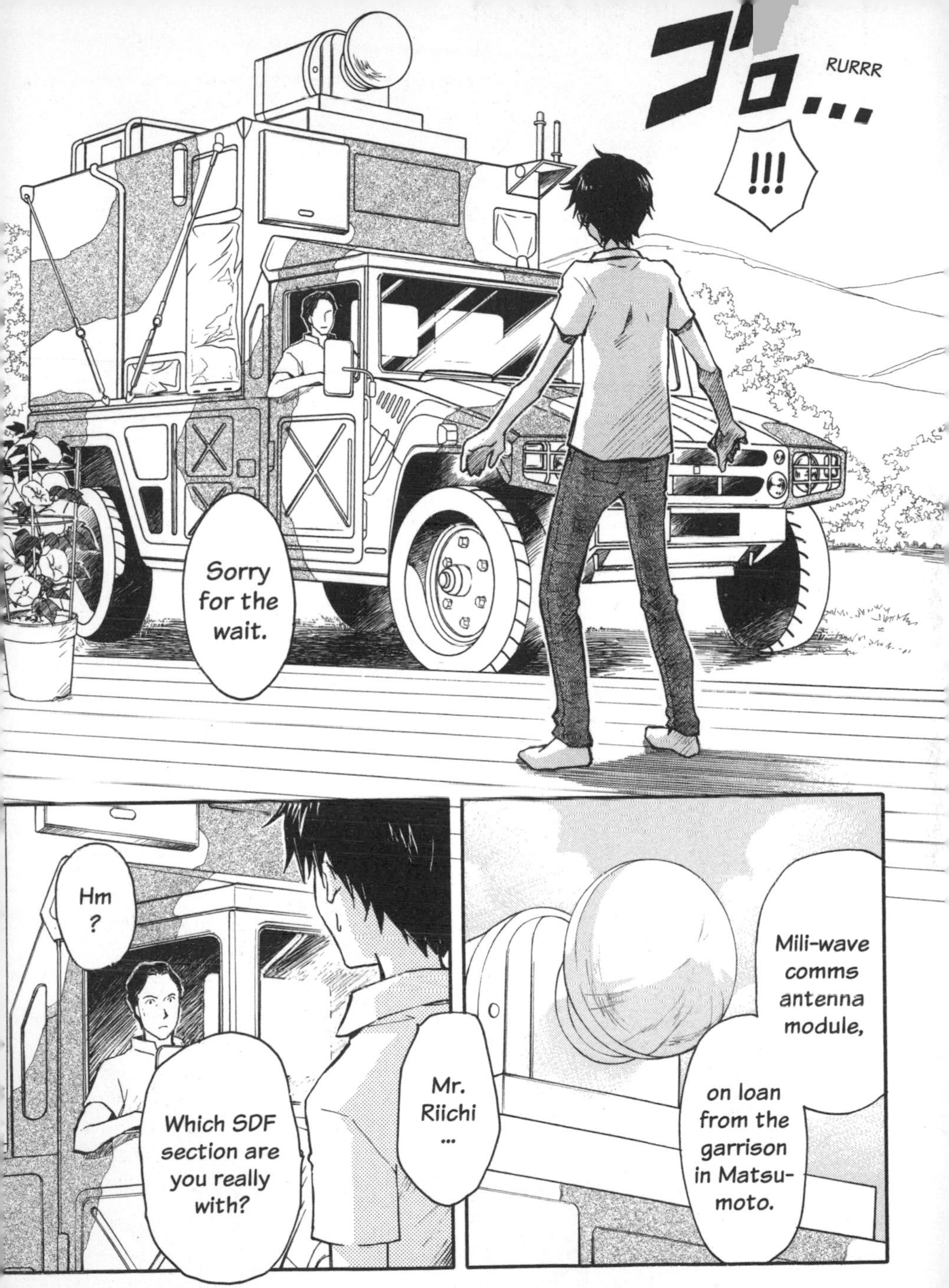
ゴロ...
RURRR
!!!
Sorry for the wait.
Mili-wave comms antenna module,
on loan from the garrison in Matsu-moto.
Mr. Riichi ...
Hm ?
Which SDF section are you really with?

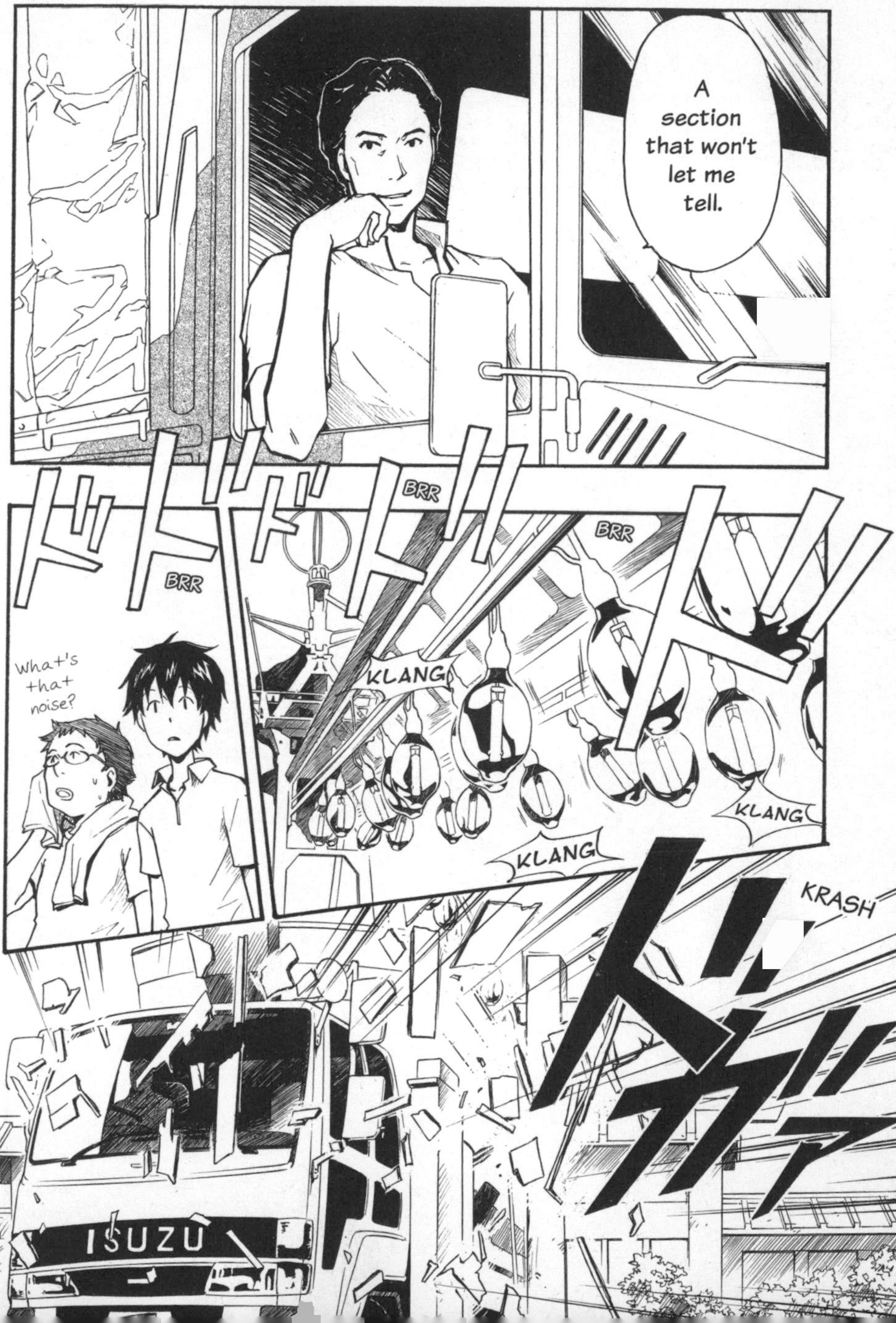
A section that won't let me tell.
BRR
BRR
KLANG
KLANG
KLANG
BRR
What's that noise?
KRASH
ISUZU

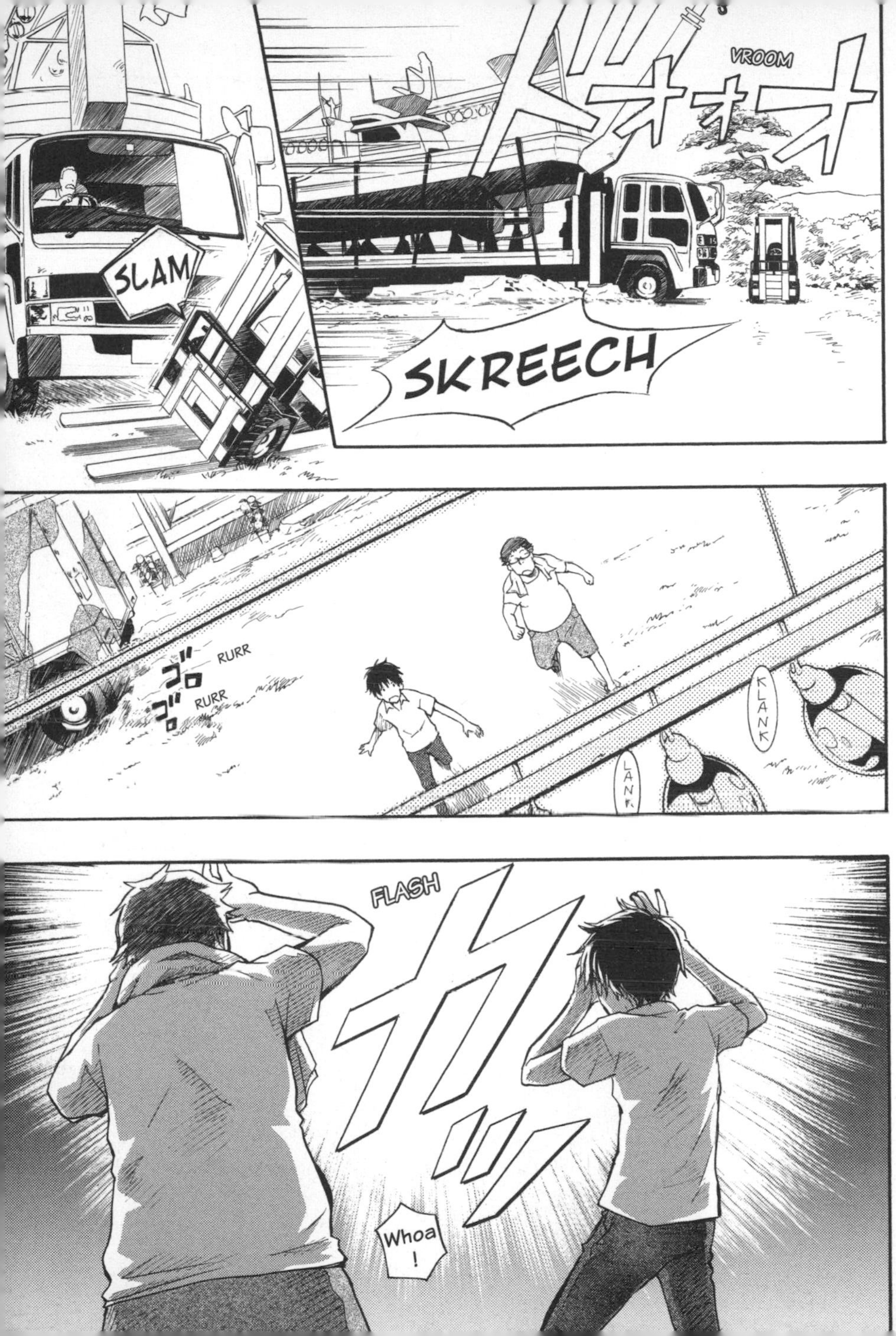
ドオォオ
VROOM
SKREECH
SLAM
KLANK
LANK
ゴロ
RURR
ゴロ
RURR
カッ
FLASH
Whoa
!

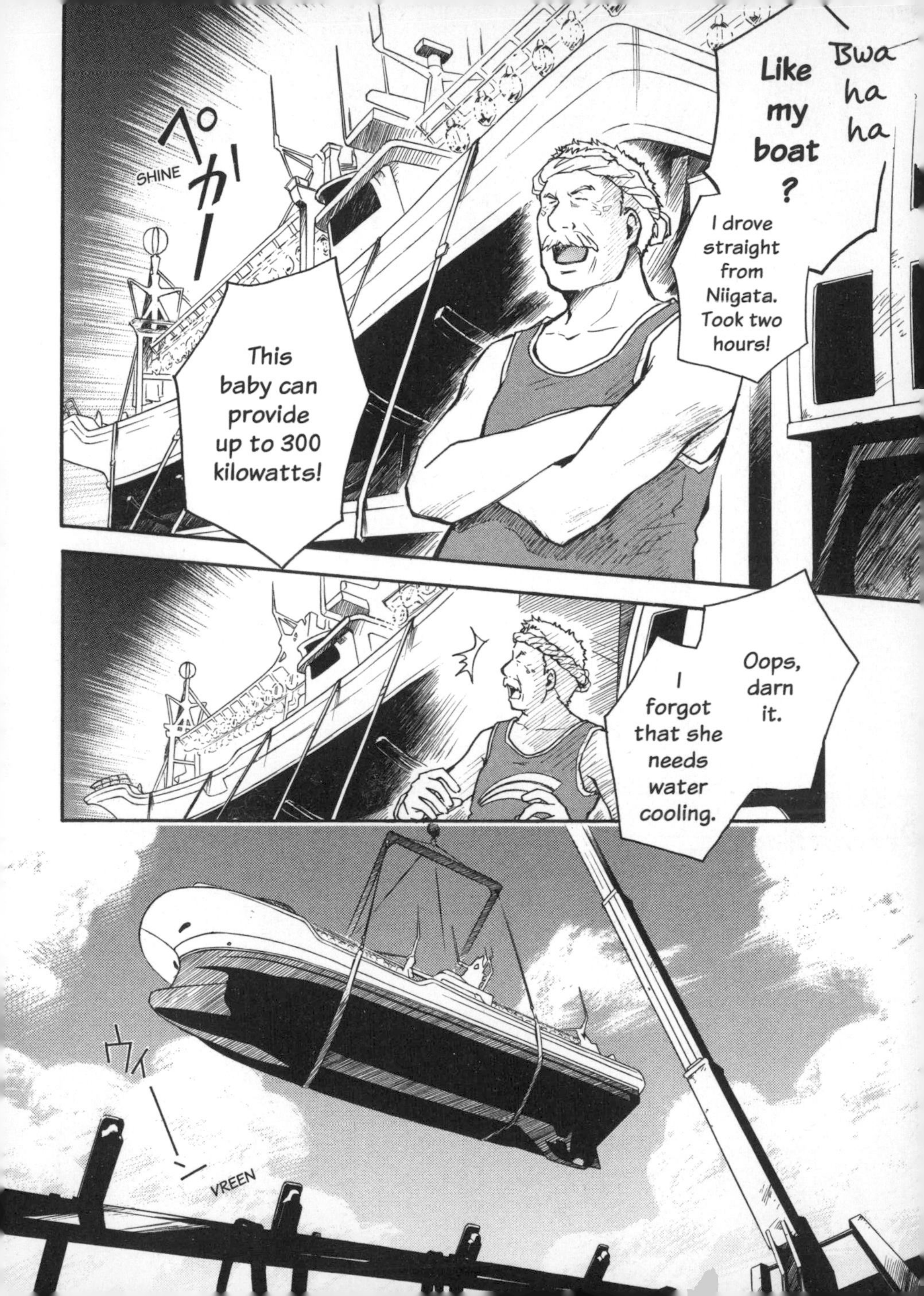
Bwa ha ha
Like my boat?
I drove straight from Niigata. Took two hours!
ペカー
SHINE
This baby can provide up to 300 kilowatts!
Oops, darn it.
I forgot that she needs water cooling.
ウィーン
VREEN

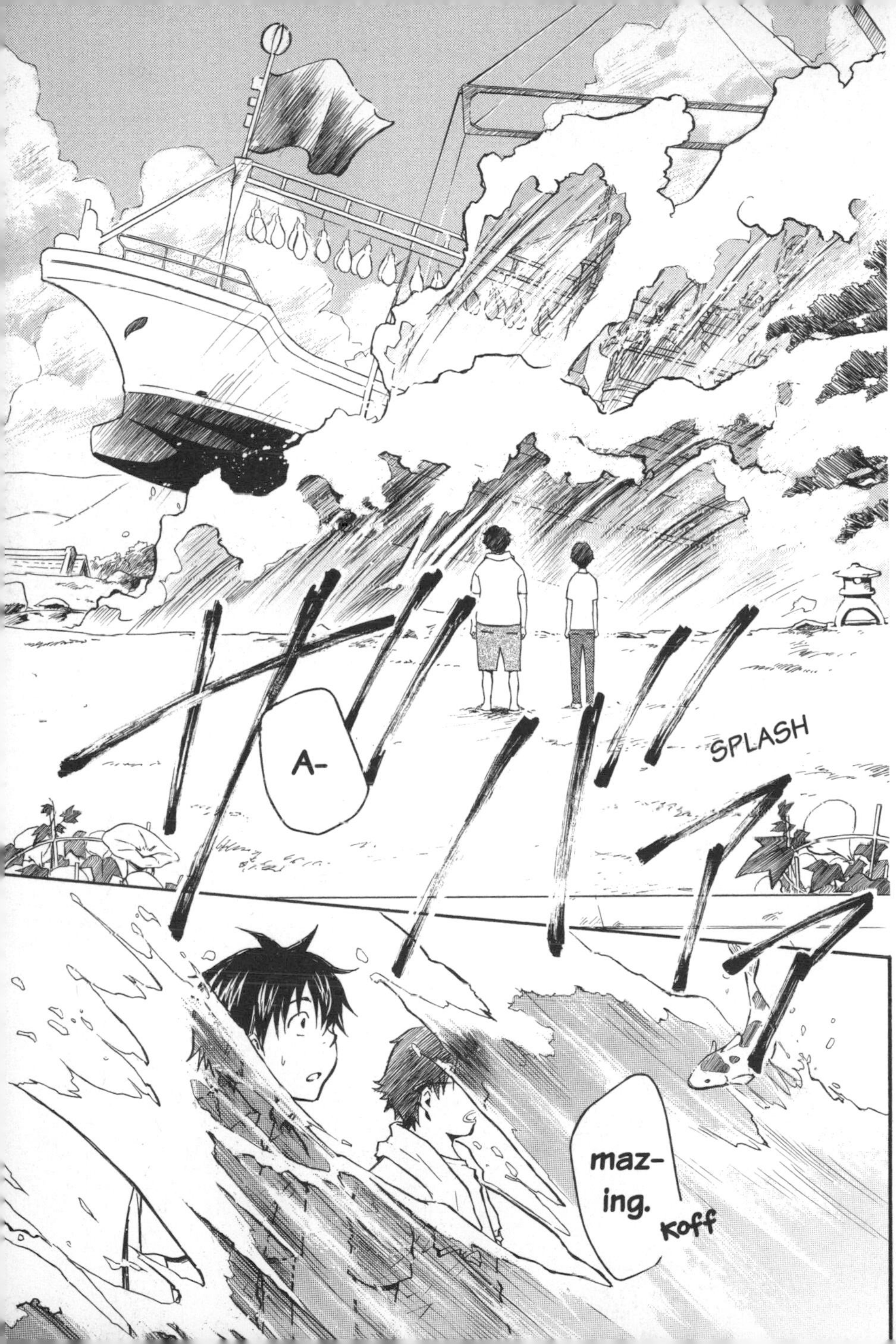
A-
SPLASH
maz-
ing.
koff

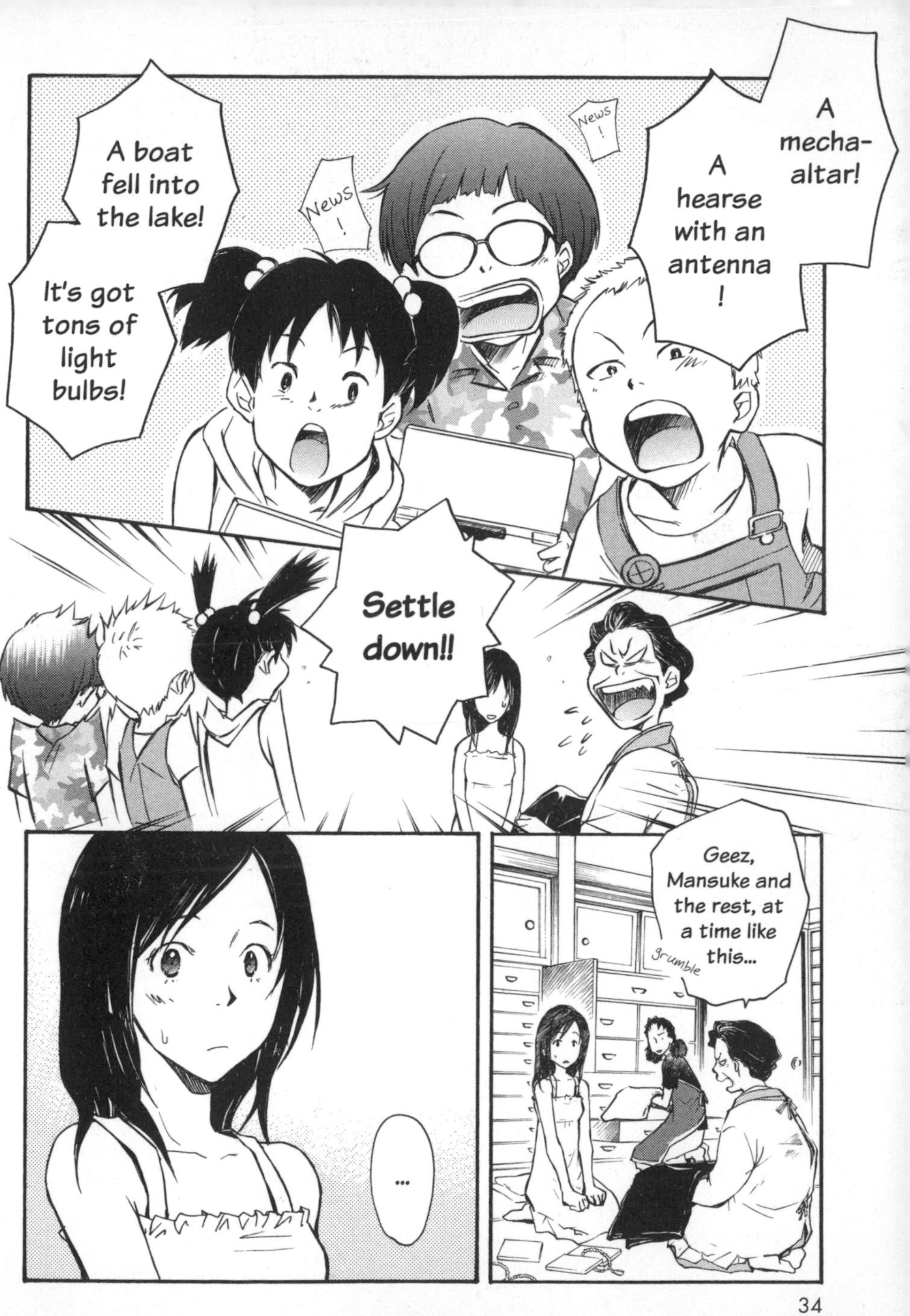
A mecha-altar!
News !
A hearse with an antenna !
A boat fell into the lake!
News !
It's got tons of light bulbs!
Settle down!!
Geez, Mansuke and the rest, at a time like this...
grumble
...

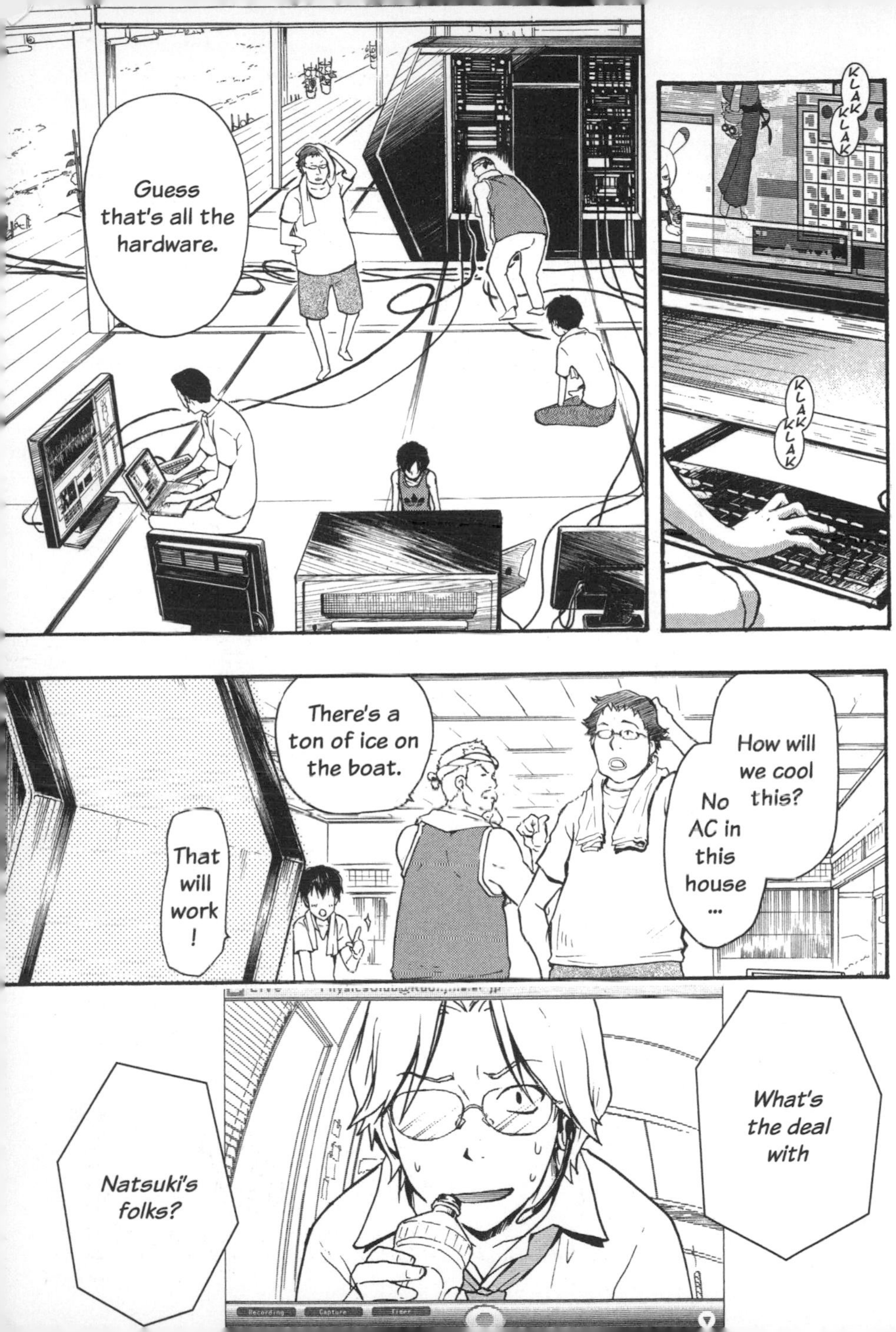
KLAK KLAK KLAK
KLAK KLAK KLAK
Guess that's all the hardware.
How will we cool this?
No AC in this house ...
There's a ton of ice on the boat.
That will work!
What's the deal with
Natsuki's folks?
Recording
Capture
Timer

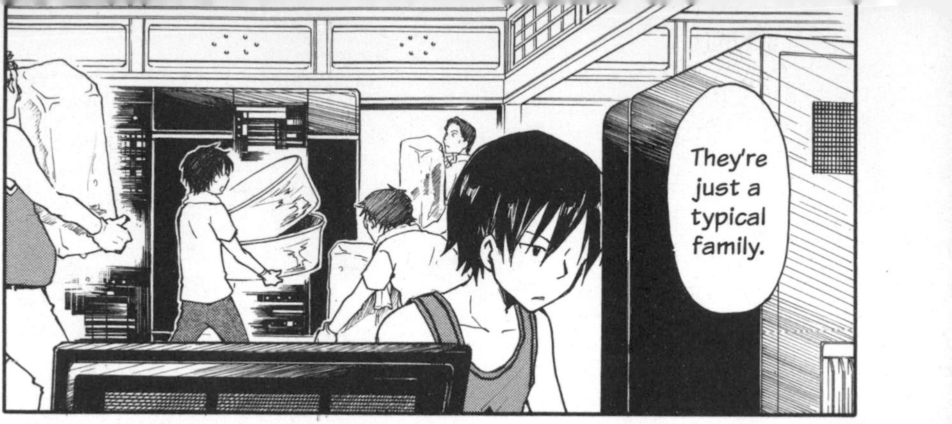
They're just a typical family.

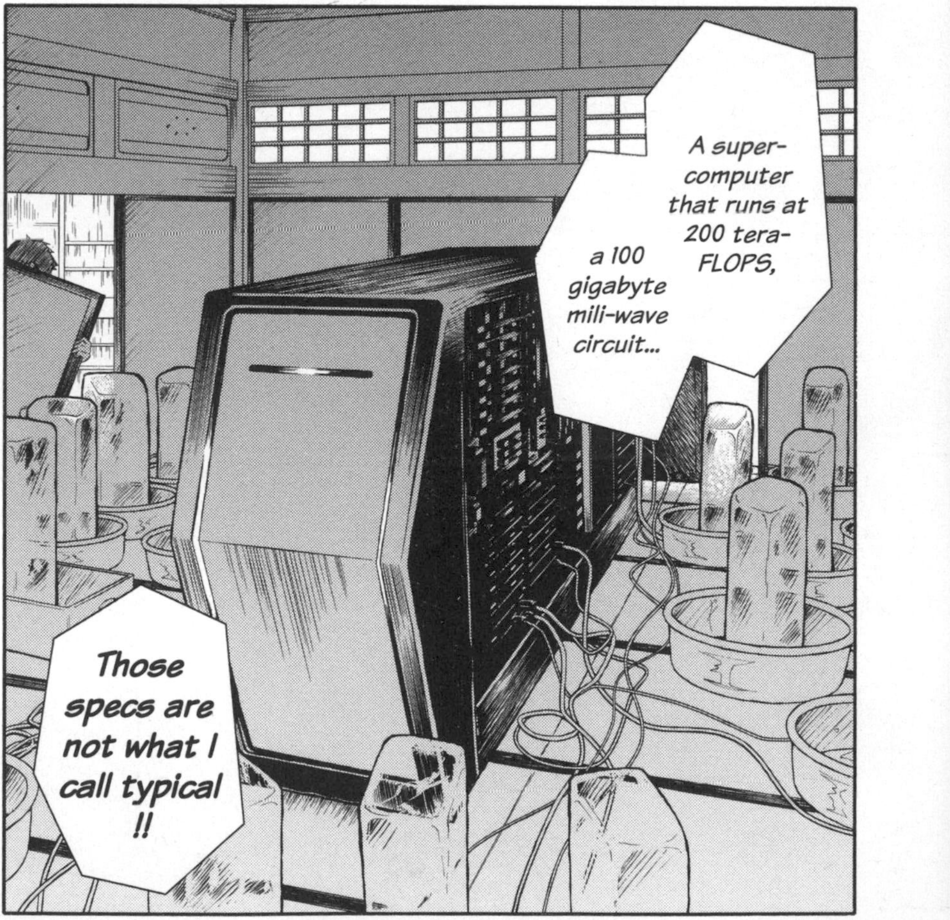
A super-computer that runs at 200 tera-FLOPS,
a 100 gigabyte mili-wave circuit...
Those specs are not what I call typical !!

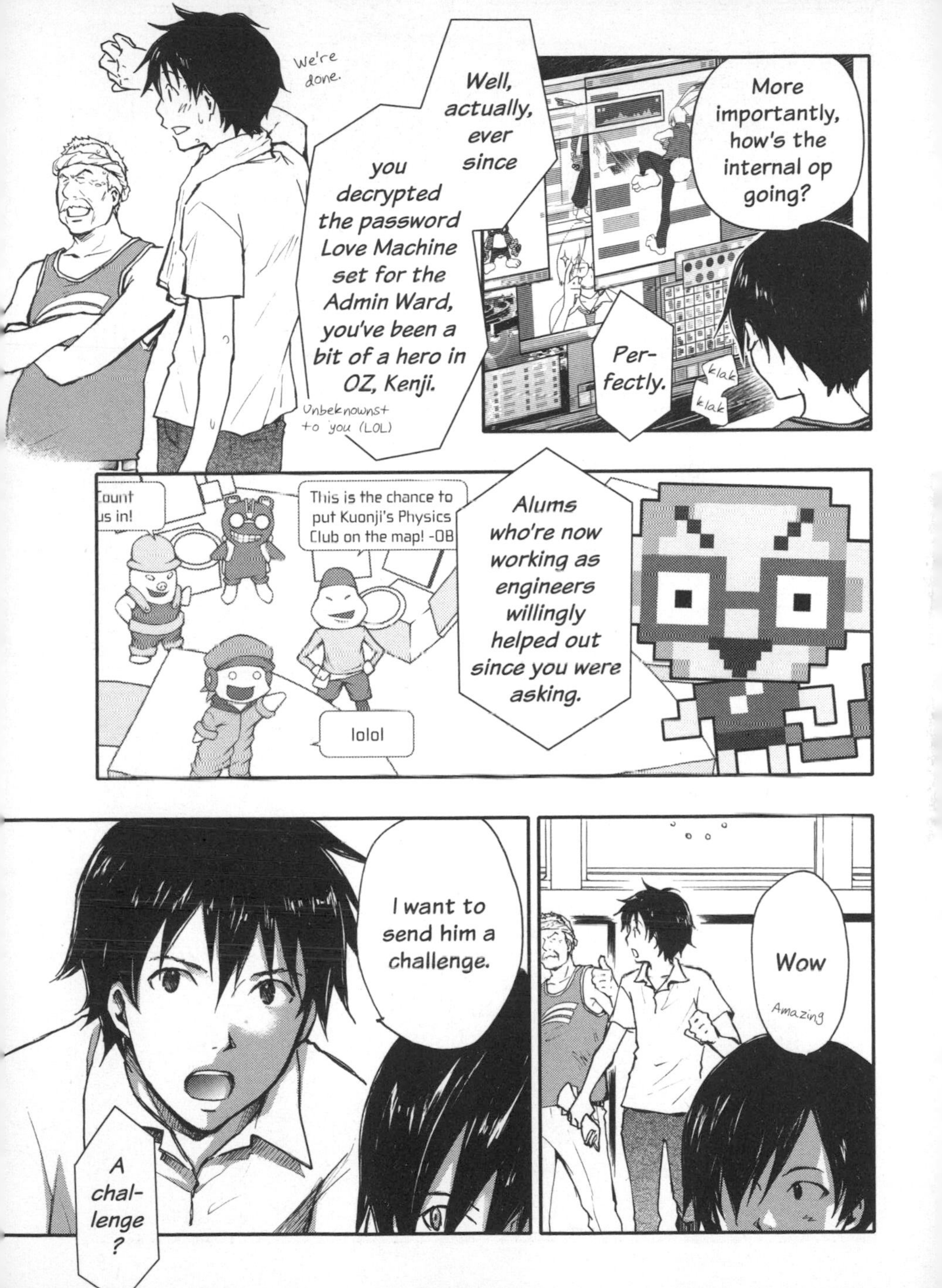
More importantly, how's the internal op going?
Per-fectly.
klak
klak
Well, actually, ever since you decrypted the password Love Machine set for the Admin Ward, you've been a bit of a hero in OZ, Kenji.
Unbeknownst to you (LOL)
We're done.
Alums who're now working as engineers willingly helped out since you were asking.
This is the chance to put Kuonji's Physics Club on the map! -OB
ount us in!
lolol
Wow
Amazing
I want to send him a challenge.
A chal-lenge?

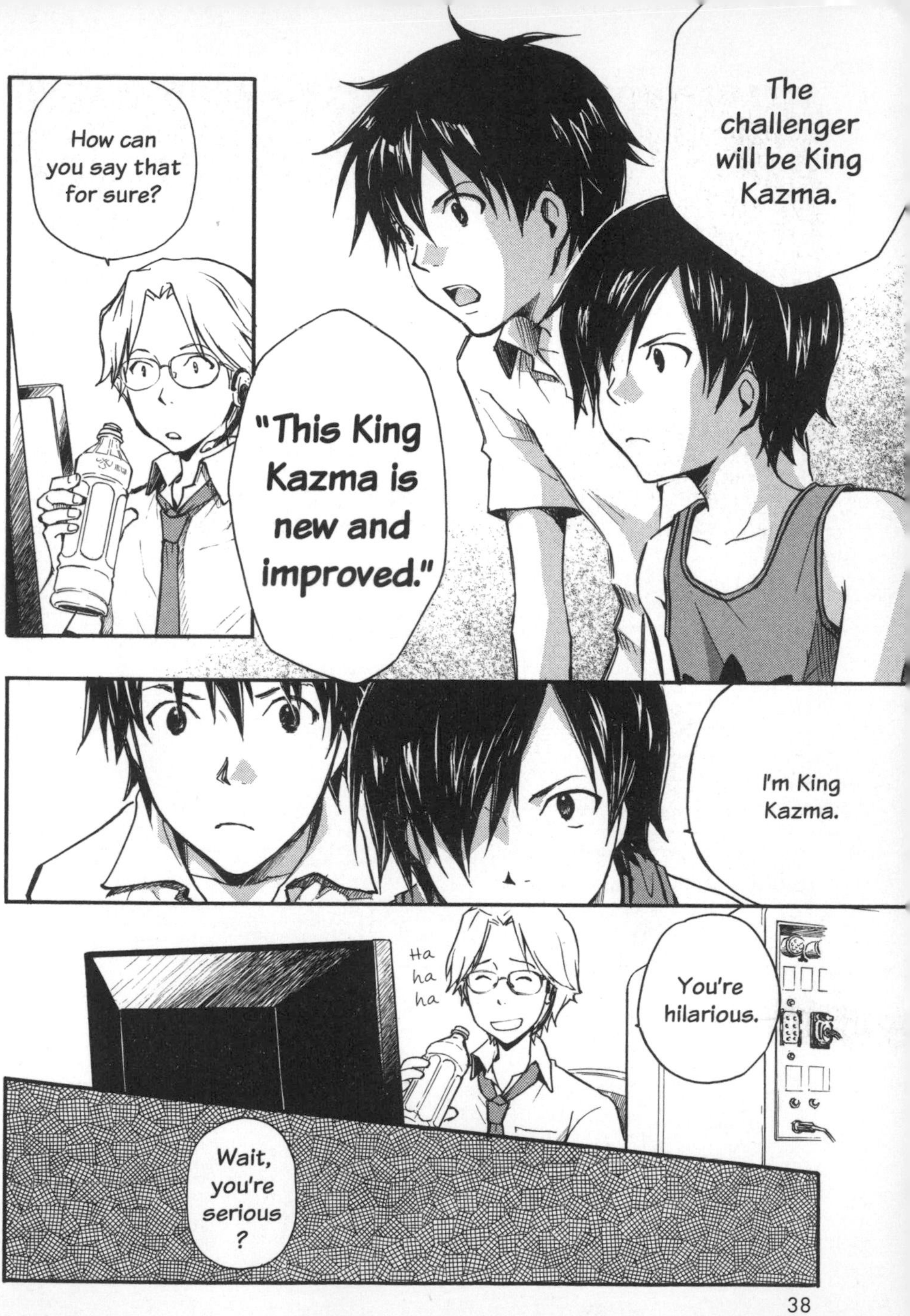
The challenger will be King Kazma.
"This King Kazma is new and improved."
How can you say that for sure?
I'm King Kazma.
You're hilarious.
Ha ha ha
Wait, you're serious?

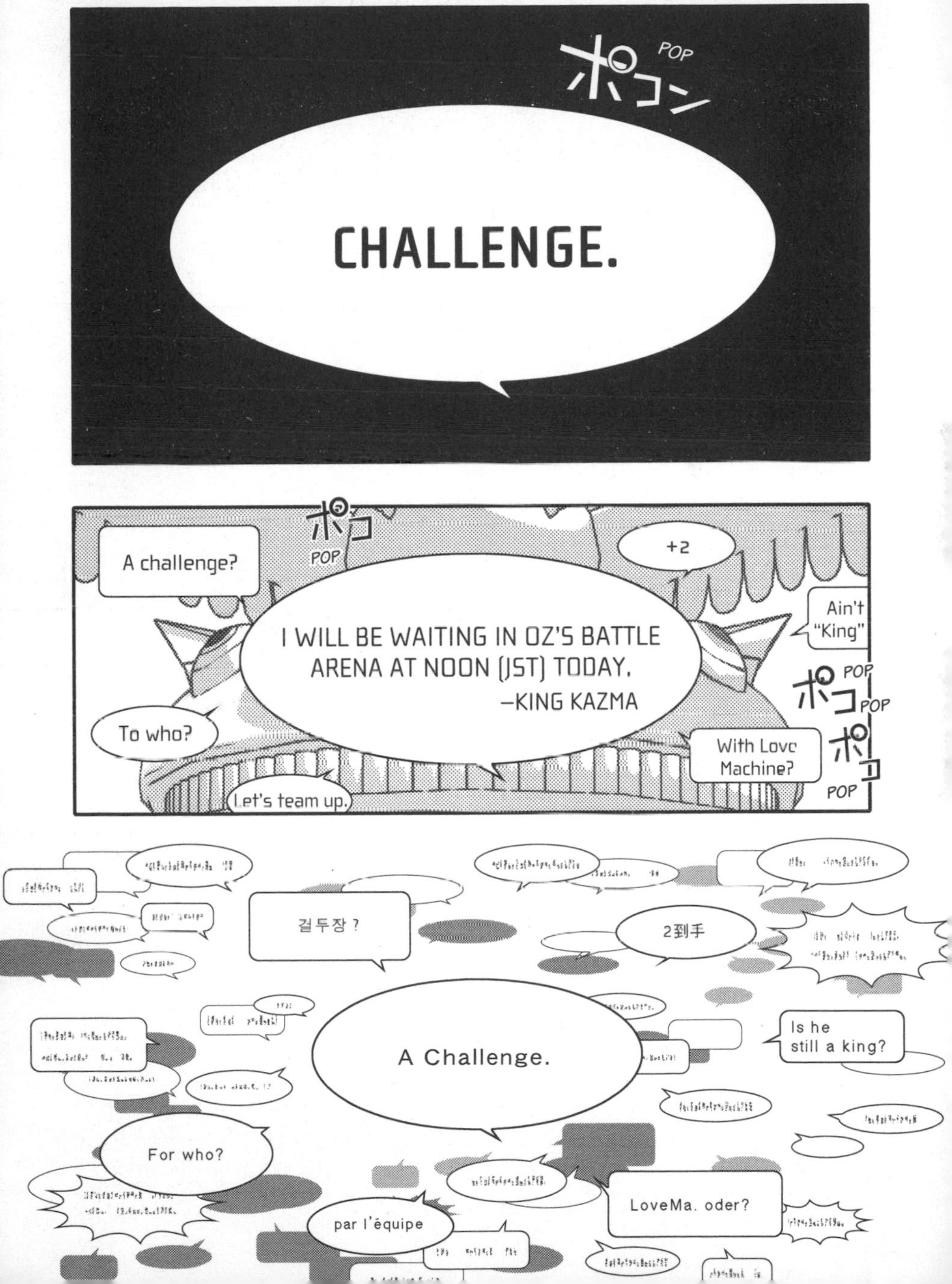
ポコン
POP
CHALLENGE.
+2
Ain't "King"
ポコ
POP
ポコ
POP
ポコ
POP
A challenge?
I WILL BE WAITING IN OZ'S BATTLE ARENA AT NOON (JST) TODAY. –KING KAZMA
With Love Machine?
To who?
Let's team up.
2到手
걸두장 ?
Is he still a king?
A Challenge.
For who?
LoveMa. oder?
par l'équipe

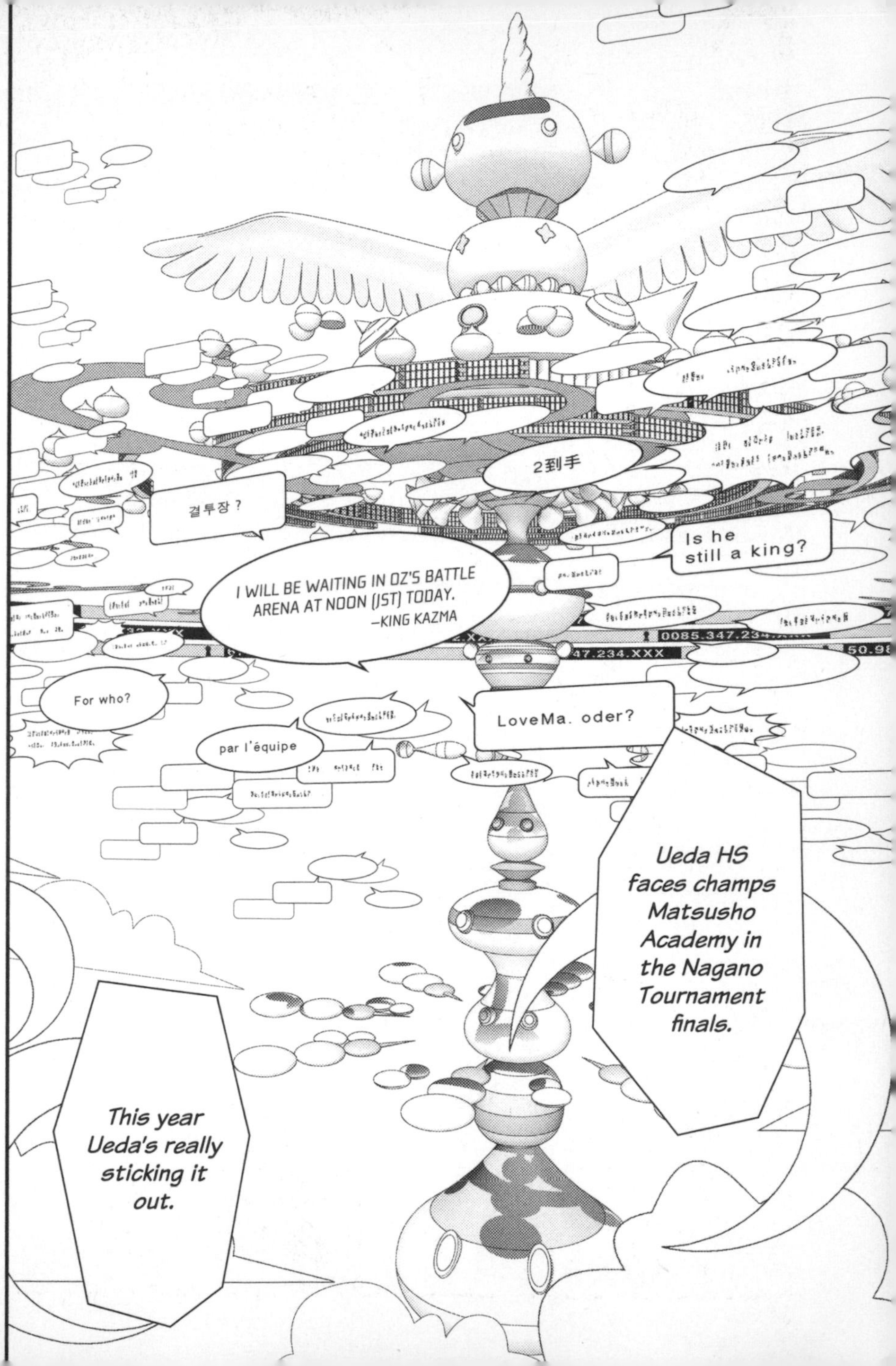
2到手
결투장 ?
Is he still a king?
I WILL BE WAITING IN OZ'S BATTLE ARENA AT NOON (JST) TODAY. —KING KAZMA
LoveMa. oder?
For who?
par l'équipe
Ueda HS faces champs Matsusho Academy in the Nagano Tournament finals.
This year Ueda's really sticking it out.

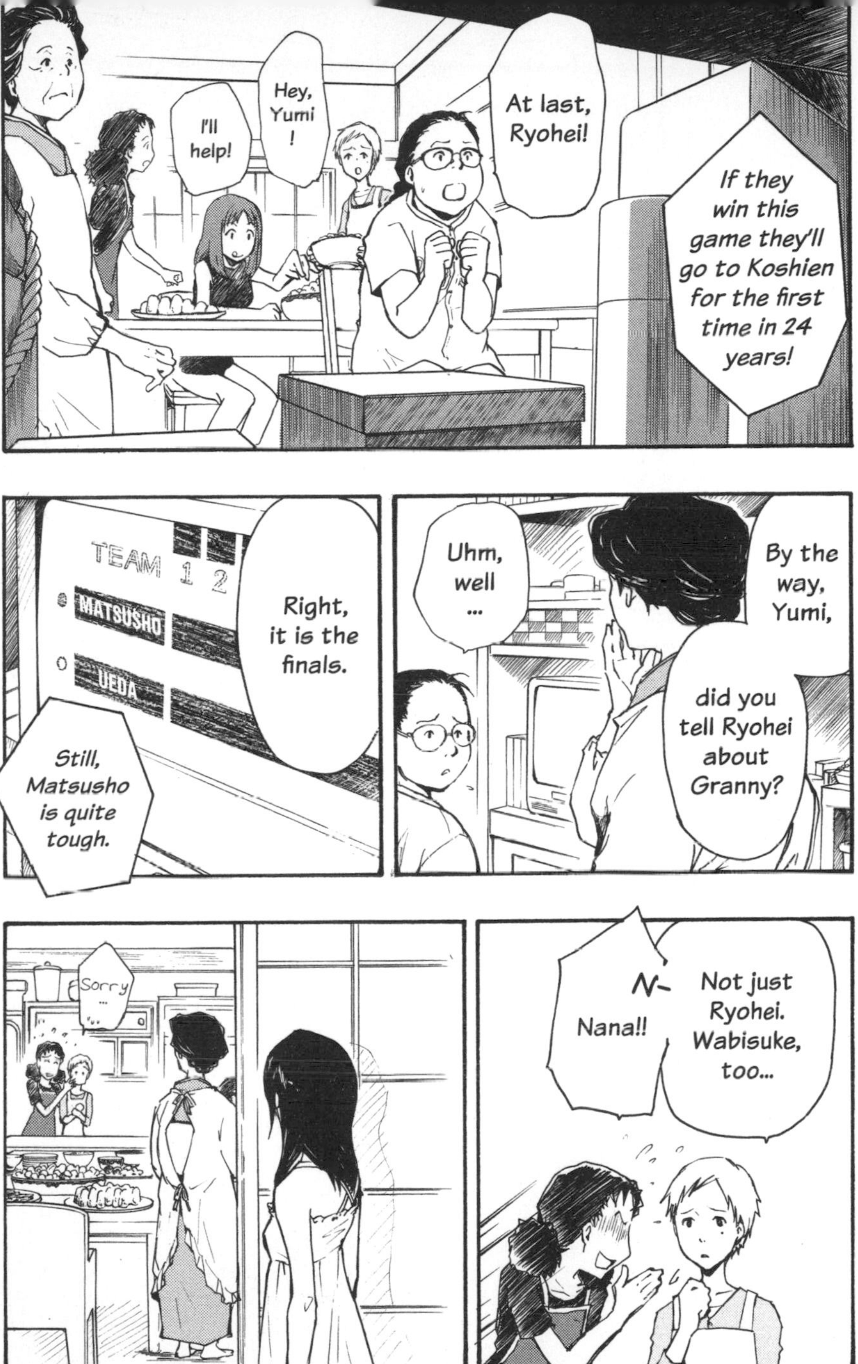
At last, Ryohei!
If they win this game they'll go to Koshien for the first time in 24 years!
Hey, Yumi!
I'll help!
By the way, Yumi,
did you tell Ryohei about Granny?
Uhm, well ...
Right, it is the finals.
TEAM 1 2
MATSUSHO
UEDA
Still, Matsusho is quite tough.
Not just Ryohei. Wabisuke, too...
N- Nana!!
Sorry ...

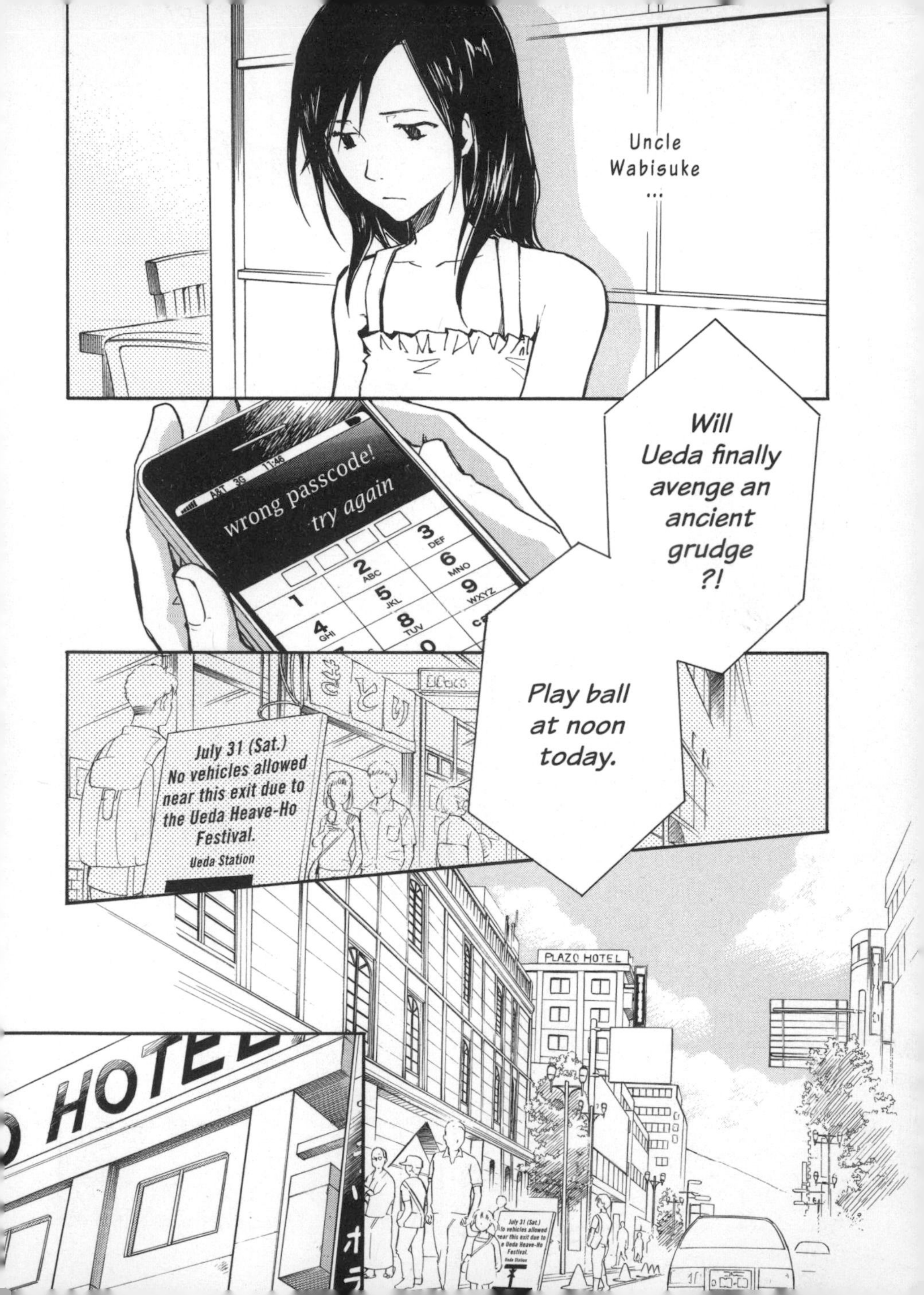

Uncle Wabisuke ...
Will Ueda finally avenge an ancient grudge ?!
wrong passcode! try again
Play ball at noon today.
July 31 (Sat.) No vehicles allowed near this exit due to the Ueda Heave-Ho Festival.
Ueda Station
PLAZO HOTEL
O HOTEL

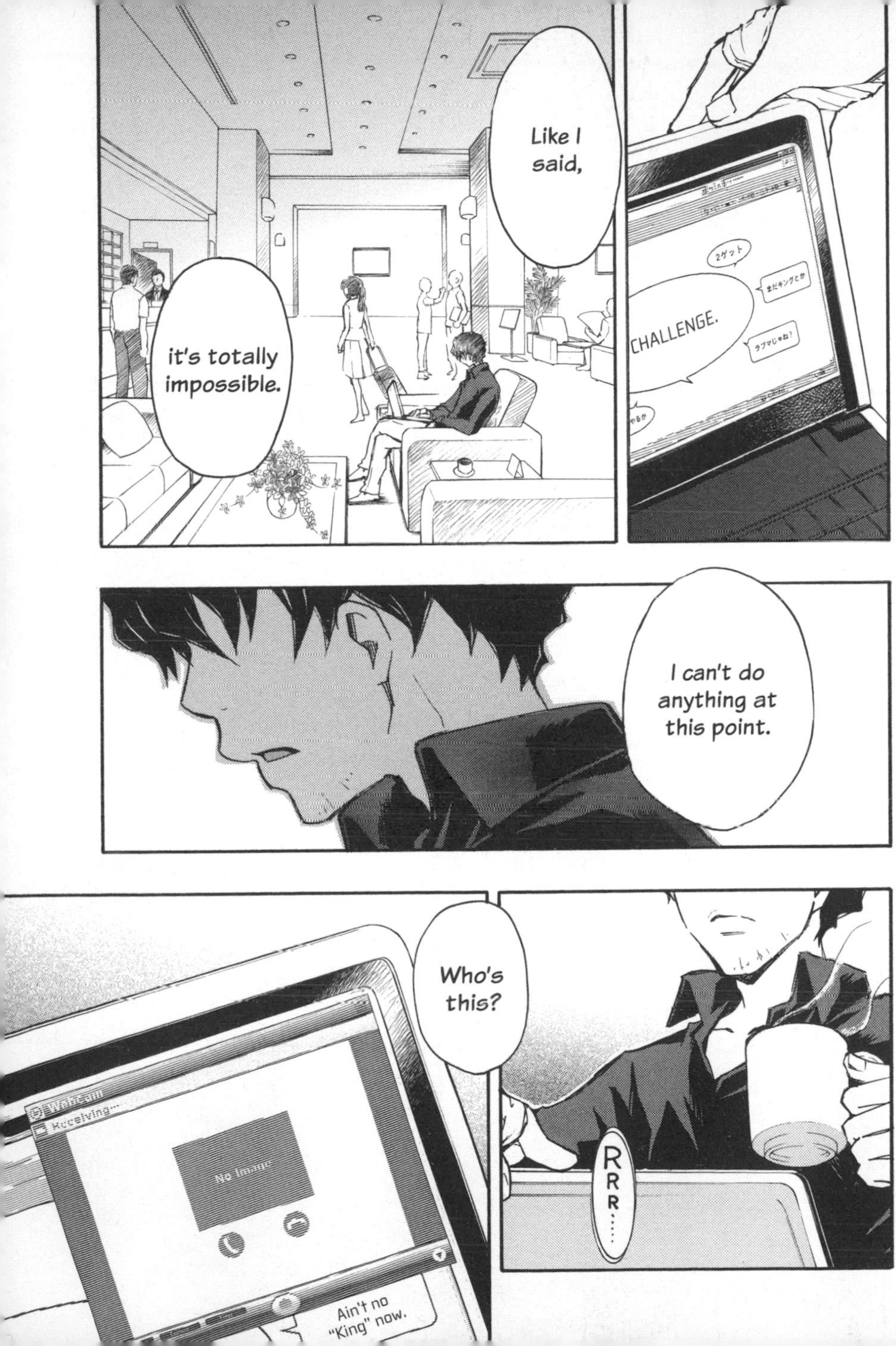
2ゲット
まだキングとか
CHALLENGE.
ラブマじゃね？
Like I said,
it's totally impossible.
I can't do anything at this point.
Who's this?
RRR.....
WebCam
Receiving...
No Image
Ain't no "King" now.

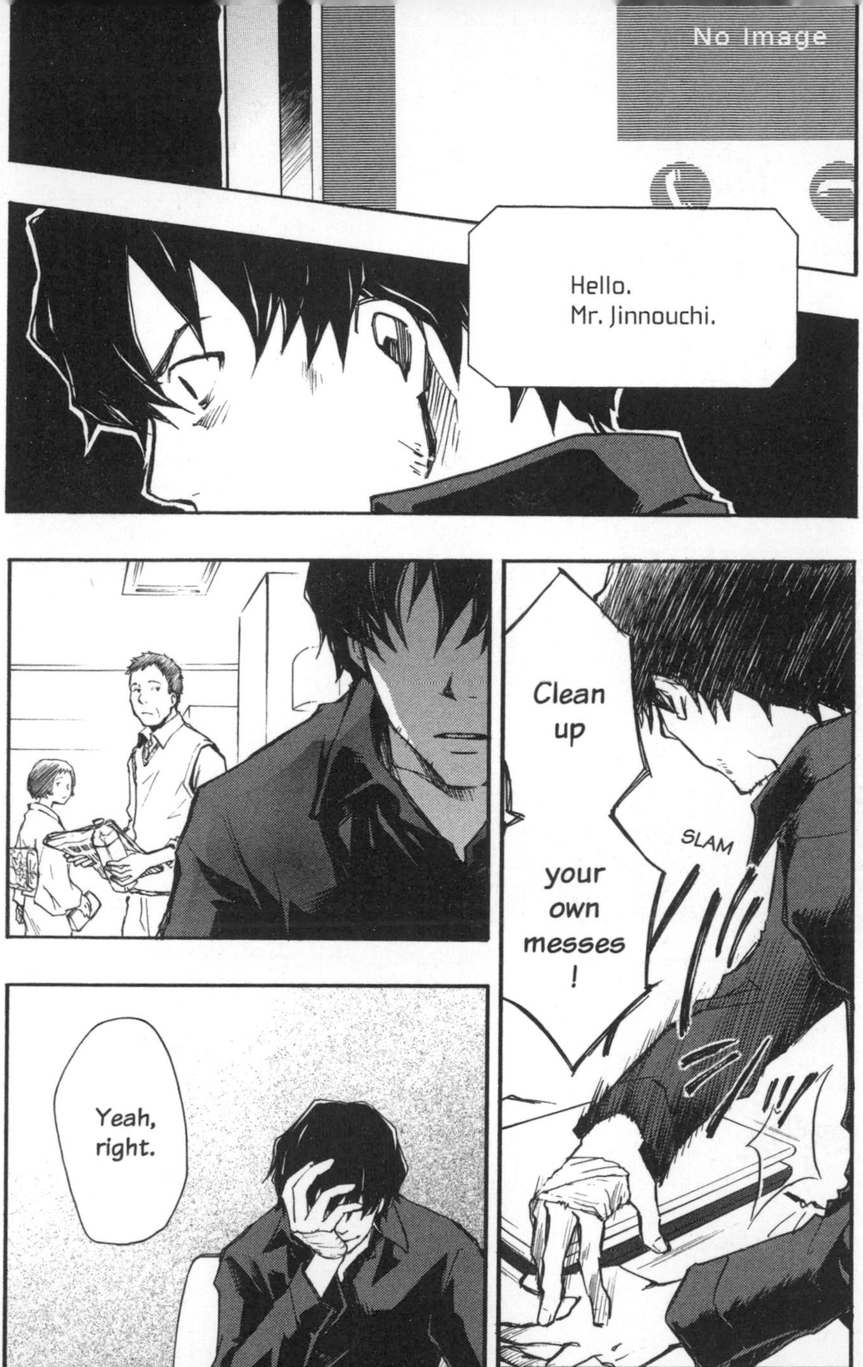
No Image
Hello. Mr. Jinnouchi.
Clean up your own messes!
SLAM
Yeah, right.

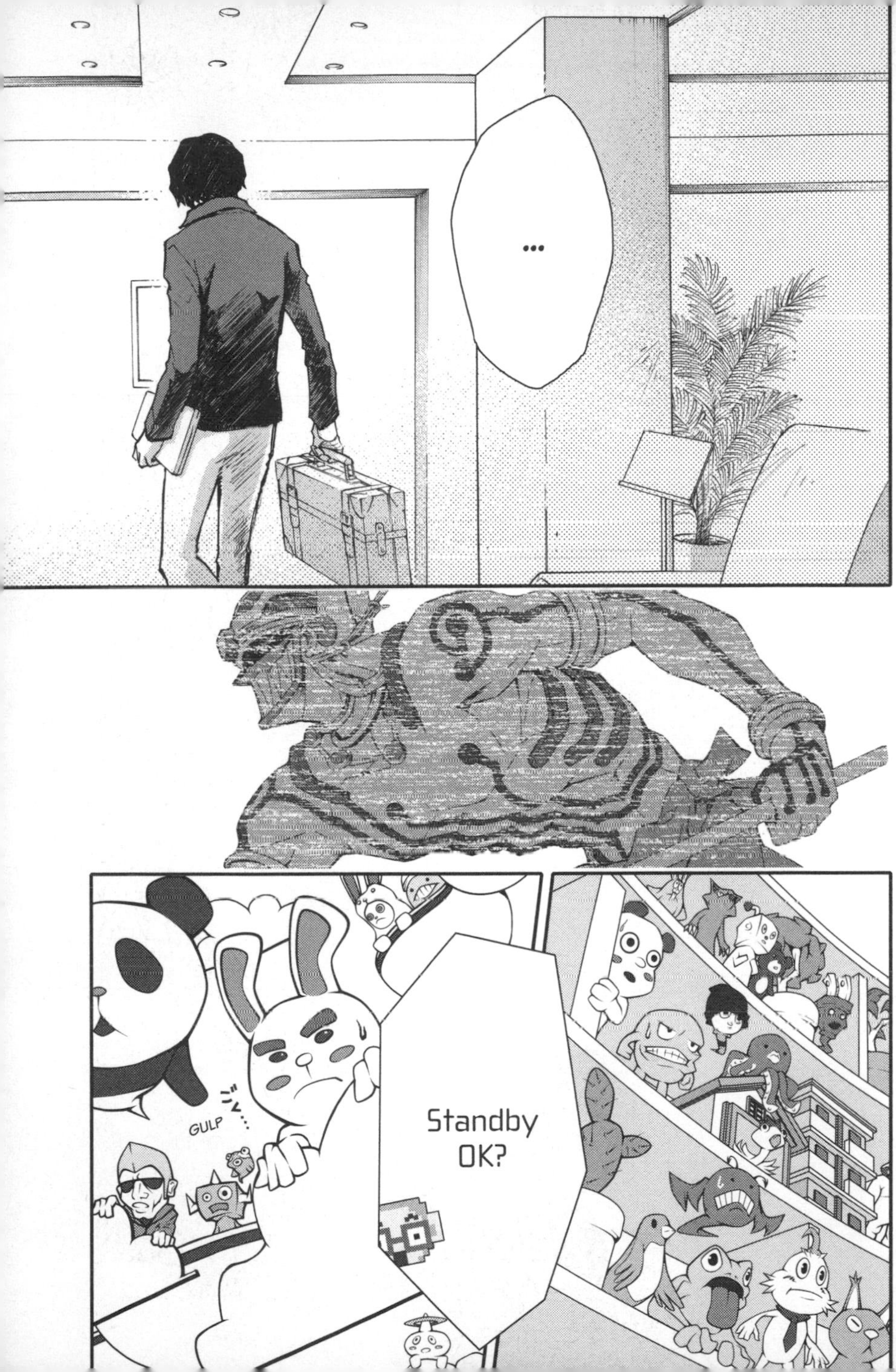
...
Standby OK?
GULP

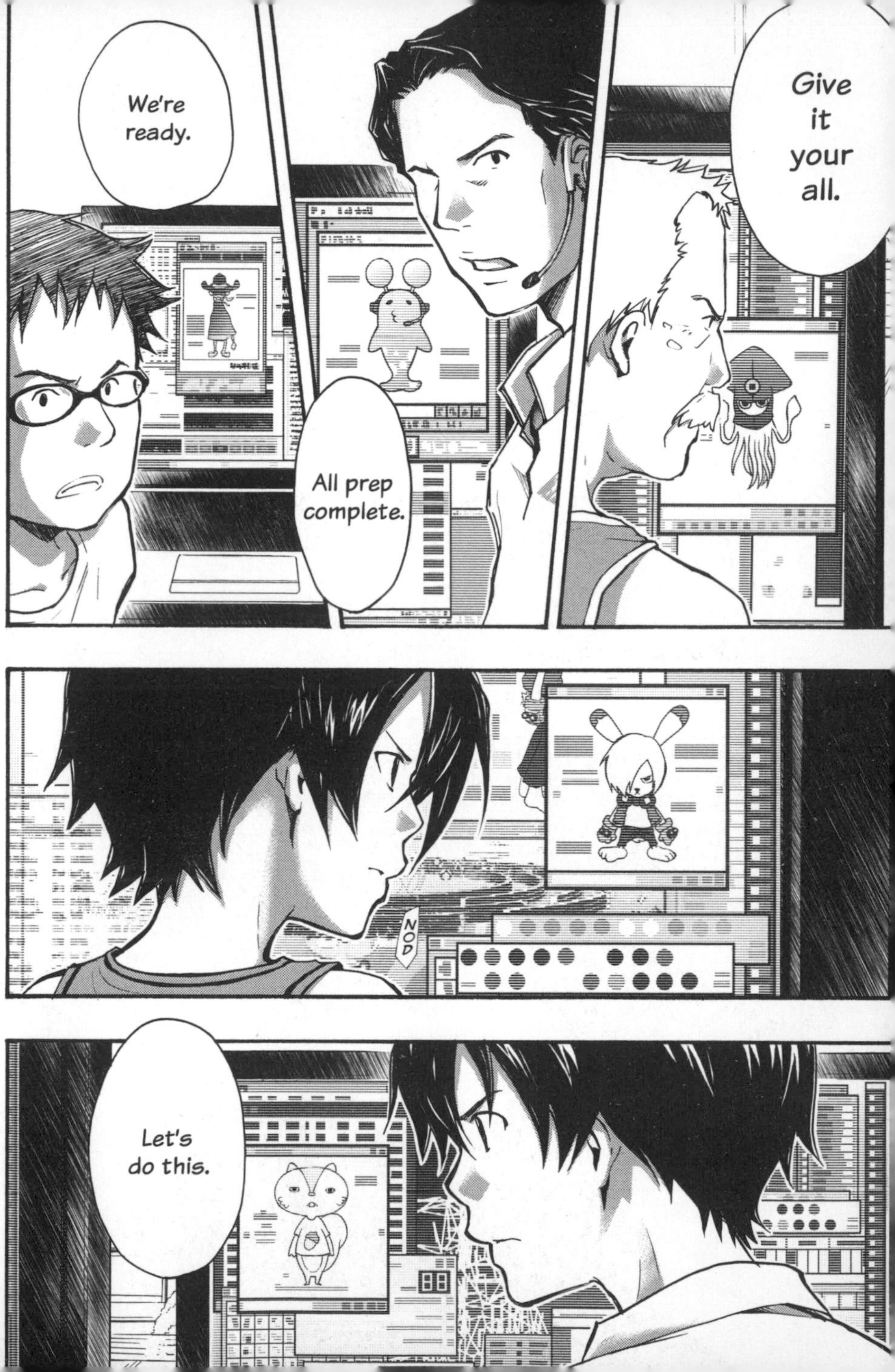
Give it your all.
All prep complete.
We're ready.
NOD
Let's do this.

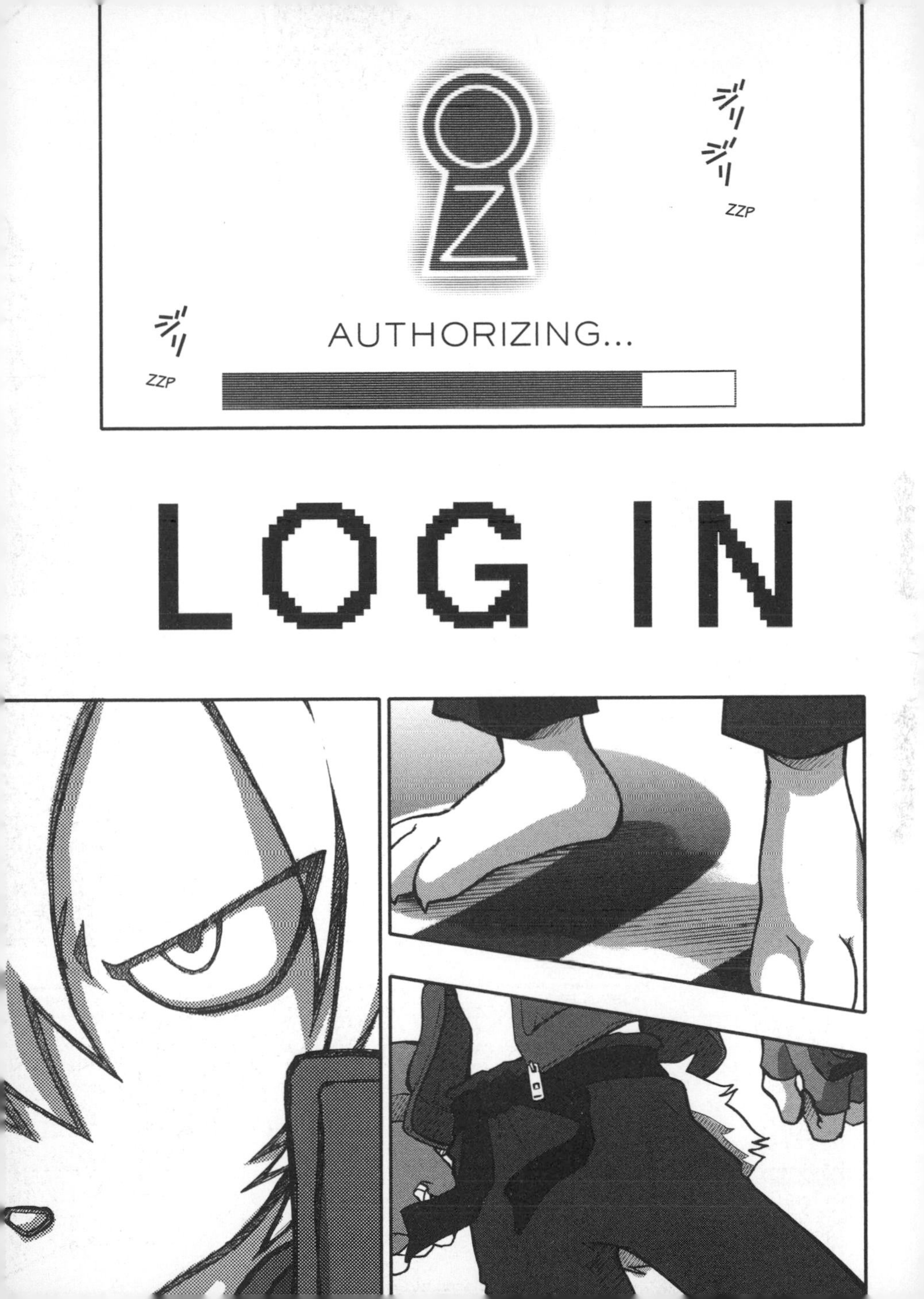
ジリ
ジリ
ZZP
AUTHORIZING...
ジリ
ZZP
LOG IN

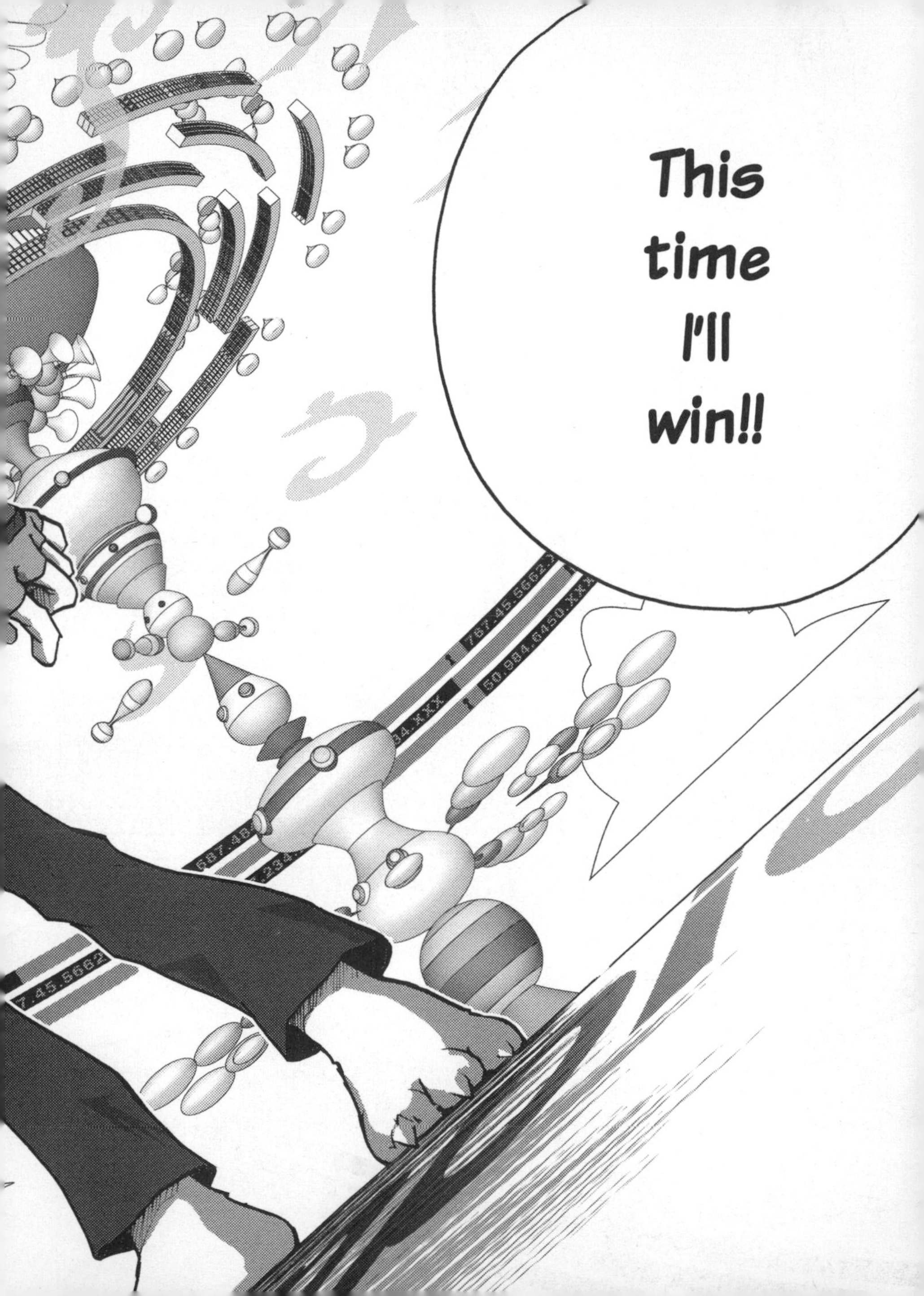
This time I'll win!!

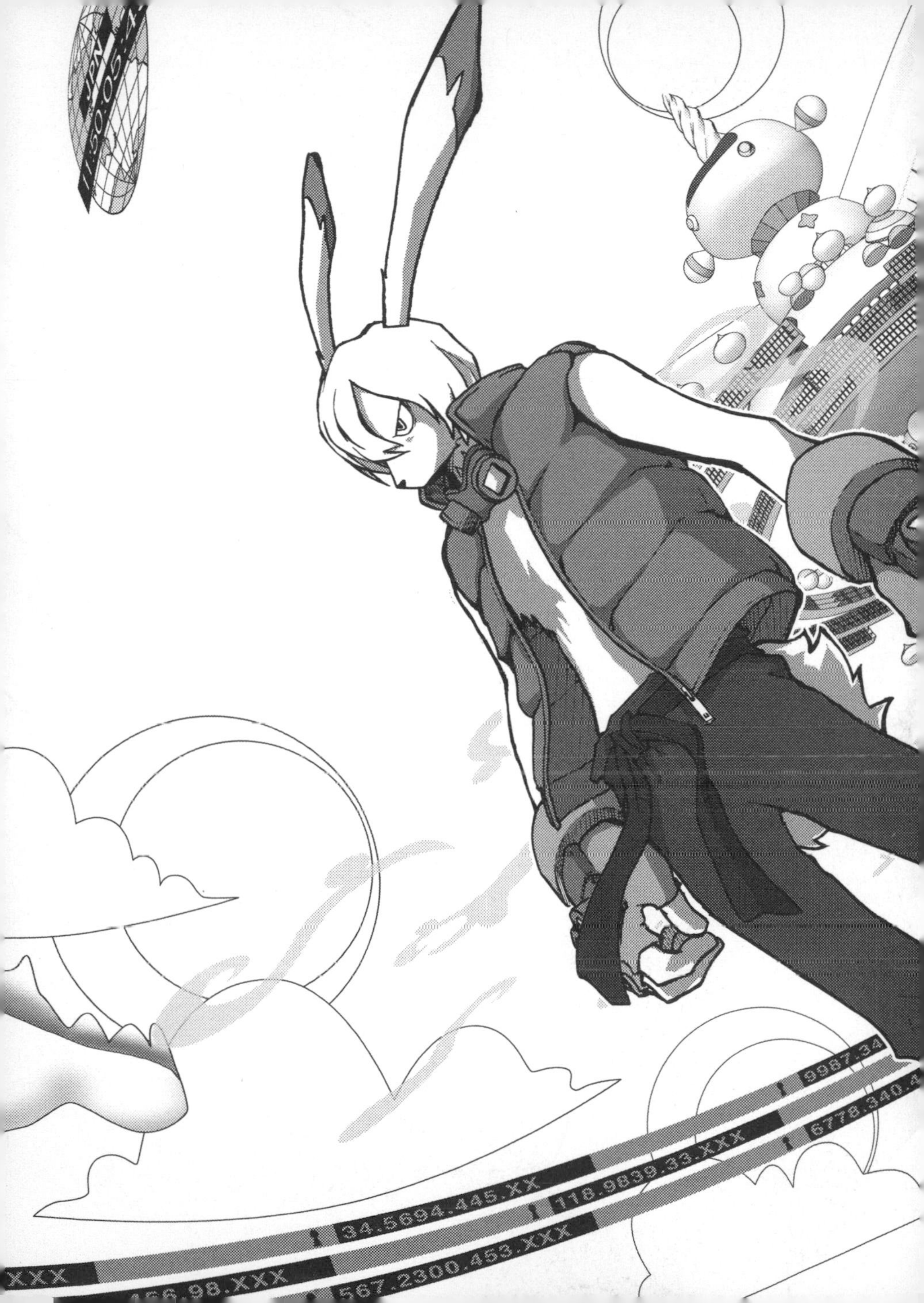
JPN
9987.34
118.9839.33.XXX
34.5694.445.XX
567.2300.453.XXX

Do not
disturb

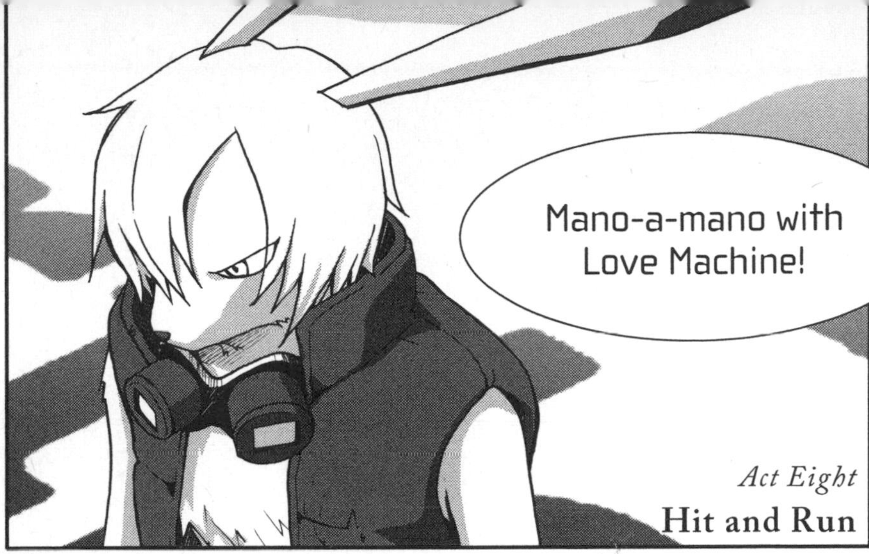
Mano-a-mano with Love Machine!
Act Eight
Hit and Run

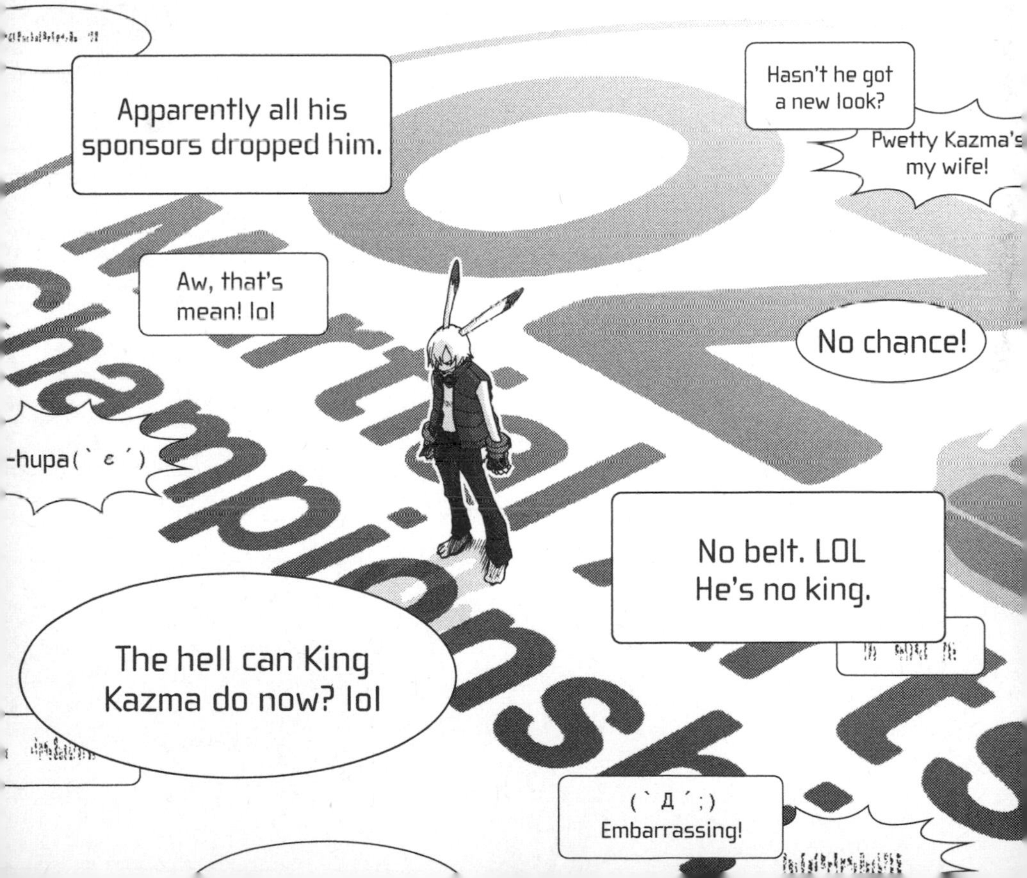
Hasn't he got a new look?
Pwetty Kazma's my wife!
Apparently all his sponsors dropped him.
No chance!
Aw, that's mean! lol
-hupa(`ε´)
No belt. LOL He's no king.
The hell can King Kazma do now? lol
(`Д´;) Embarrassing!

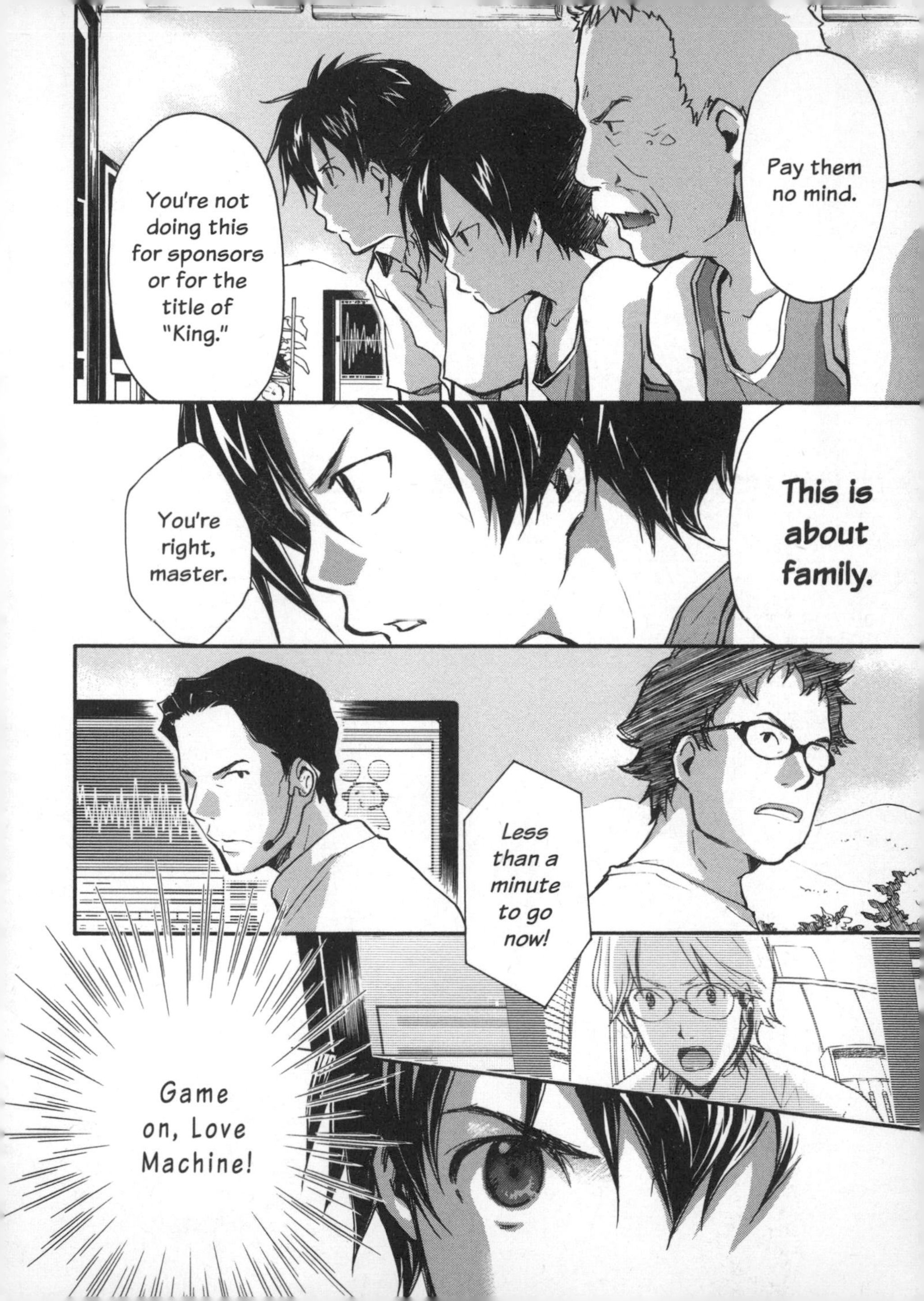
Pay them no mind.
You're not doing this for sponsors or for the title of "King."
This is about family.
You're right, master.
Less than a minute to go now!
Game on, Love Machine!

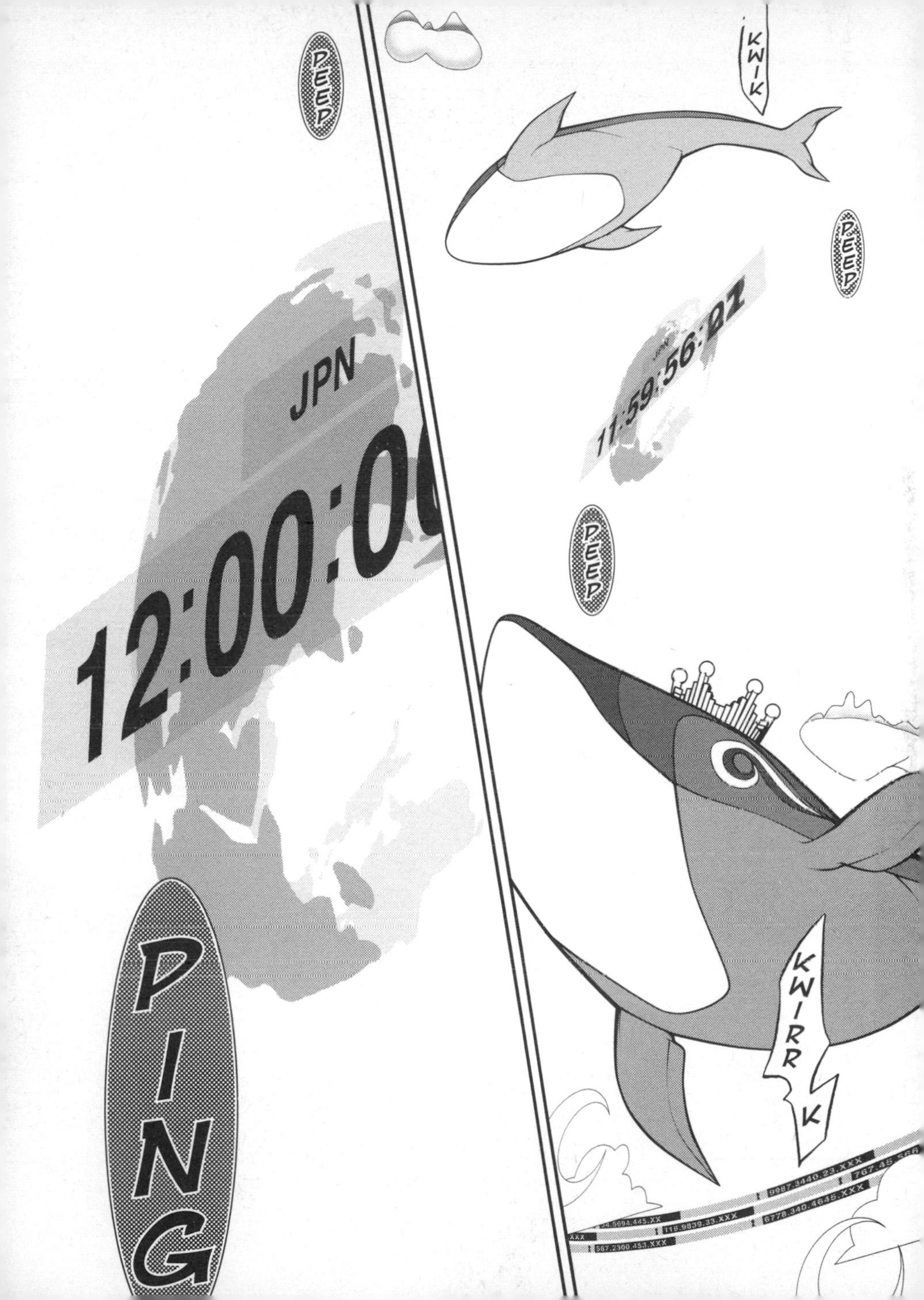
KWIK
PEEP
JPN
11:59:56
PEEP
KWIRR K
JPN
12:00:0
PEEP
PING

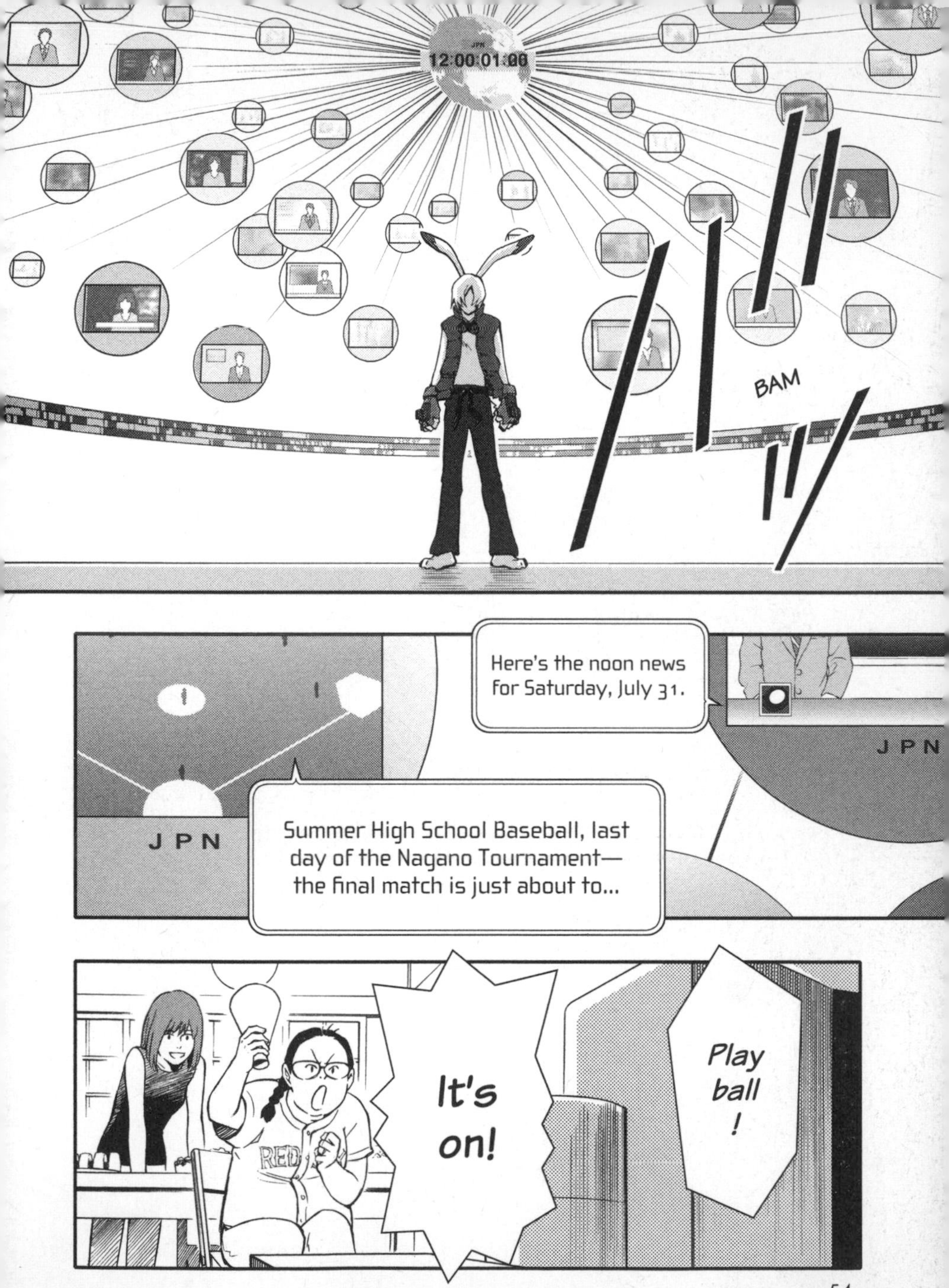
JPN
12:00:01:00
BAM
Here's the noon news for Saturday, July 31.
JPN
JPN
Summer High School Baseball, last day of the Nagano Tournament—the final match is just about to...
Play ball!
It's on!
RED

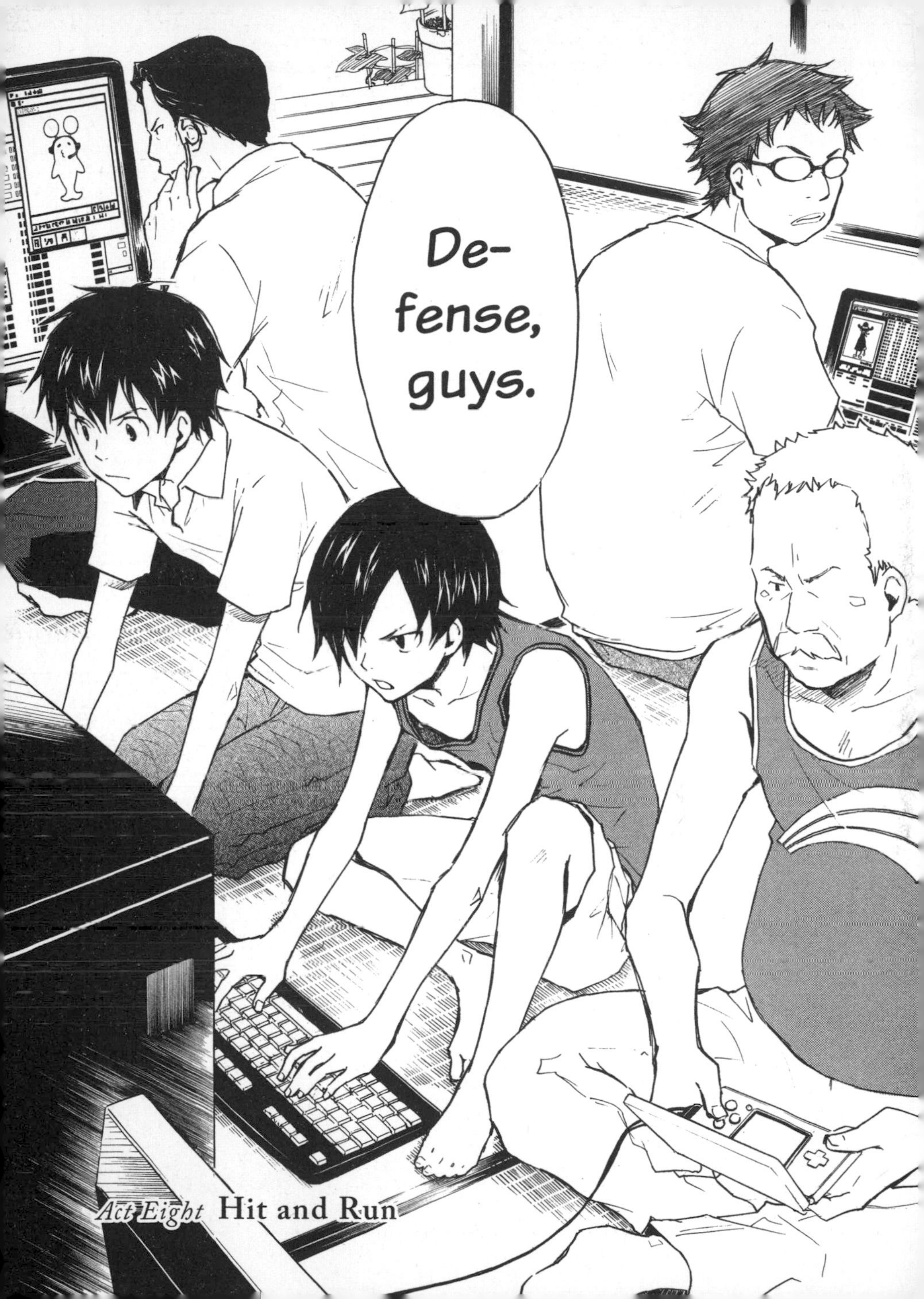
De-fense, guys.
Act Eight Hit and Run

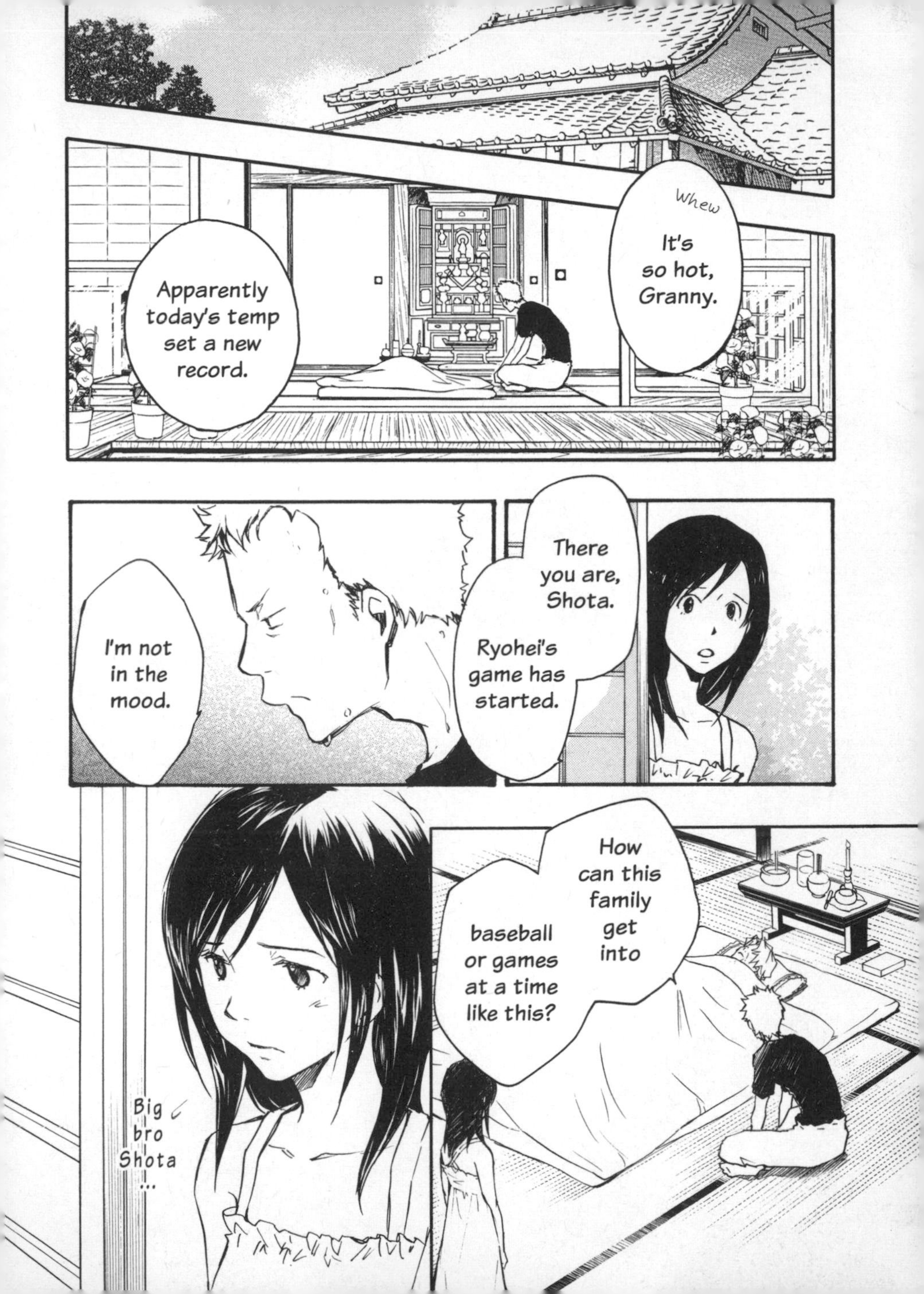
Whew
It's so hot, Granny.
Apparently today's temp set a new record.
There you are, Shota.
Ryohei's game has started.
I'm not in the mood.
How can this family get into baseball or games at a time like this?
Big bro Shota...

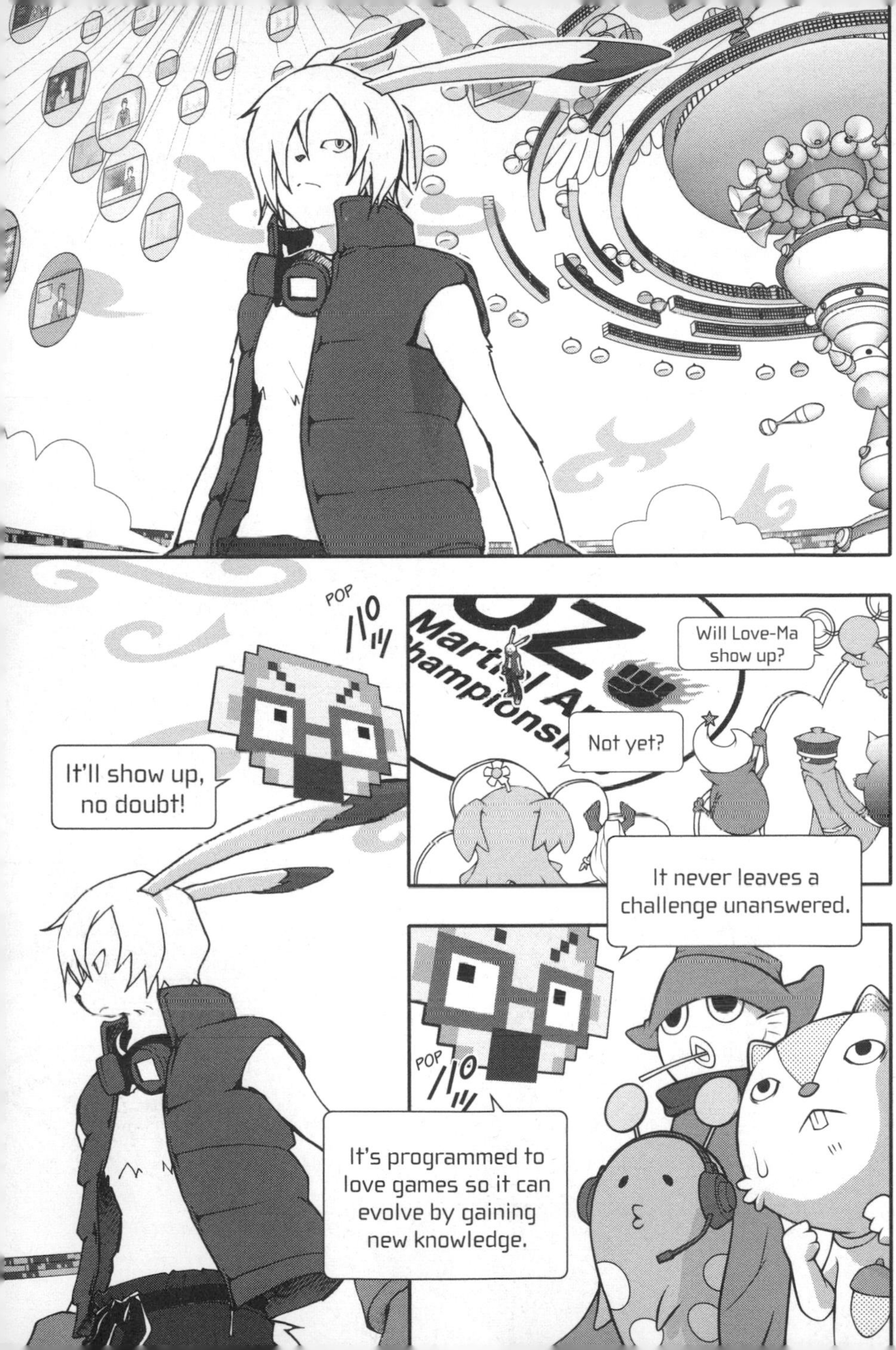
Will Love-Ma show up?
Not yet?
It never leaves a challenge unanswered.
POP
It's programmed to love games so it can evolve by gaining new knowledge.
POP
It'll show up, no doubt!

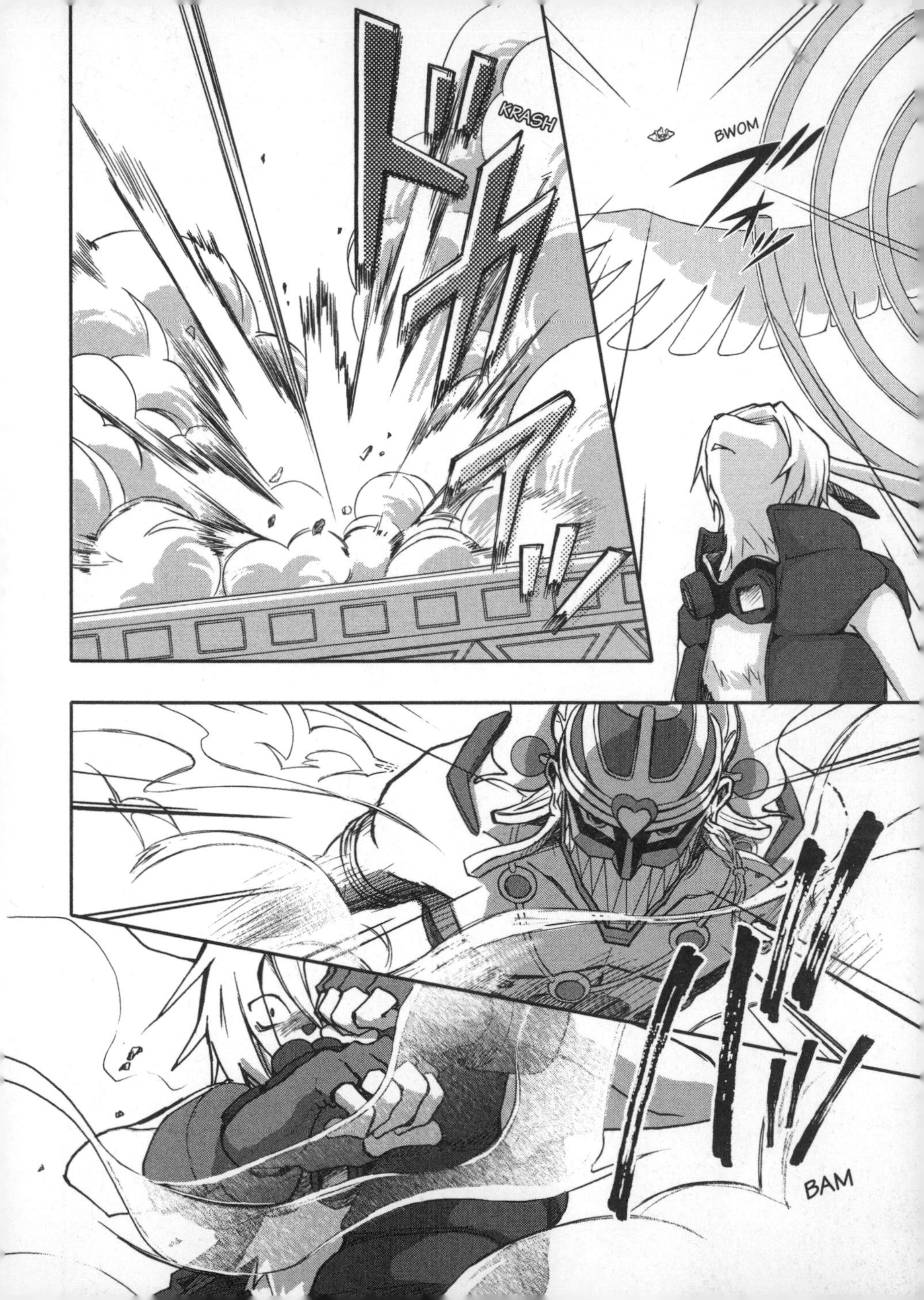
BWOM
KRASH
BAM

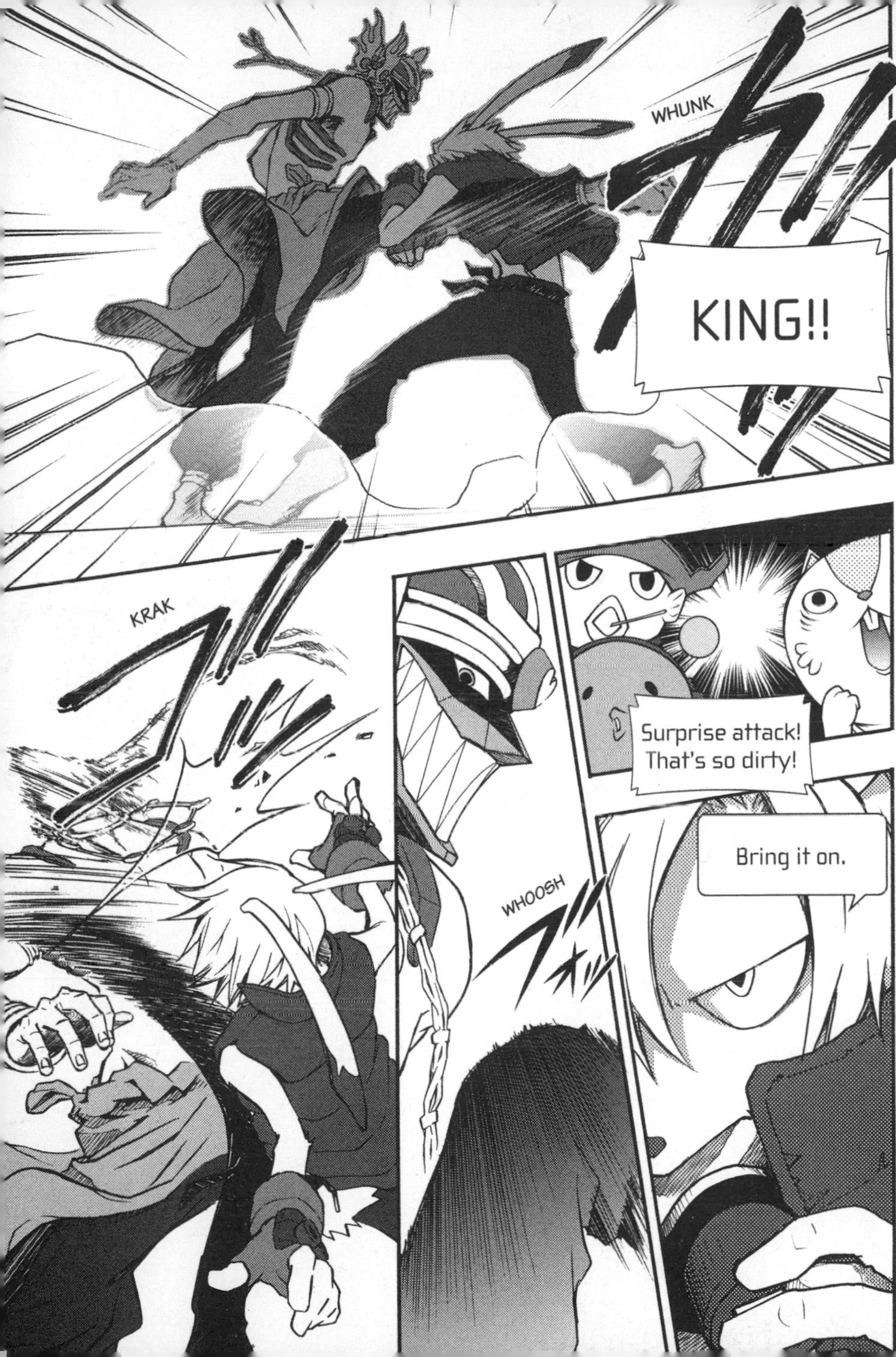
WHUNK
KING!!
Surprise attack! That's so dirty!
Bring it on.
WHOOSH
KRAK

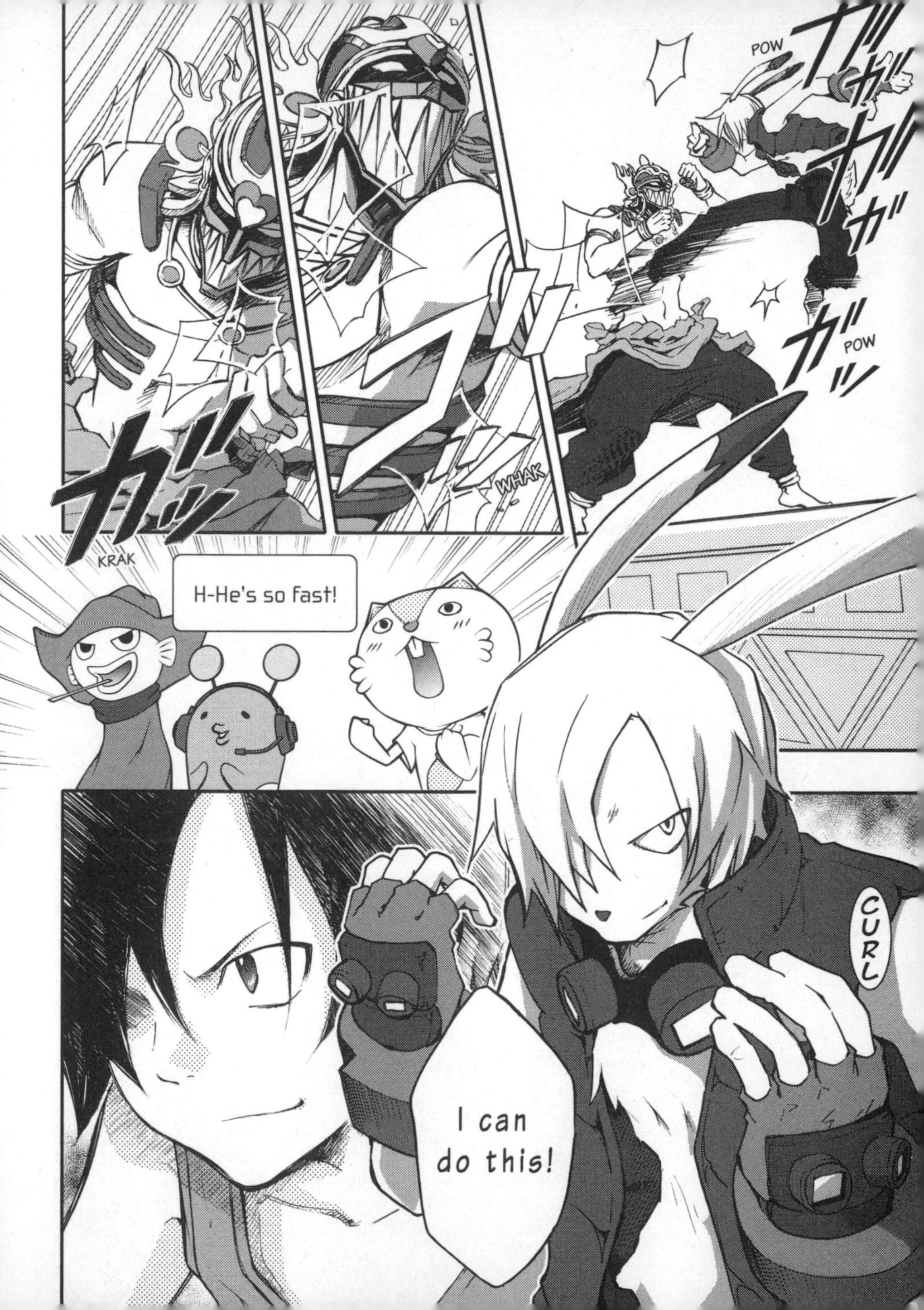
POW
POW
WHAK
KRAK
H-He's so fast!
CURL
I can do this!

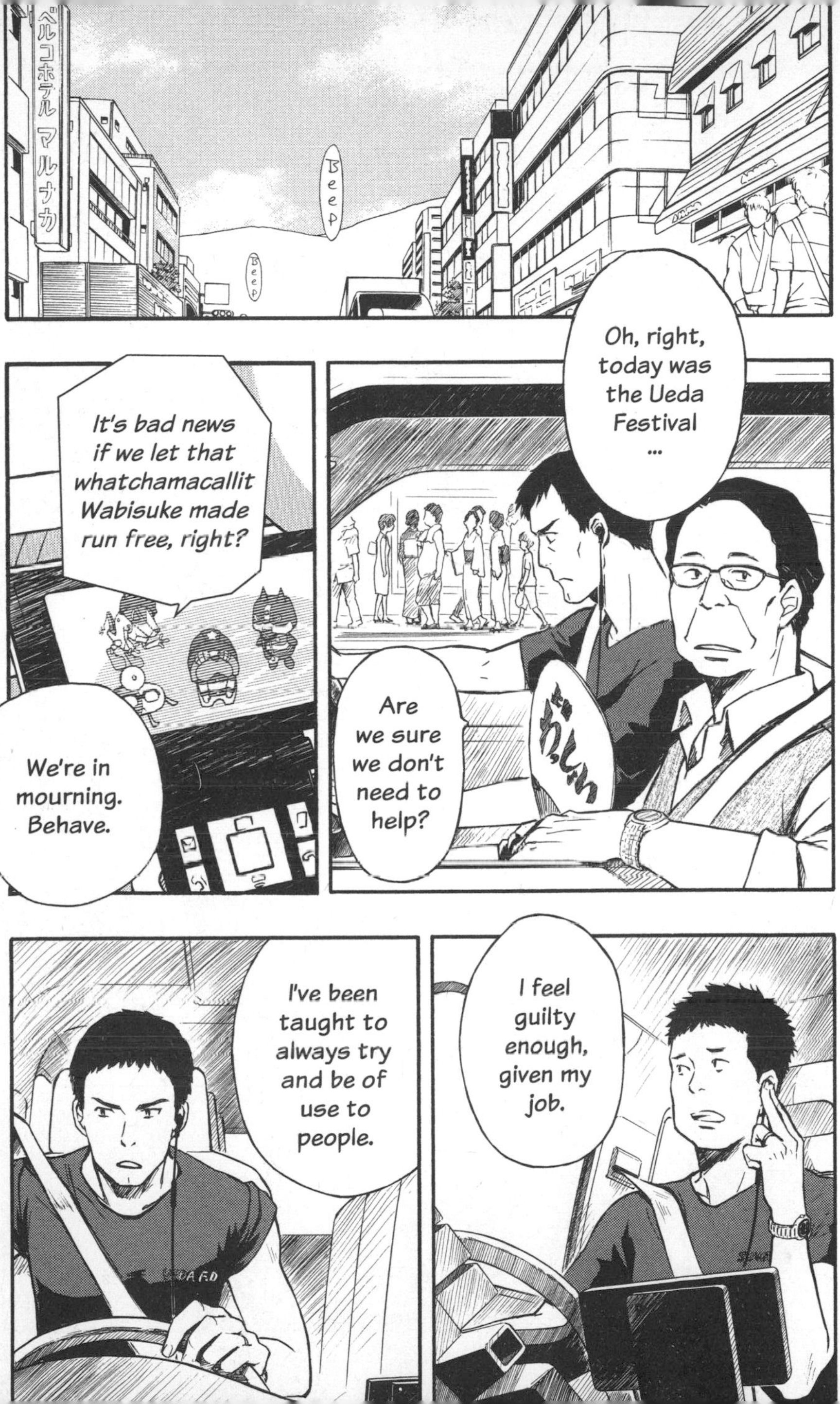
Beep
Beep
ベルコホテル マルナカ
Oh, right, today was the Ueda Festival ...
Are we sure we don't need to help?
It's bad news if we let that whatchamacallit Wabisuke made run free, right?
We're in mourning. Behave.
I feel guilty enough, given my job.
I've been taught to always try and be of use to people.

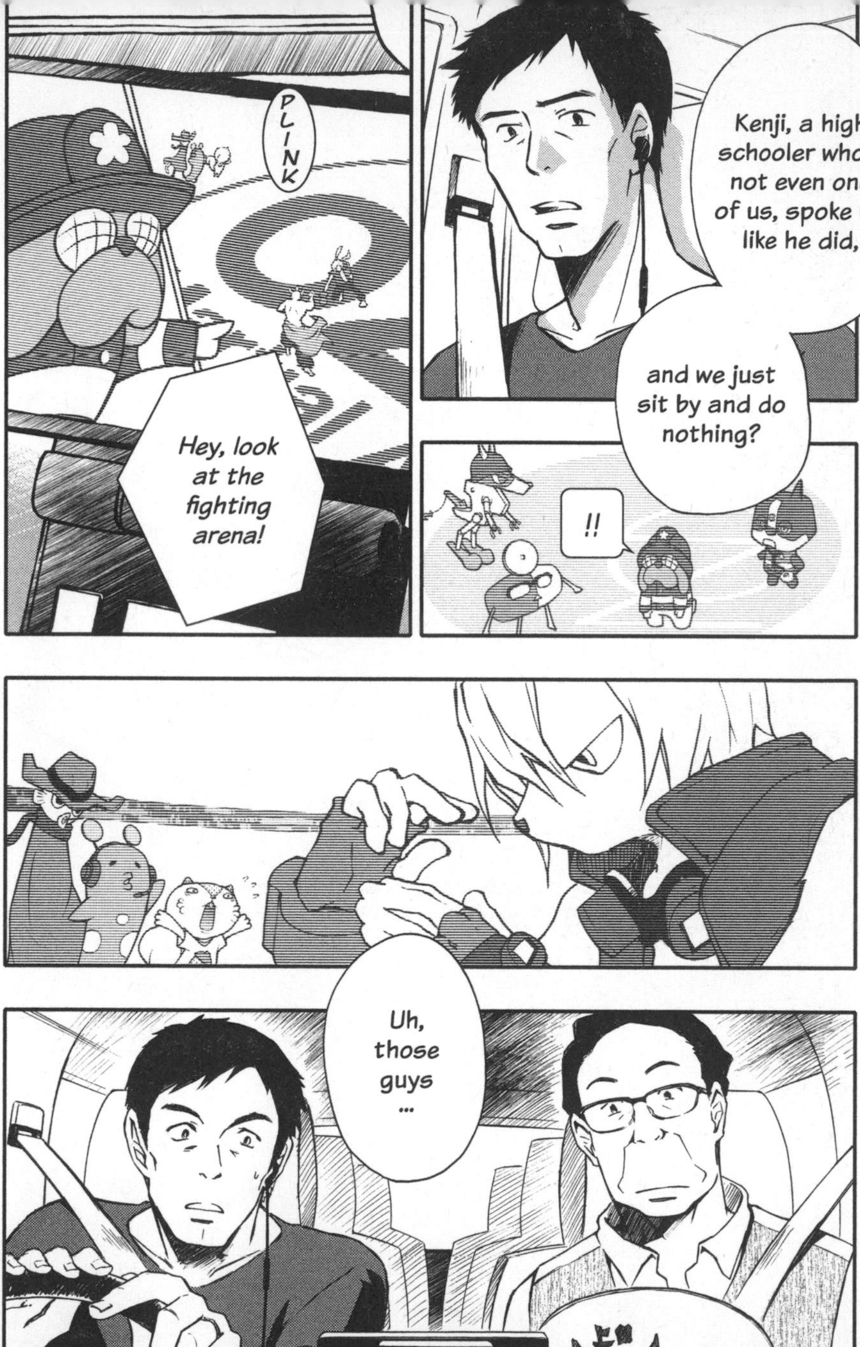
Kenji, a high schooler who's not even one of us, spoke up like he did,
and we just sit by and do nothing?
!!
PLINK
Hey, look at the fighting arena!
Uh, those guys ...

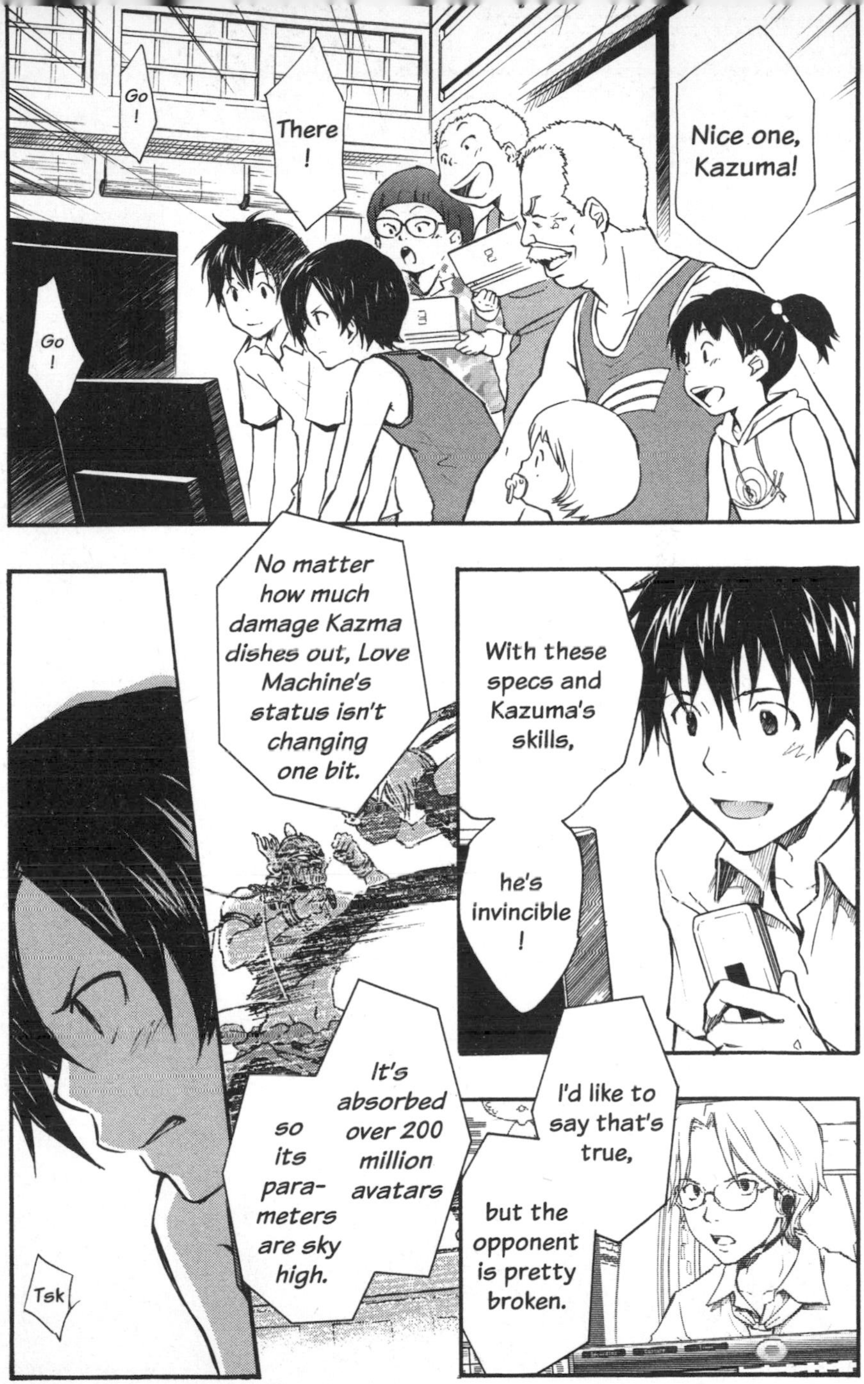
Nice one, Kazuma!
There!
Go!
Go!
With these specs and Kazuma's skills,
he's invincible!
I'd like to say that's true,
but the opponent is pretty broken.
No matter how much damage Kazma dishes out, Love Machine's status isn't changing one bit.
It's absorbed over 200 million avatars
so its parameters are sky high.
Tsk

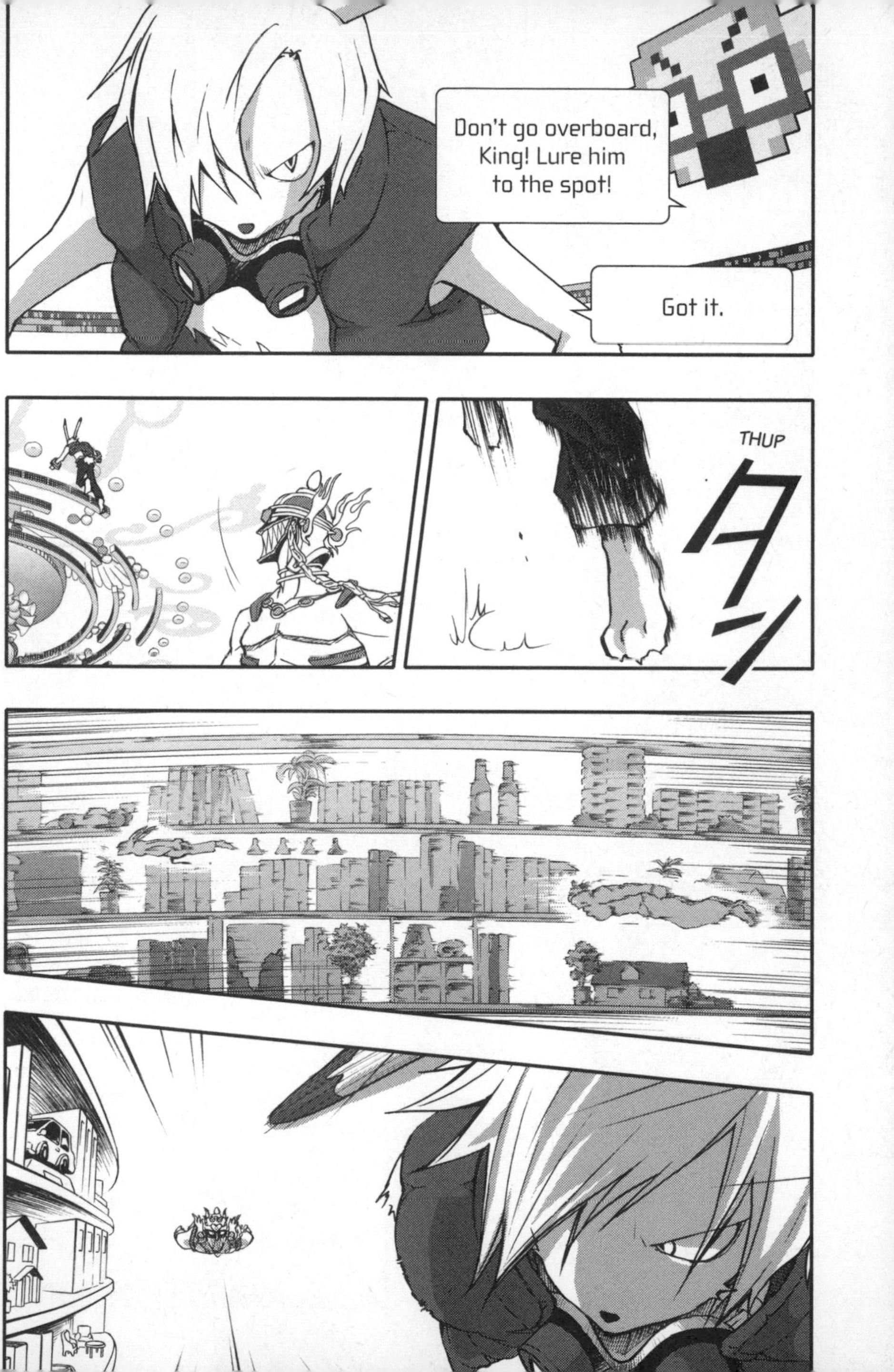
Don't go overboard, King! Lure him to the spot!
Got it.
THUP
タン

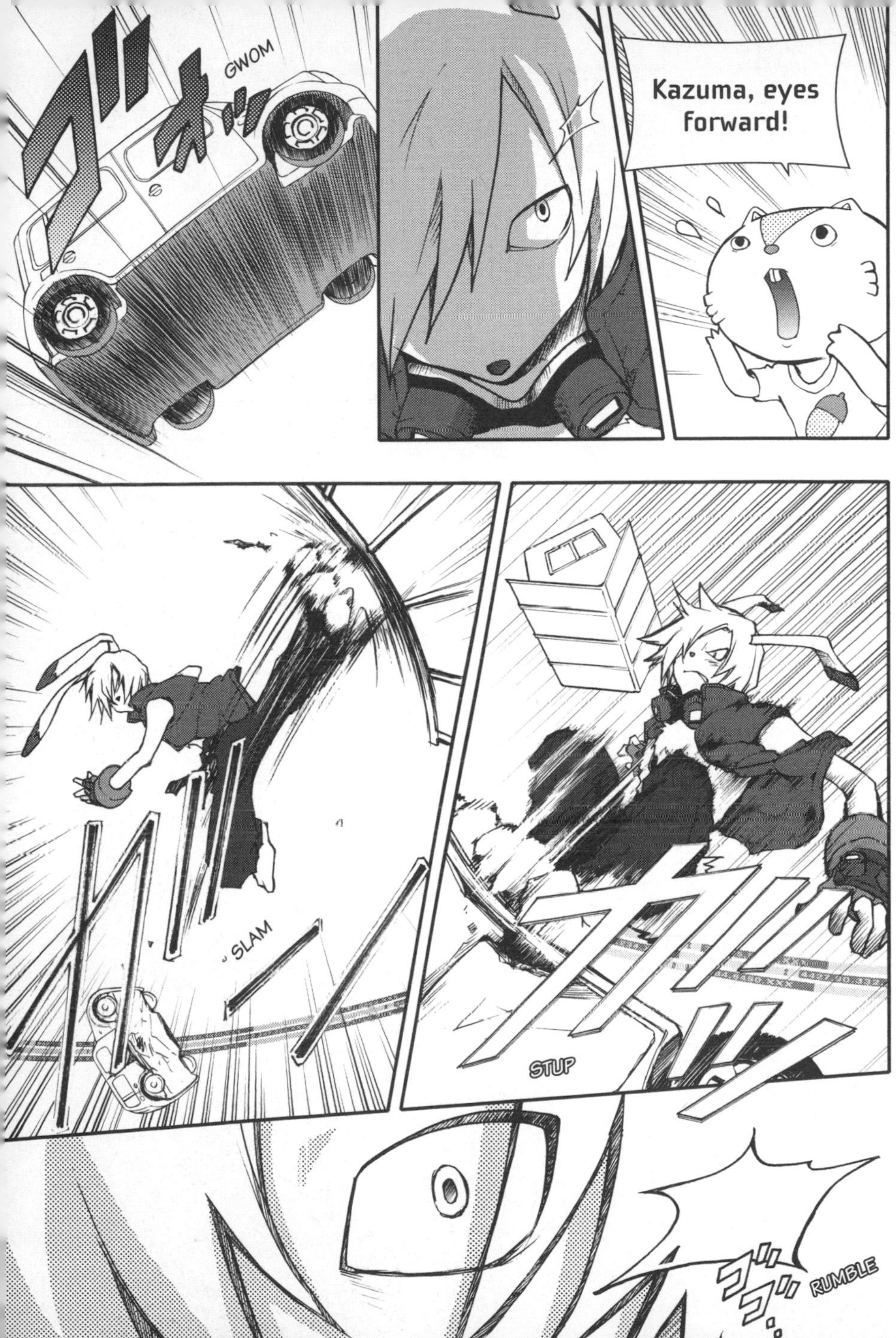
Kazuma, eyes forward!
GWOM
STUP
SLAM
RUMBLE

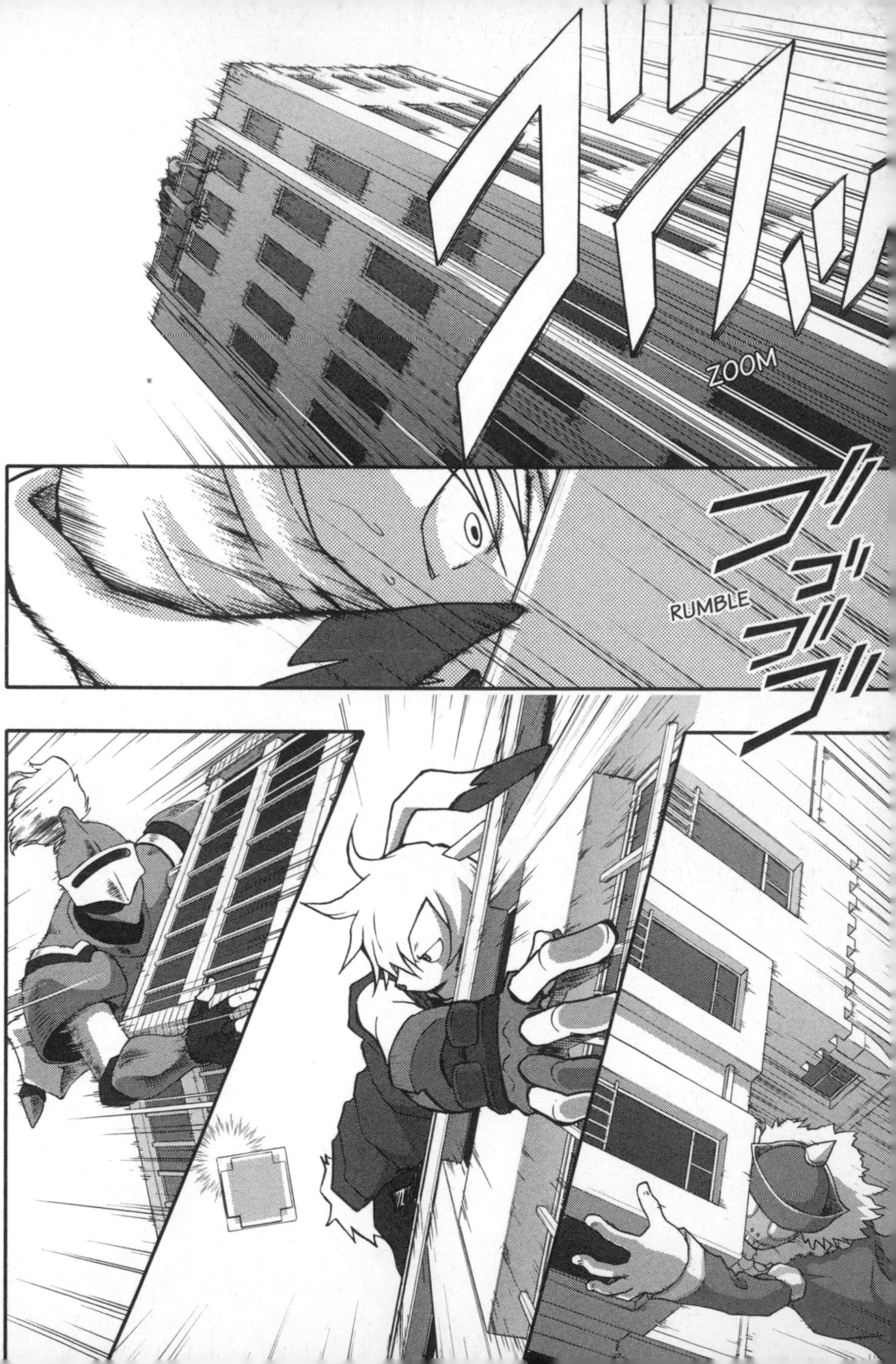
ZOOM
ゴゴゴゴ
RUMBLE

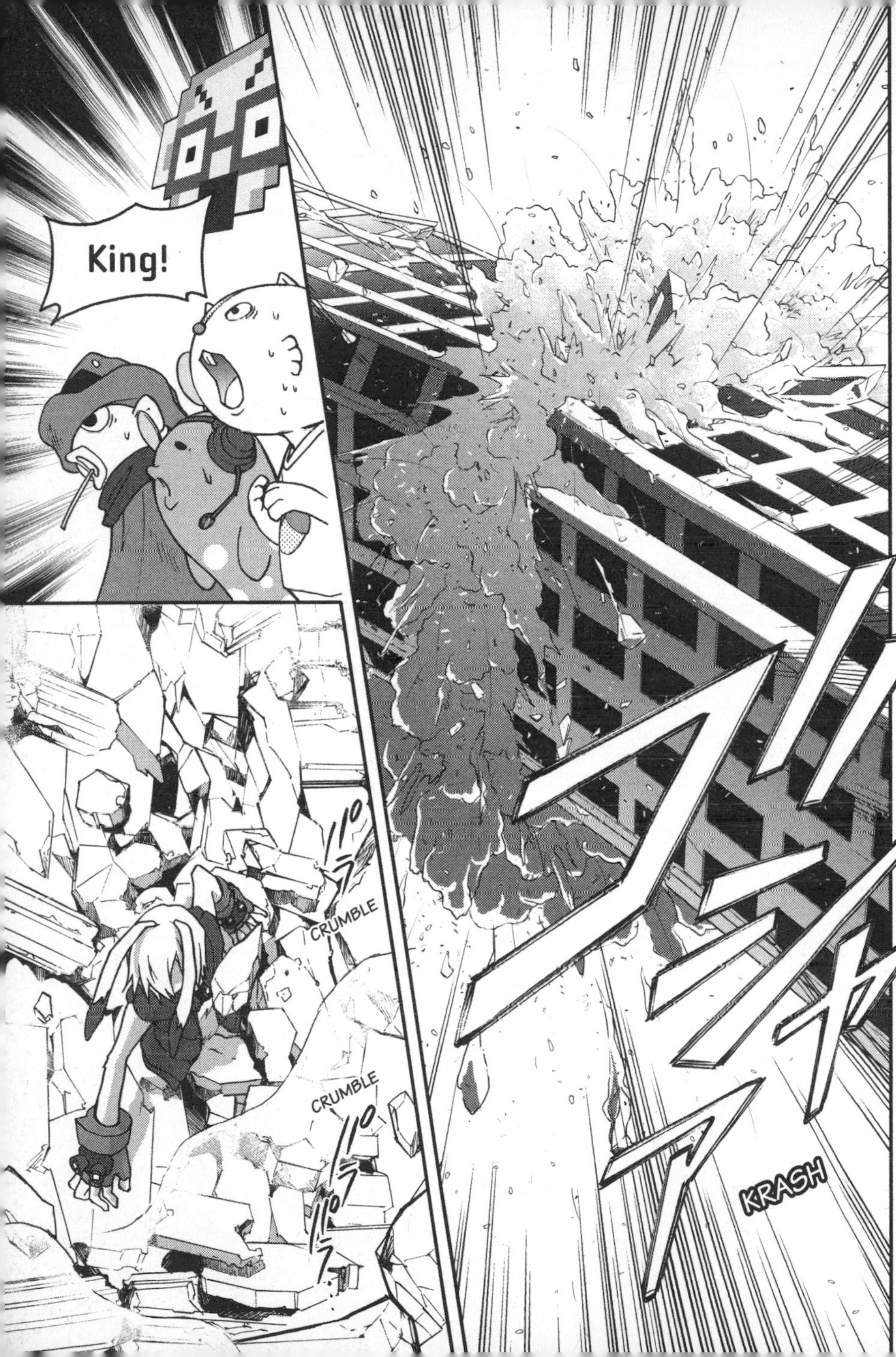
KRASH
King!
CRUMBLE
CRUMBLE

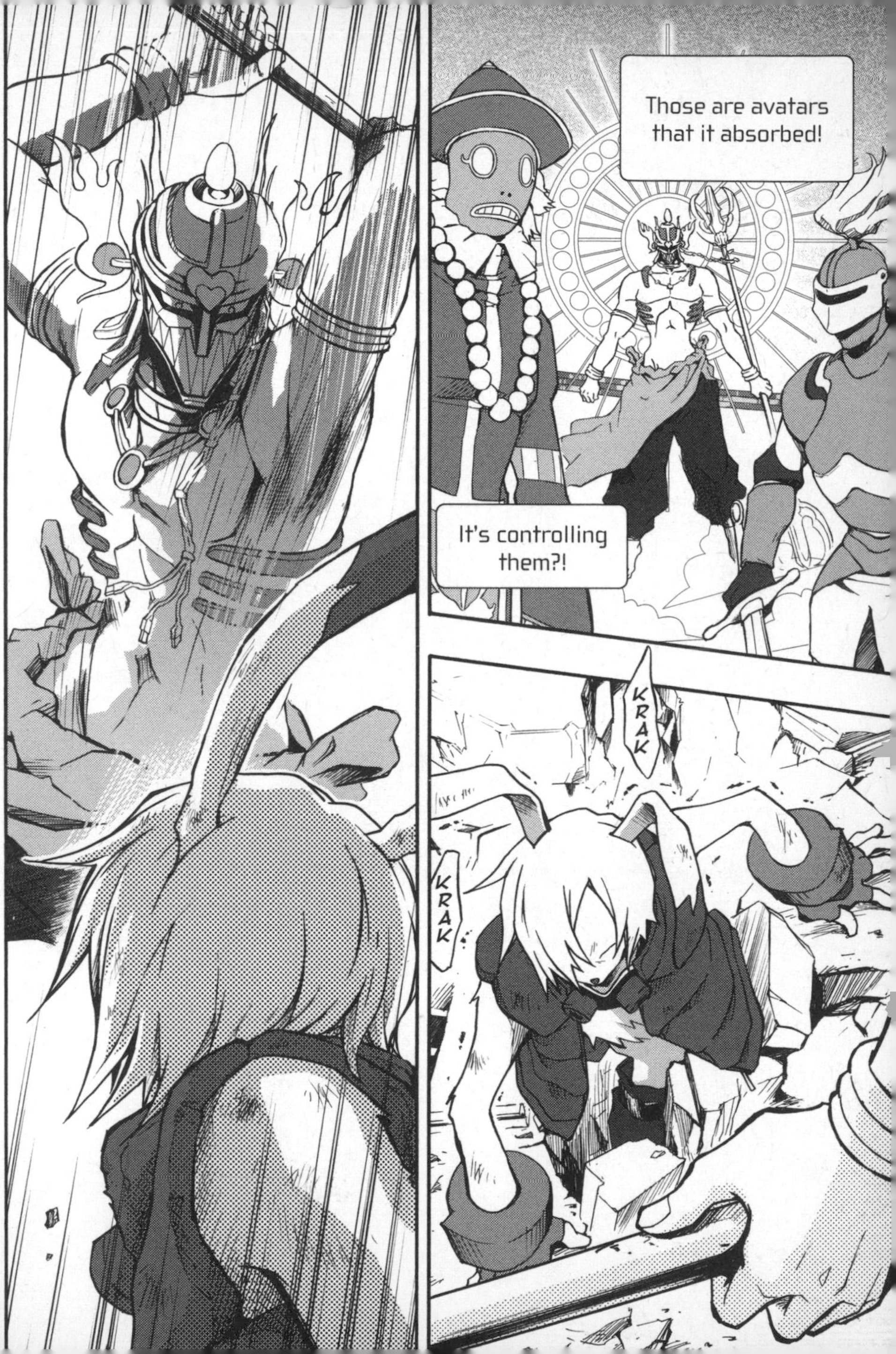
Those are avatars that it absorbed!
It's controlling them?!
KRAK
KRAK

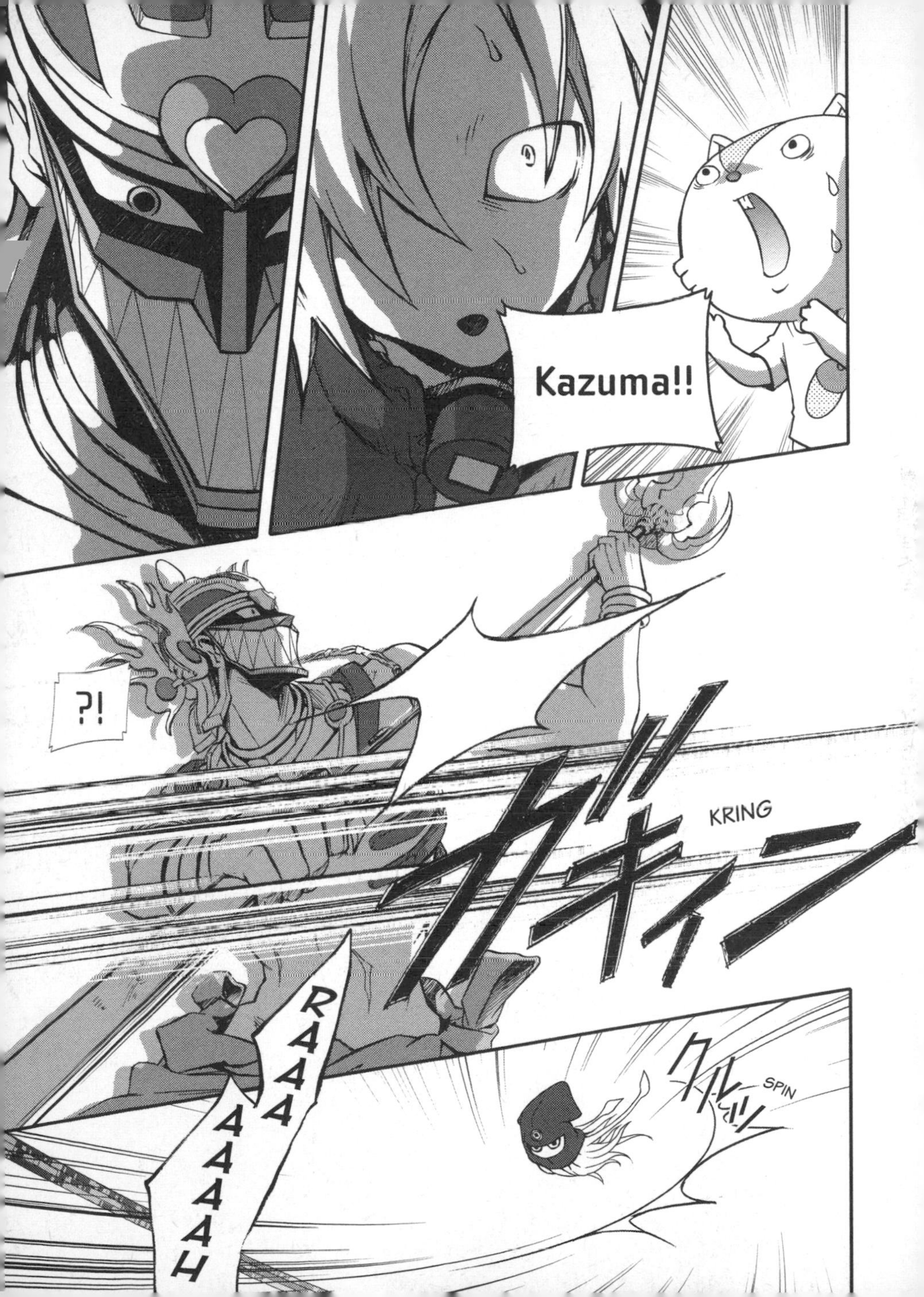
Kazuma!!
?!
KRING
SPIN
RAAAAAAAH

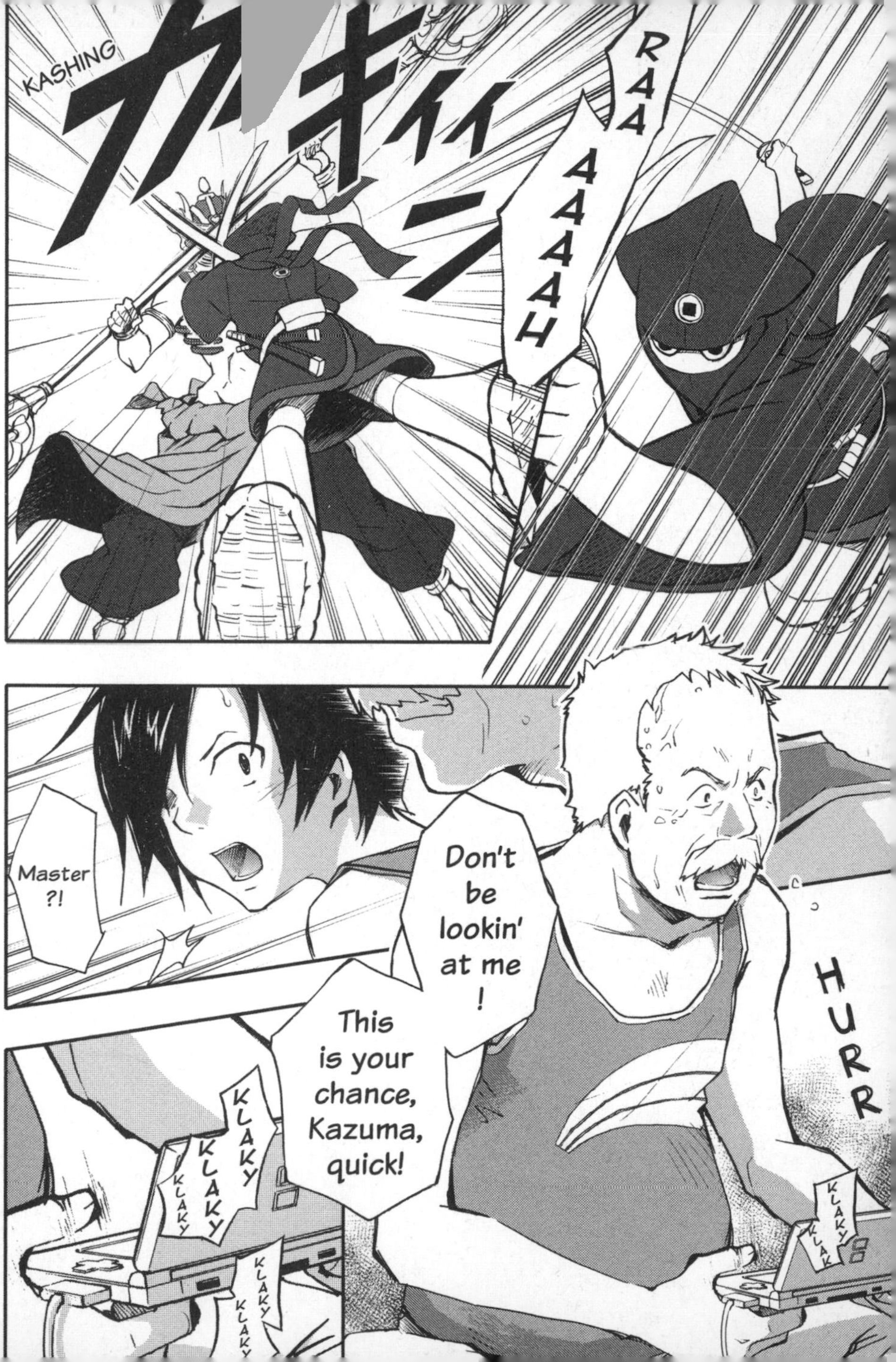
RAA
AAAAH
KASHING
Don't be lookin' at me!
This is your chance, Kazuma, quick!
HURR
KLAKY KLAKY KLAK
Master?!
KLAKY KLAKY KLAKY
KLAKY KLAKY KLAKY

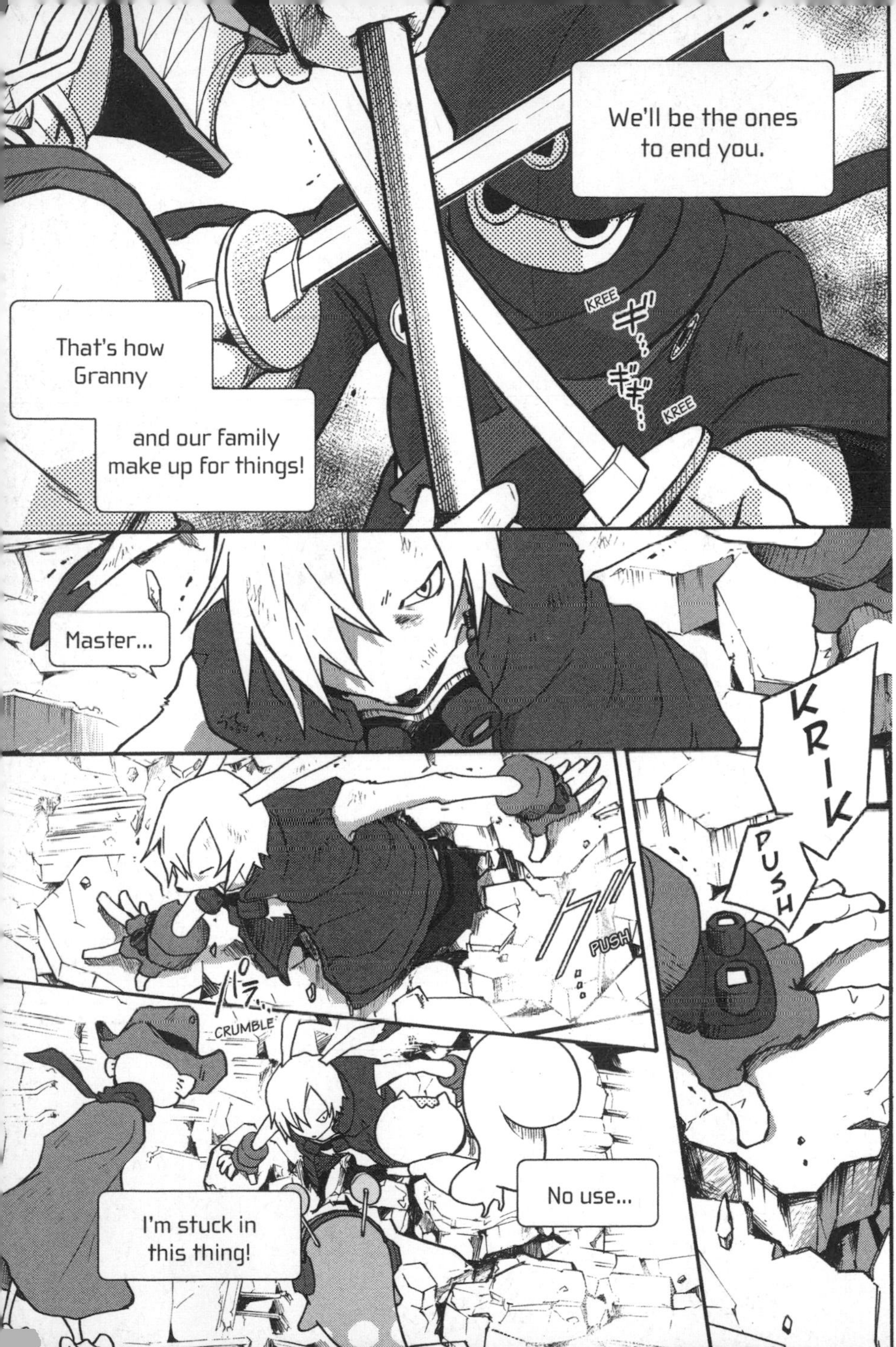

We'll be the ones to end you.
KREE
ギ…
ギギ…
KREE
That's how Granny
and our family make up for things!
Master...
KRIK
PUSH
PUSH
CRUMBLE
No use...
I'm stuck in this thing!

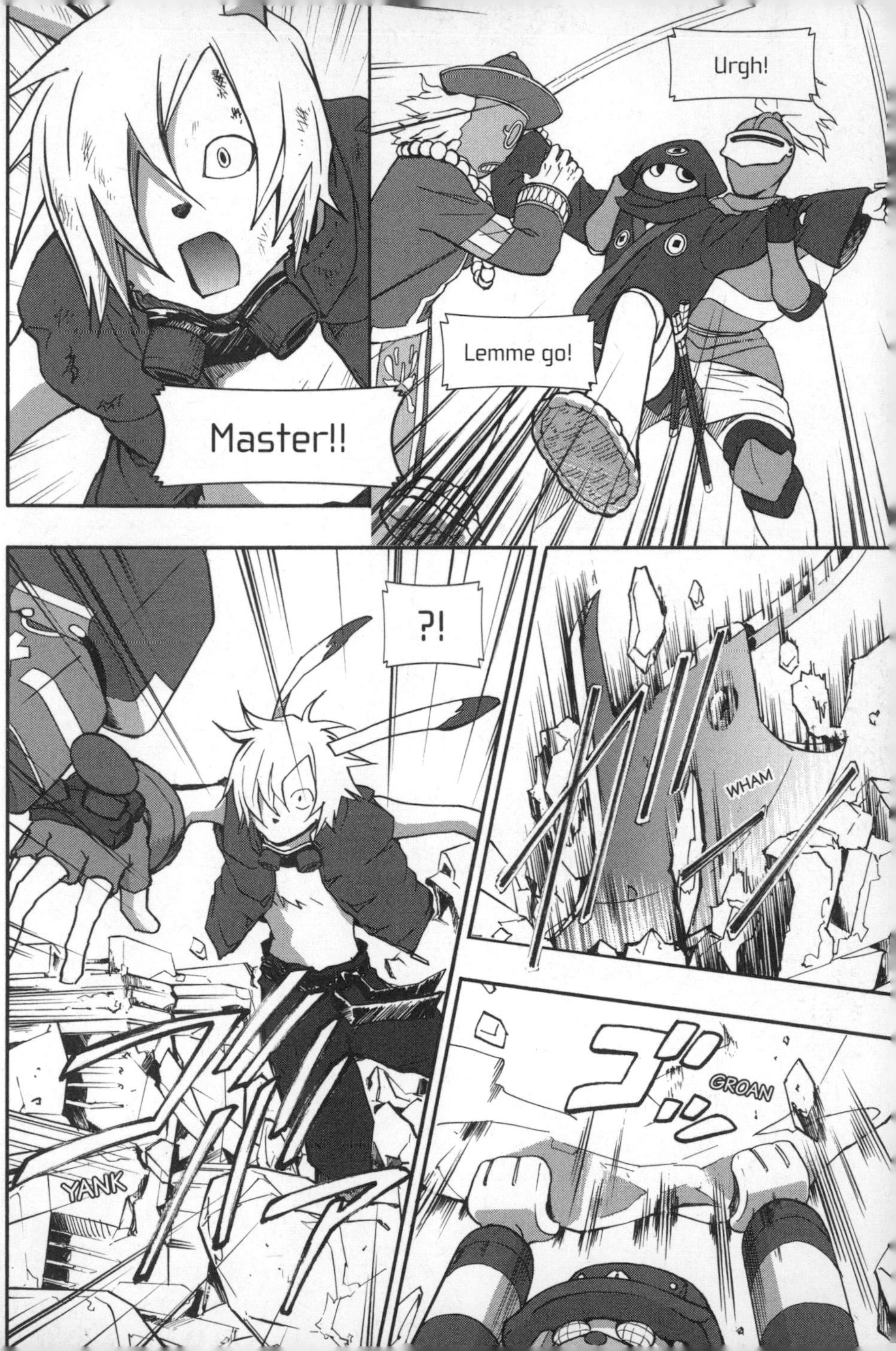
Urgh!
Lemme go!
Master!!
WHAM
GROAN
?!
YANK

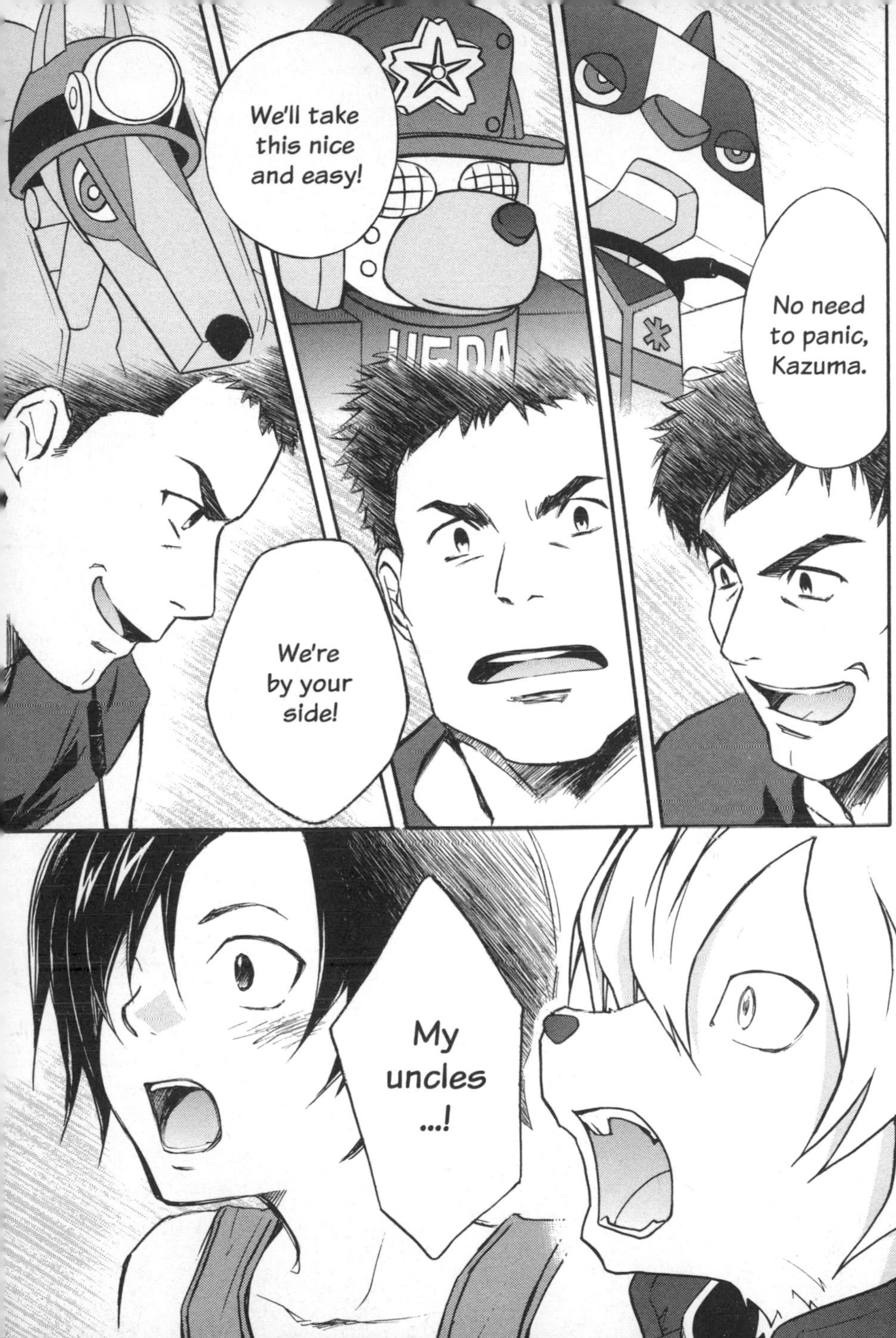
No need to panic, Kazuma.
We'll take this nice and easy!
We're by your side!
My uncles ...!

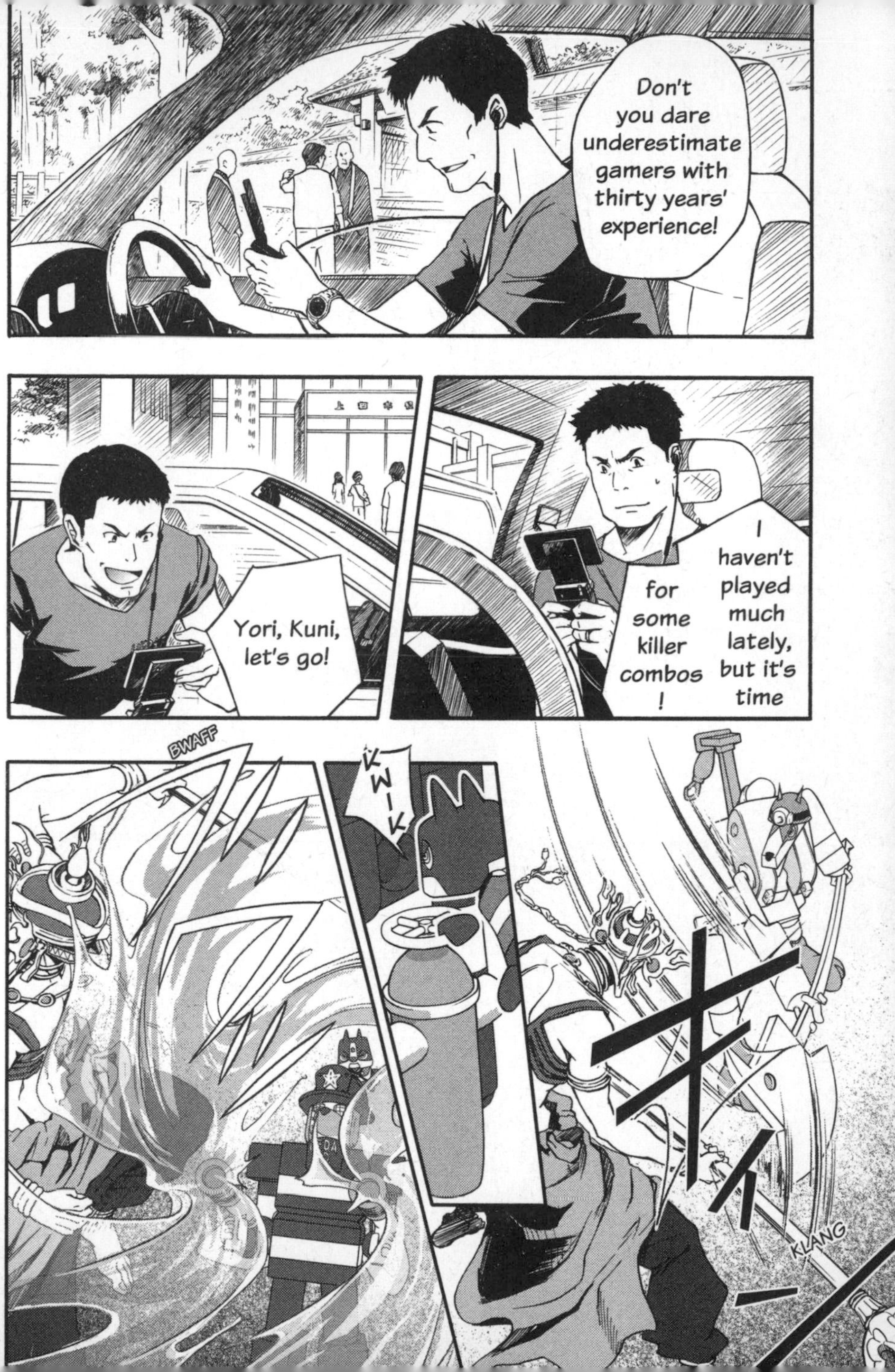
Don't you dare underestimate gamers with thirty years' experience!
I haven't played much lately, but it's time
for some killer combos!
Yori, Kuni, let's go!
KLANG
KWIK
BWAFF

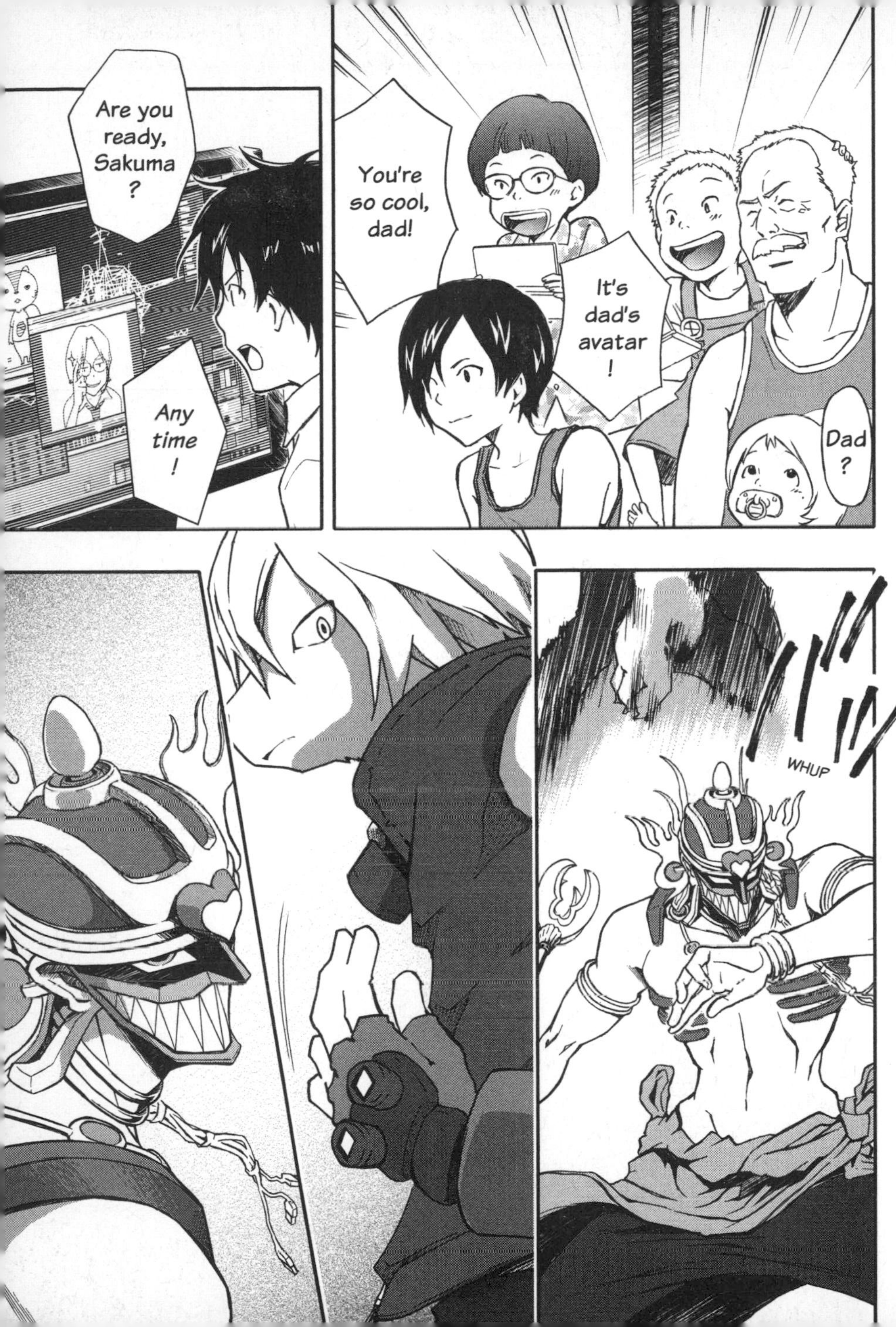
You're so cool, dad!
It's dad's avatar!
Dad?
Are you ready, Sakuma?
Any time!
WHUP

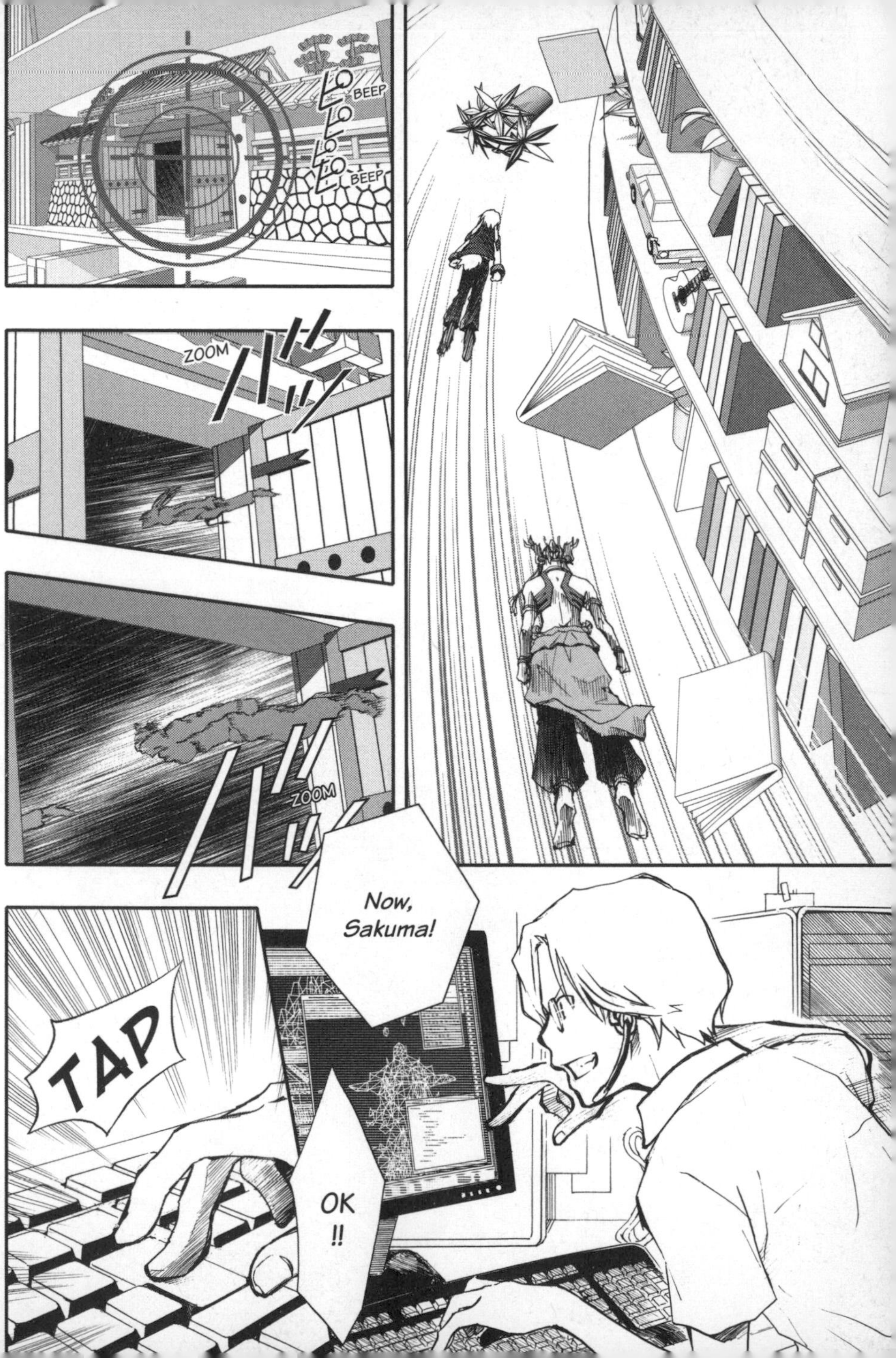
BEEP
BEEP
ZOOM
ZOOM
Now, Sakuma!
TAP
OK !!

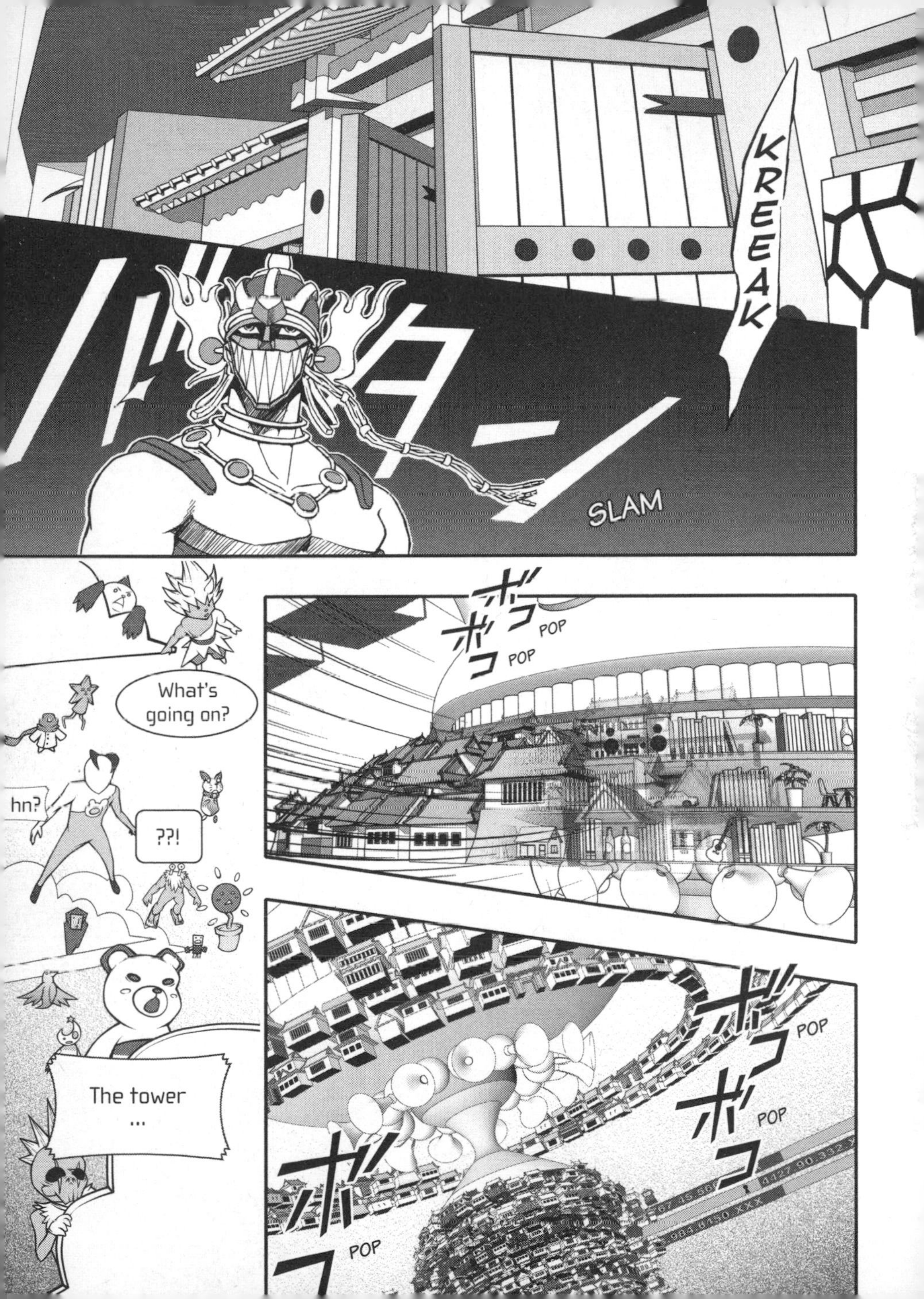
KREEAK
バターン
SLAM
ボコ ボコ
POP POP
ボコ ボコ
POP POP
ボコ
POP
What's going on?
hn?
??!
The tower ...

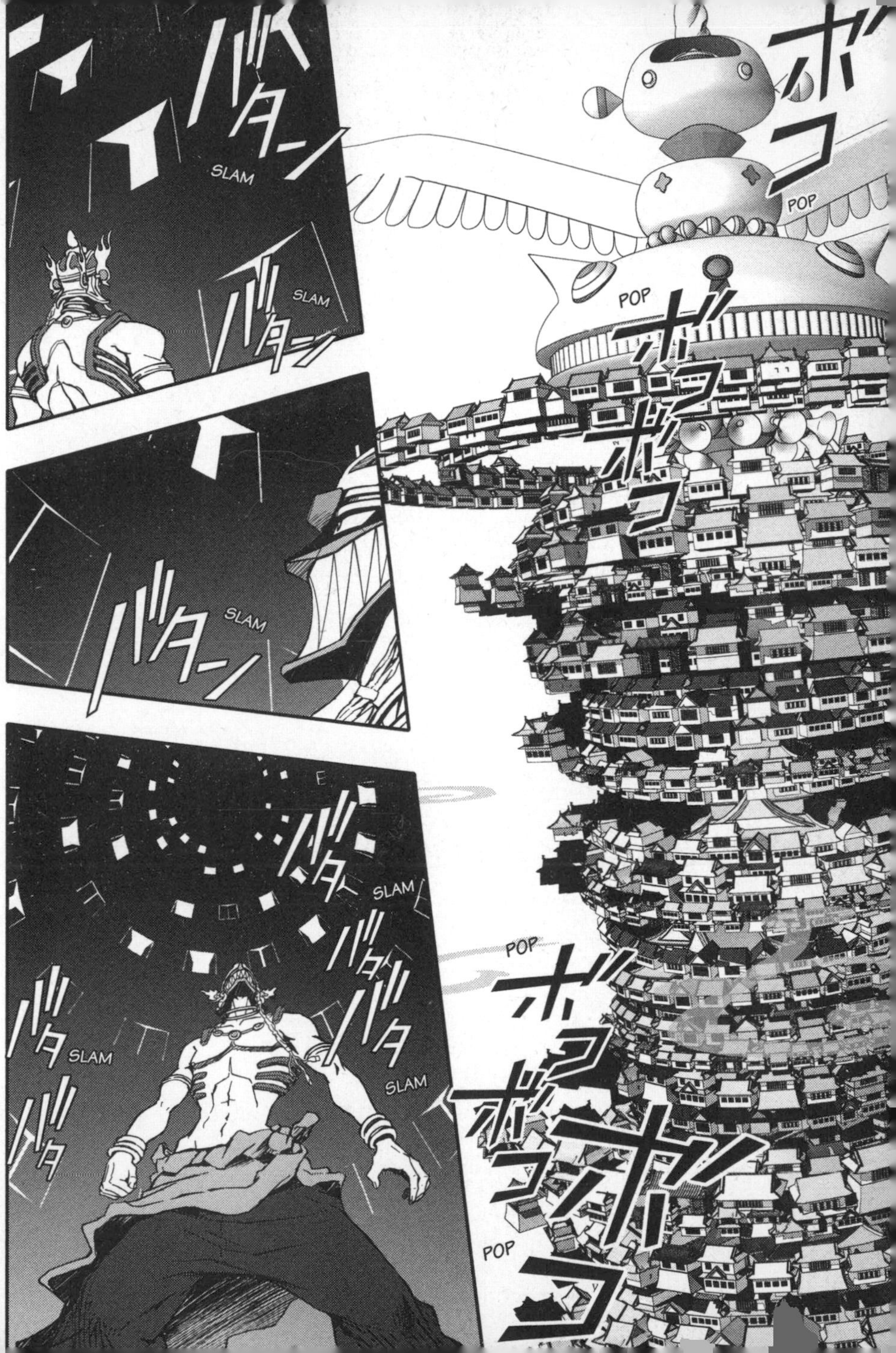

POP
POP
POP
POP
SLAM
SLAM
SLAM
SLAM
SLAM
SLAM

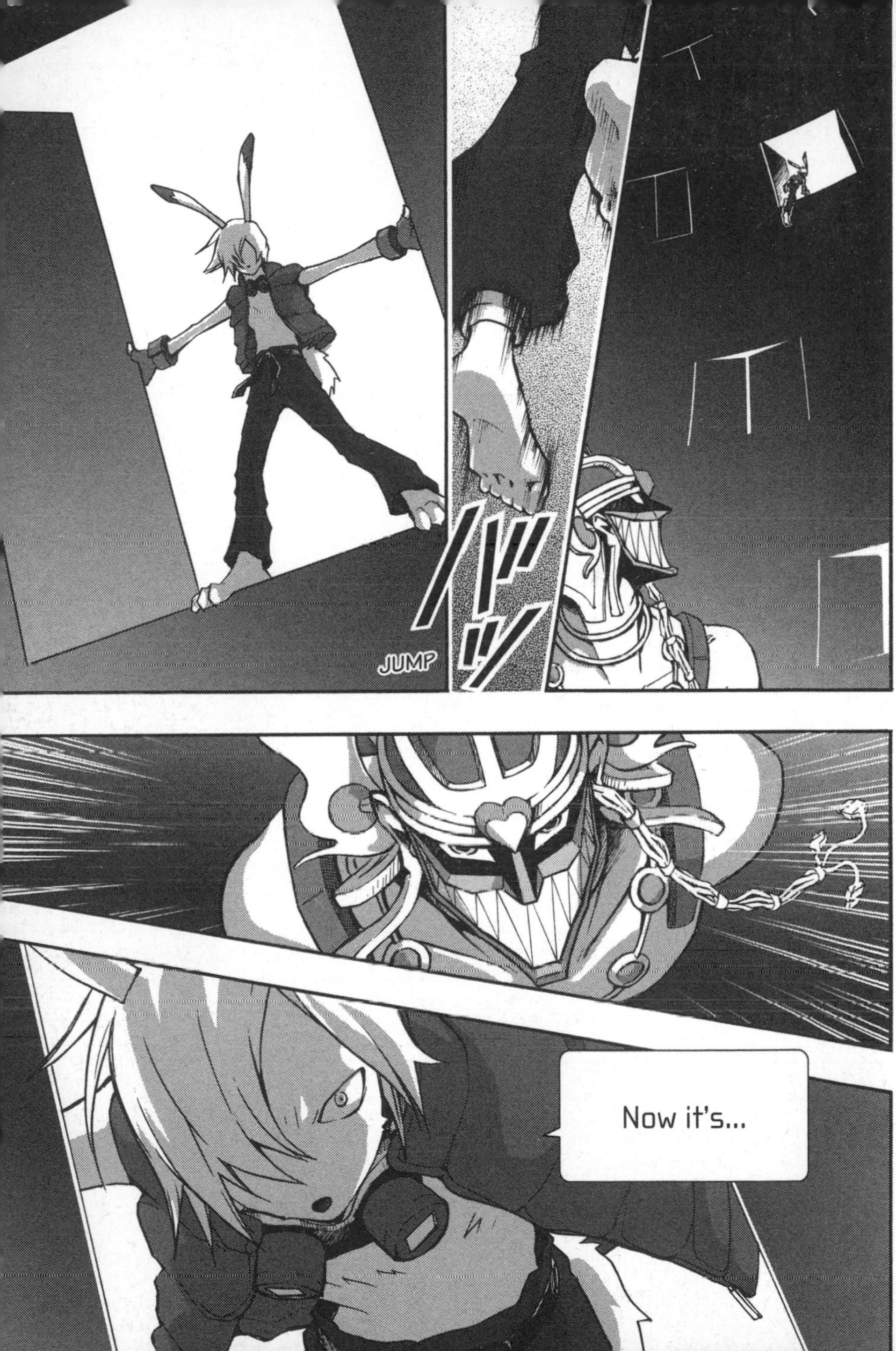
バッ
JUMP
Now it's...

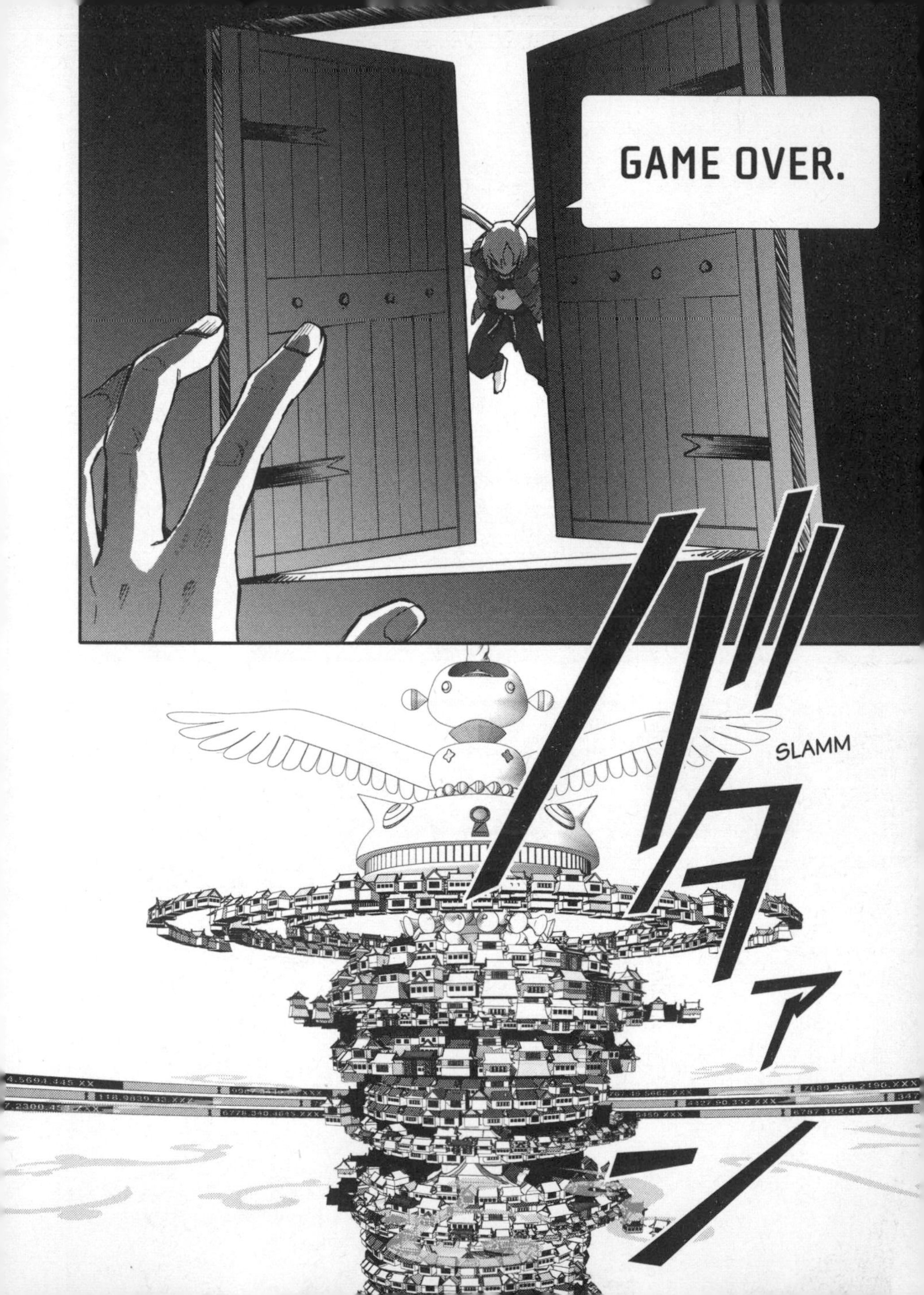
GAME OVER.
SLAMM

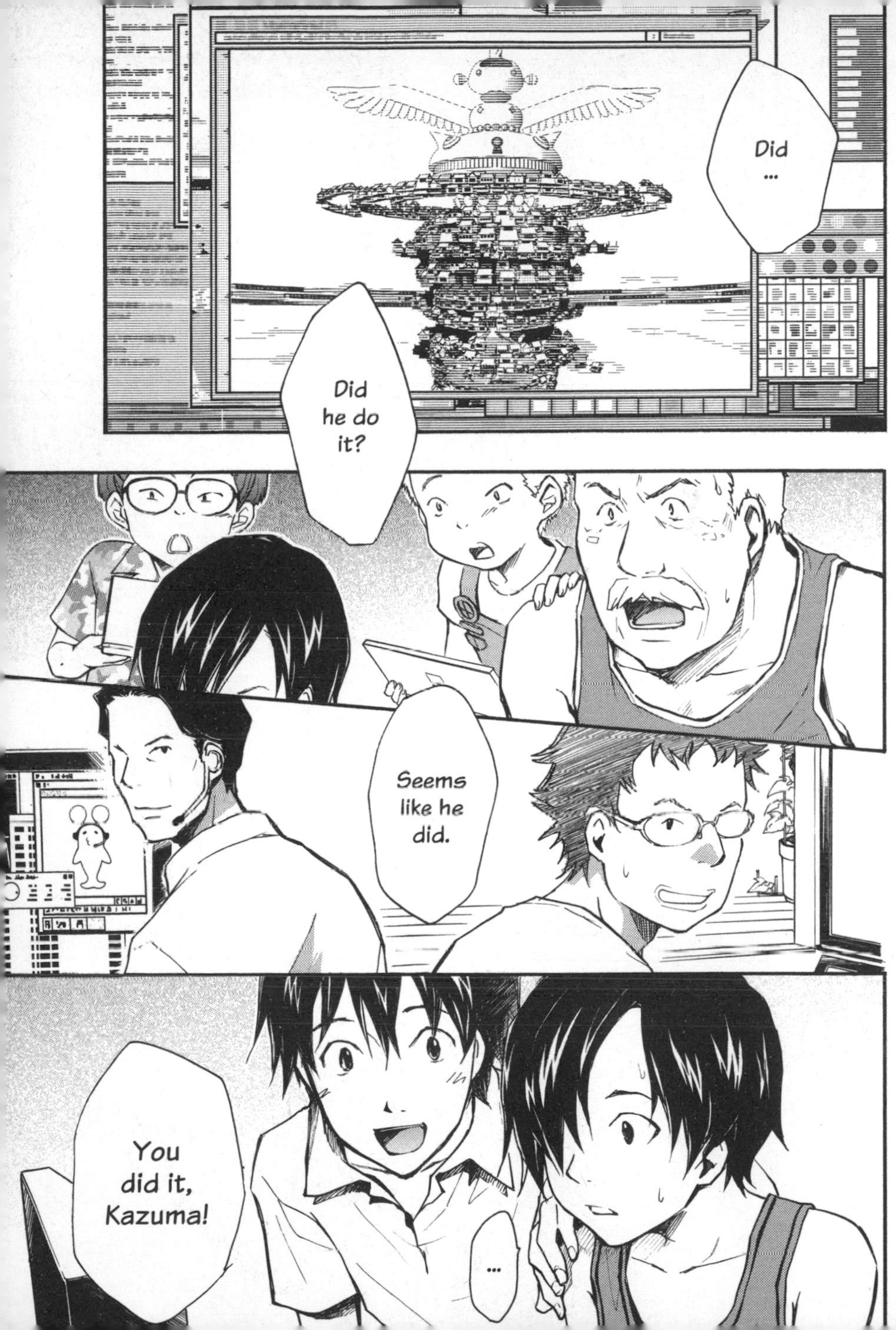
Did ...
Did he do it?
Seems like he did.
You did it, Kazuma!
...

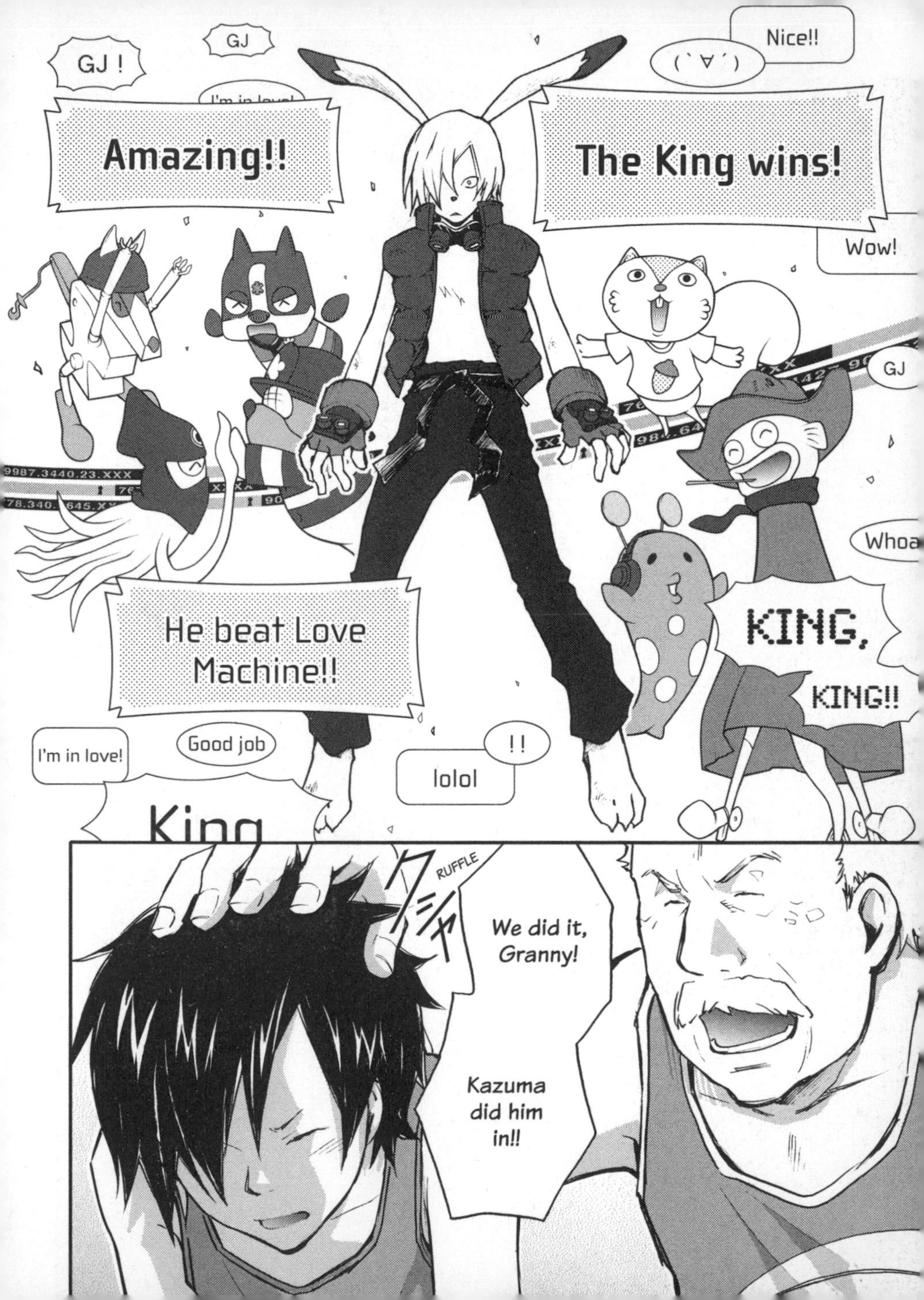
Nice!!
(´∀`)
The King wins!
Wow!
GJ
GJ
GJ !
Amazing!!
Whoa
KING,
KING!!
!!
lolol
Good job
I'm in love!
He beat Love Machine!!
King
クシャ
RUFFLE
We did it, Granny!
Kazuma did him in!!

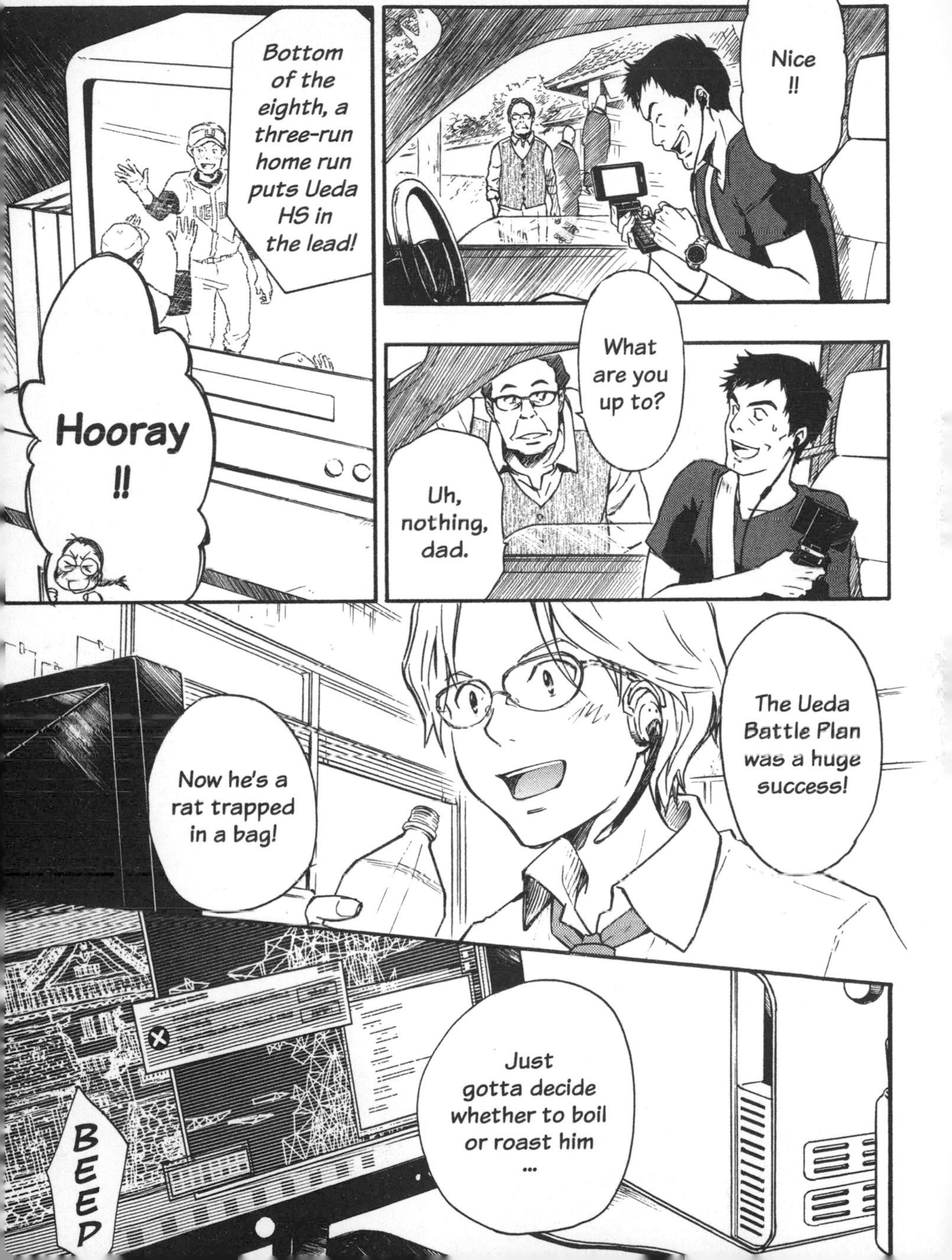
Nice !!
What are you up to?
Uh, nothing, dad.
Bottom of the eighth, a three-run home run puts Ueda HS in the lead!
Hooray !!
The Ueda Battle Plan was a huge success!
Now he's a rat trapped in a bag!
Just gotta decide whether to boil or roast him ...
BEEEP

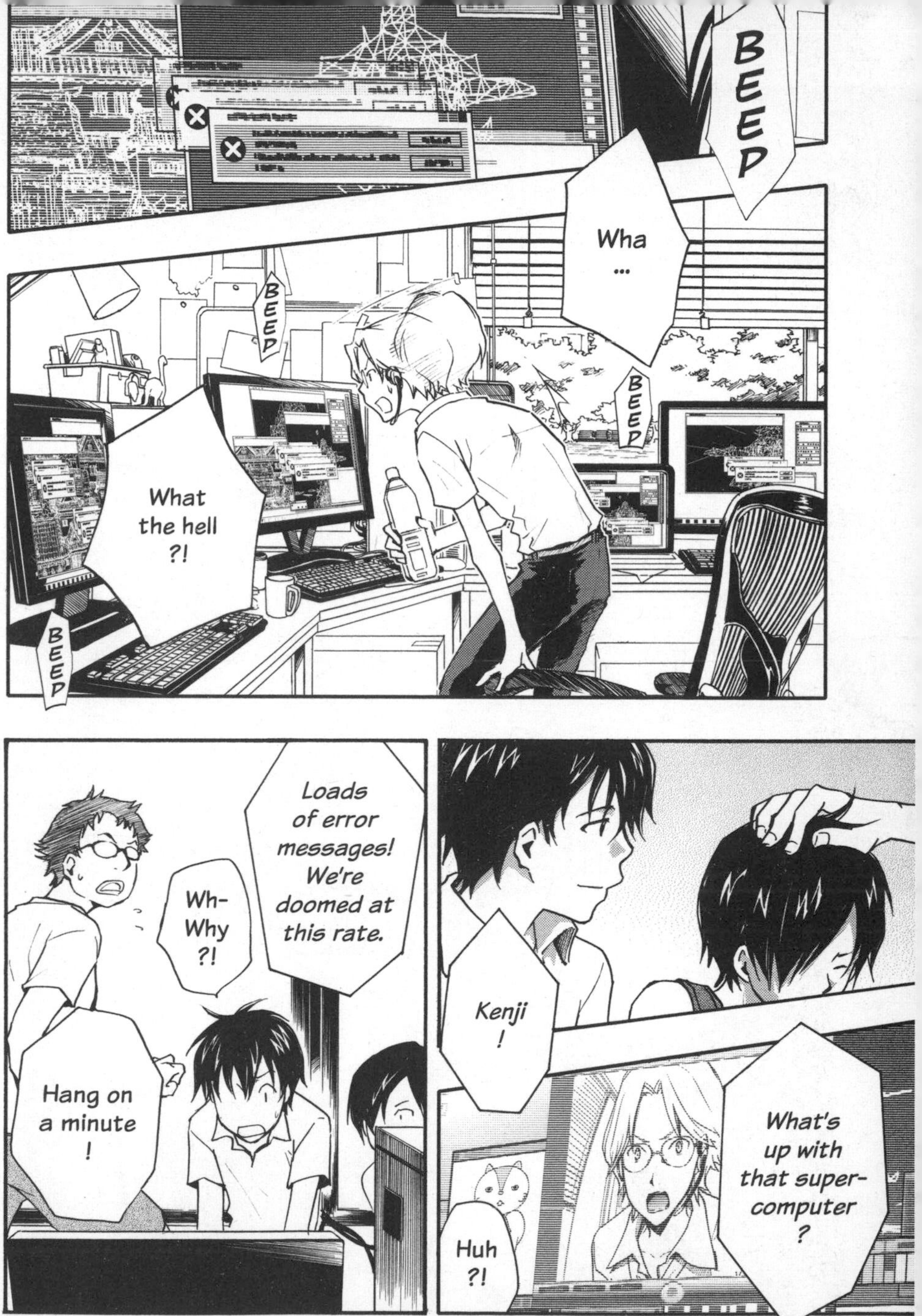
BEEP
Wha ...
BEEP
BEEP
What the hell ?!
BEEP
Kenji !
What's up with that super-computer ?
Huh ?!
Loads of error messages! We're doomed at this rate.
Wh- Why ?!
Hang on a minute !

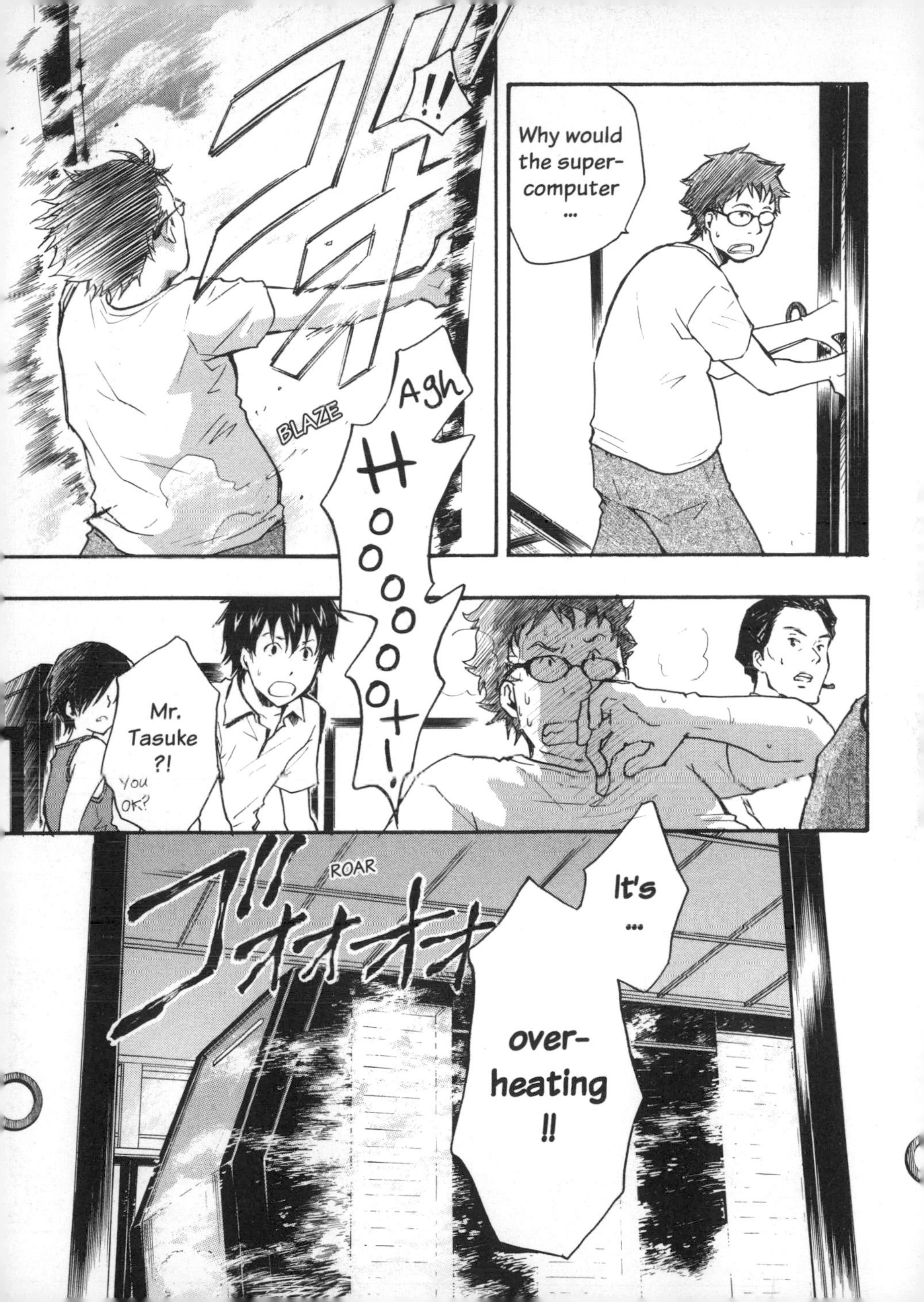
Why would the super-computer ...
!!
BLAZE
Agh
Hooooooot!
Mr. Tasuke ?!
You OK?
ROAR
It's ...
over-heating !!

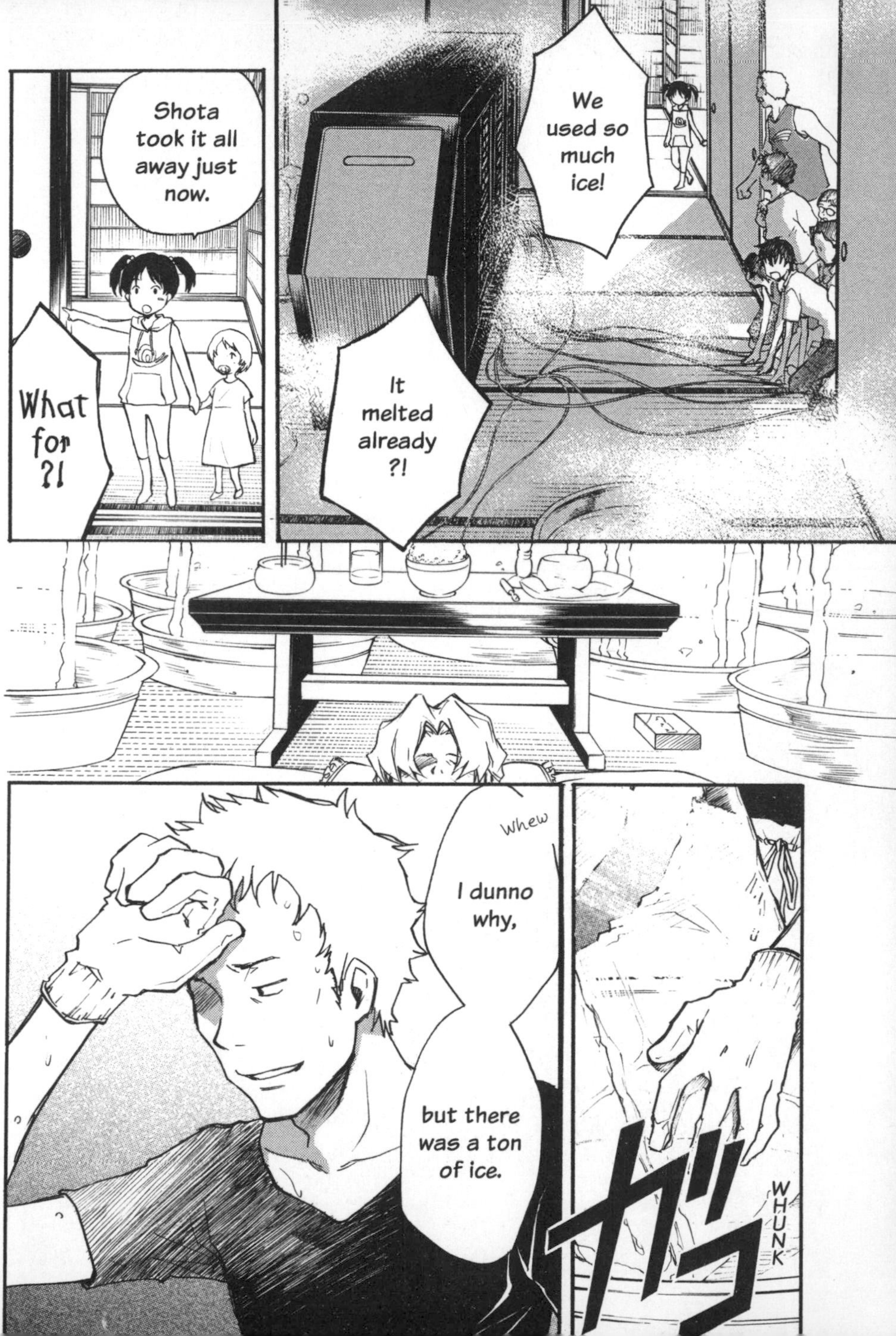
We used so much ice!
It melted already?!
Shota took it all away just now.
What for?!
WHUNK
Whew
I dunno why,
but there was a ton of ice.

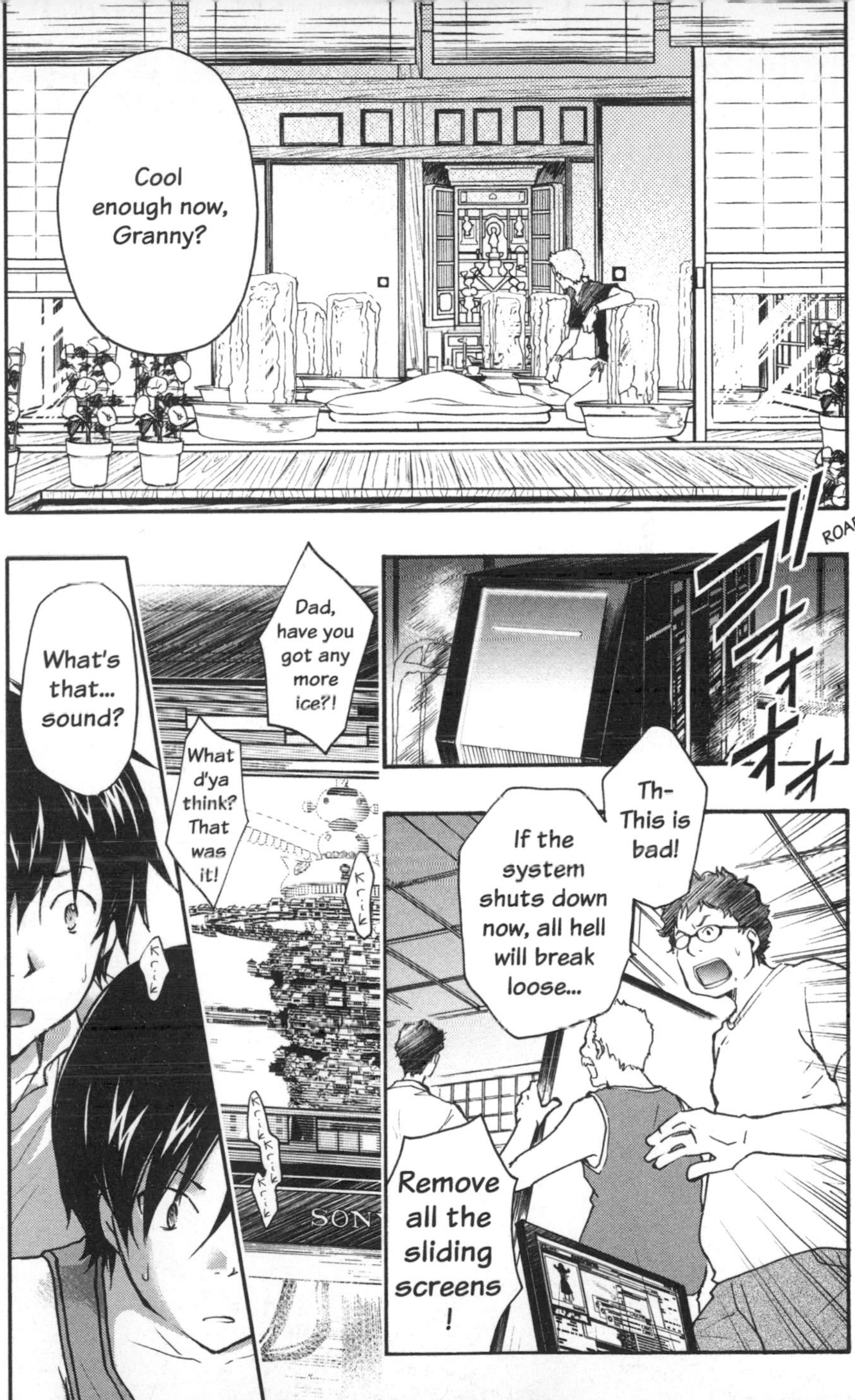
Cool enough now, Granny?
ROAR
Th- This is bad!
If the system shuts down now, all hell will break loose...
Remove all the sliding screens!
Dad, have you got any more ice?!
What d'ya think? That was it!
What's that... sound?

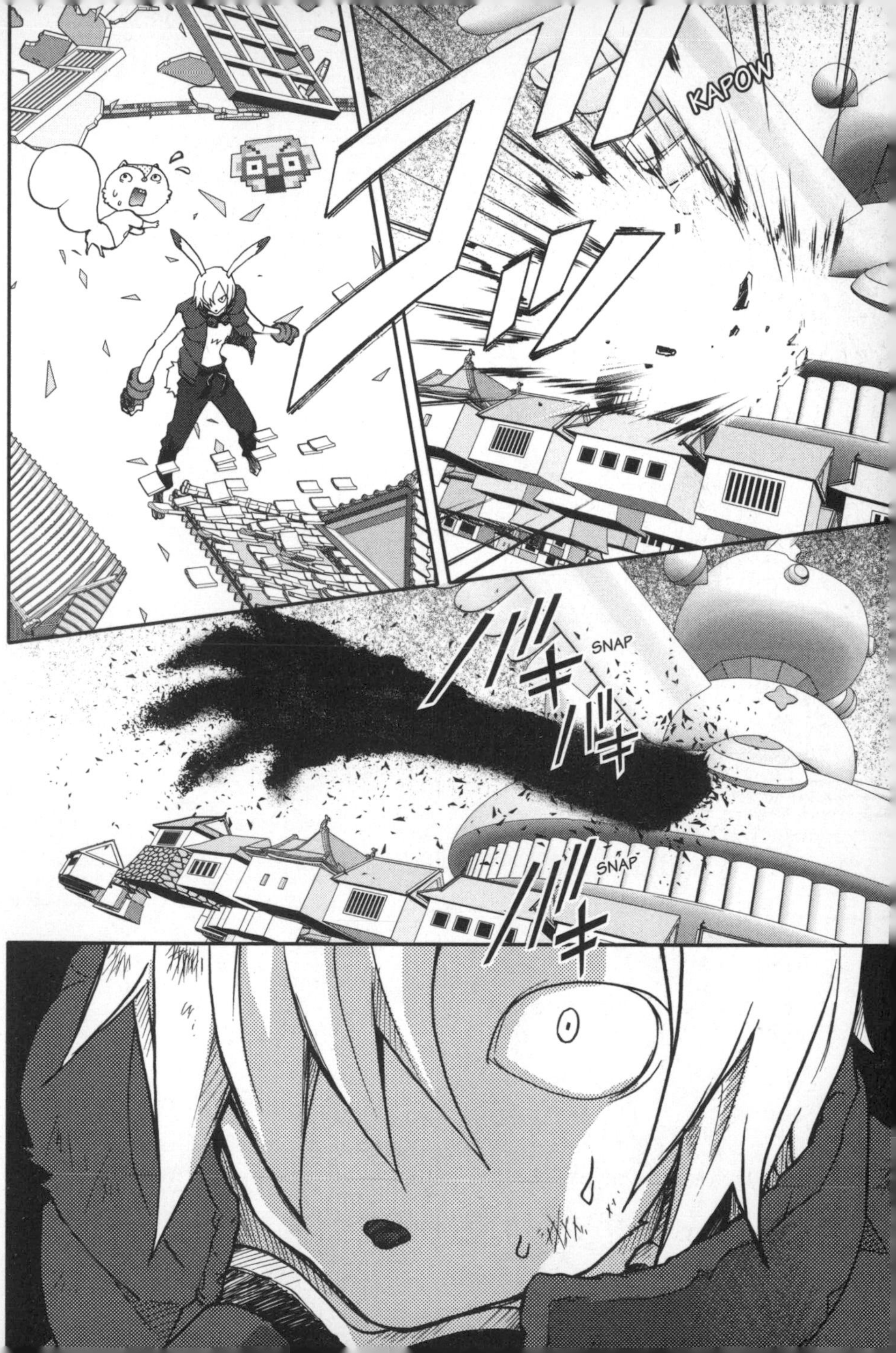
KAPOW
SNAP
SNAP

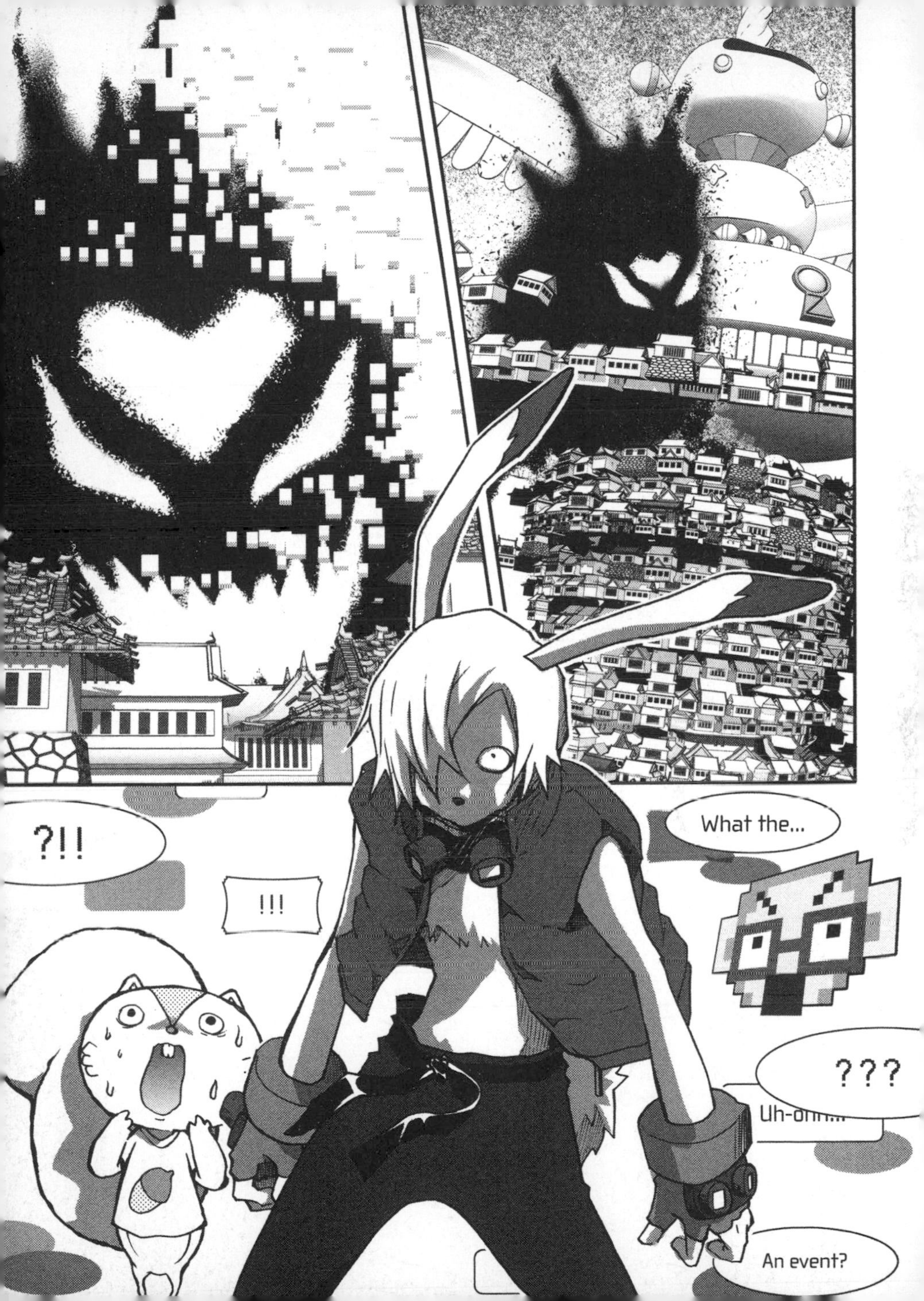
What the...
?!!
!!!
???
Uh-oh
An event?

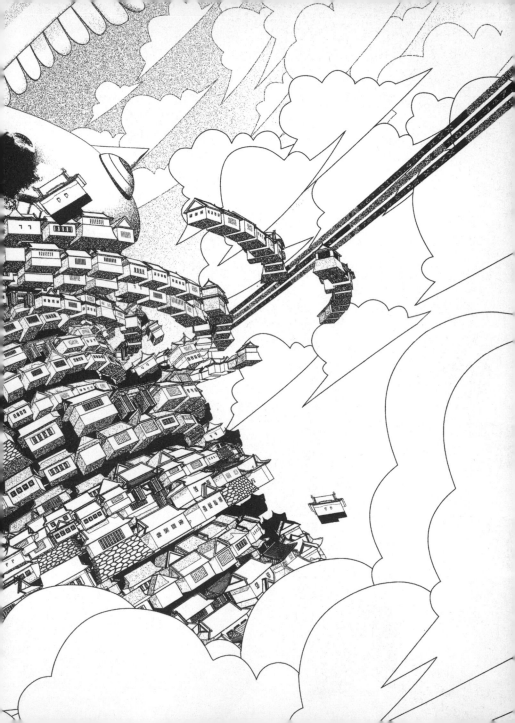

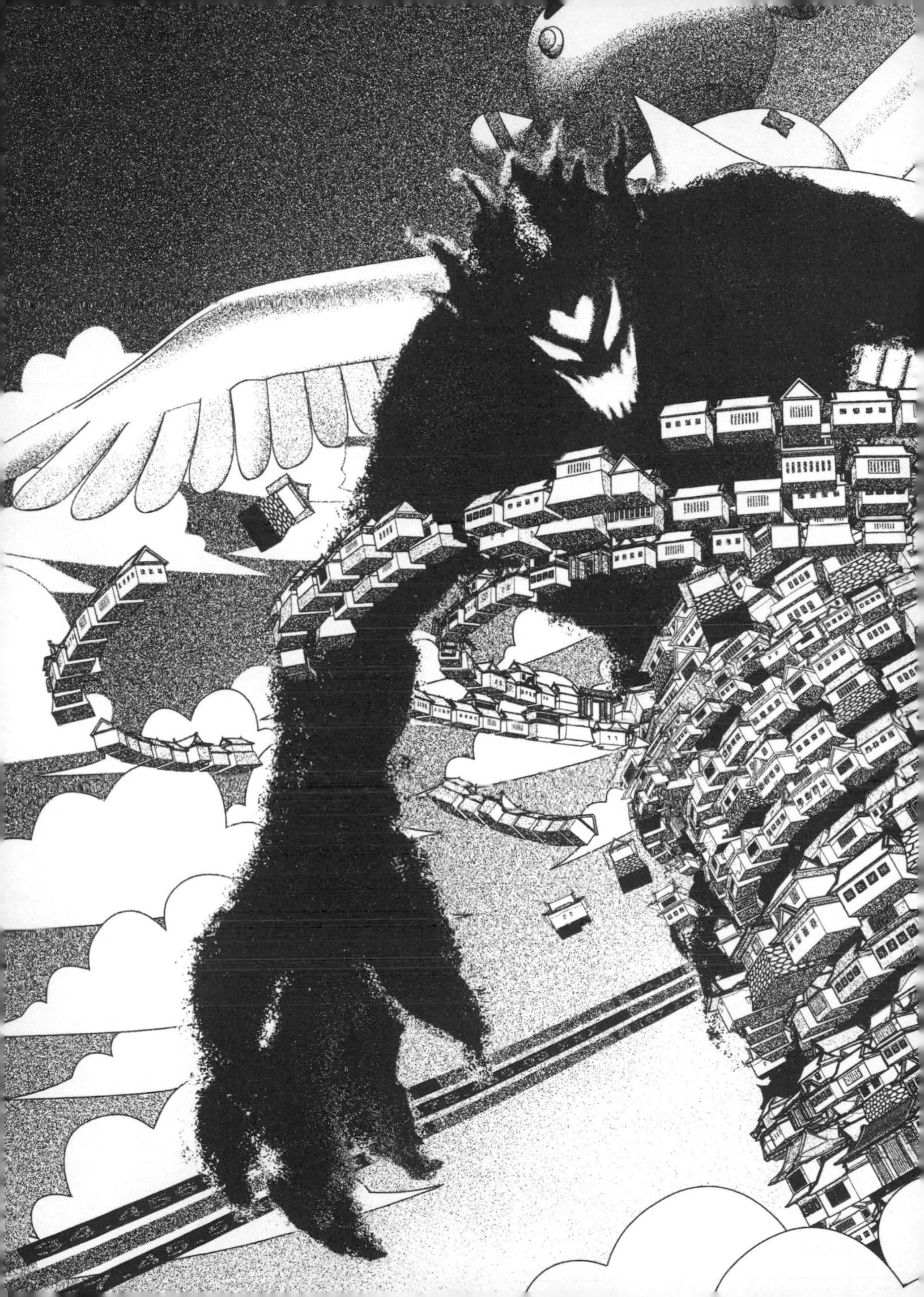

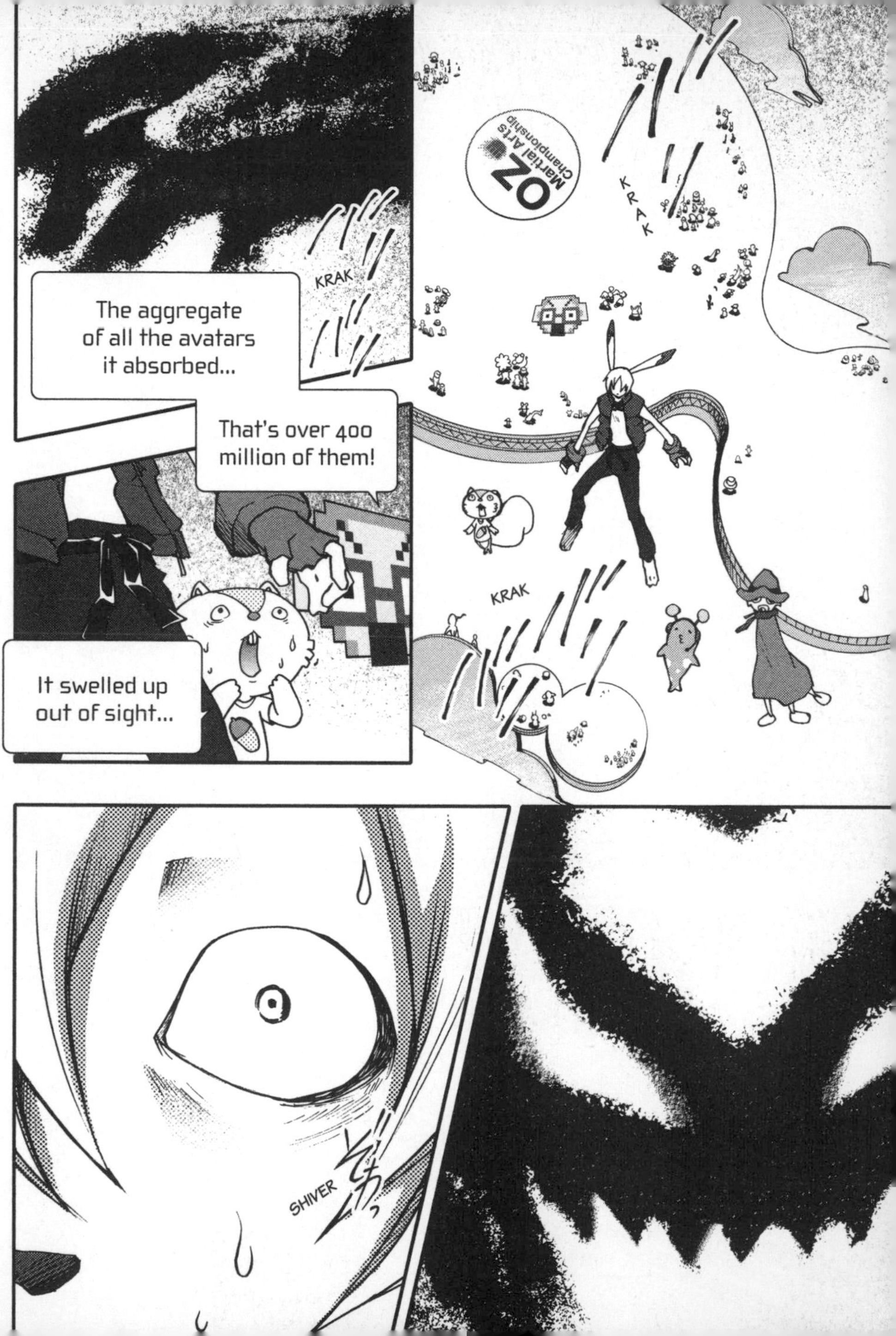
OZ
Martial Arts
Championship
KRAK
KRAK
KRAK
The aggregate of all the avatars it absorbed...
That's over 400 million of them!
It swelled up out of sight...
SHIVER

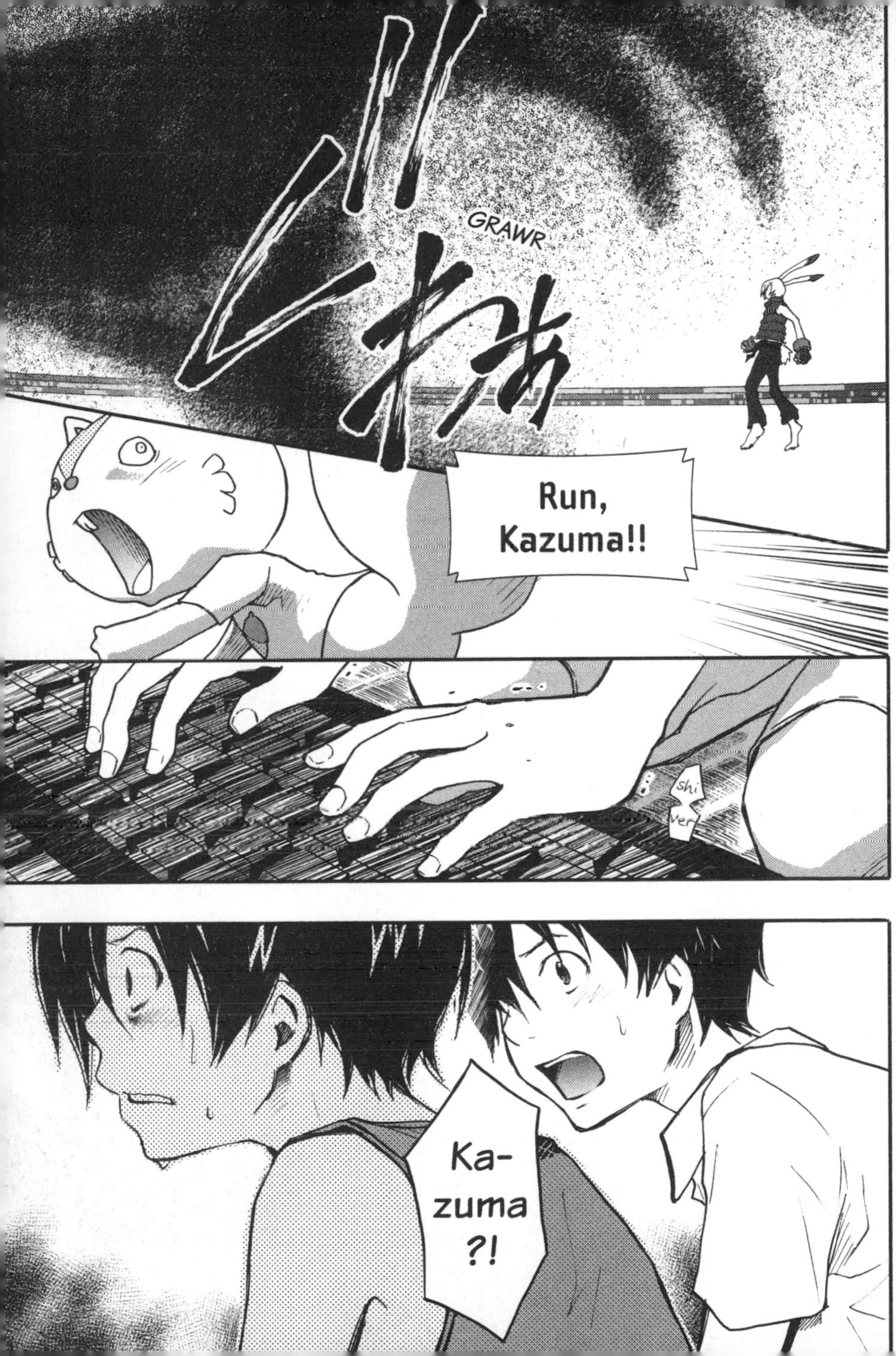
GRAWR
Run, Kazuma!!
shi ver
Ka- zuma ?!

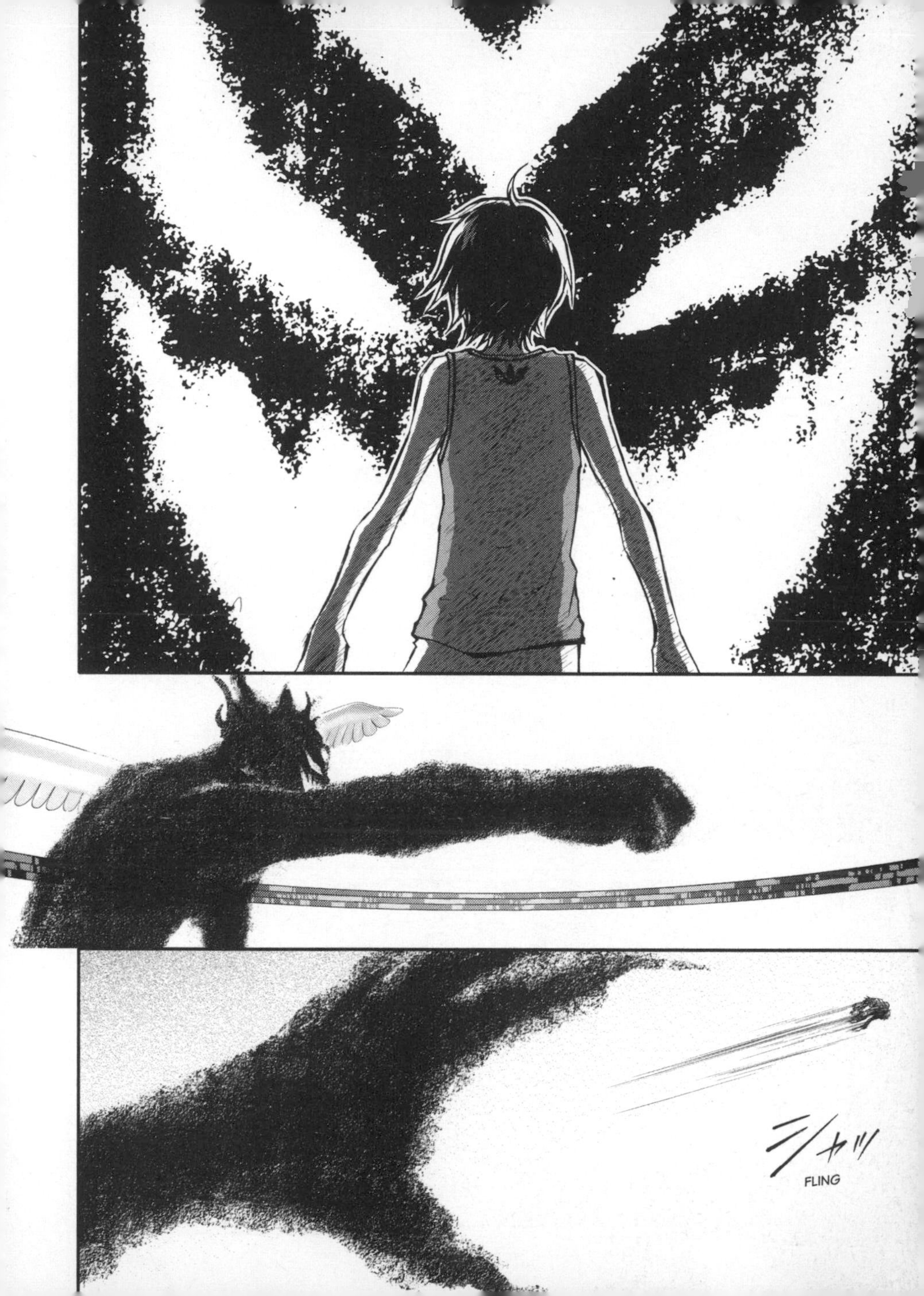
シャツ
FLING

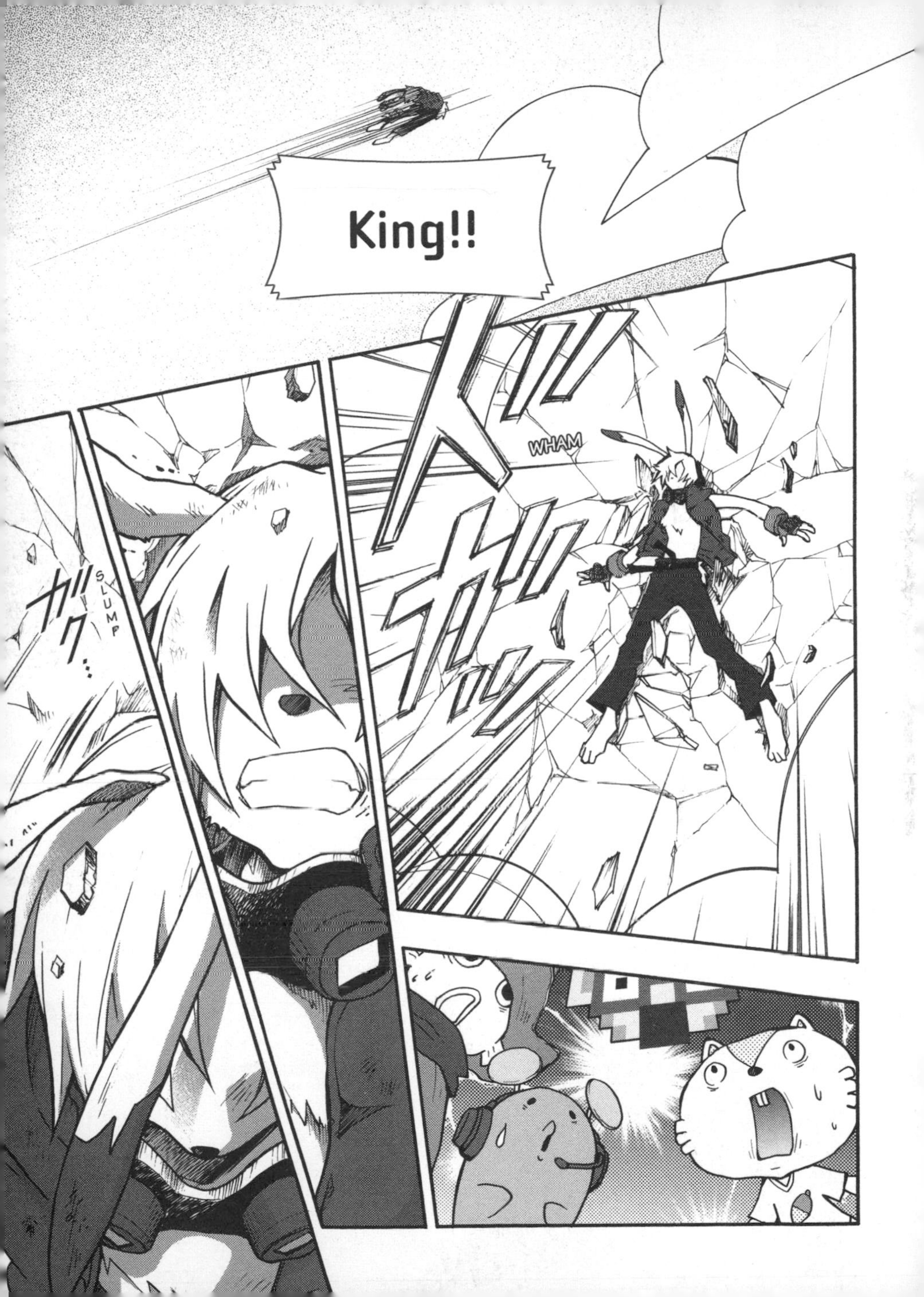
King!!
WHAM
SLUMP

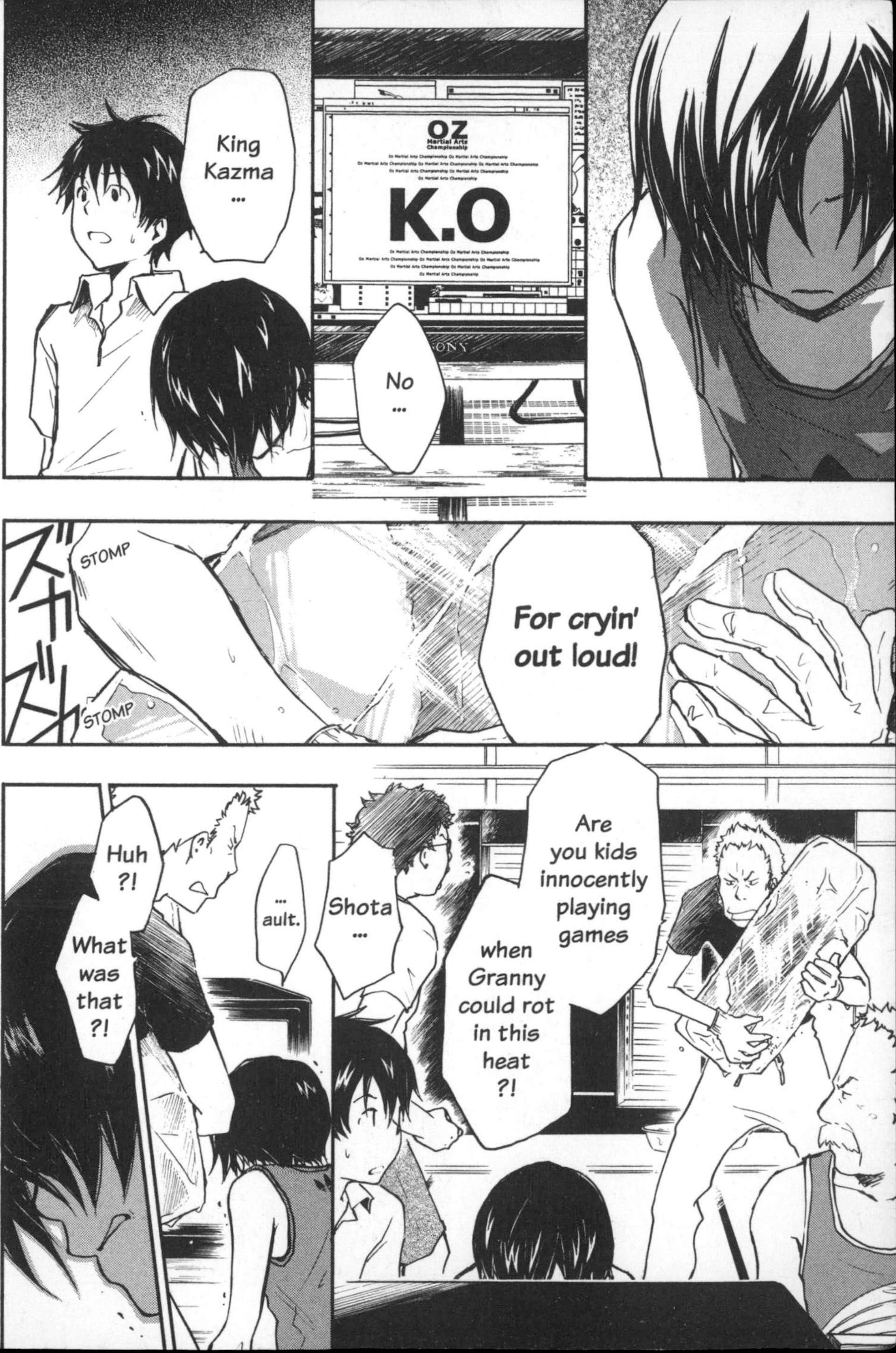
OZ
Martial Arts Championship
K.O
No ...
King Kazma ...
For cryin' out loud!
STOMP
STOMP
Are you kids innocently playing games
when Granny could rot in this heat?!
Shota ...
... ault.
Huh?!
What was that?!

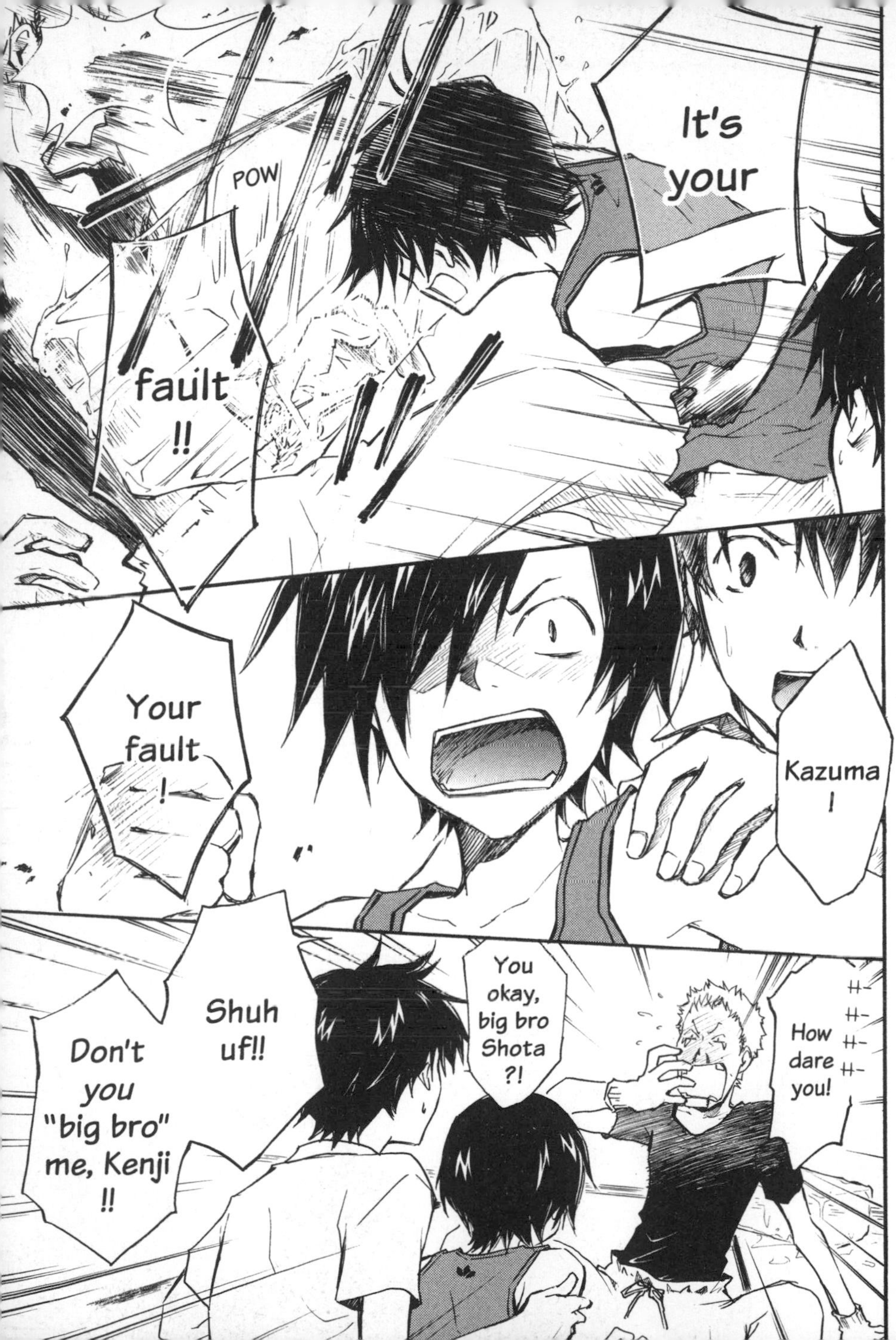
It's your
POW
fault !!
Kazuma !
Your fault !
H- H- H- H-
How dare you!
You okay, big bro Shota ?!
Shuh uf!!
Don't you "big bro" me, Kenji !!

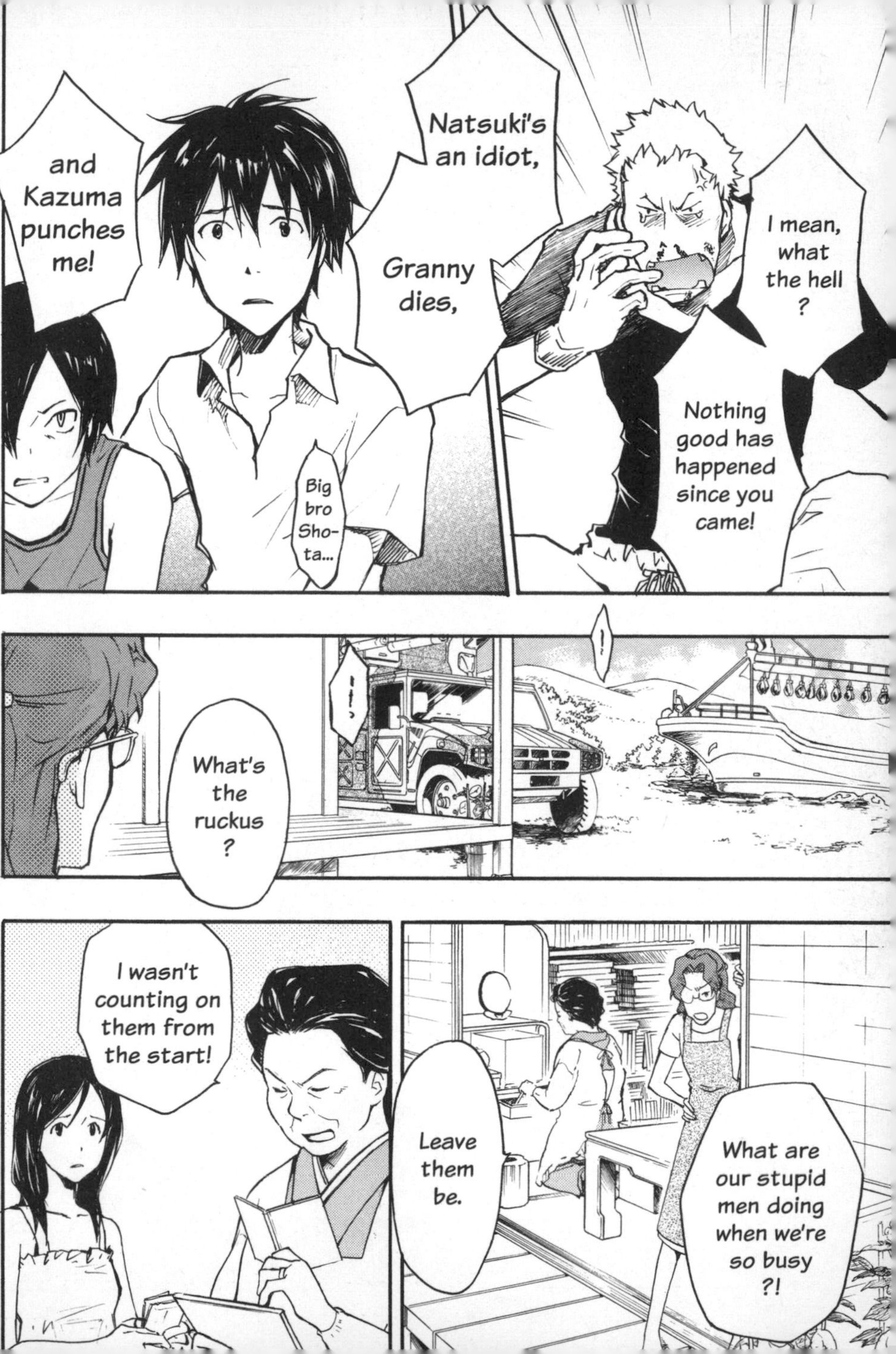
I mean, what the hell ?
Nothing good has happened since you came!
Natsuki's an idiot,
Granny dies,
and Kazuma punches me!
Big bro Shota...
!
What's the ruckus ?
What are our stupid men doing when we're so busy ?!
Leave them be.
I wasn't counting on them from the start!

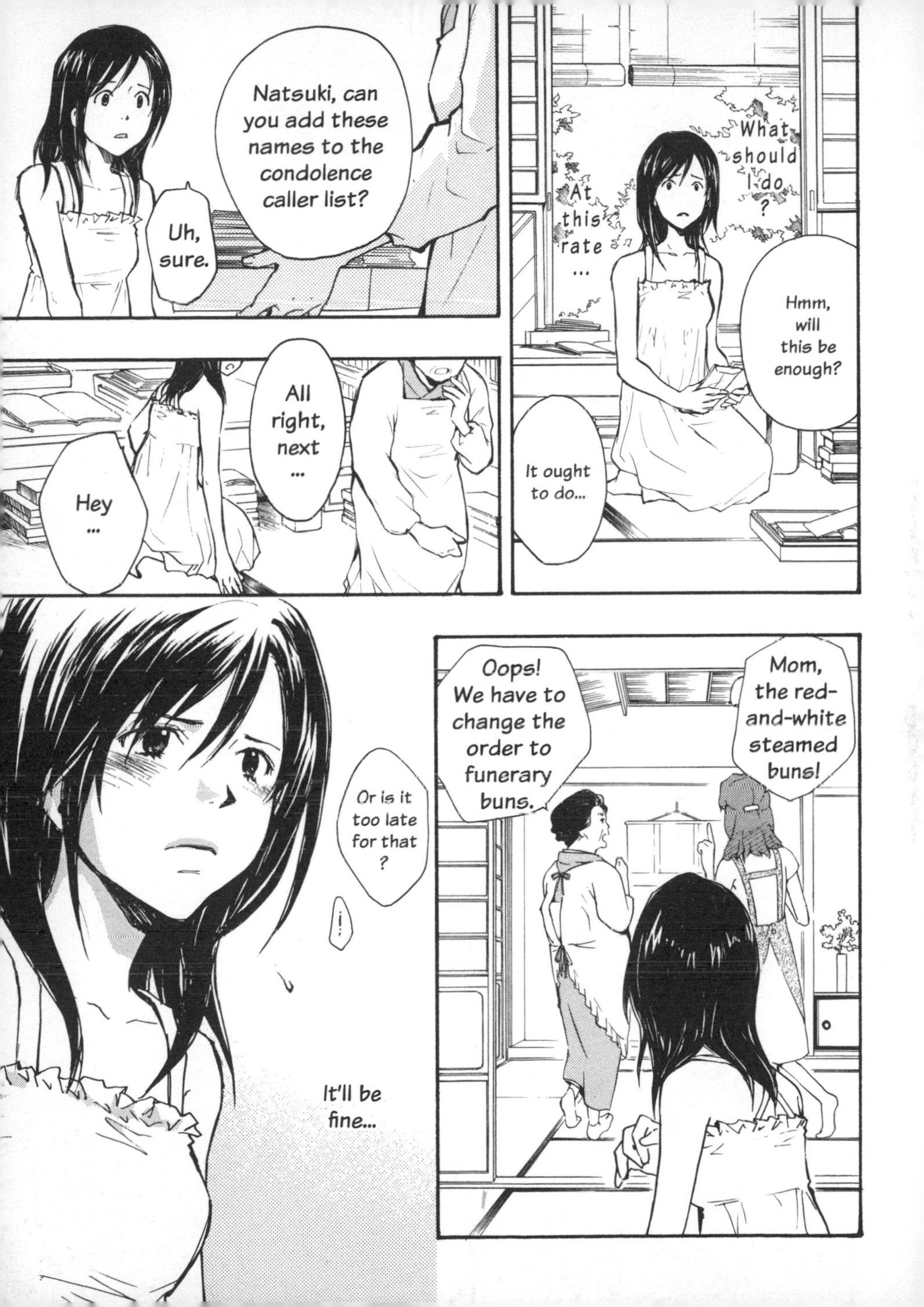
What should I do?
At this rate...
Hmm, will this be enough?
It ought to do...
Natsuki, can you add these names to the condolence caller list?
Uh, sure.
All right, next...
Hey...
Mom, the red-and-white steamed buns!
Oops! We have to change the order to funerary buns.
Or is it too late for that?
!
It'll be fine...

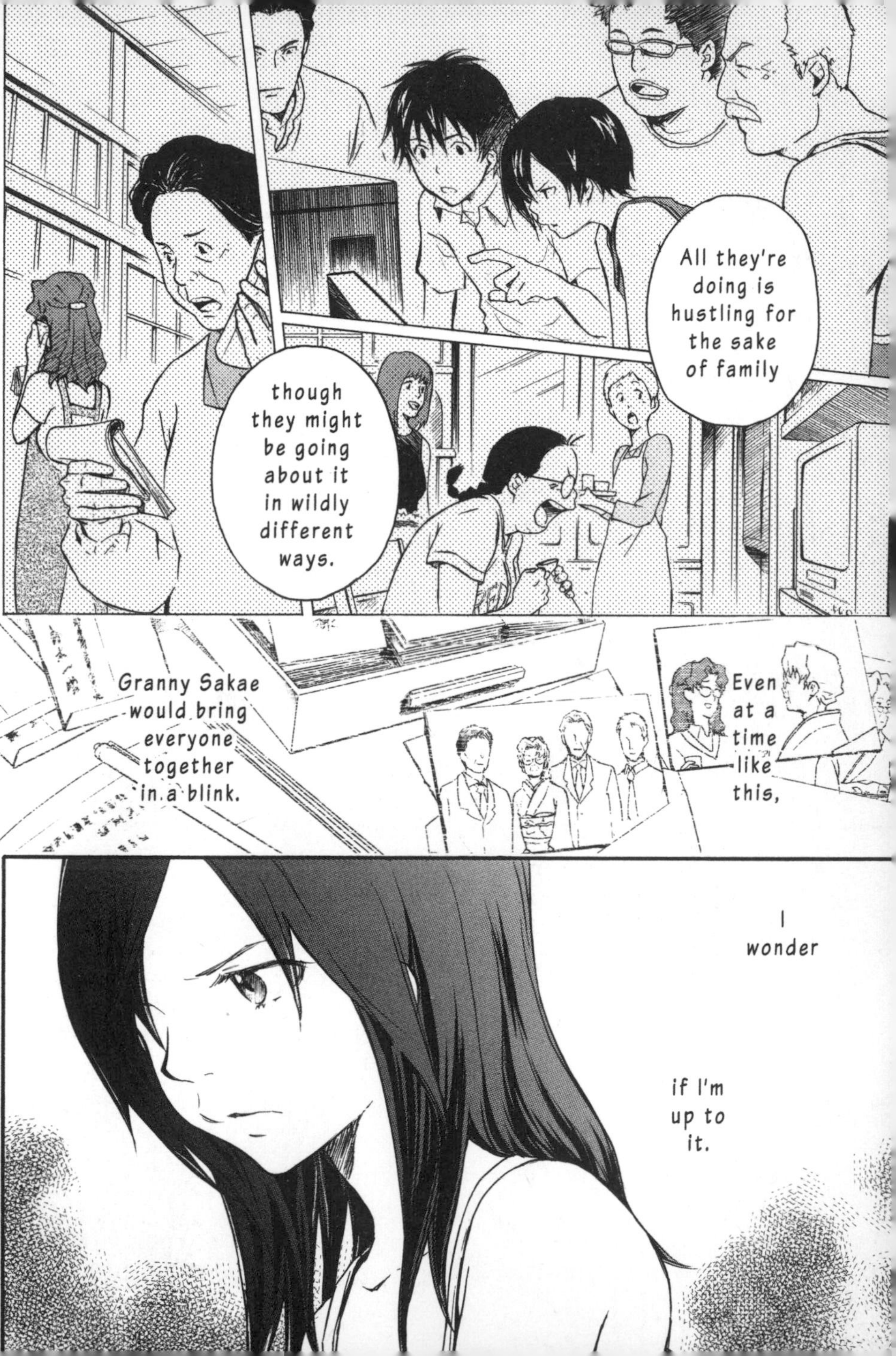
All they're doing is hustling for the sake of family
though they might be going about it in wildly different ways.
Even at a time like this,
Granny Sakae would bring everyone together in a blink.
I wonder
if I'm up to it.

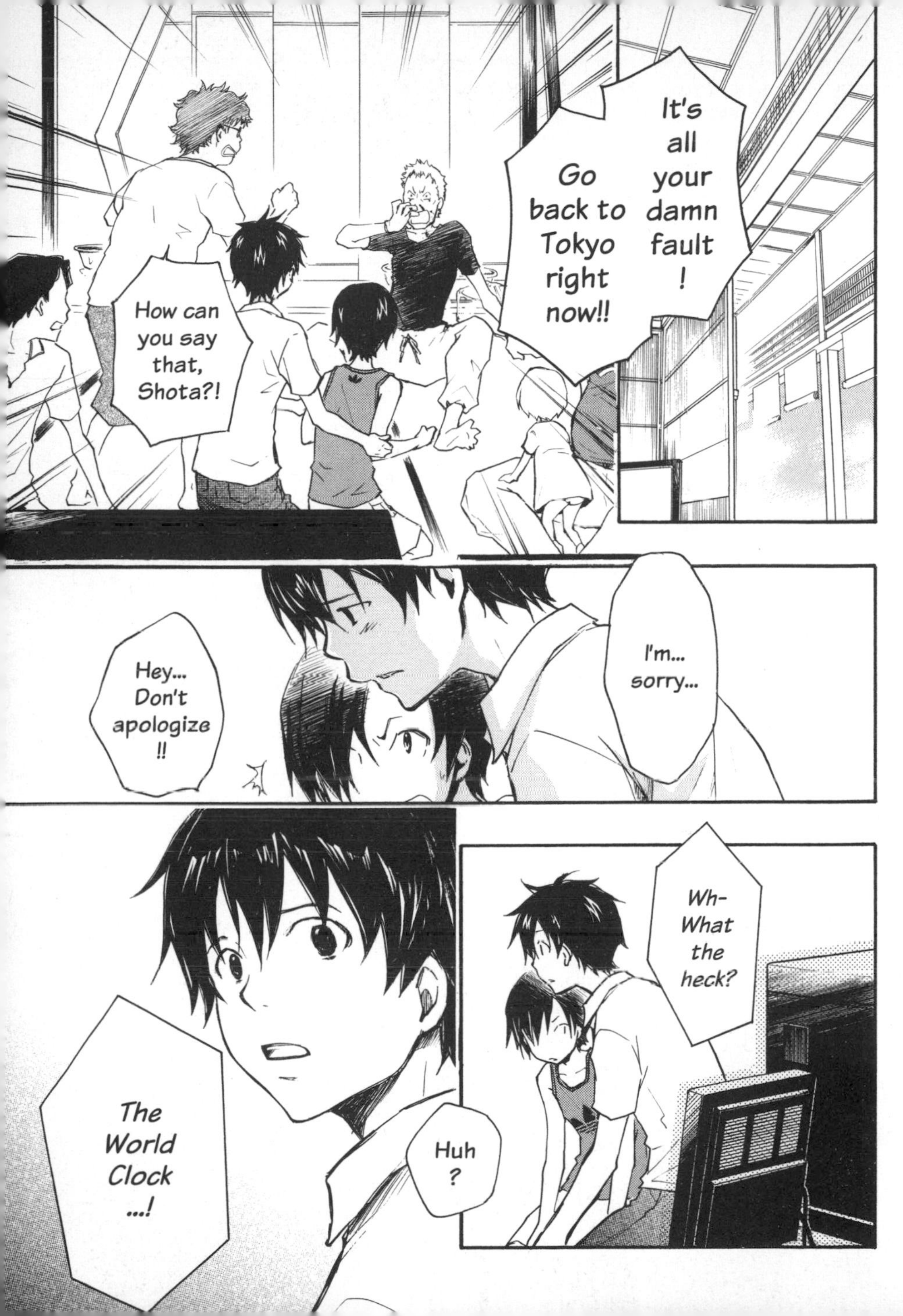
It's all your damn fault!
Go back to Tokyo right now!!
How can you say that, Shota?!
I'm... sorry...
Hey... Don't apologize!!
Wh- What the heck?
Huh?
The World Clock...!

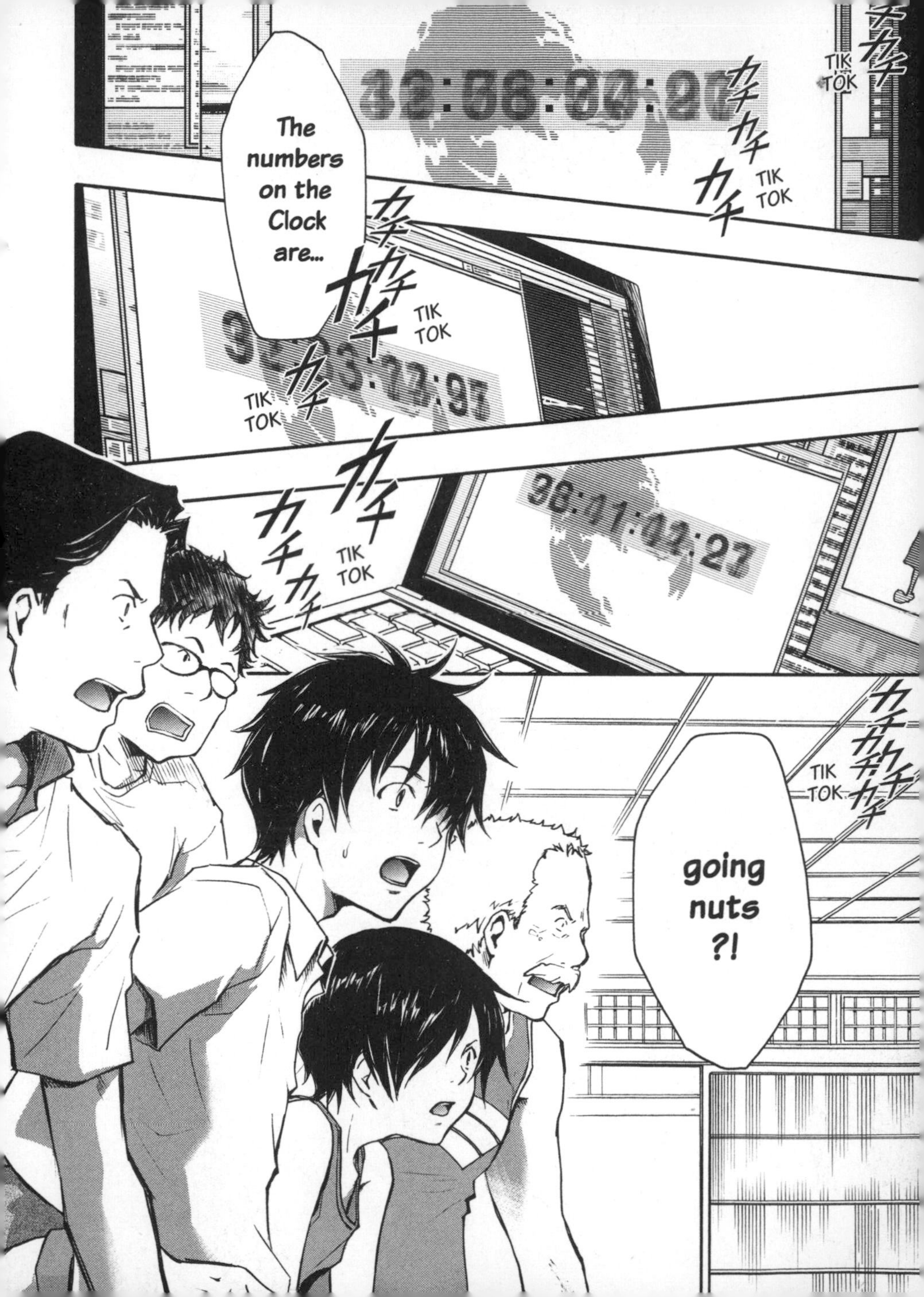
TIK TOK
TIK TOK
The numbers on the Clock are...
TIK TOK
TIK TOK
TIK TOK
TIK TOK
going nuts ?!

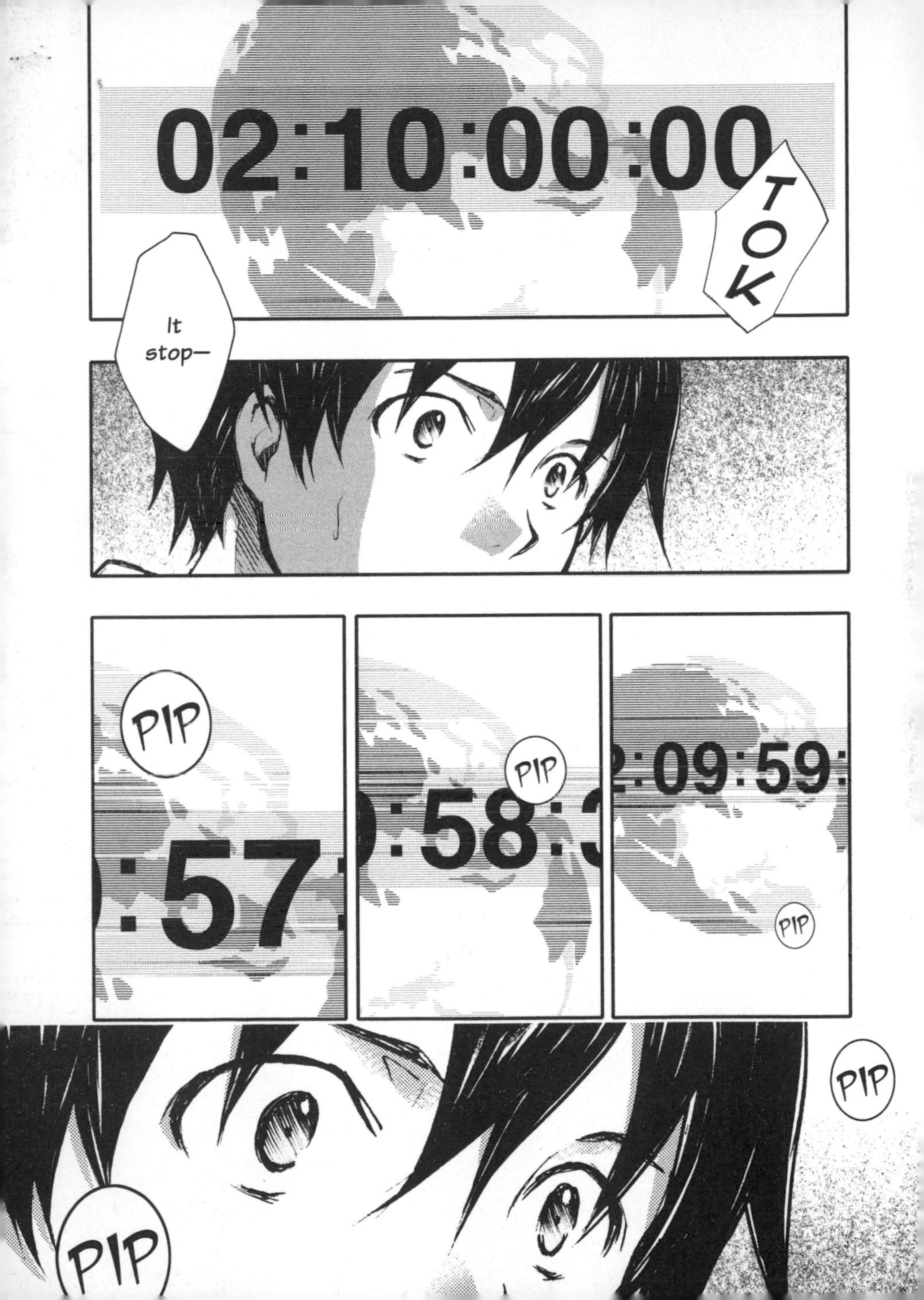
02:10:00:00
TOK
It stop—
2:09:59:
PIP
PIP
:58:
PIP
:57:
PIP
PIP

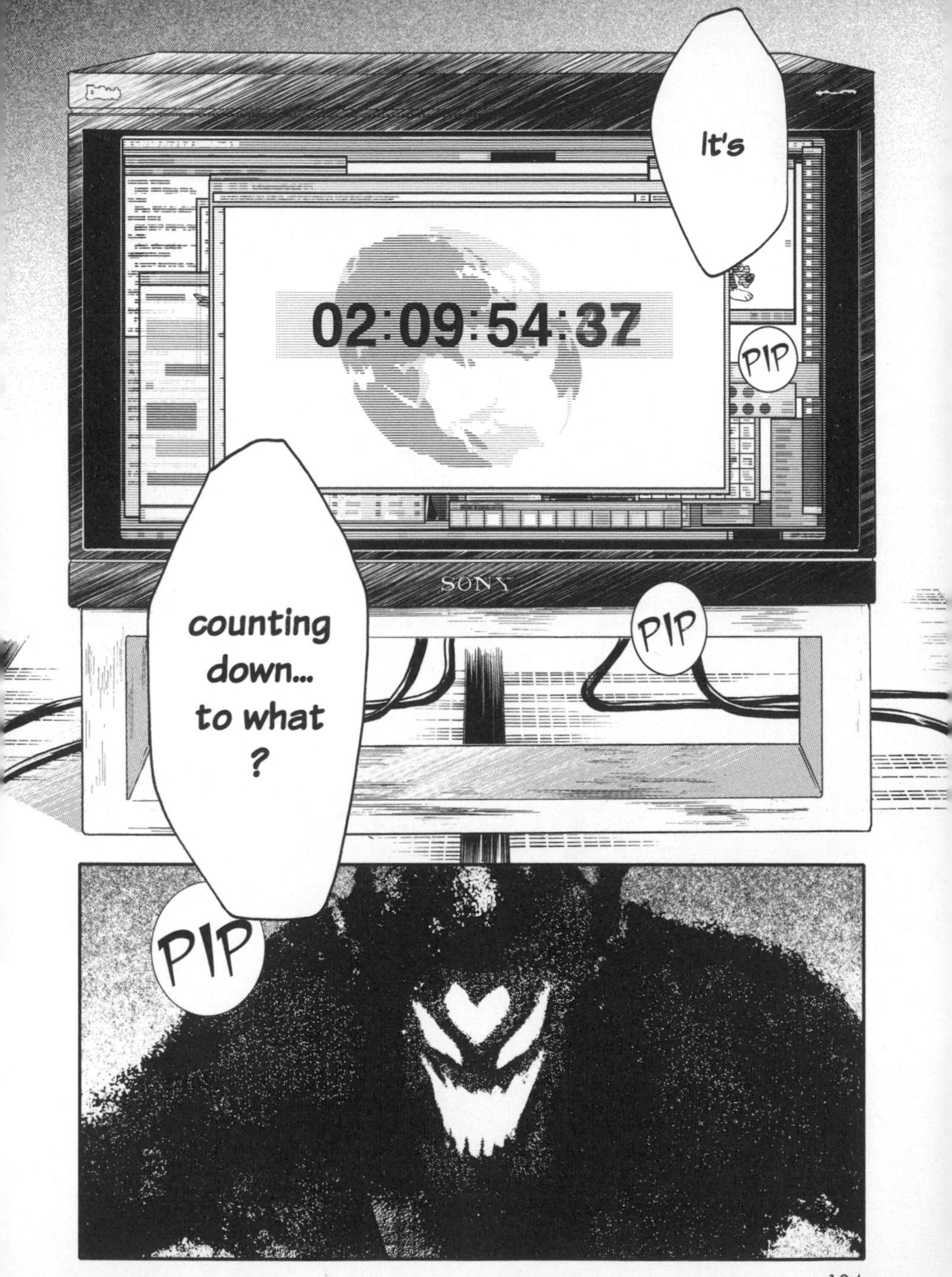
It's
PIP
02:09:54:37
counting down... to what ?
SONY
PIP
PIP

SUMMER WARS

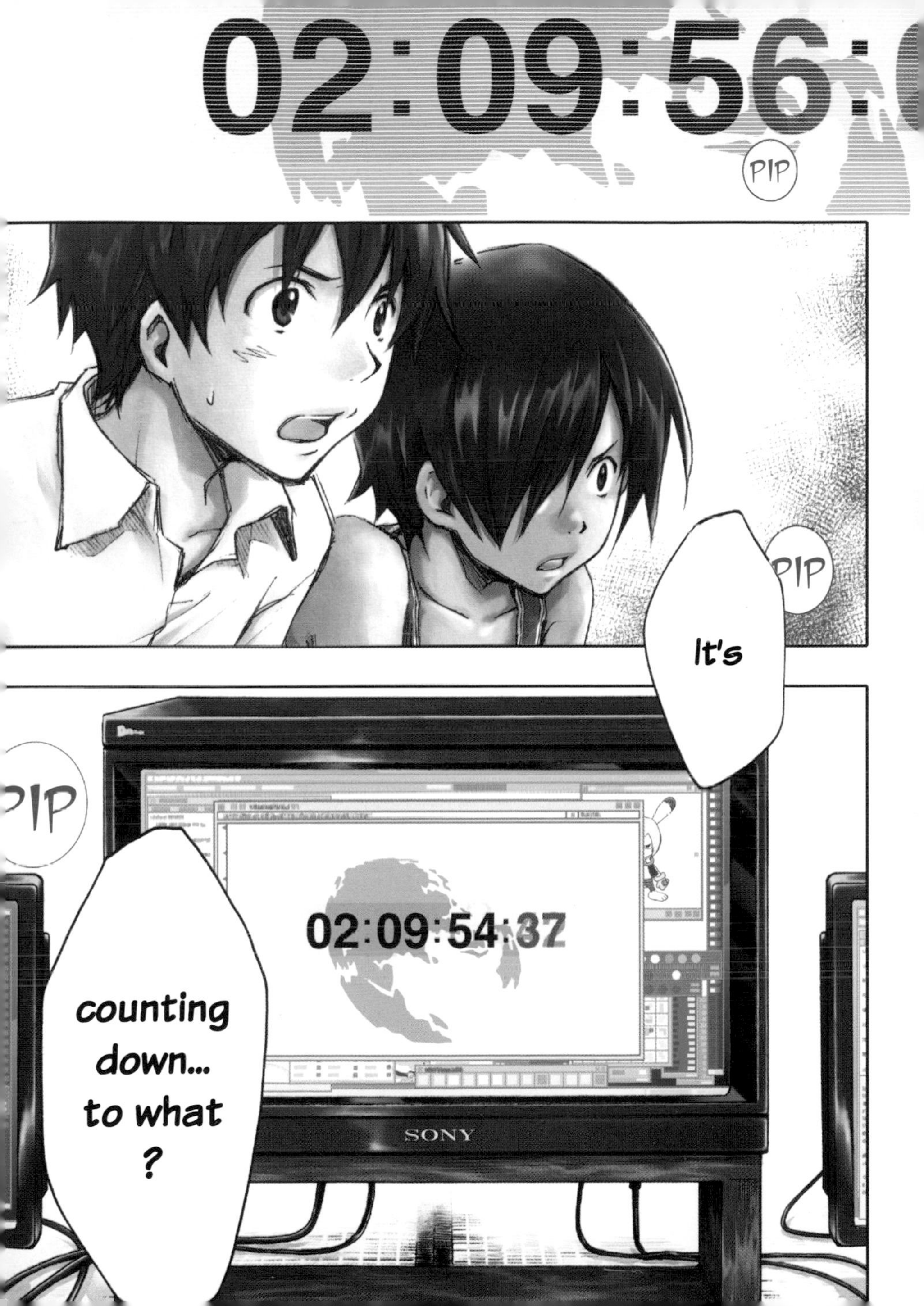
02:09:56:
PIP
PIP
It's
PIP
02:09:54:37
counting down... to what ?
SONY

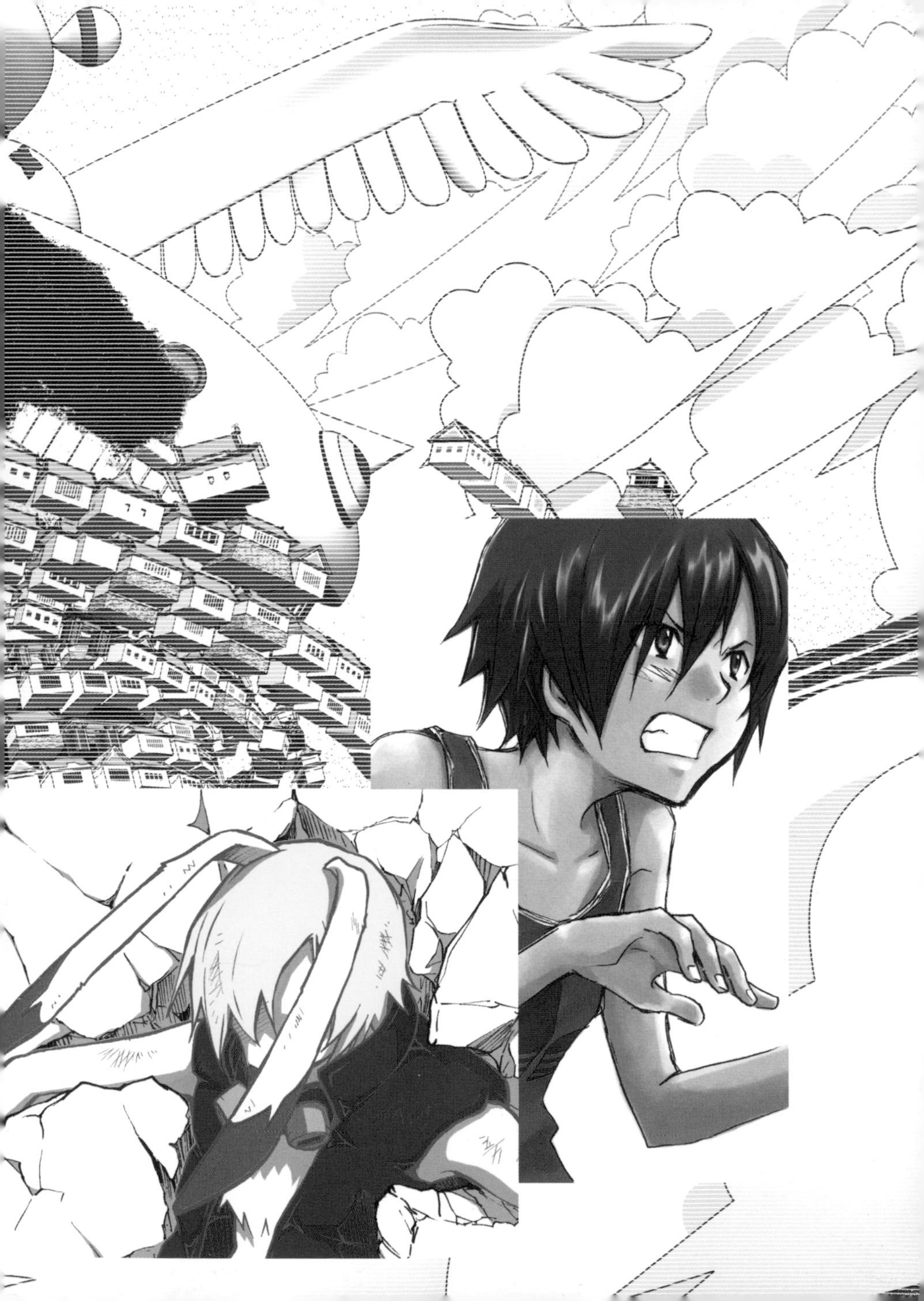

Act Nine Time Limit

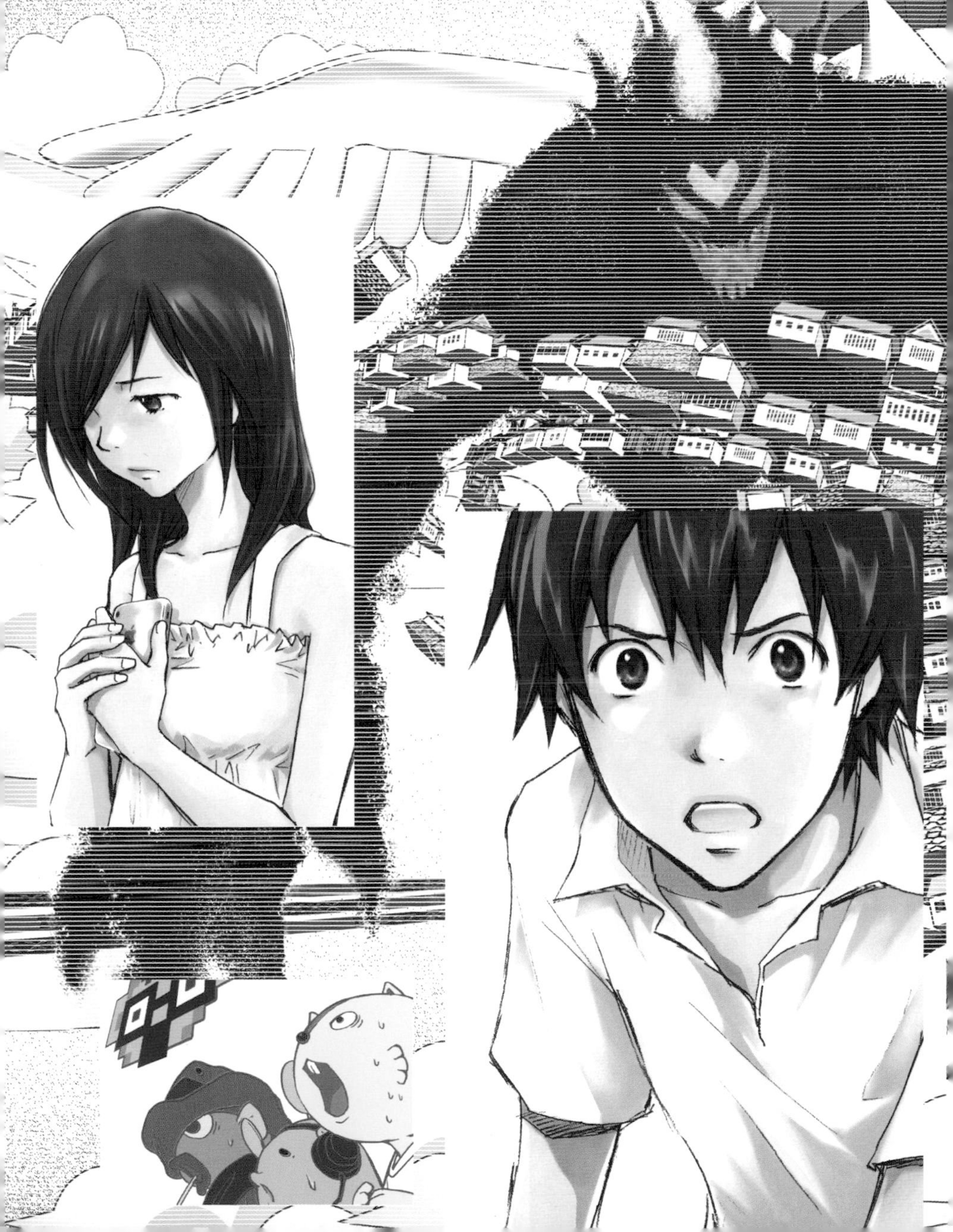

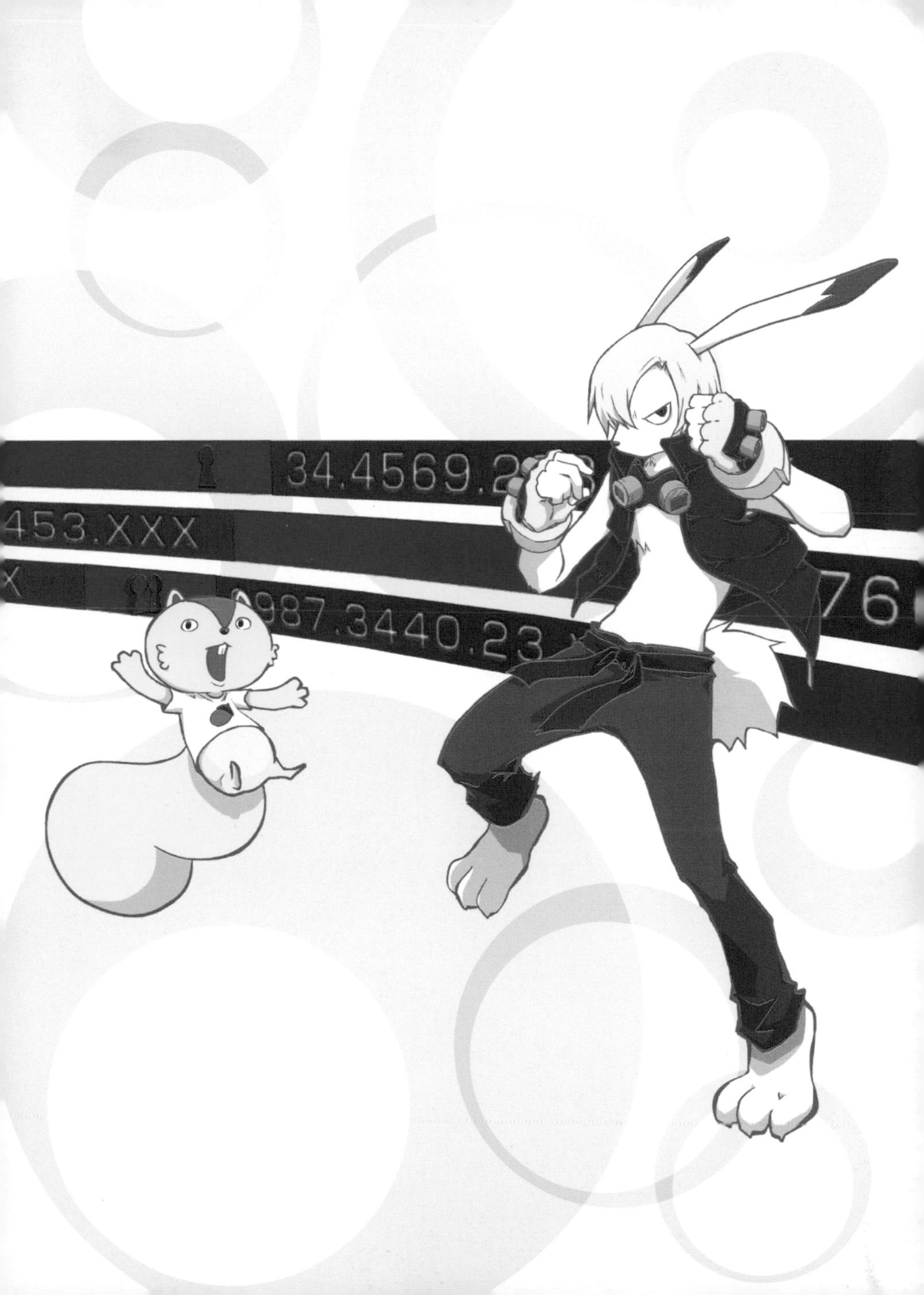
34.4569.2
453.XXX
987.3440.23
76

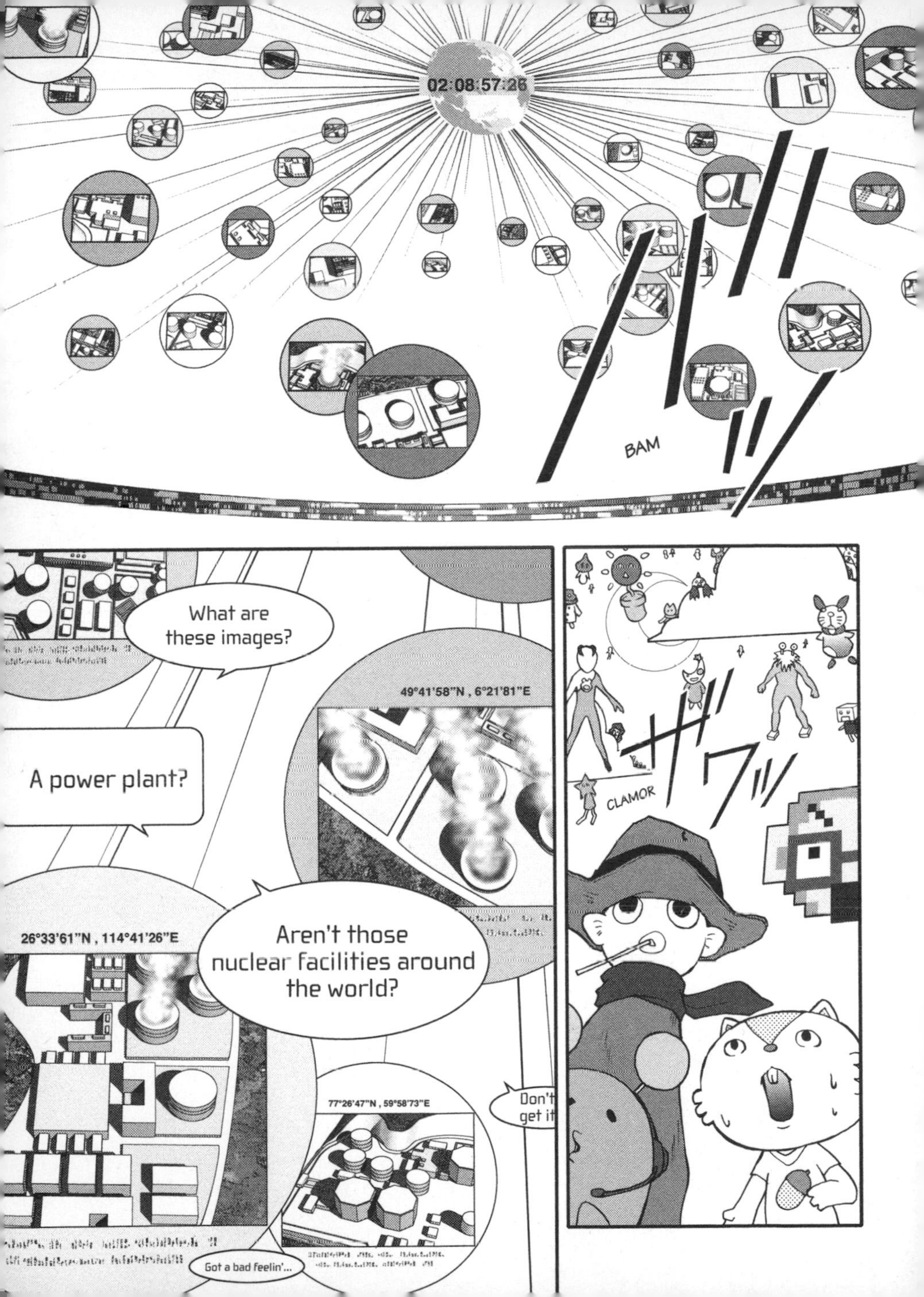
02:08:57:26
BAM
CLAMOR
What are these images?
49°41'58"N , 6°21'81"E
A power plant?
Aren't those nuclear facilities around the world?
26°33'61"N , 114°41'26"E
Don't get it
77°26'47"N , 59°58'73"E
Got a bad feelin'...

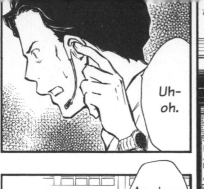

Uh-oh.

Why nuclear power plants?

An alarm has gone off on the U.S. military's covert circuit.

Japan's asteroid probe "Wild Eagle"

has gone rogue and is falling toward Earth.

What is it?

Huh ?!

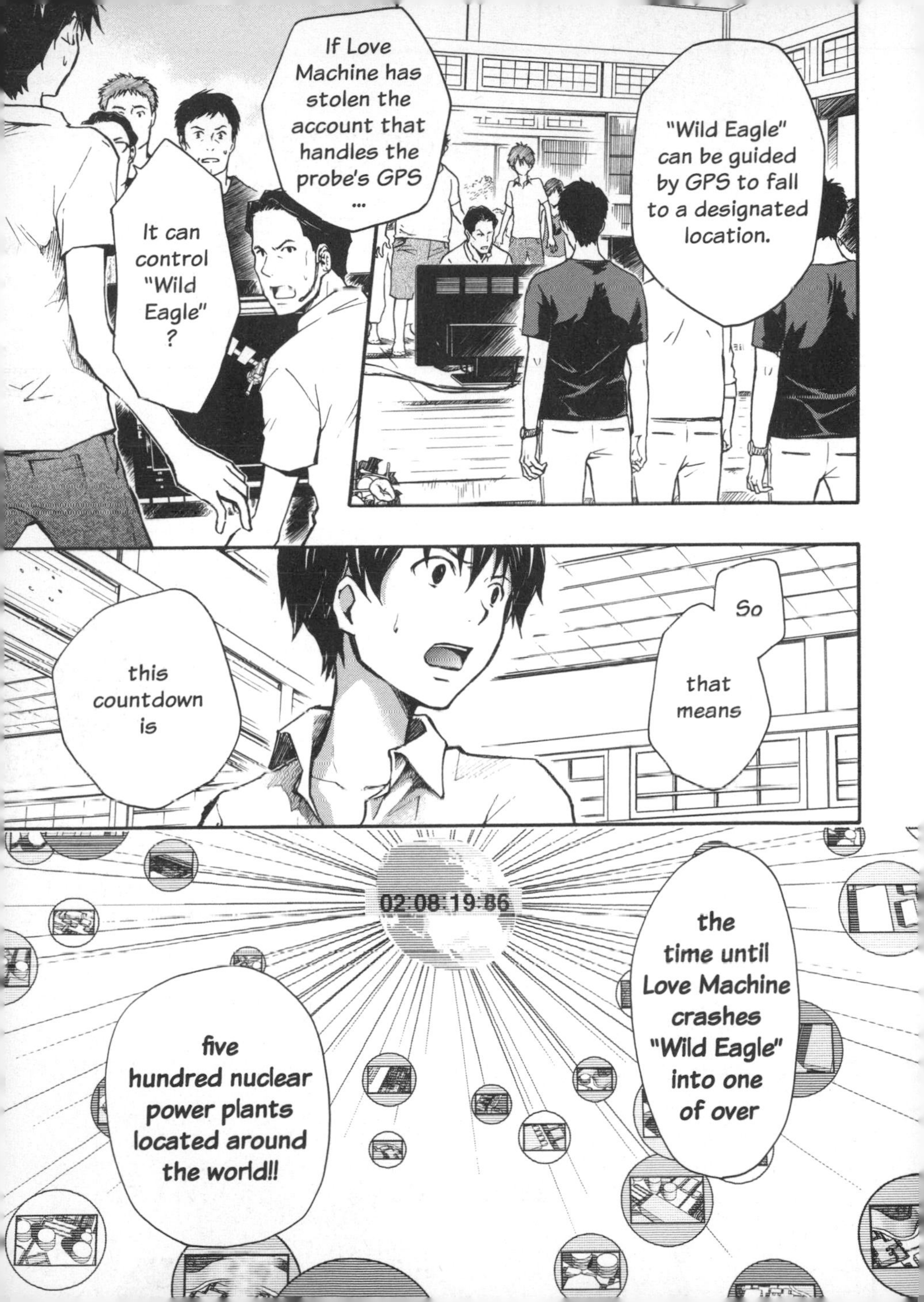
"Wild Eagle" can be guided by GPS to fall to a designated location.
If Love Machine has stolen the account that handles the probe's GPS ...
It can control "Wild Eagle" ?
So that means
this countdown is
02:08:19:86
the time until Love Machine crashes "Wild Eagle" into one of over
five hundred nuclear power plants located around the world!!

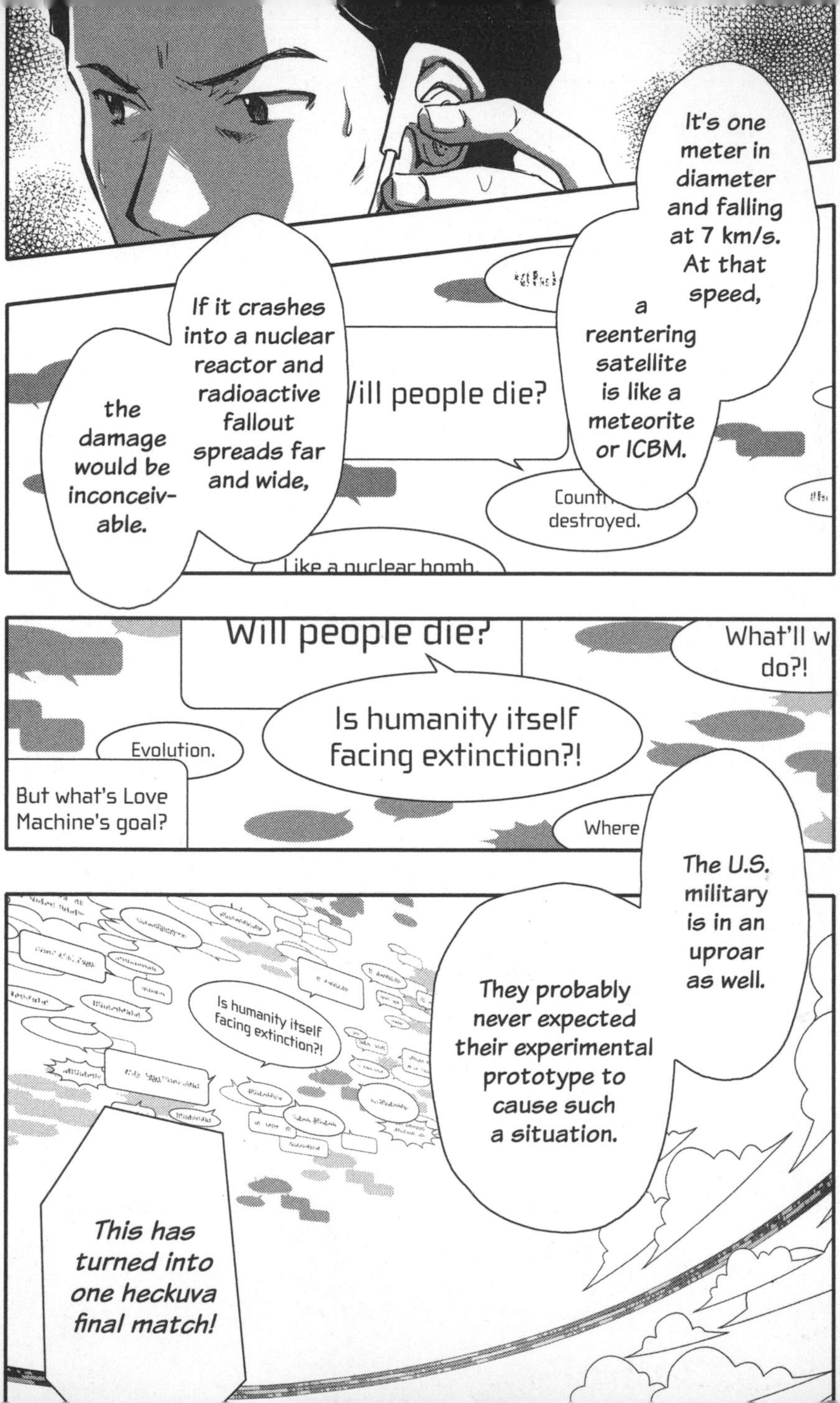

It's one meter in diameter and falling at 7 km/s. At that speed,
a reentering satellite is like a meteorite or ICBM.
If it crashes into a nuclear reactor and radioactive fallout spreads far and wide,
the damage would be inconceivable.
Will people die?
destroyed.
Will people die?
Is humanity itself facing extinction?!
Evolution.
But what's Love Machine's goal?
Where
The U.S. military is in an uproar as well.
They probably never expected their experimental prototype to cause such a situation.
Is humanity itself facing extinction?!
This has turned into one heckuva final match!

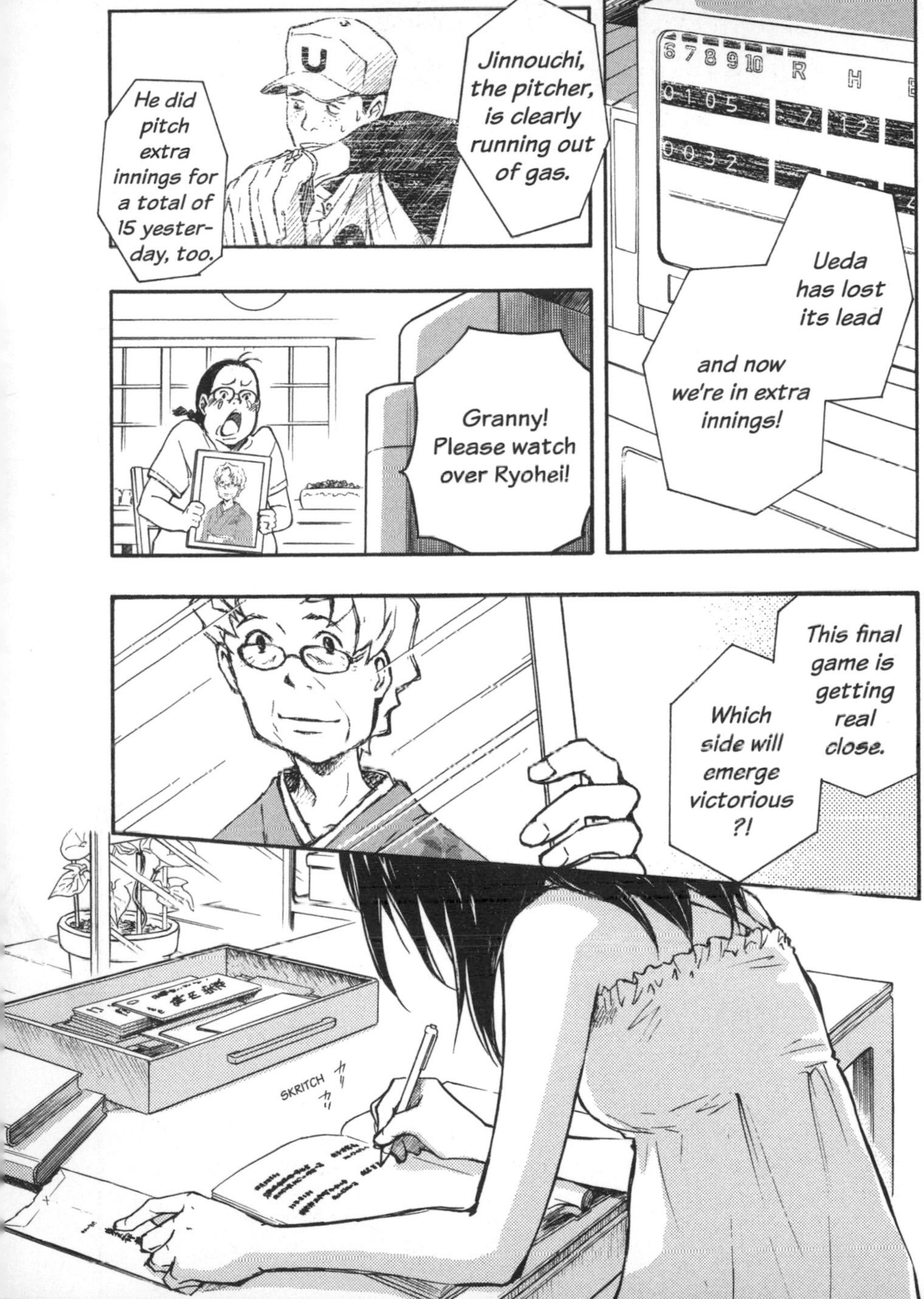
Ueda has lost its lead
and now we're in extra innings!
Jinnouchi, the pitcher, is clearly running out of gas.
He did pitch extra innings for a total of 15 yesterday, too.
Granny! Please watch over Ryohei!
This final game is getting real close.
Which side will emerge victorious?!
SKRITCH

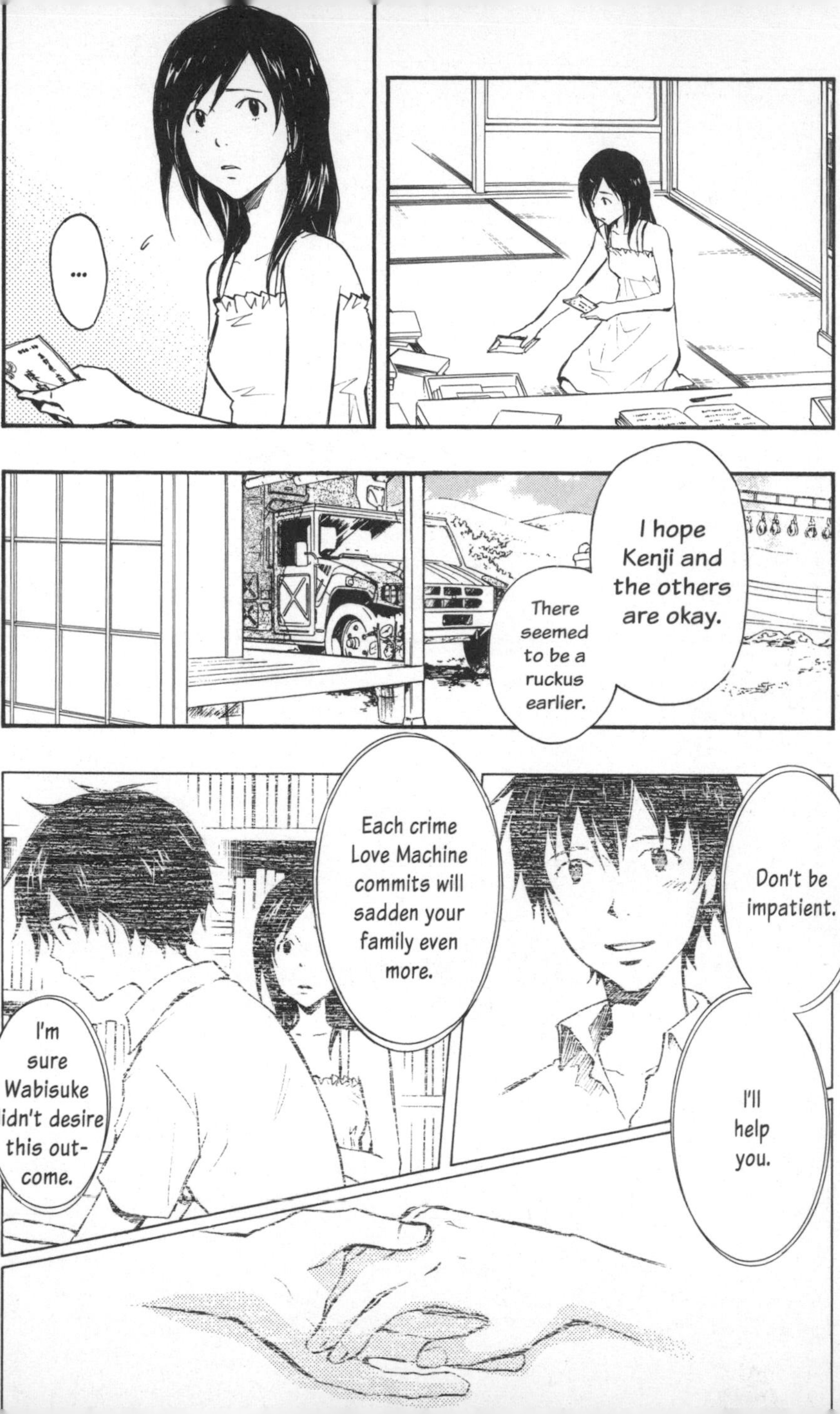
...
I hope Kenji and the others are okay.
There seemed to be a ruckus earlier.
Don't be impatient.
I'll help you.
Each crime Love Machine commits will sadden your family even more.
I'm sure Wabisuke didn't desire this out-come.

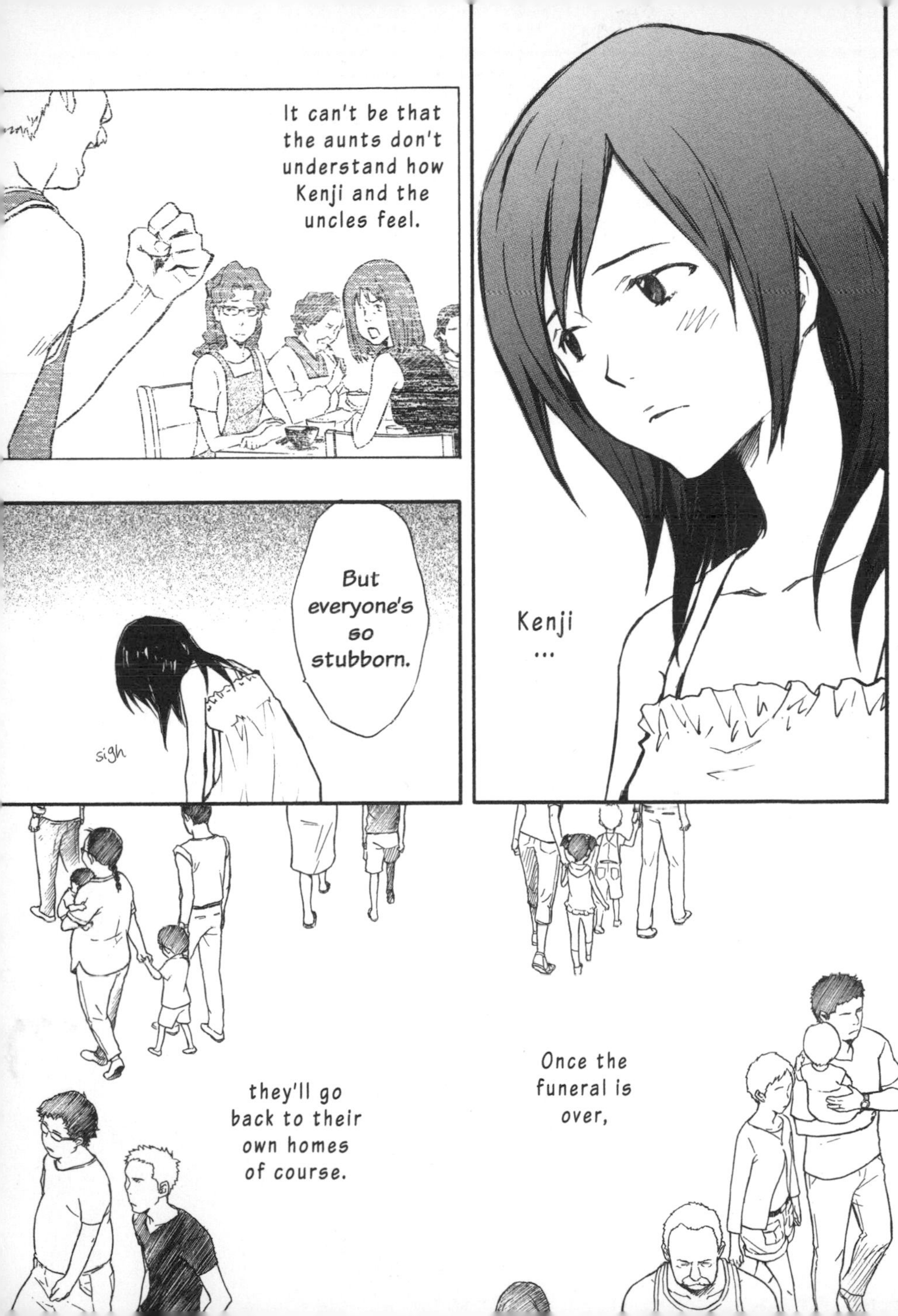
Kenji ...
It can't be that the aunts don't understand how Kenji and the uncles feel.
But everyone's so stubborn.
sigh
Once the funeral is over,
they'll go back to their own homes of course.

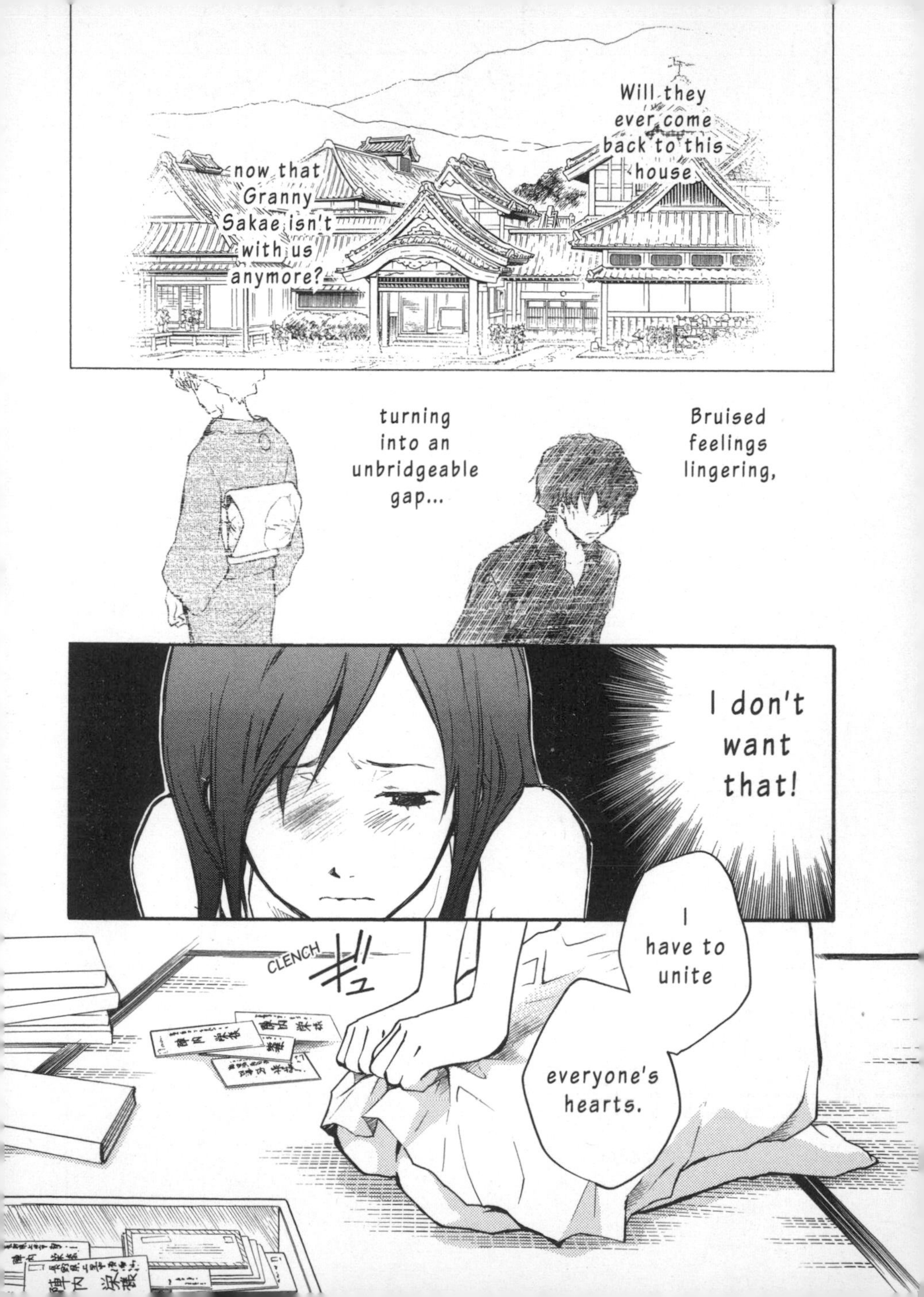
Will they ever come back to this house
now that Granny Sakae isn't with us anymore?
Bruised feelings lingering,
turning into an unbridgeable gap...
I don't want that!
I have to unite
everyone's hearts.
CLENCH

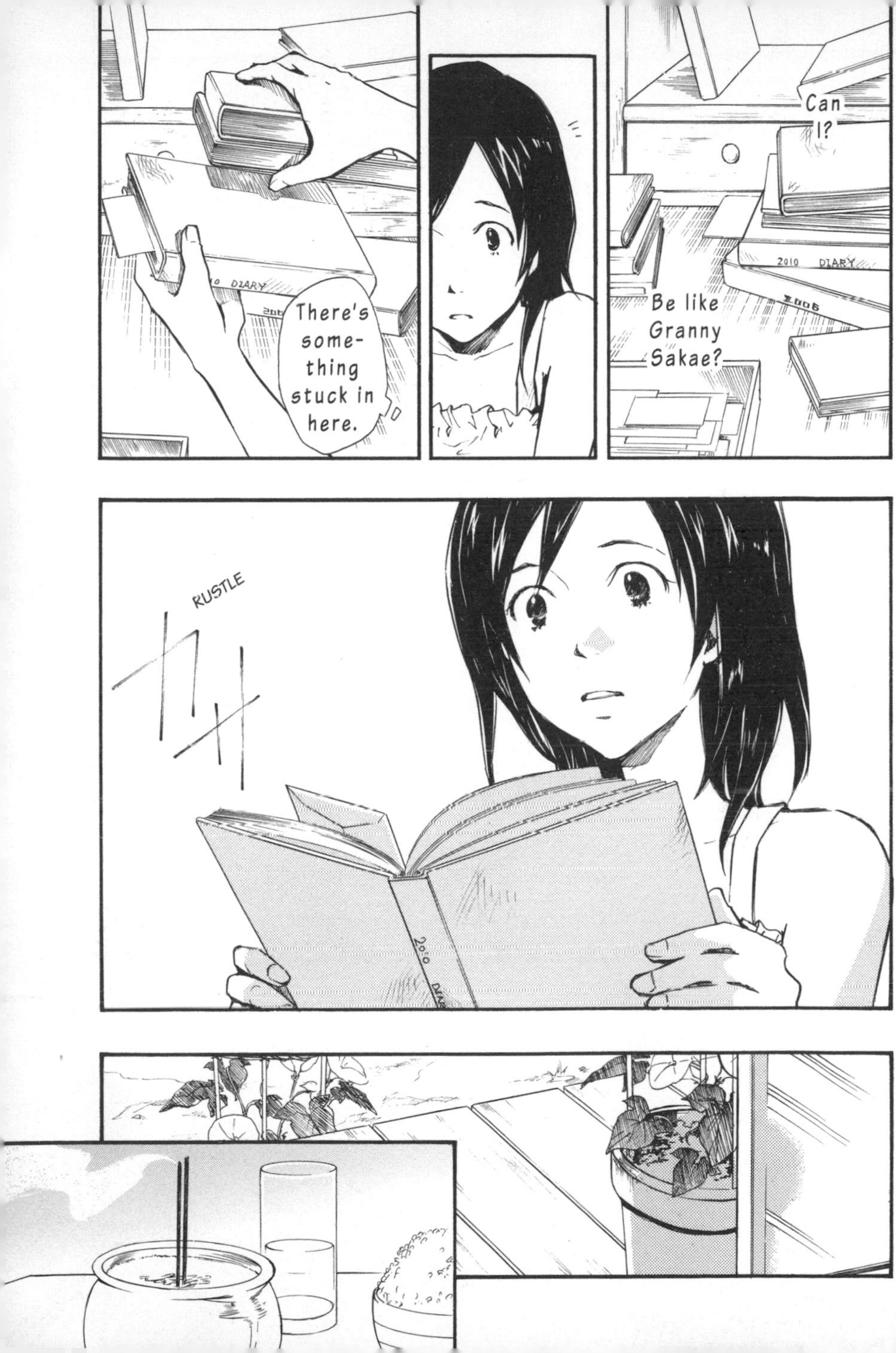
Can I?
Be like Granny Sakae?
2010 DIARY
There's some-thing stuck in here.
RUSTLE

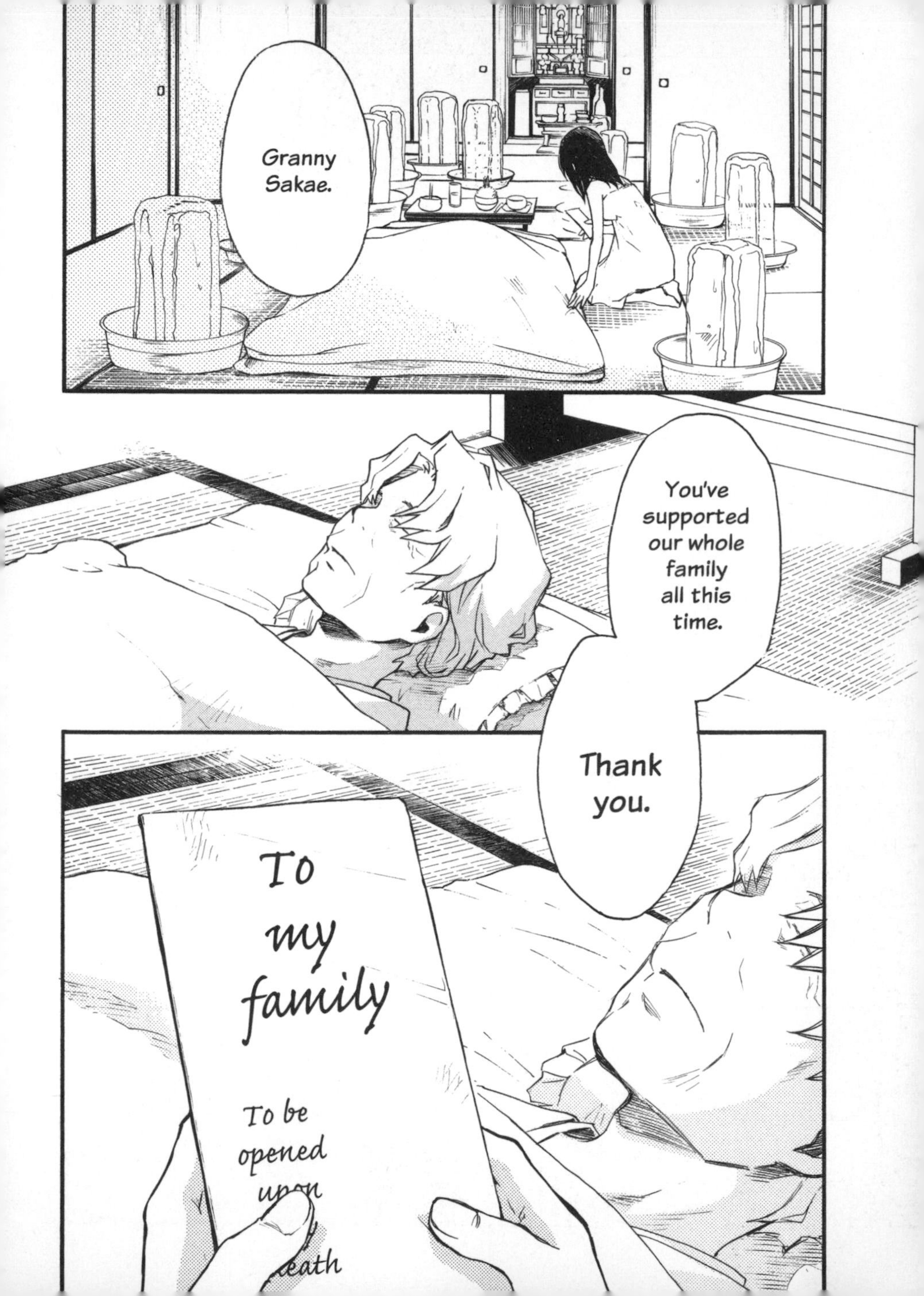
Granny Sakae.
You've supported our whole family all this time.
Thank you.
To my family
To be opened

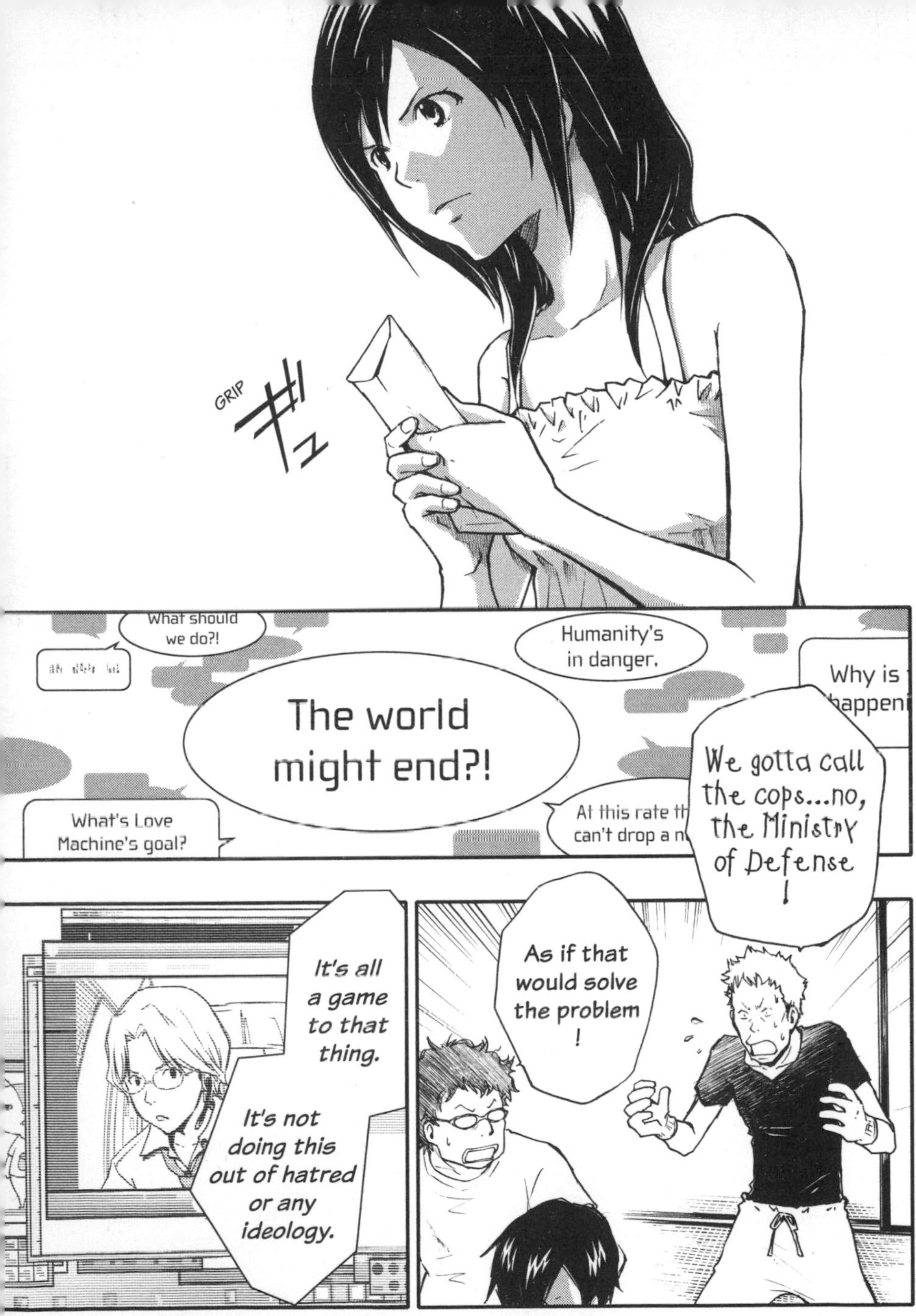

GRIP
Why is
Humanity's in danger.
What should we do?!
The world might end?!
At this rate th can't drop a n
What's Love Machine's goal?
We gotta call the cops...no, the Ministry of Defense!
As if that would solve the problem!
It's all a game to that thing.
It's not doing this out of hatred or any ideology.

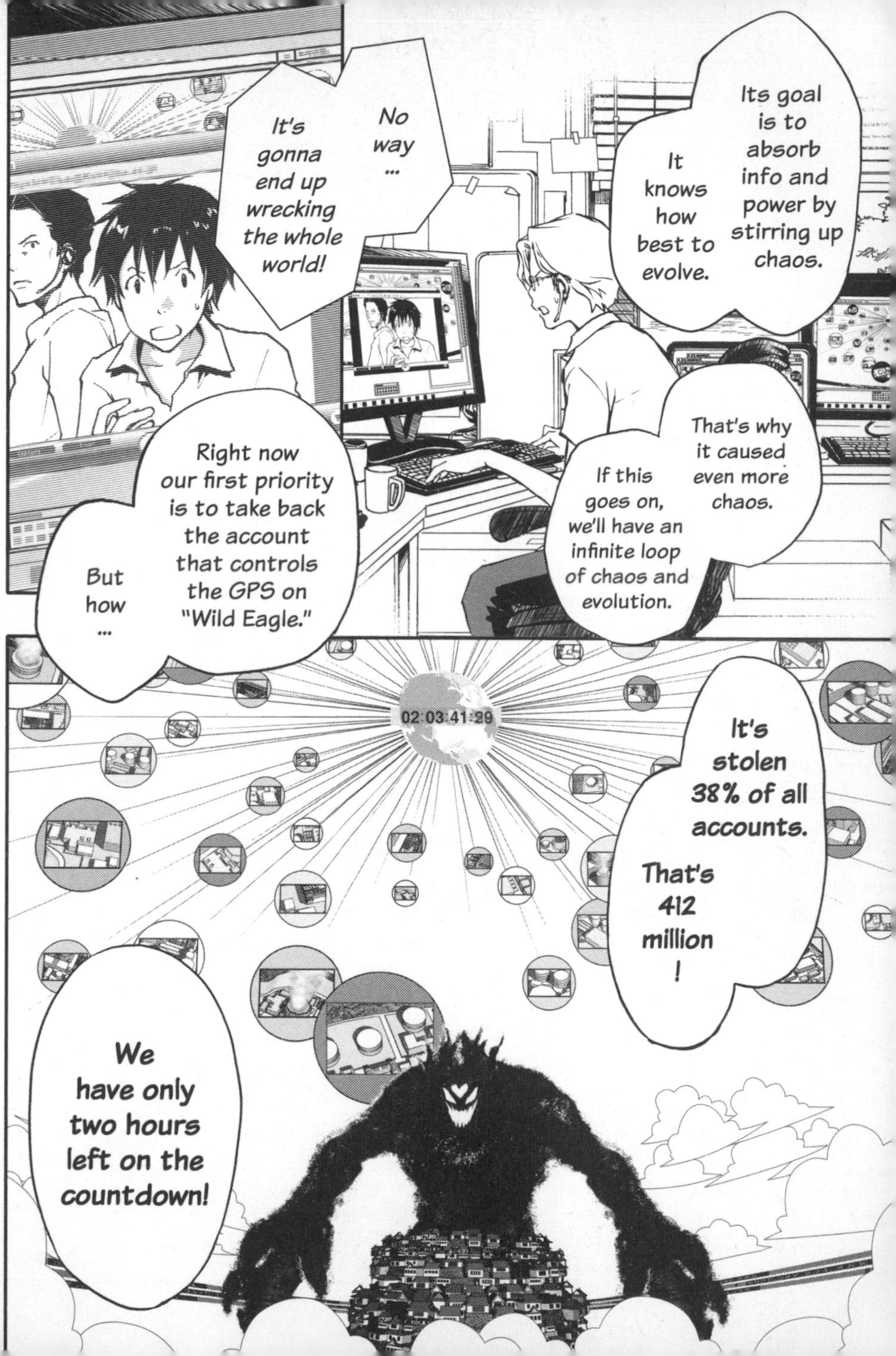
Its goal is to absorb info and power by stirring up chaos.
It knows how best to evolve.
No way ...
It's gonna end up wrecking the whole world!
That's why it caused even more chaos.
If this goes on, we'll have an infinite loop of chaos and evolution.
Right now our first priority is to take back the account that controls the GPS on "Wild Eagle."
But how ...
02:03:41:29
It's stolen 38% of all accounts.
That's 412 million!
We have only two hours left on the countdown!

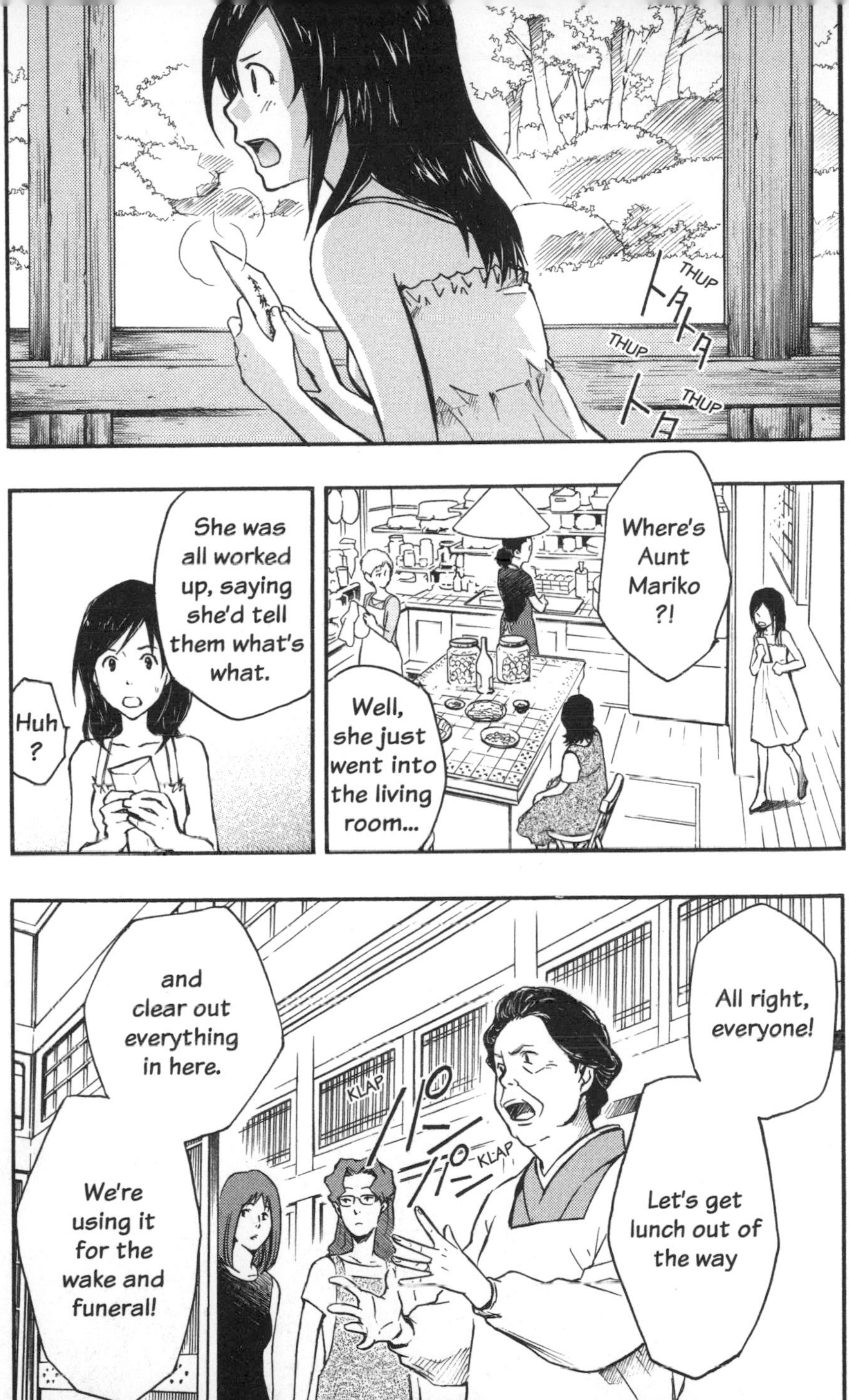
THUP
トタトタ
THUP
THUP
トタ
Where's Aunt Mariko ?!
Well, she just went into the living room...
She was all worked up, saying she'd tell them what's what.
Huh ?
All right, everyone!
Let's get lunch out of the way
and clear out everything in here.
We're using it for the wake and funeral!
KLAP
KLAP

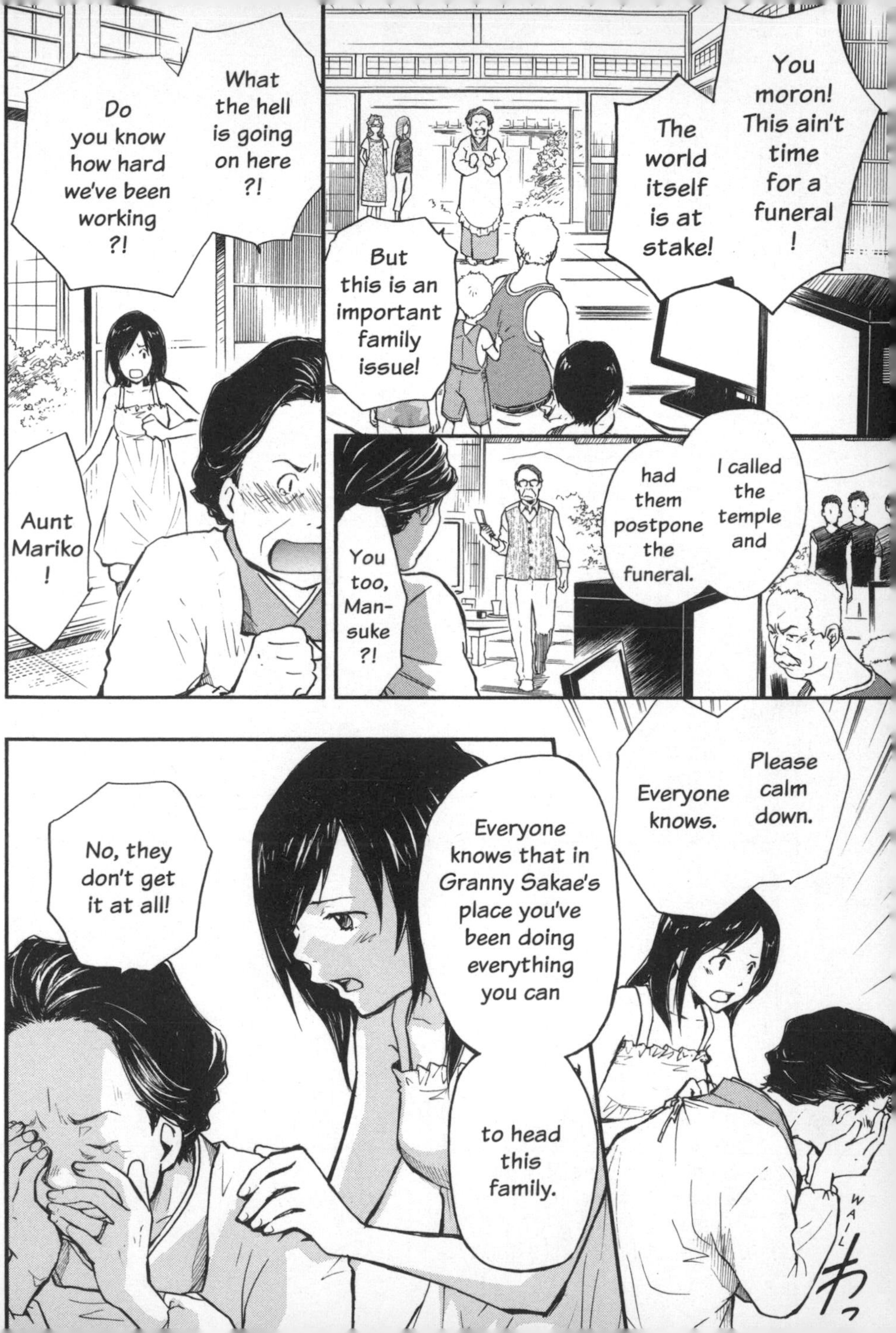
You moron! This ain't time for a funeral!
The world itself is at stake!
But this is an important family issue!
I called the temple and
had them postpone the funeral.
You too, Man-suke?!
What the hell is going on here?!
Do you know how hard we've been working?!
Aunt Mariko!
Please calm down.
Everyone knows.
Everyone knows that in Granny Sakae's place you've been doing everything you can
to head this family.
No, they don't get it at all!
WAIL

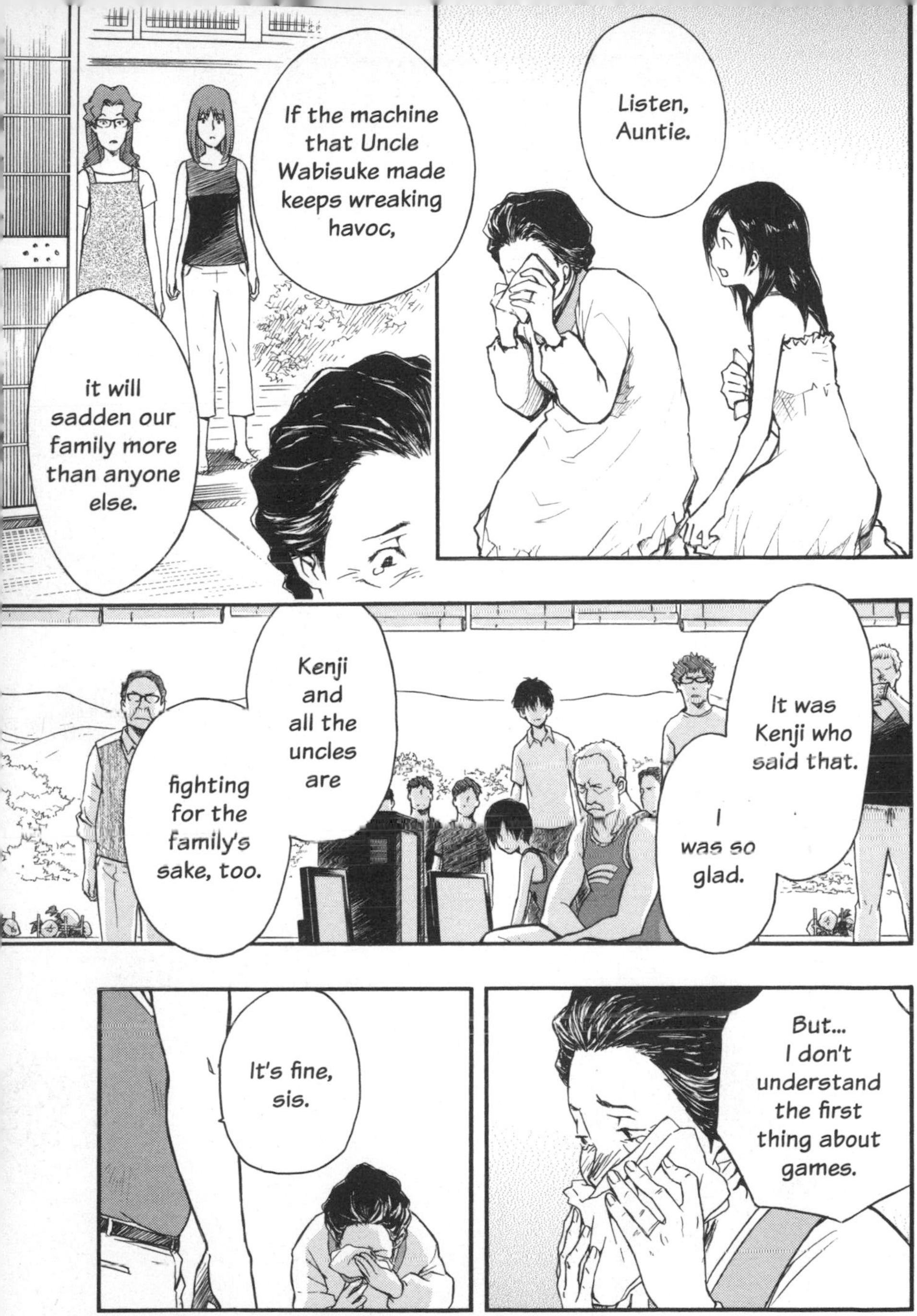
Listen, Auntie.
If the machine that Uncle Wabisuke made keeps wreaking havoc,
it will sadden our family more than anyone else.
It was Kenji who said that.
I was so glad.
Kenji and all the uncles are
fighting for the family's sake, too.
But... I don't understand the first thing about games.
It's fine, sis.

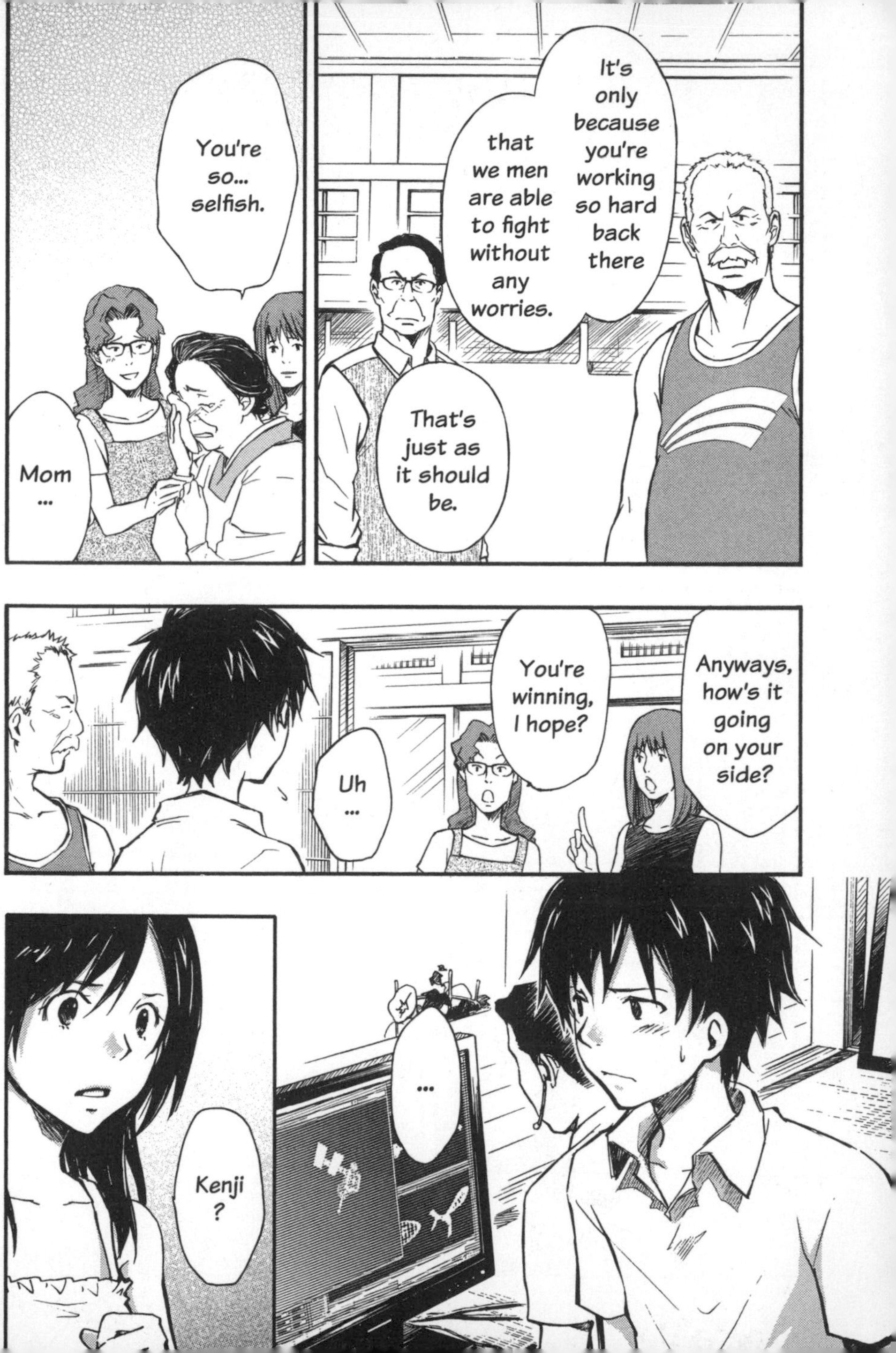
It's only because you're working so hard back there
that we men are able to fight without any worries.
That's just as it should be.
You're so... selfish.
Mom ...
Anyways, how's it going on your side?
You're winning, I hope?
Uh ...
...
Kenji ?

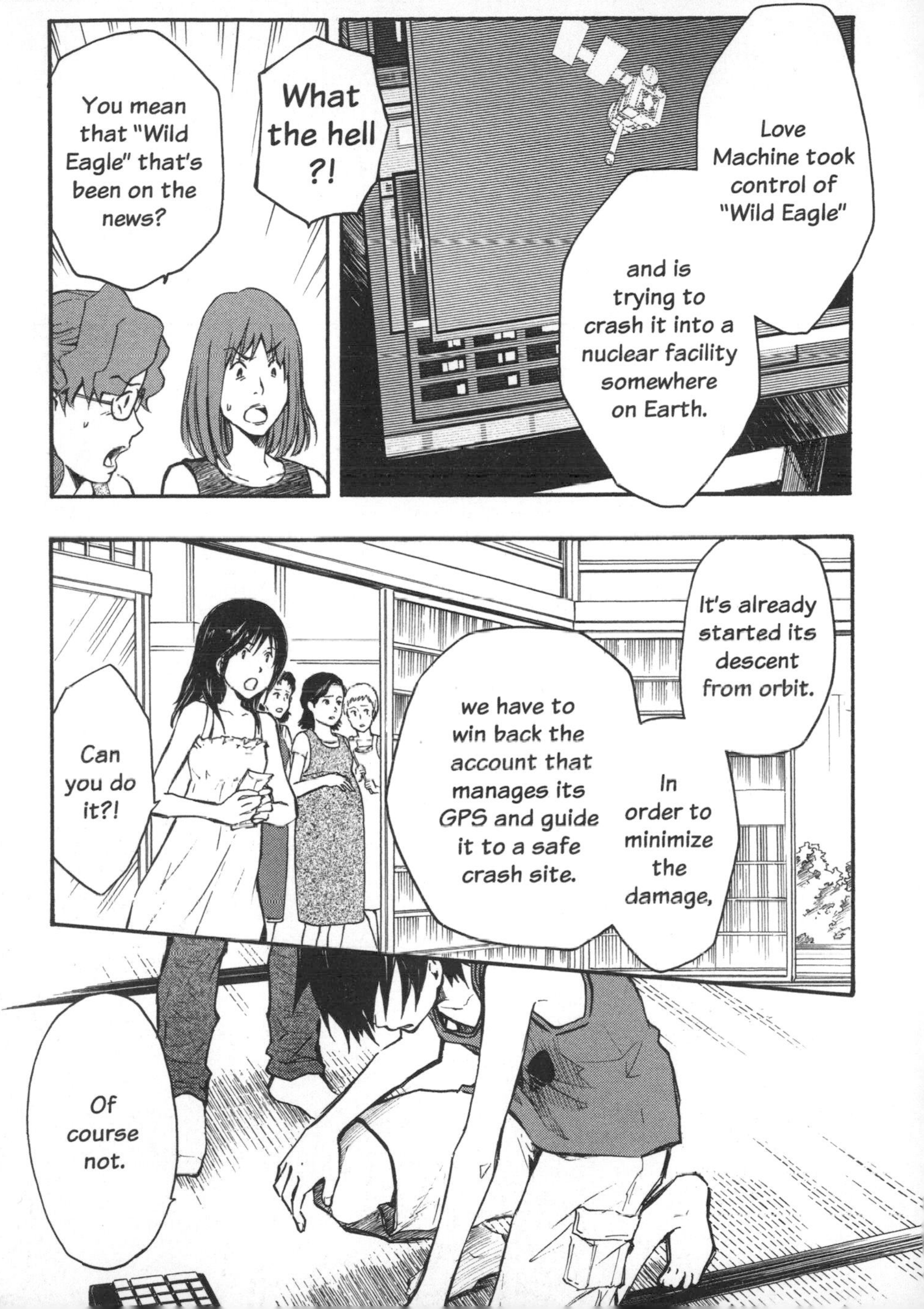
Love Machine took control of "Wild Eagle"
and is trying to crash it into a nuclear facility somewhere on Earth.
What the hell ?!
You mean that "Wild Eagle" that's been on the news?
It's already started its descent from orbit.
In order to minimize the damage,
we have to win back the account that manages its GPS and guide it to a safe crash site.
Can you do it?!
Of course not.

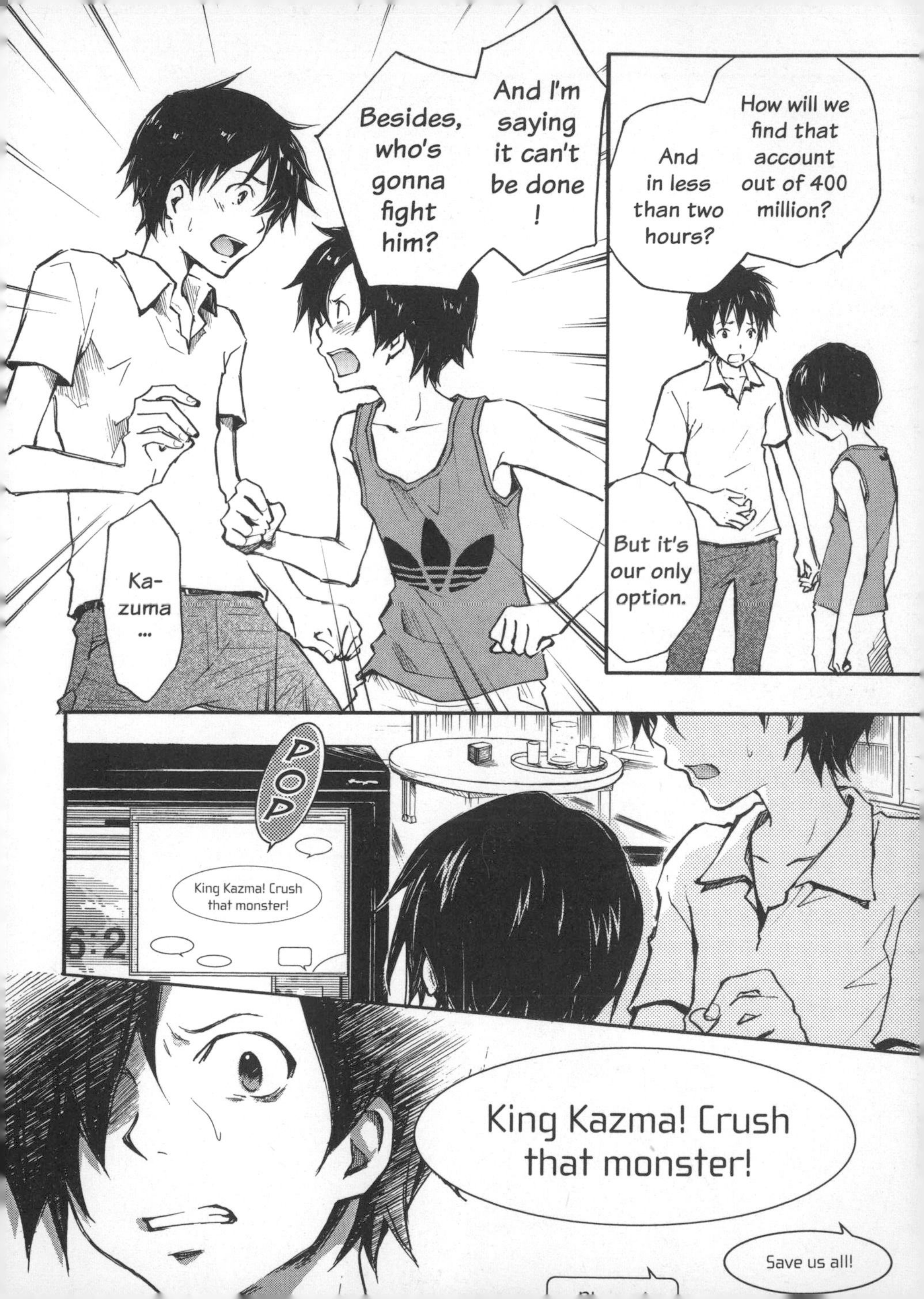
How will we find that account out of 400 million?
And in less than two hours?
But it's our only option.
And I'm saying it can't be done!
Besides, who's gonna fight him?
Ka-zuma...
POP
King Kazma! Crush that monster!
King Kazma! Crush that monster!
Save us all!

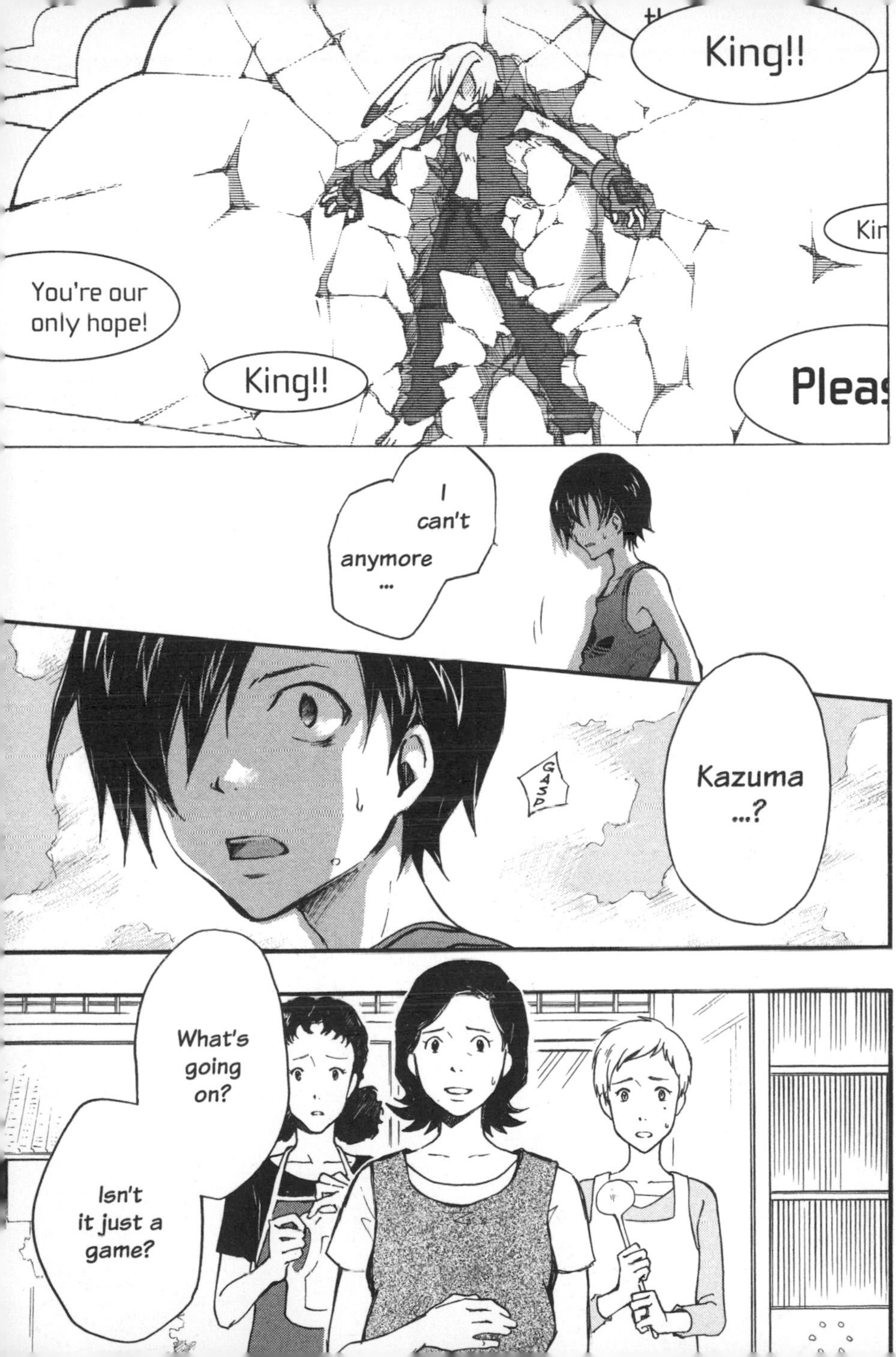
King!!
Kin
Pleas
King!!
You're our only hope!
I can't anymore ...
Kazuma ...?
GASP
What's going on?
Isn't it just a game?

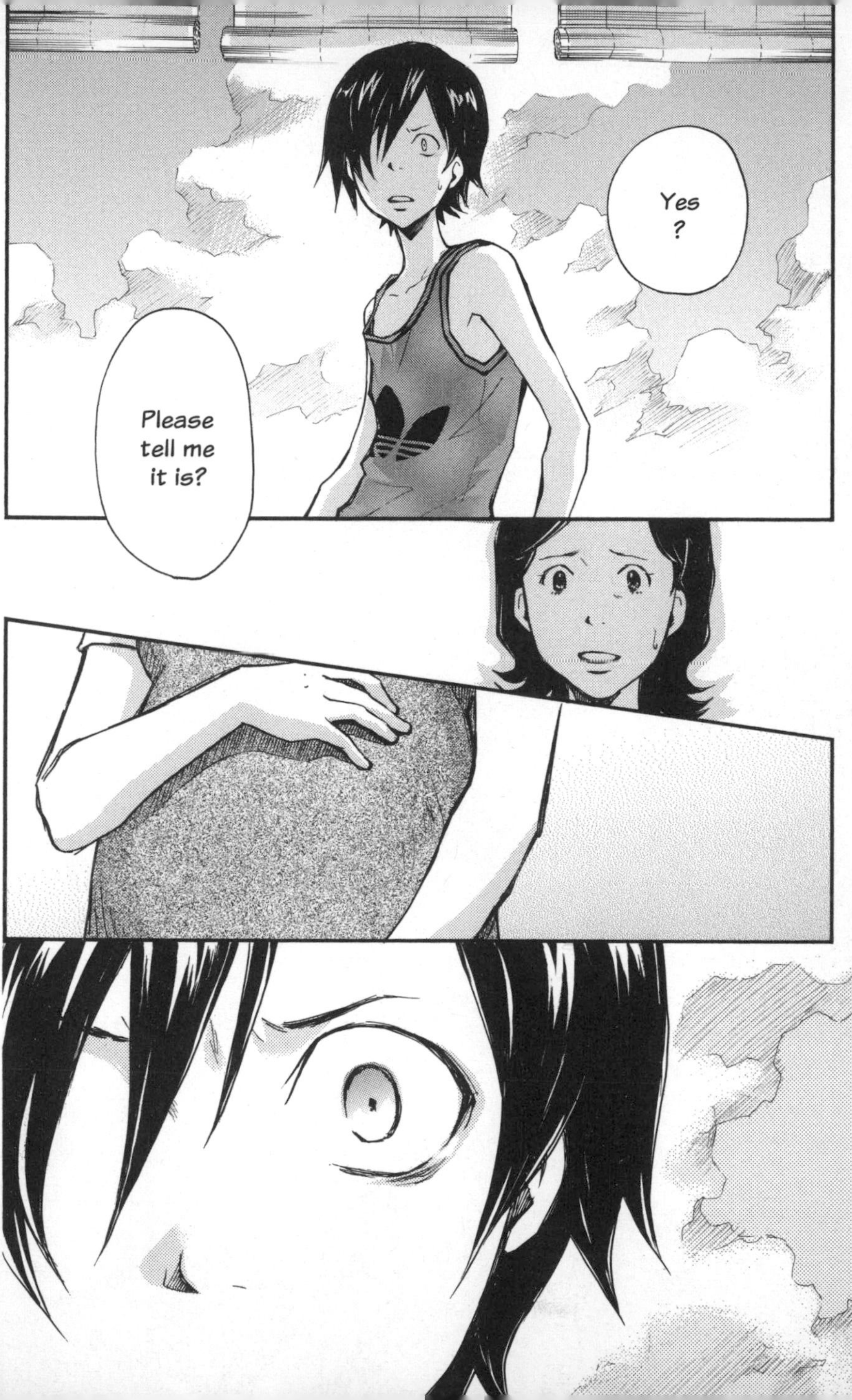
Yes ?
Please tell me it is?

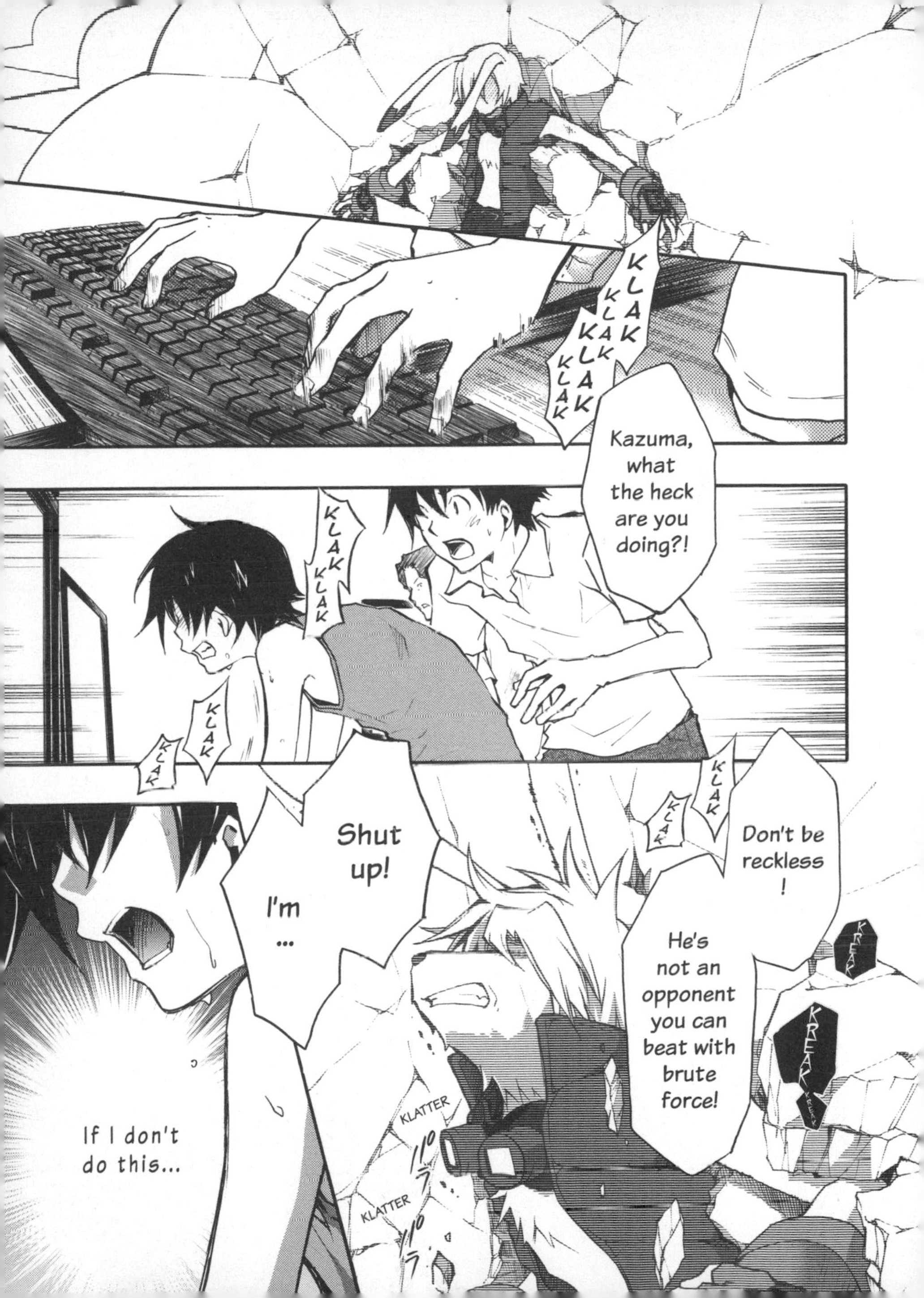
KLAK KLAK KLAK KLAK
Kazuma, what the heck are you doing?!
KLAK KLAK
KLAK KLAK
KLAK KLAK
Don't be reckless!
He's not an opponent you can beat with brute force!
KREAK KREAK
Shut up!
I'm ...
KLATTER KLATTER
If I don't do this...

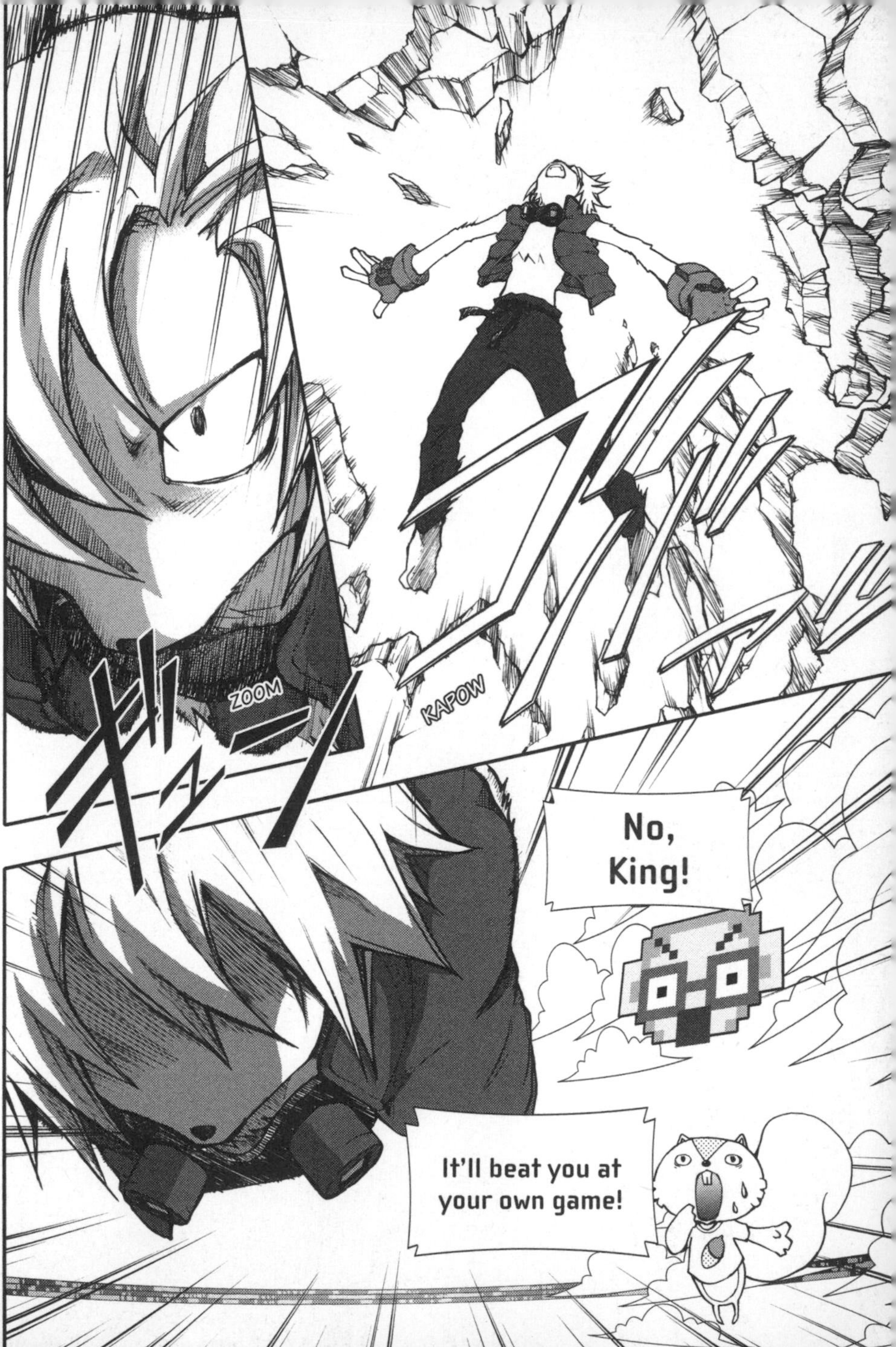
KAPOW
ZOOM
No, King!
It'll beat you at your own game!

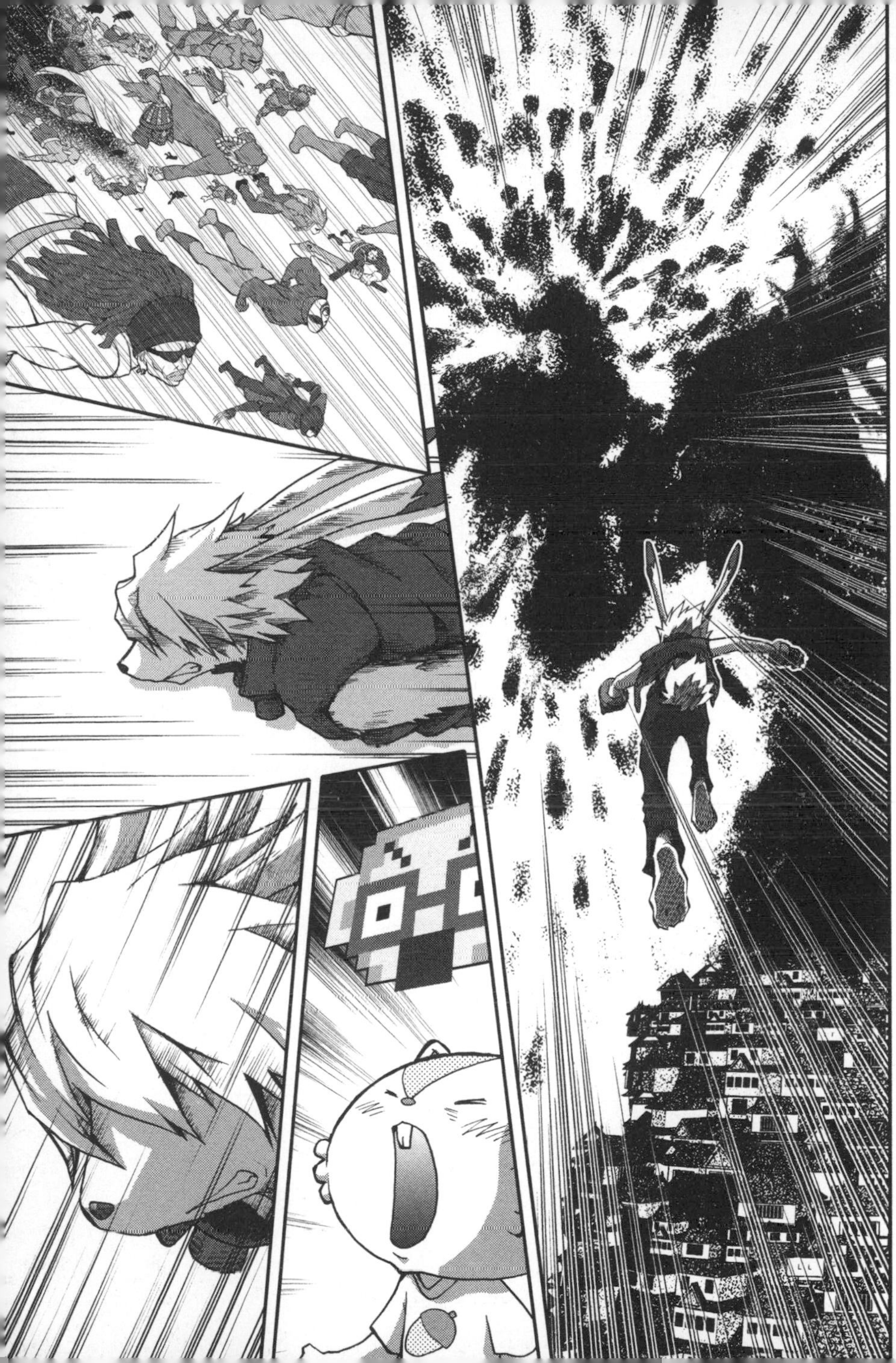

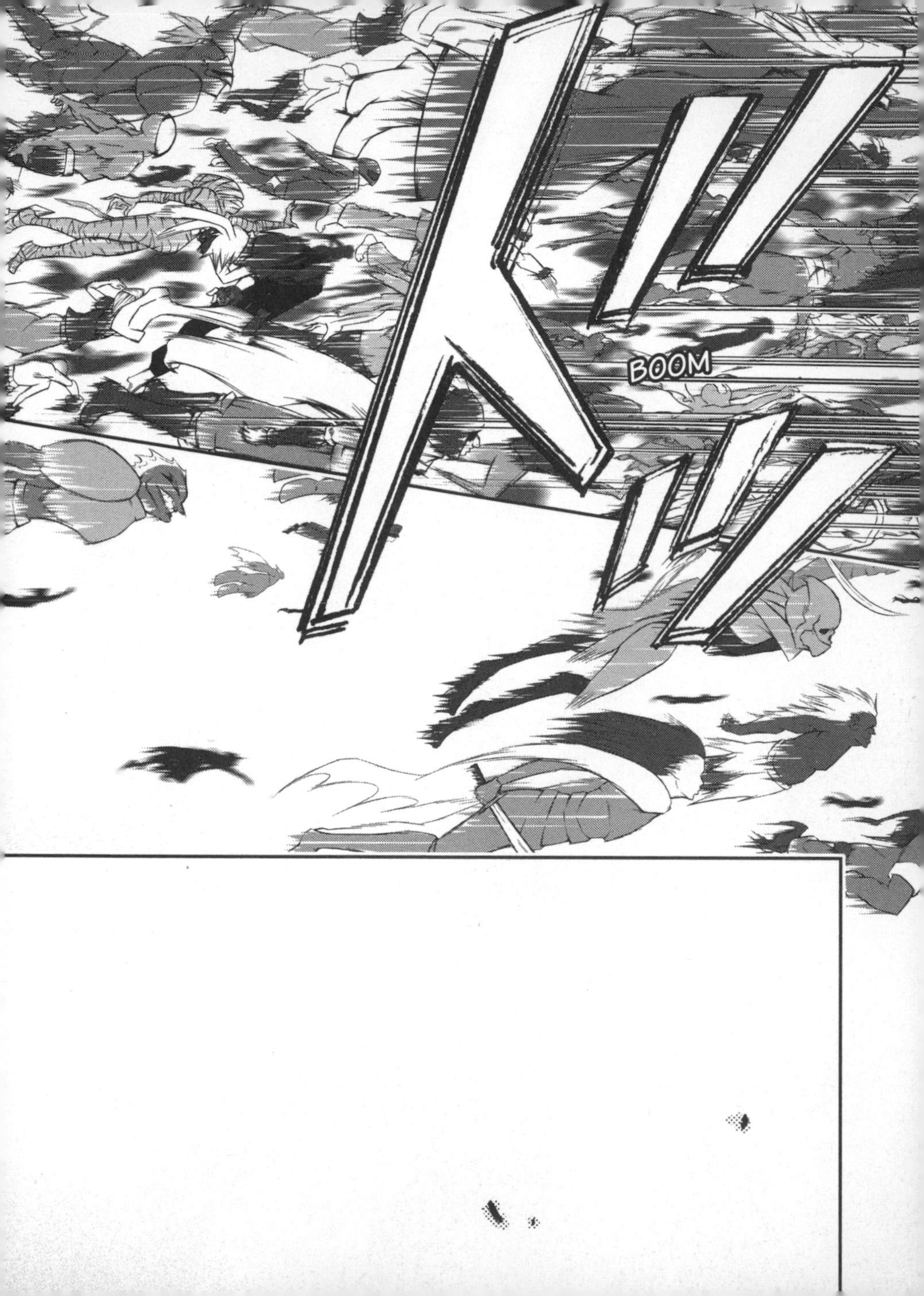
BOOM

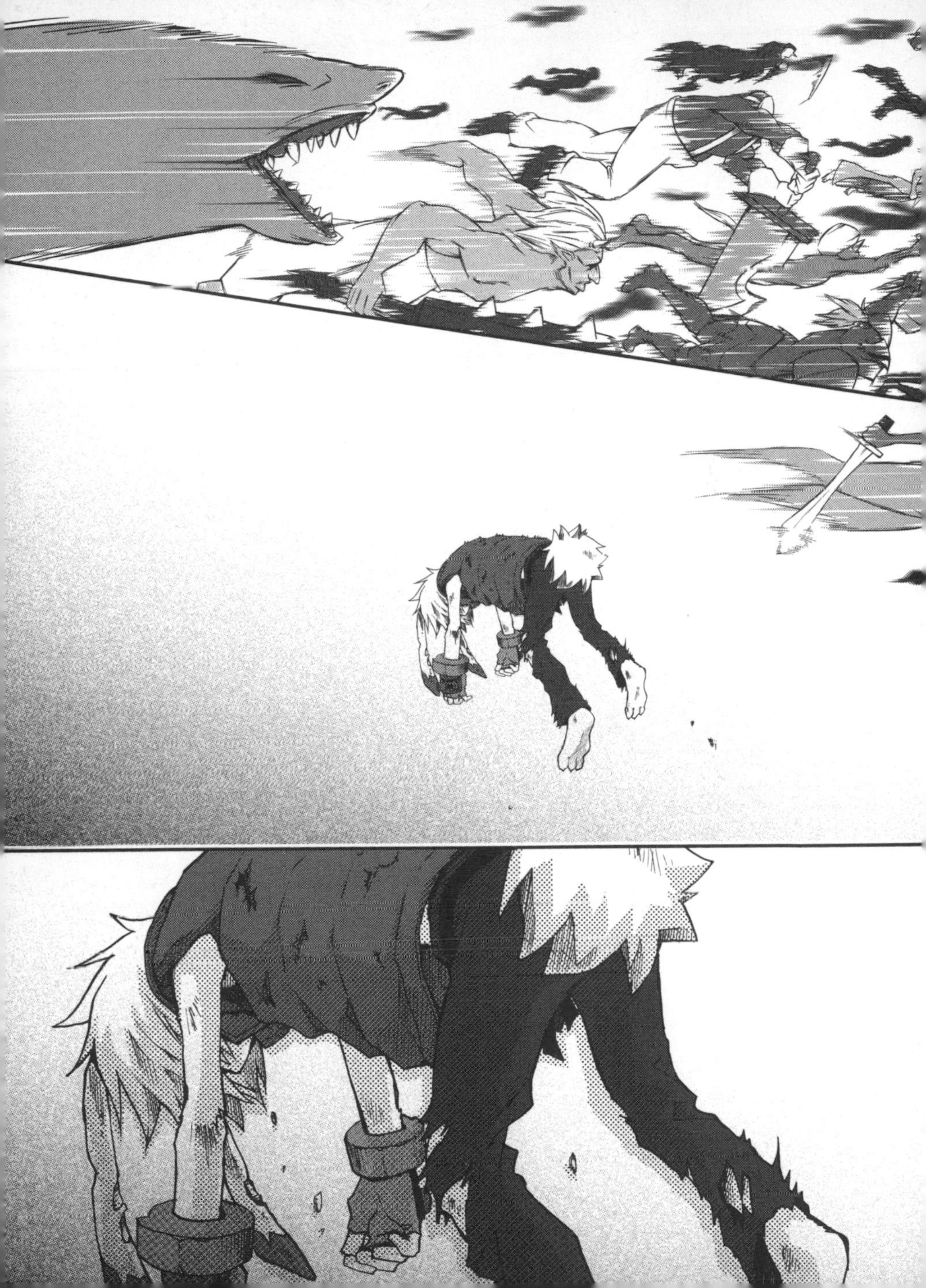

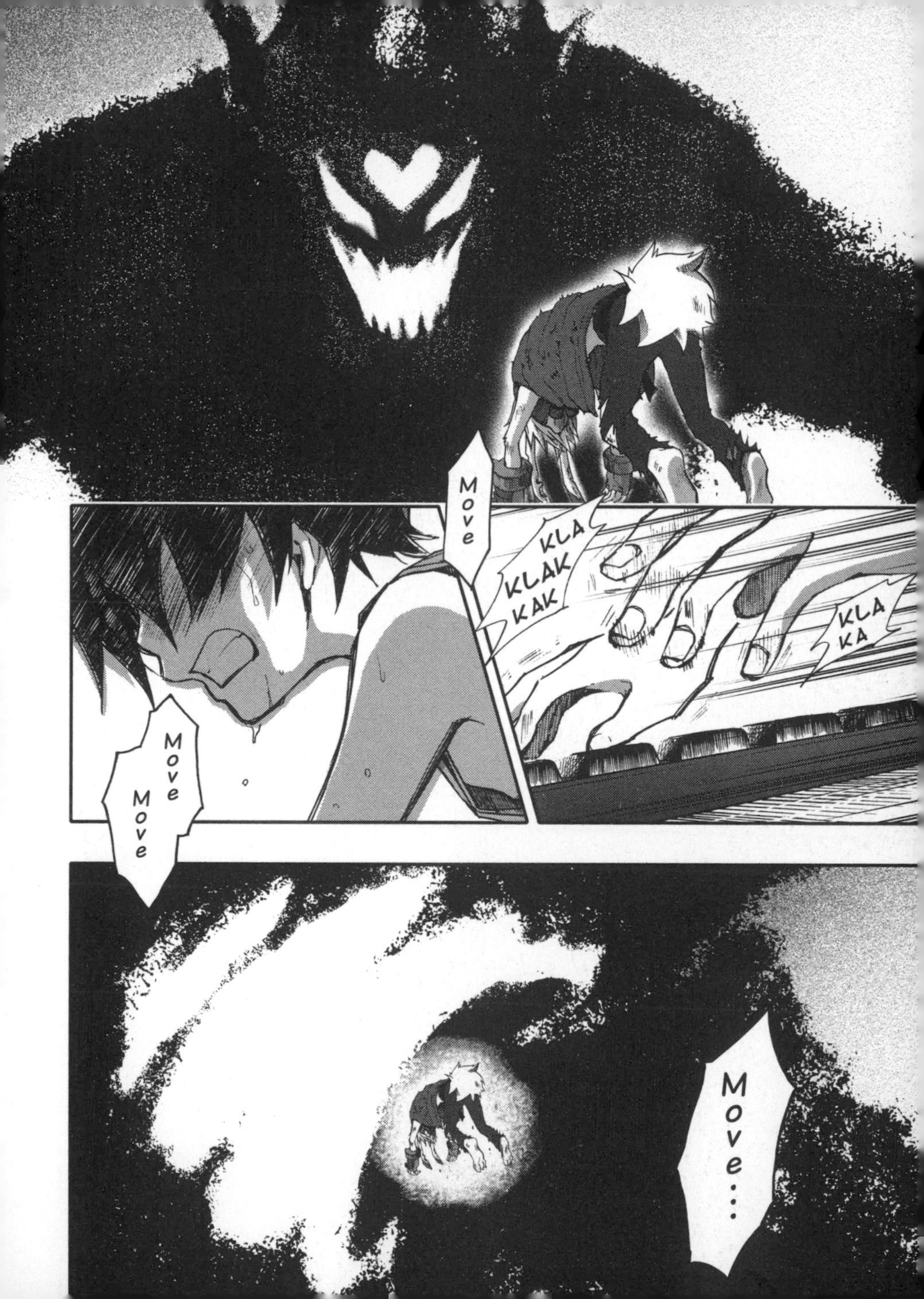
Move
KLA KLAK KAK
KLA KA
Move
Move
Move...

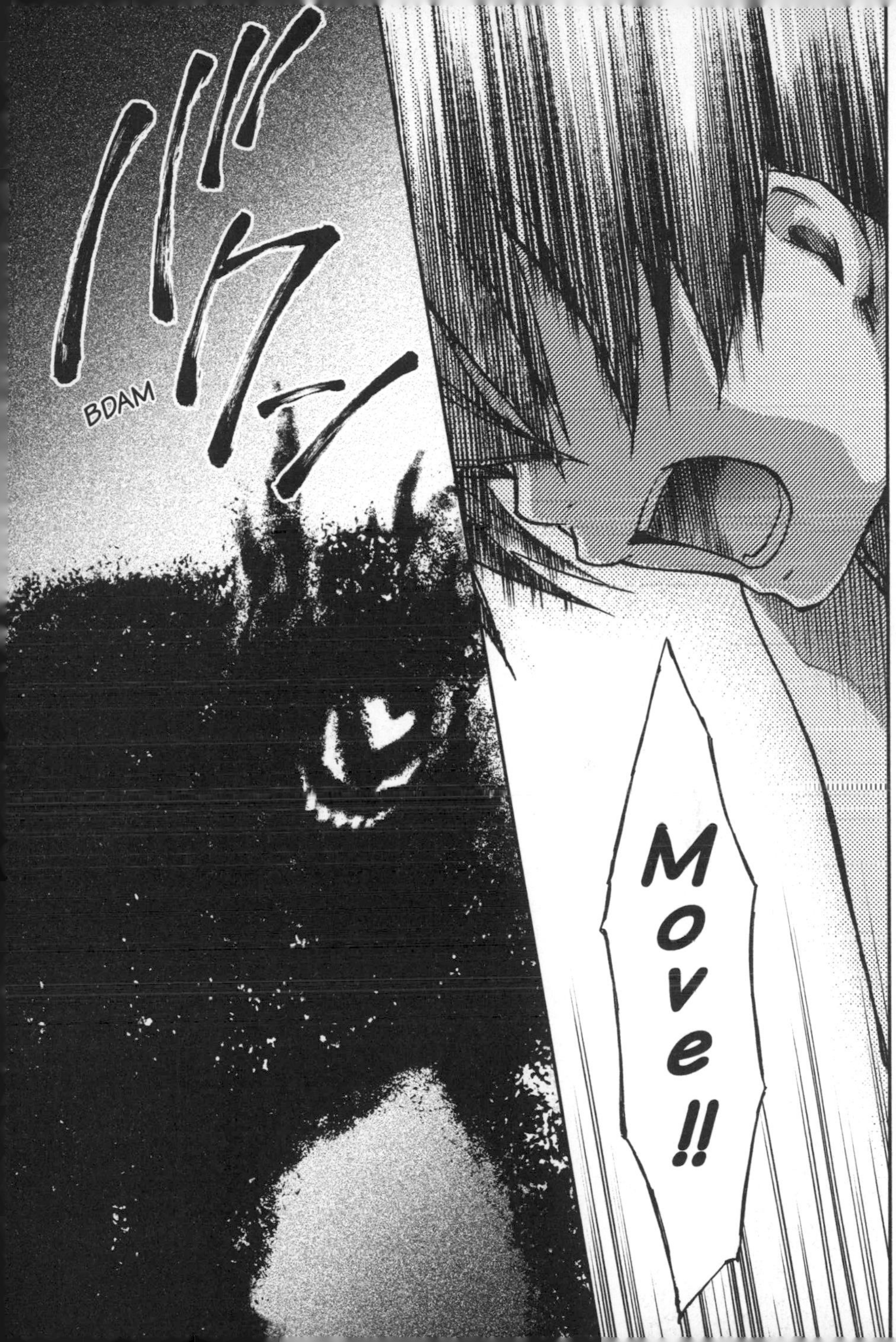
Move!!
BDAM

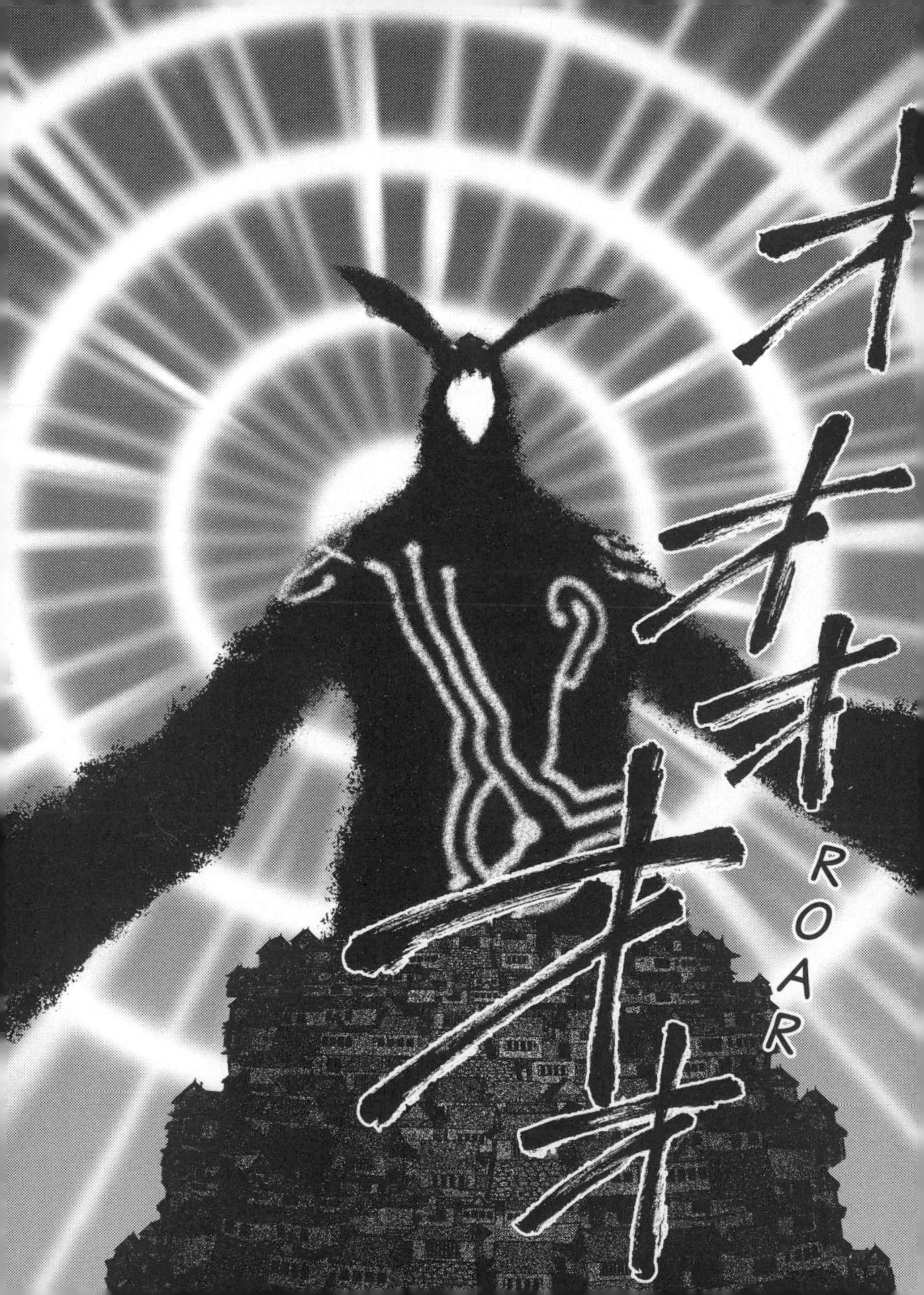
オオオオ
ROAR

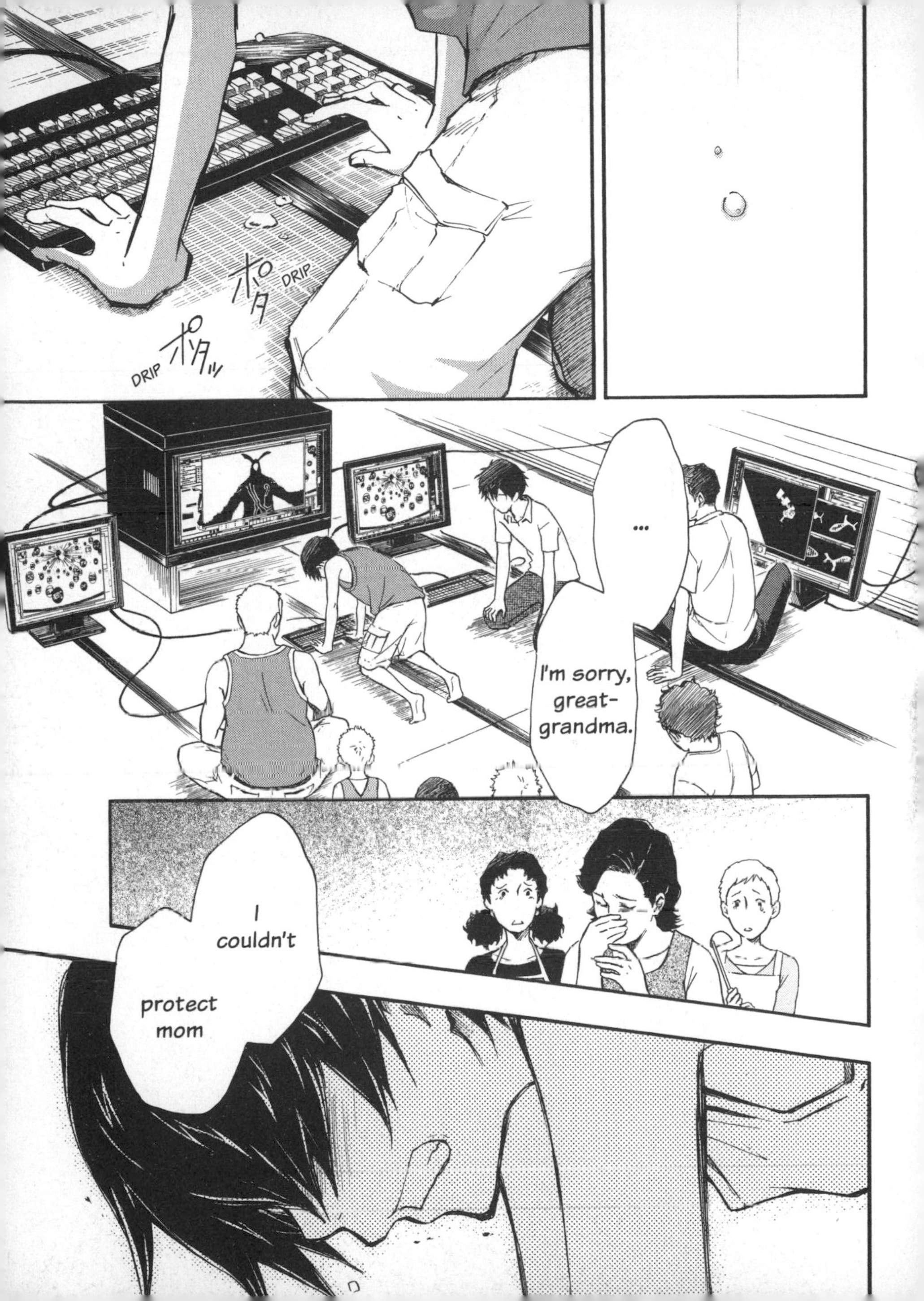

ポタ
DRIP
ポタッ
DRIP
...
I'm sorry, great-grandma.
I couldn't protect mom

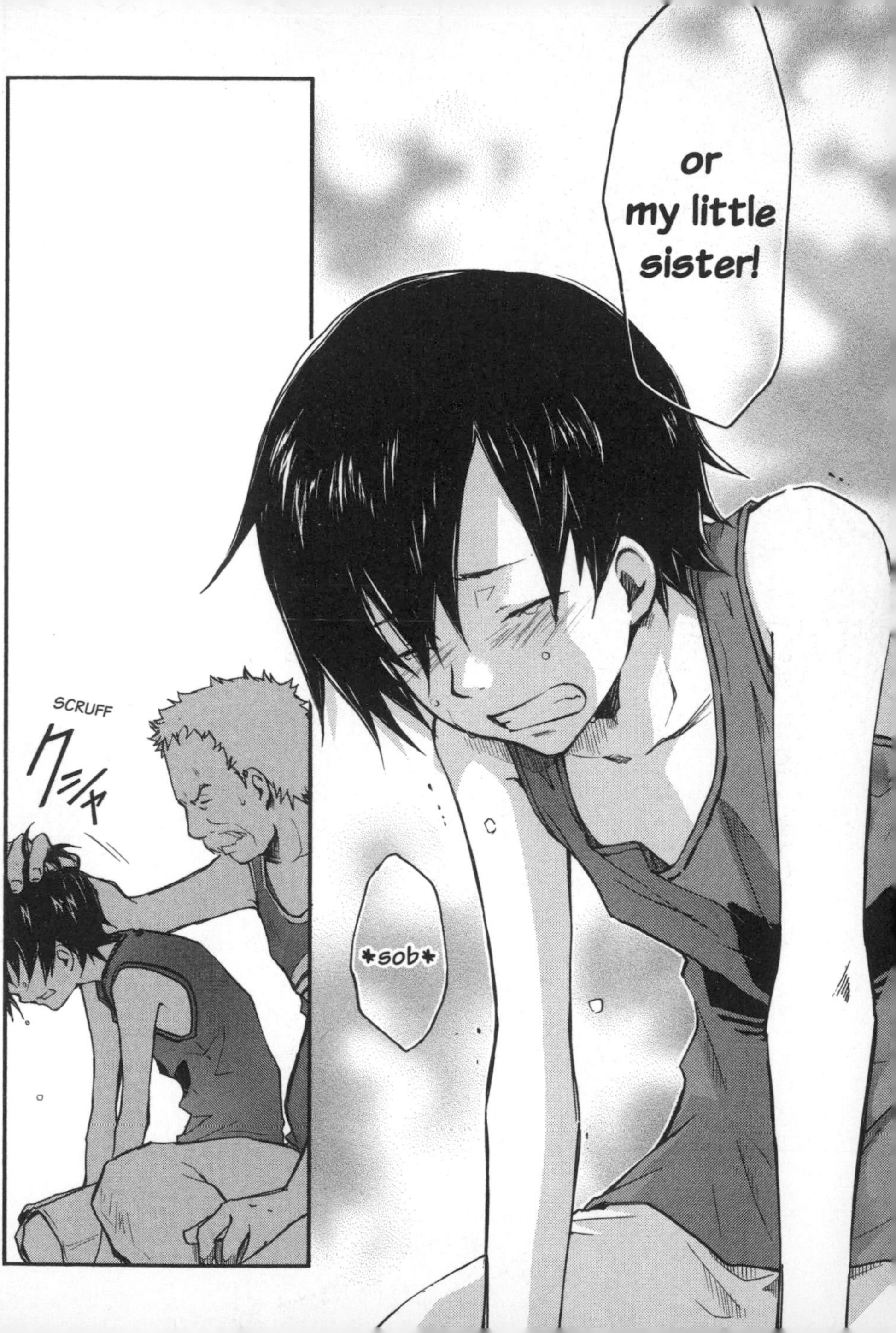
or my little sister!
sob
SCRUFF
クシャ

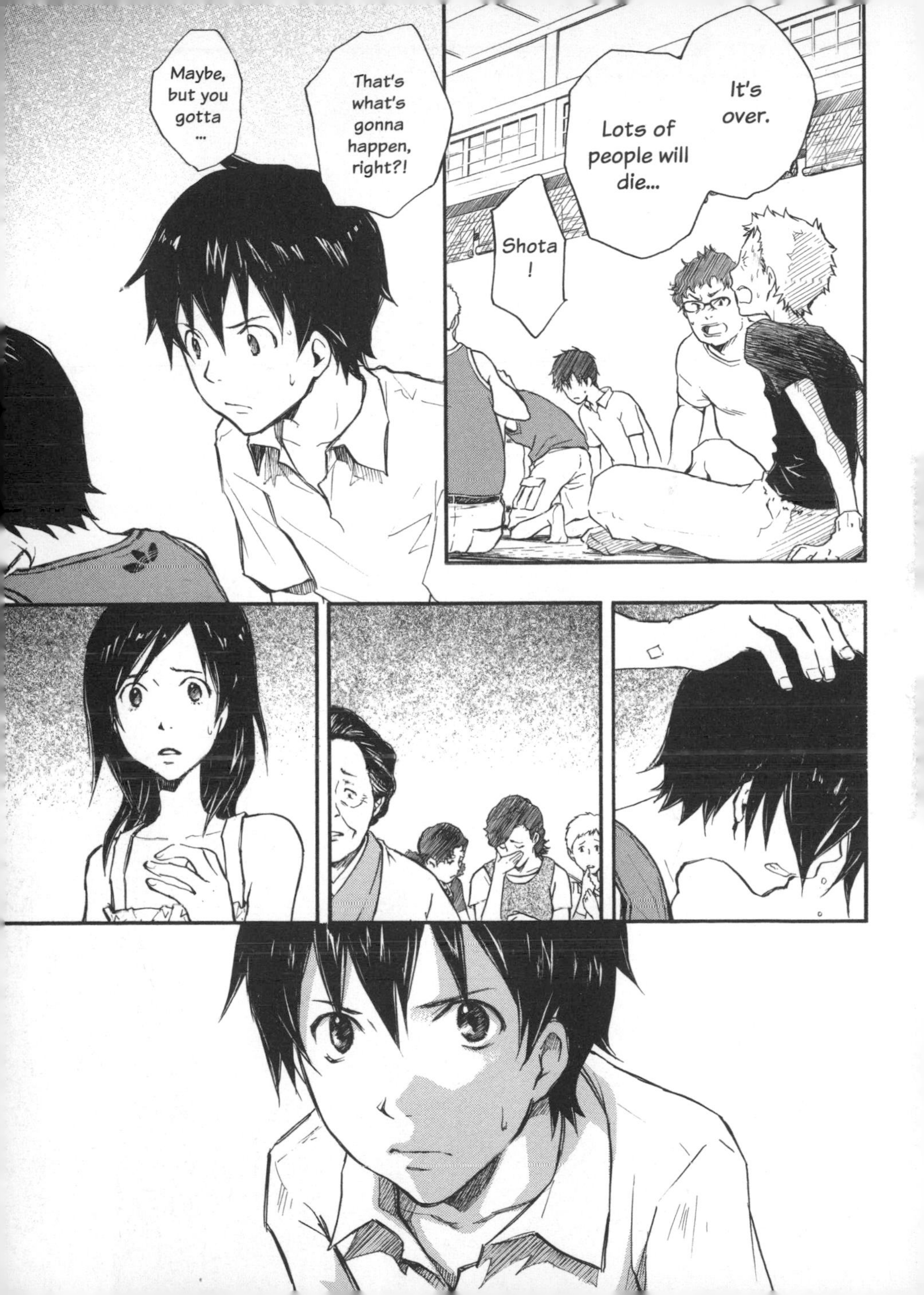
It's over.
Lots of people will die...
Shota!
That's what's gonna happen, right?!
Maybe, but you gotta ...

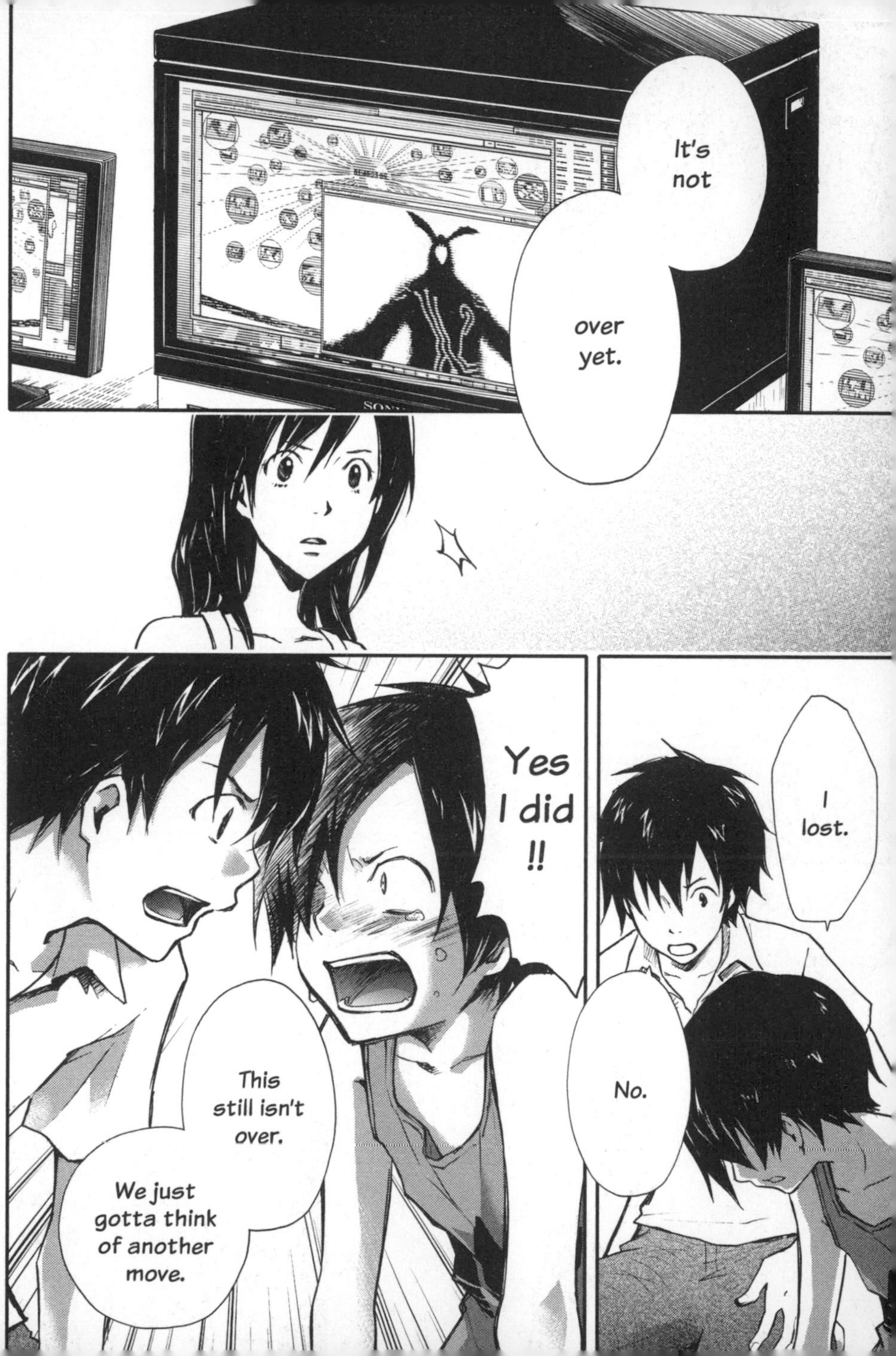
It's not over yet.
I lost.
No.
Yes I did!!
This still isn't over.
We just gotta think of another move.

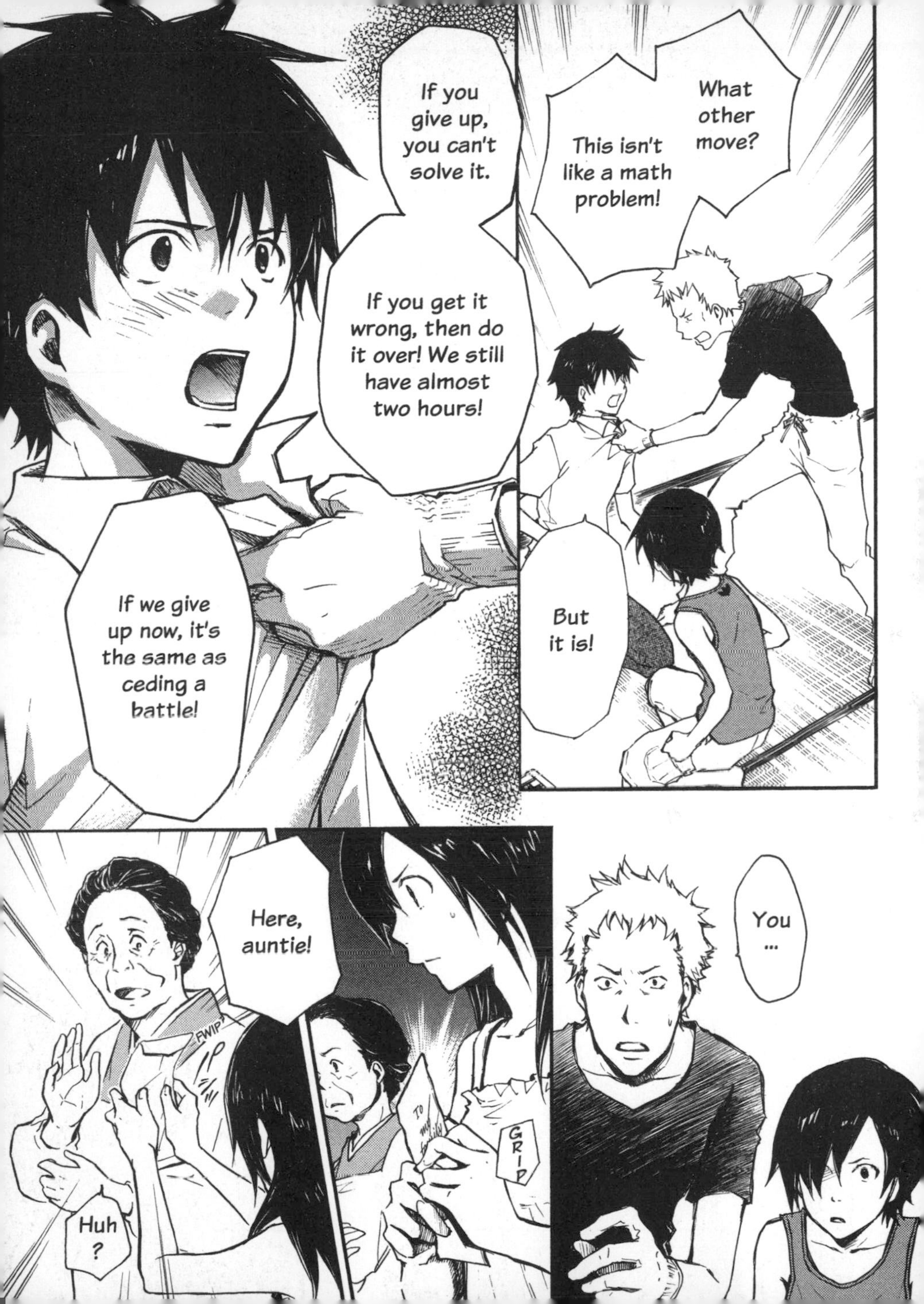
What other move?
This isn't like a math problem!
But it is!
If you give up, you can't solve it.
If you get it wrong, then do it over! We still have almost two hours!
If we give up now, it's the same as ceding a battle!
You ...
Here, auntie!
FWIP
GRIP
Huh?

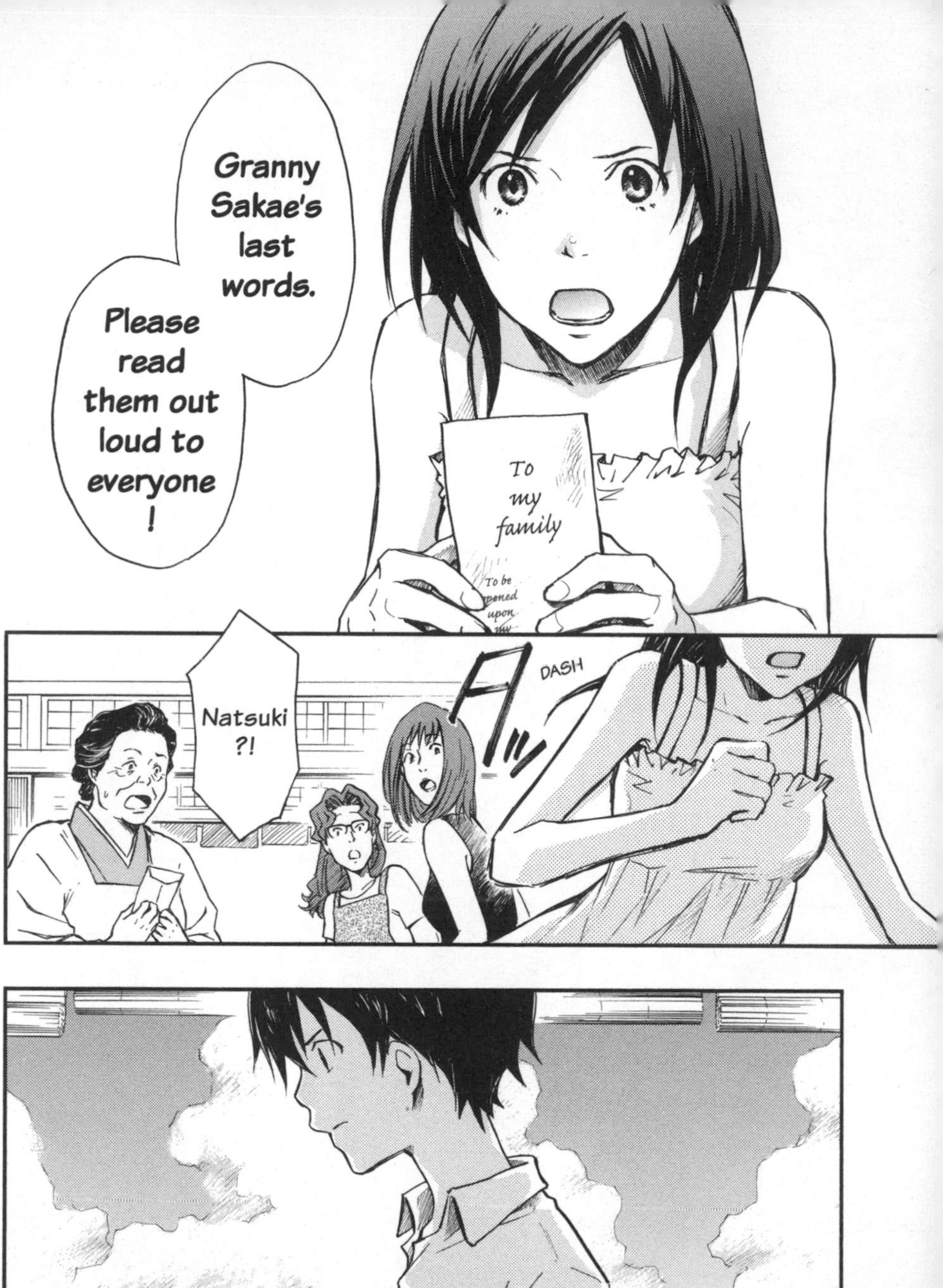
Granny Sakae's last words. Please read them out loud to everyone!
To my family
To be opened upon
DASH
Natsuki?!

Act Ten To My Family

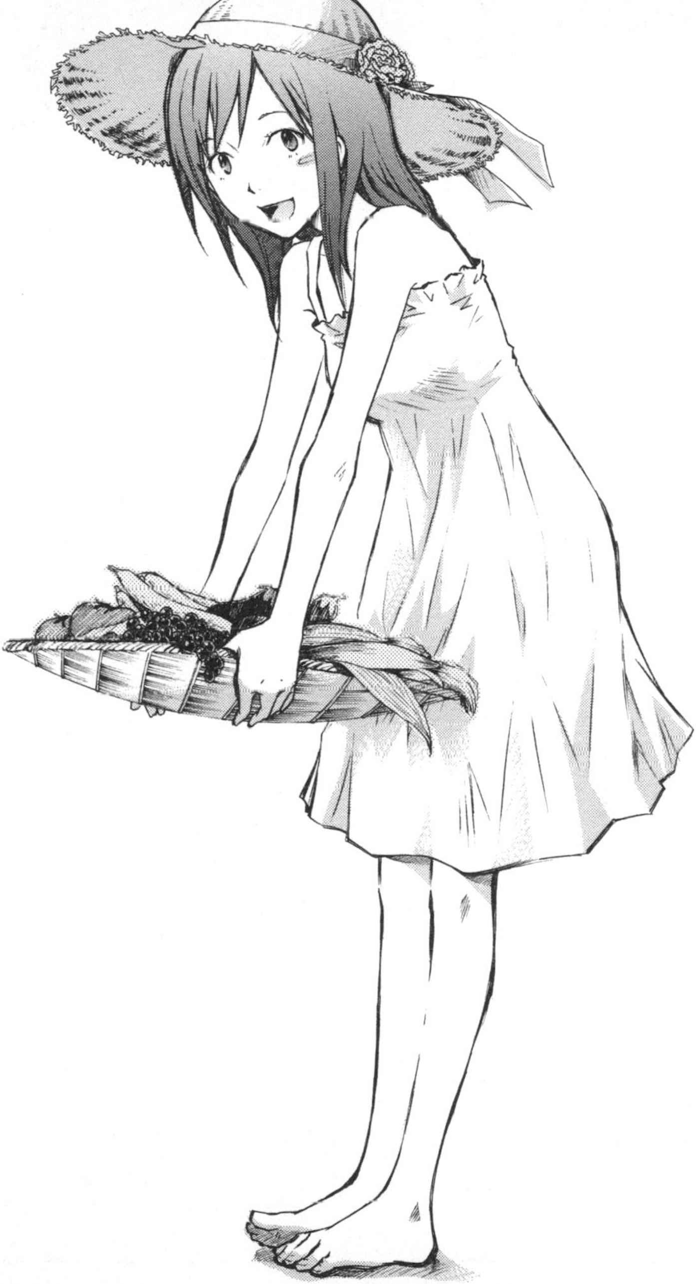

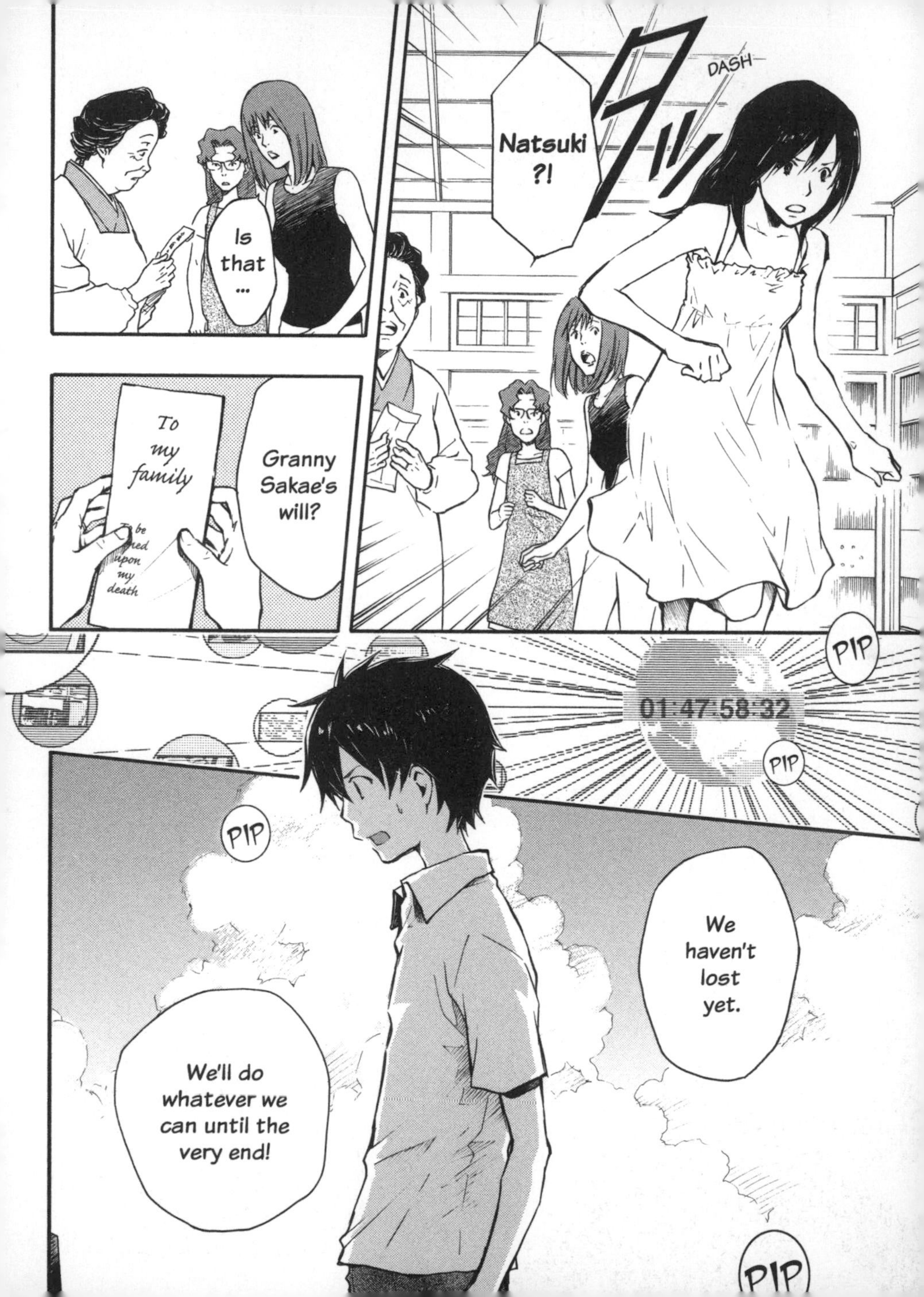

DASH
Natsuki ?!
Is that ...
To my family
upon my death
Granny Sakae's will?
PIP
01:47:58:32
PIP
PIP
We haven't lost yet.
We'll do whatever we can until the very end!
PIP

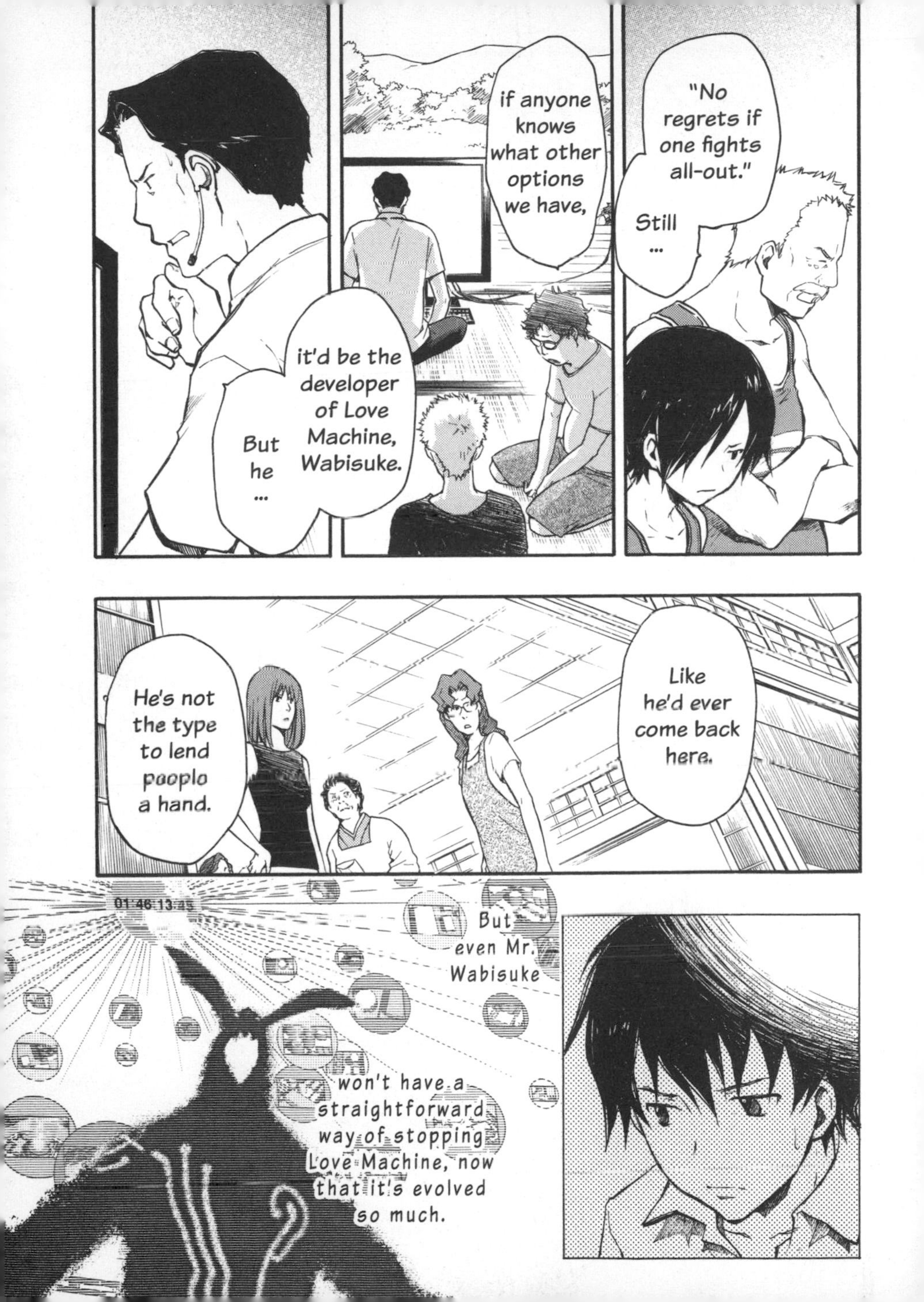
"No regrets if one fights all-out."
Still ...
if anyone knows what other options we have,
it'd be the developer of Love Machine, Wabisuke.
But he ...
Like he'd ever come back here.
He's not the type to lend people a hand.
01:46:13:45
But even Mr. Wabisuke
won't have a straightforward way of stopping Love Machine, now that it's evolved so much.

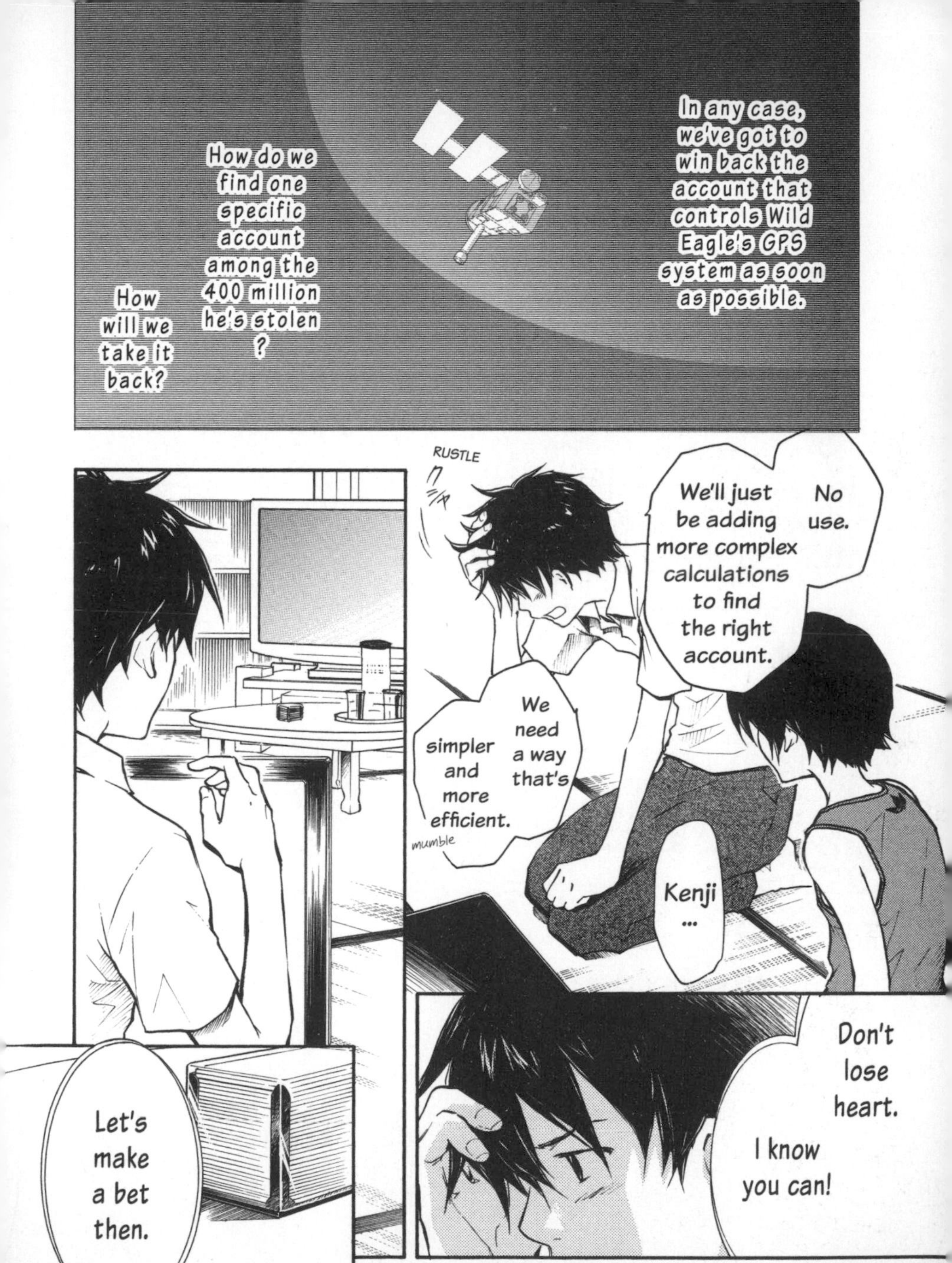
In any case, we've got to win back the account that controls Wild Eagle's GPS system as soon as possible.
How do we find one specific account among the 400 million he's stolen ?
How will we take it back?
RUSTLE
No use.
We'll just be adding more complex calculations to find the right account.
We need a way that's simpler and more efficient.
mumble
Kenji ...
Don't lose heart.
I know you can!
Let's make a bet then.

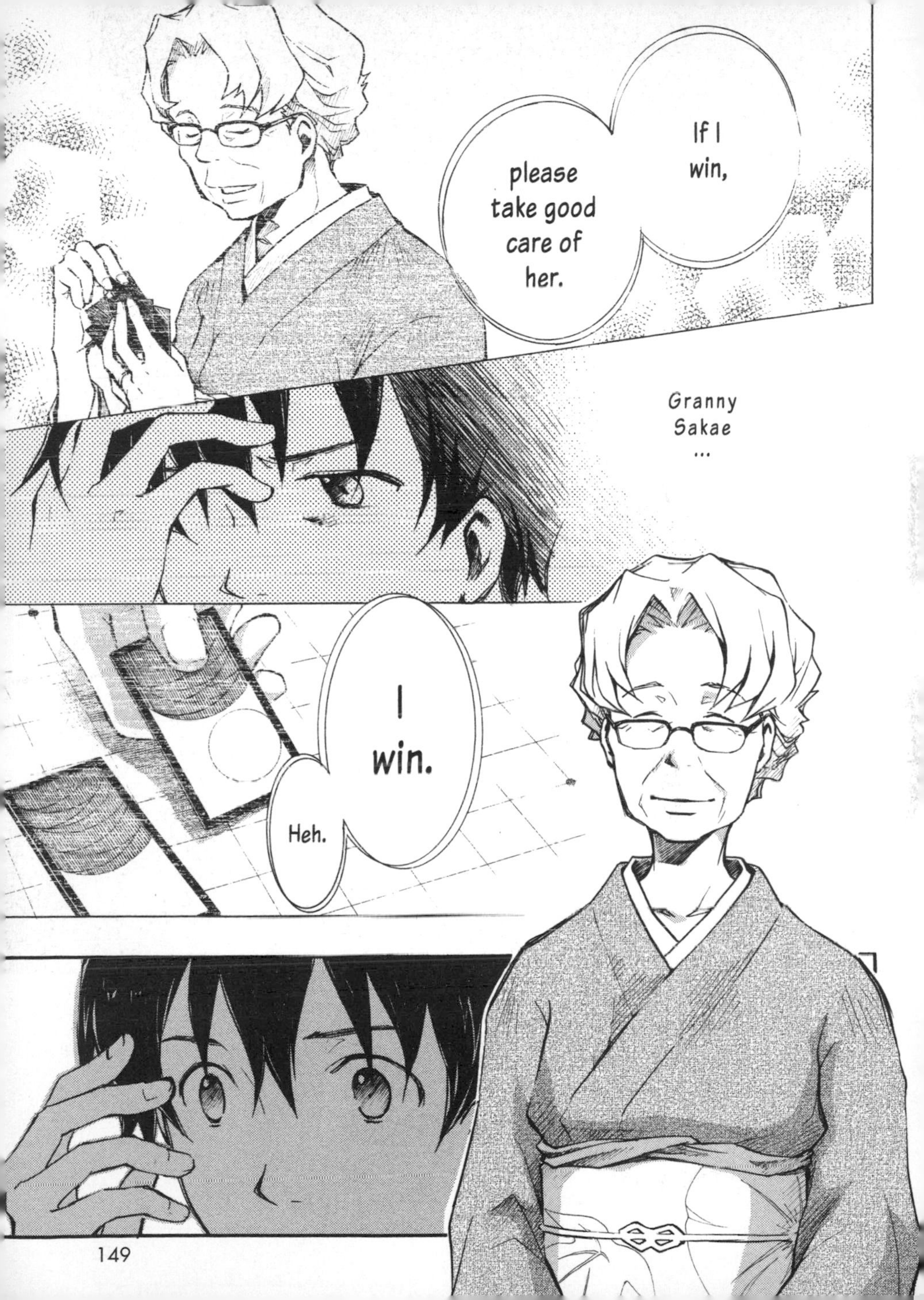
If I win,
please take good care of her.
Granny Sakae ...
I win.
Heh.

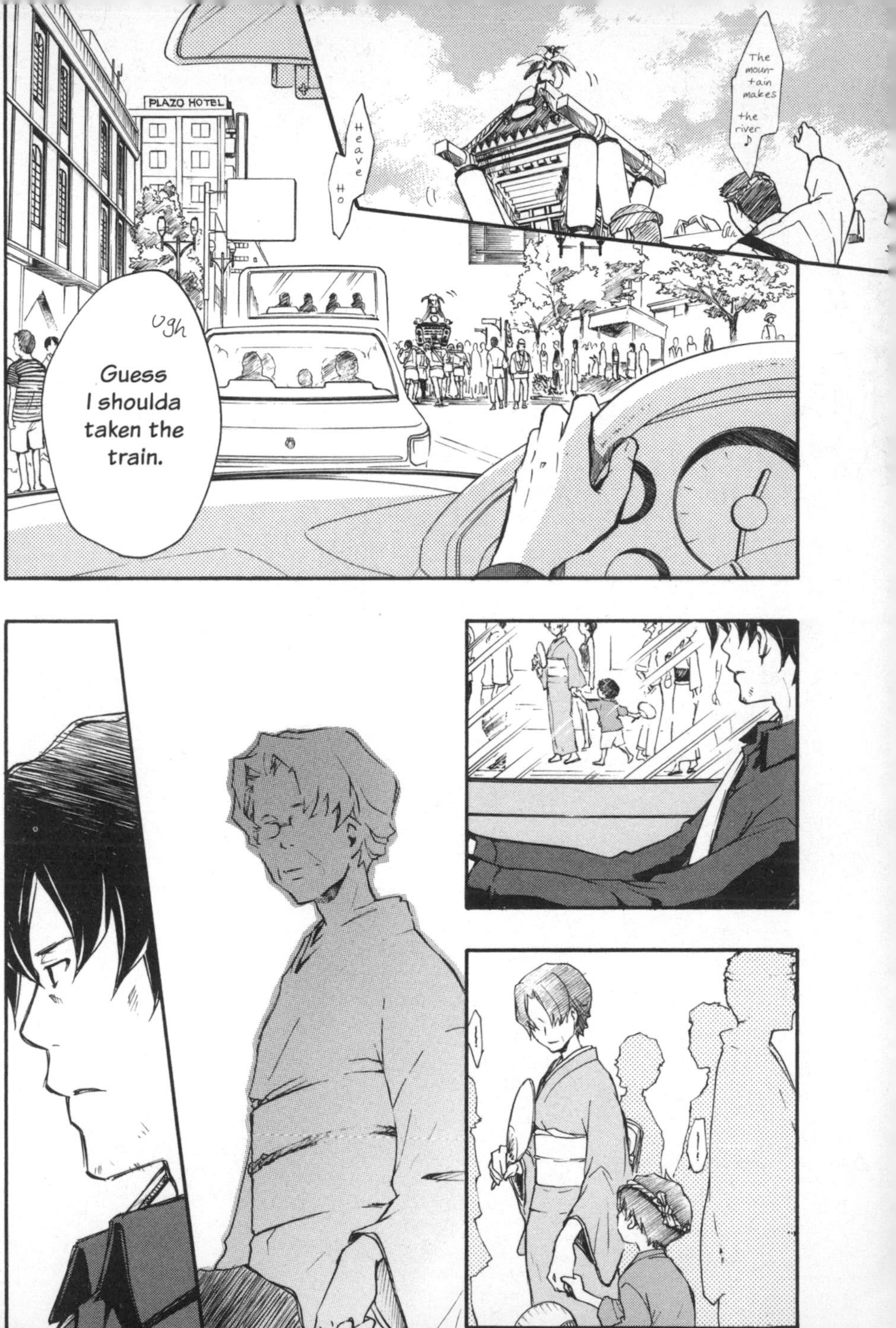
The moun-tain makes the river ♪
Heave Ho
Ugh
Guess I shoulda taken the train.
!
!

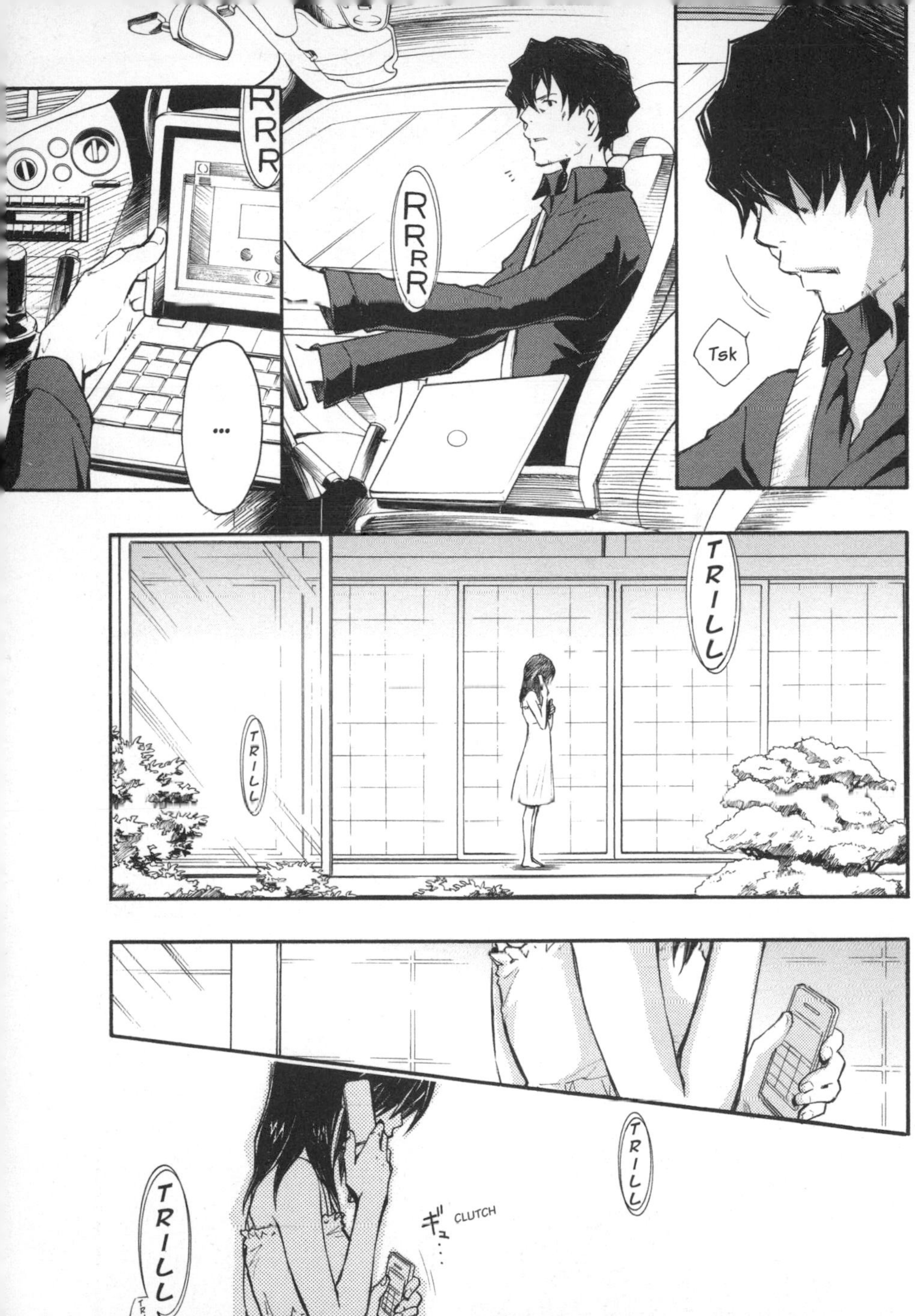
Tsk
RRRR
RRR
...
TRILL
TRILL
TRILL
ギュ
CLUTCH
TRILL
TRILL

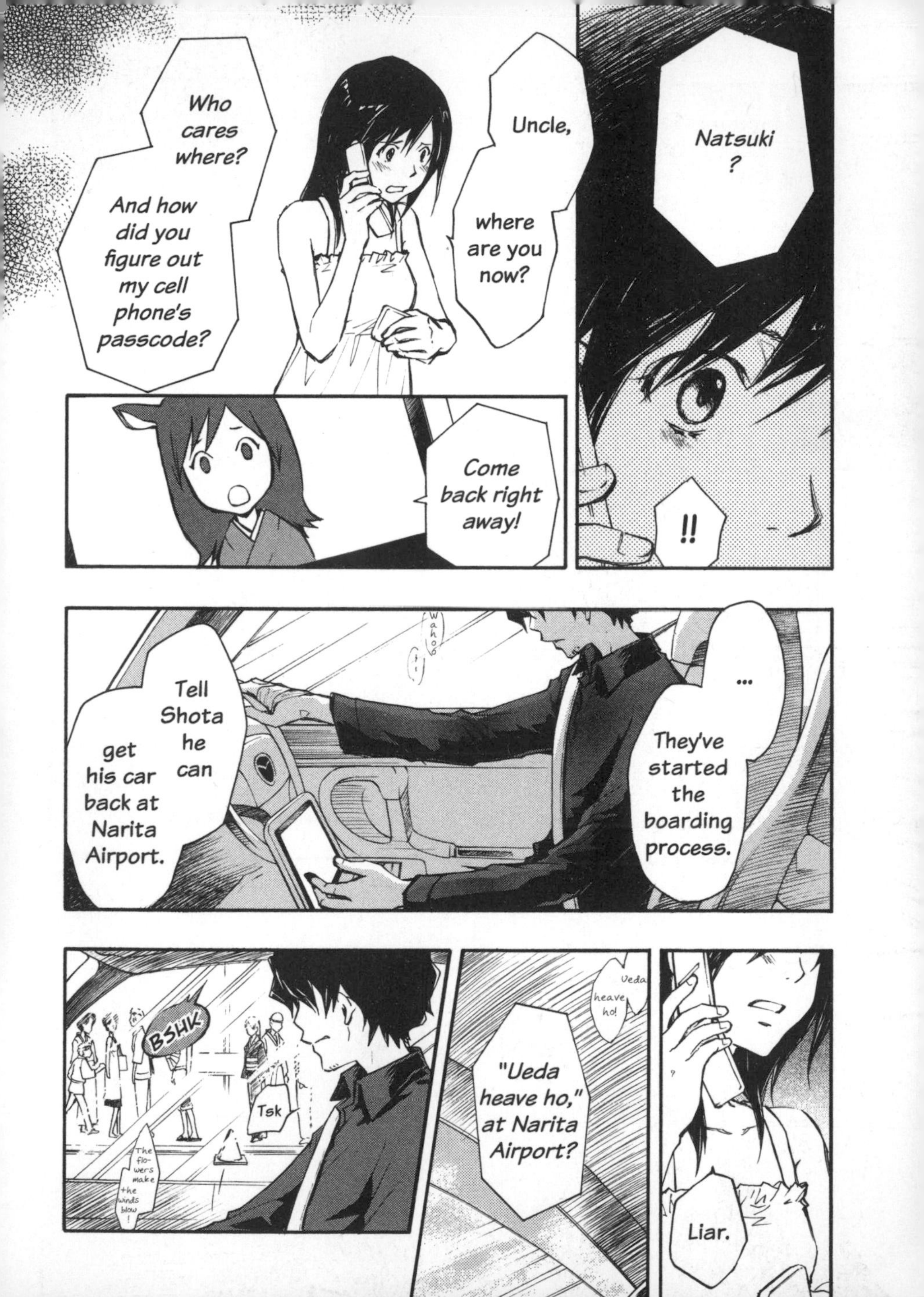
Natsuki?
!!
Uncle, where are you now?
Who cares where? And how did you figure out my cell phone's passcode?
Come back right away!
... They've started the boarding process.
Wahoo
Tell Shota he can get his car back at Narita Airport.
Liar.
Ueda heave ho!
"Ueda heave ho," at Narita Airport?
BSHK
Tsk
The flowers make the winds blow!

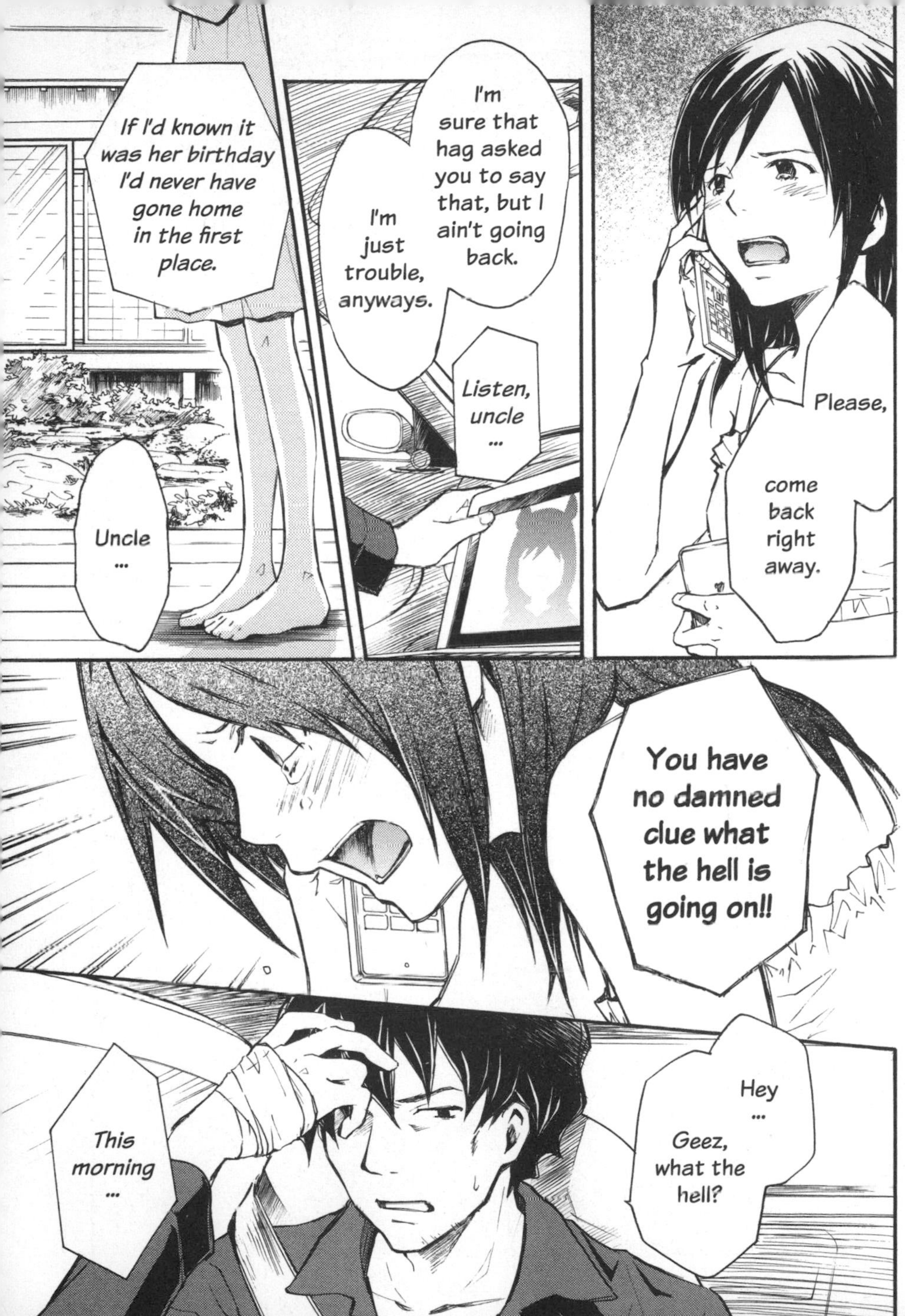
Please,
come back right away.
I'm sure that hag asked you to say that, but I ain't going back.
I'm just trouble, anyways.
Listen, uncle ...
If I'd known it was her birthday I'd never have gone home in the first place.
Uncle ...
You have no damned clue what the hell is going on!!
Hey ...
Geez, what the hell?
This morning ...

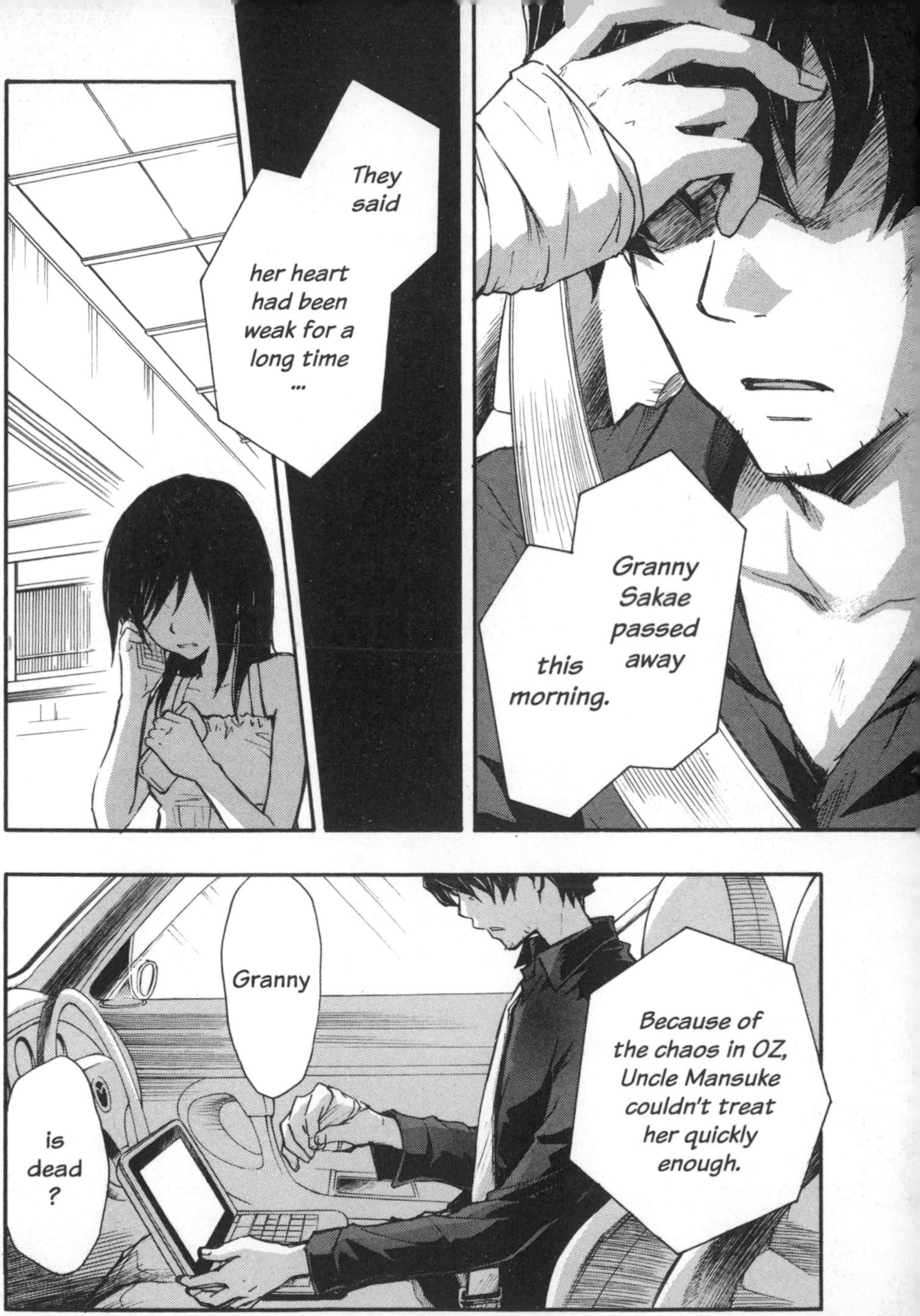
Granny Sakae passed away this morning.
They said
her heart had been weak for a long time ...
Because of the chaos in OZ, Uncle Mansuke couldn't treat her quickly enough.
Granny
is dead ?

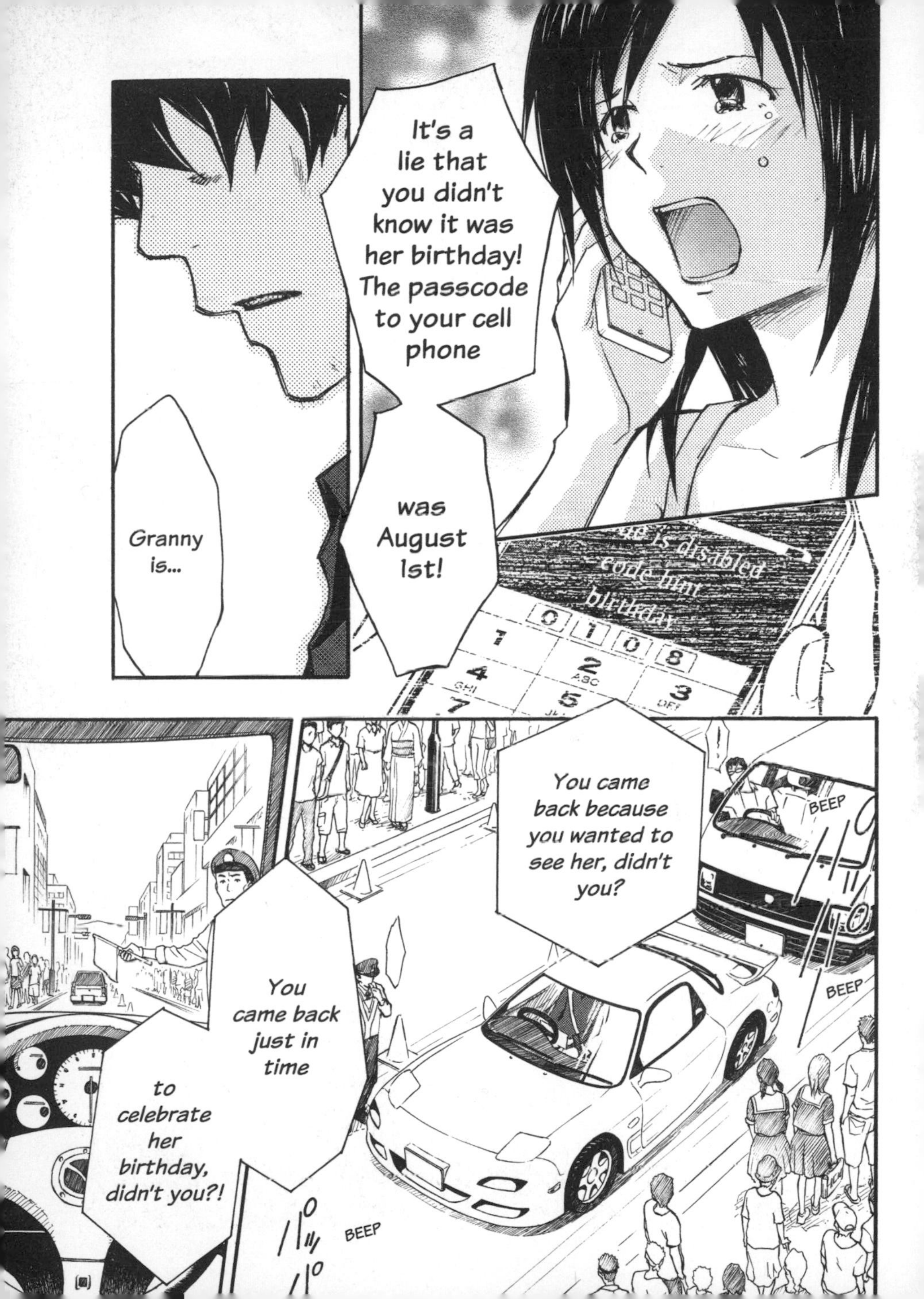
It's a lie that you didn't know it was her birthday! The passcode to your cell phone
was August 1st!
0108
Granny is...
You came back because you wanted to see her, didn't you?
BEEP
BEEP
You came back just in time
to celebrate her birthday, didn't you?!
BEEP

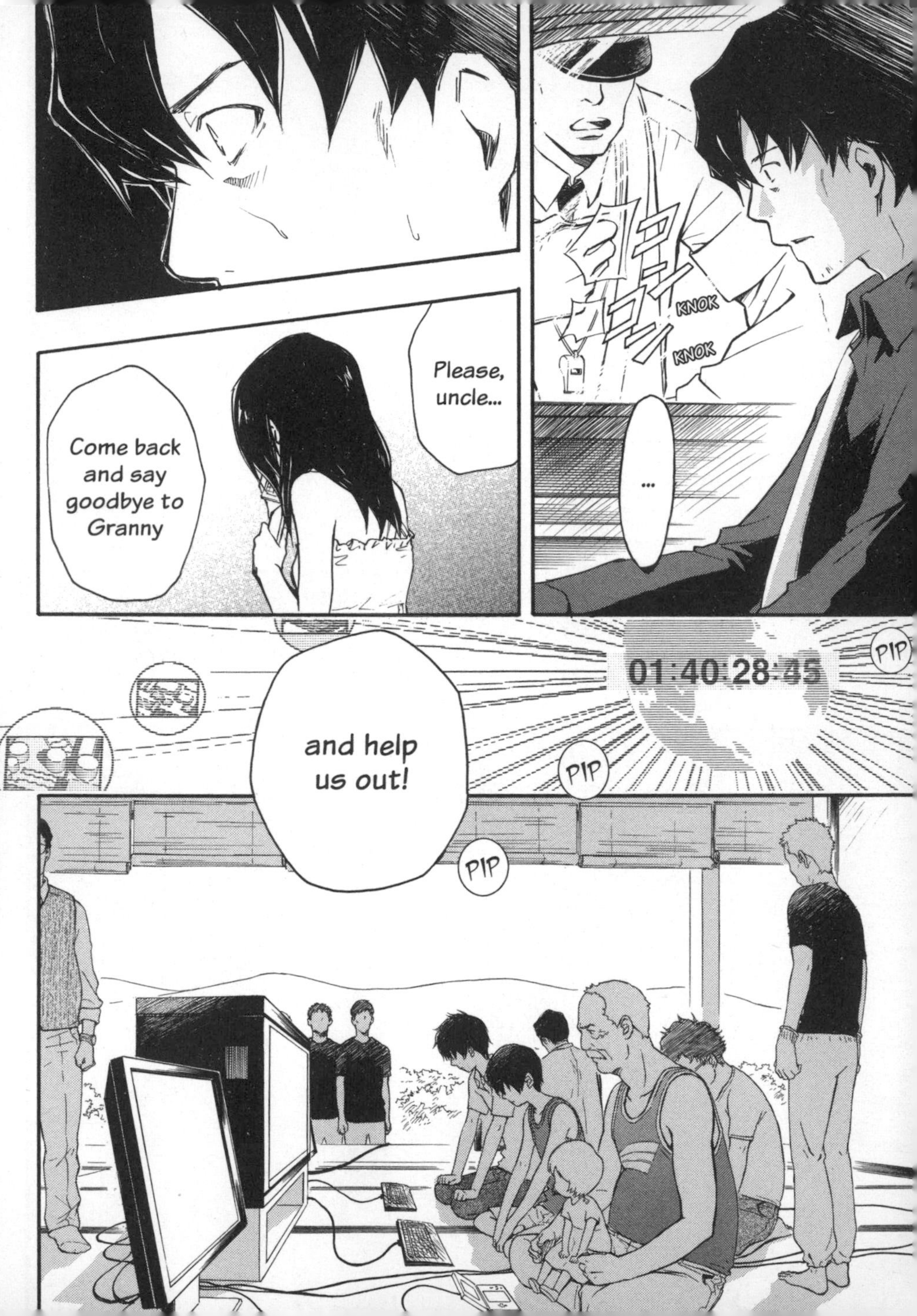
KNOK
KNOK
...
Please, uncle...
Come back and say goodbye to Granny
PIP
01:40:28:45
and help us out!
PIP
PIP

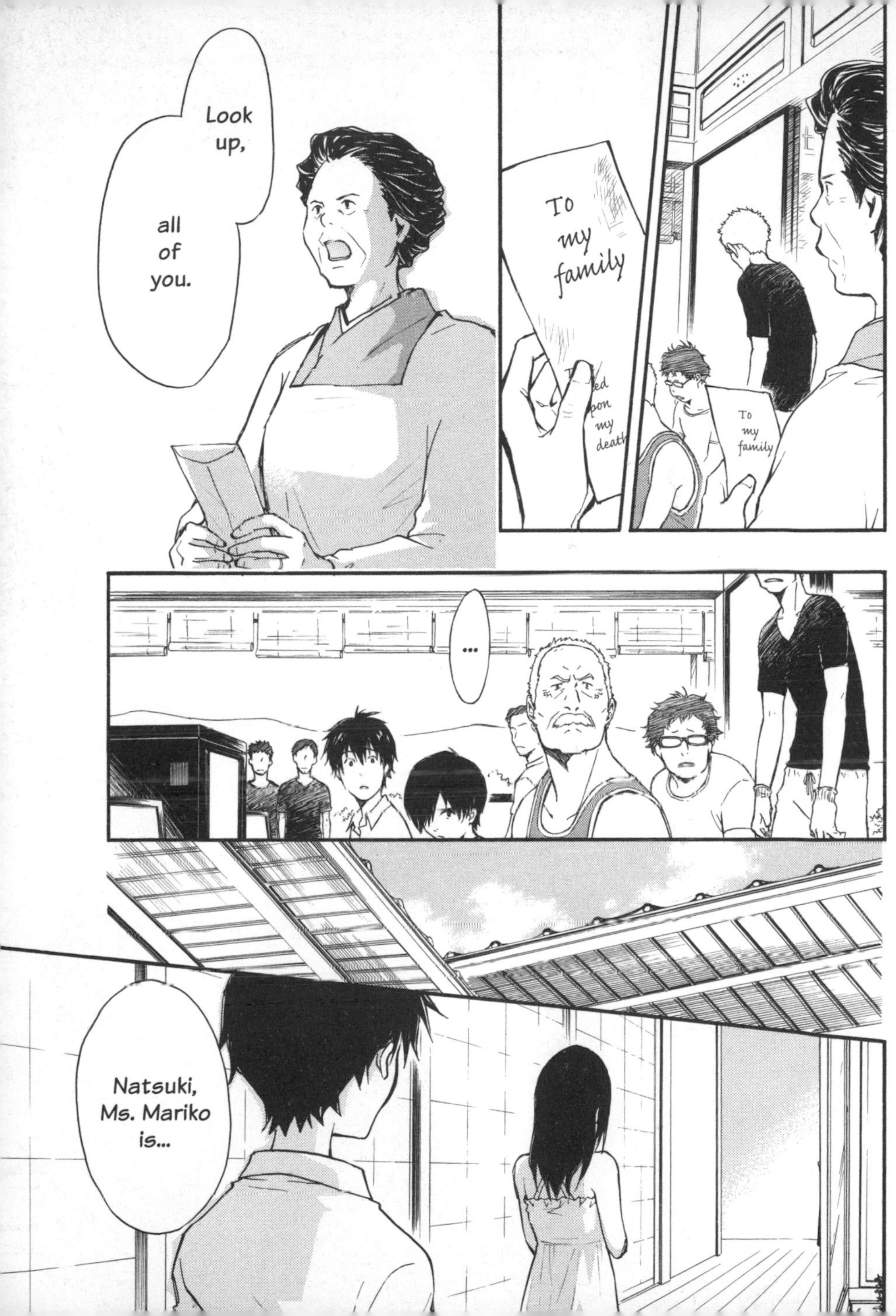
To my family
To my family
my death
Look up,
all of you.
...
Natsuki, Ms. Mariko is...

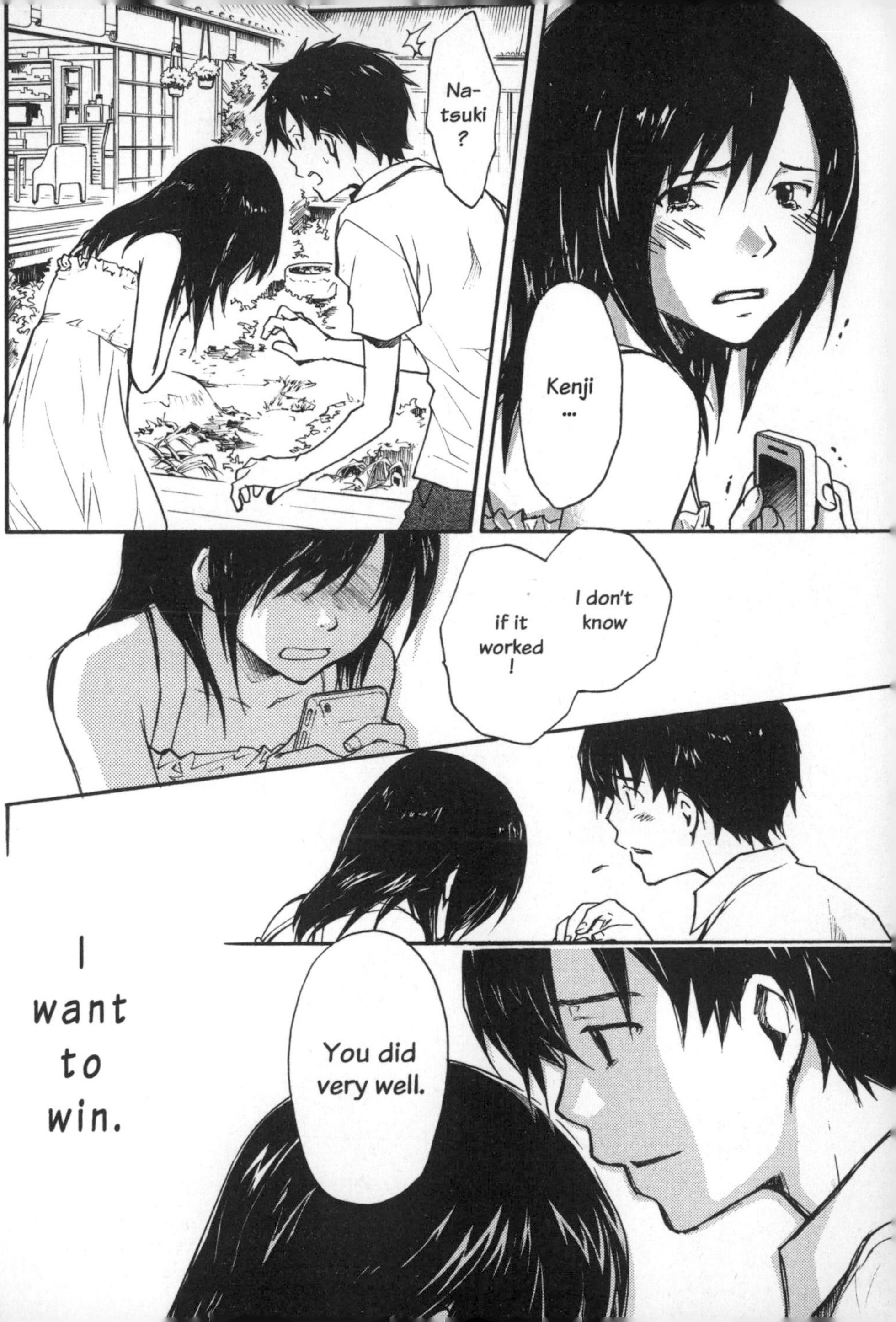
Kenji ...
Na-tsuki ?
I don't know if it worked !
You did very well.
I want to win.

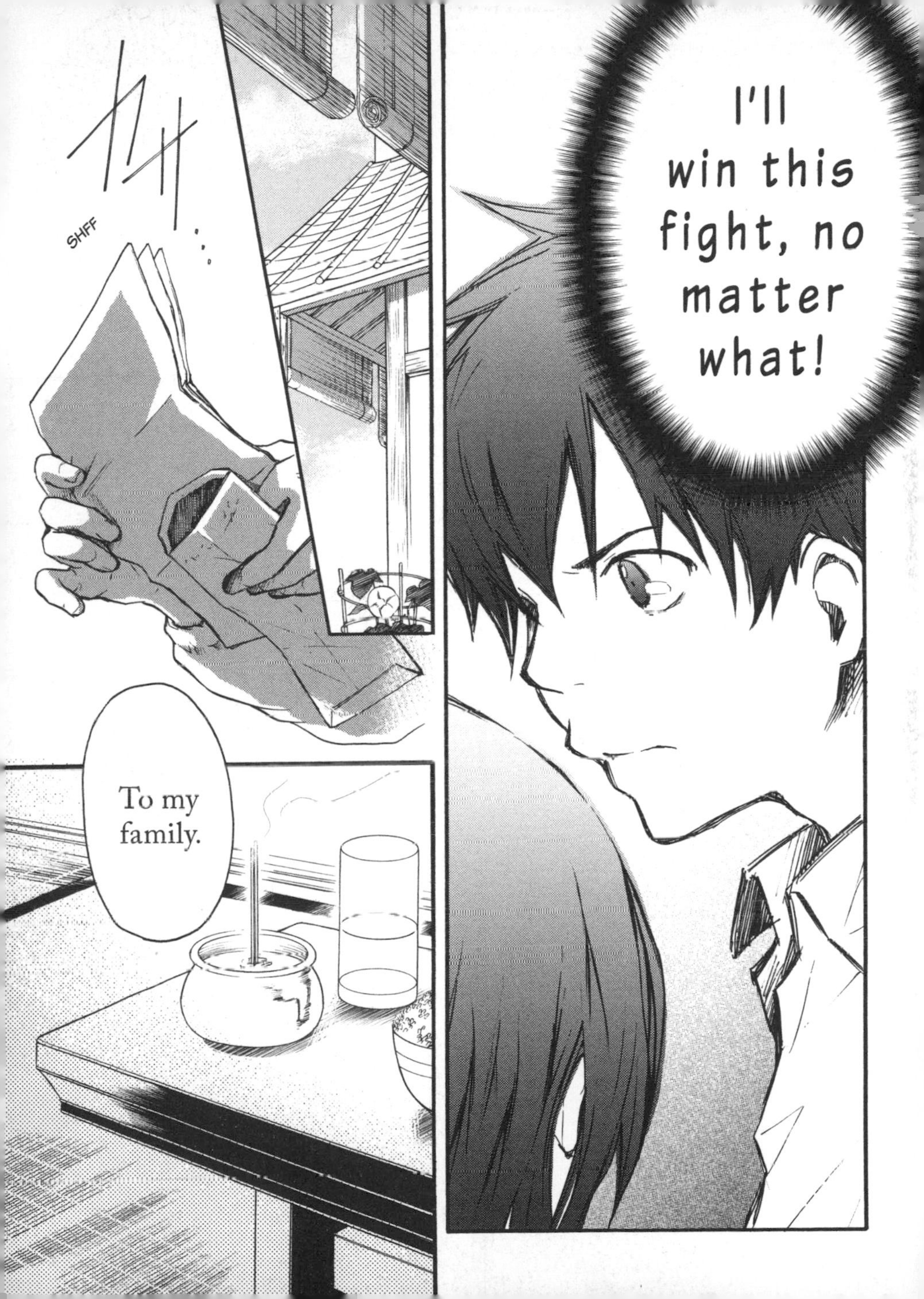
I'll win this fight, no matter what!
SHFF
To my family.

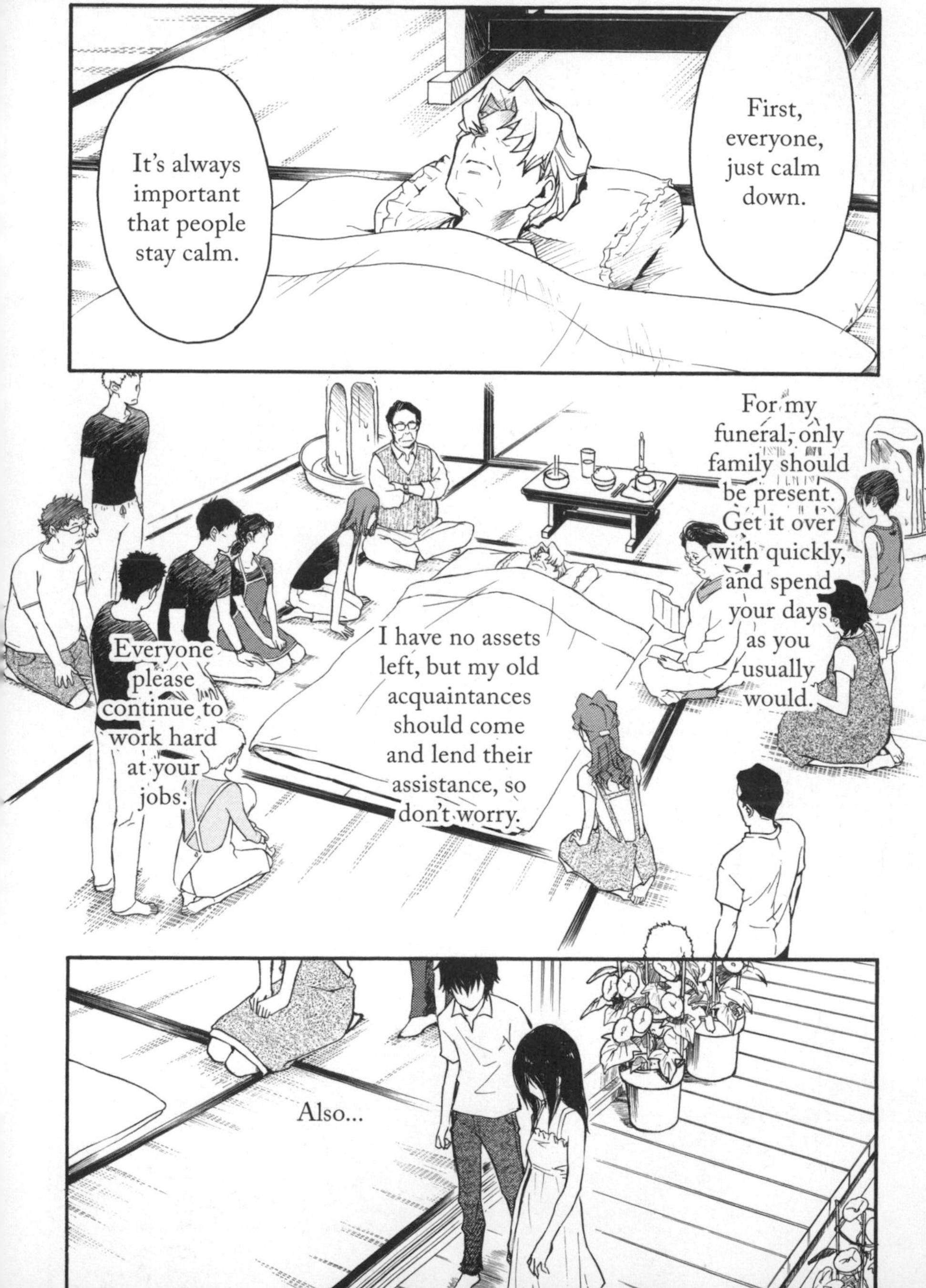
First, everyone, just calm down.
It's always important that people stay calm.
For my funeral, only family should be present. Get it over with quickly, and spend your days as you usually would.
I have no assets left, but my old acquaintances should come and lend their assistance, so don't worry.
Everyone please continue to work hard at your jobs.
Also...

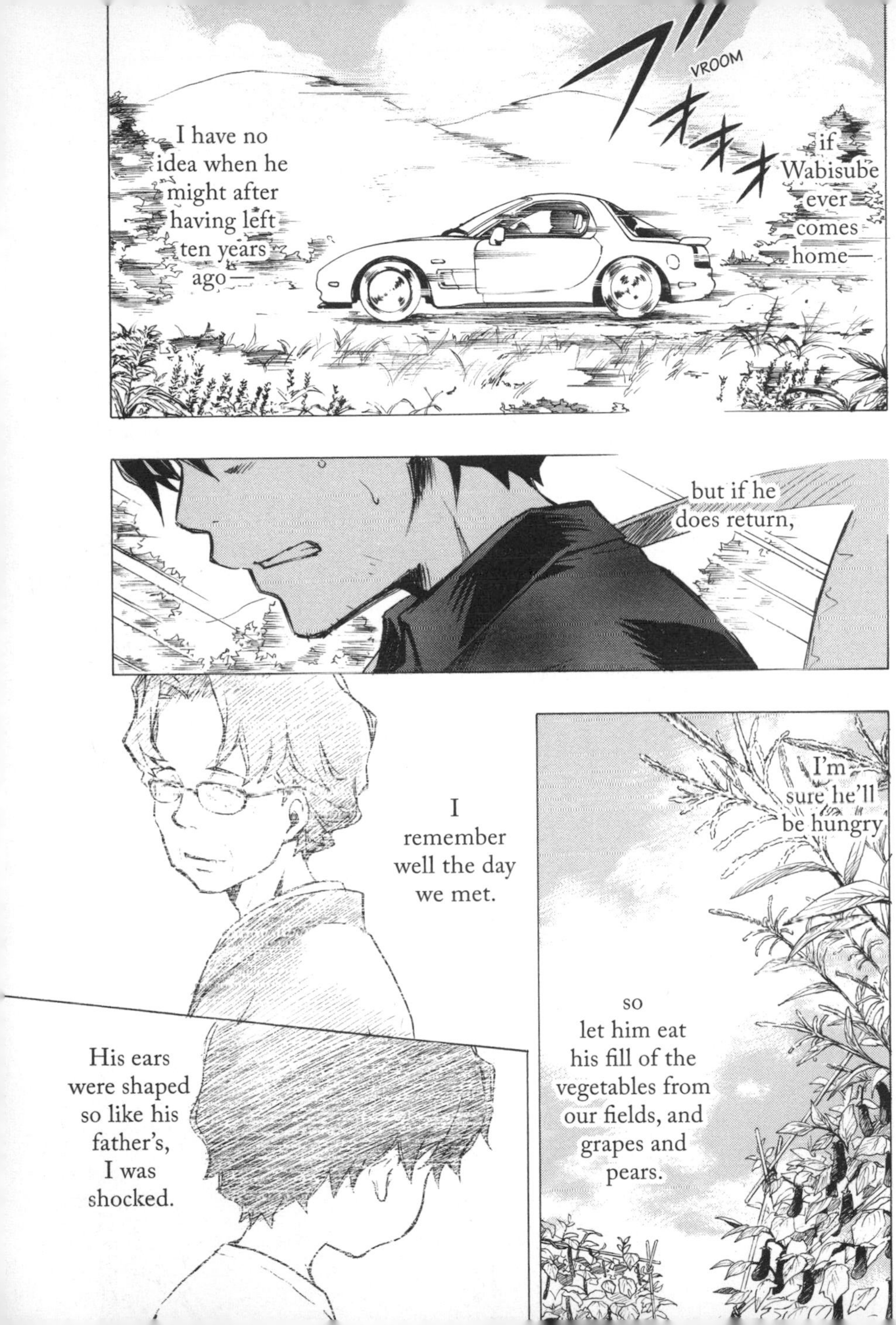
VROOM
if Wabisube ever comes home—
I have no idea when he might after having left ten years ago—
but if he does return,
I'm sure he'll be hungry
so let him eat his fill of the vegetables from our fields, and grapes and pears.
I remember well the day we met.
His ears were shaped so like his father's, I was shocked.

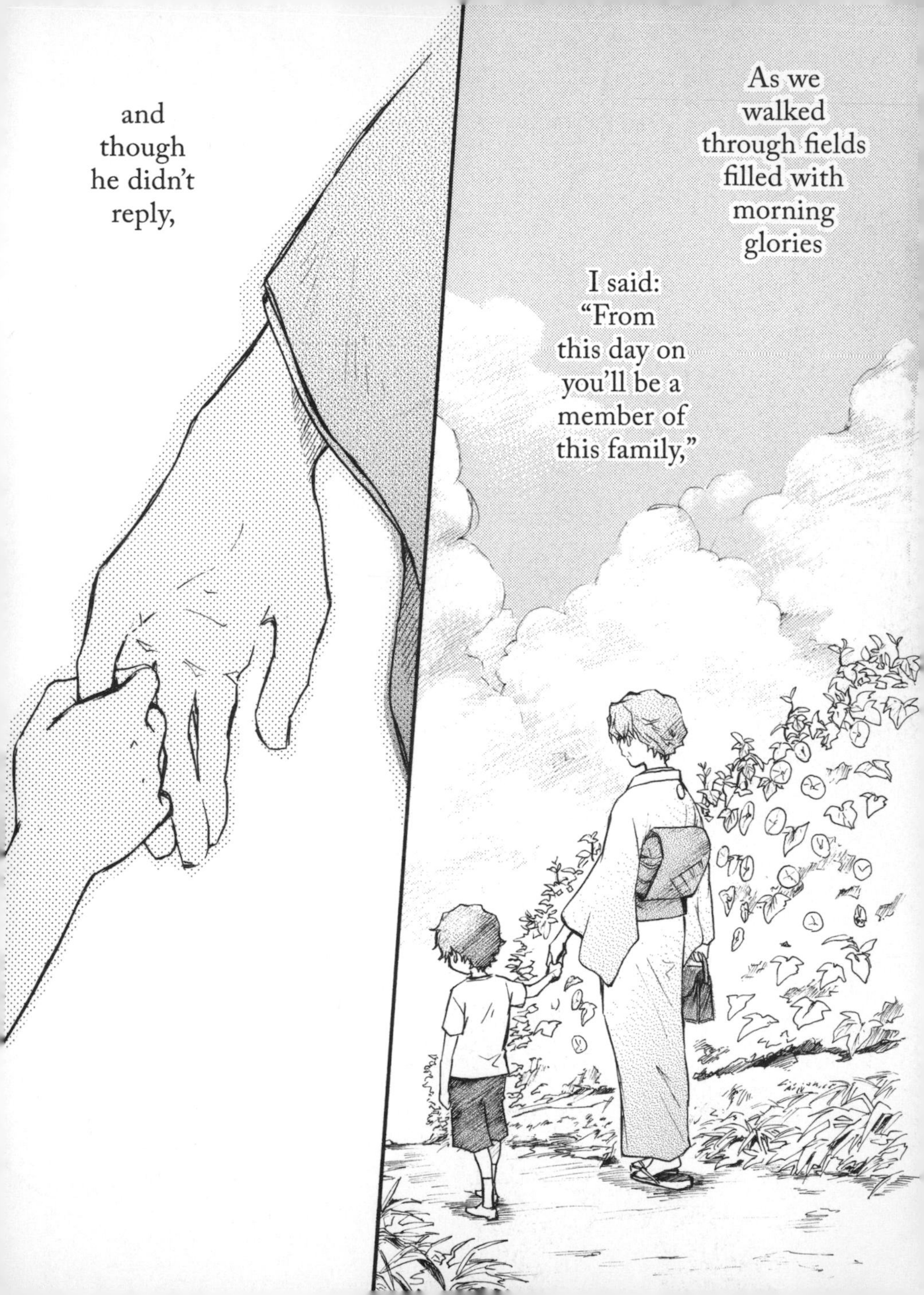
As we walked through fields filled with morning glories
I said: "From this day on you'll be a member of this family,"
and though he didn't reply,

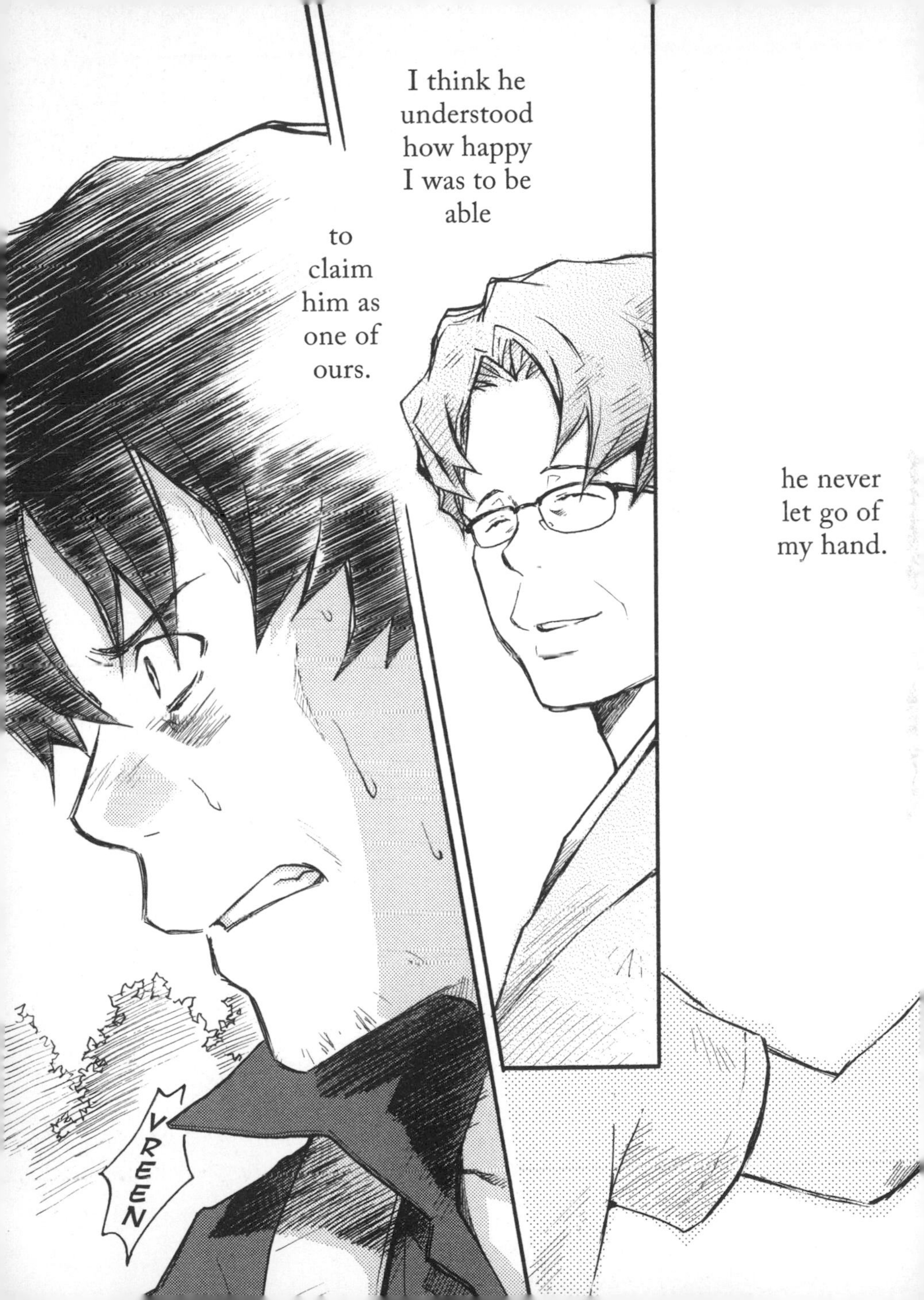
he never let go of my hand.
I think he understood how happy I was to be able
to claim him as one of ours.
VREEN

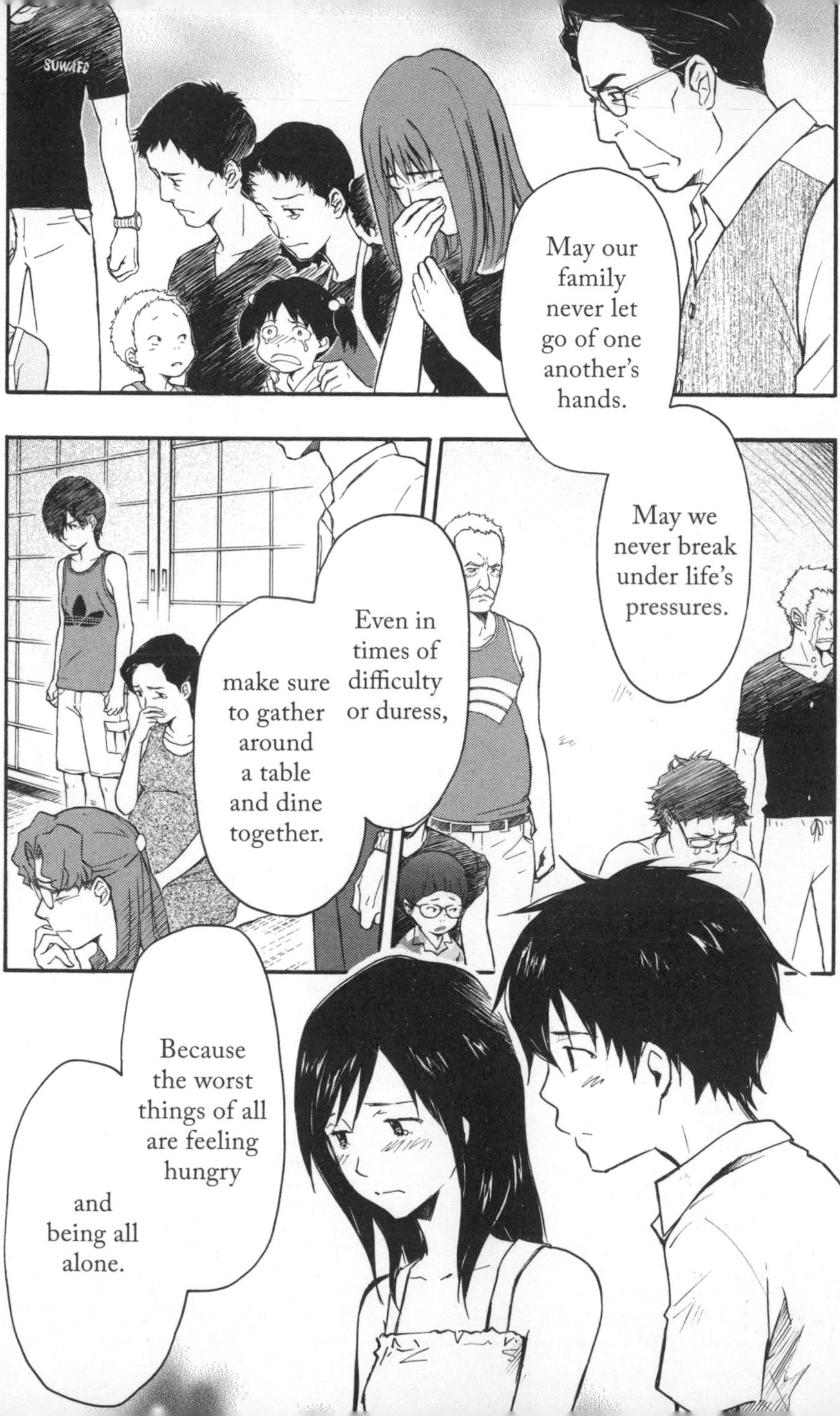
May our family never let go of one another's hands.
May we never break under life's pressures.
Even in times of difficulty or duress,
make sure to gather around a table and dine together.
Because the worst things of all are feeling hungry
and being all alone.

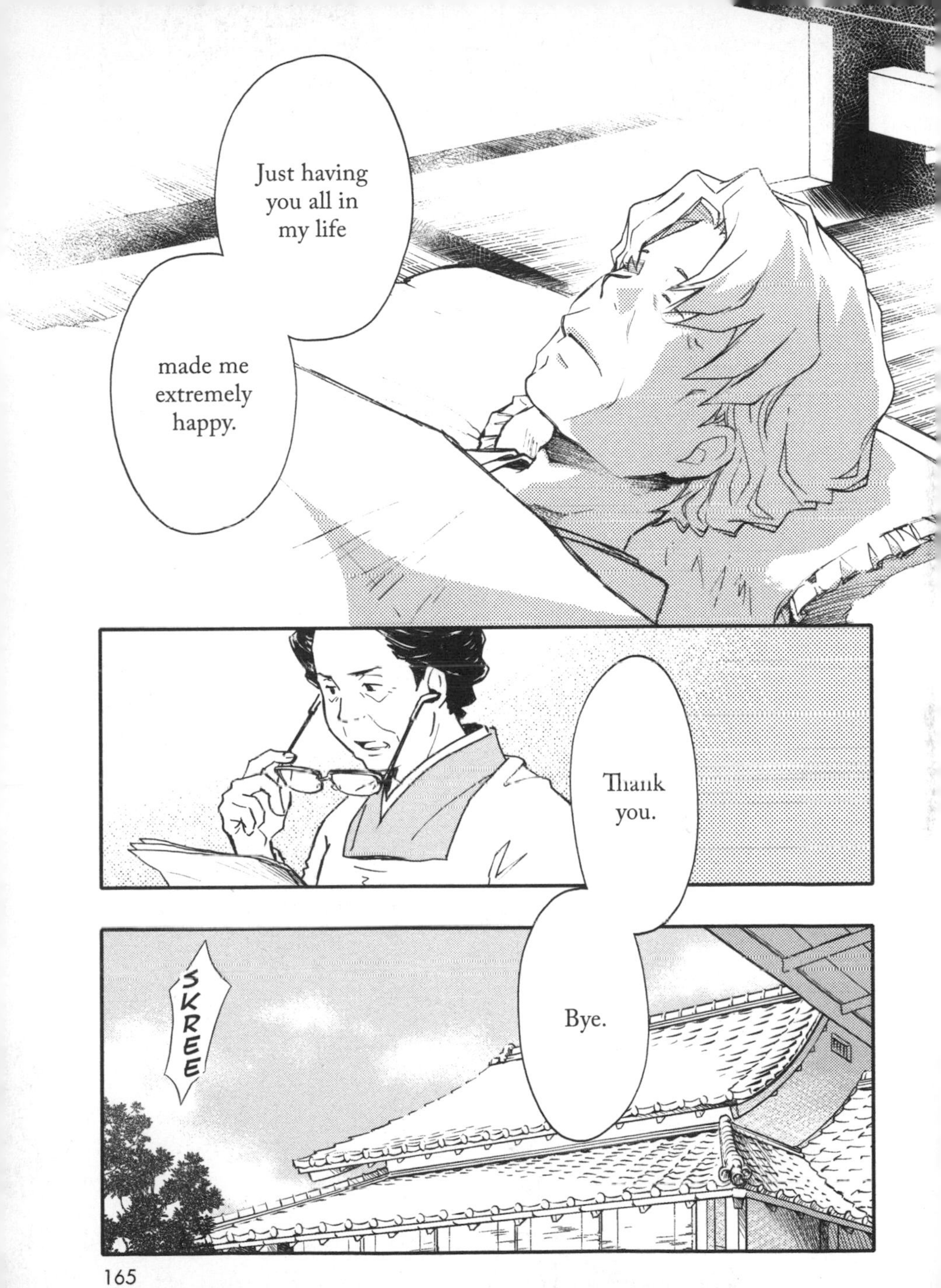
Just having you all in my life
made me extremely happy.
Thank you.
Bye.
SKREE

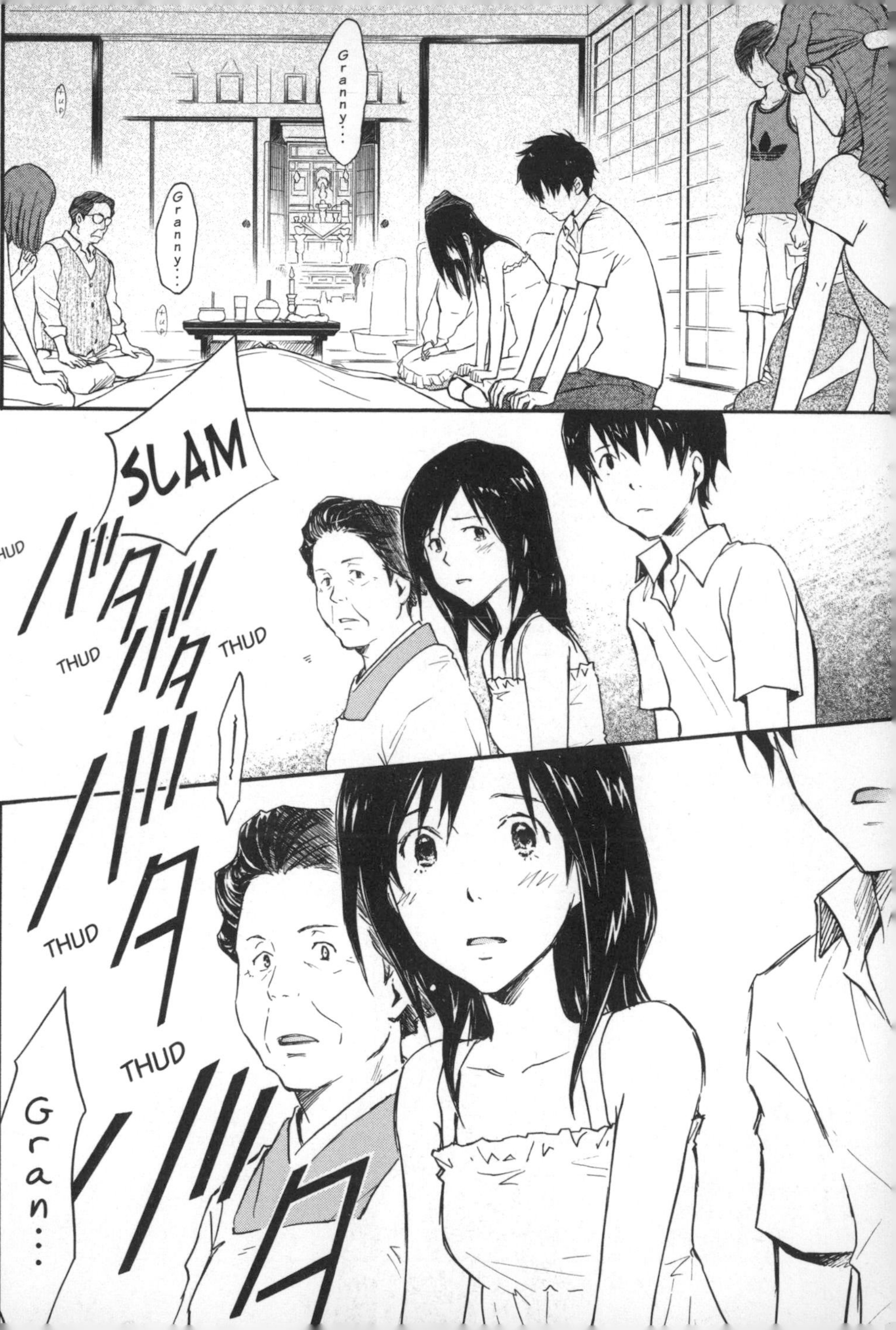

Granny...
Granny...
tup
tup
SLAM
THUD
THUD
THUD
!
THUD
THUD
Gran...

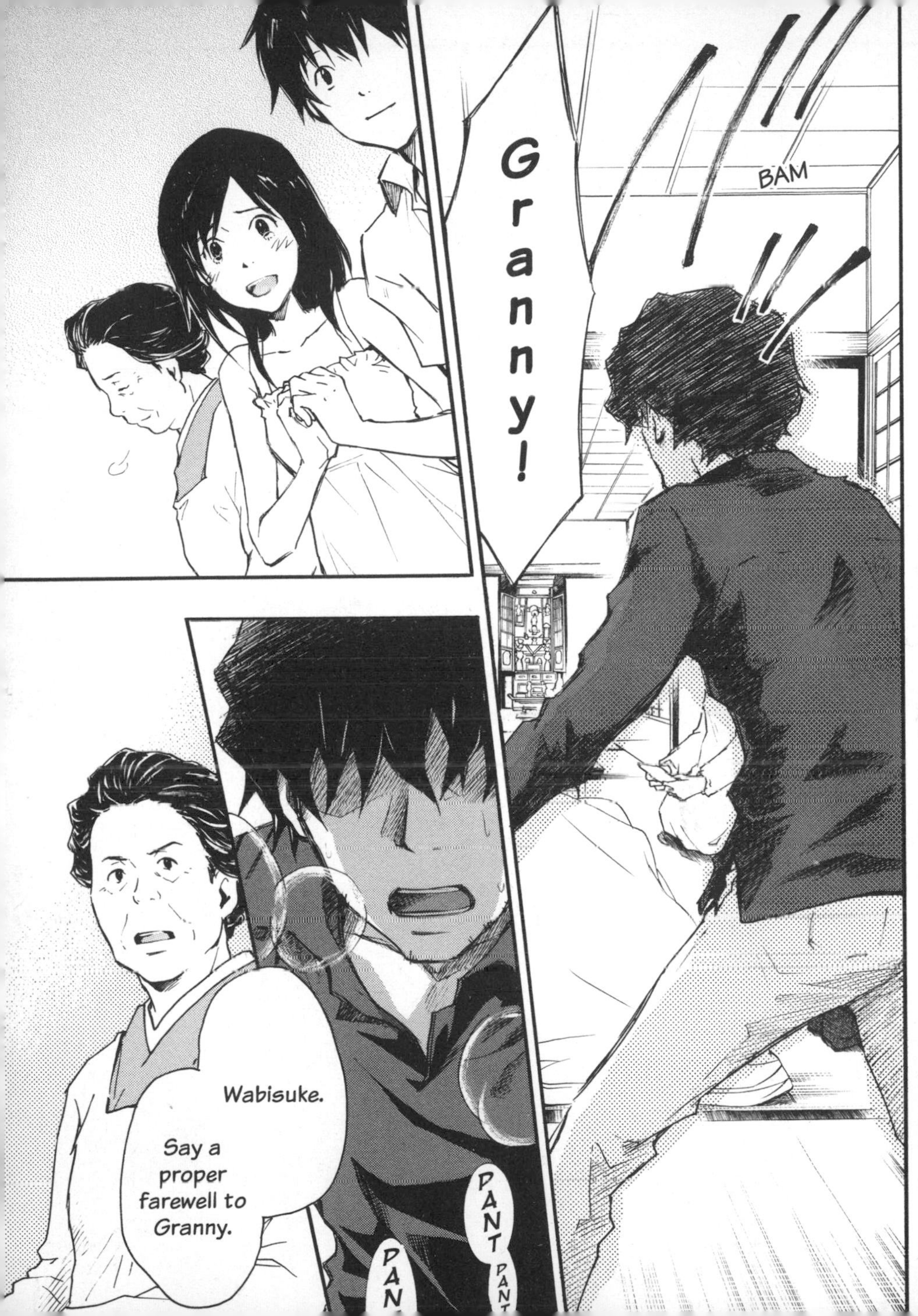
Grannny!
BAM
PANT
PANT
Wabisuke.
Say a proper farewell to Granny.

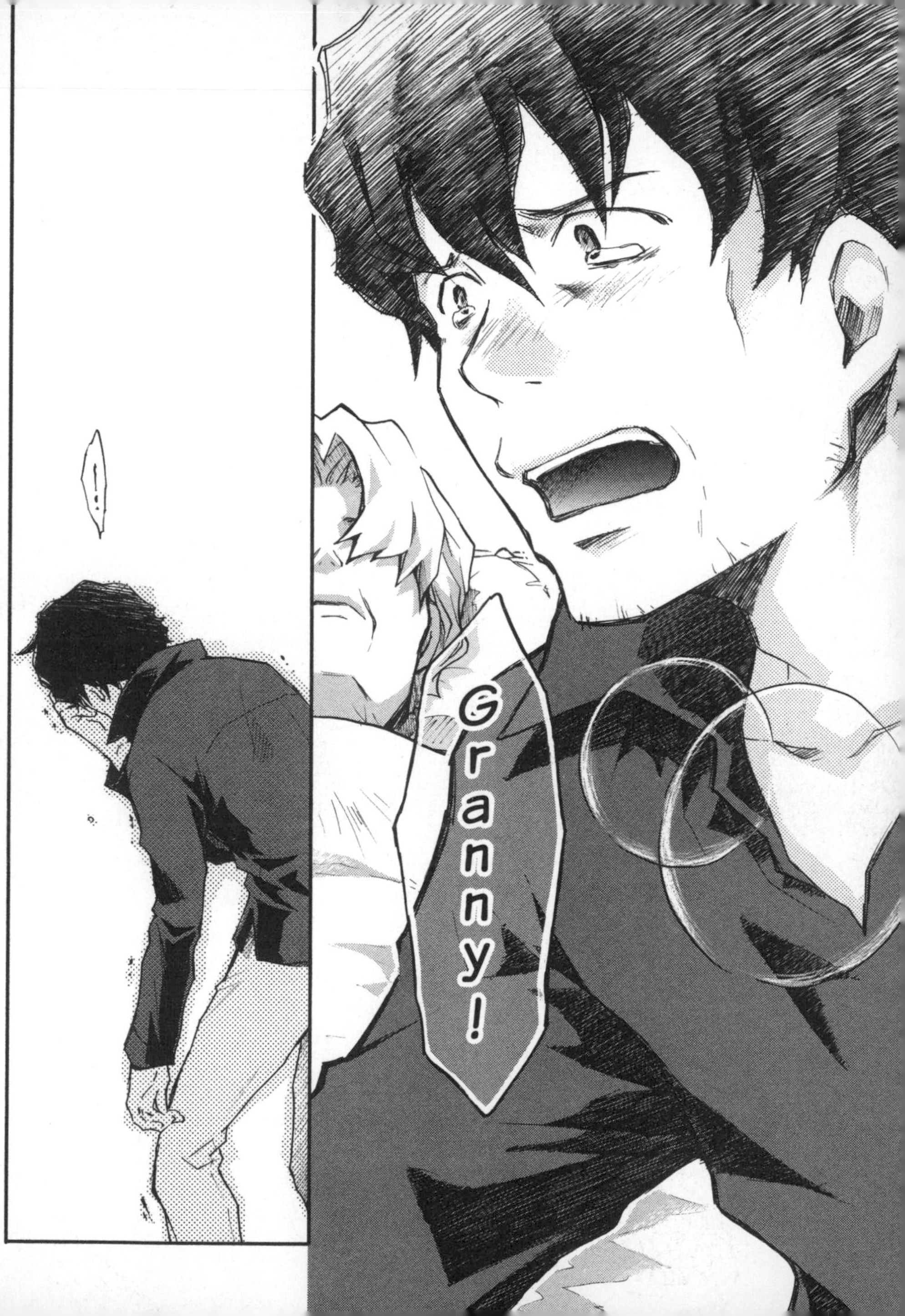
Granny!
!

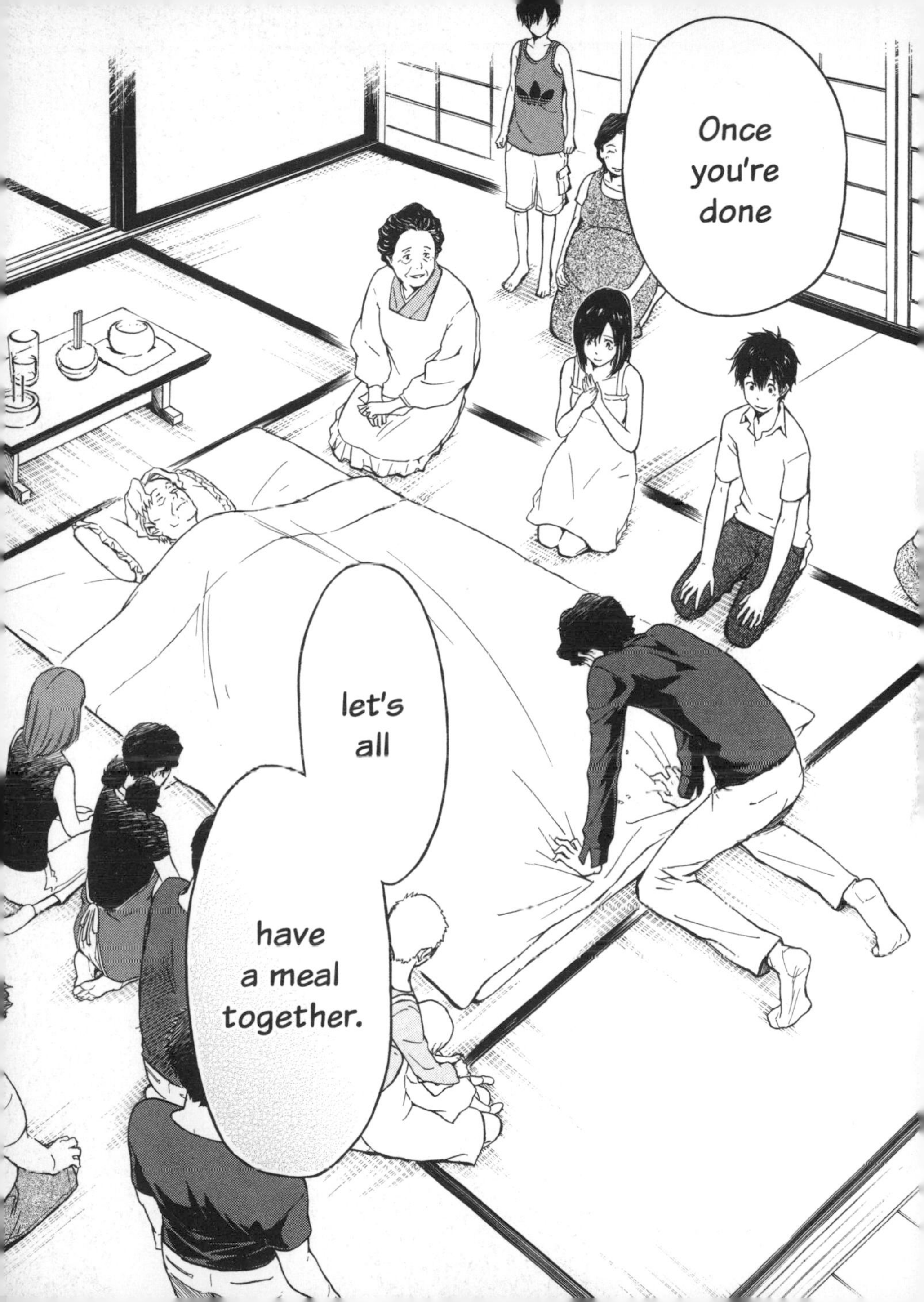
Once you're done
let's all have a meal together.

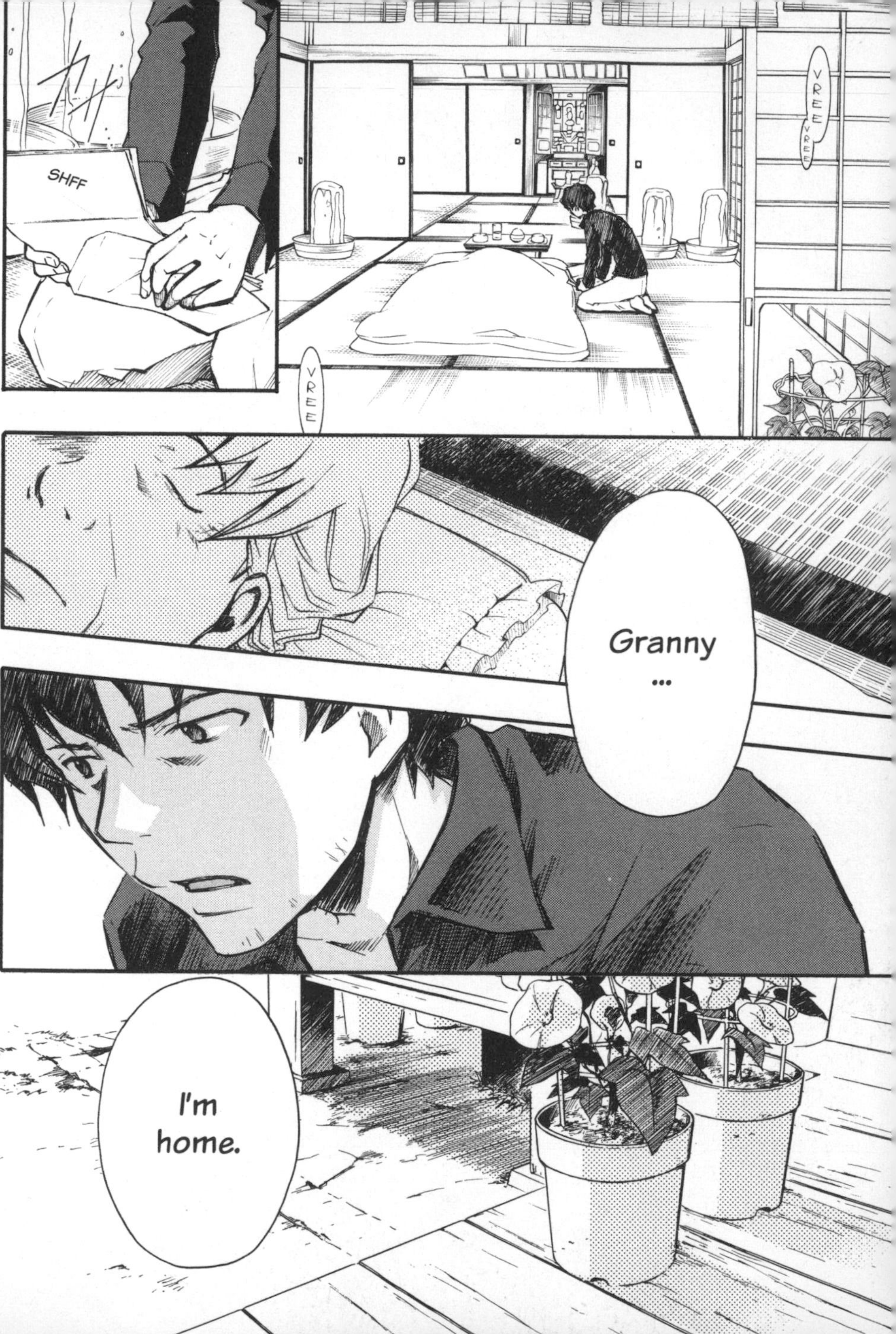

VREE
VREE
VREE
SHFF
Granny ...
I'm home.

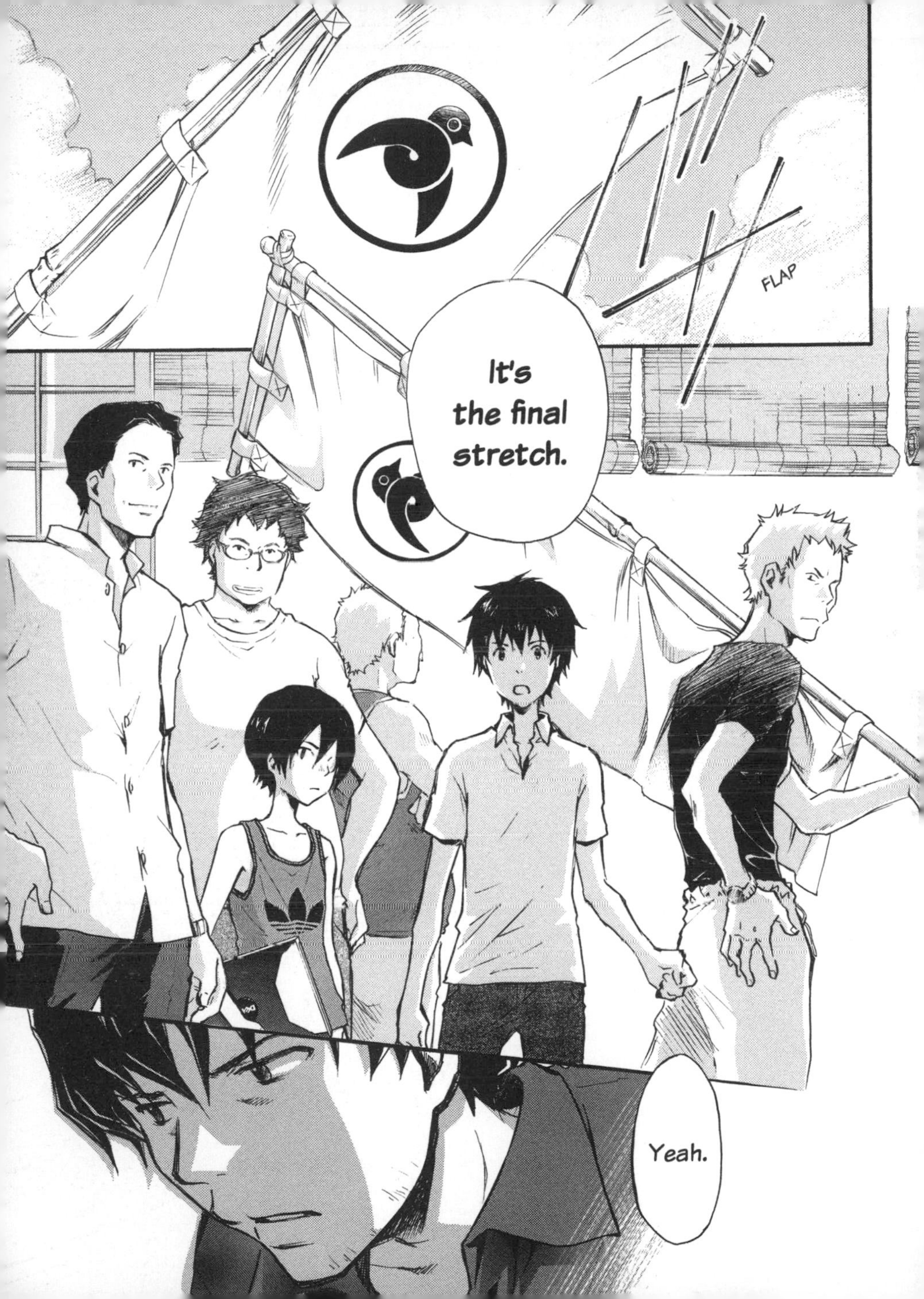
FLAP
It's the final stretch.
Yeah.

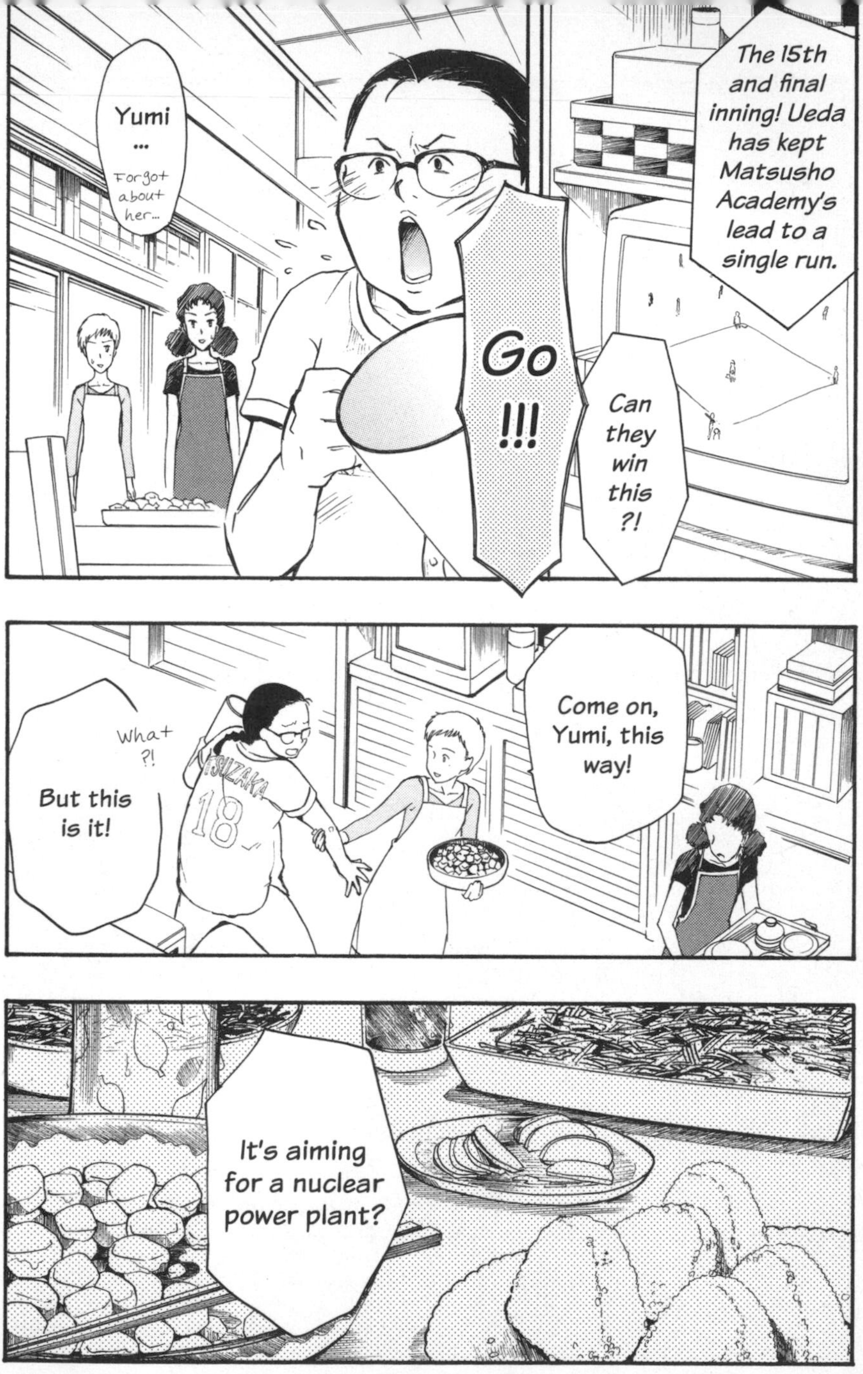

The 15th and final inning! Ueda has kept Matsusho Academy's lead to a single run.
Can they win this ?!
Go !!!
Yumi ...
Forgot about her...
Come on, Yumi, this way!
What ?!
But this is it!
It's aiming for a nuclear power plant?

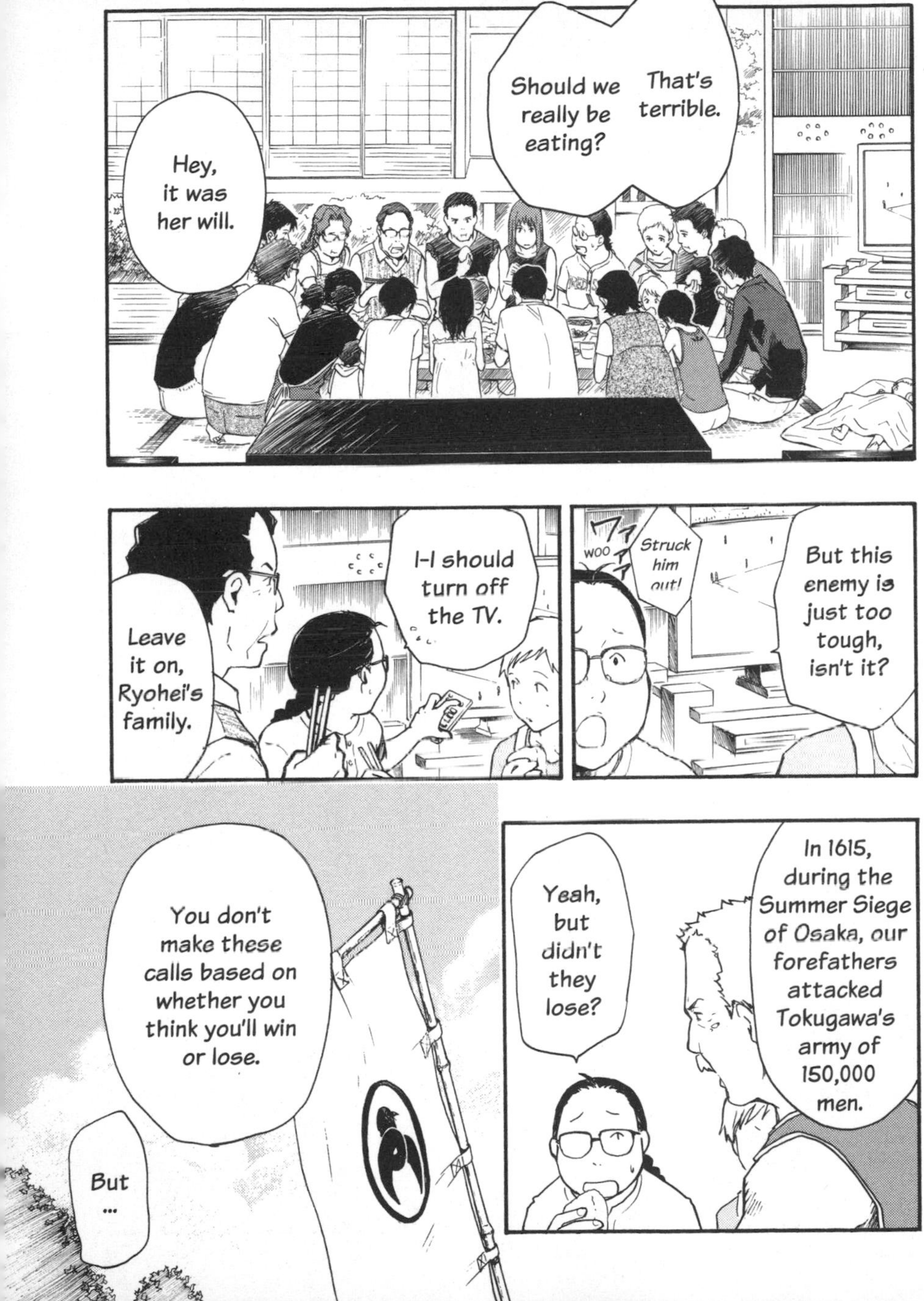
That's terrible.
Should we really be eating?
Hey, it was her will.
But this enemy is just too tough, isn't it?
Struck him out!
WOO
I-I should turn off the TV.
Leave it on, Ryohei's family.
In 1615, during the Summer Siege of Osaka, our forefathers attacked Tokugawa's army of 150,000 men.
Yeah, but didn't they lose?
You don't make these calls based on whether you think you'll win or lose.
But ...

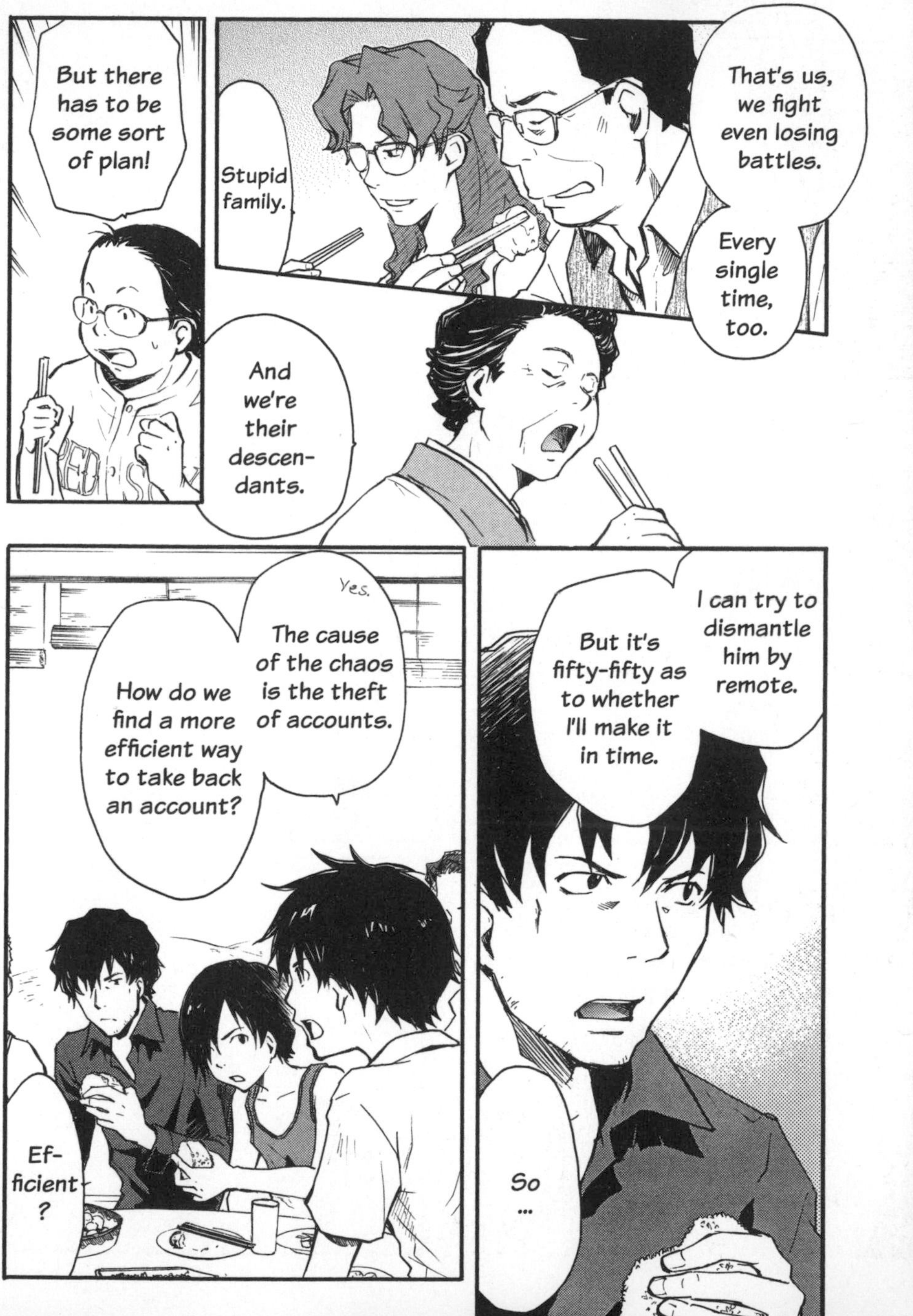
That's us, we fight even losing battles.
Every single time, too.
Stupid family.
But there has to be some sort of plan!
And we're their descendants.
I can try to dismantle him by remote.
But it's fifty-fifty as to whether I'll make it in time.
So ...
Yes.
The cause of the chaos is the theft of accounts.
How do we find a more efficient way to take back an account?
Ef-ficient?

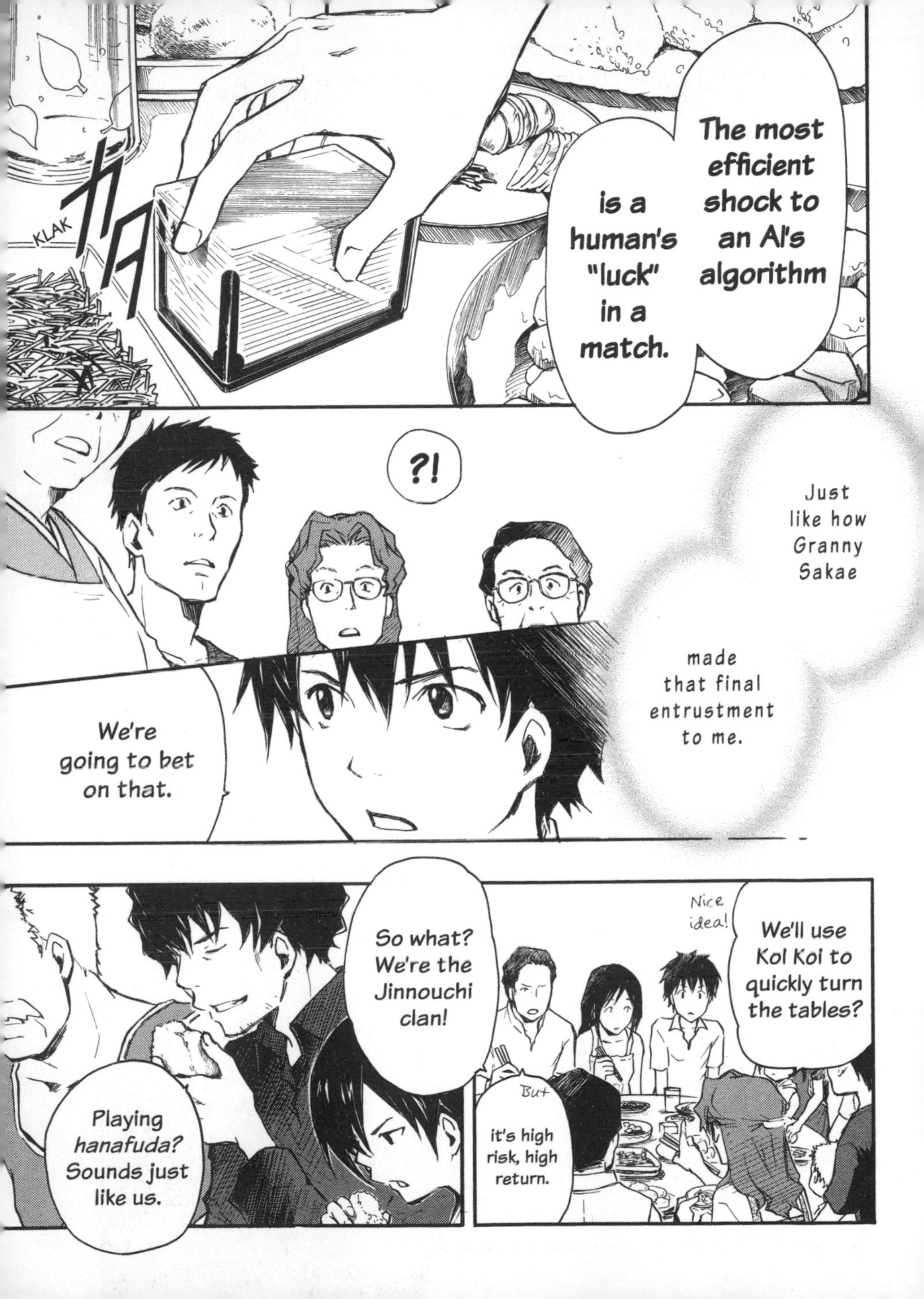
The most efficient shock to an AI's algorithm is a human's "luck" in a match.
KLAK
?!
Just like how Granny Sakae made that final entrustment to me.
We're going to bet on that.
We'll use Koi Koi to quickly turn the tables?
Nice idea!
But it's high risk, high return.
So what? We're the Jinnouchi clan!
Playing hanafuda? Sounds just like us.

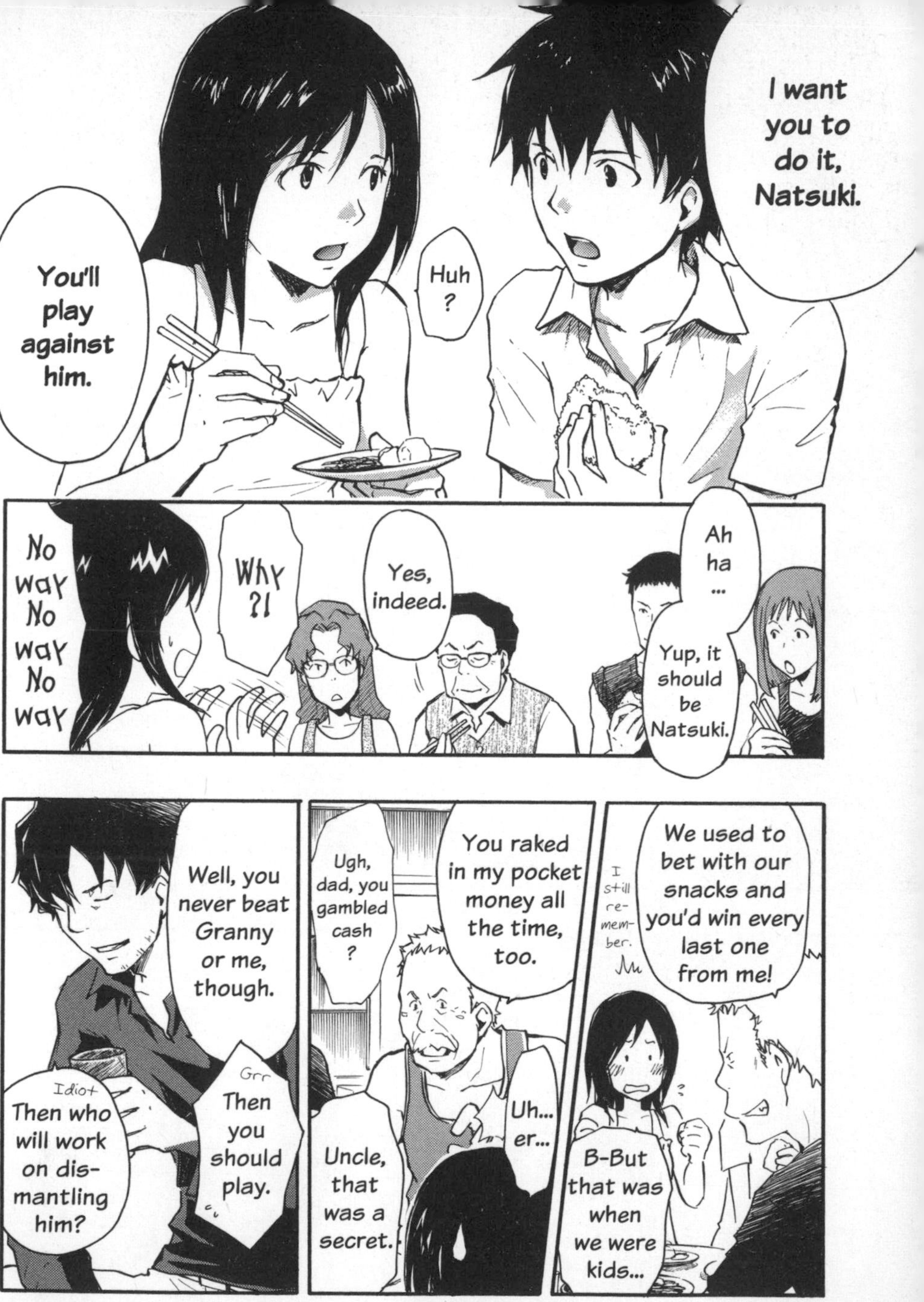
I want you to do it, Natsuki.
Huh?
You'll play against him.
Ah ha...
Yup, it should be Natsuki.
Yes, indeed.
Why?!
No way No way No way No way
We used to bet with our snacks and you'd win every last one from me!
I still re-member.
B-But that was when we were kids...
You raked in my pocket money all the time, too.
Ugh, dad, you gambled cash?
Uh... er...
Uncle, that was a secret.
Well, you never beat Granny or me, though.
Grr
Then you should play.
Idiot
Then who will work on dis-mantling him?

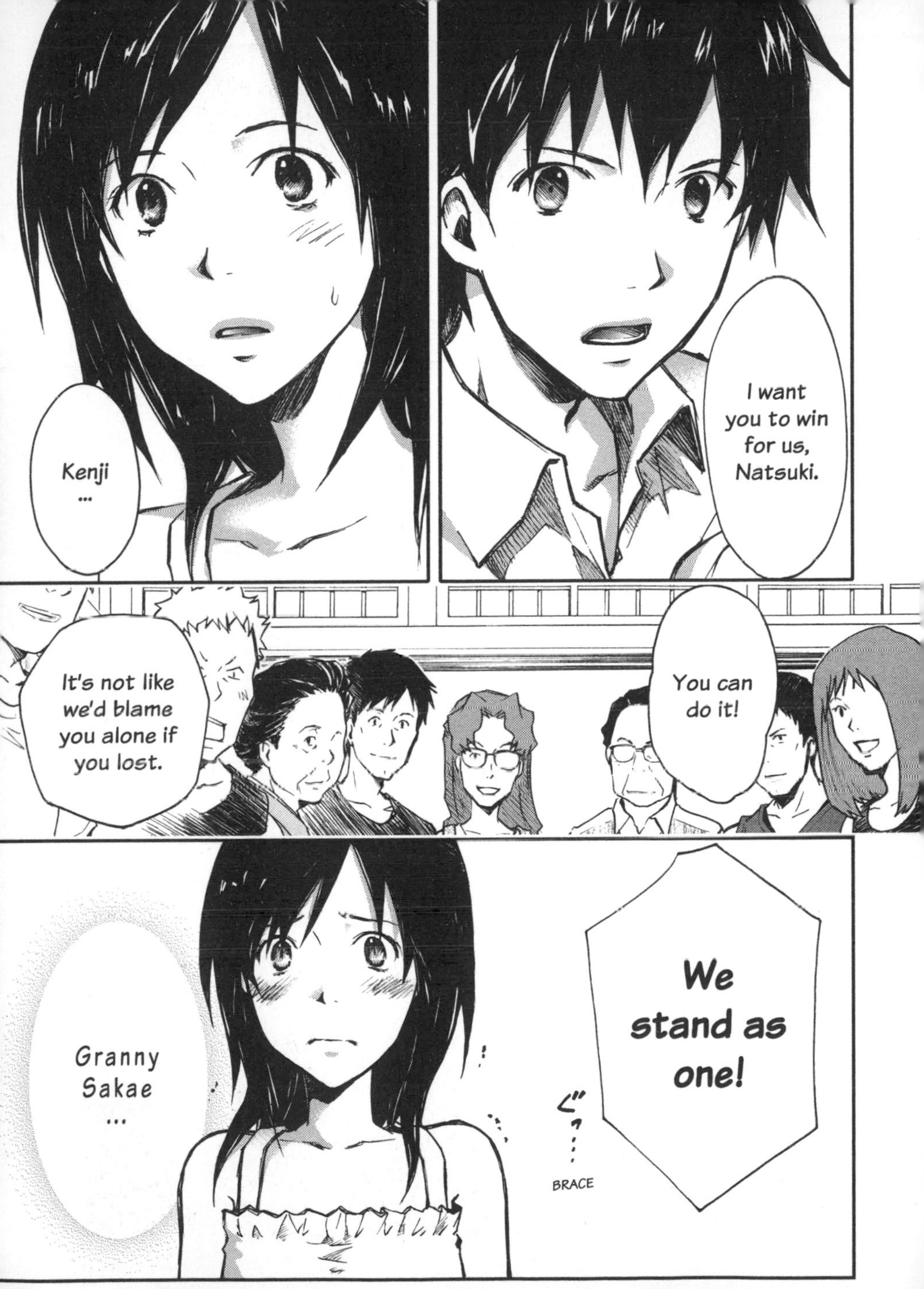
I want you to win for us, Natsuki.
Kenji ...
You can do it!
It's not like we'd blame you alone if you lost.
We stand as one!
ぐっ
BRACE
Granny Sakae ...

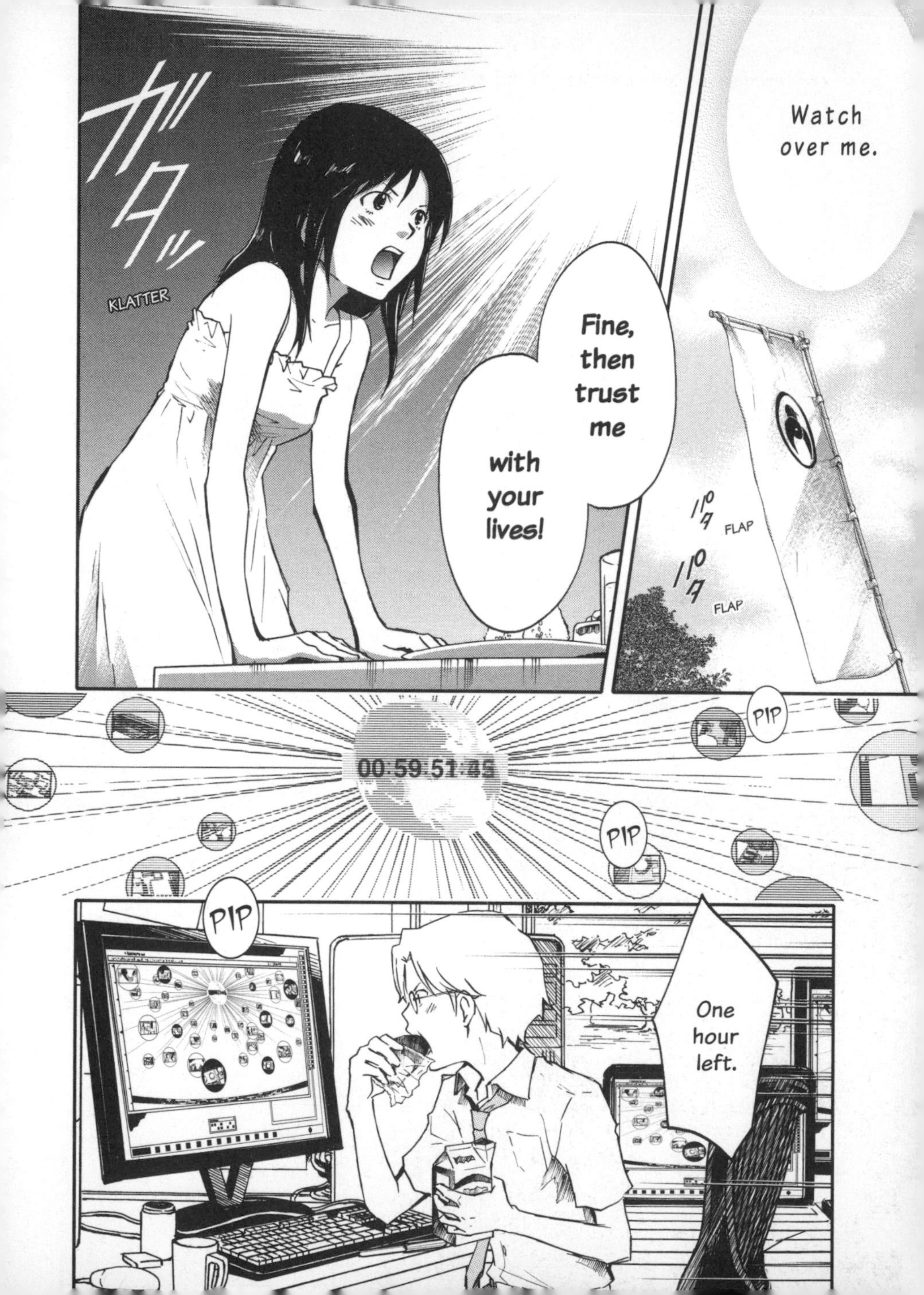
Watch over me.
パタ
FLAP
パタ
FLAP
Fine, then trust me with your lives!
ガタッ
KLATTER
PIP
00:59:51:45
PIP
PIP
One hour left.

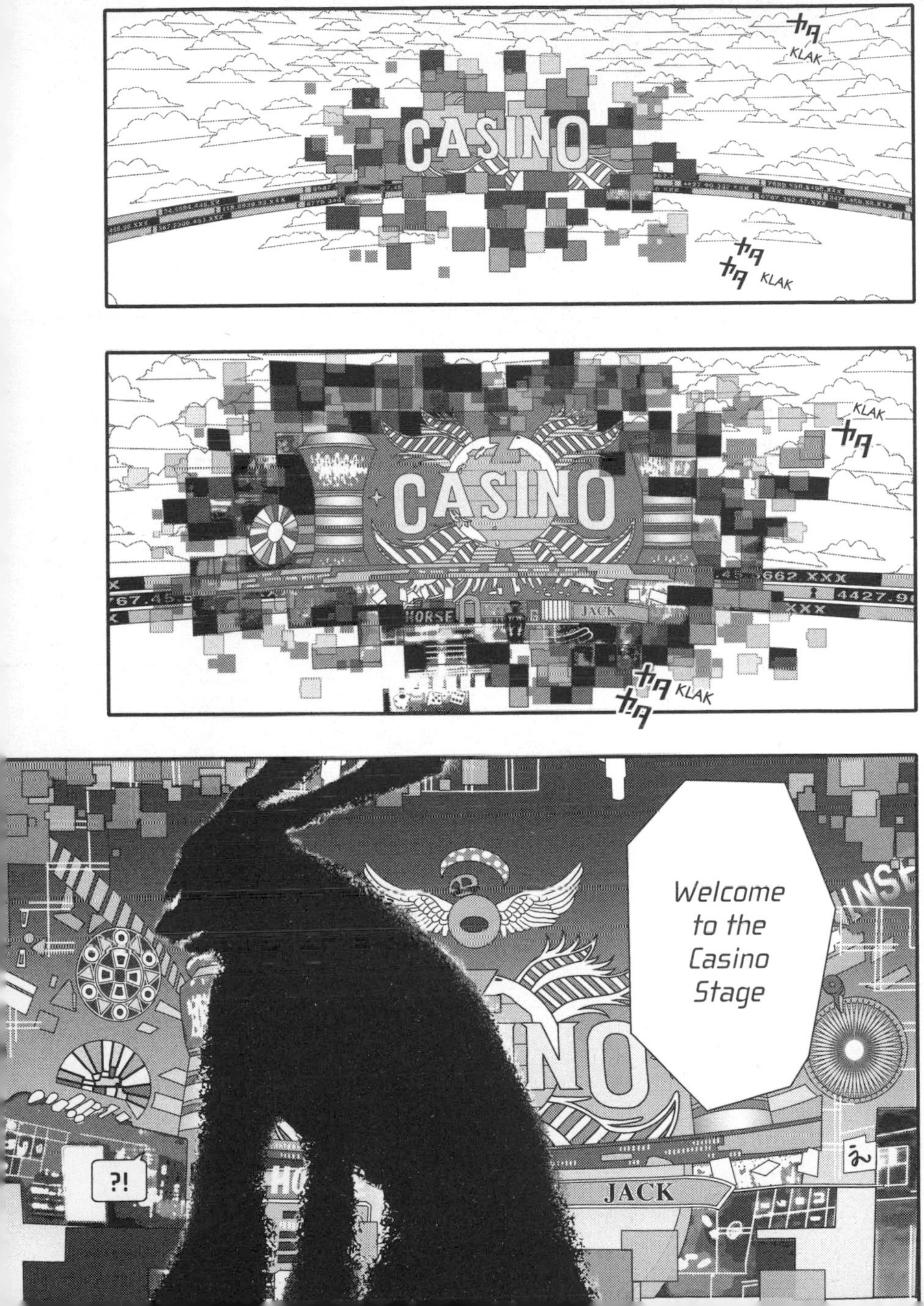

ガタ
KLAK
CASINO
ガタガタ
KLAK
KLAK
ガタ
CASINO
HORSE
JACK
ガタガタ
KLAK
Welcome to the Casino Stage
JACK
?!

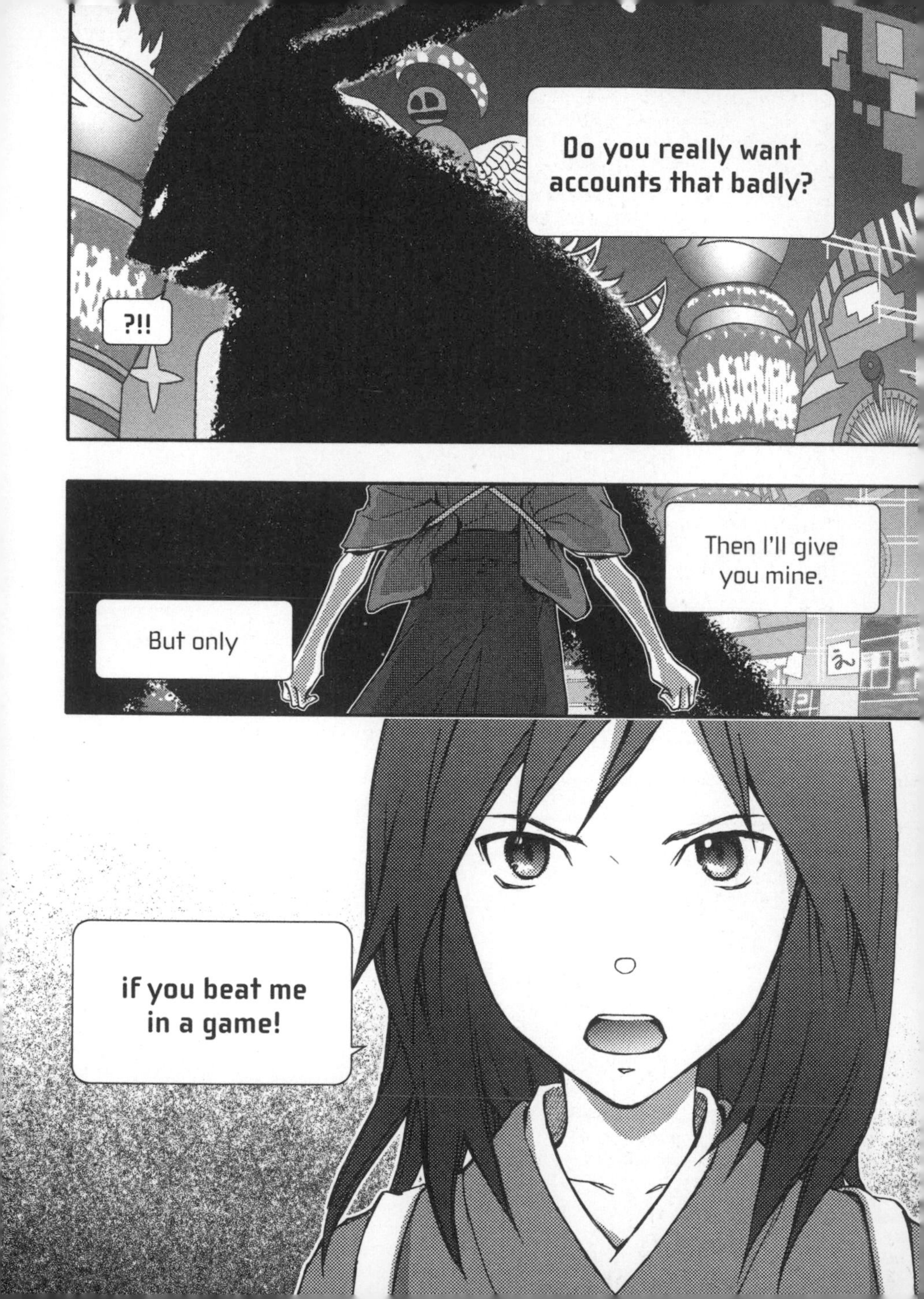
Do you really want accounts that badly?
?!!
Then I'll give you mine.
But only
if you beat me in a game!

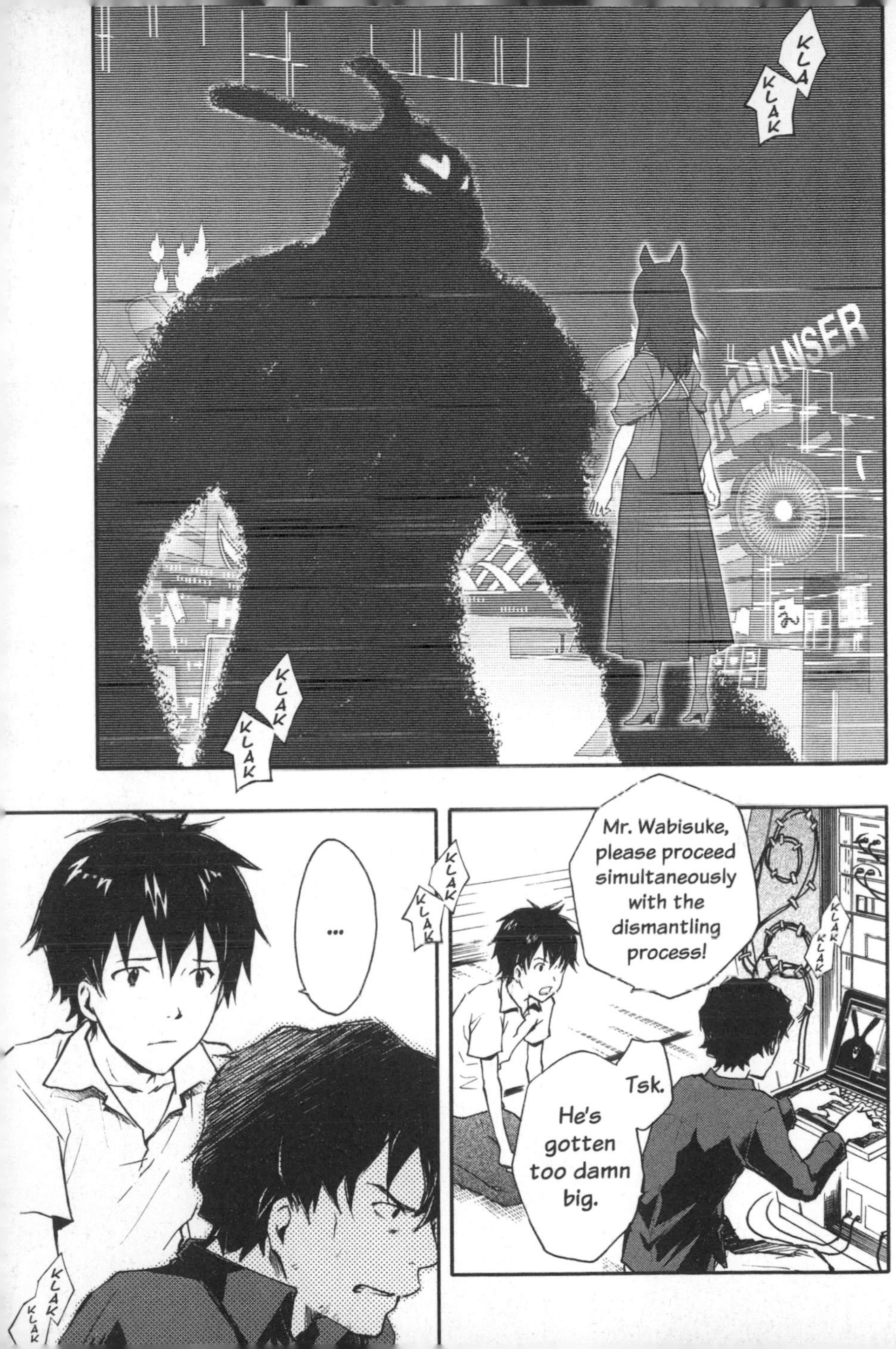
KLAK KLAK KLA
KLAK KLAK KLAK
Mr. Wabisuke, please proceed simultaneously with the dismantling process!
KLAK KLAK
Tsk.
He's gotten too damn big.
KLAK KLAK KLAK
...
KLAK KLAK

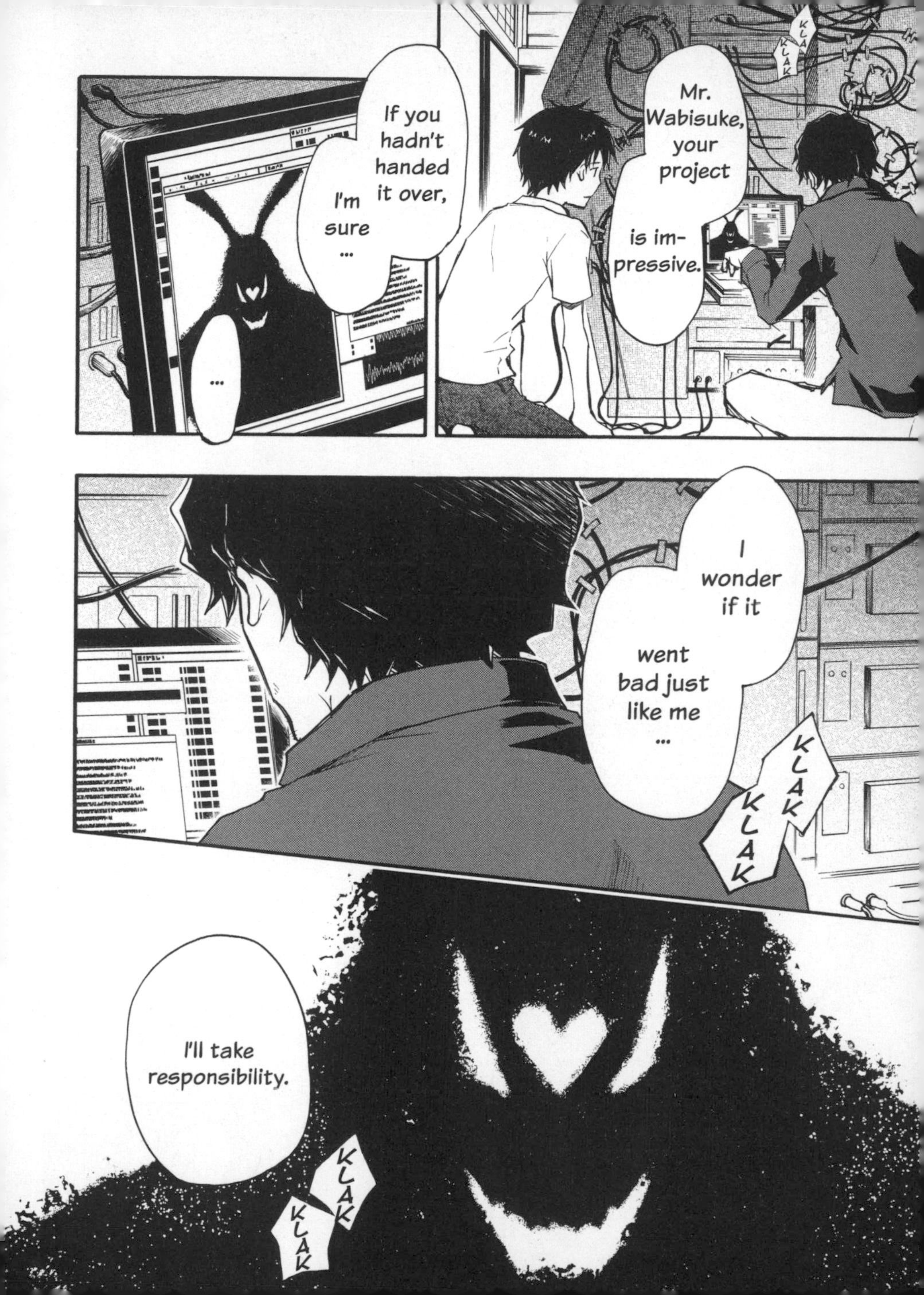
KLA KLAK
Mr. Wabisuke, your project is impressive.
If you hadn't handed it over, I'm sure ...
...
I wonder if it went bad just like me ...
KLAK KLAK
I'll take responsibility.
KLAK KLAK

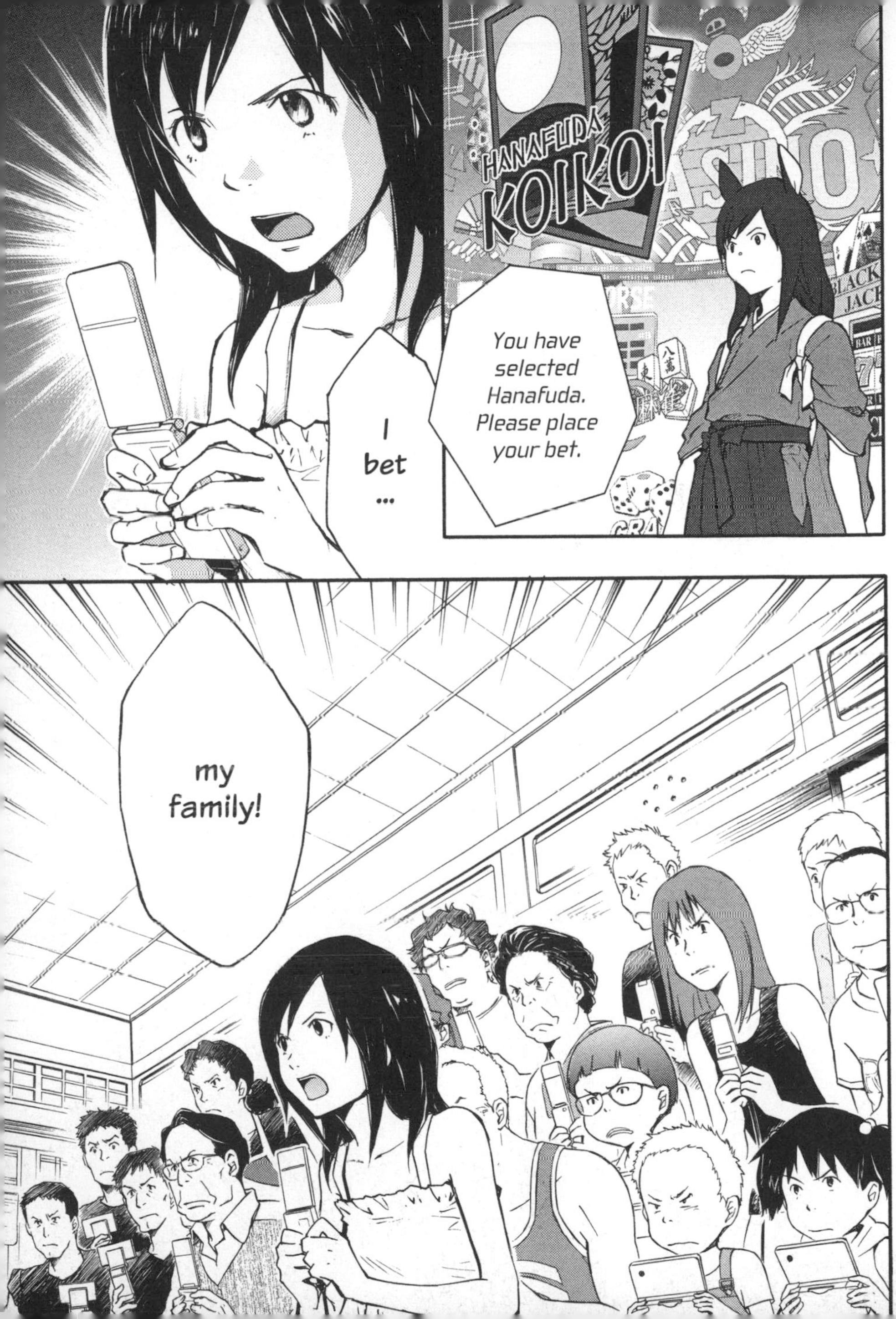
HANAFUDA KOIKOI
BLACK JACK
You have selected Hanafuda. Please place your bet.
I bet ...
my family!

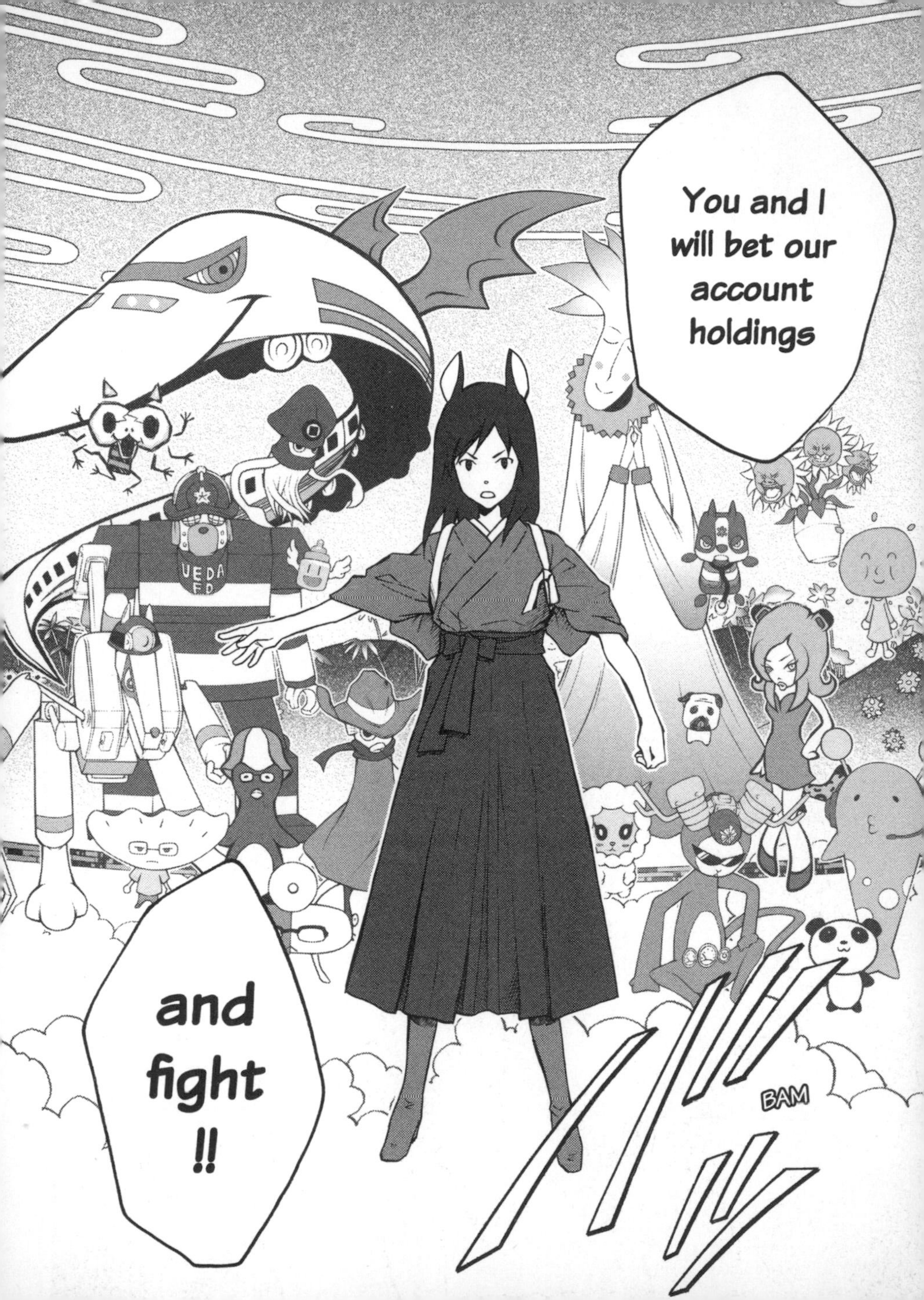
You and I will bet our account holdings
and fight !!
BAM
UEDA FD

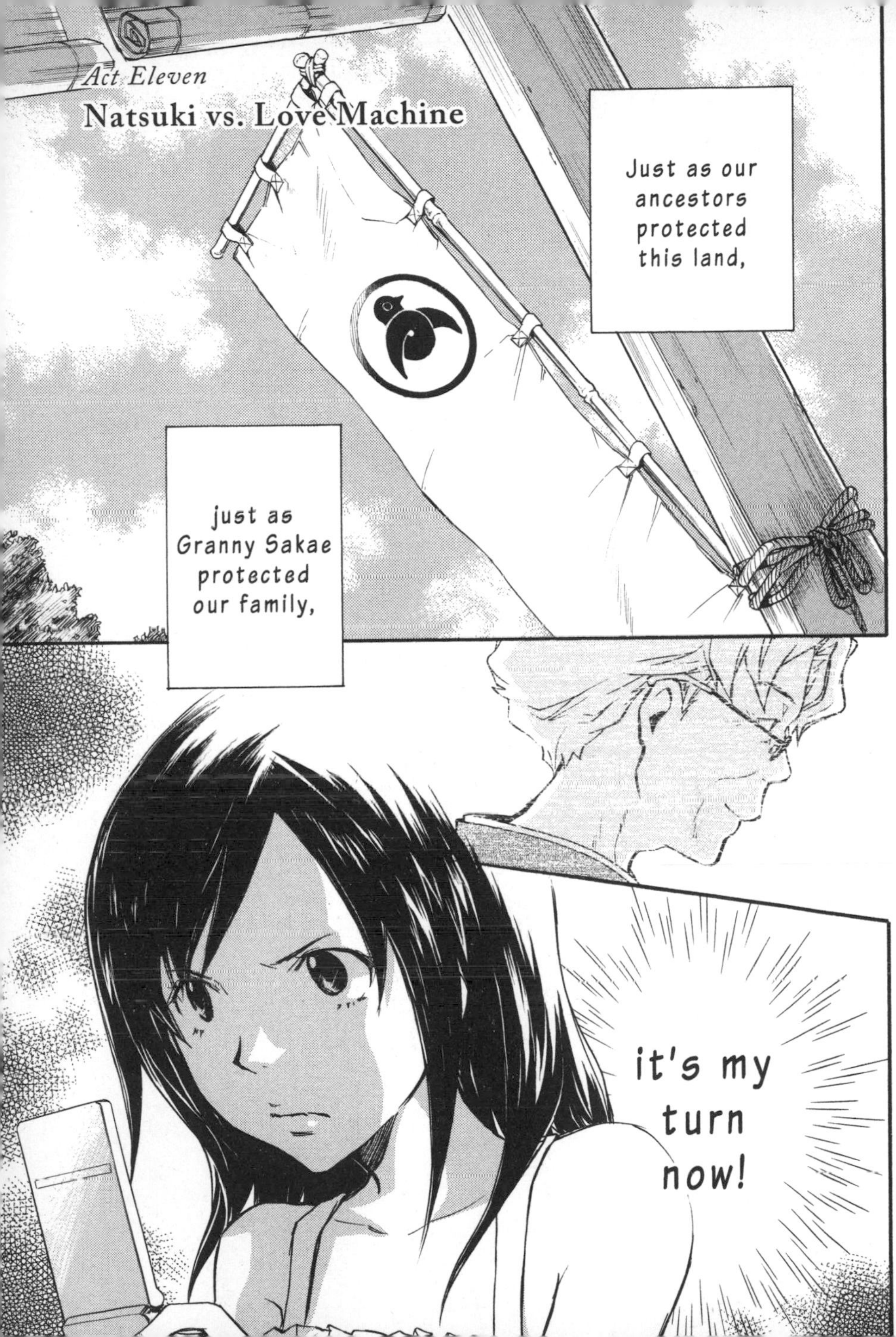
Act Eleven
Natsuki vs. Love Machine
Just as our ancestors protected this land,
just as Granny Sakae protected our family,
it's my turn now!

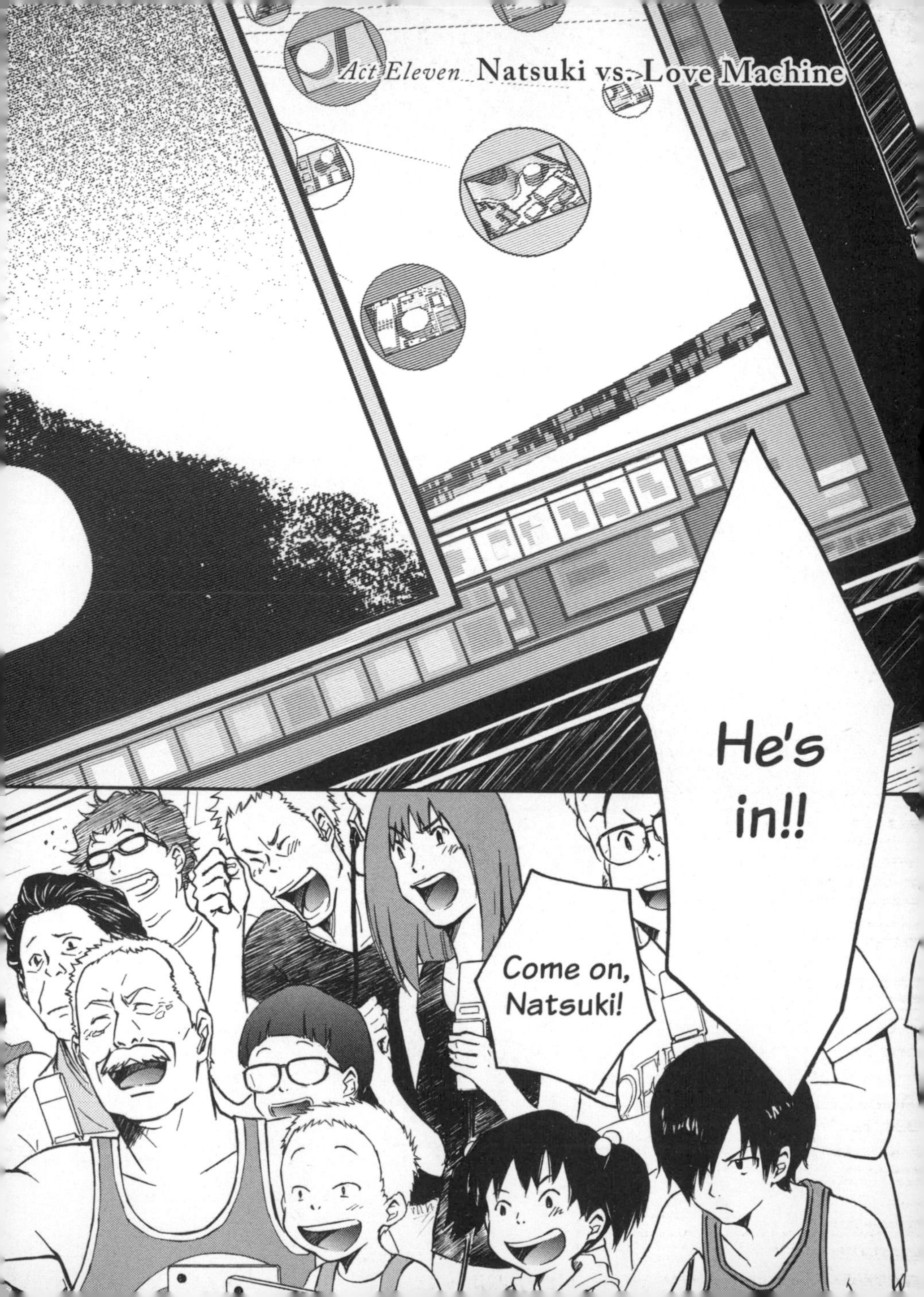
Act Eleven Natsuki vs. Love Machine
He's in!!
Come on, Natsuki!

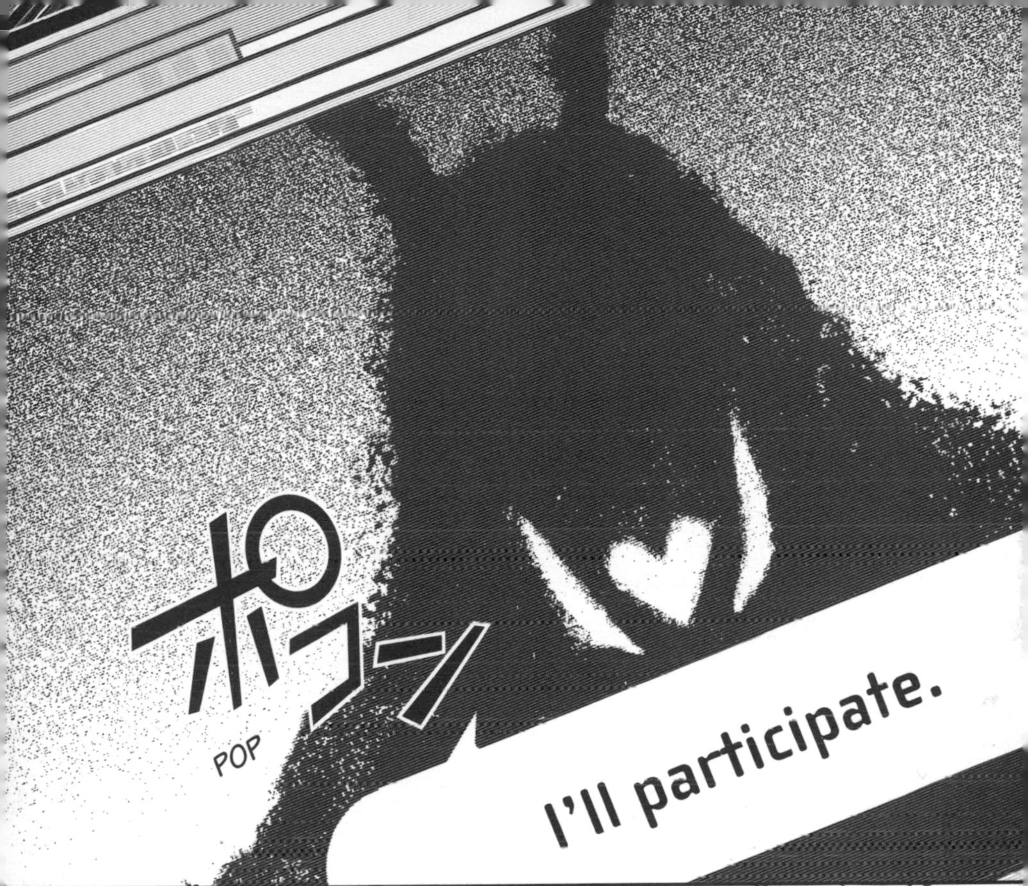
ポコーン
POP
I'll participate.
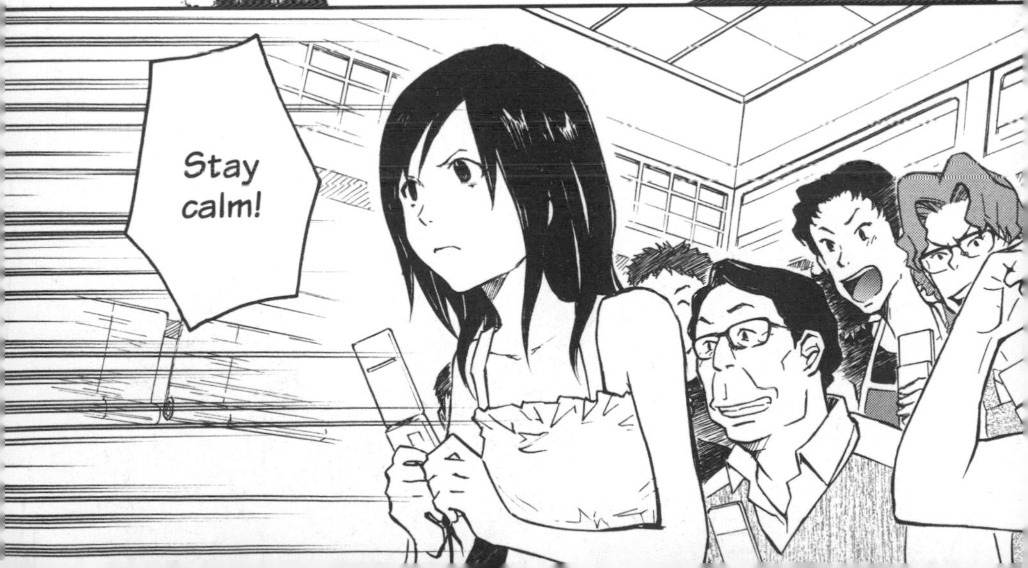
Stay calm!

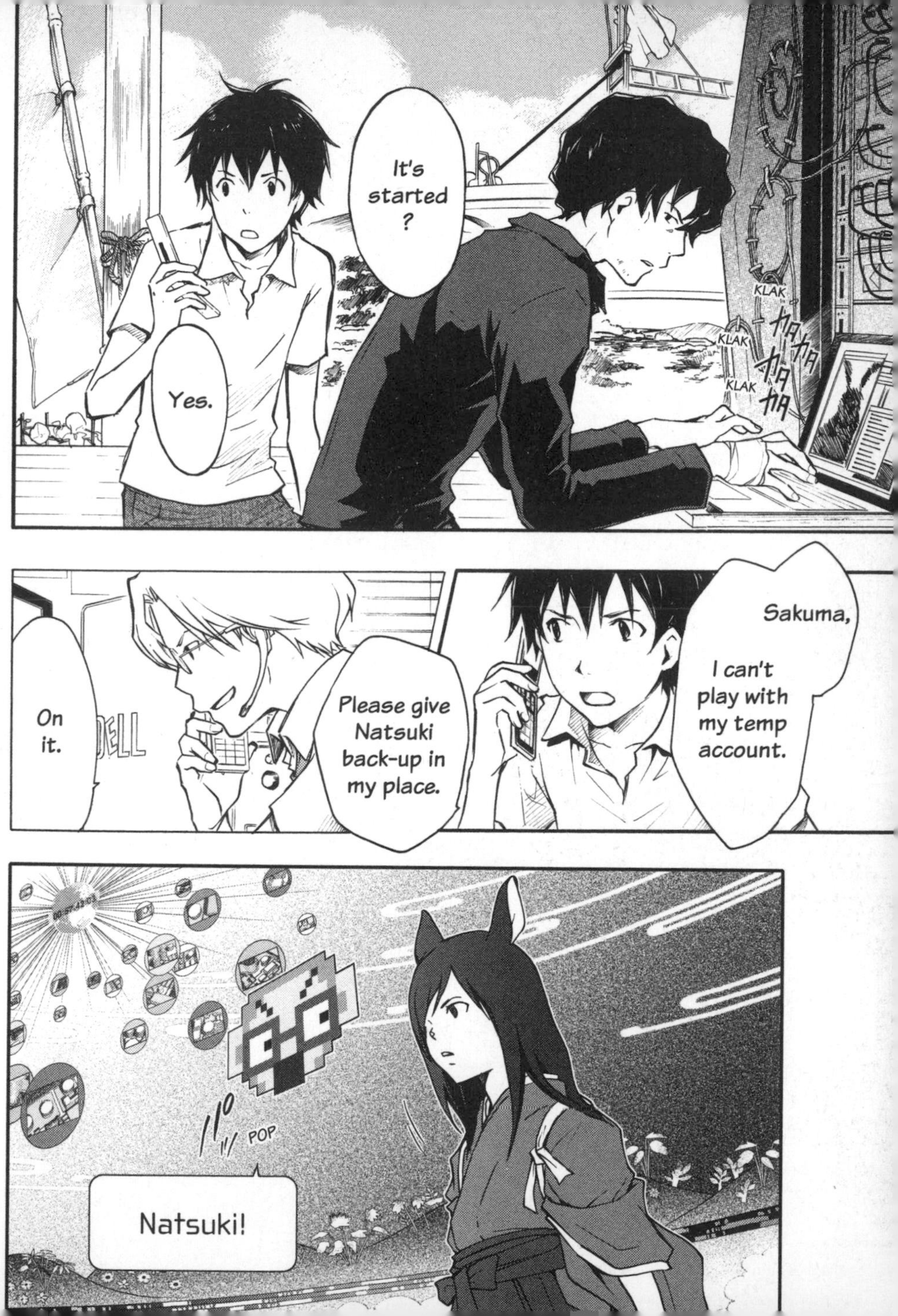
It's started ?
Yes.
KLAK
KLAK
KLAK
Sakuma, I can't play with my temp account.
Please give Natsuki back-up in my place.
On it.
DELL
POP
Natsuki!

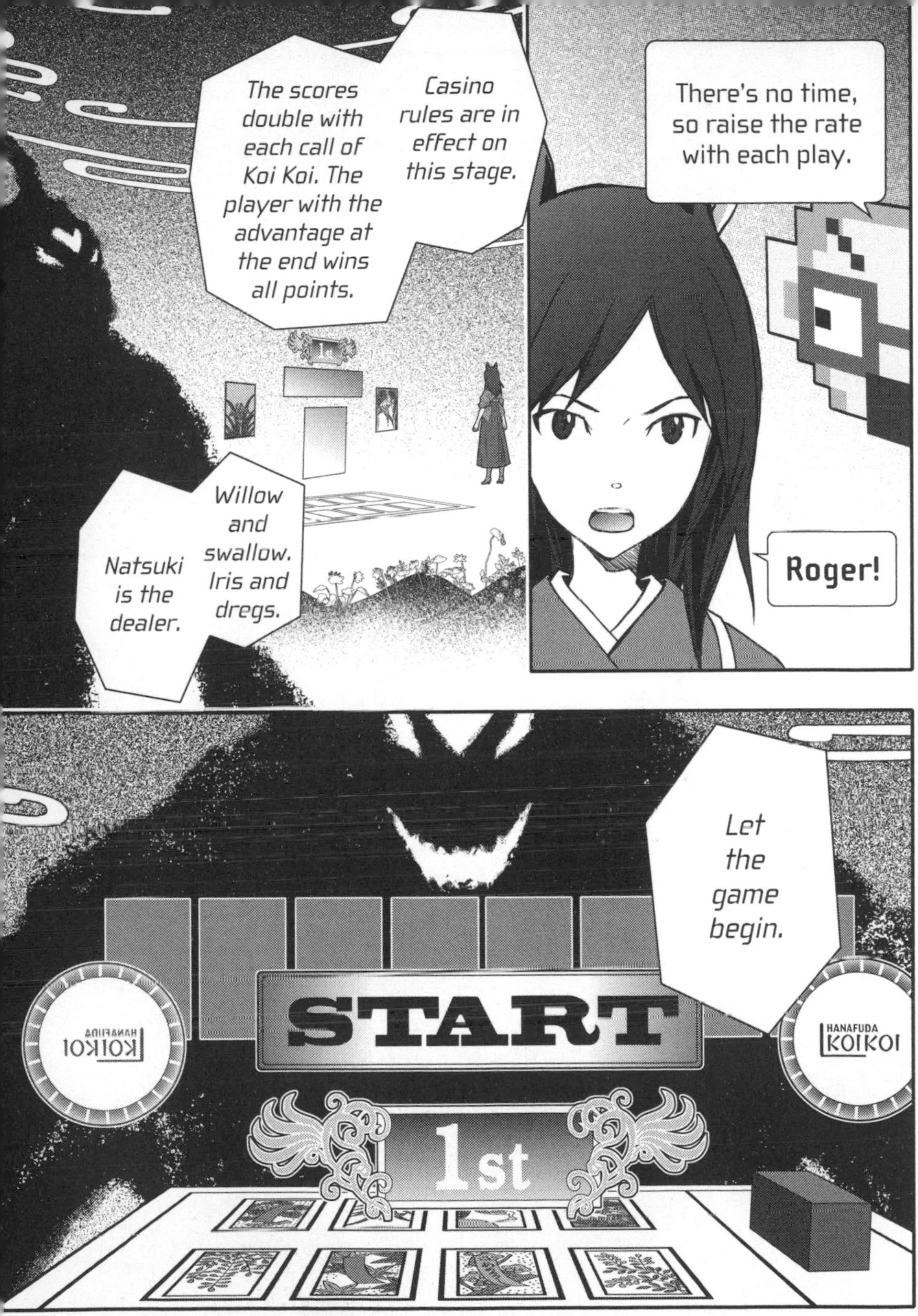
There's no time, so raise the rate with each play.
Roger!
Casino rules are in effect on this stage.
The scores double with each call of Koi Koi. The player with the advantage at the end wins all points.
Willow and swallow. Iris and dregs.
Natsuki is the dealer.
Let the game begin.
START
HANAFUDA KOIKOI
1st

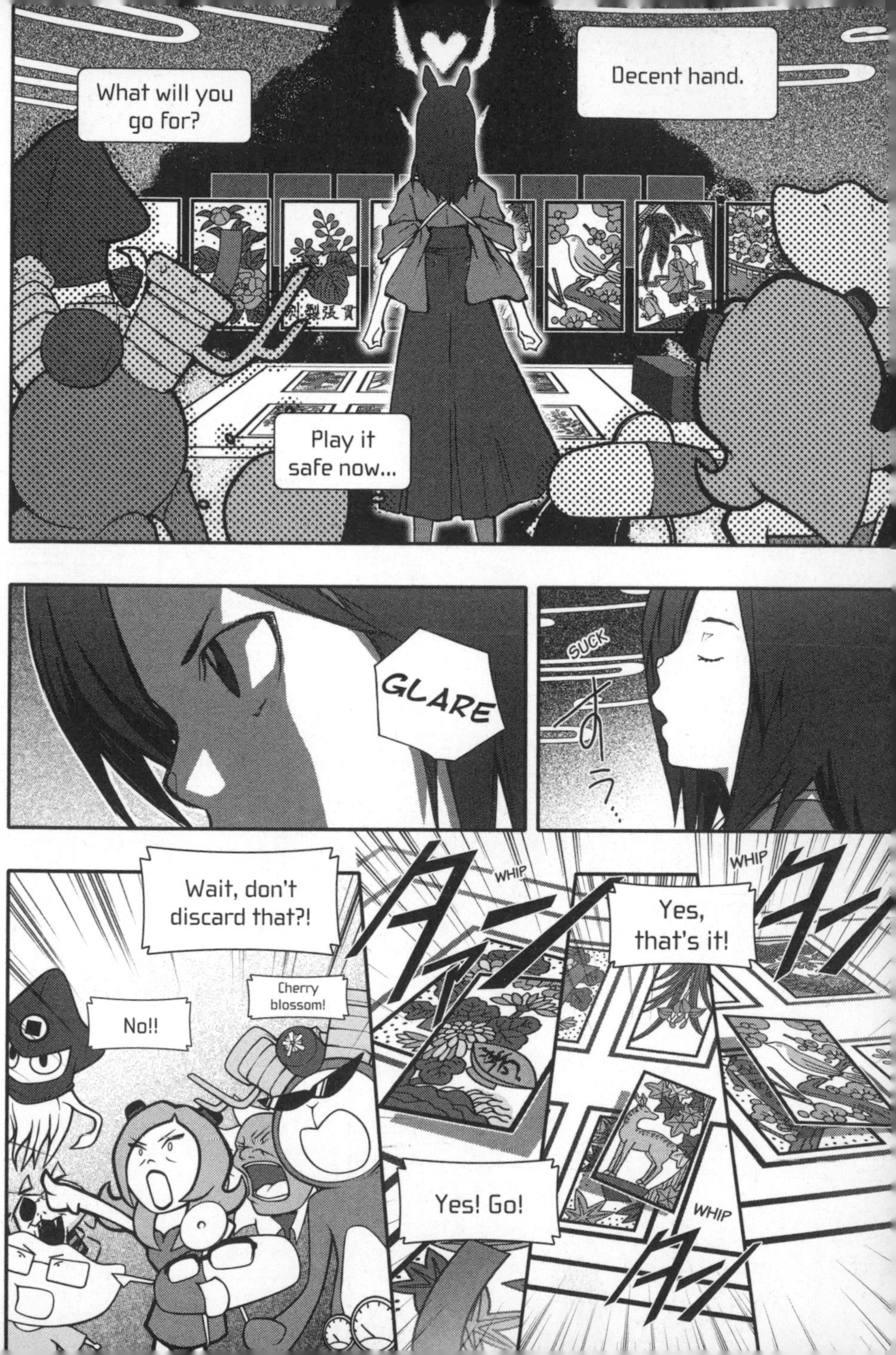
Decent hand.
What will you go for?
Play it safe now...
SUCK
GLARE
WHIP
Yes, that's it!
WHIP
Yes! Go!
WHIP
Wait, don't discard that?!
Cherry blossom!
No!!

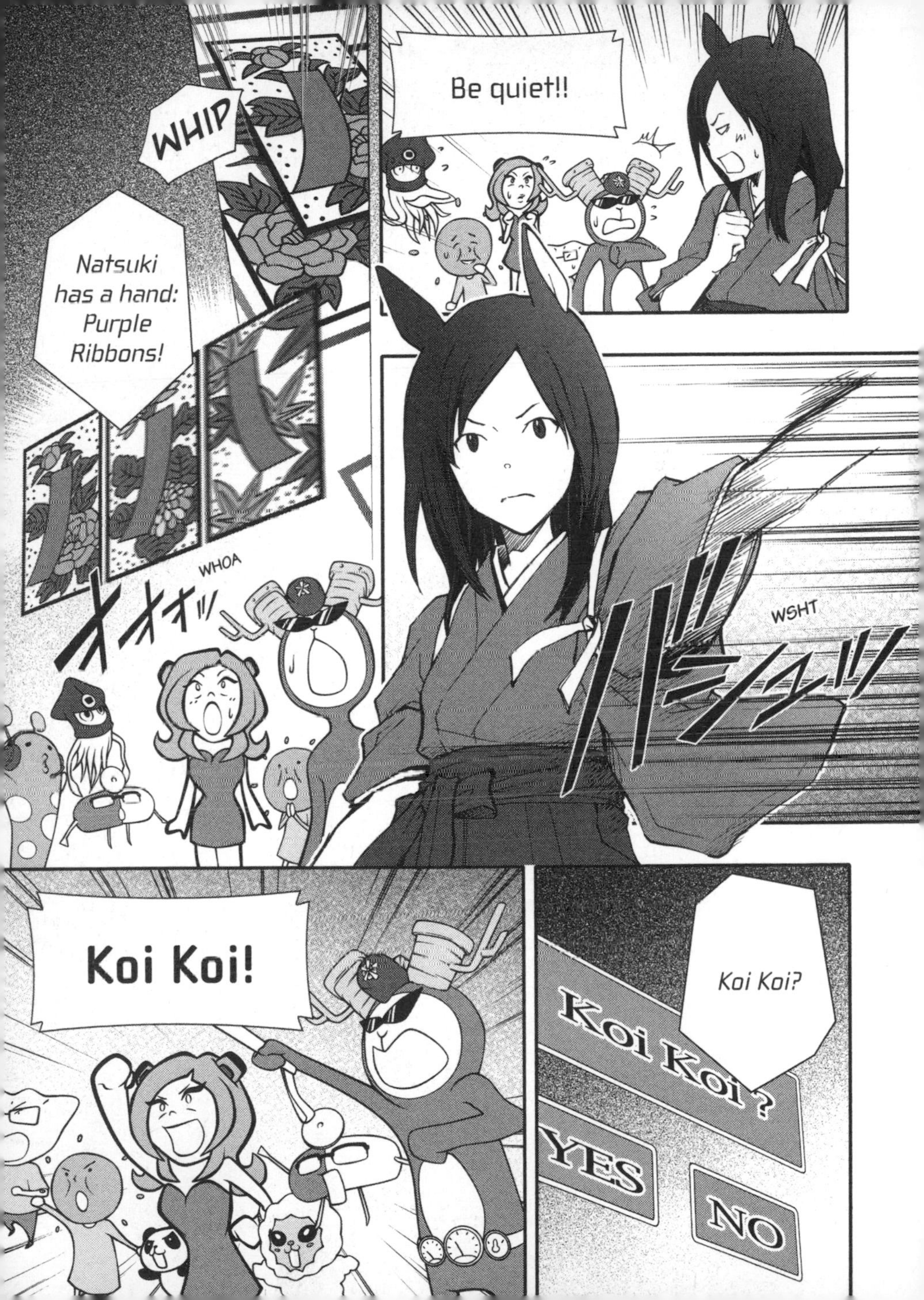
Be quiet!!
WHIP
Natsuki has a hand: Purple Ribbons!
WSHT
WHOA
Koi Koi?
Koi Koi ?
YES
NO
Koi Koi!

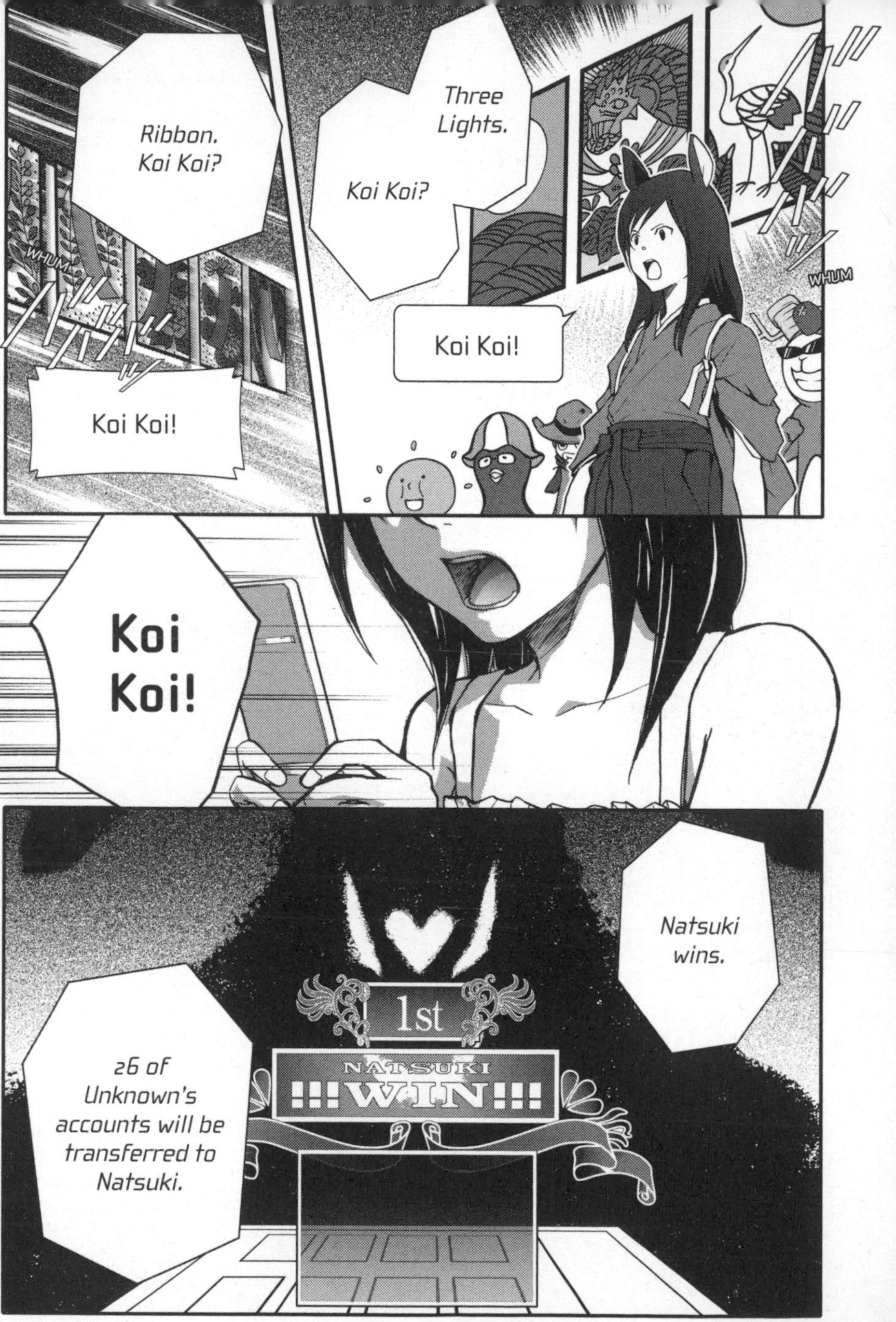
Three Lights.
Koi Koi?
WHUM
Koi Koi!
Ribbon. Koi Koi?
WHUM
Koi Koi!
Koi Koi!
Natsuki wins.
1st
NATSUKI
!!!WIN!!!
26 of Unknown's accounts will be transferred to Natsuki.

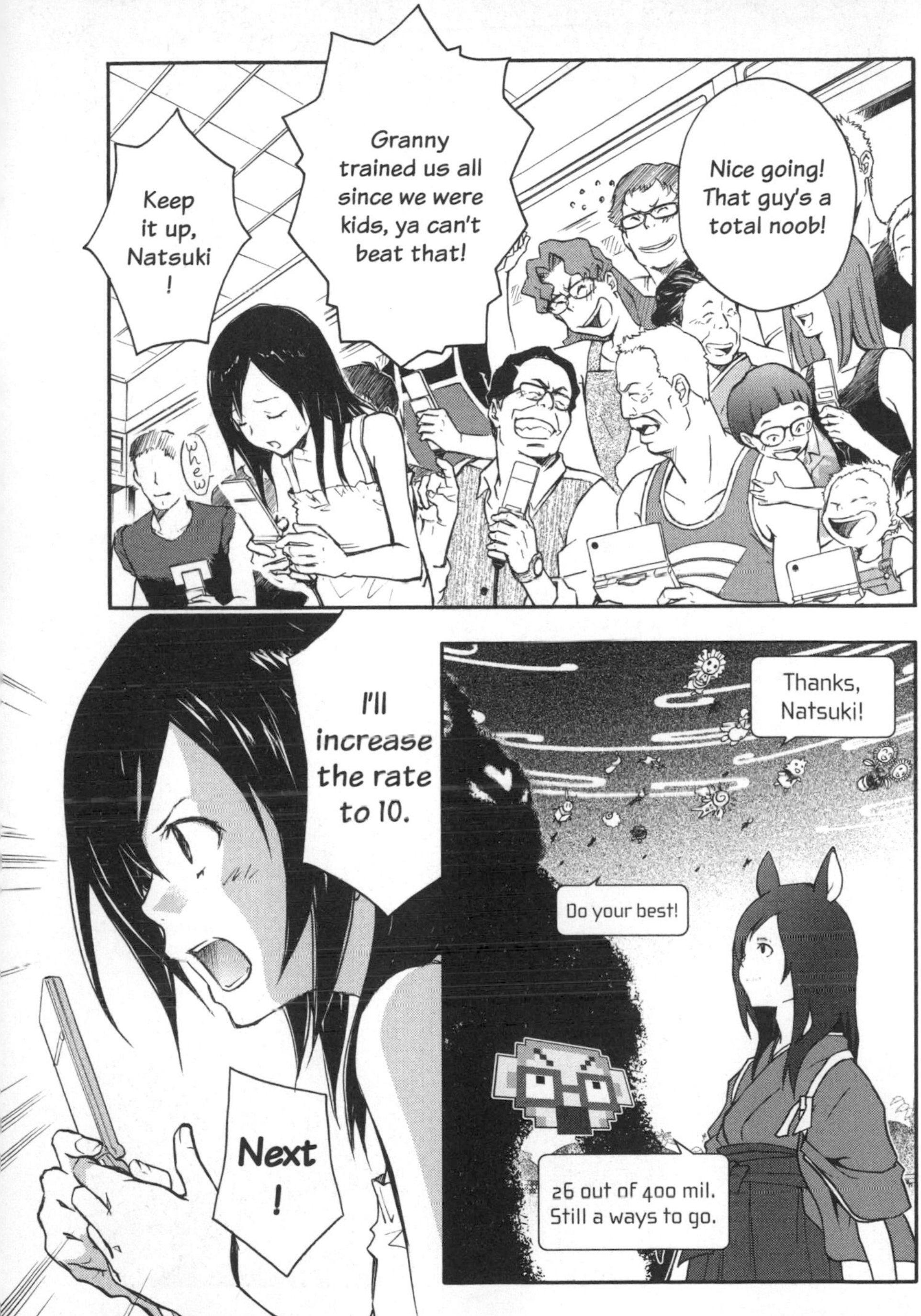
Nice going! That guy's a total noob!
Granny trained us all since we were kids, ya can't beat that!
Keep it up, Natsuki!
whew
Thanks, Natsuki!
Do your best!
26 out of 400 mil. Still a ways to go.
I'll increase the rate to 10.
Next!

Seeds.

Three Lights.

WHUM

WHUM

WHUM

Boar, Deer, Butterfly.

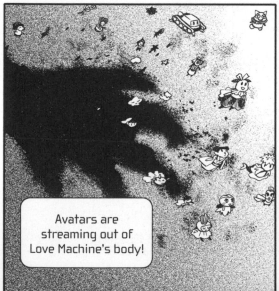

Avatars are streaming out of Love Machine's body!

21 wins in a row...

Wow...

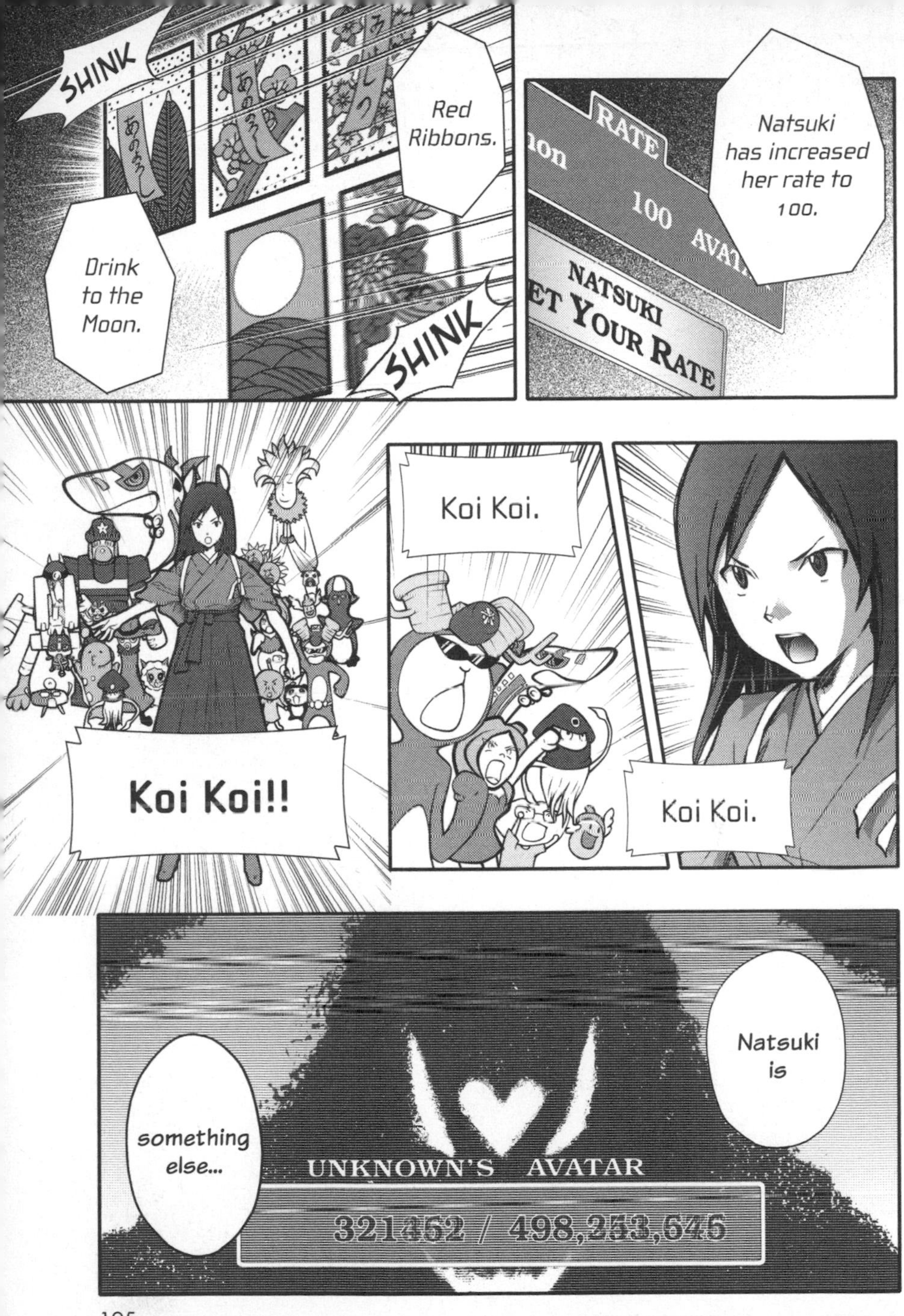
RATE
100
NATSUKI
ET YOUR RATE
Natsuki has increased her rate to 100.
Red Ribbons.
SHINK
あのよろし
Drink to the Moon.
SHINK
Koi Koi.
Koi Koi.
Koi Koi!!
Natsuki is
something else...
UNKNOWN'S AVATAR
321452 / 498,253,646

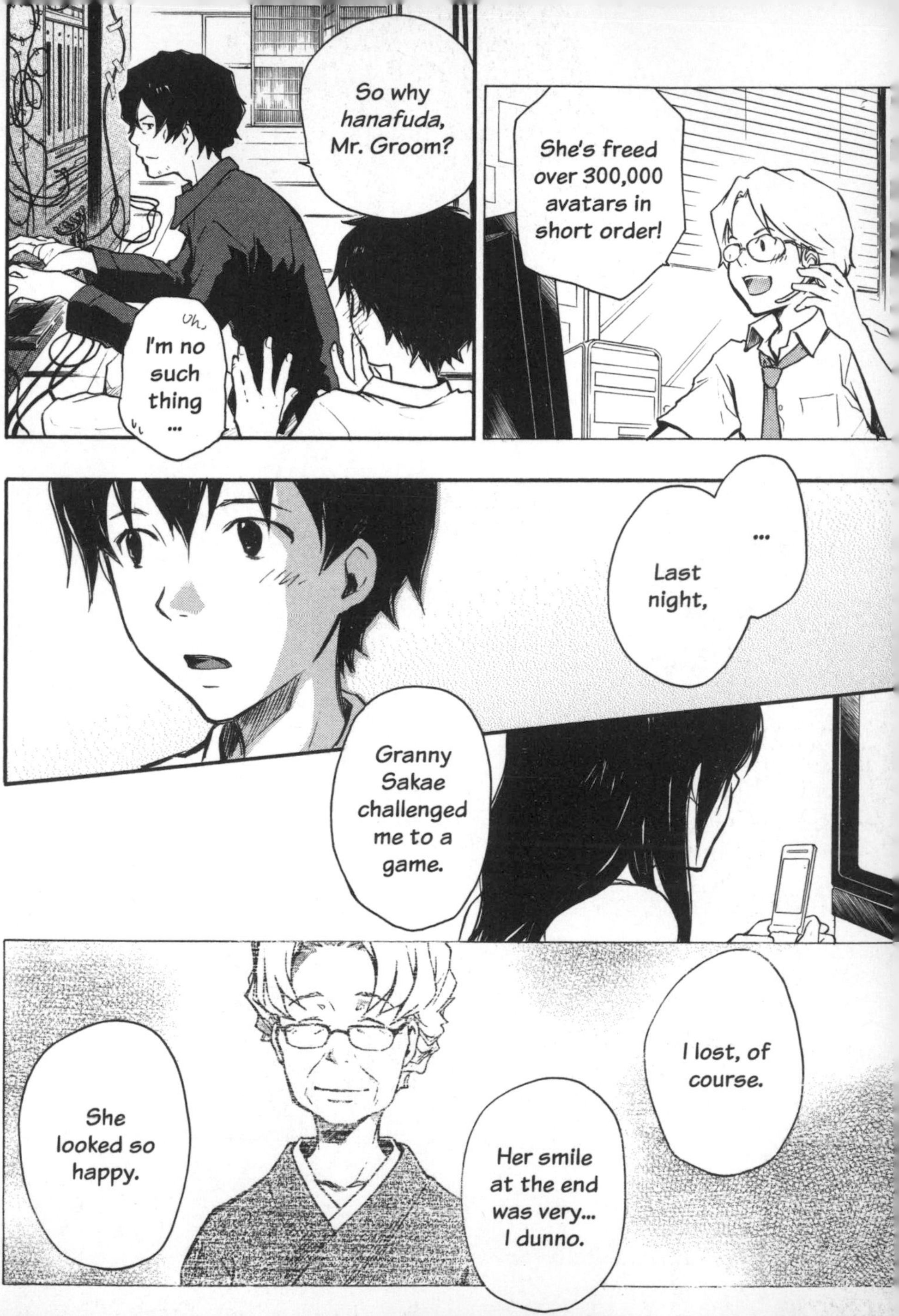
She's freed over 300,000 avatars in short order!
So why *hanafuda*, Mr. Groom?
I'm no such thing...
... Last night,
Granny Sakae challenged me to a game.
I lost, of course.
Her smile at the end was very... I dunno.
She looked so happy.

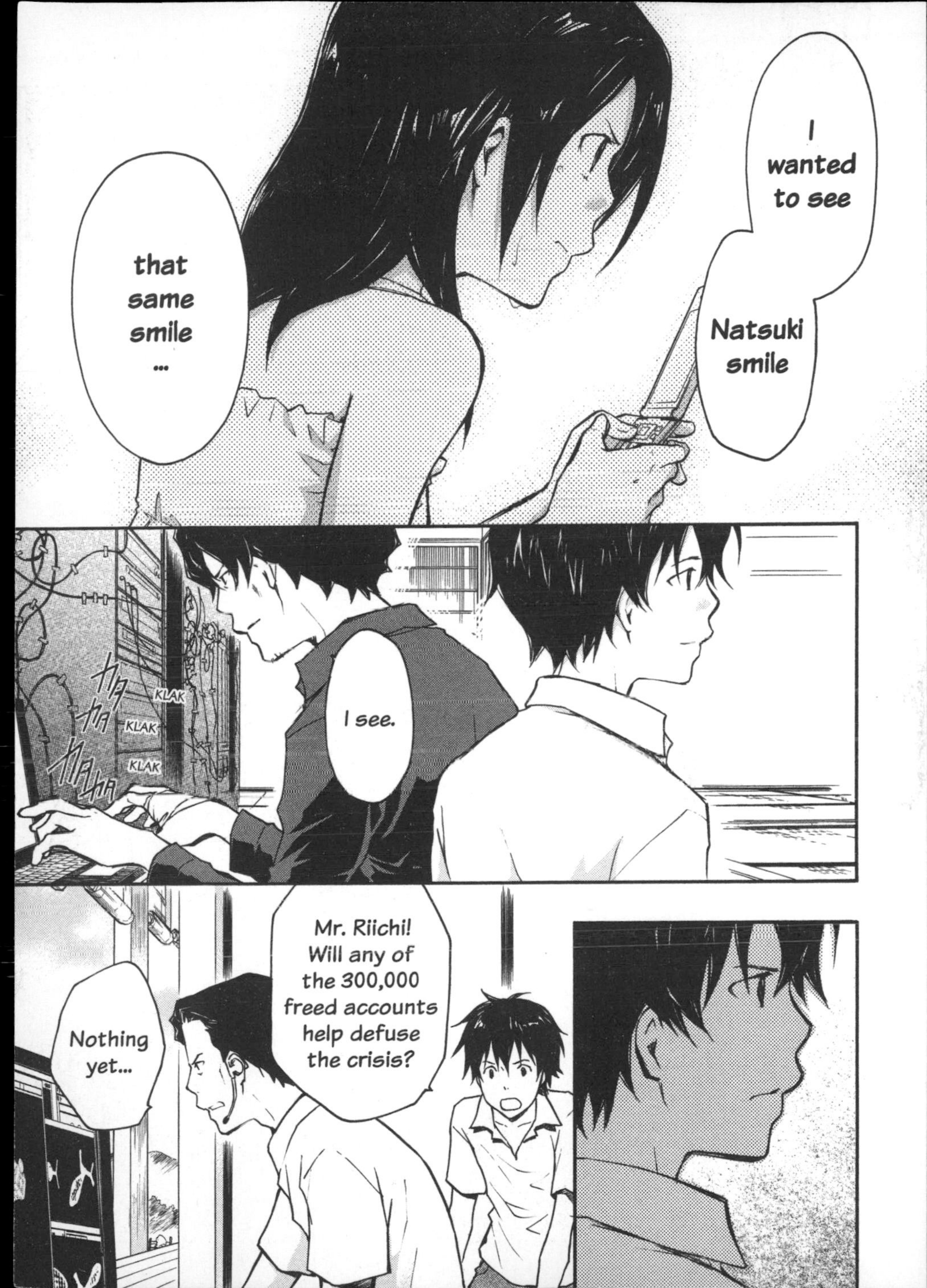
I wanted to see Natsuki smile
that same smile ...
I see.
KLAK
KLAK
KLAK
Mr. Riichi! Will any of the 300,000 freed accounts help defuse the crisis?
Nothing yet...

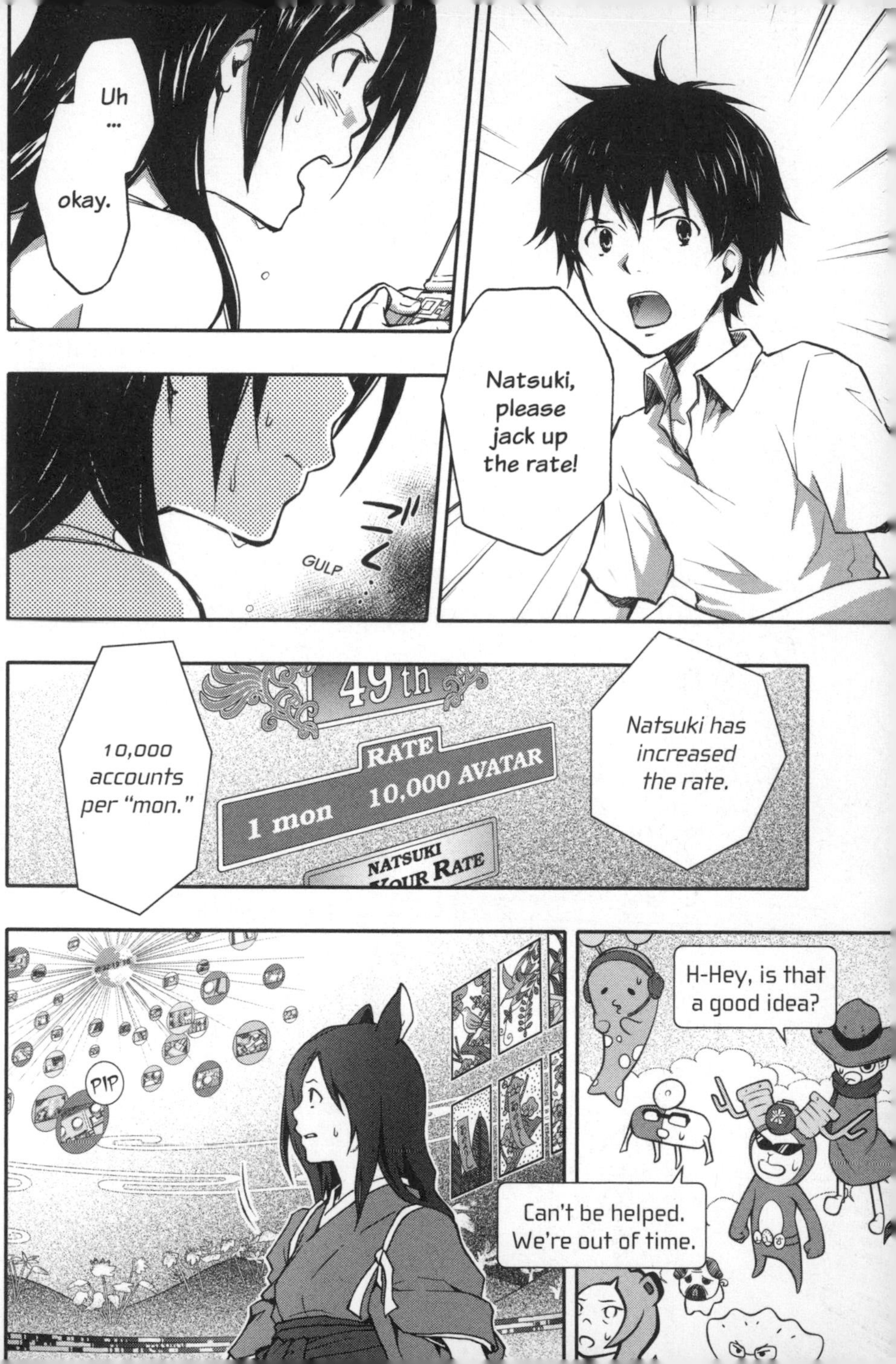

Natsuki, please jack up the rate!
Uh ... okay.
GULP
Natsuki has increased the rate.
49th
RATE
1 mon 10,000 AVATAR
NATSUKI YOUR RATE
10,000 accounts per "mon."
H-Hey, is that a good idea?
Can't be helped. We're out of time.
PIP

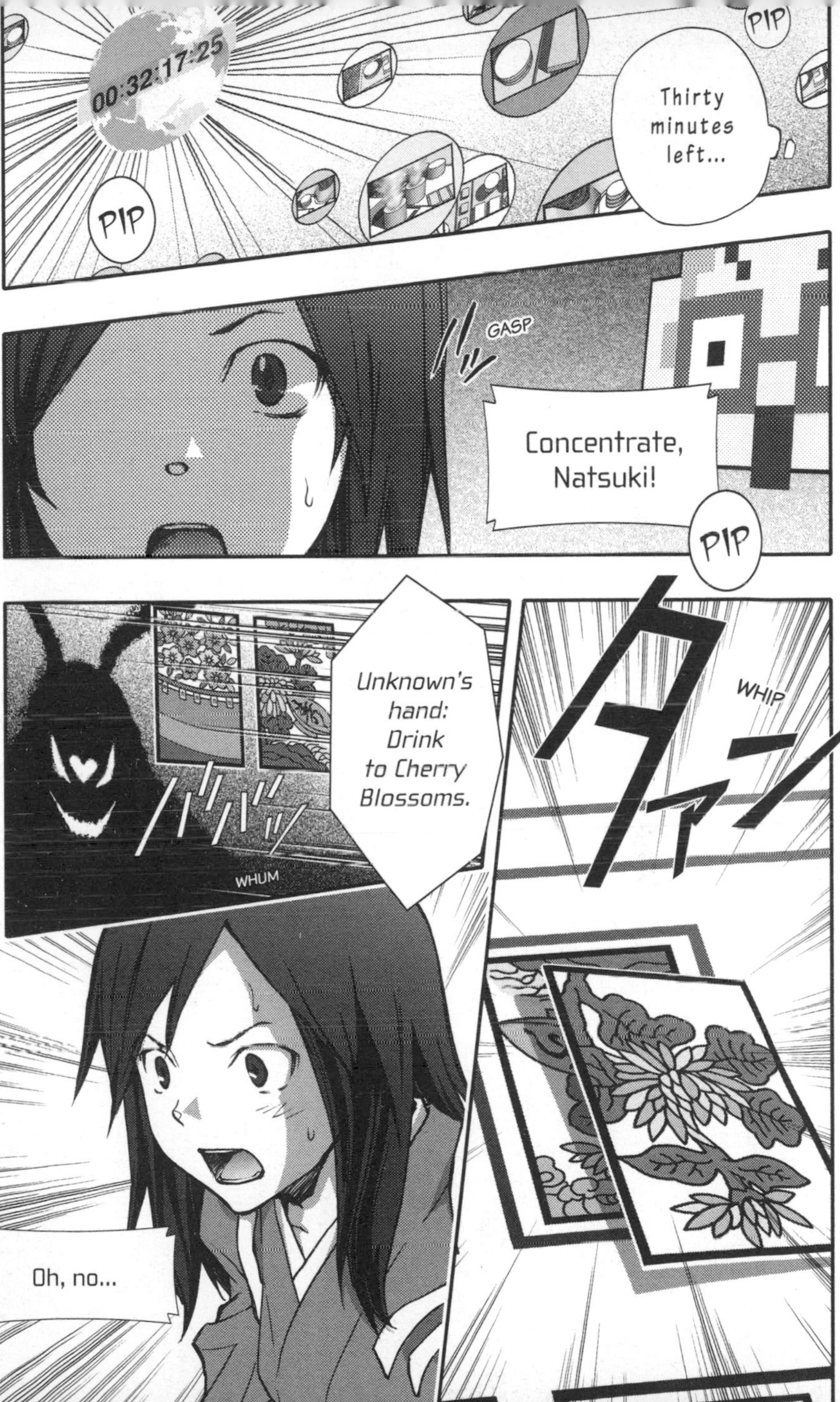
PIP
Thirty minutes left...
00:32:17:25
PIP
GASP
Concentrate, Natsuki!
PIP
WHIP
Unknown's hand: Drink to Cherry Blossoms.
WHUM
Oh, no...

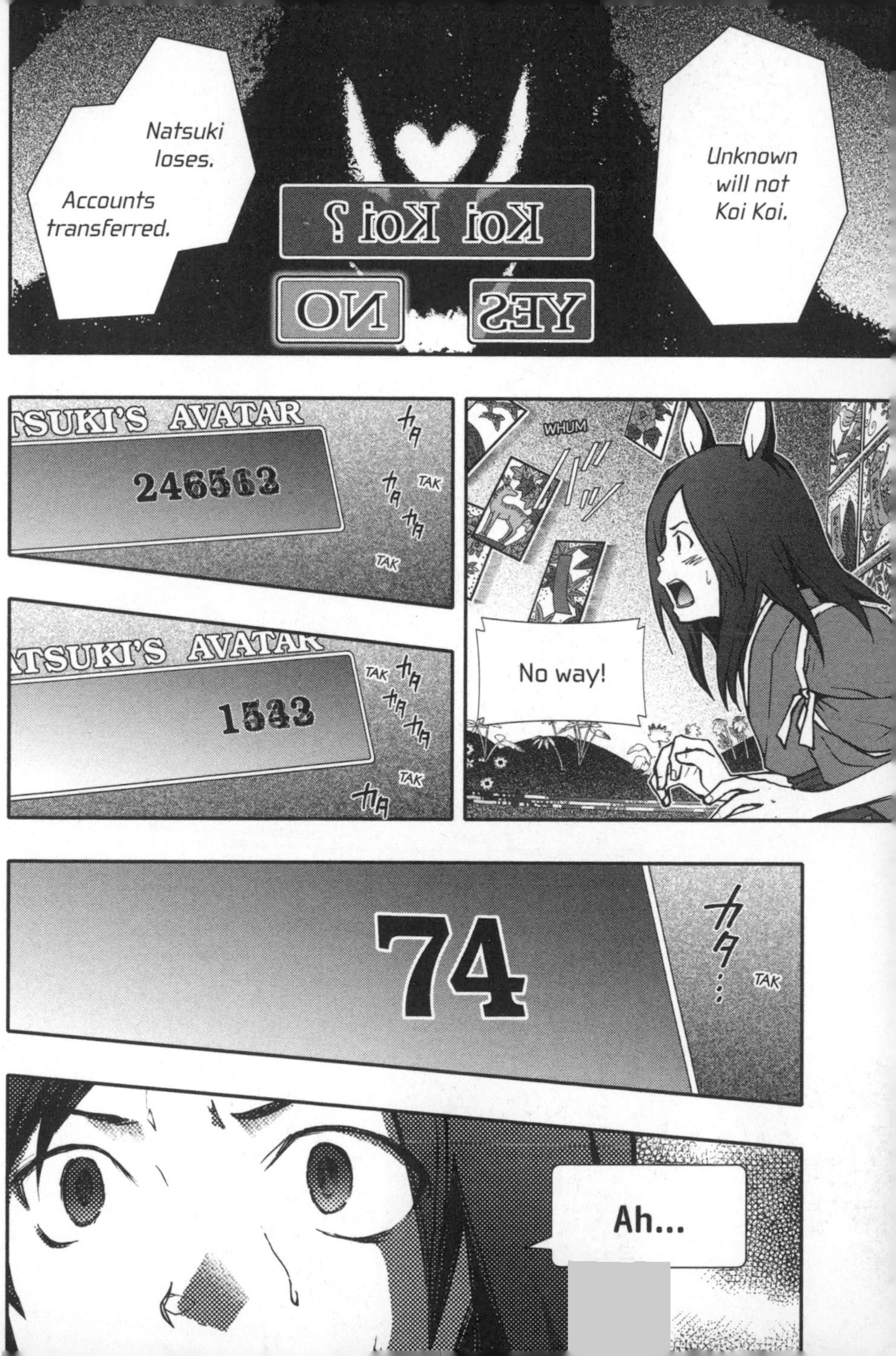
Unknown will not Koi Koi.
Koi Koi ?
YES
NO
Natsuki loses.
Accounts transferred.
WHUM
No way!
TSUKI'S AVATAR
TAK
TAK
ATSUKI'S AVATAR
TAK
TAK
74
TAK
Ah...

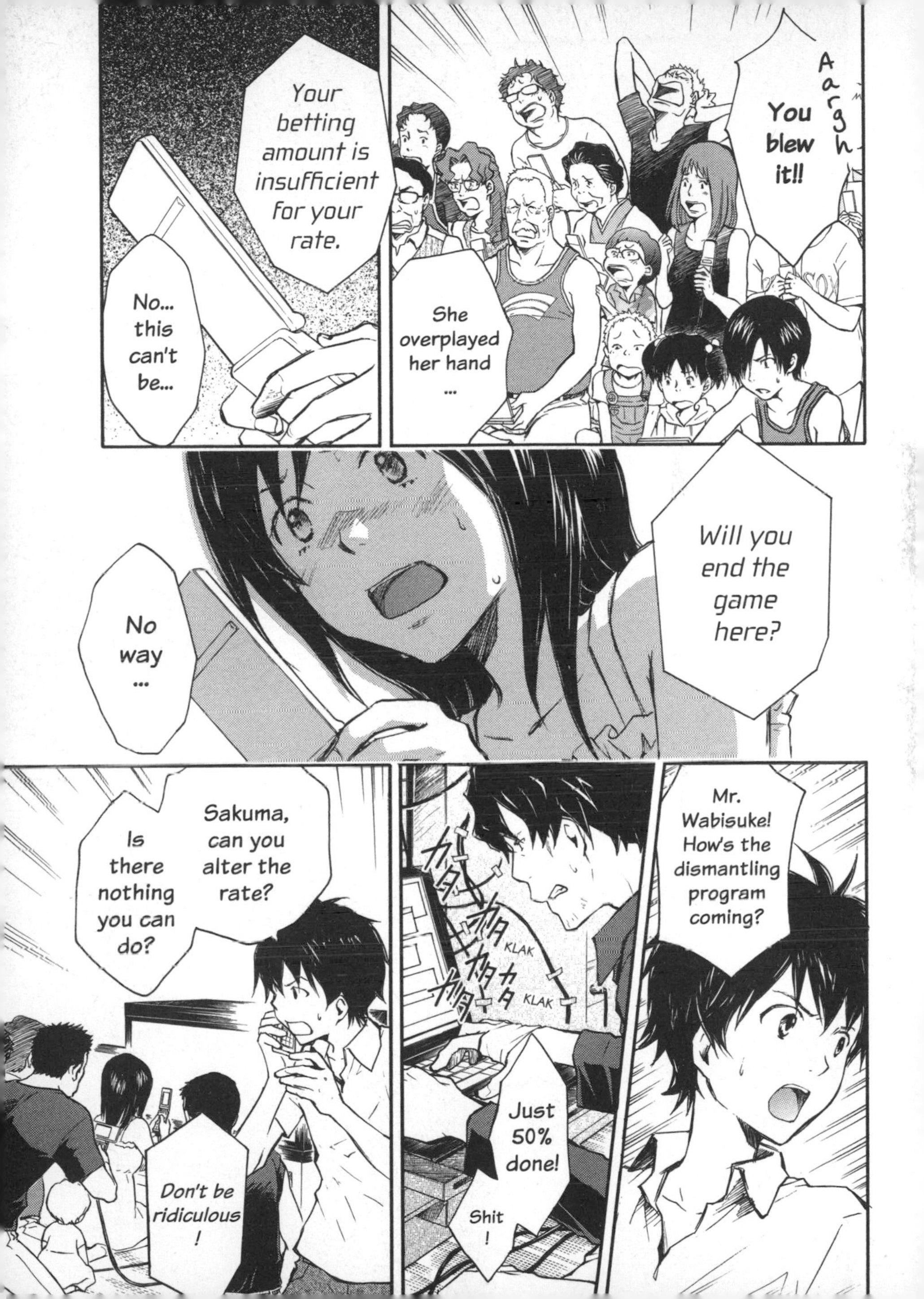
Aargh
You blew it!!
She overplayed her hand ...
Your betting amount is insufficient for your rate.
No... this can't be...
Will you end the game here?
No way ...
Mr. Wabisuke! How's the dismantling program coming?
KLAK
KLAK
Just 50% done!
Shit !
Sakuma, can you alter the rate?
Is there nothing you can do?
Don't be ridiculous !

PIP

Your betting amount is insufficient.

Will you end the game here?

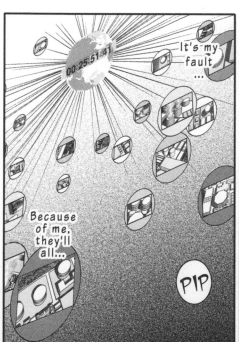

00:25:51:41

It's my fault...

Because of me, they'll all...

PIP

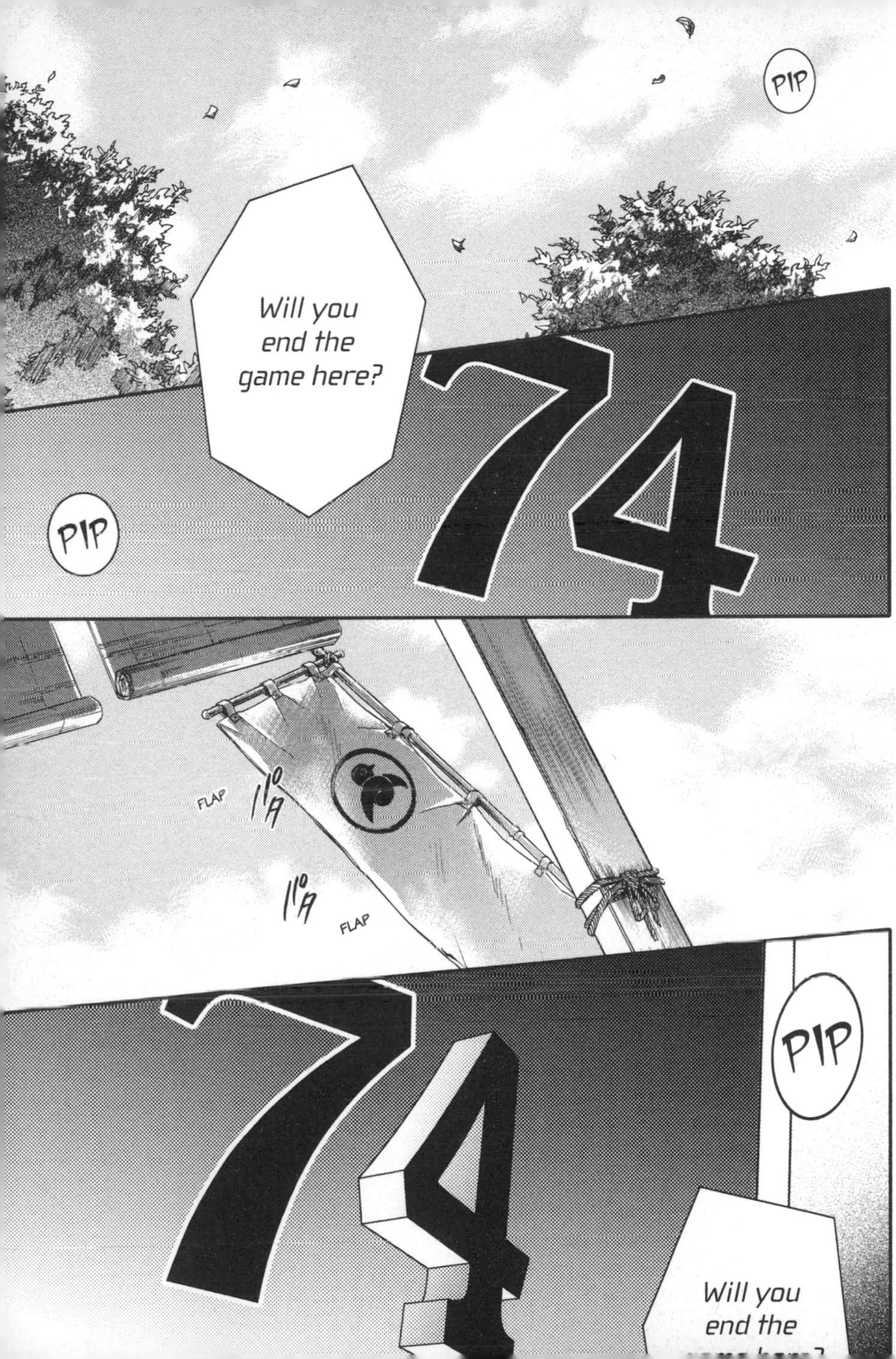
PIP
Will you end the game here?
PIP
FLAP
FLAP
PIP
Will you end the

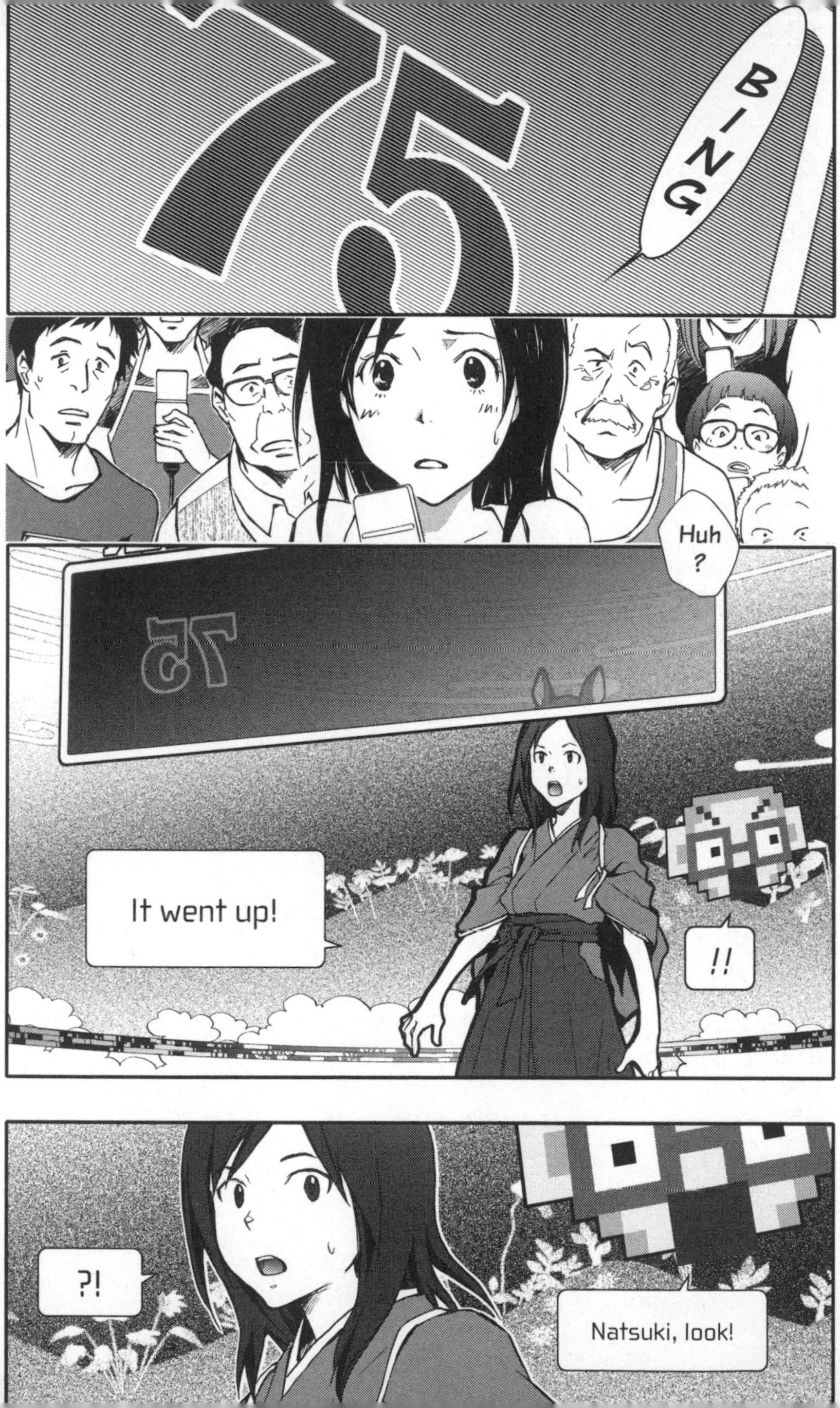
75
BING
Huh?
75
It went up!
!!
Natsuki, look!
?!

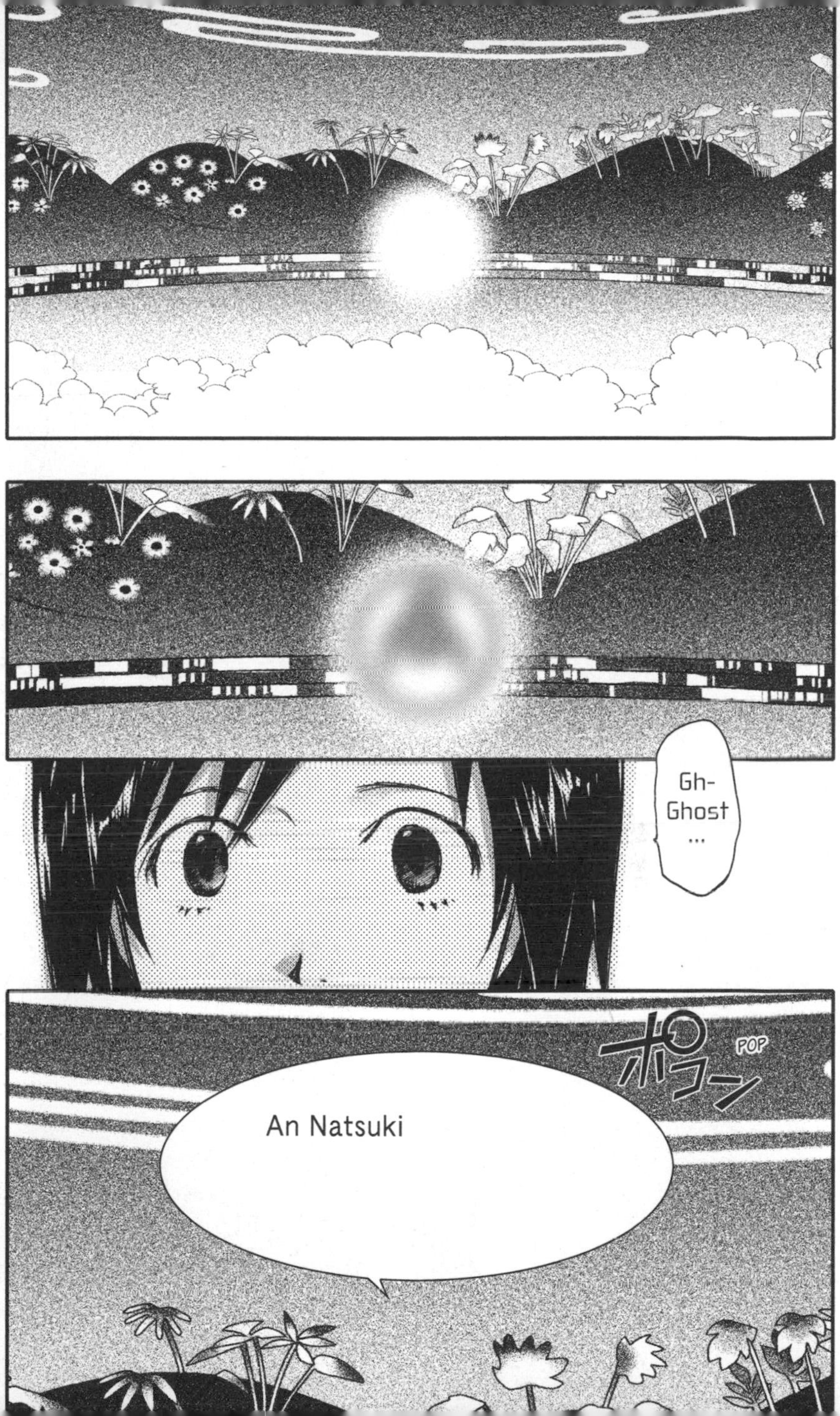
Gh- Ghost ...
ポコン
POP
An Natsuki

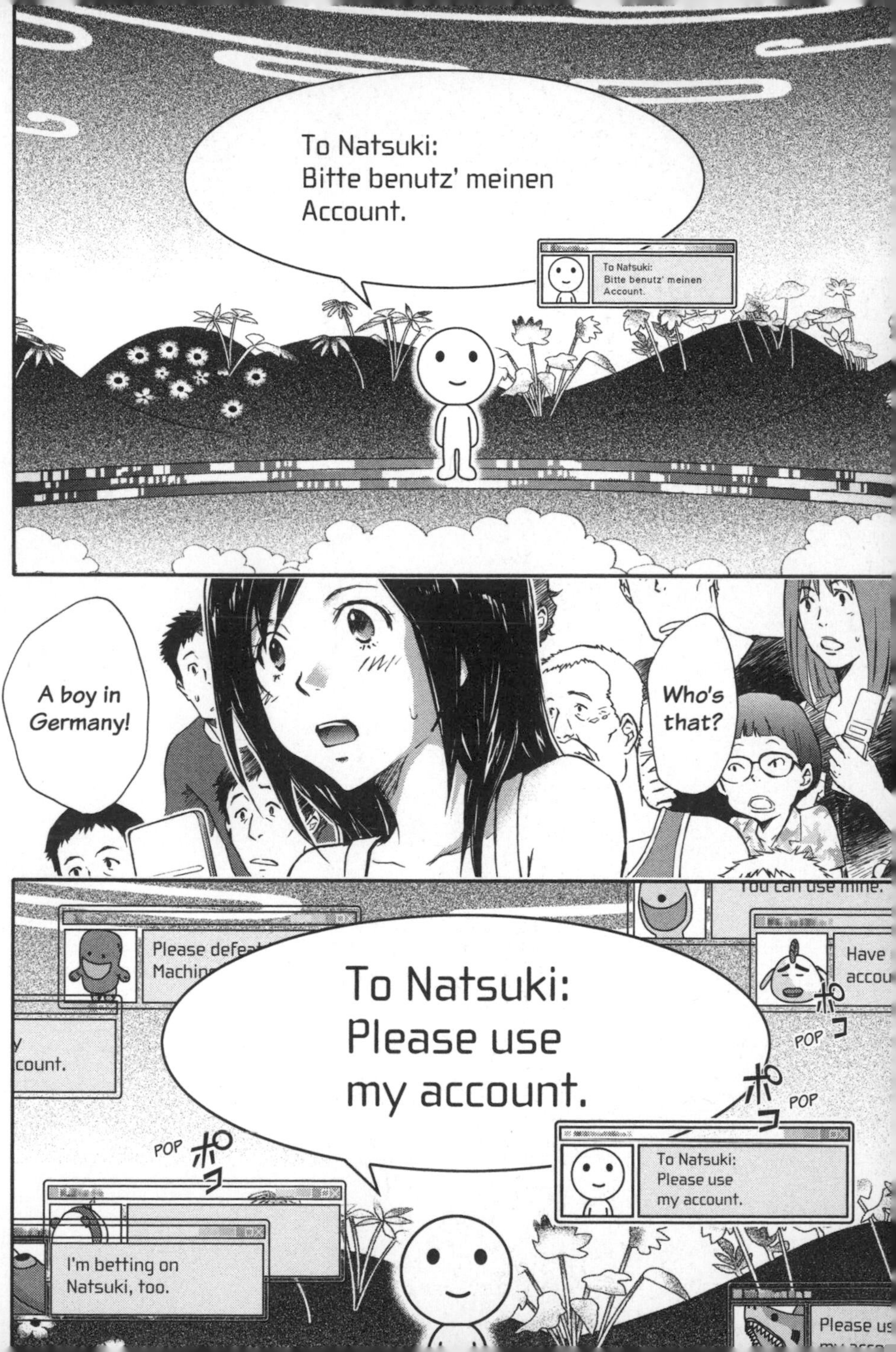

To Natsuki:
Bitte benutz' meinen
Account.
To Natsuki:
Bitte benutz' meinen
Account.
Who's that?
A boy in Germany!
POP
POP
To Natsuki:
Please use
my account.
To Natsuki:
Please use
my account.
POP
I'm betting on
Natsuki, too.

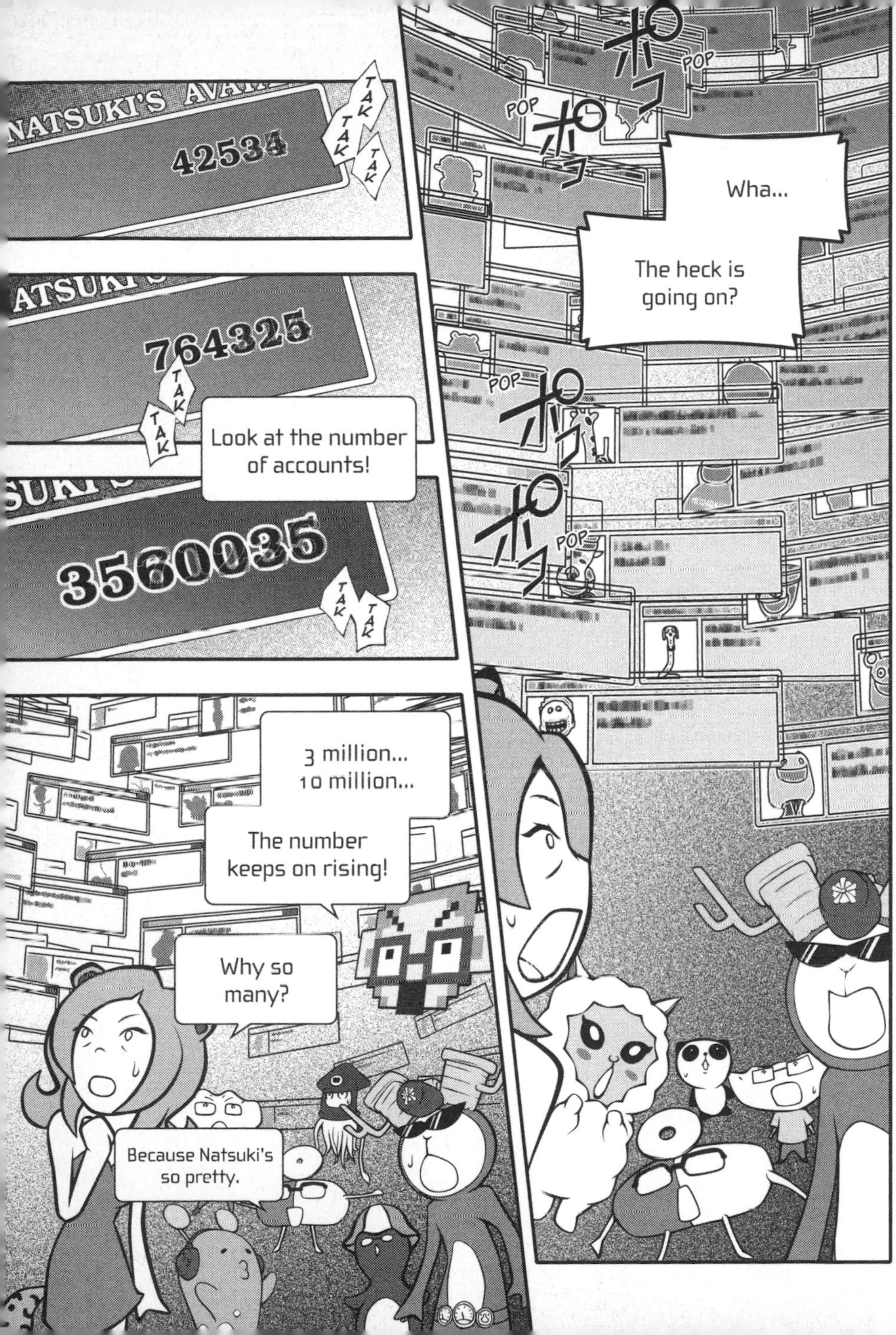
POP
POP
Wha...
The heck is going on?
POP
POP
NATSUKI'S AVAT
42534
TAK TAK TAK
ATSUKI'S
764325
TAK TAK
Look at the number of accounts!
SUKI'S
3560035
TAK TAK
3 million... 10 million...
The number keeps on rising!
Why so many?
Because Natsuki's so pretty.

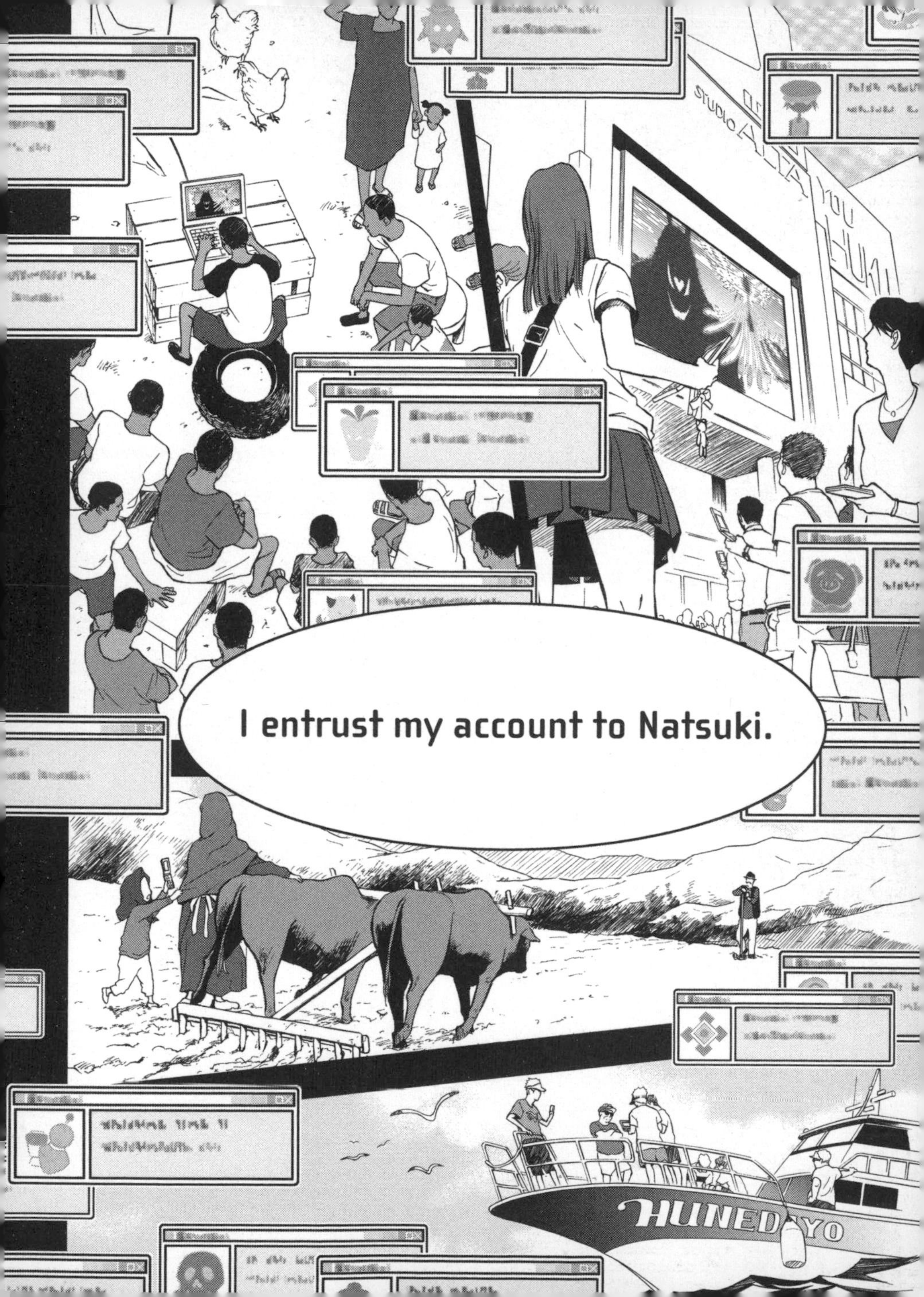
I entrust my account to Natsuki.

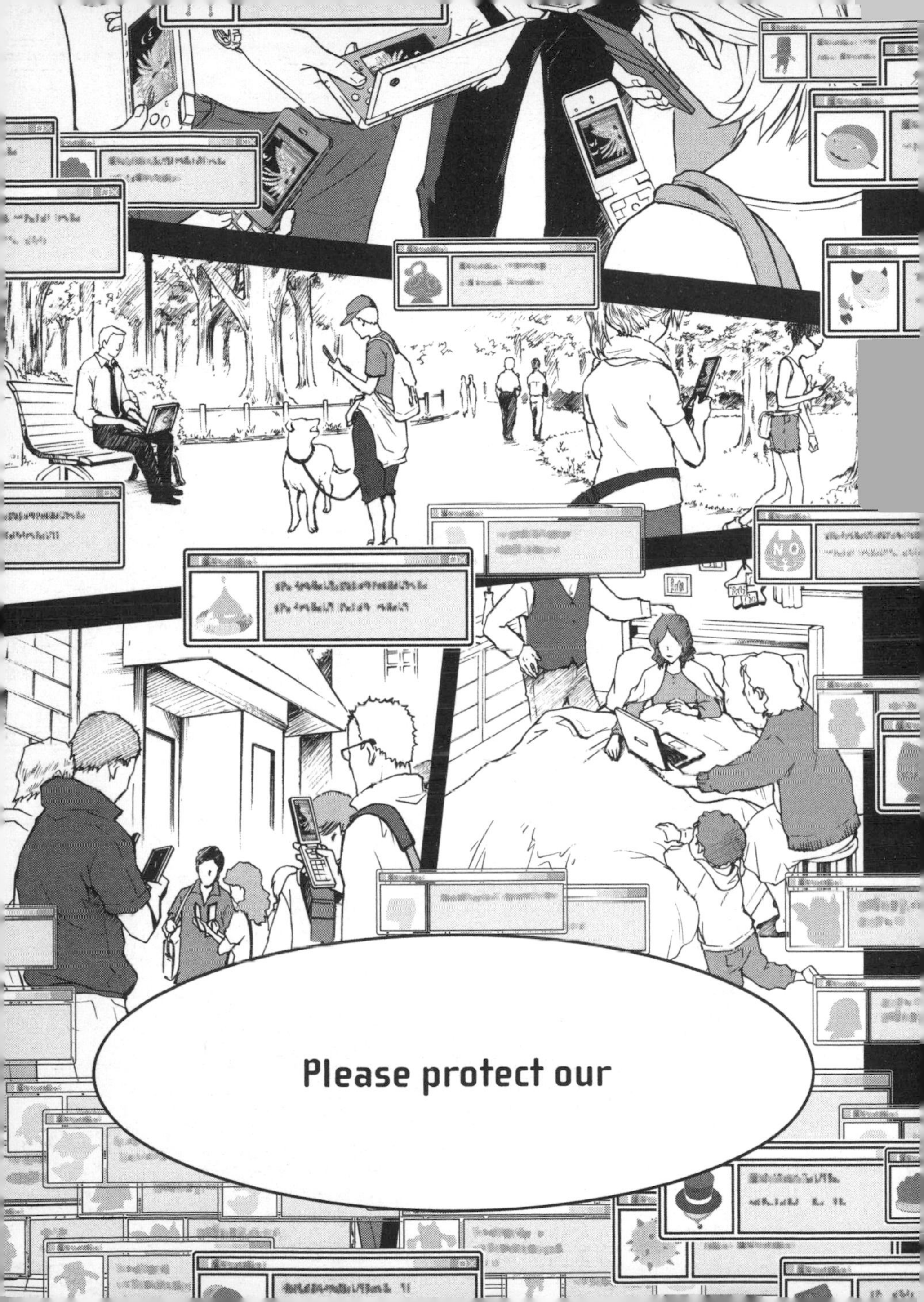
Please protect our

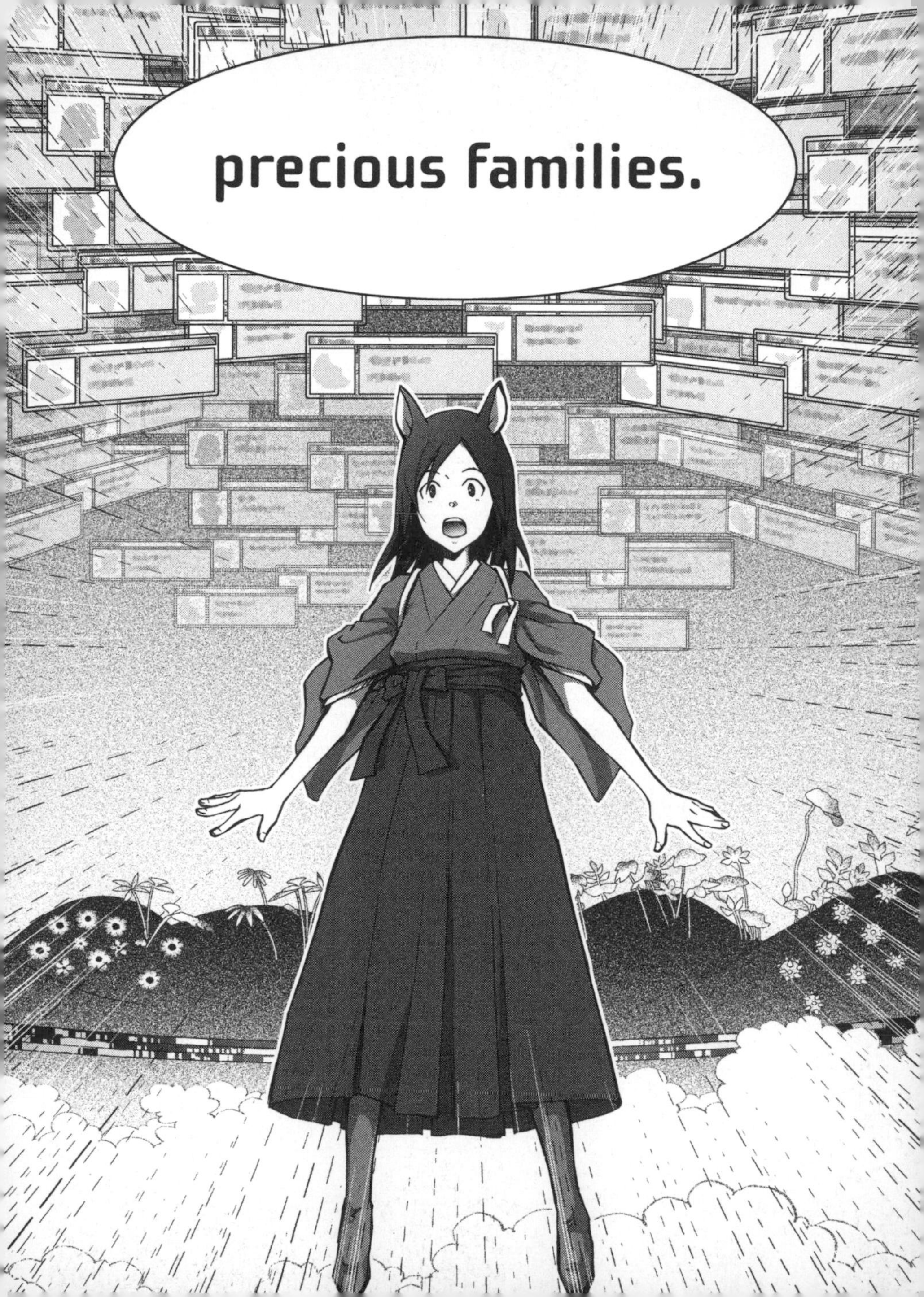
precious families.

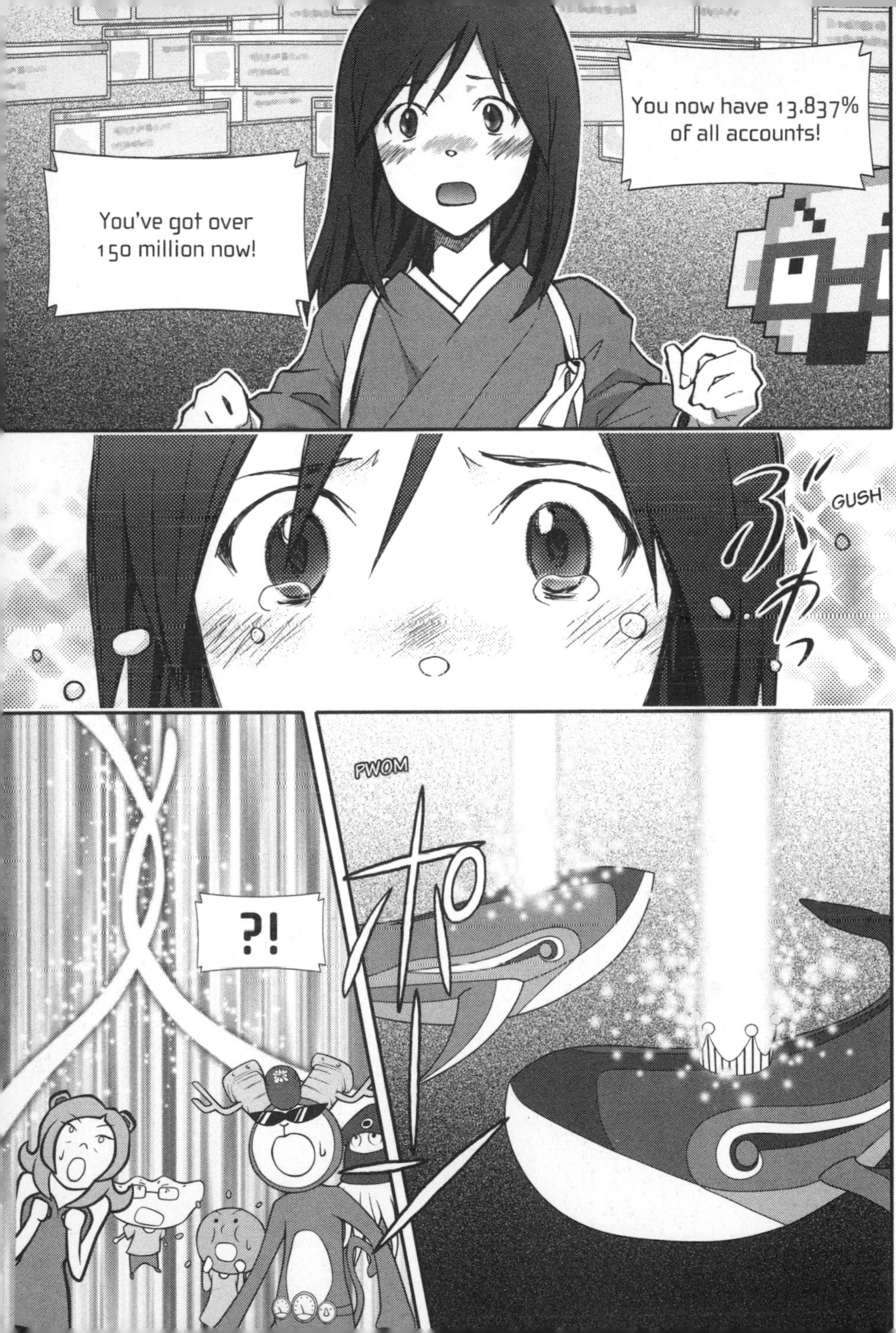

You now have 13.837% of all accounts!
You've got over 150 million now!
GUSH
PWOM
?!

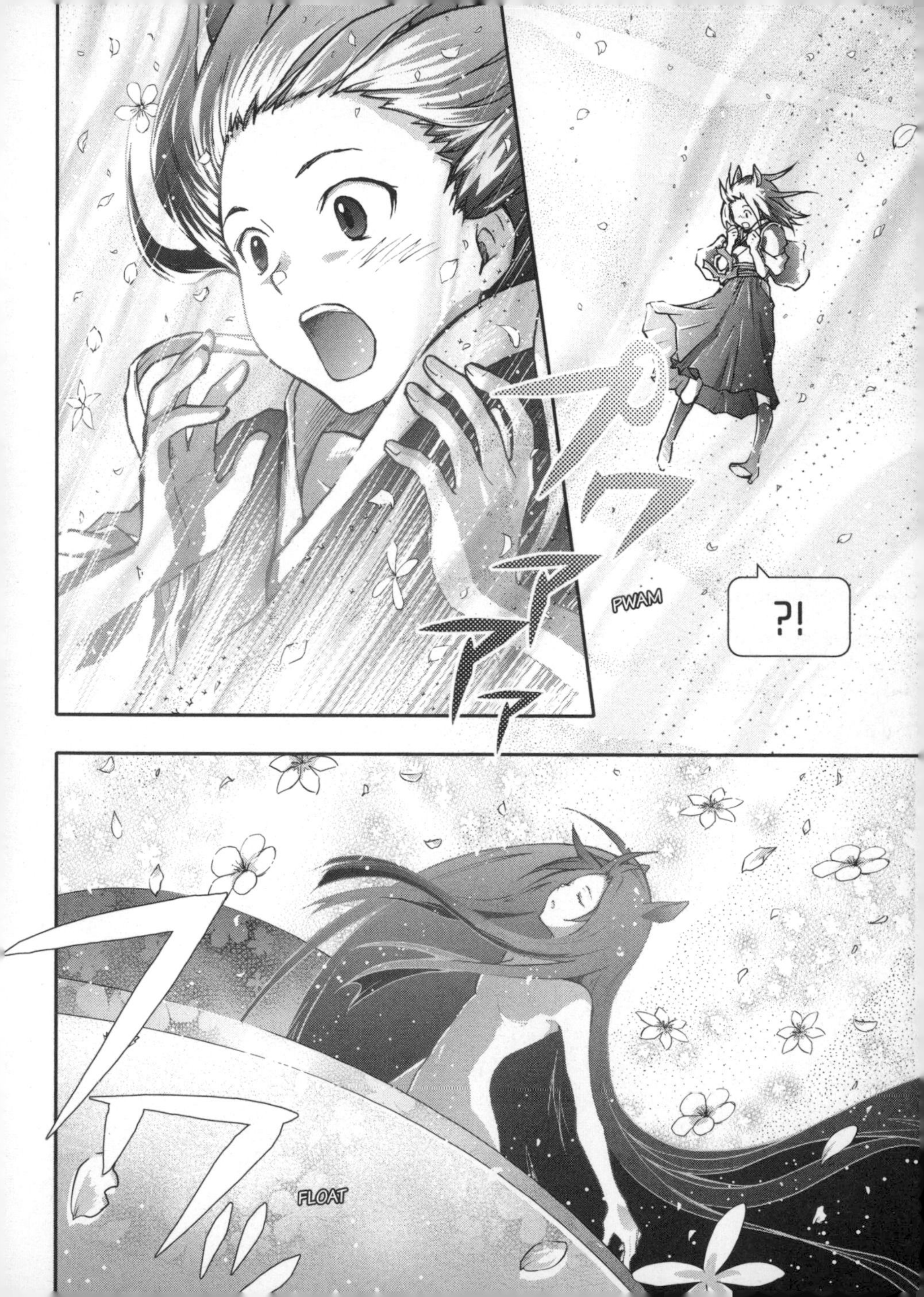
?!
PWAM
FLOAT

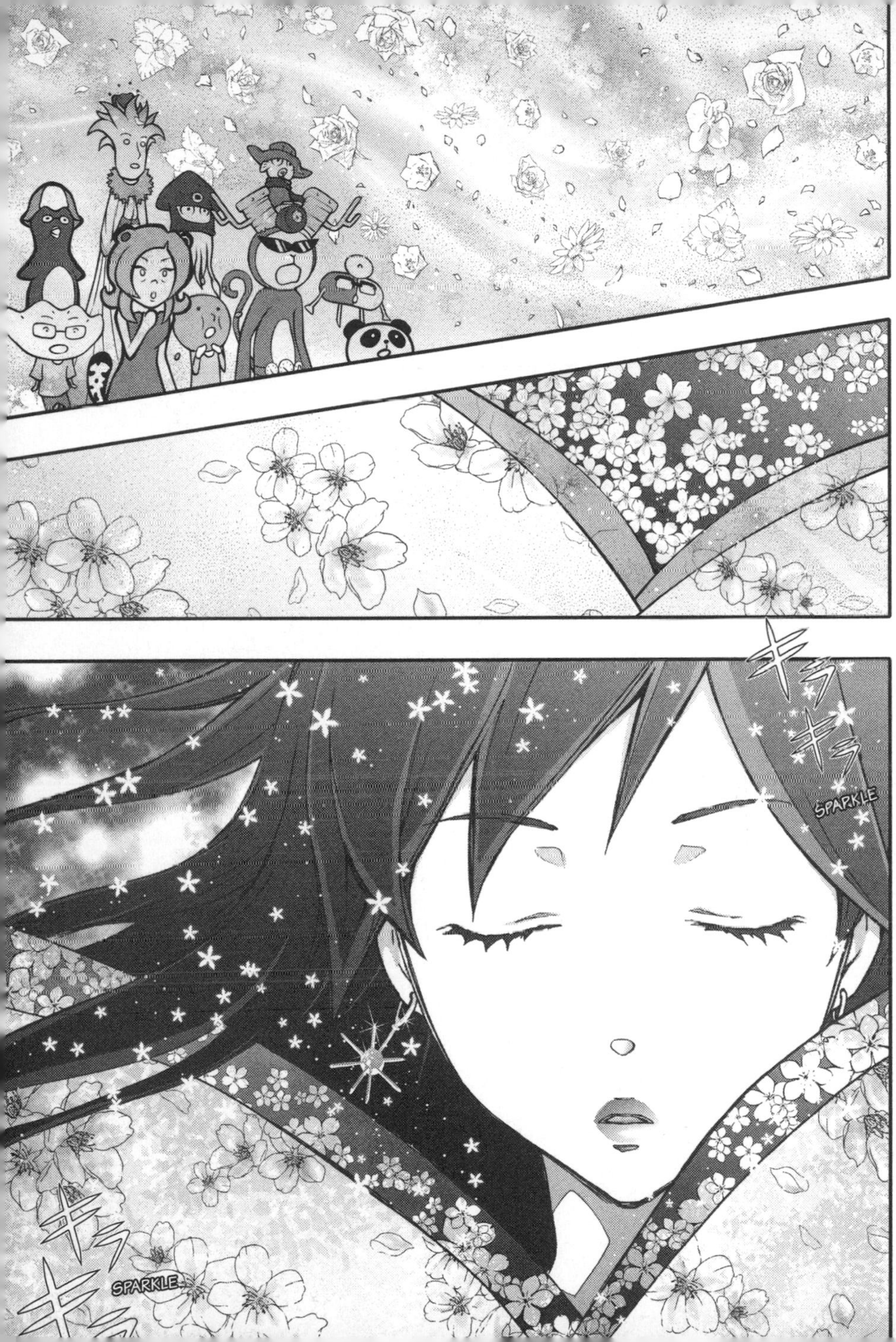

SPARKLE
SPARKLE

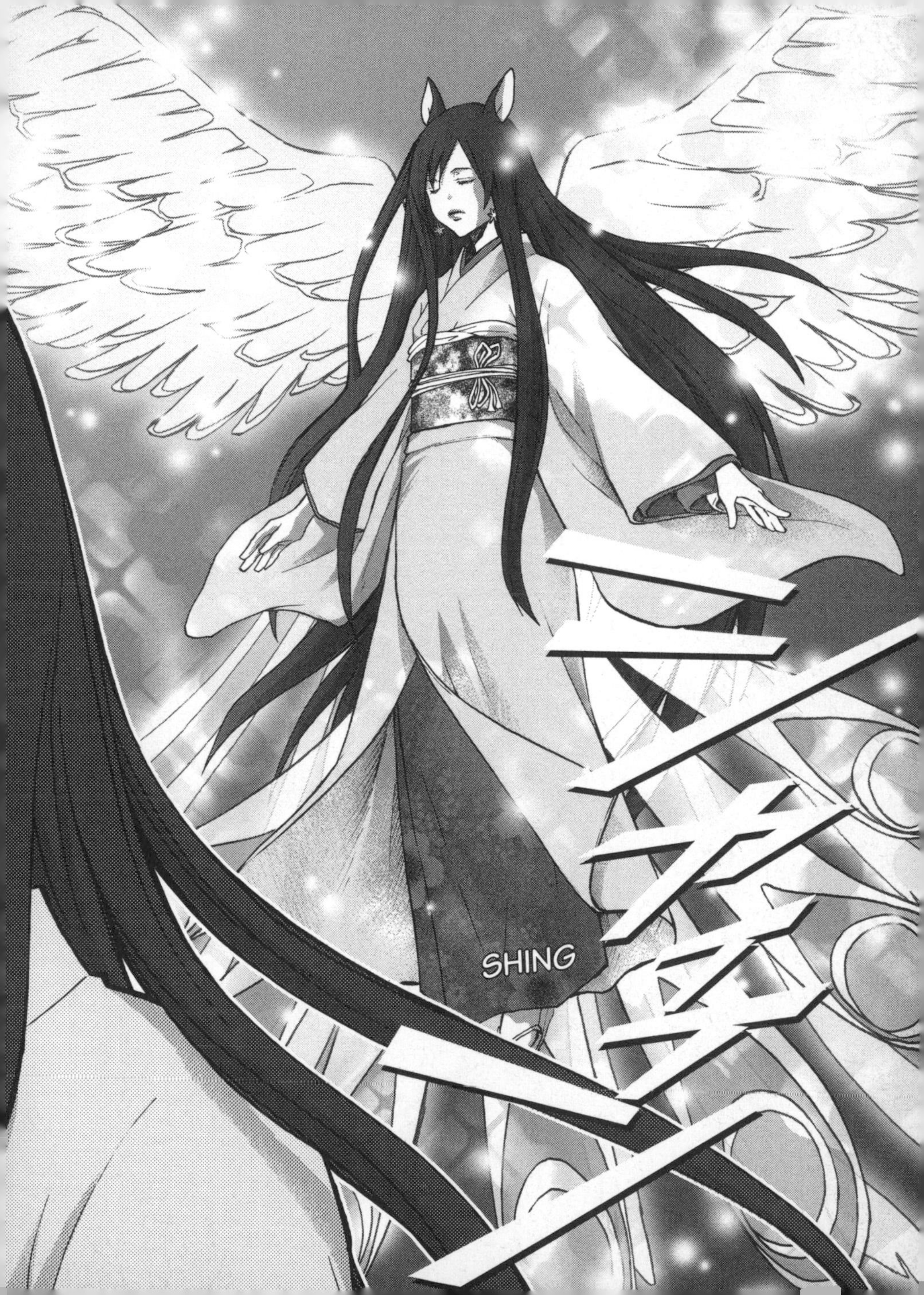
SHING

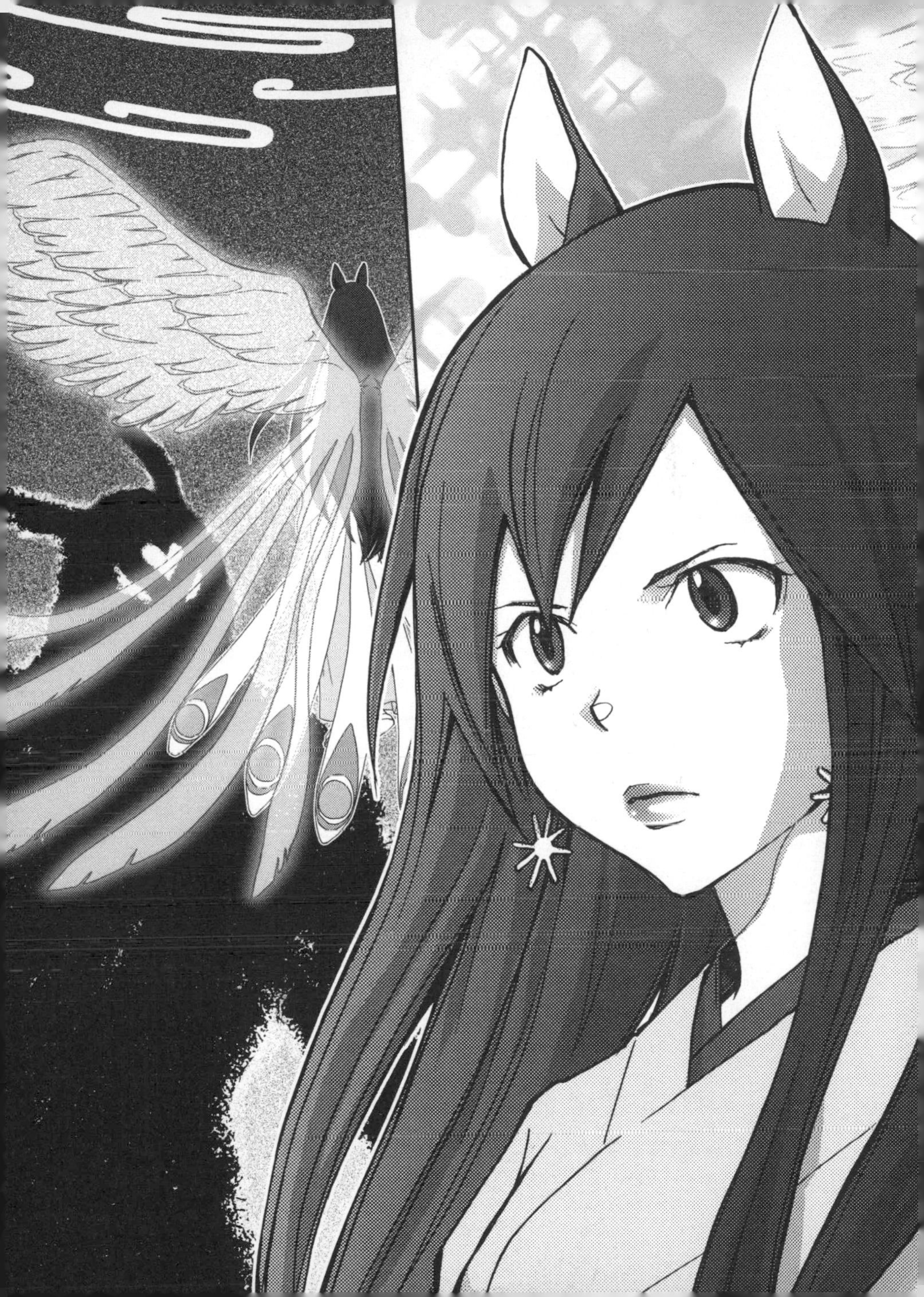

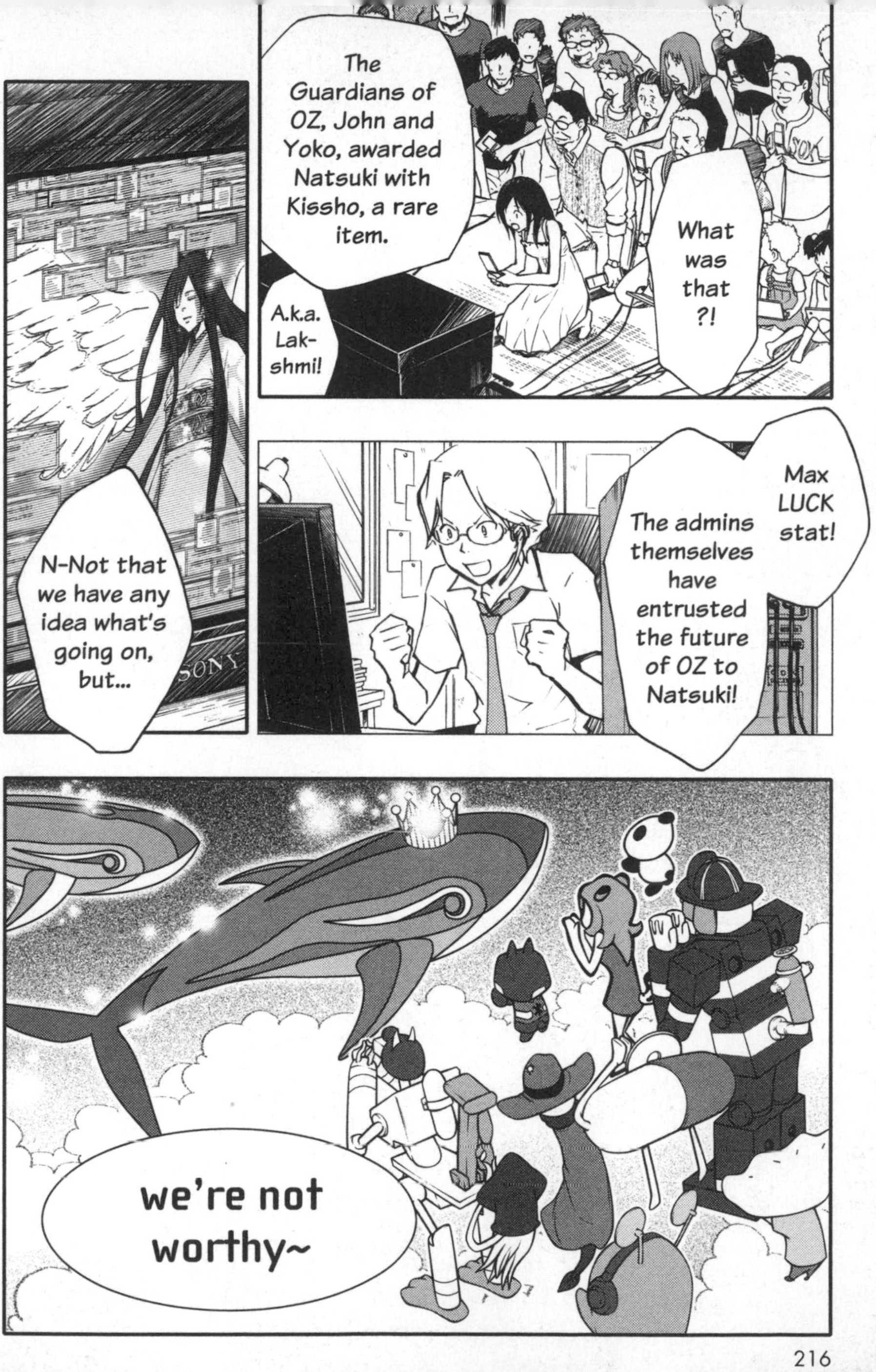
What was that ?!
The Guardians of OZ, John and Yoko, awarded Natsuki with Kissho, a rare item.
A.k.a. Lakshmi!
Max LUCK stat!
The admins themselves have entrusted the future of OZ to Natsuki!
N-Not that we have any idea what's going on, but...
SONY
we're not worthy~

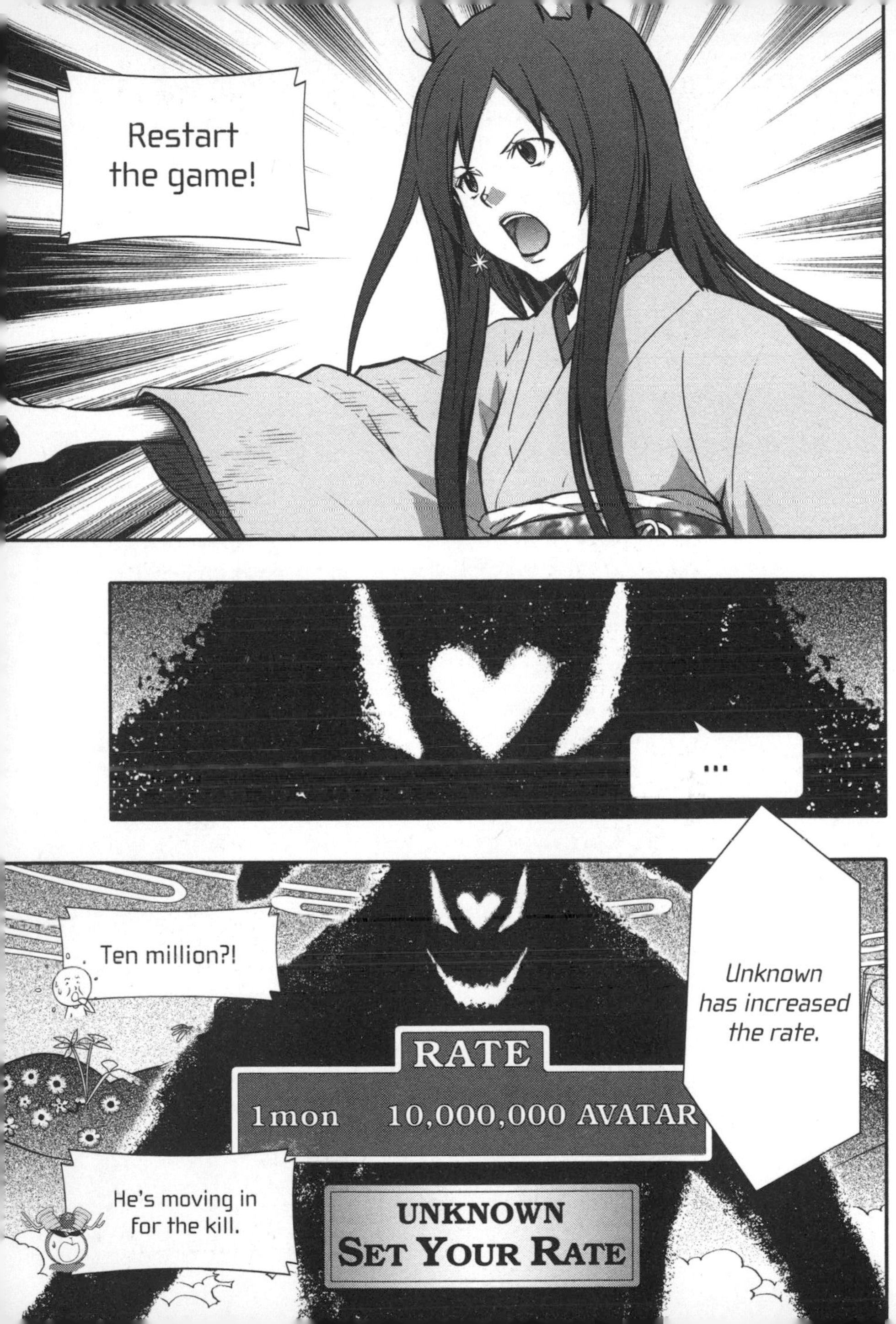
Restart the game!
...
Unknown has increased the rate.
Ten million?!
RATE
1mon 10,000,000 AVATAR
UNKNOWN
SET YOUR RATE
He's moving in for the kill.

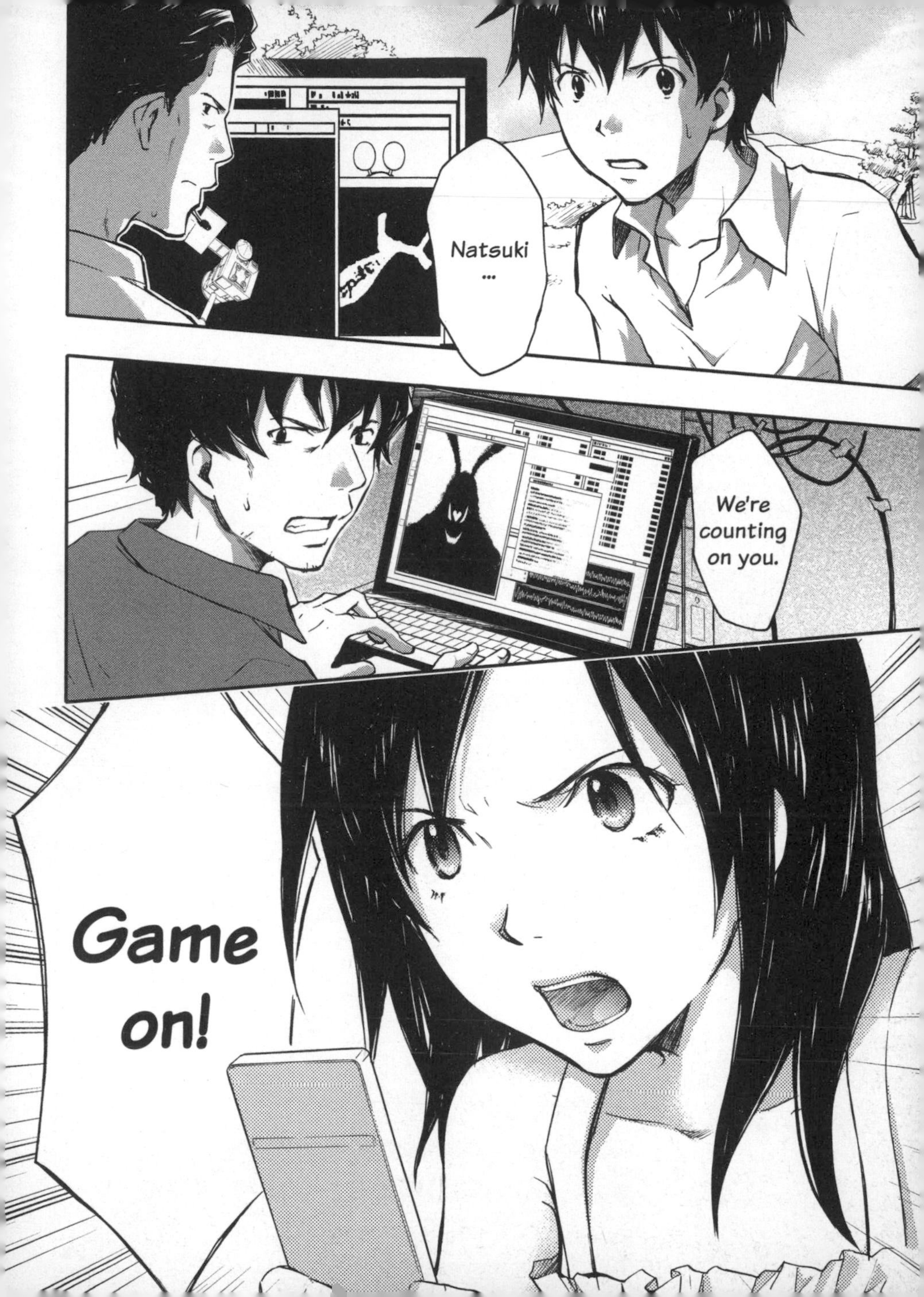
Natsuki
...
We're counting on you.
Game on!

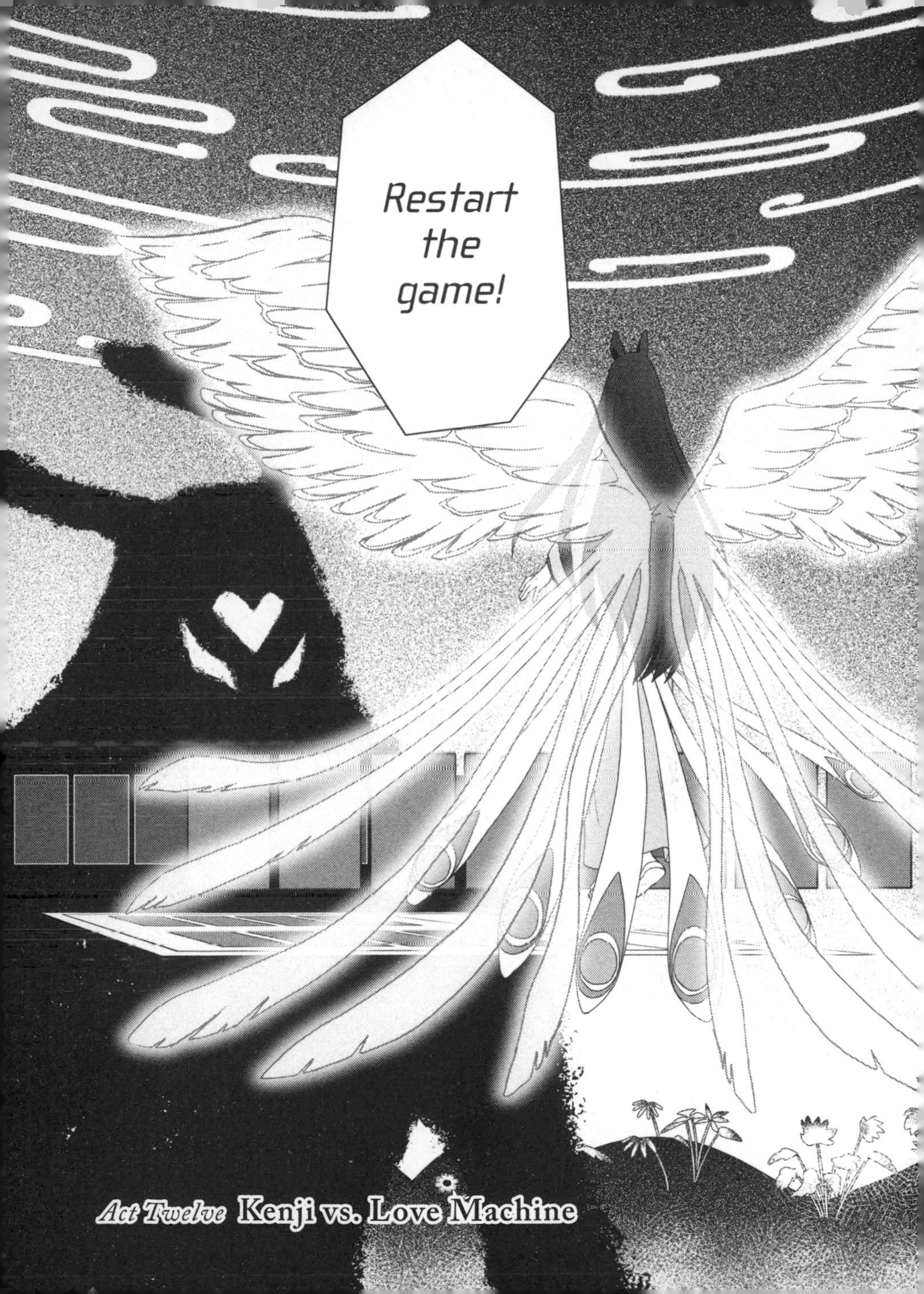
Restart the game!
Act Twelve Kenji vs. Love Machine

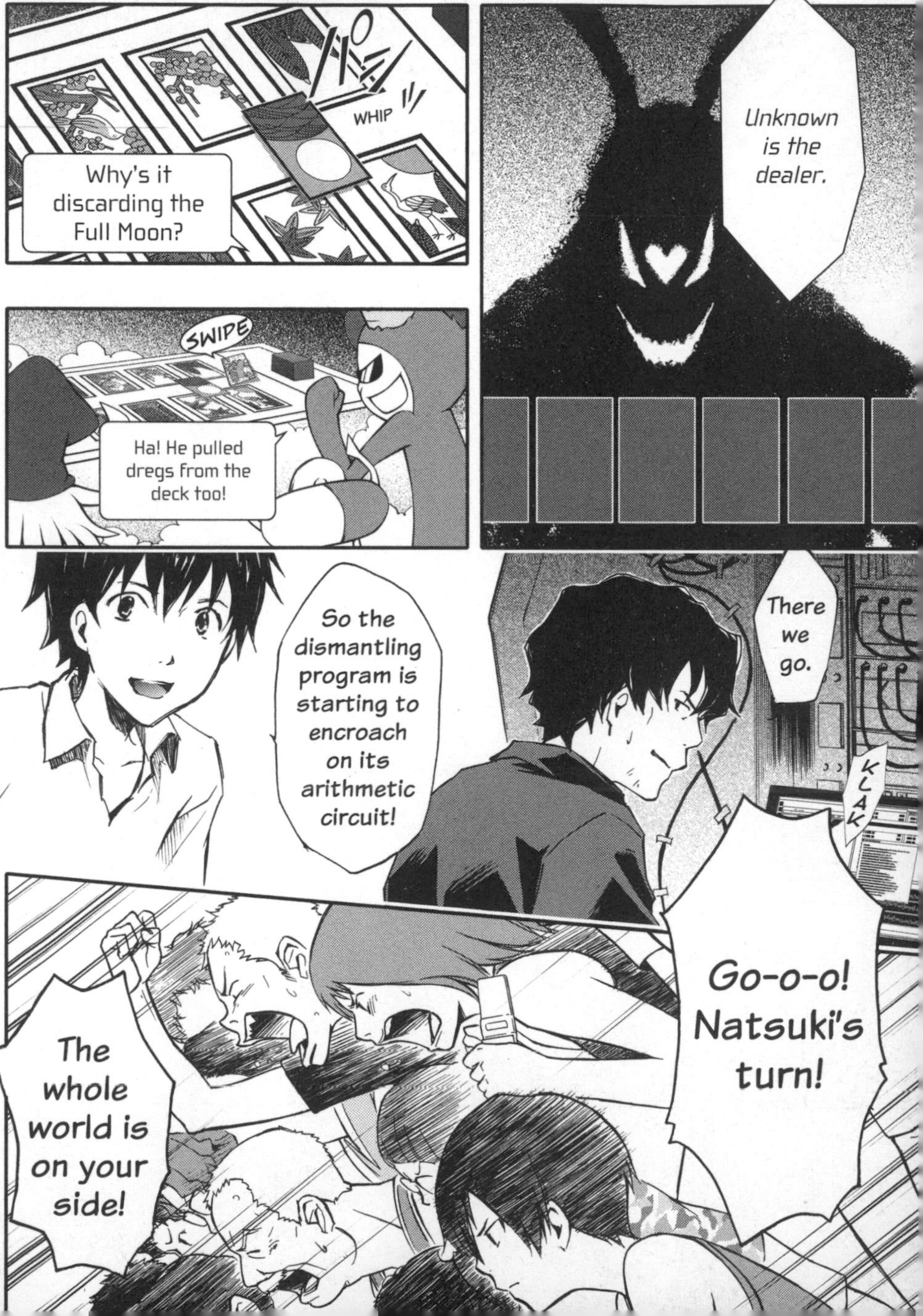
Unknown is the dealer.
WHIP
Why's it discarding the Full Moon?
SWIPE
Ha! He pulled dregs from the deck too!
There we go.
KLAK
So the dismantling program is starting to encroach on its arithmetic circuit!
Go-o-o! Natsuki's turn!
The whole world is on your side!

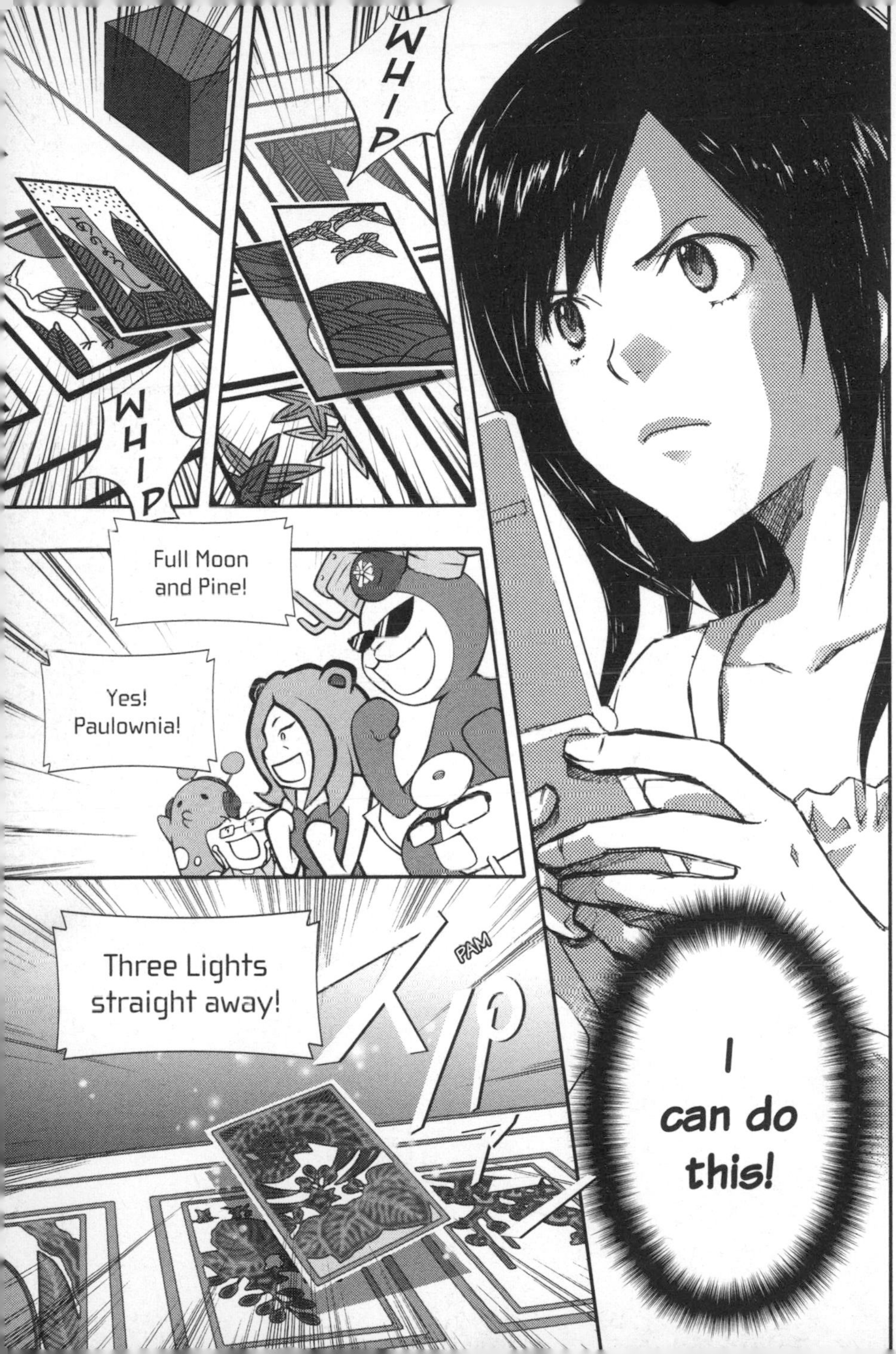
I can do this!
WHIP
WHIP
Full Moon and Pine!
Yes! Paulownia!
Three Lights straight away!
PAM

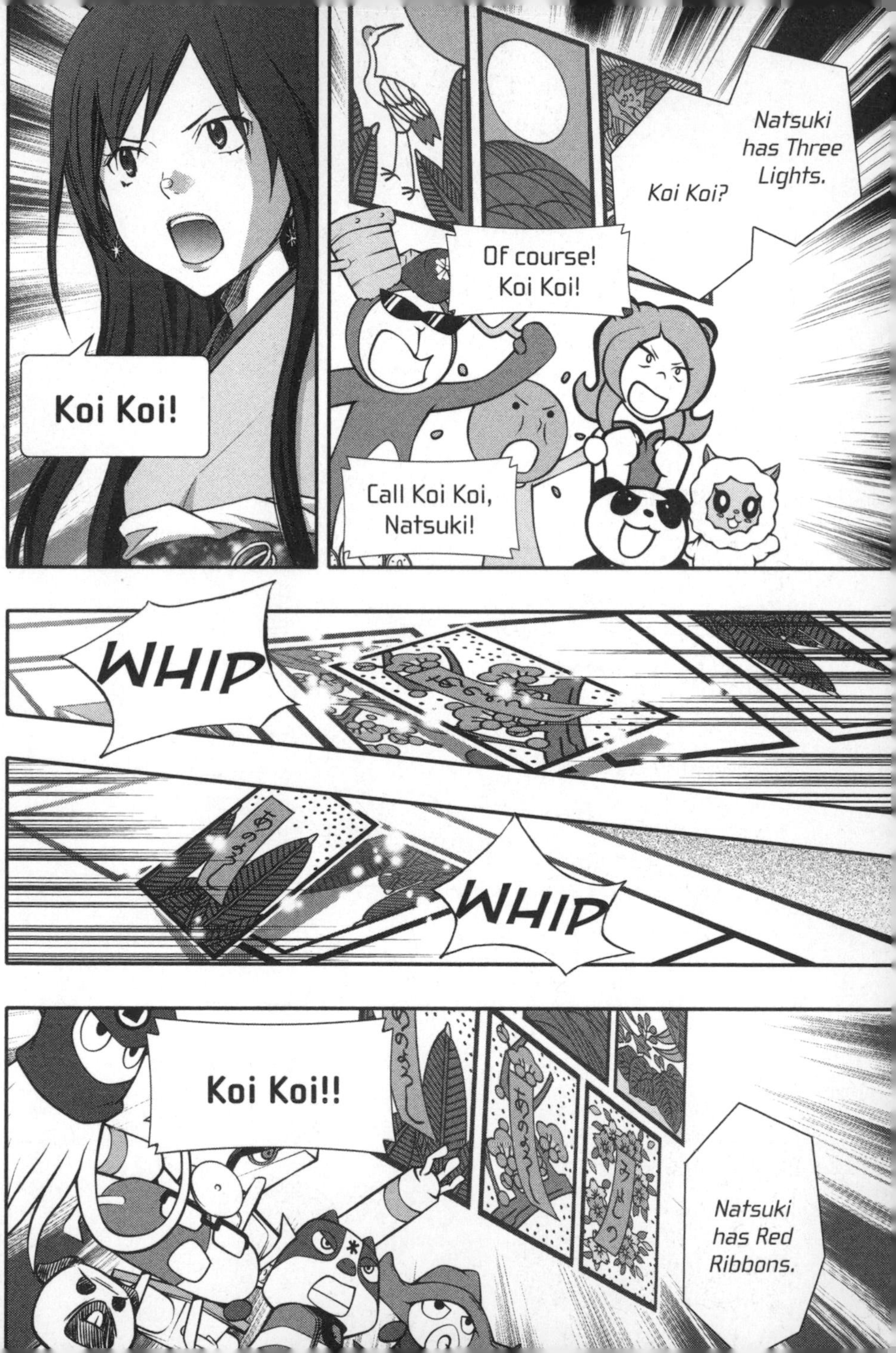
Natsuki has Three Lights.
Koi Koi?
Of course! Koi Koi!
Call Koi Koi, Natsuki!
Koi Koi!
WHIP
WHIP
Natsuki has Red Ribbons.
Koi Koi!!

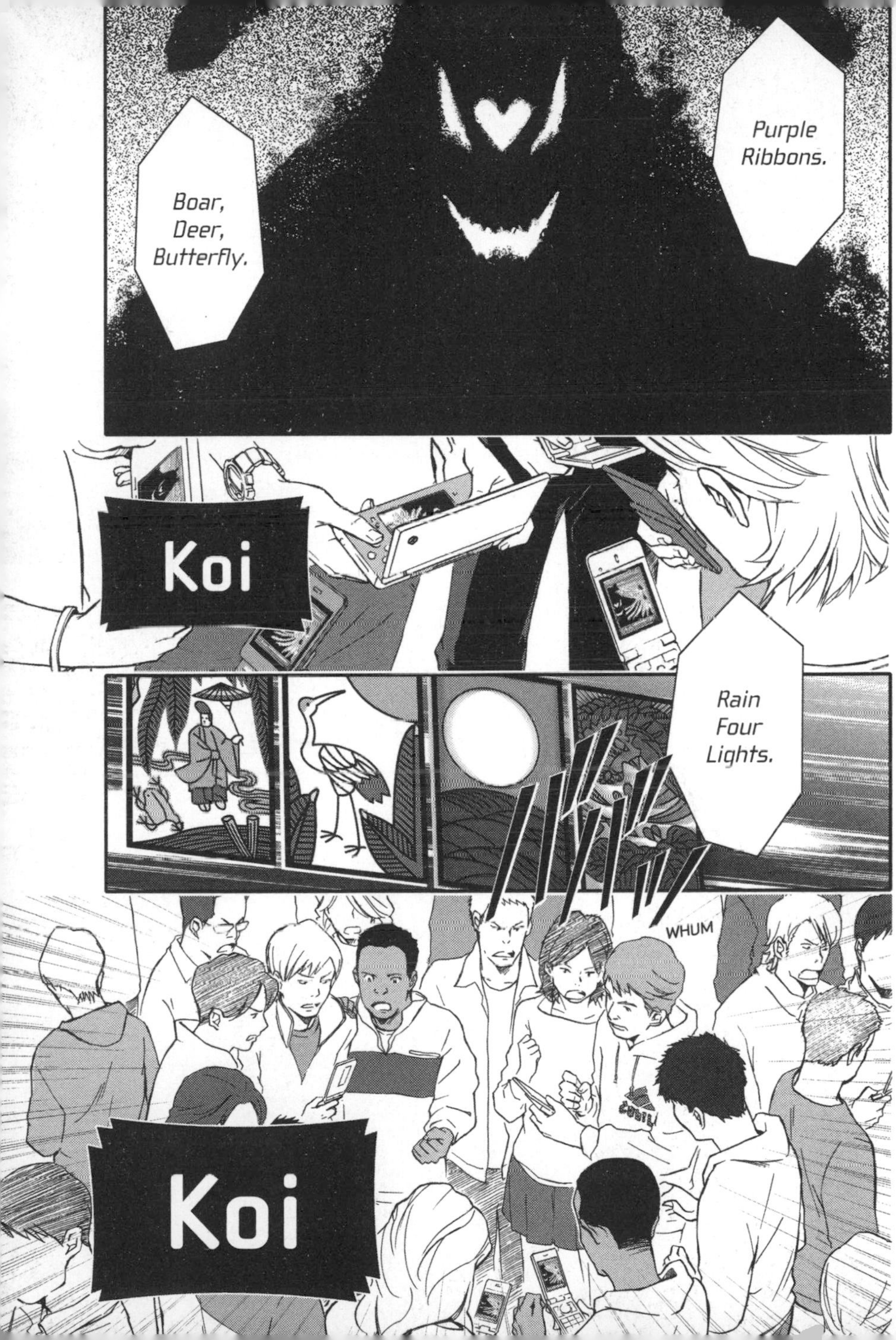
Purple Ribbons.
Boar, Deer, Butterfly.
Koi
Rain Four Lights.
WHUM
Koi

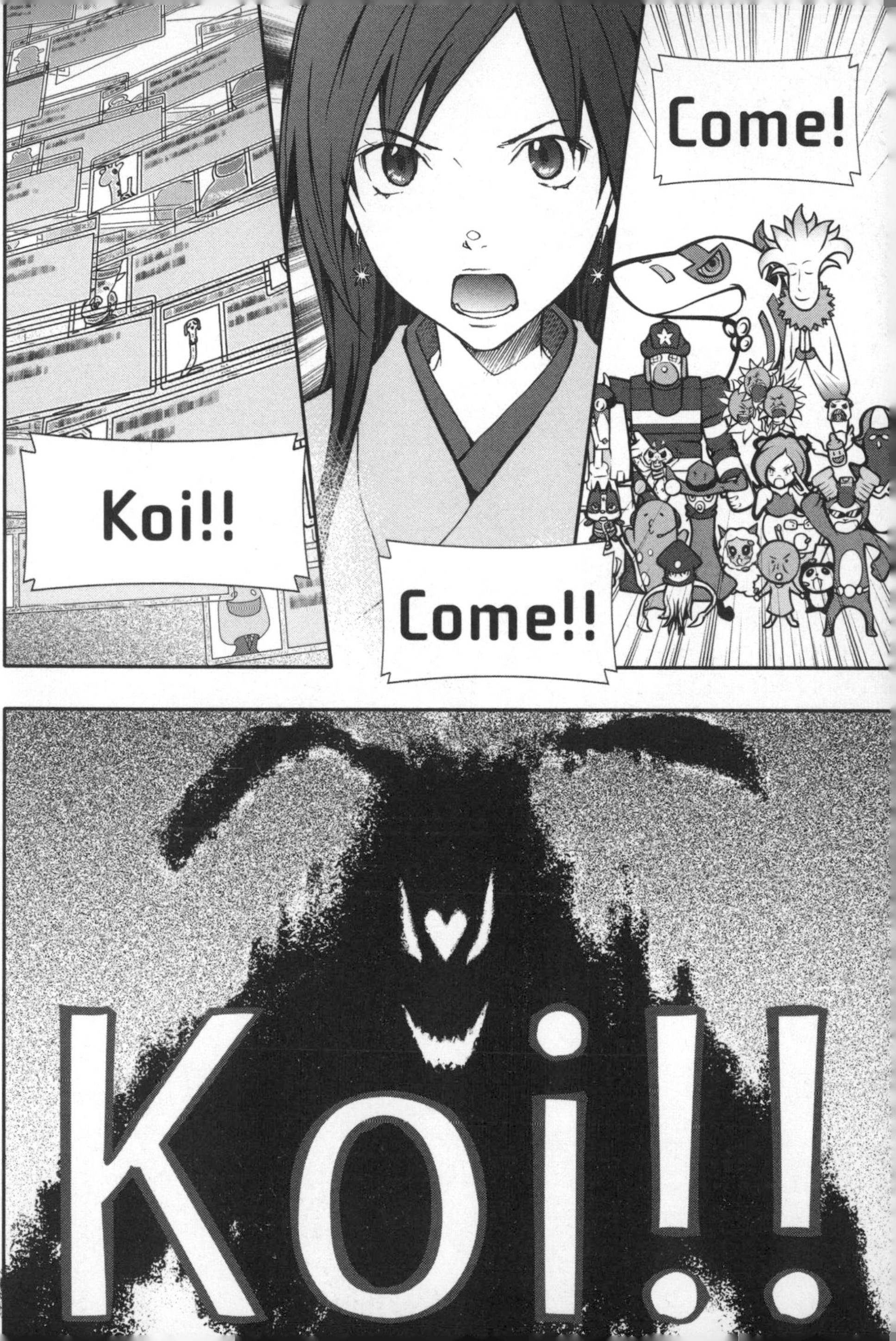
Come!
Come!!
Koi!!
Koi!!

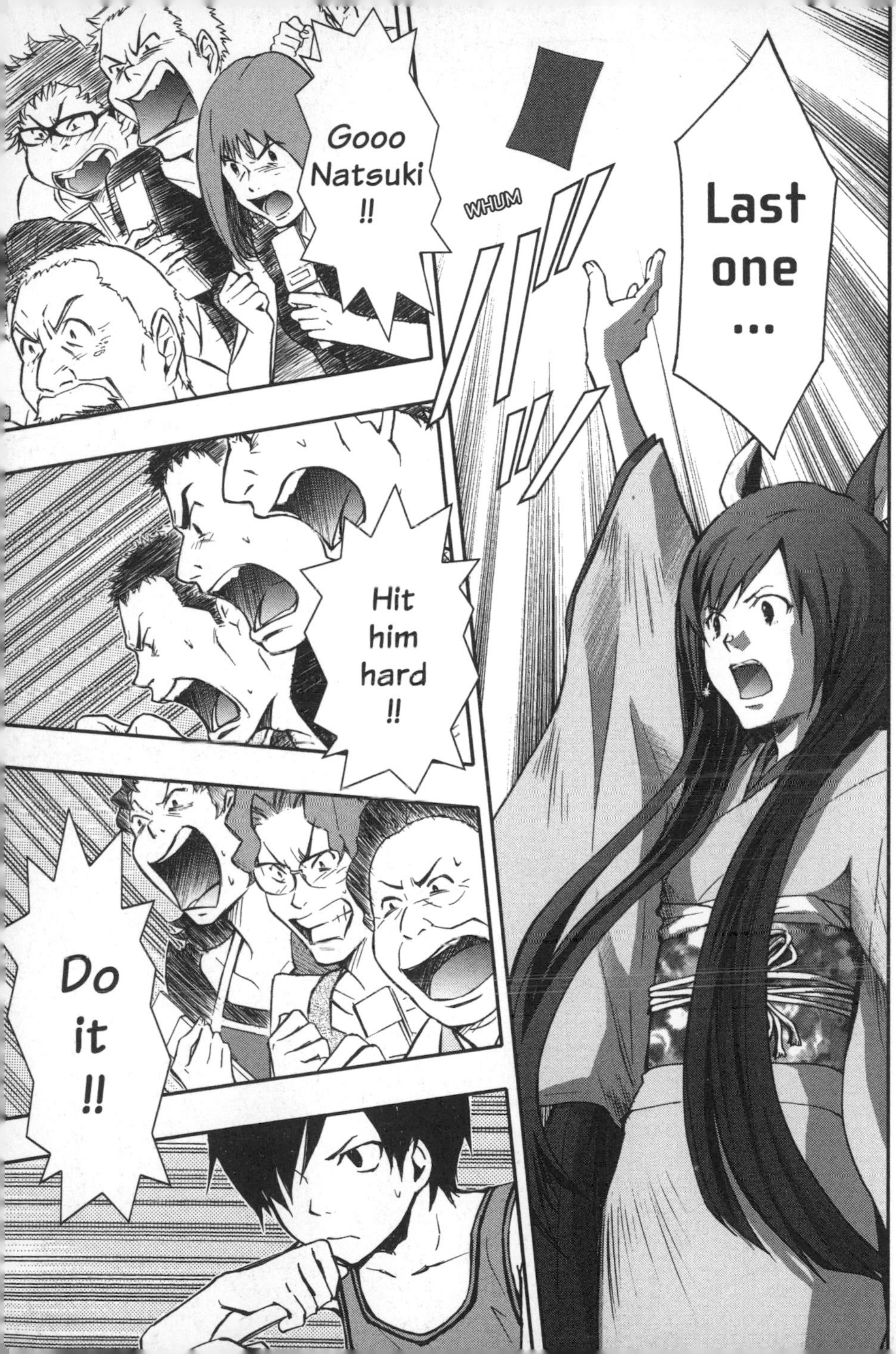
Last one ...
WHUM
Gooo Natsuki !!
Hit him hard !!
Do it !!

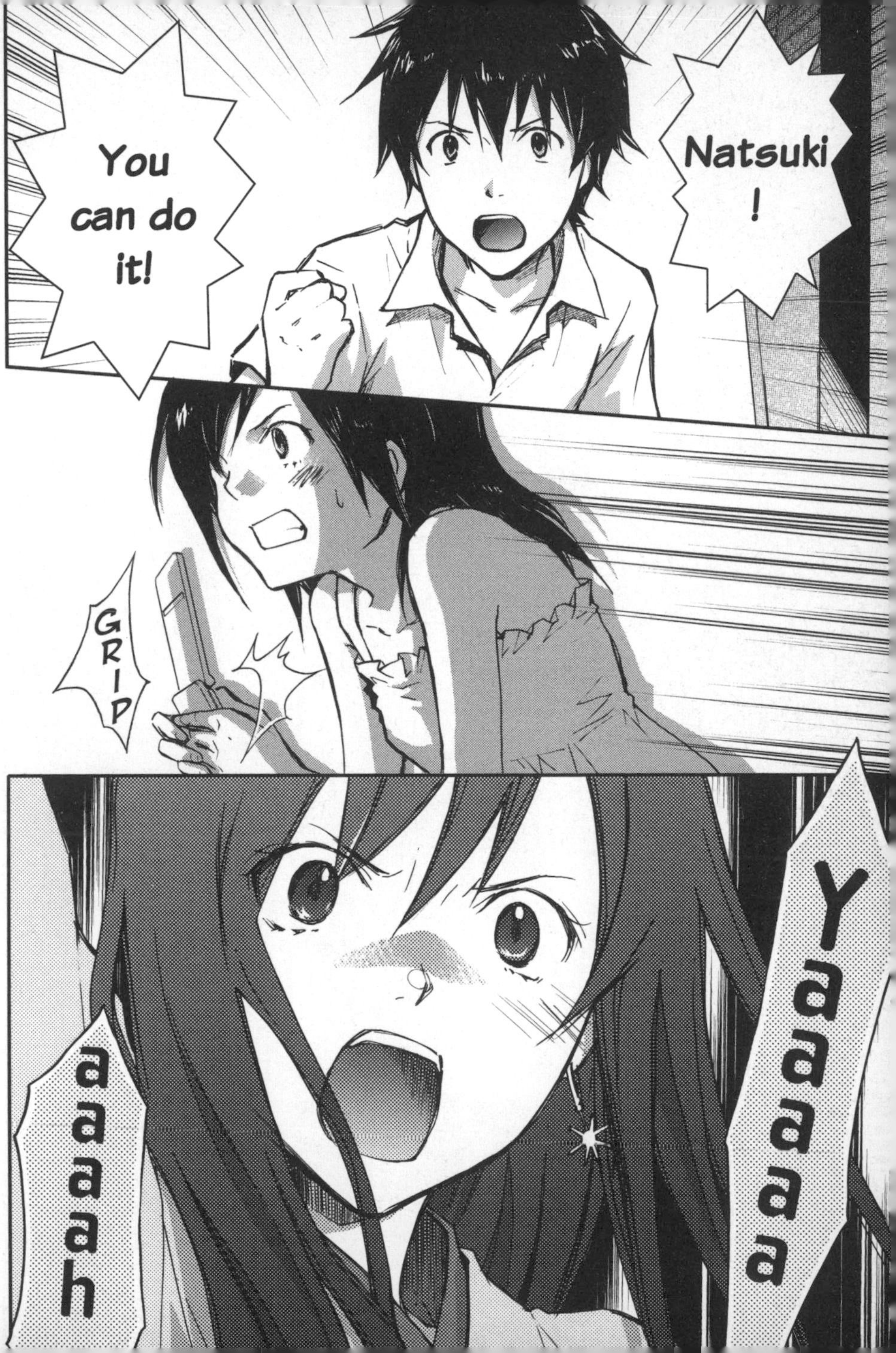
Natsuki!
You can do it!
GRIP
Yaaaaa
aaaaah

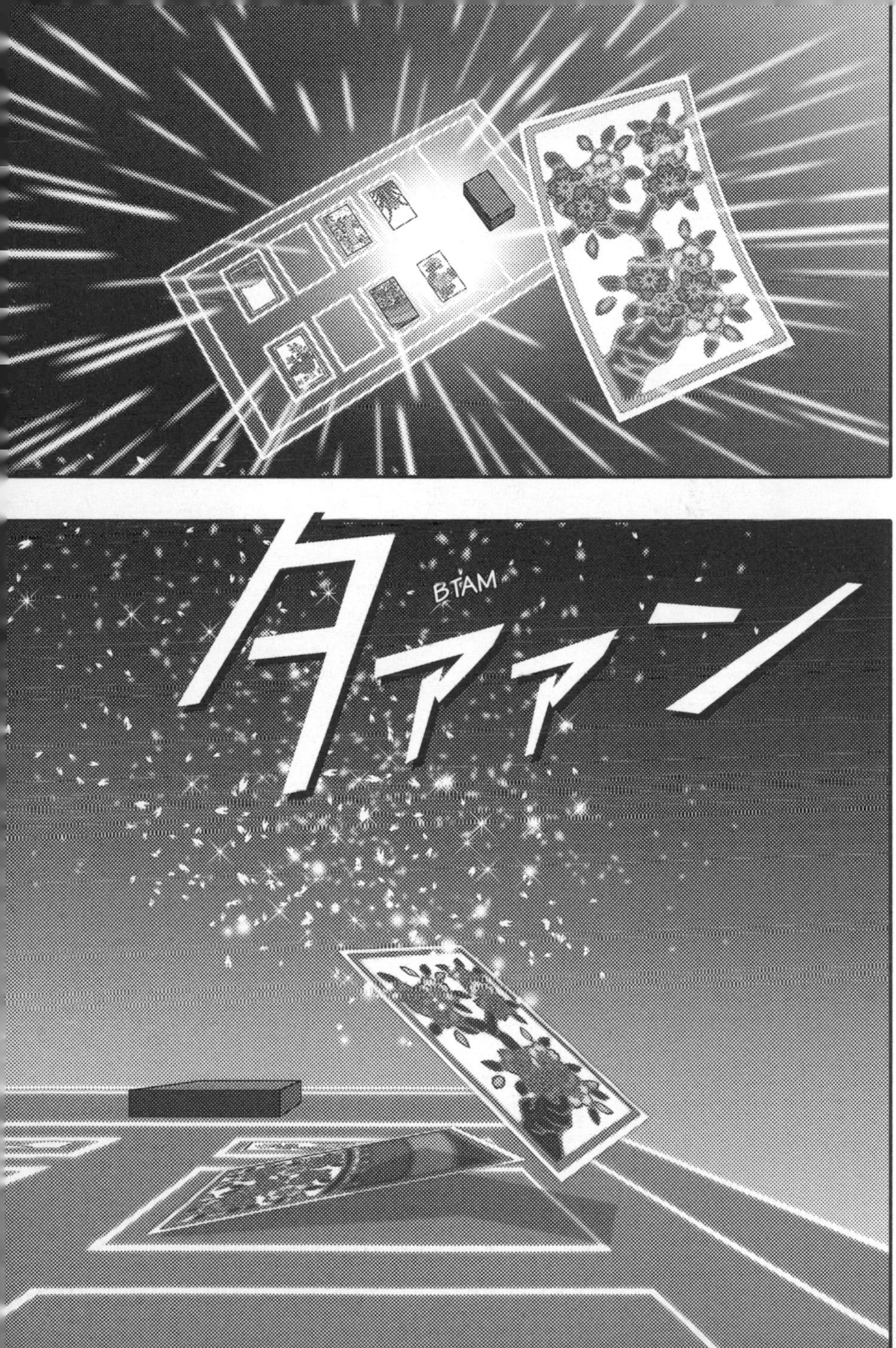
タァァーン
BTAM

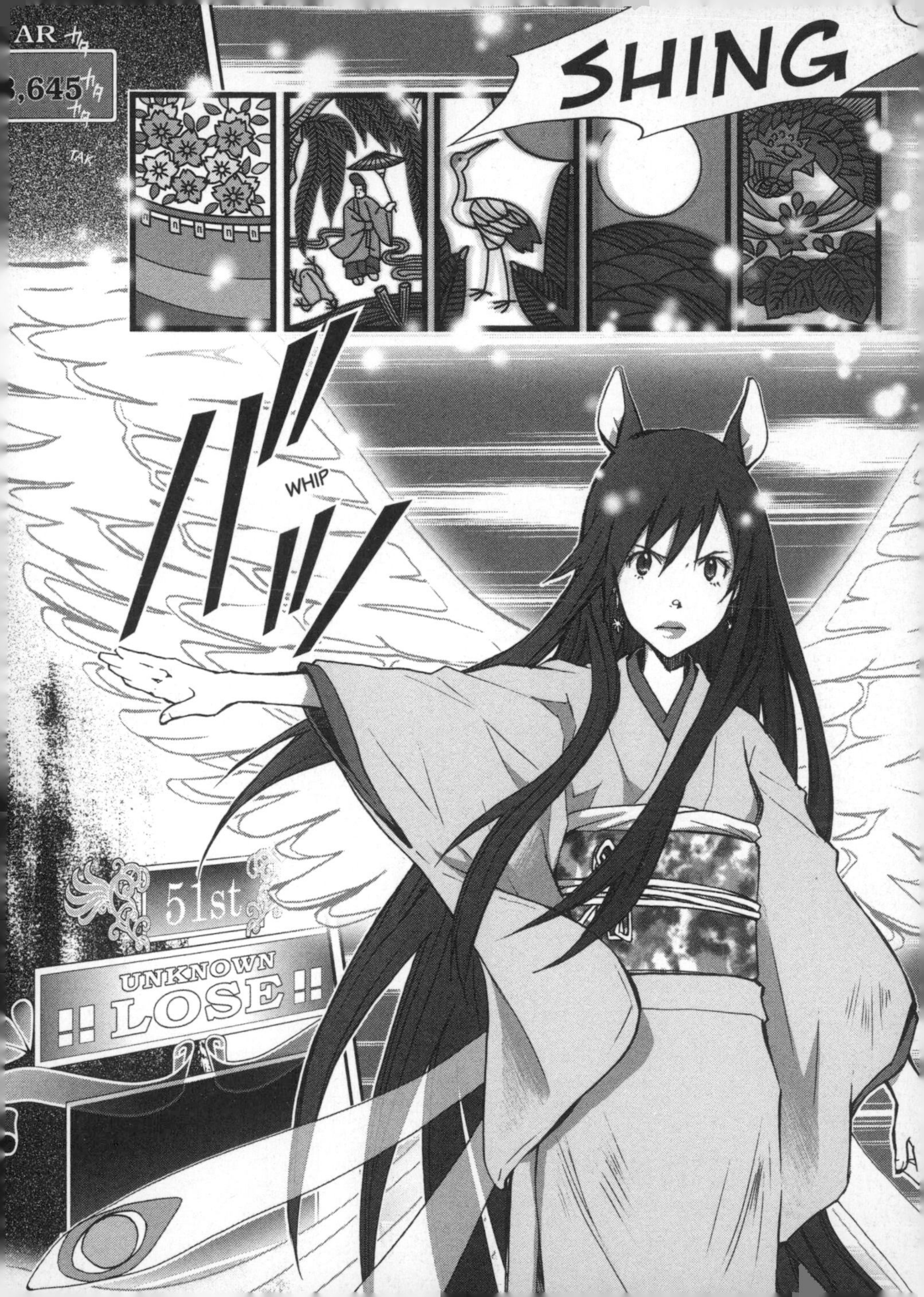
AR
3,645
TAK
SHING
WHIP
51st
UNKNOWN
LOSE

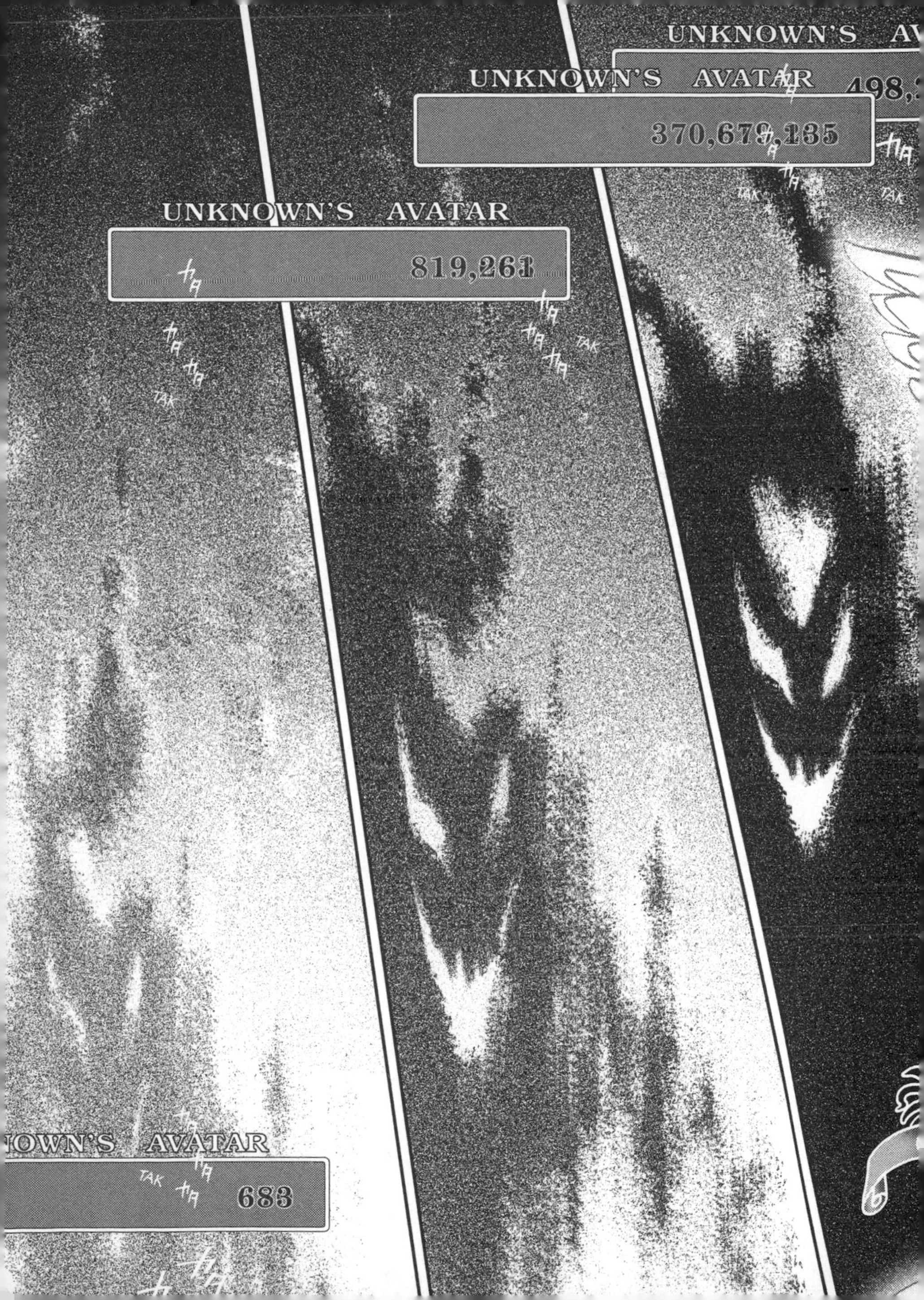
UNKNOWN'S AV
498,
UNKNOWN'S AVATAR
370,679,135
TAK
TAK
UNKNOWN'S AVATAR
819,261
TAK
TAK
OWN'S AVATAR
TAK
683

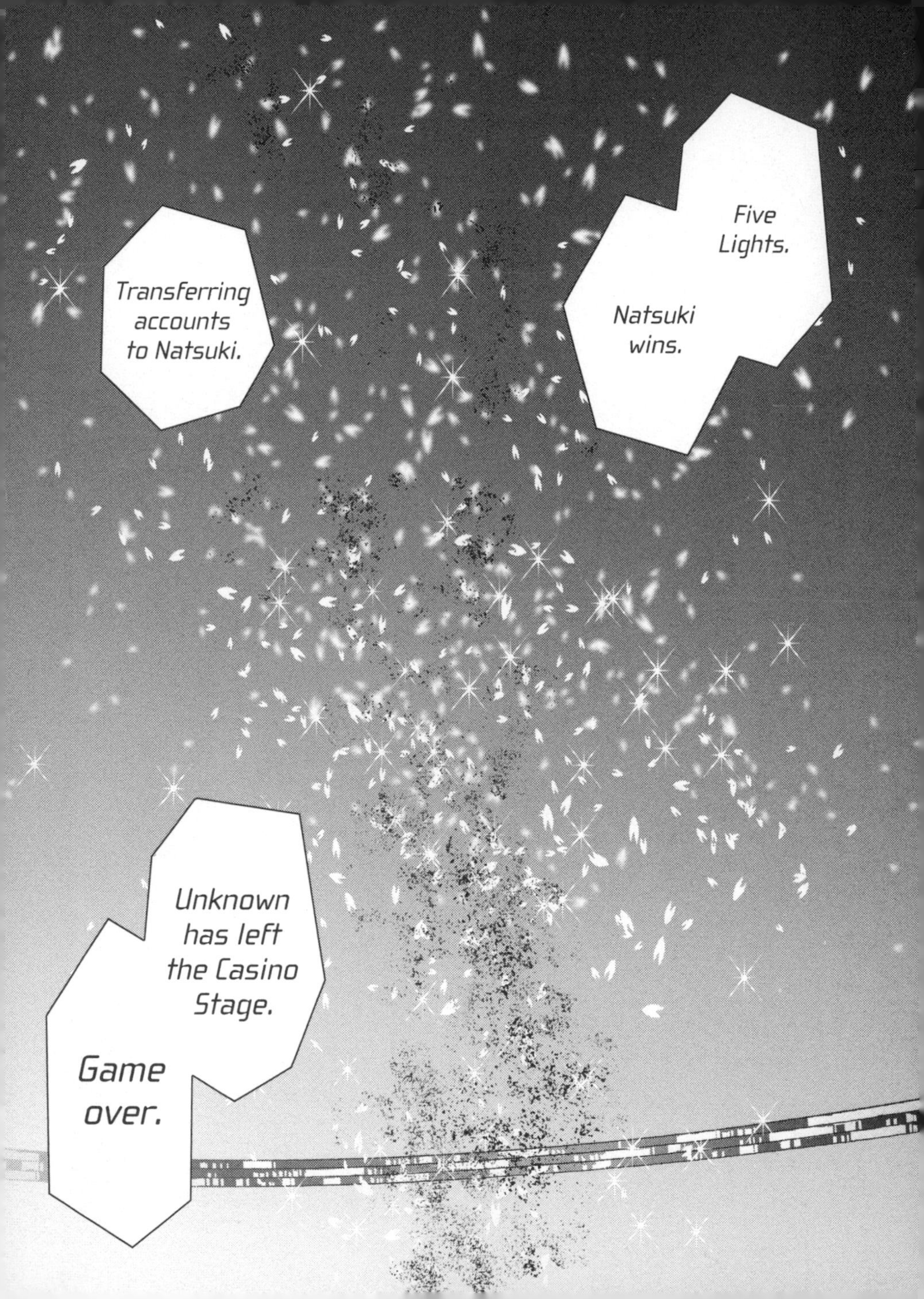
Five Lights.
Natsuki wins.
Transferring accounts to Natsuki.
Unknown has left the Casino Stage.
Game over.

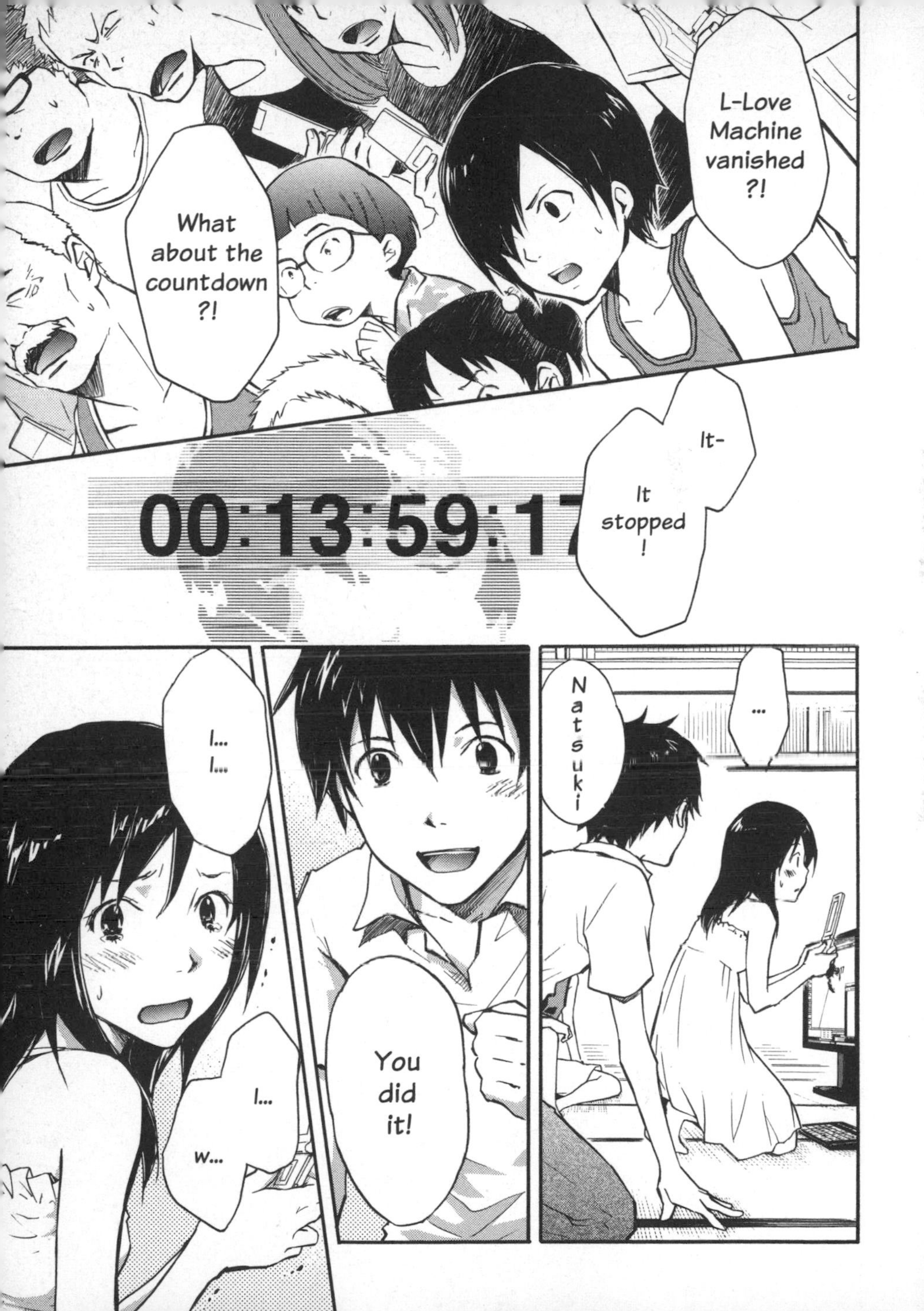
L-Love Machine vanished ?!
What about the countdown ?!
It-
It stopped !
00:13:59:17
...
Natsuki
You did it!
I... I...
I... w...

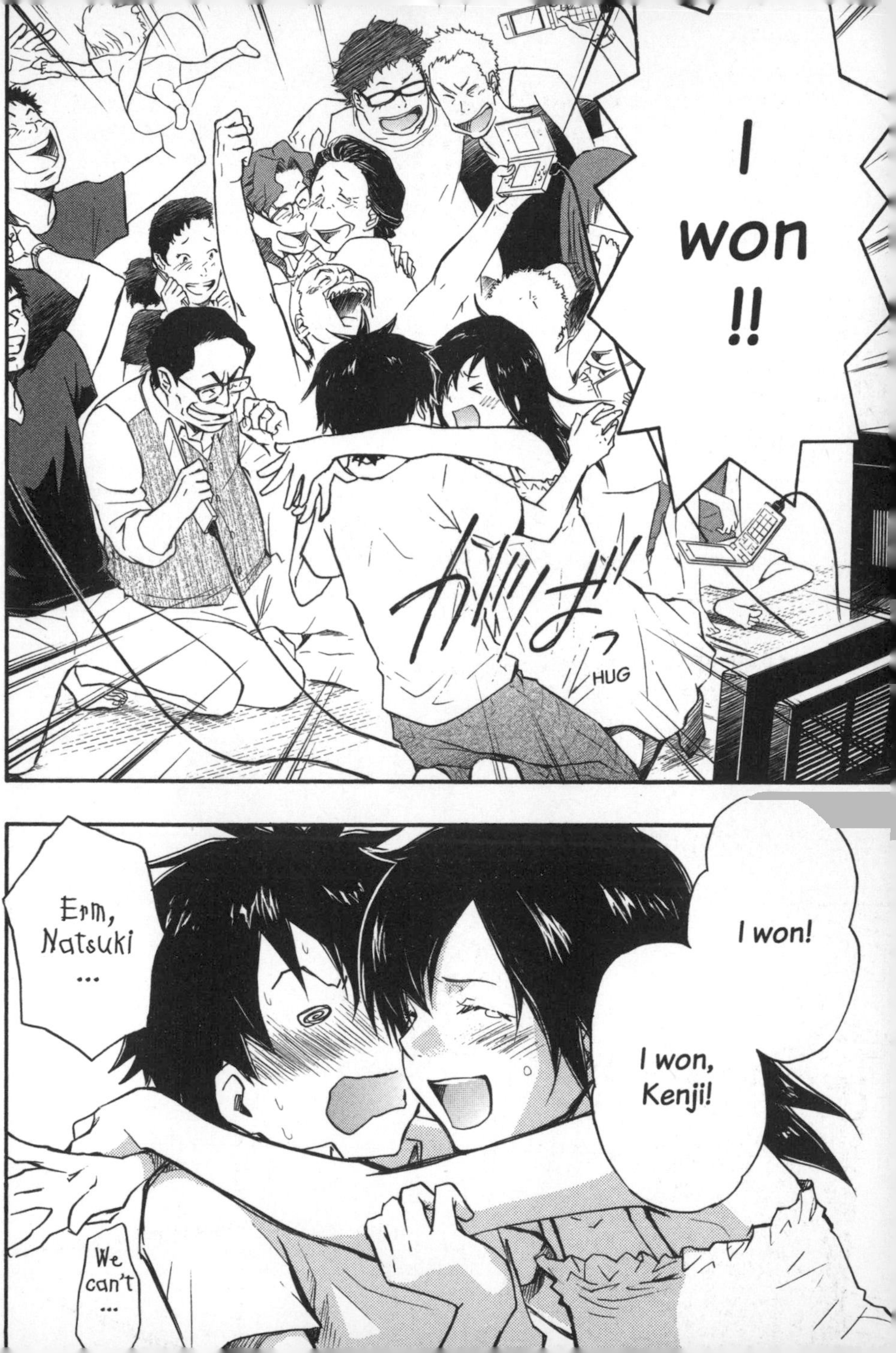
I won !!
HUG
I won!
I won, Kenji!
Erm, Natsuki ...
We can't ...

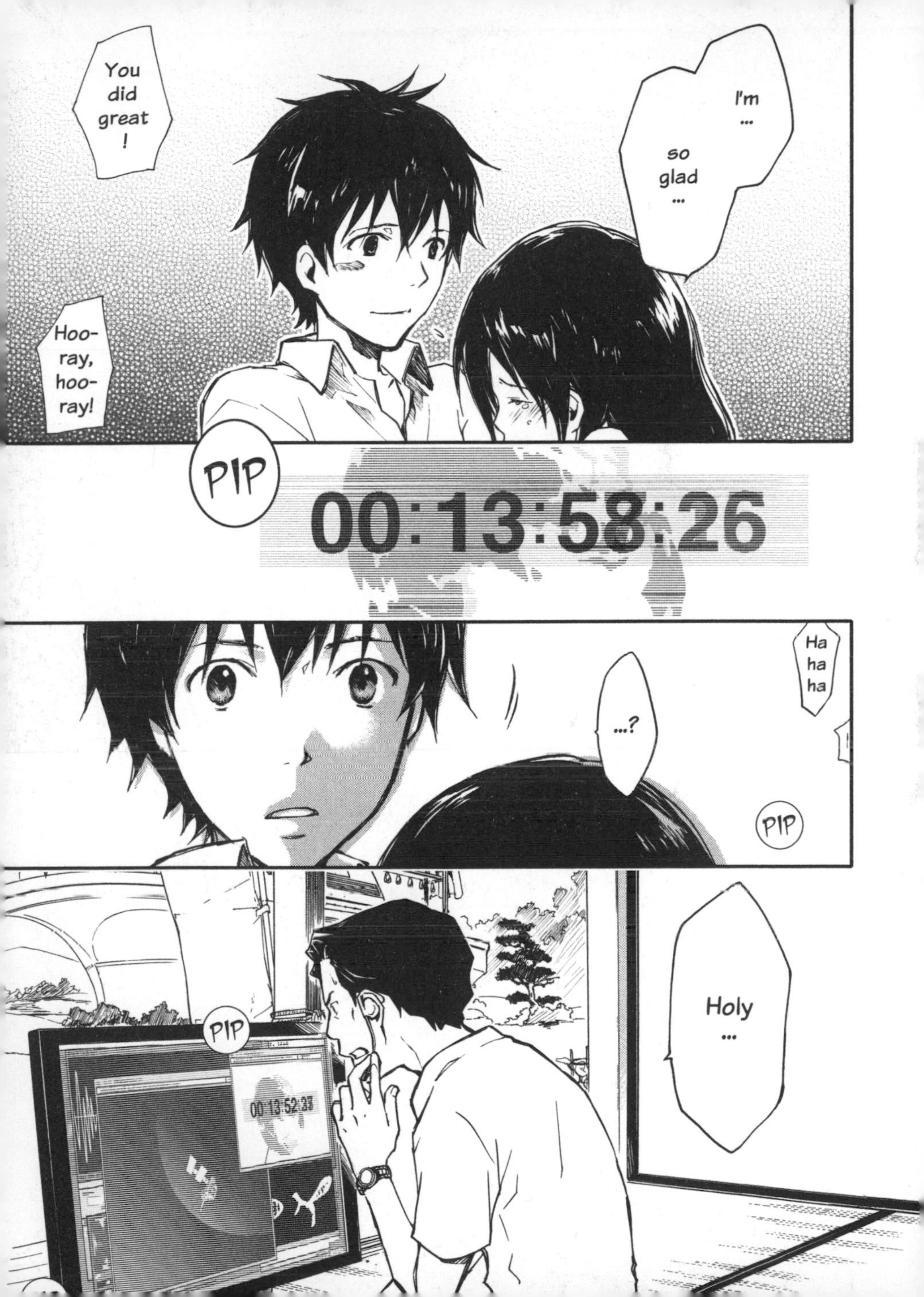
I'm ... so glad ...
You did great!
Hooray, hooray!
PIP
00:13:58:26
Ha ha ha
...?
PIP
Holy ...
PIP
00:13:52:37

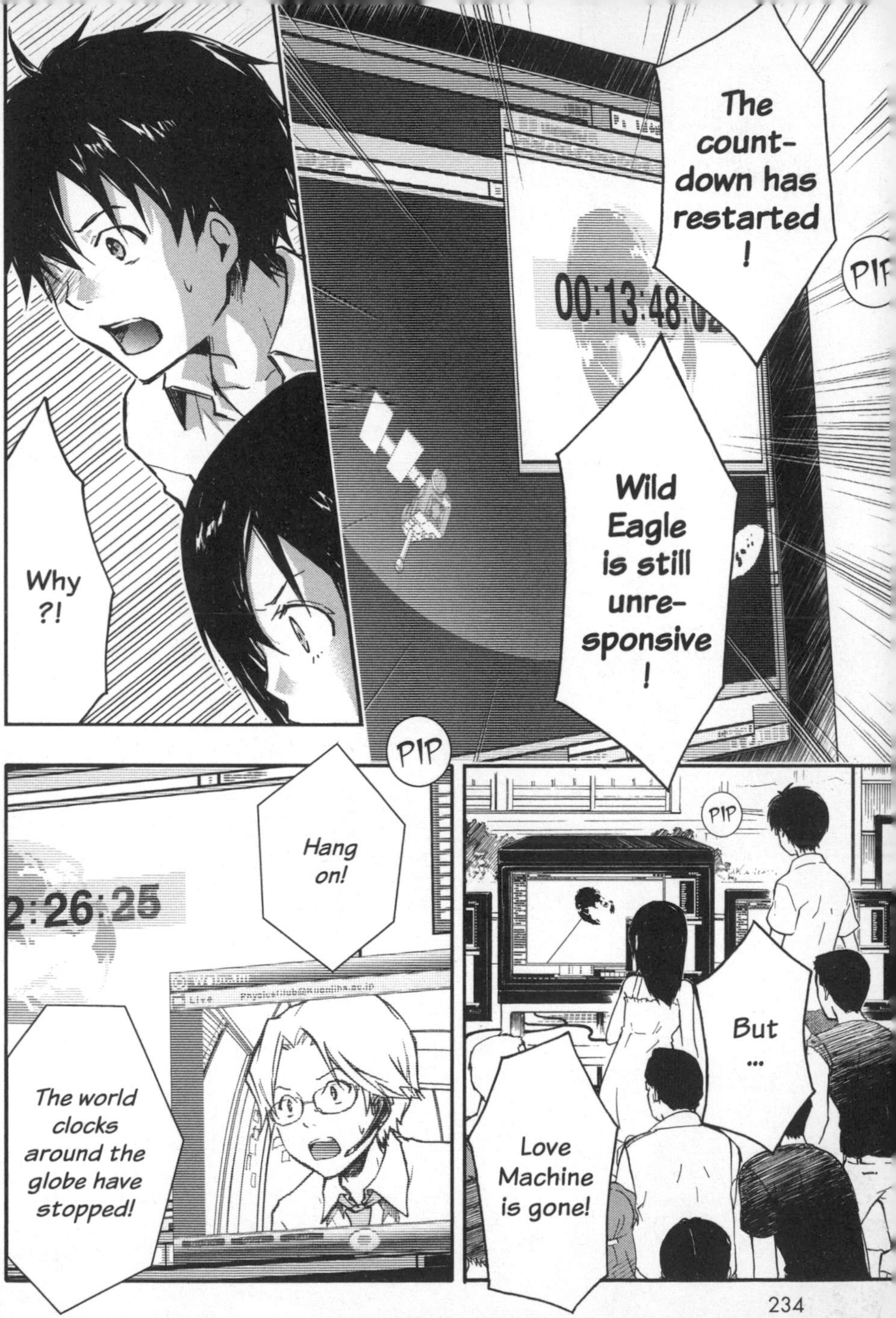
The count-down has restarted!
PIP
00:13:48:02
Wild Eagle is still unre-sponsive!
Why?!
PIP
PIP
But ...
Love Machine is gone!
Hang on!
2:26:25
The world clocks around the globe have stopped!

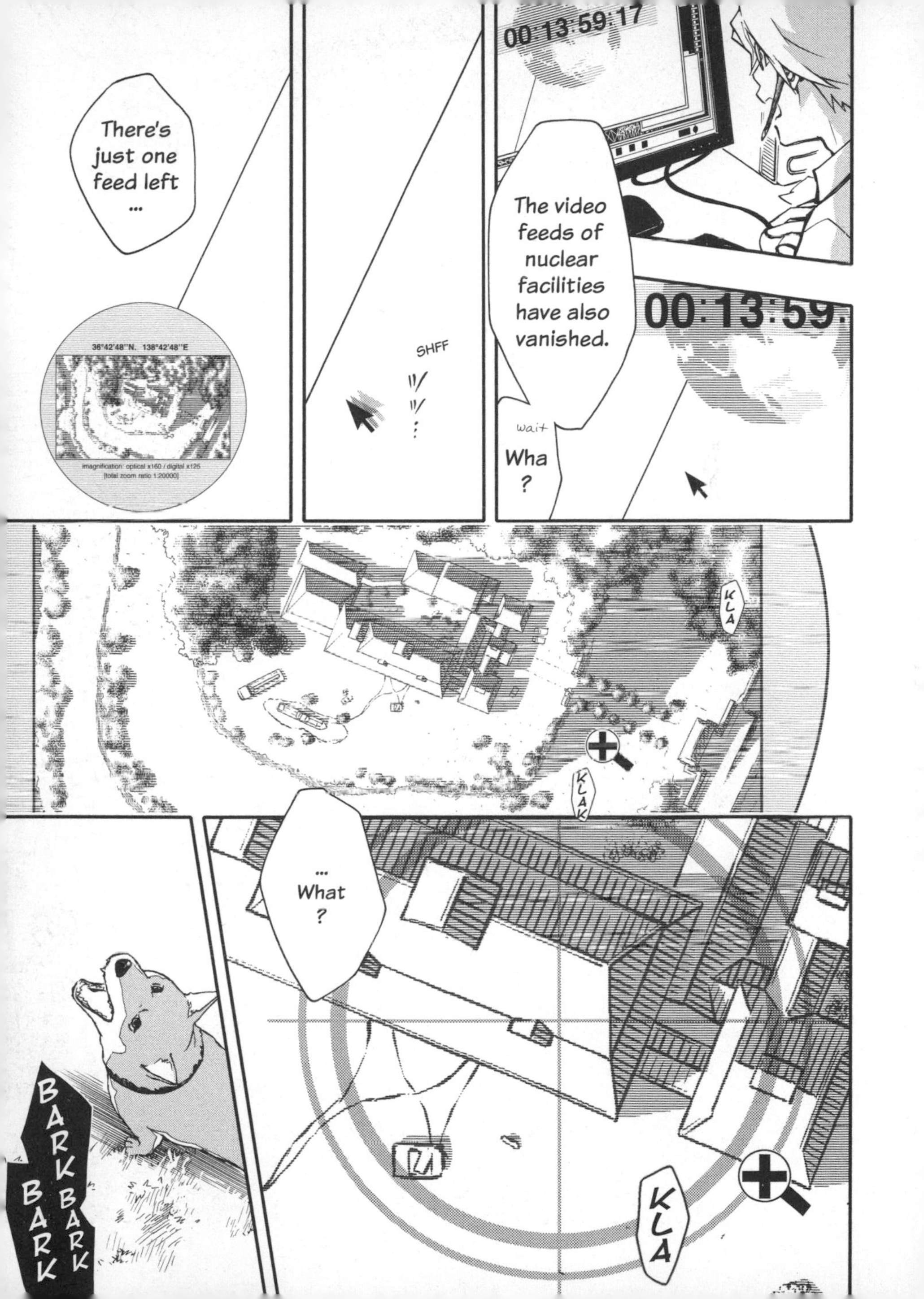
00:13:59:17
The video feeds of nuclear facilities have also vanished.
00:13:59.
wait
Wha ?
SHFF
There's just one feed left ...
36°42'48''N. 138°42'48''E
imagnification: optical x160 / digital x125
[total zoom ratio 1:20000]
KLA
KLAK
... What ?
KLA
BARK BARK BARK BARK

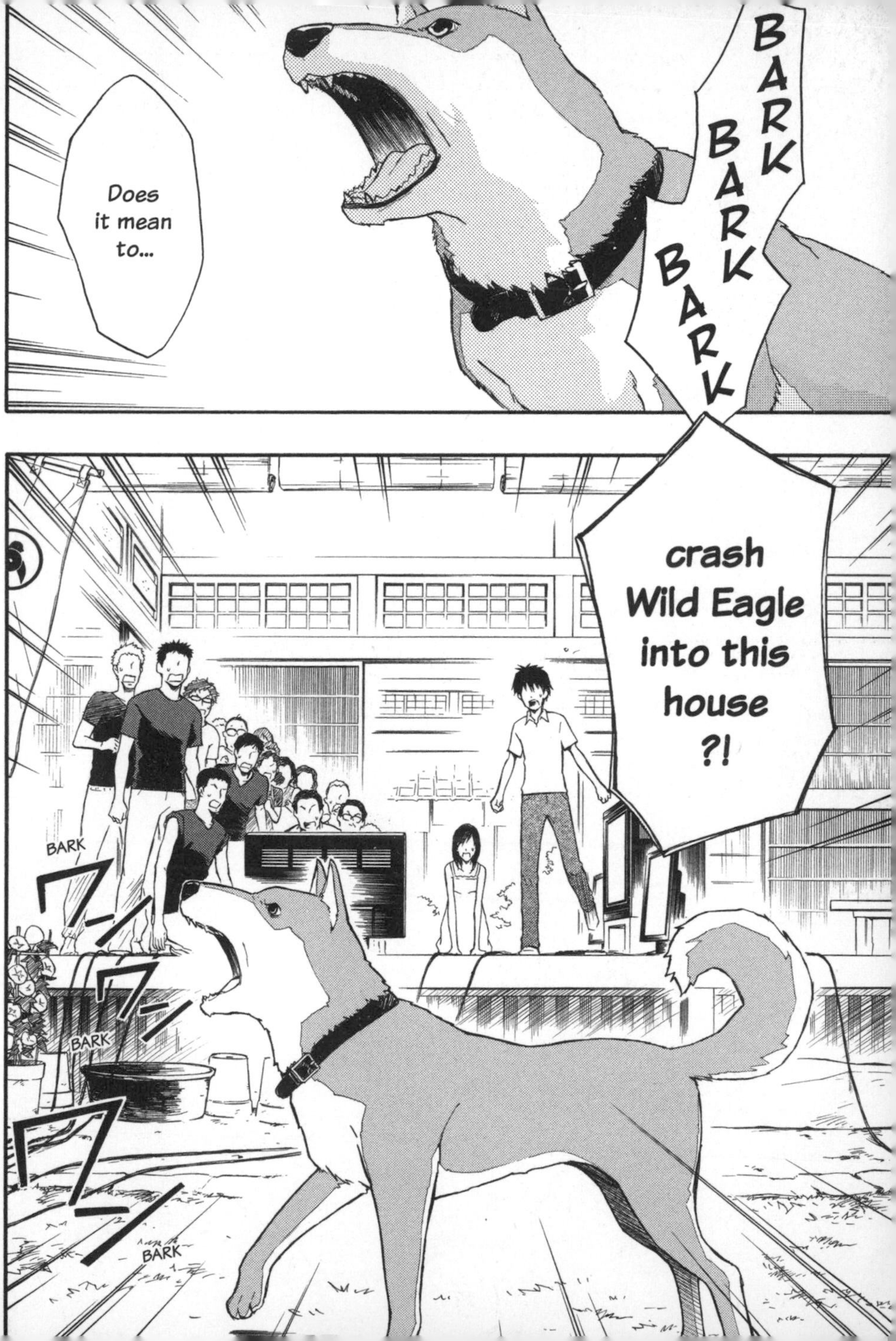
BARK BARK BARK
Does it mean to...
crash Wild Eagle into this house ?!
BARK
BARK
BARK

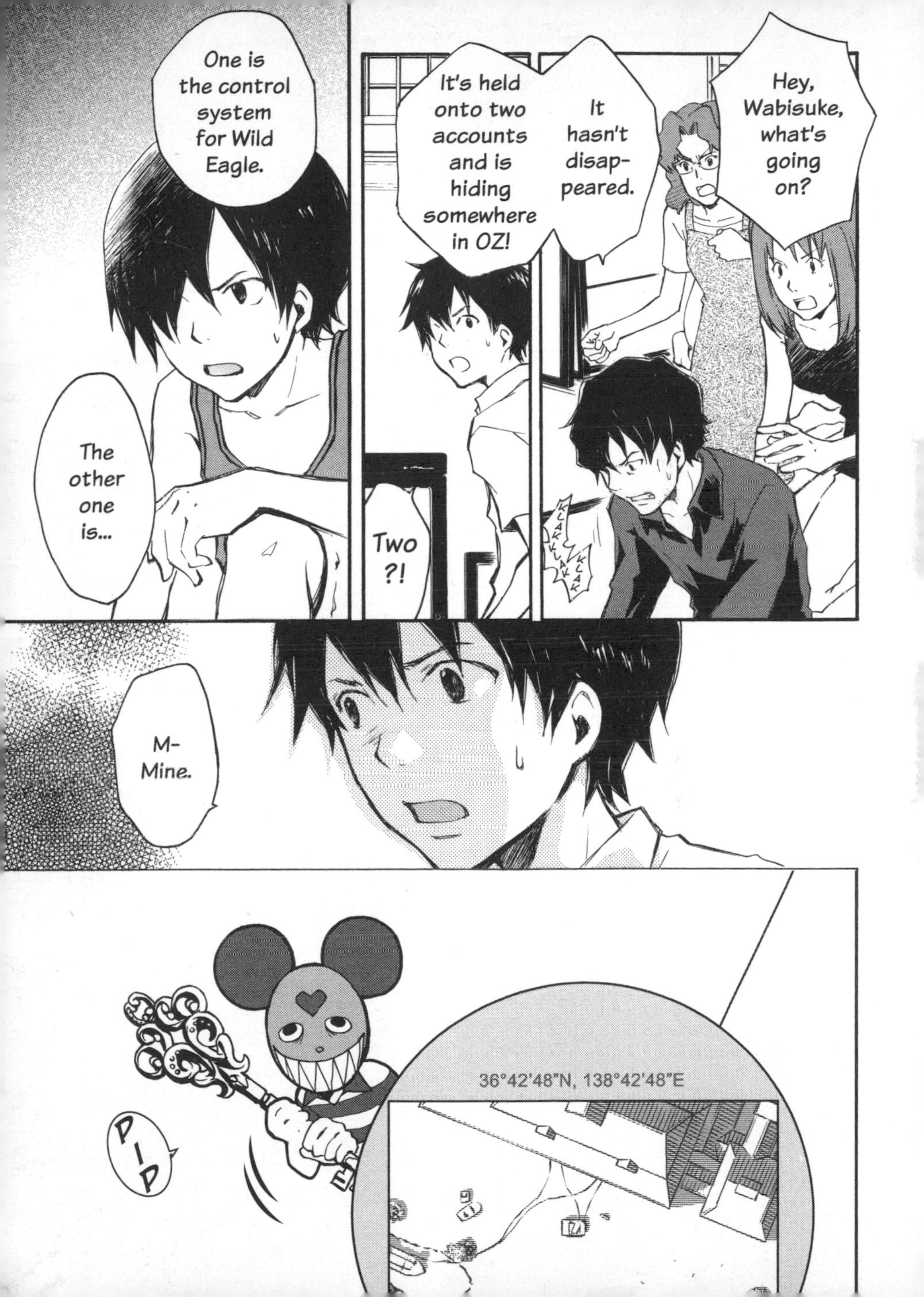
Hey, Wabisuke, what's going on?
It hasn't disappeared.
It's held onto two accounts and is hiding somewhere in OZ!
KLAK KLAK KLAK KLAK
Two?!
One is the control system for Wild Eagle.
The other one is...
M- Mine.
36°42'48"N, 138°42'48"E
PIP

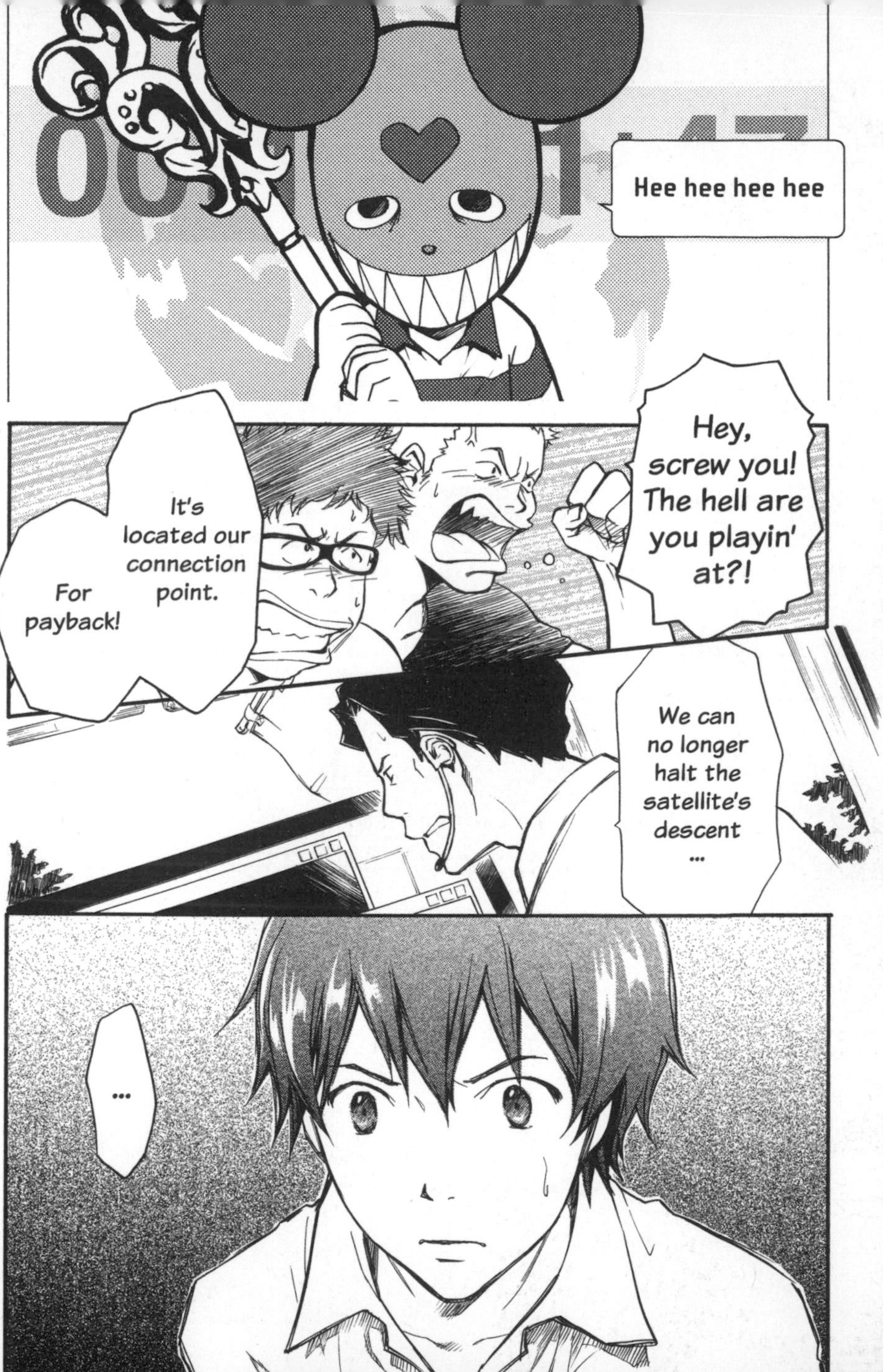
Hee hee hee hee
Hey, screw you! The hell are you playin' at?!
It's located our connection point.
For payback!
We can no longer halt the satellite's descent ...
...

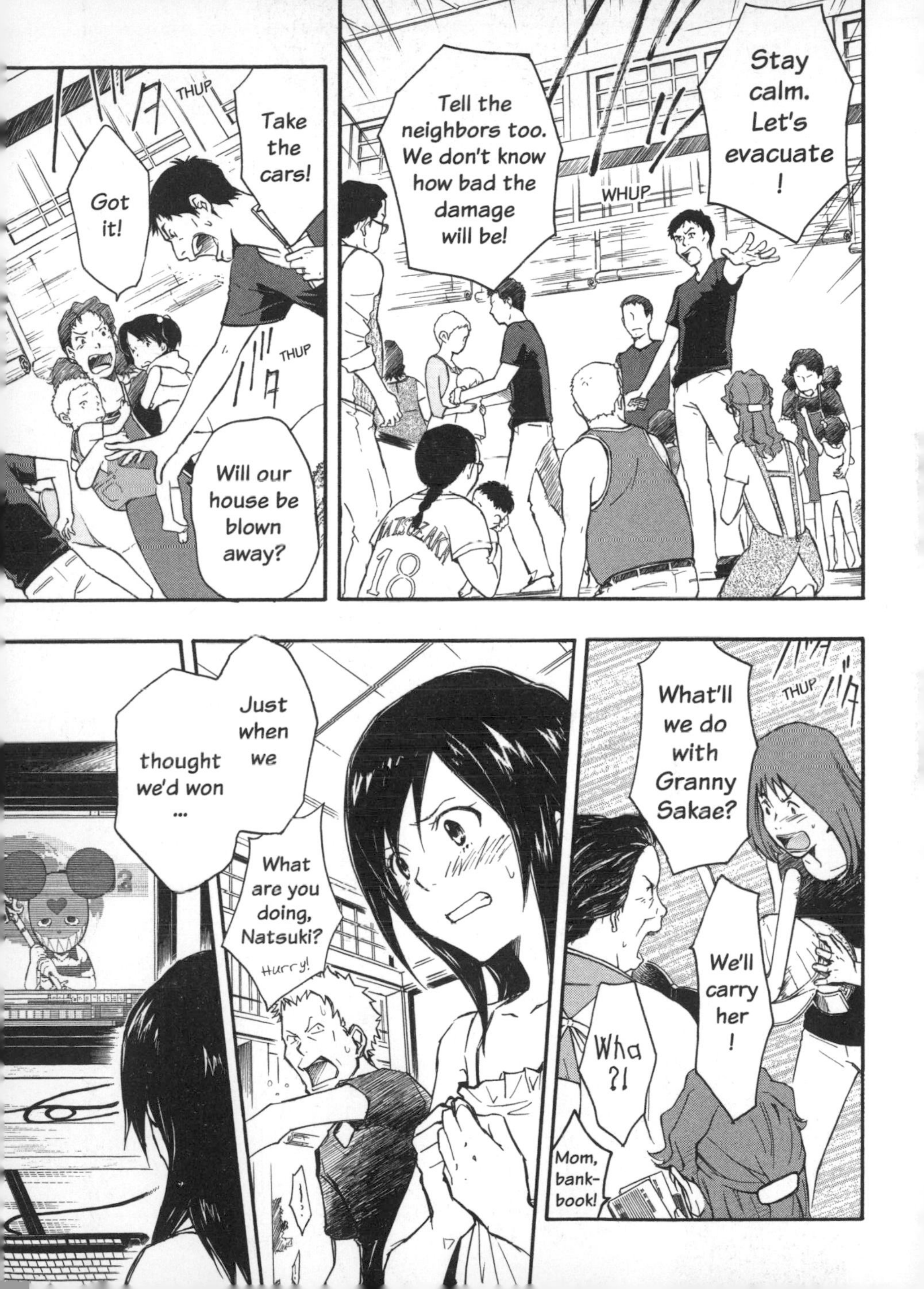
Stay calm. Let's evacuate!
Tell the neighbors too. We don't know how bad the damage will be!
WHUP
THUP
Take the cars!
Got it!
THUP
Will our house be blown away?
THUP
What'll we do with Granny Sakae?
We'll carry her!
Wha?!
Mom, bank-book!
Just when we thought we'd won...
What are you doing, Natsuki?
Hurry!

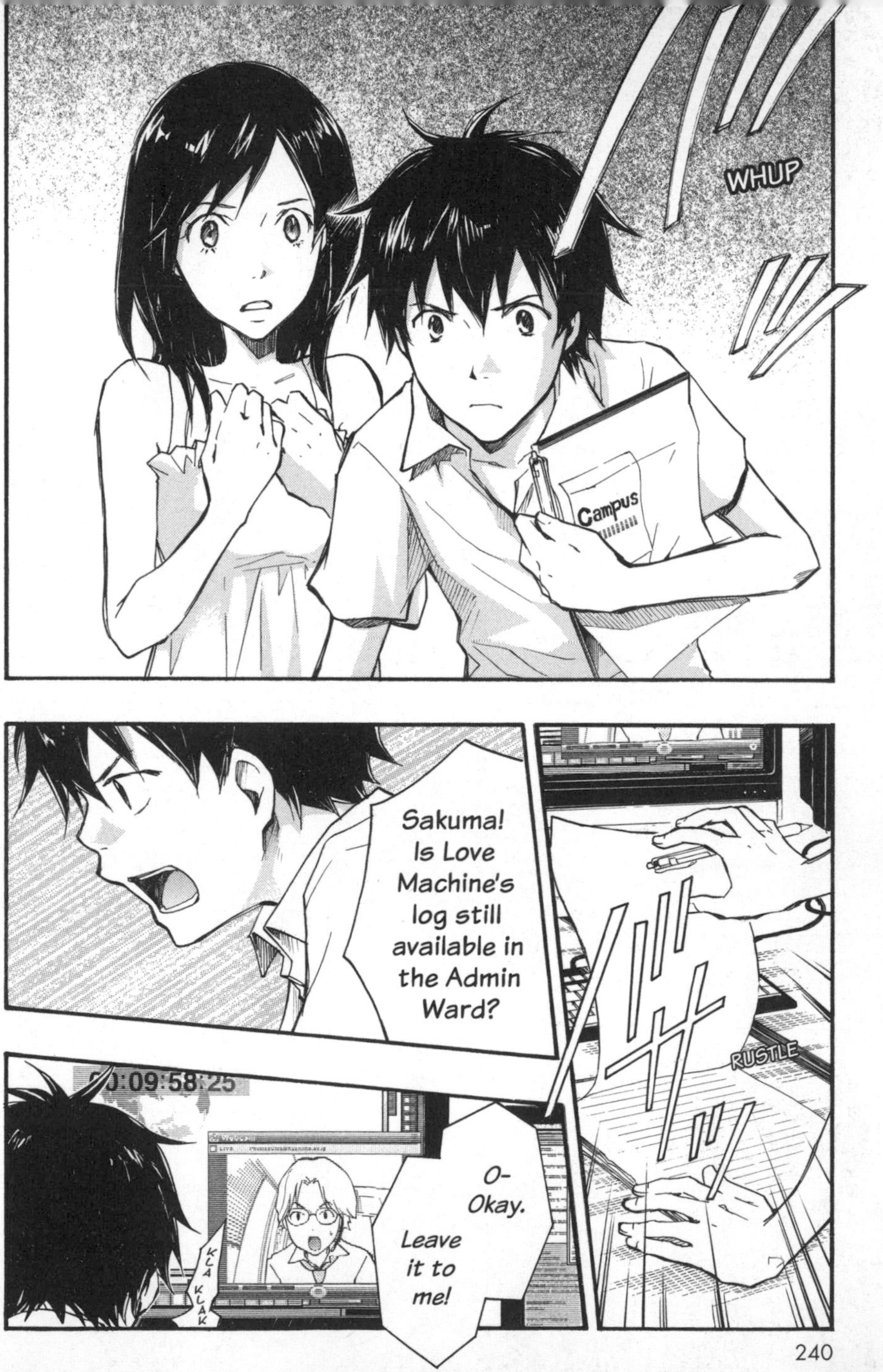
WHUP
Campus
RUSTLE
Sakuma! Is Love Machine's log still available in the Admin Ward?
O- Okay. Leave it to me!
0:09:58:25
KLA KLAK

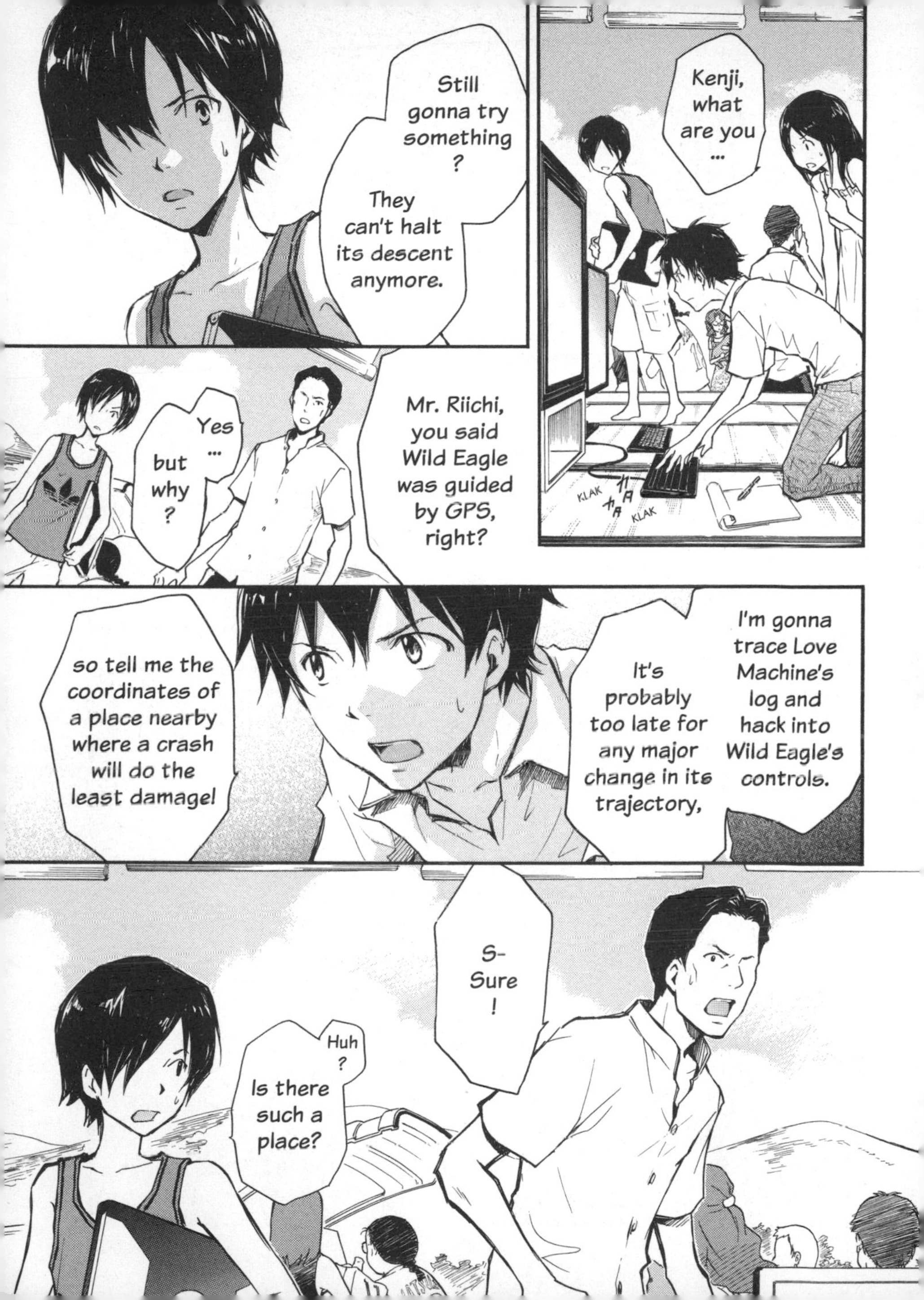
Kenji, what are you ...
KLAK
KLAK
Still gonna try something?
They can't halt its descent anymore.
Mr. Riichi, you said Wild Eagle was guided by GPS, right?
Yes ...
but why?
I'm gonna trace Love Machine's log and hack into Wild Eagle's controls.
It's probably too late for any major change in its trajectory,
so tell me the coordinates of a place nearby where a crash will do the least damage!
S-Sure!
Huh?
Is there such a place?

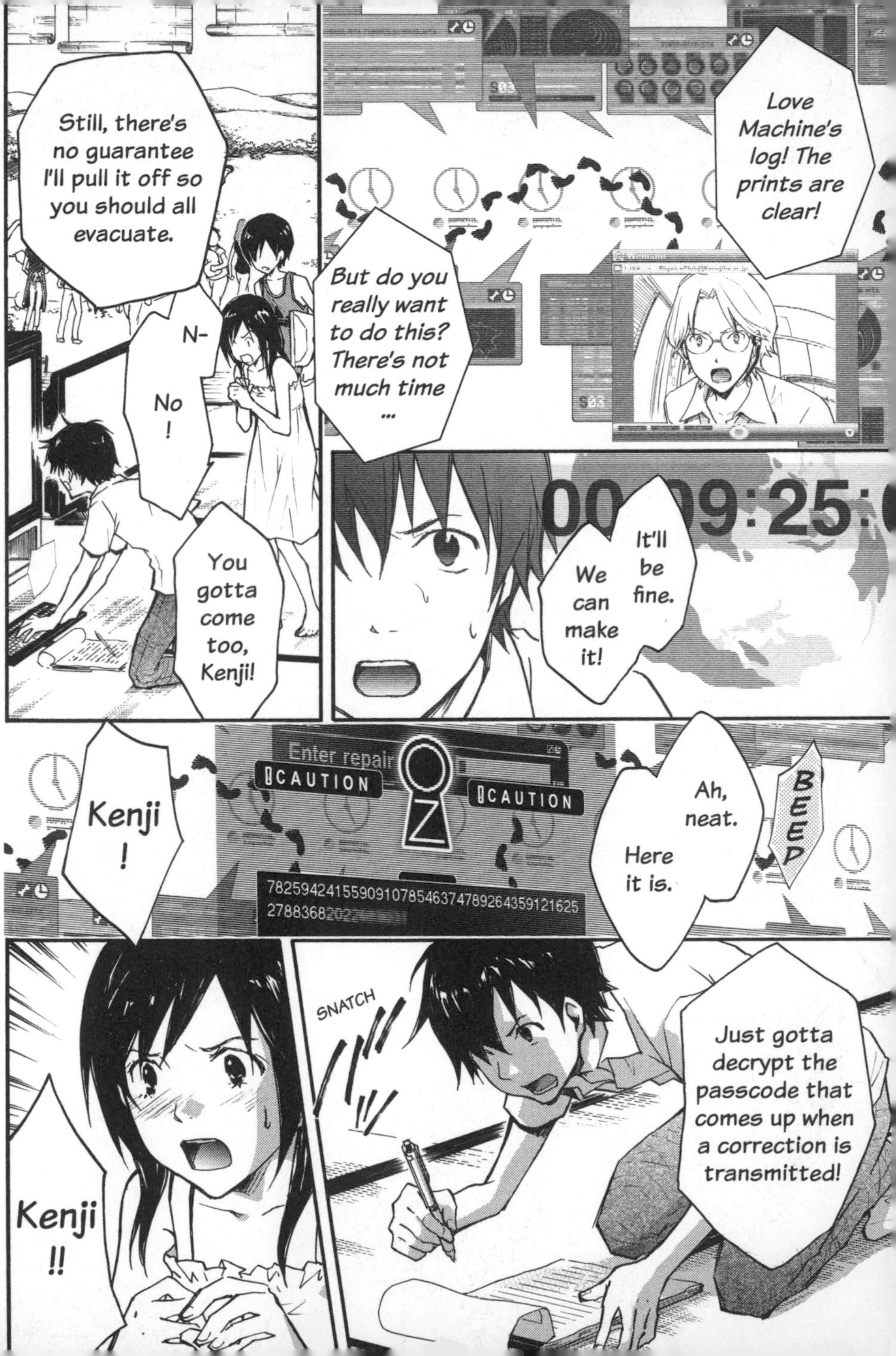
Love Machine's log! The prints are clear!
But do you really want to do this? There's not much time ...
It'll be fine.
We can make it!
Still, there's no guarantee I'll pull it off so you should all evacuate.
N-
No!
You gotta come too, Kenji!
Ah, neat.
Here it is.
BEEP
Enter repair
CAUTION
CAUTION
782594241559091078546374789264359121625
2788368202
Kenji!
SNATCH
Just gotta decrypt the passcode that comes up when a correction is transmitted!
Kenji!!

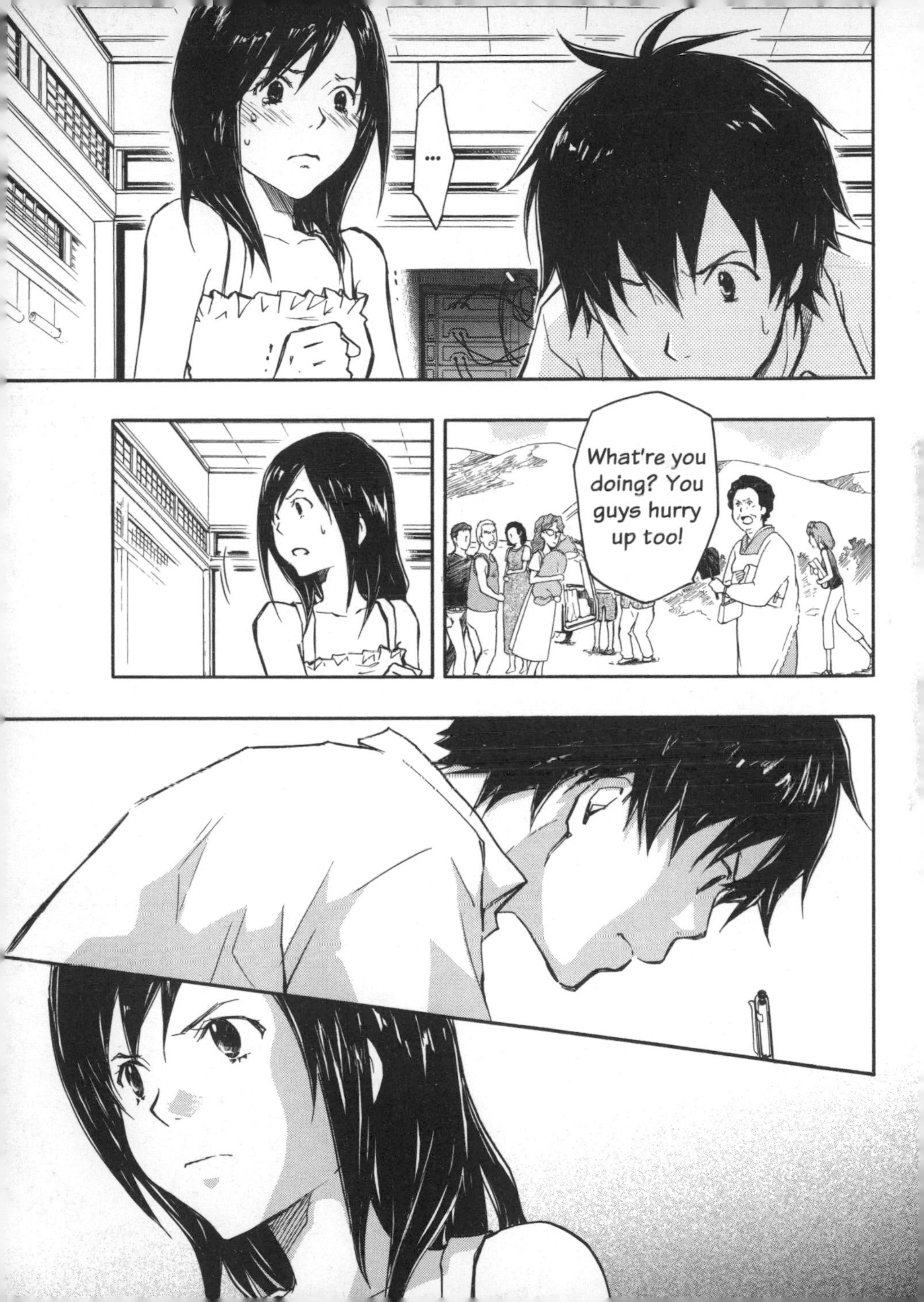
...
What're you doing? You guys hurry up too!

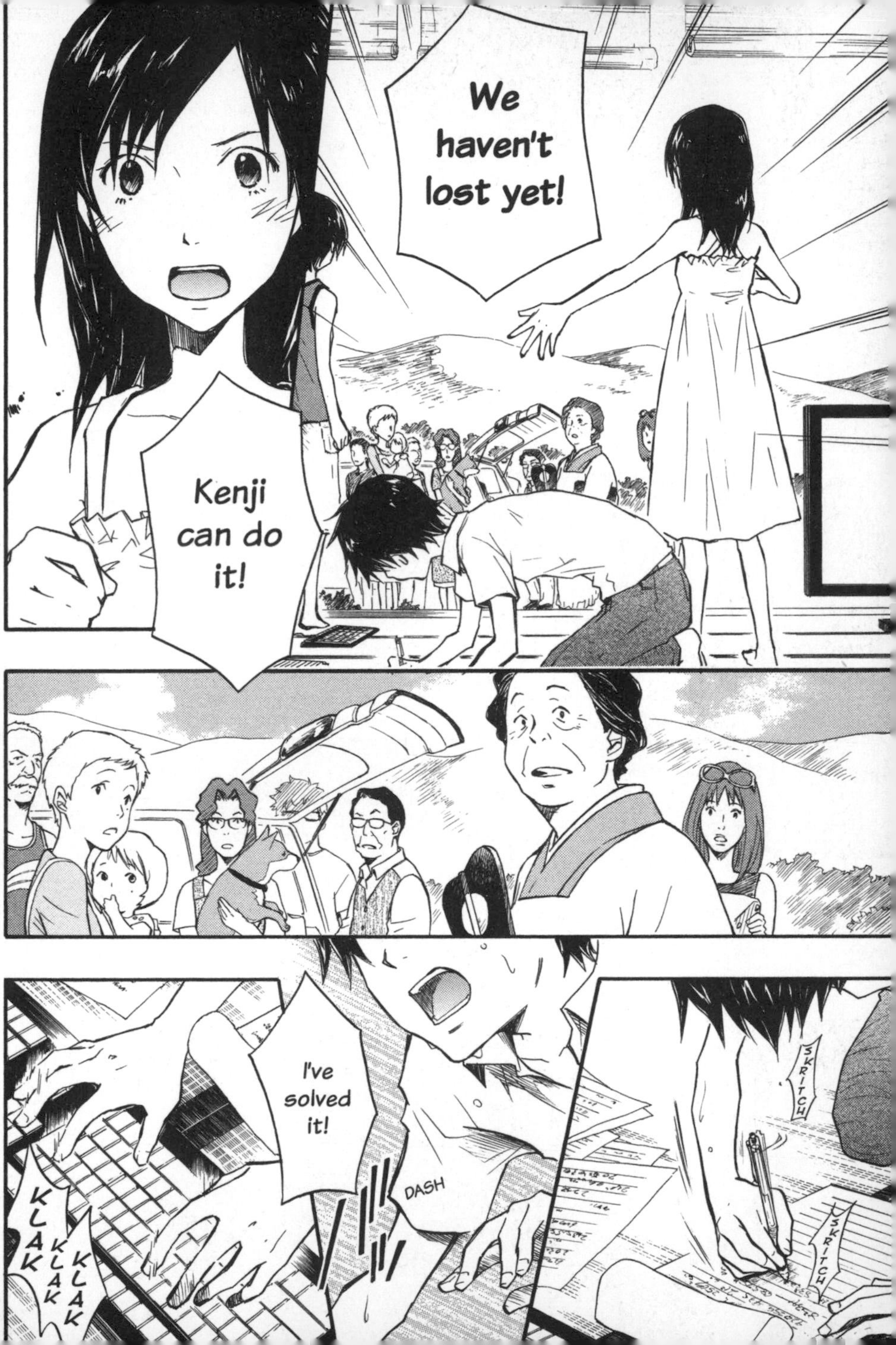
We haven't lost yet!
Kenji can do it!
SKRITCH
SKRITCH
I've solved it!
DASH
KLAK KLAK KLAK

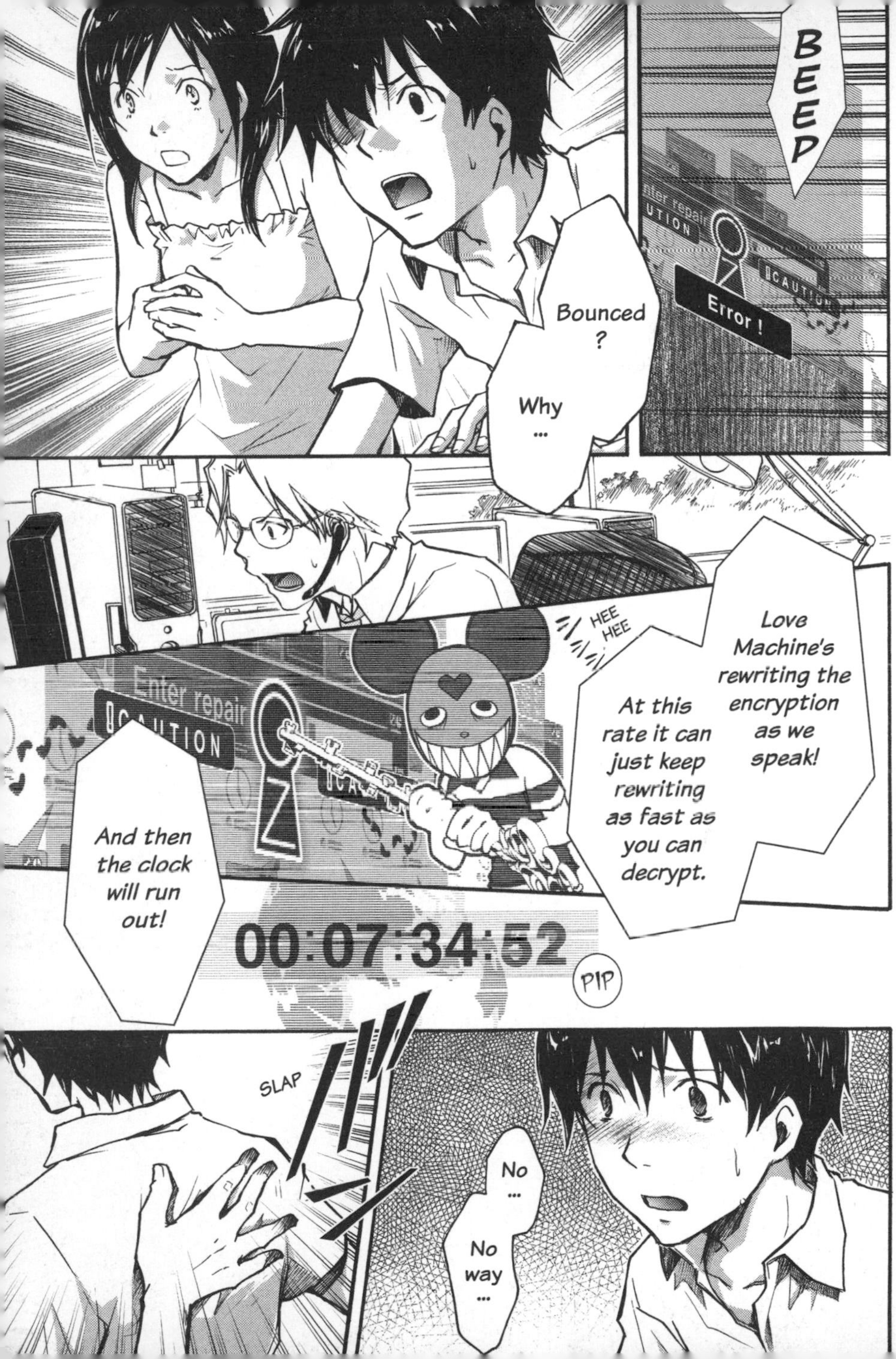

BEED
Error !
Bounced ?
Why ...
Love Machine's rewriting the encryption as we speak!
At this rate it can just keep rewriting as fast as you can decrypt.
HEE HEE
Enter repair
CAUTION
And then the clock will run out!
00:07:34:52
PIP
No ...
No way ...
SLAP

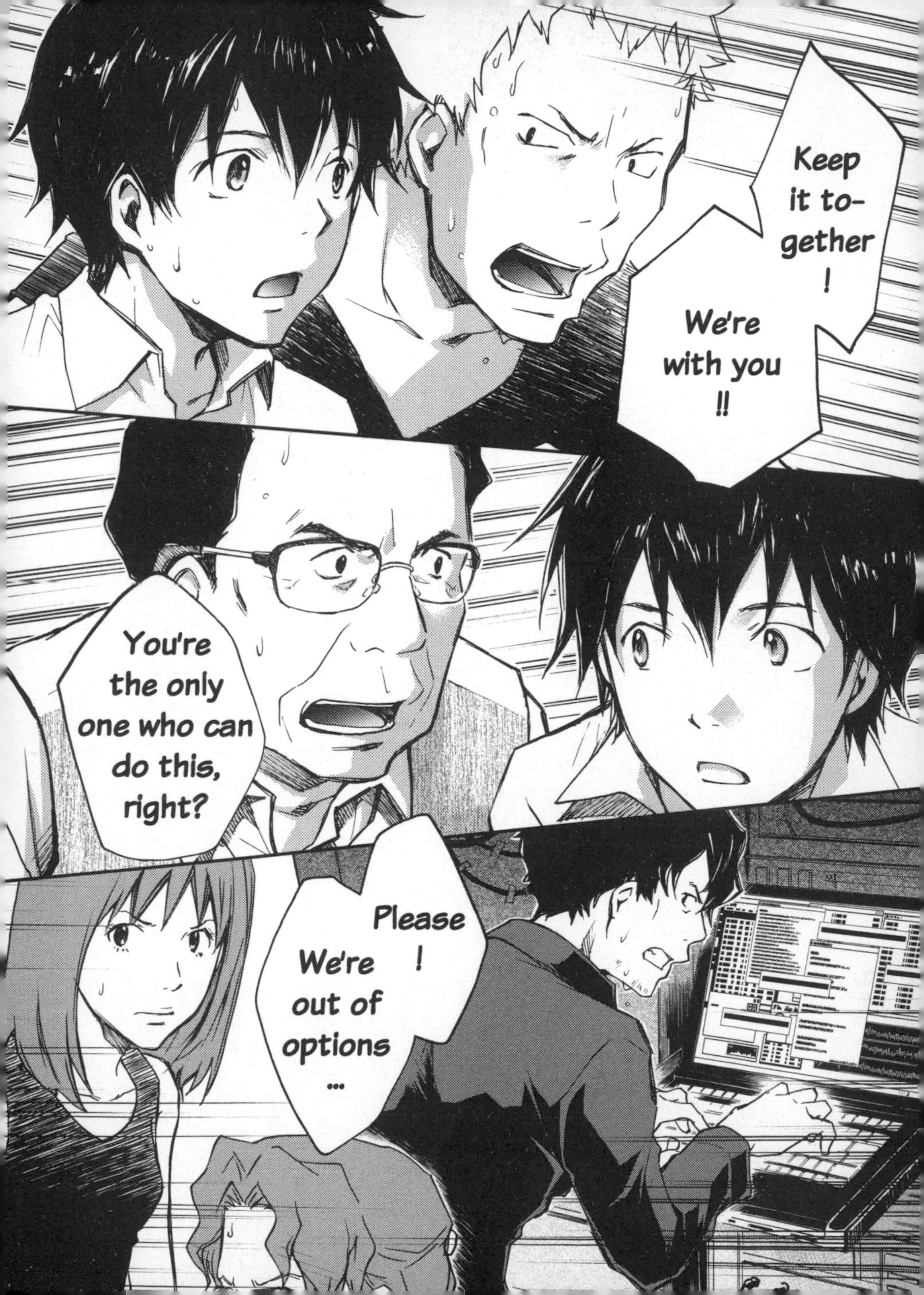
Keep it to-gether!
We're with you!!
You're the only one who can do this, right?
Please!
We're out of options...

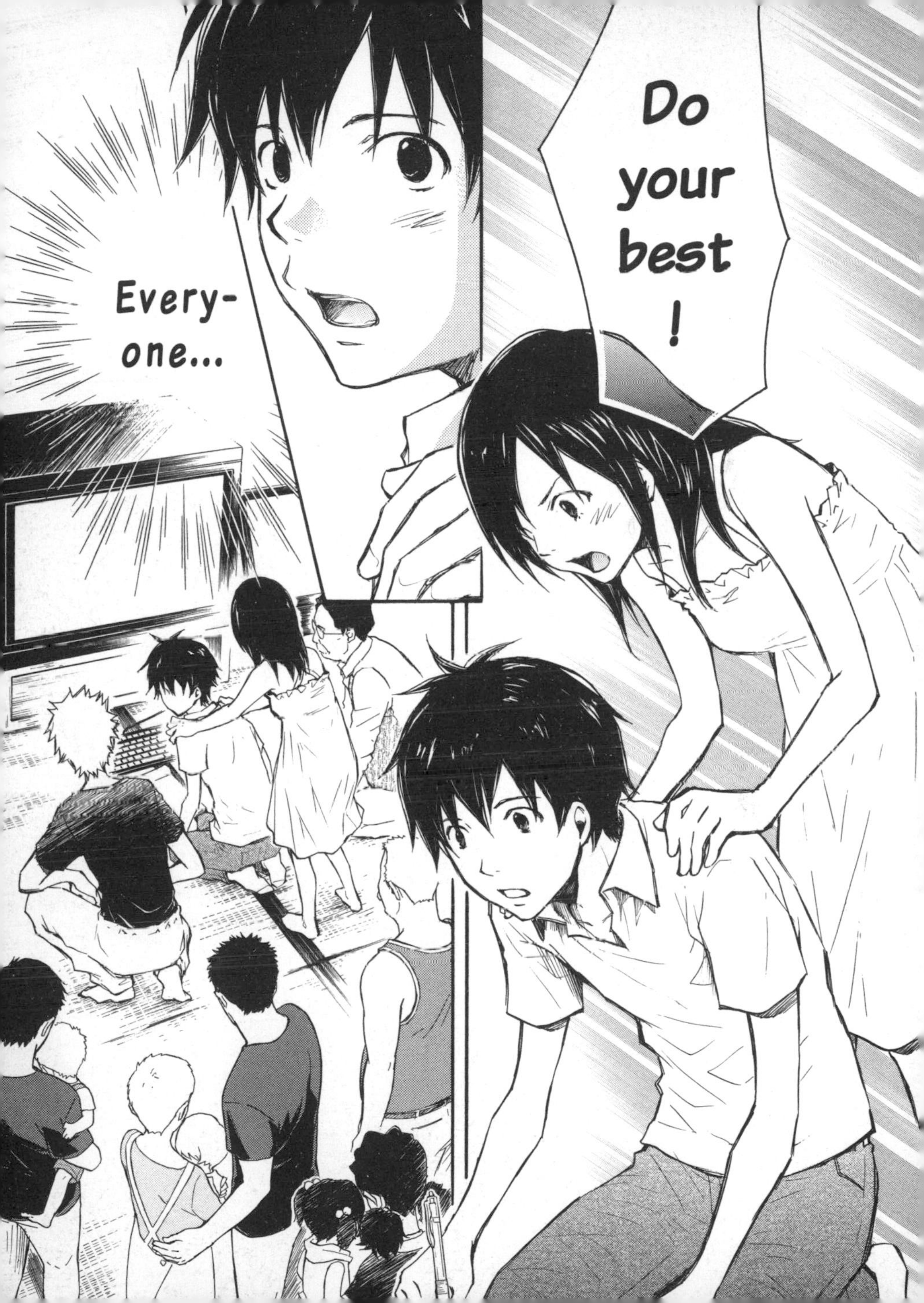
Do your best!
Every-one...

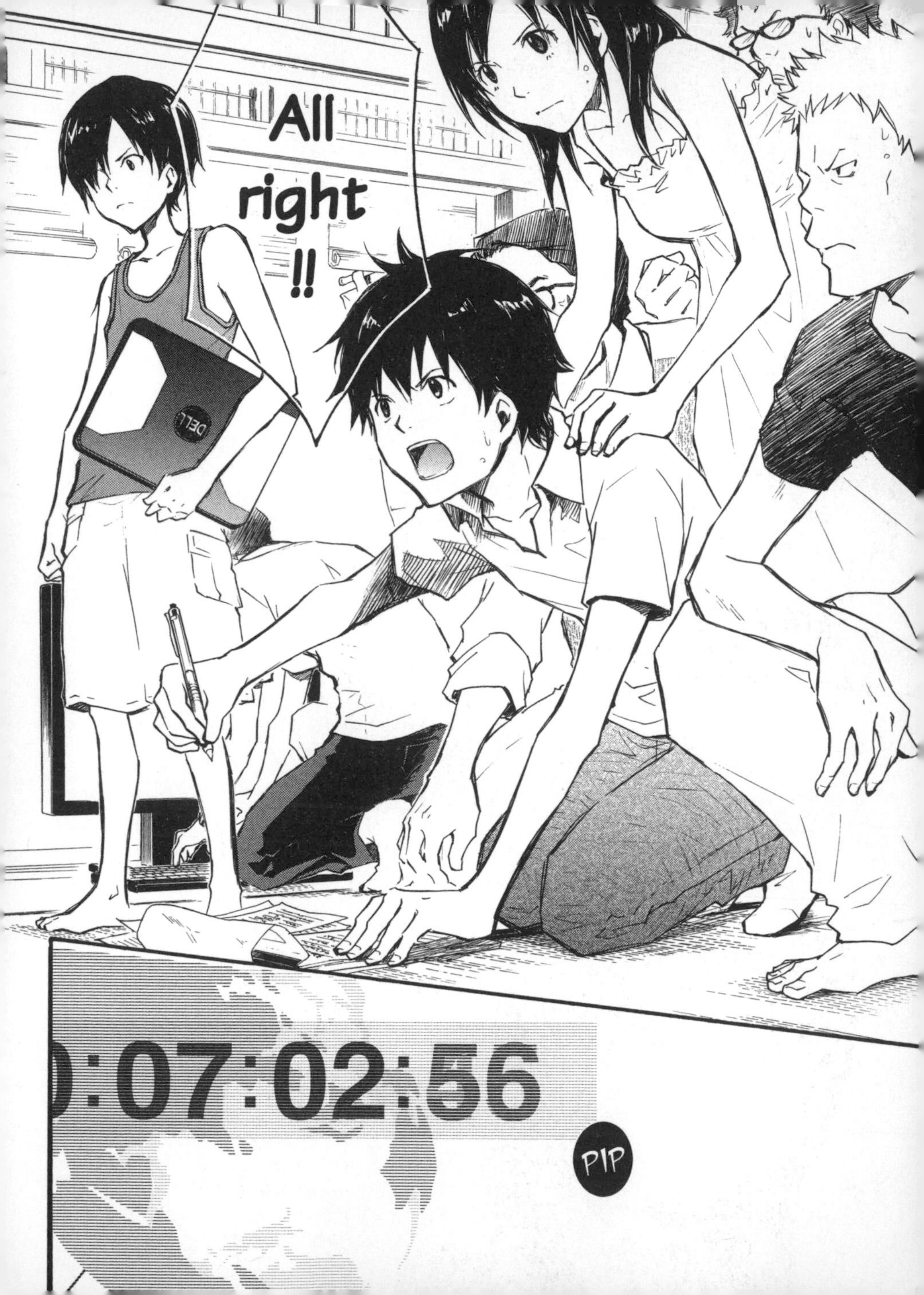
All right !!
0:07:02:56
PIP

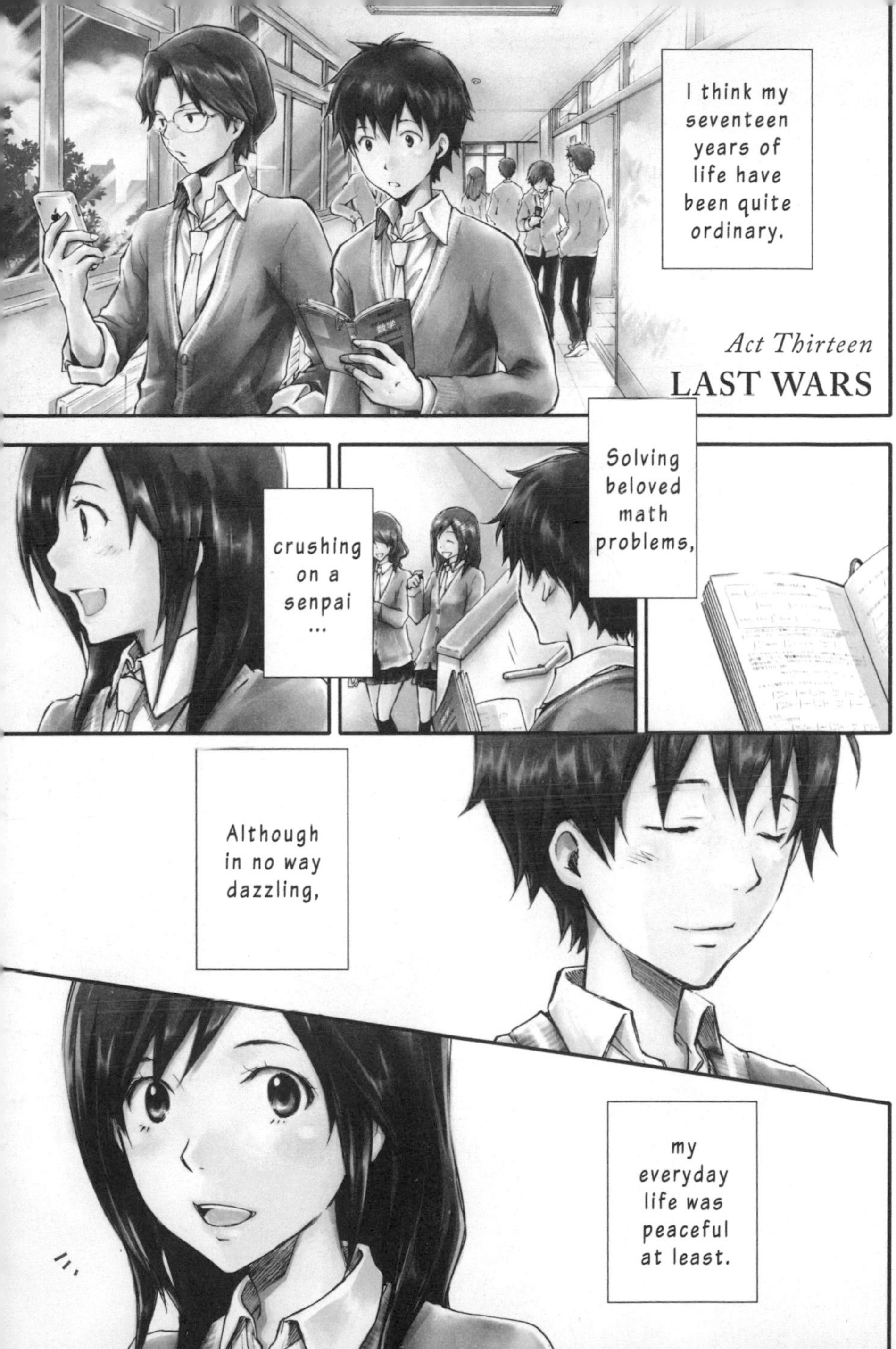
I think my seventeen years of life have been quite ordinary.
Act Thirteen
LAST WARS
Solving beloved math problems,
crushing on a senpai ...
Although in no way dazzling,
my everyday life was peaceful at least.

Act Thirteen LAST WARS

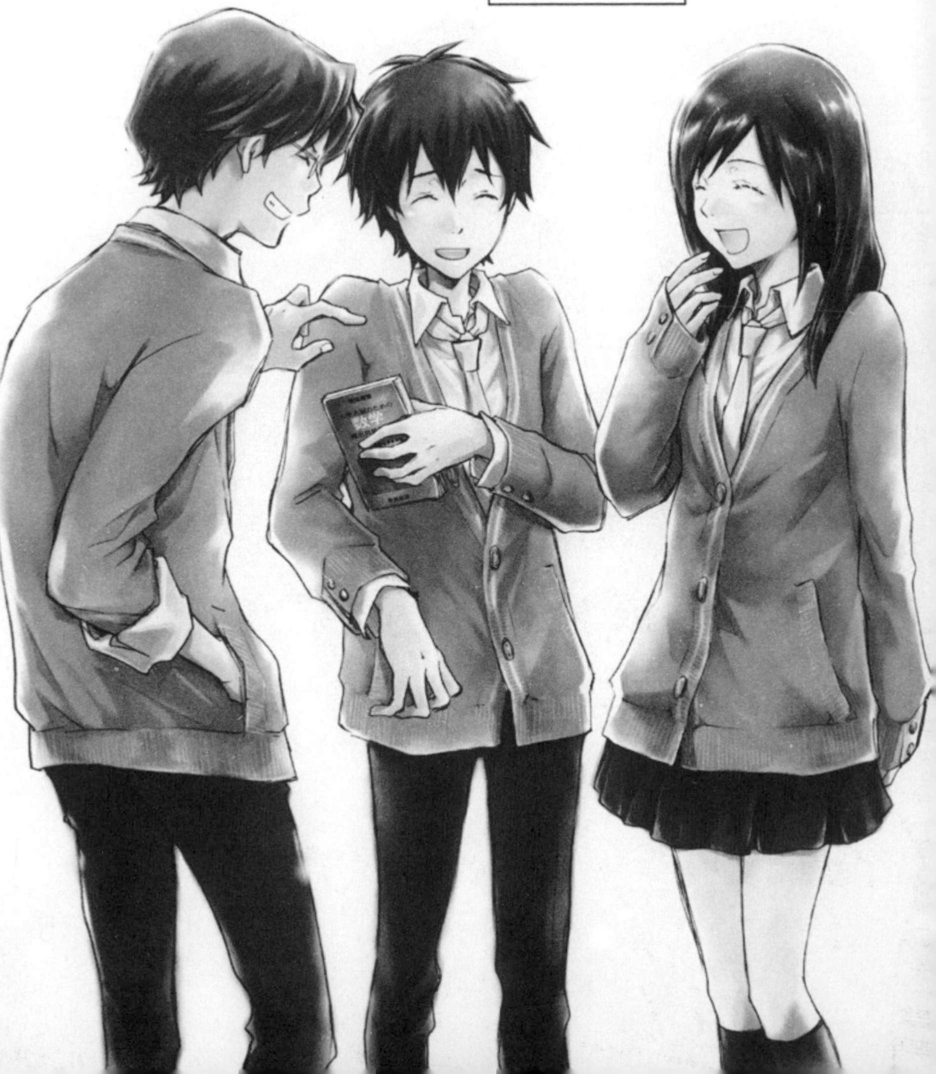
That hottest summer ever,
an event rocked my entire world—

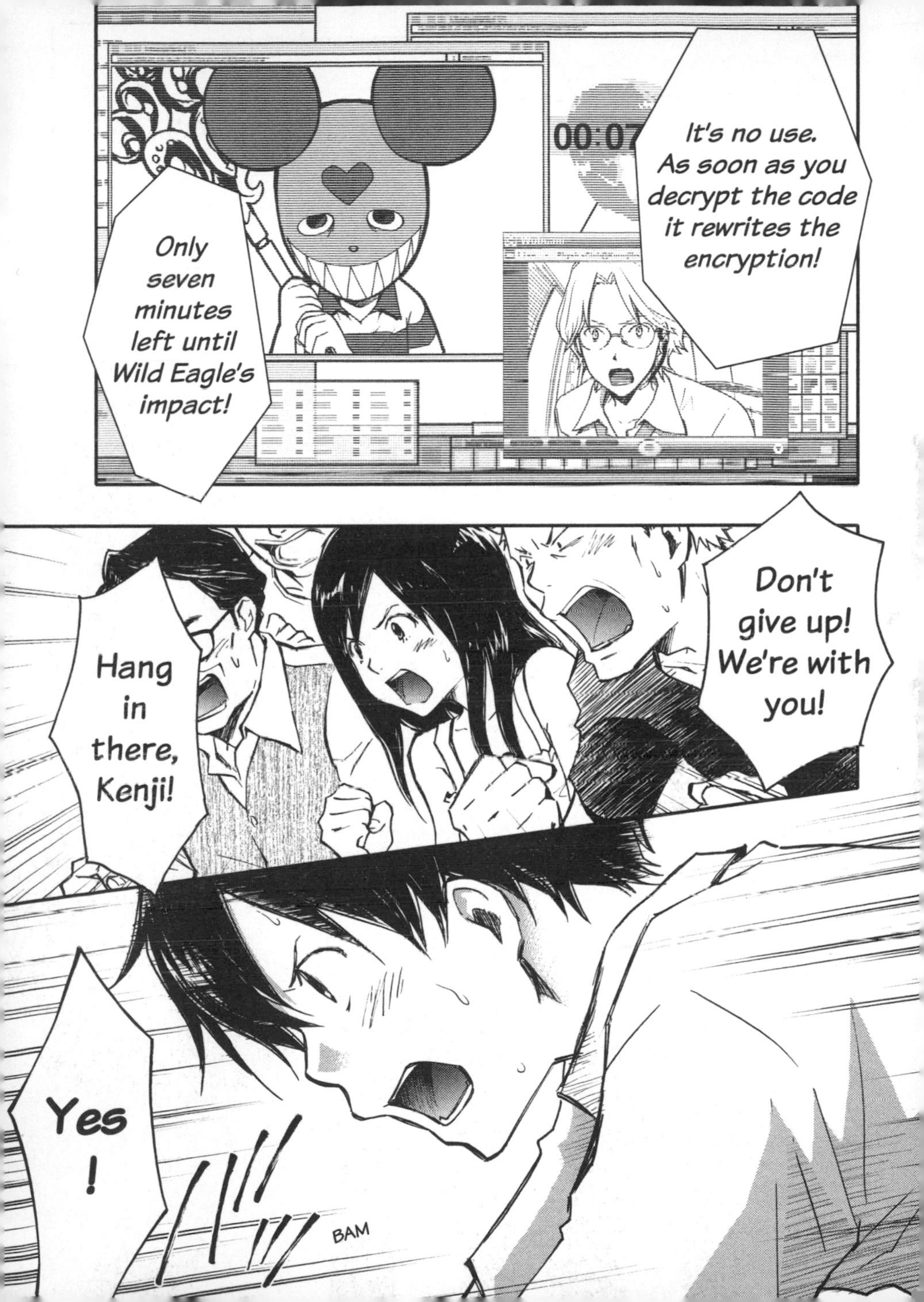
00:07
It's no use. As soon as you decrypt the code it rewrites the encryption!
Only seven minutes left until Wild Eagle's impact!
Don't give up! We're with you!
Hang in there, Kenji!
Yes!
BAM

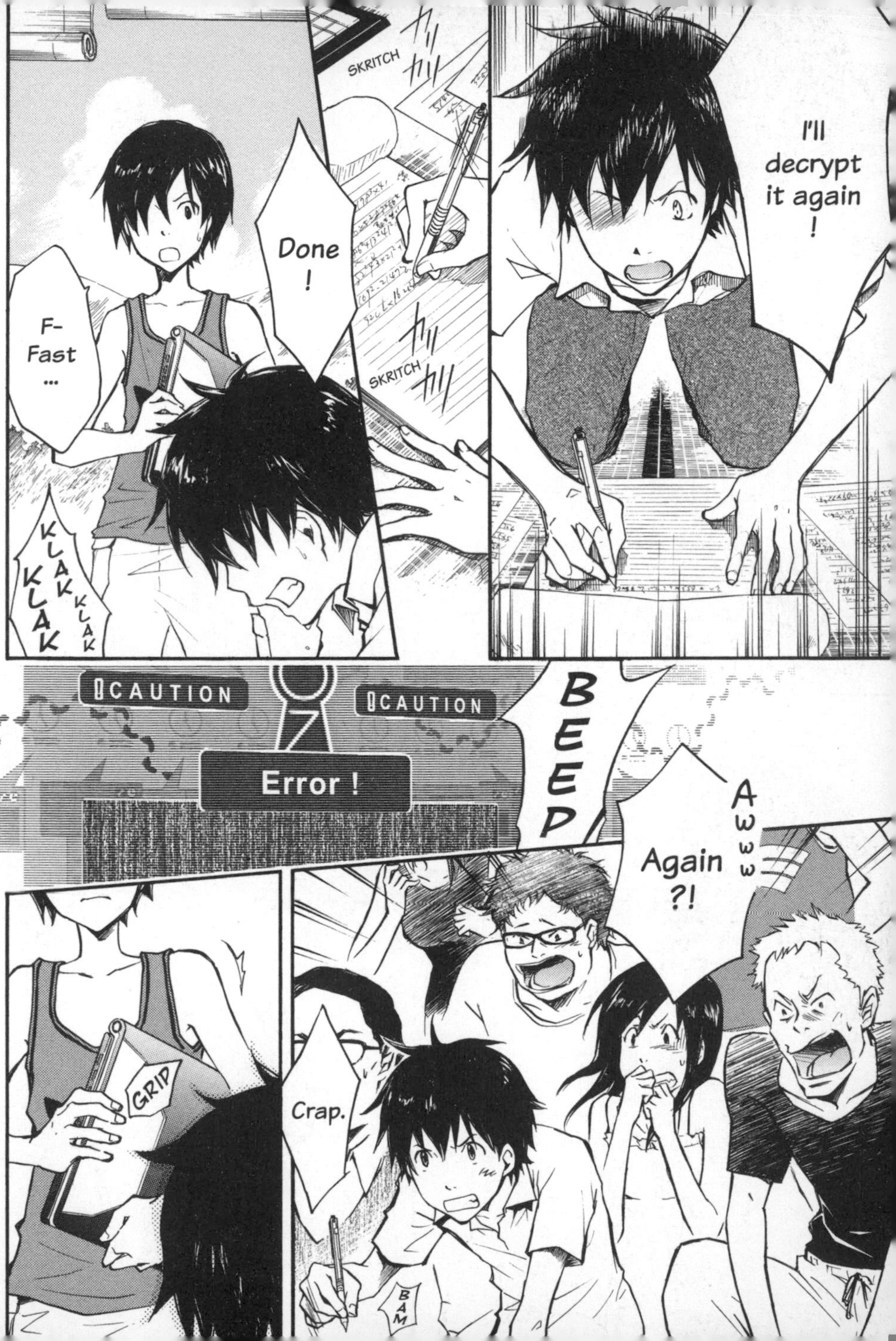

I'll decrypt it again!
SKRITCH
SKRITCH
Done!
F- Fast ...
KLAK KLAK KLAK KLAK
BEEP
CAUTION
CAUTION
Error !
Awww
Again?!
Crap.
BAM
GRIP

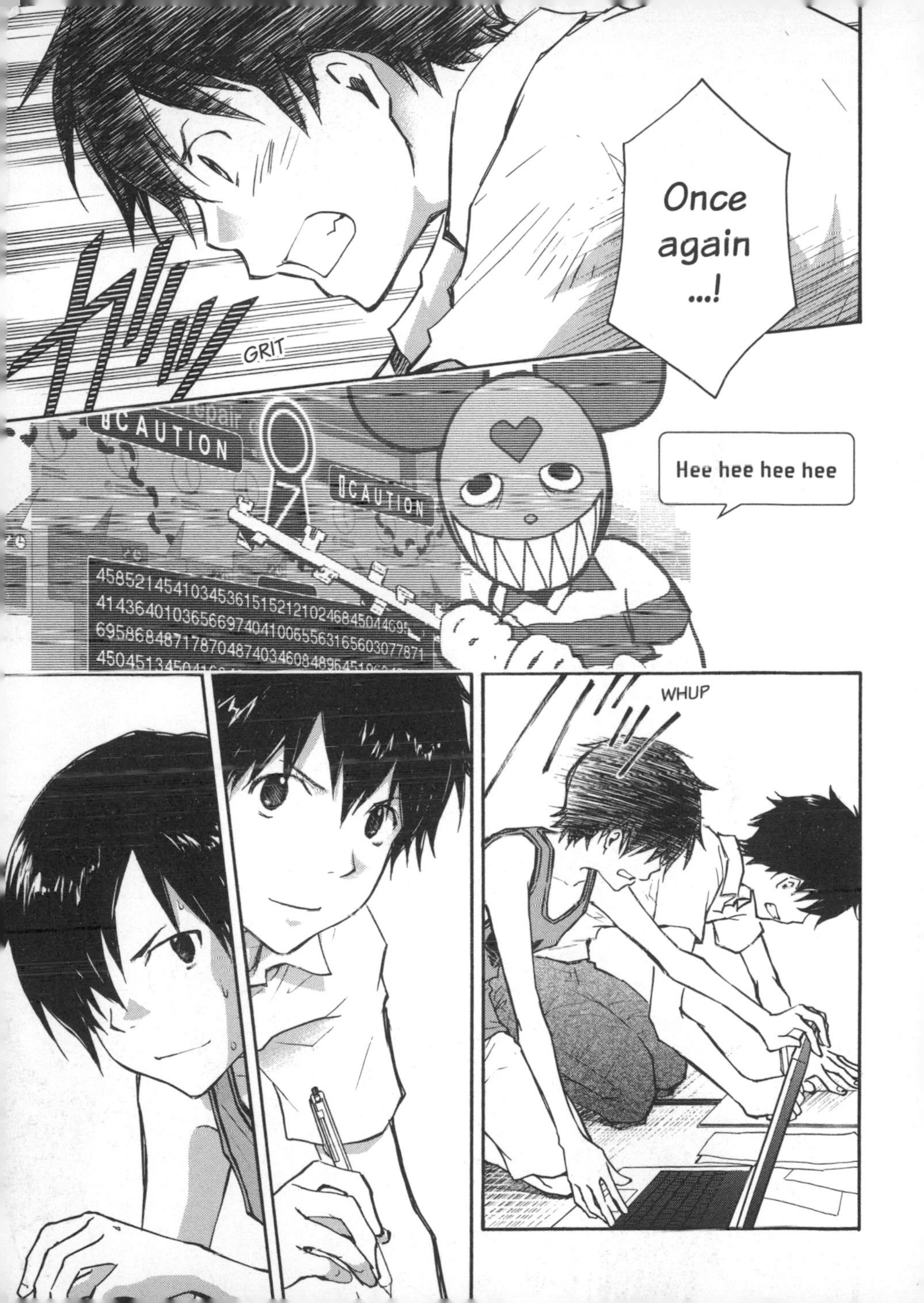
Once again ...!
GRIT
Hee hee hee hee
CAUTION
CAUTION
WHUP

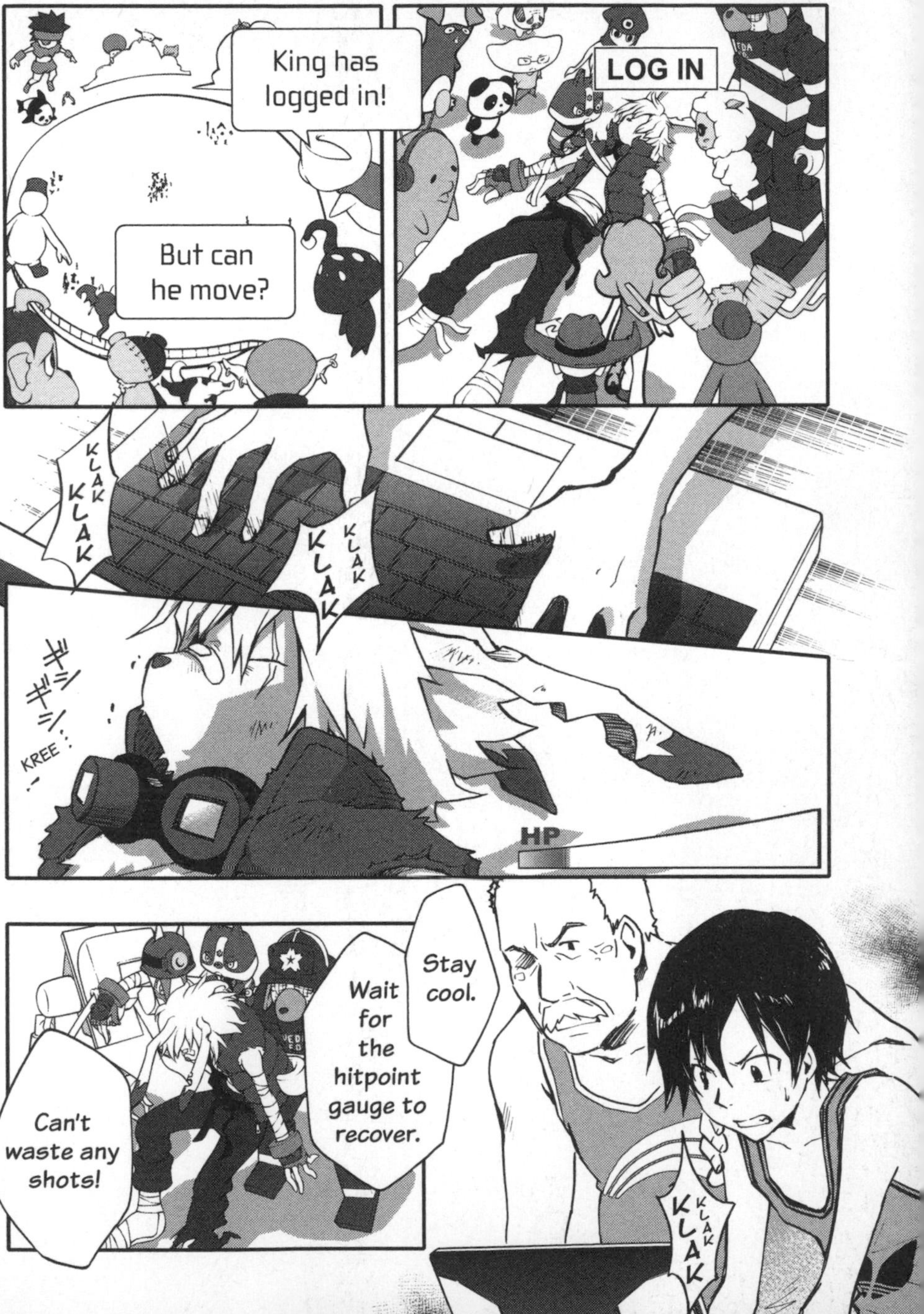
LOG IN
King has logged in!
But can he move?
KLAK KLAK
KLAK KLAK
ギシ ギシ…
KREE
HP
Stay cool.
Wait for the hitpoint gauge to recover.
KLAK KLAK
Can't waste any shots!

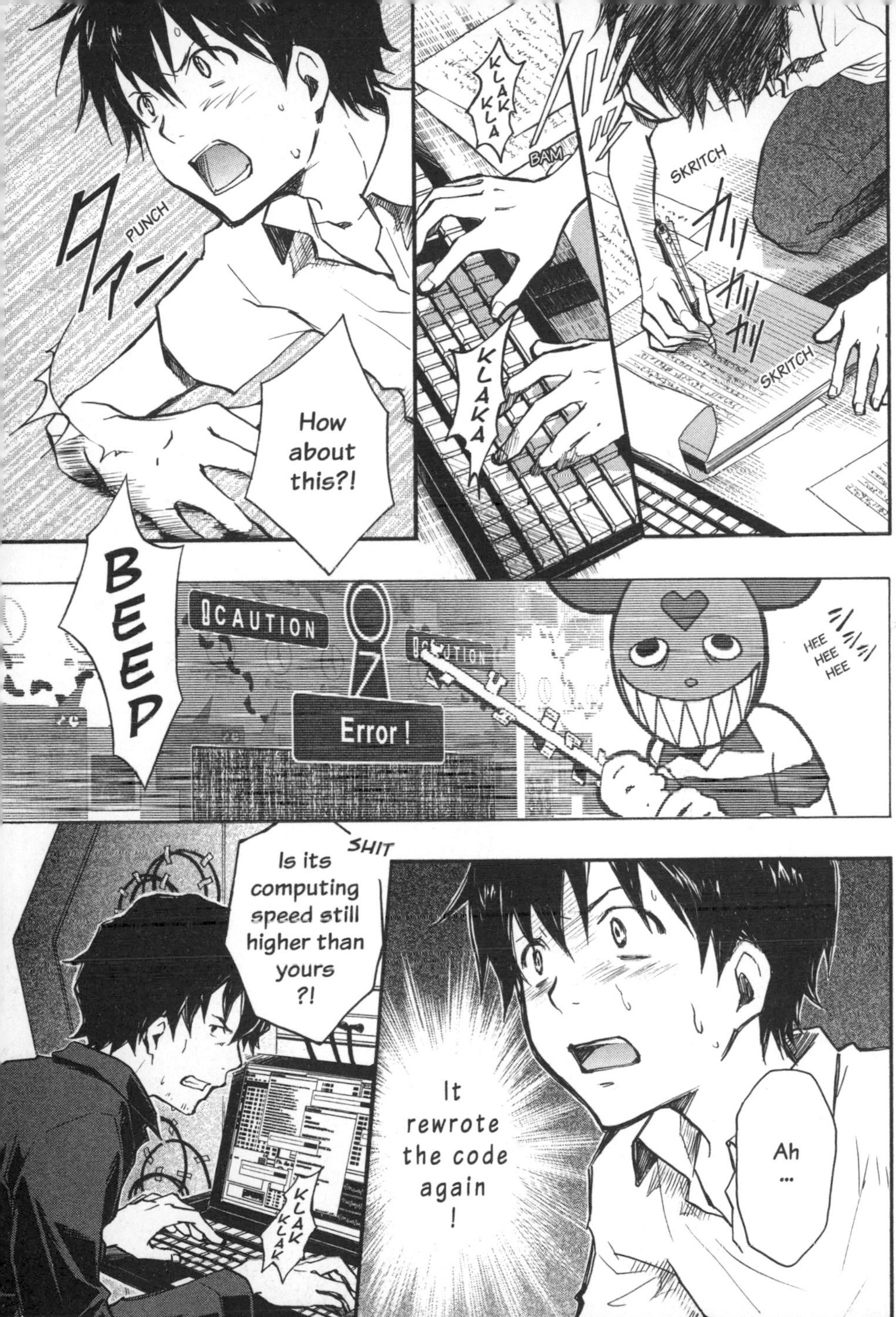

SKRITCH
SKRITCH
KLAK KLA
BAM
KLAKA
PUNCH
How about this?!
HEE HEE HEE
CAUTION
CAUTION
Error !
BEEP
Ah ...
It rewrote the code again !
SHIT
Is its computing speed still higher than yours ?!
KLAK KLAK

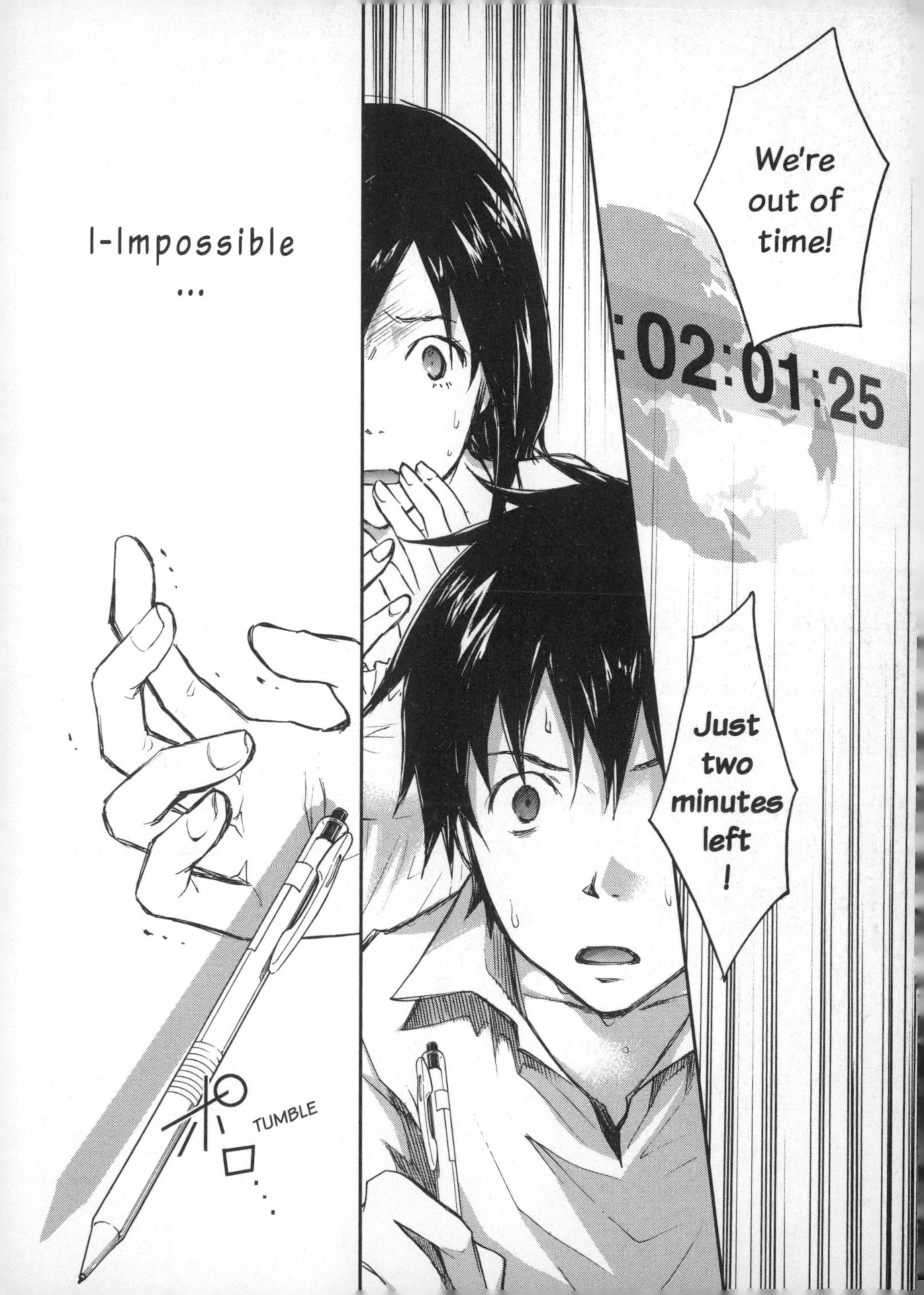
We're out of time!
02:01:25
Just two minutes left!
I-Impossible ...
TUMBLE

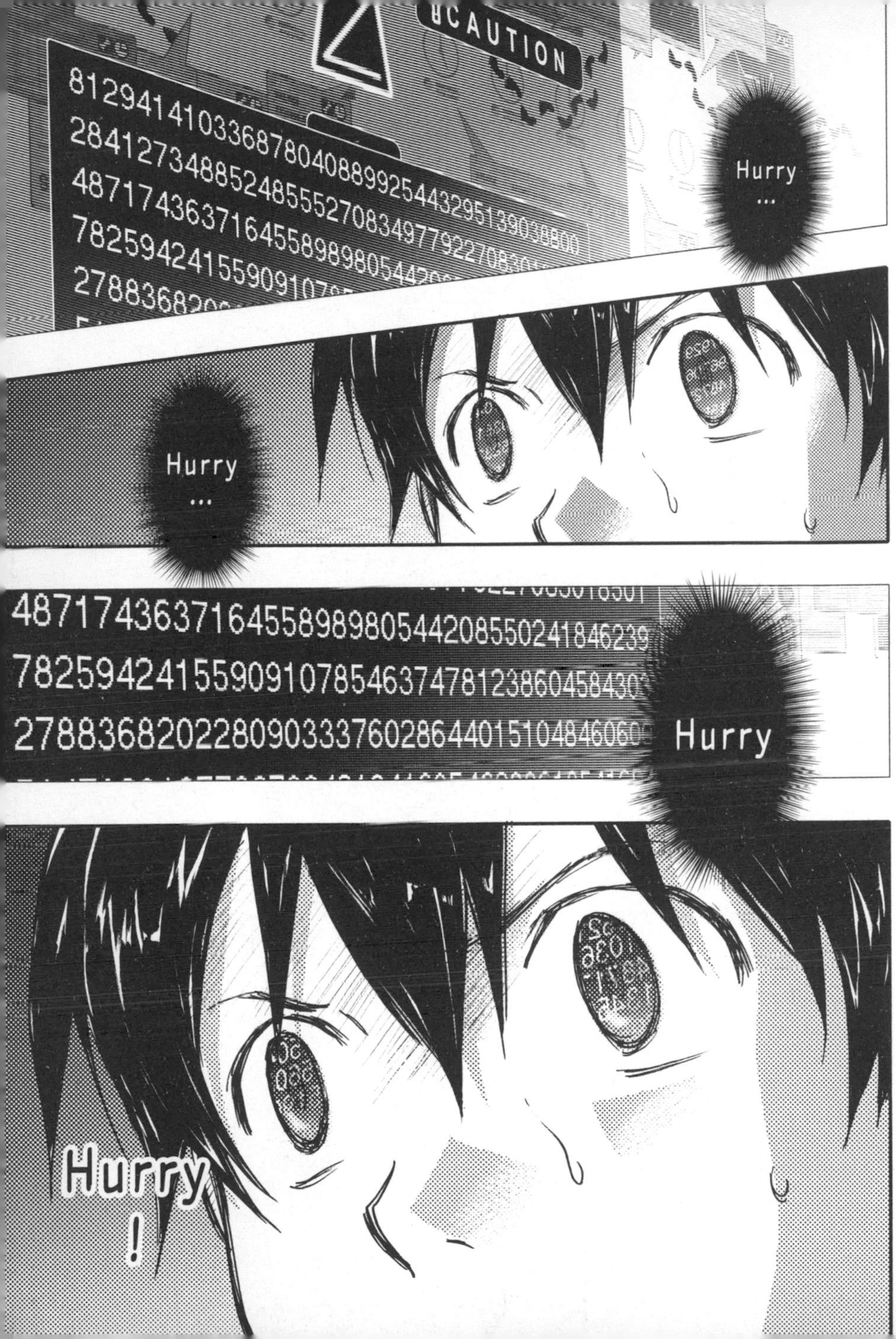
CAUTION
Hurry …
Hurry …
487174363716455898980544208550241846239
782594241559091078546374781238604584309
278836820228090333760286440151048460606
Hurry
Hurry !

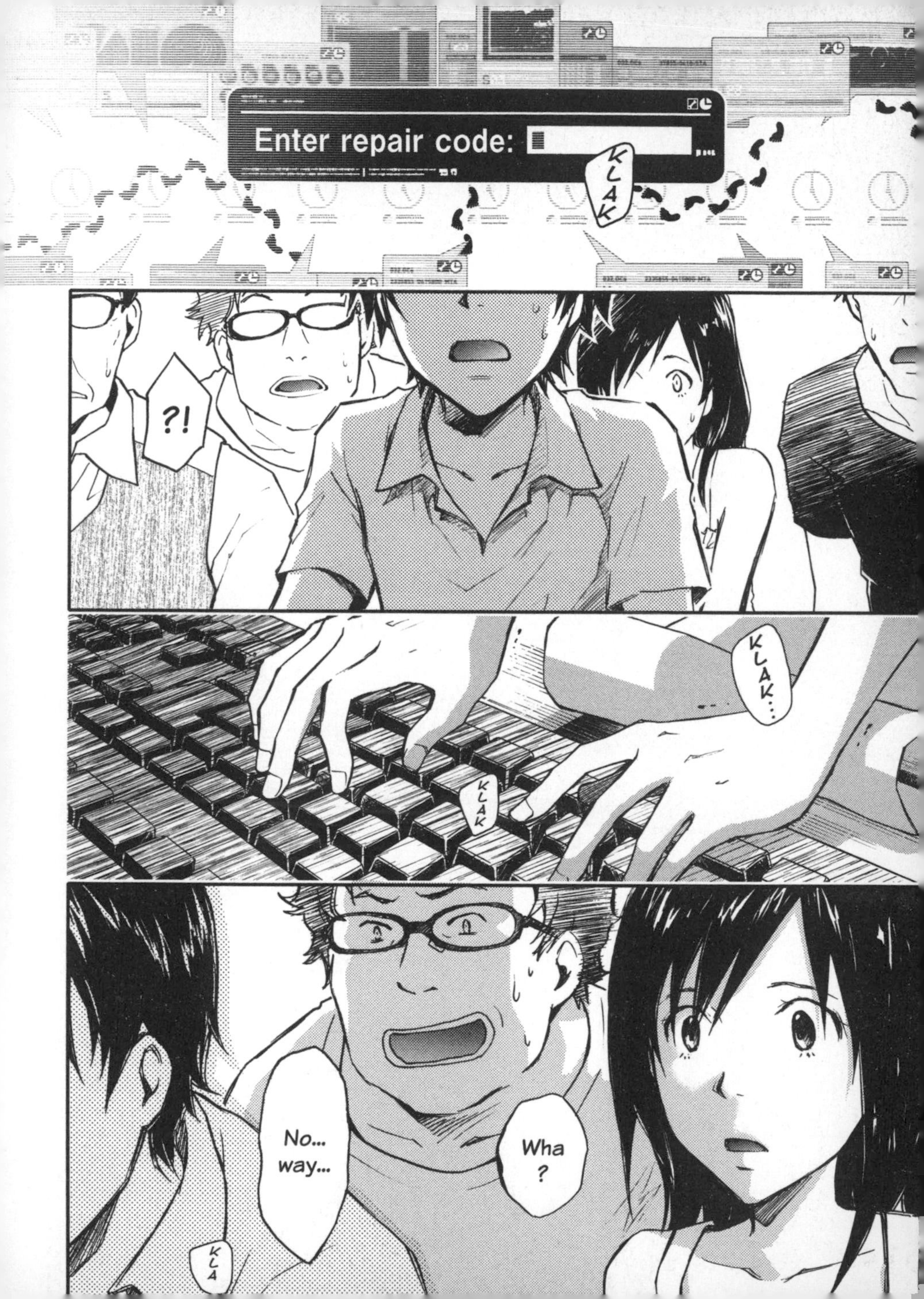
Enter repair code:
KLAK
?!
KLAK...
KLAK
Wha ?
No... way...
KLA

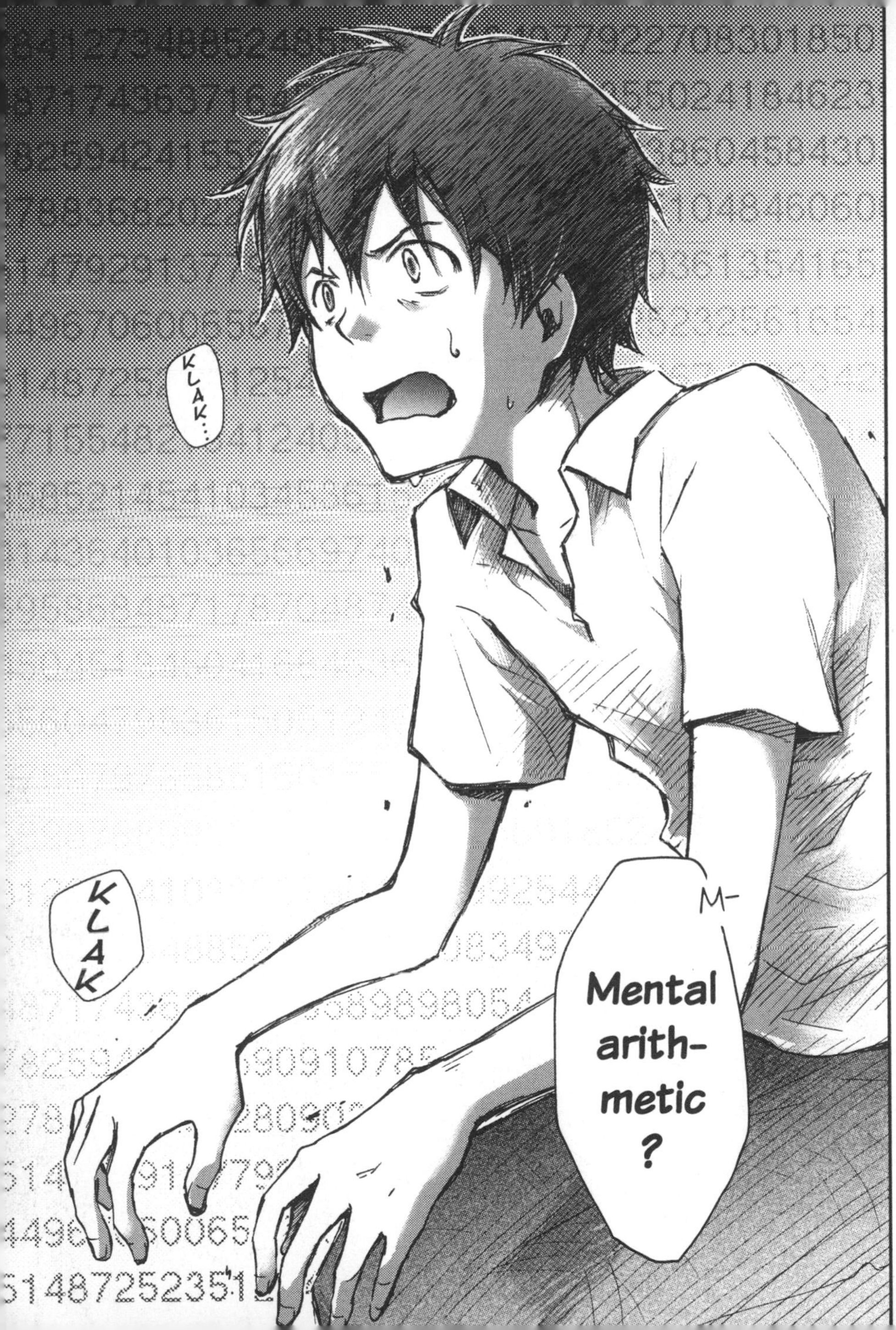
KLAK...
M-
Mental arith-metic?
KLAK

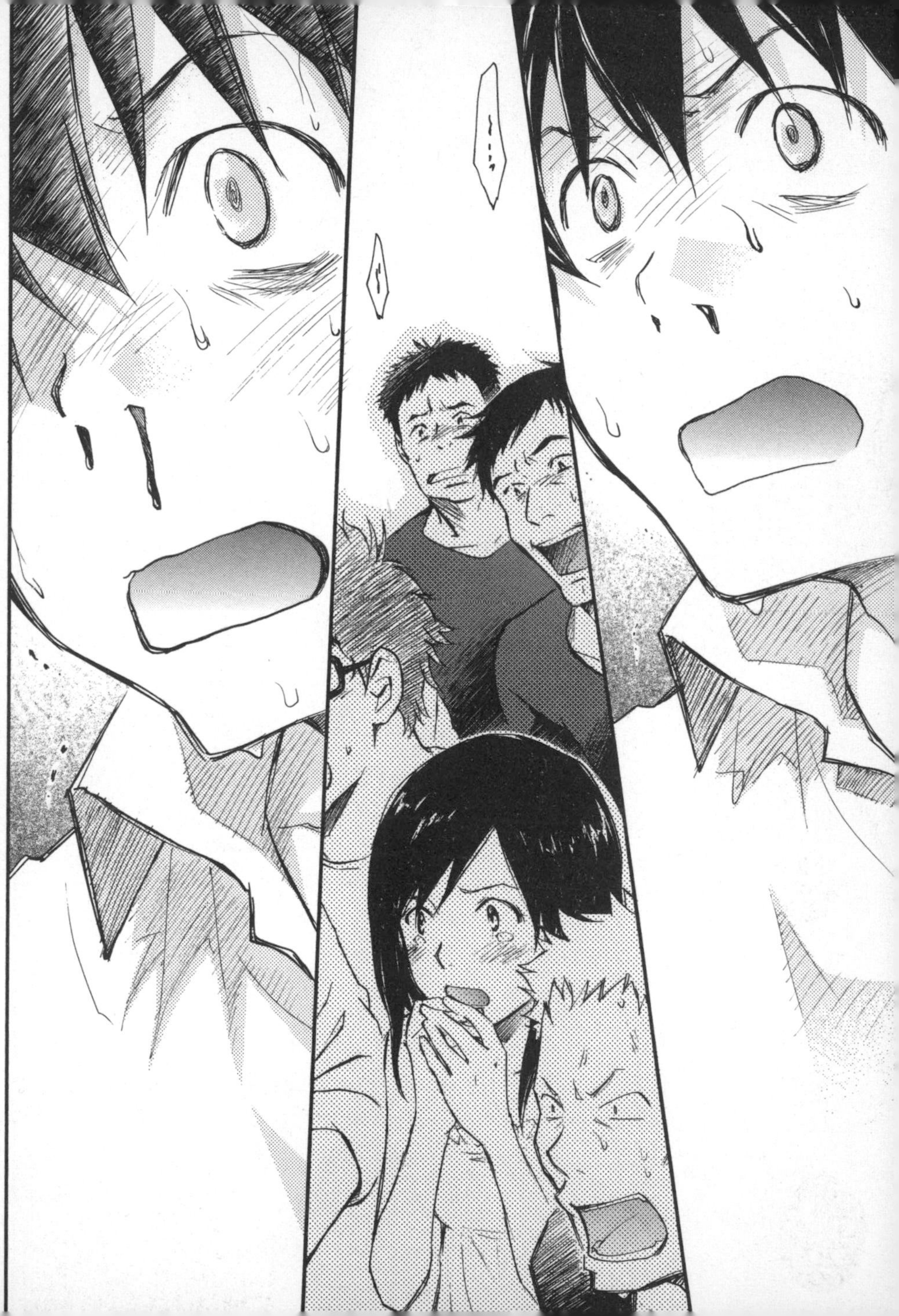

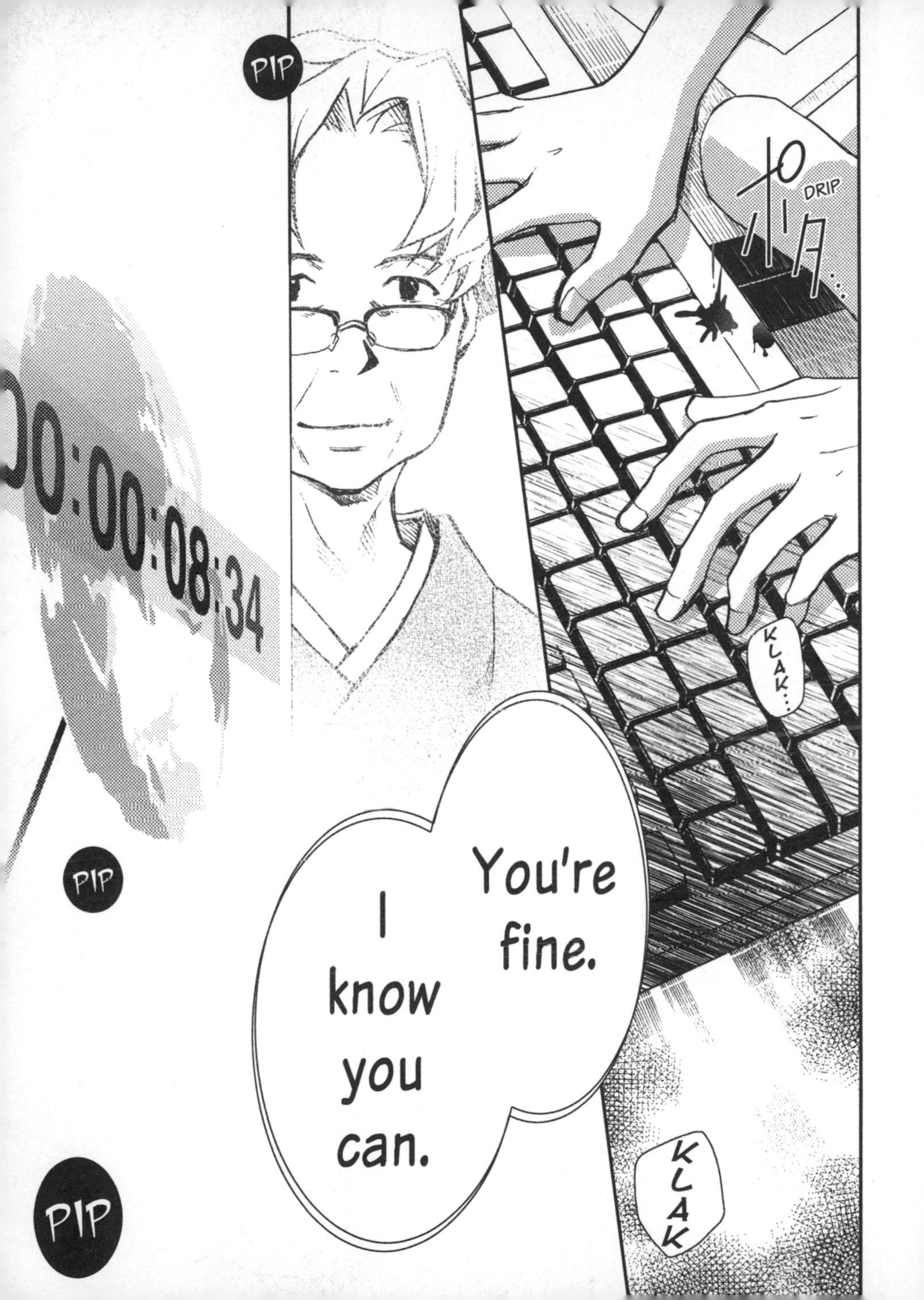

ポタ…
DRIP
KLAK…
PIP
You're fine.
I know you can.
KLAK
00:00:08:34
PIP
PIP

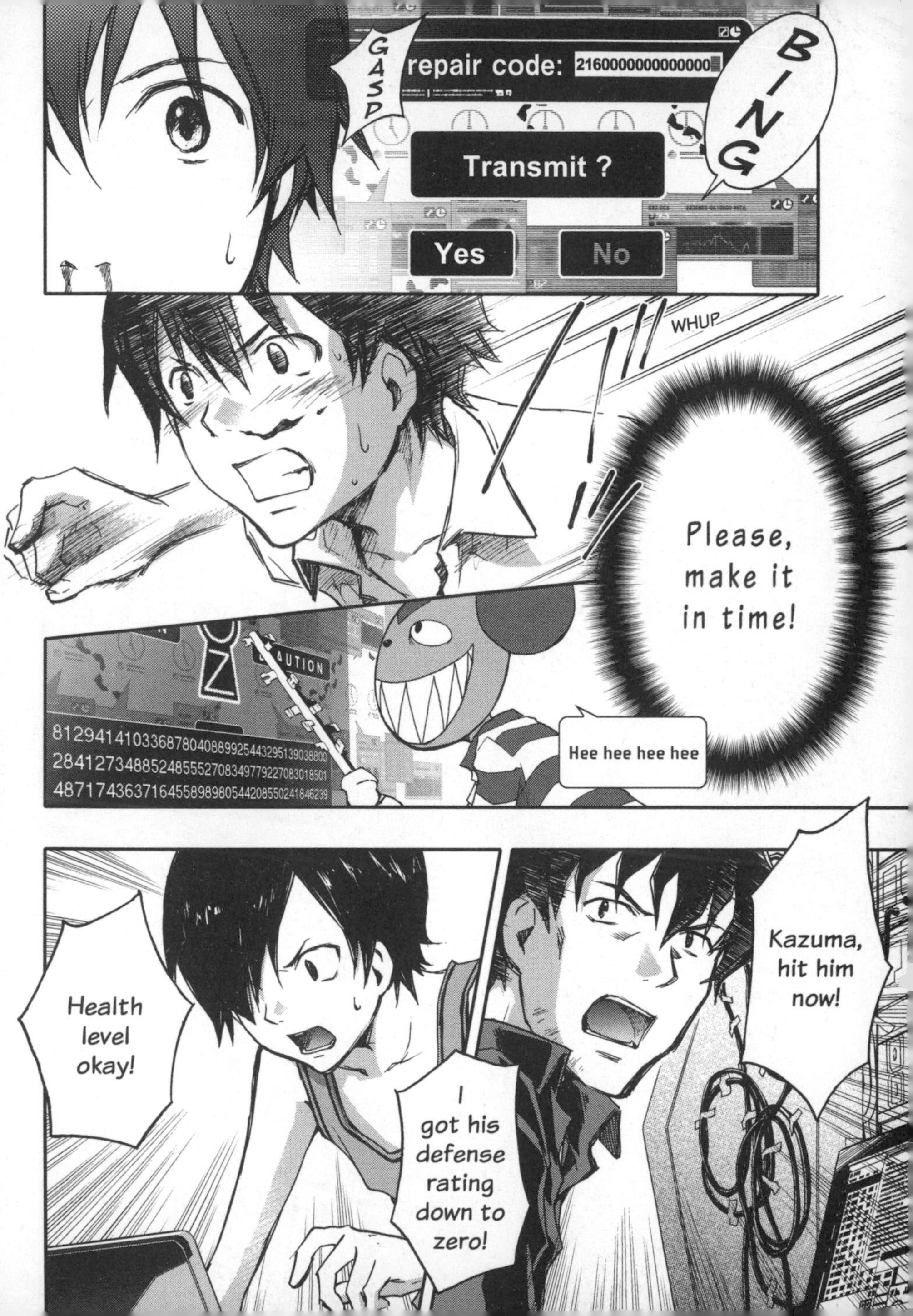
BING
GASP
repair code: 2160000000000000
Transmit ?
Yes
No
WHUP
Please, make it in time!
Hee hee hee hee
81294141033687804088992544329513903880 0
28412734885248555270834977922708301850 1
48717436371645589898054420855024184623 9
Kazuma, hit him now!
Health level okay!
I got his defense rating down to zero!

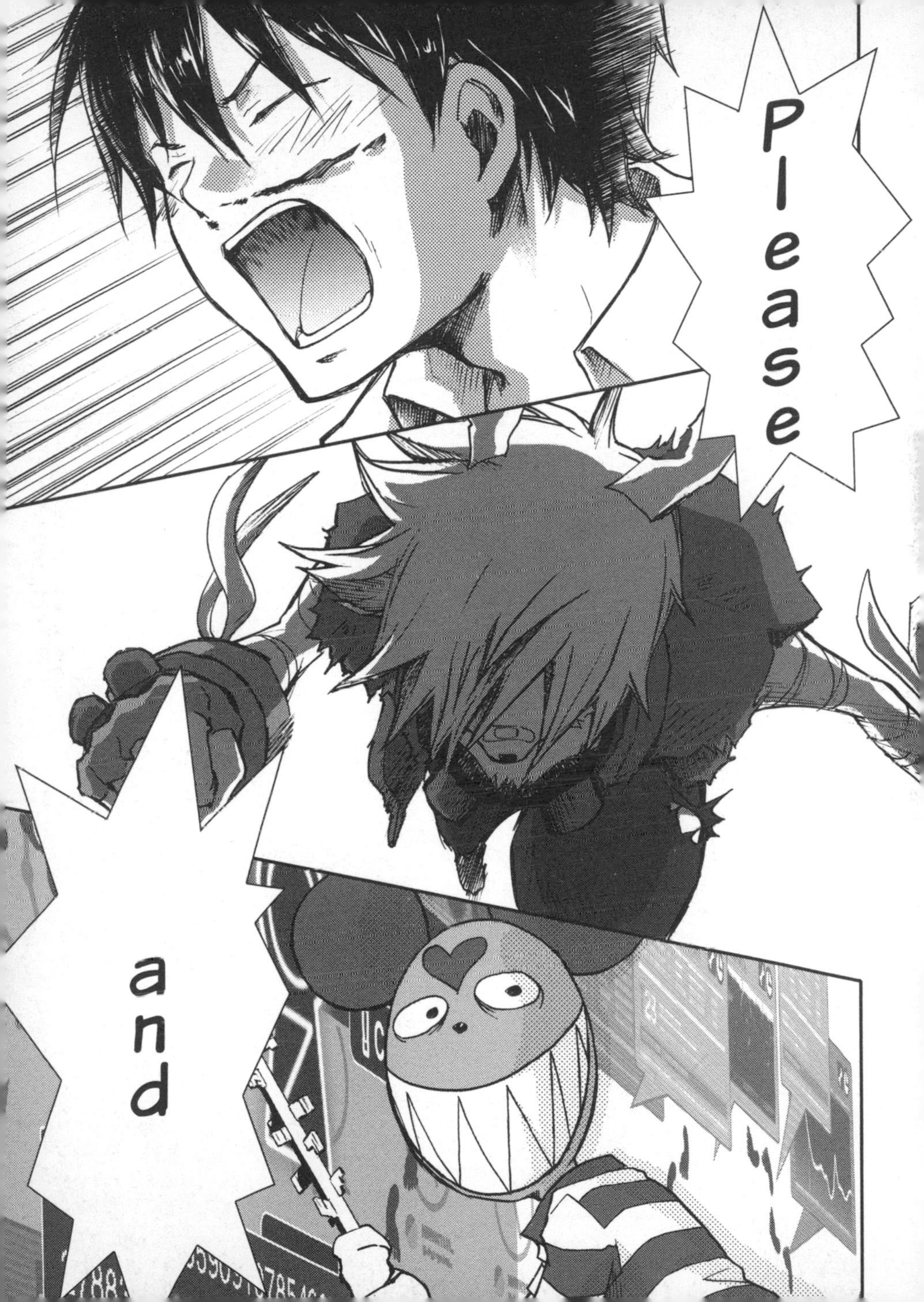
Please
and

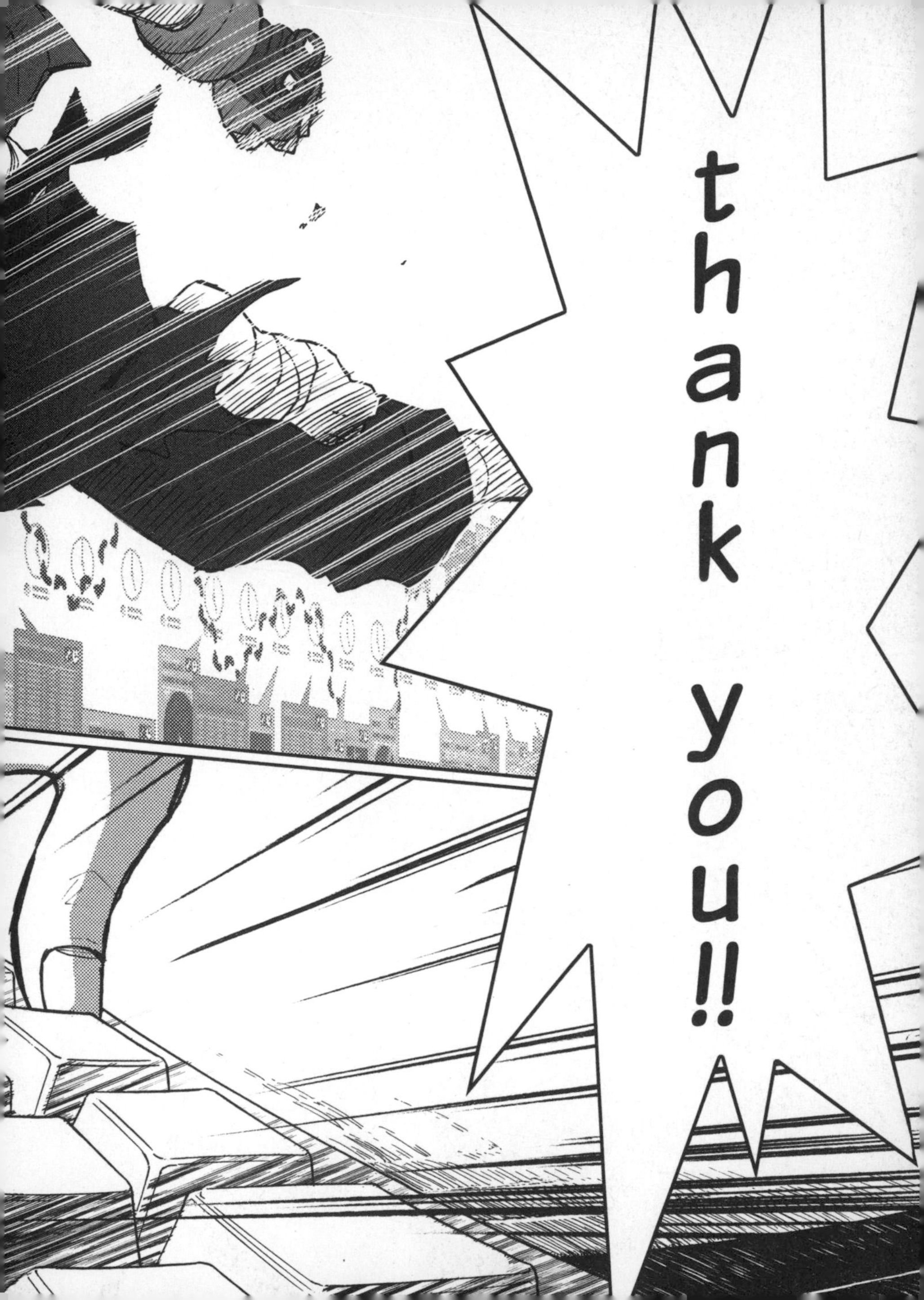
thank you!!

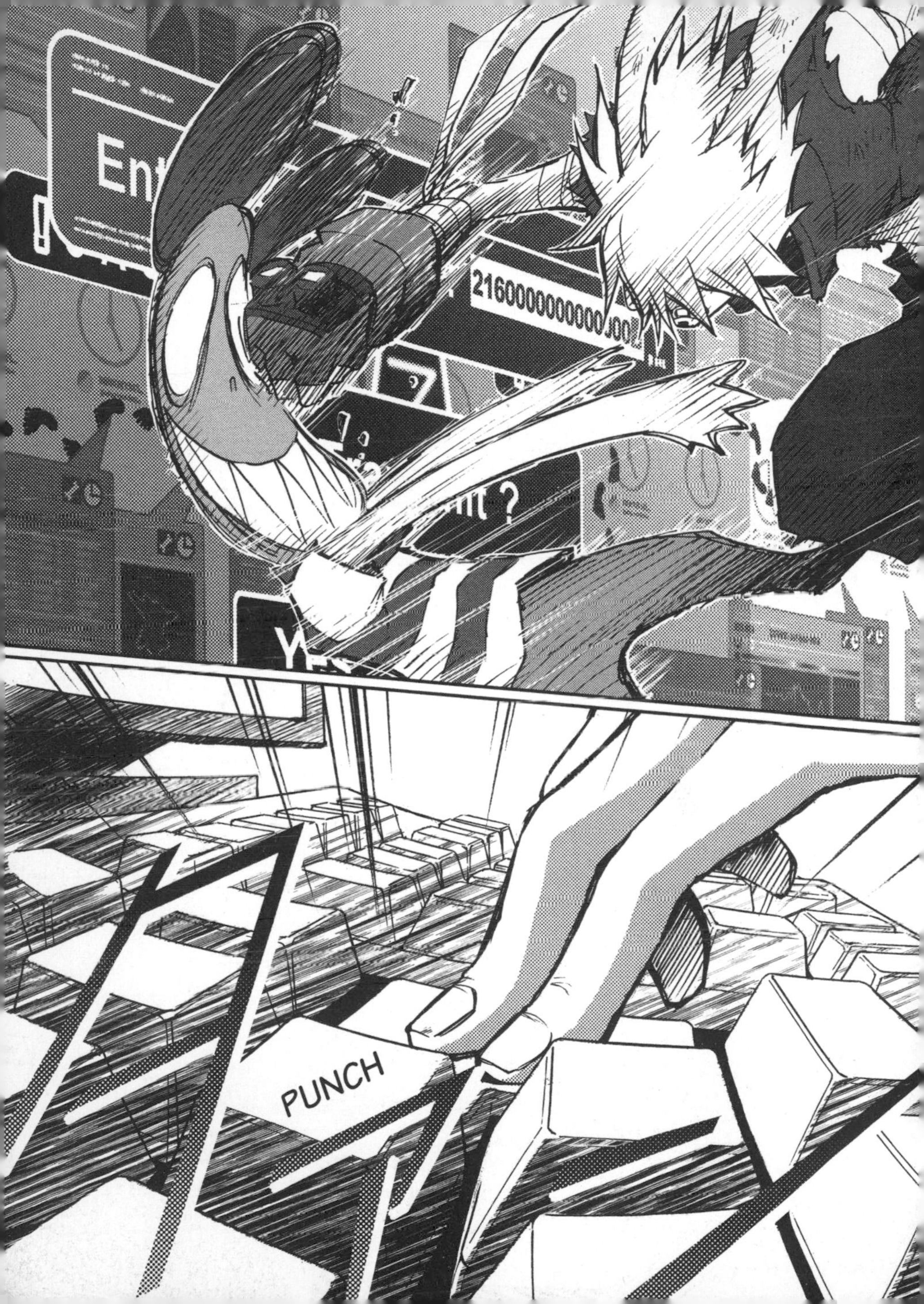

2160000000000J00
Ent
nt ?
PUNCH

TIK
カチ
Processing...
カチ
TIK
TIK
カチ
Processing...
カチ
カチ
TIK

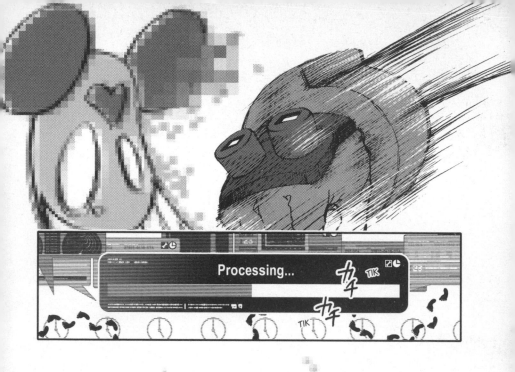

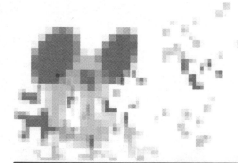

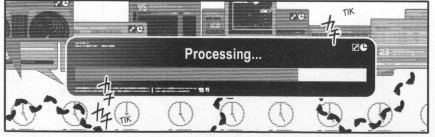

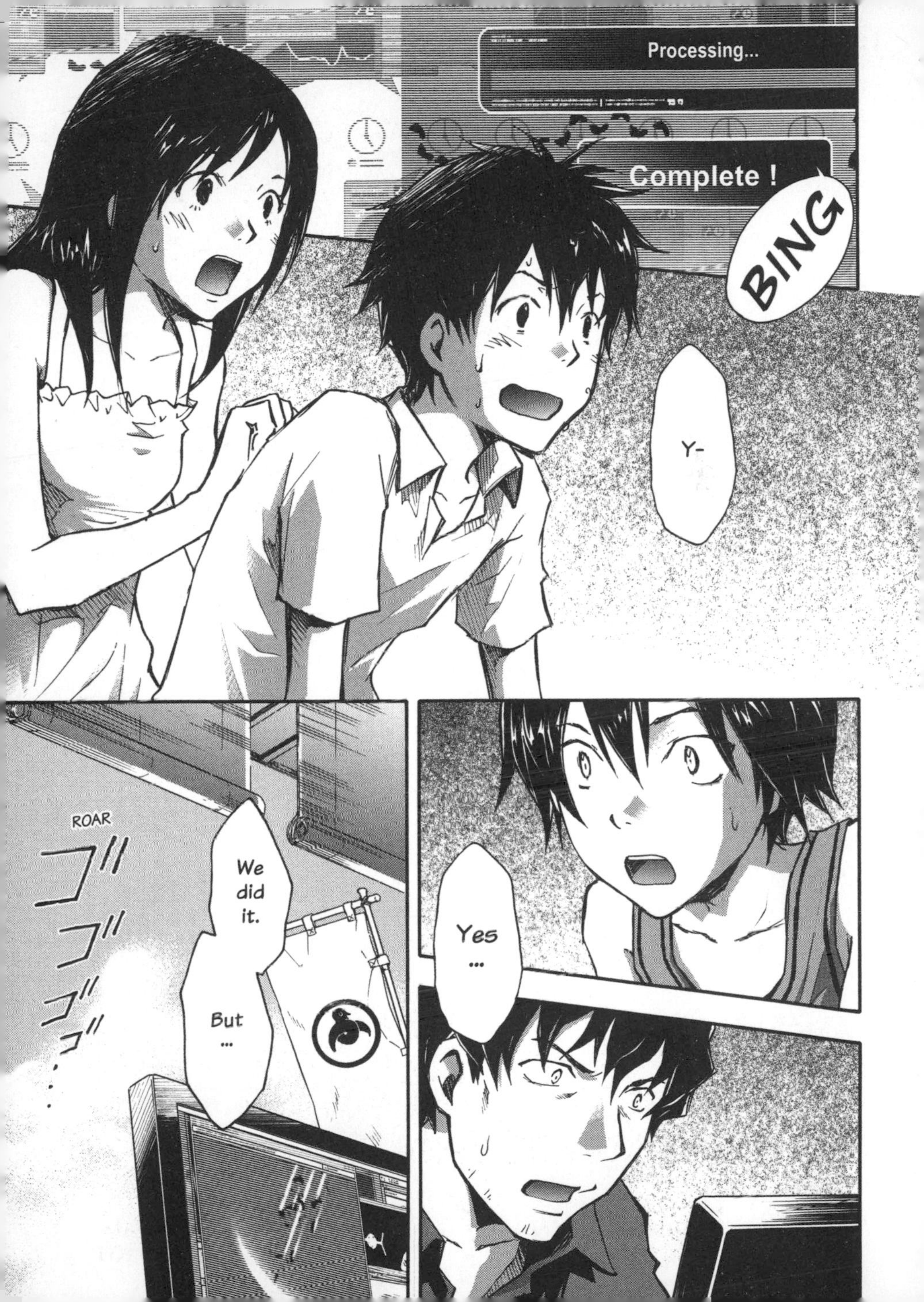

Processing...
Complete !
BING
Y-
Yes ...
We did it.
But ...
ROAR
ゴゴゴゴ...

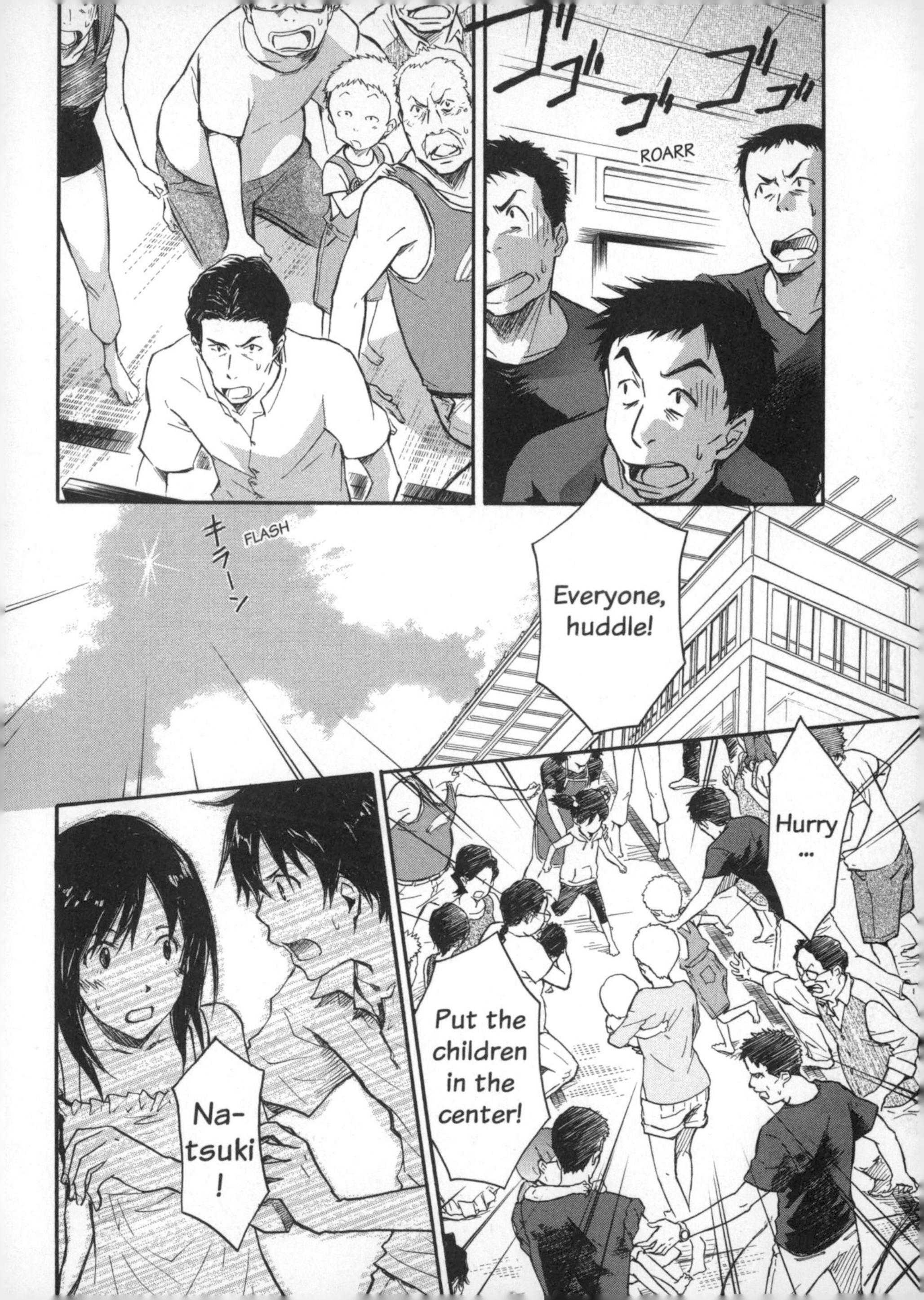
ゴゴゴゴゴ
ROARR
Everyone, huddle!
キラーン
FLASH
Hurry ...
Put the children in the center!
Na-tsuki!

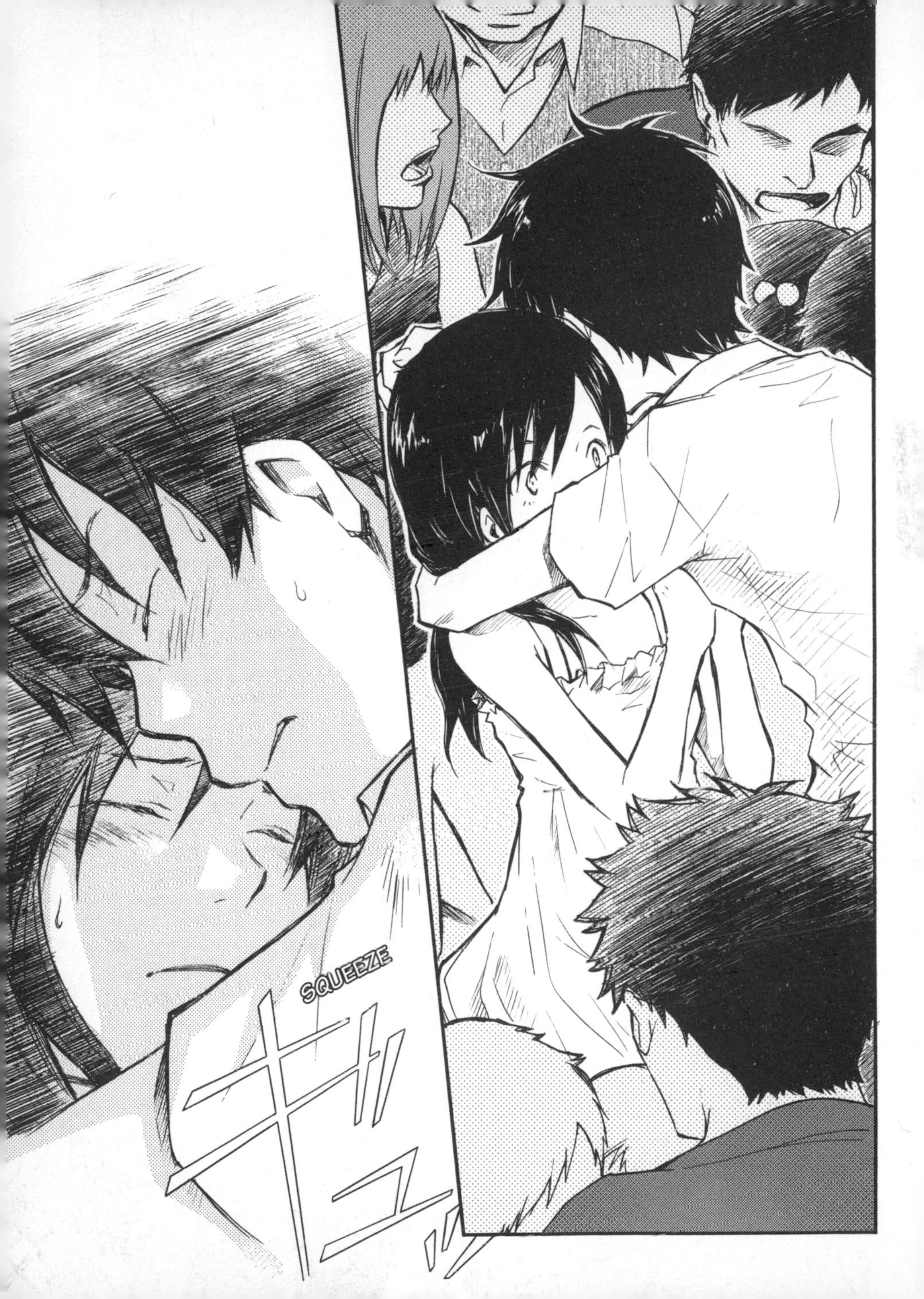
SQUEEZE
ギュッ

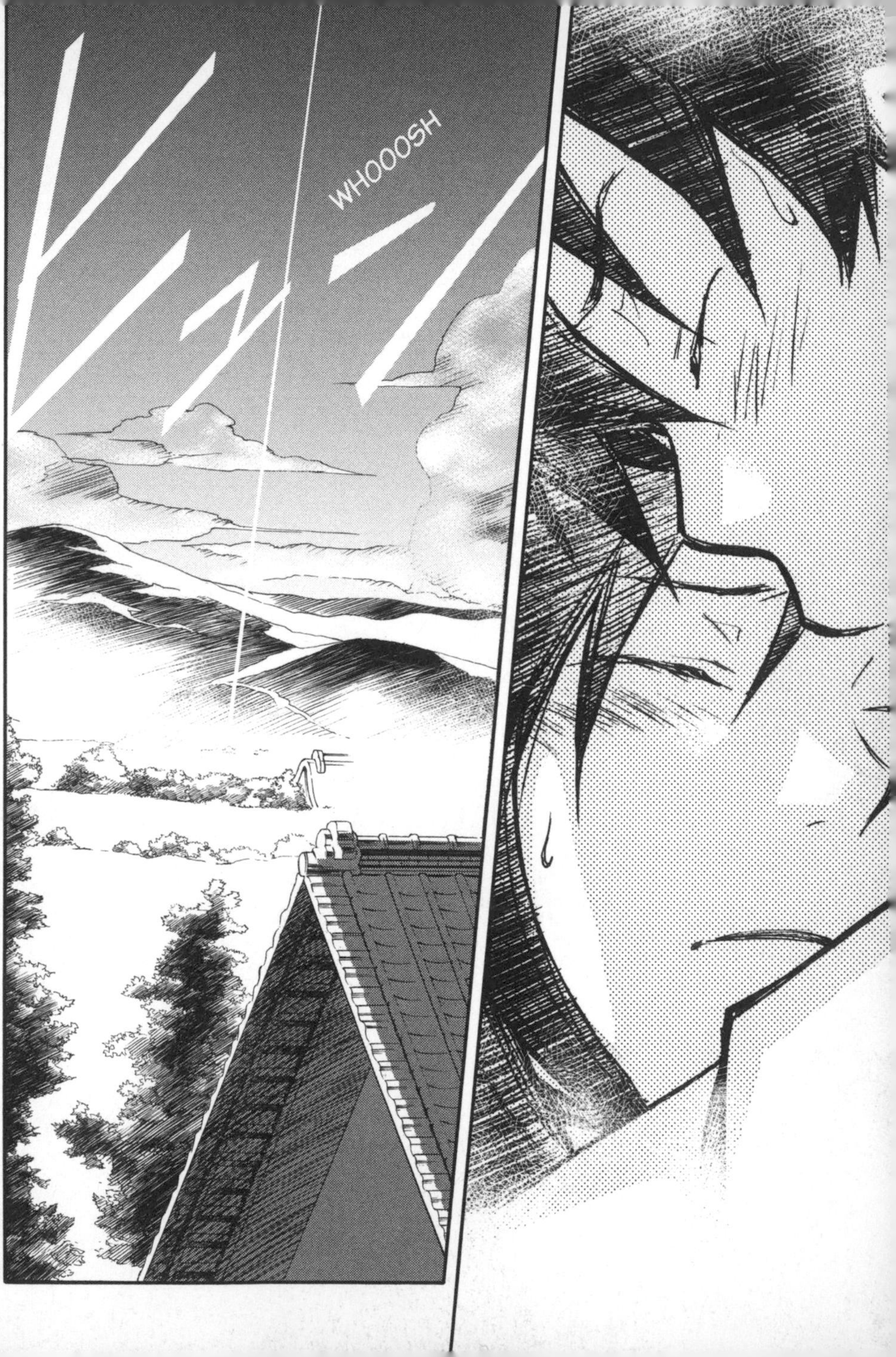
WHOOOSH

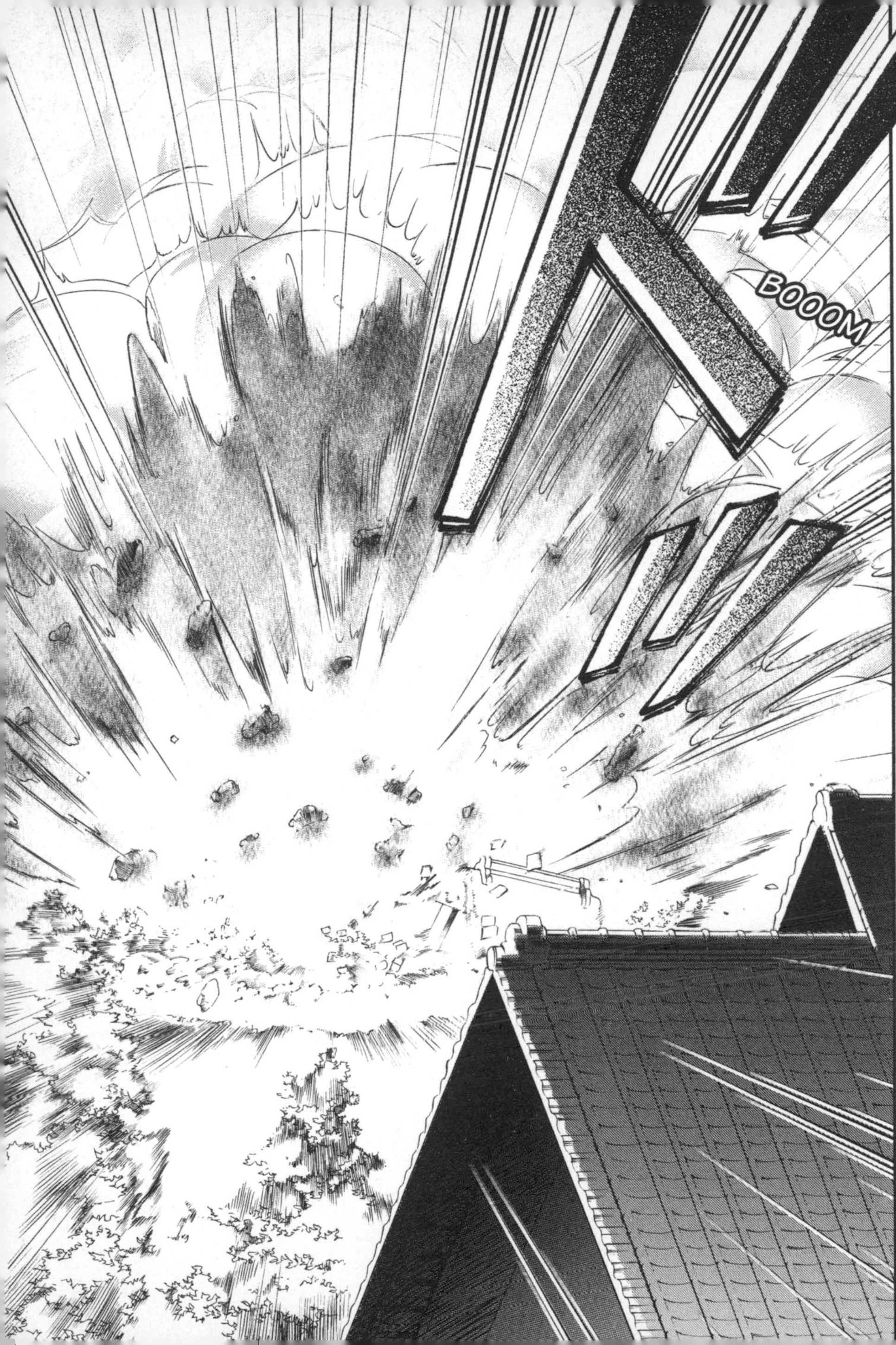
BOOOM

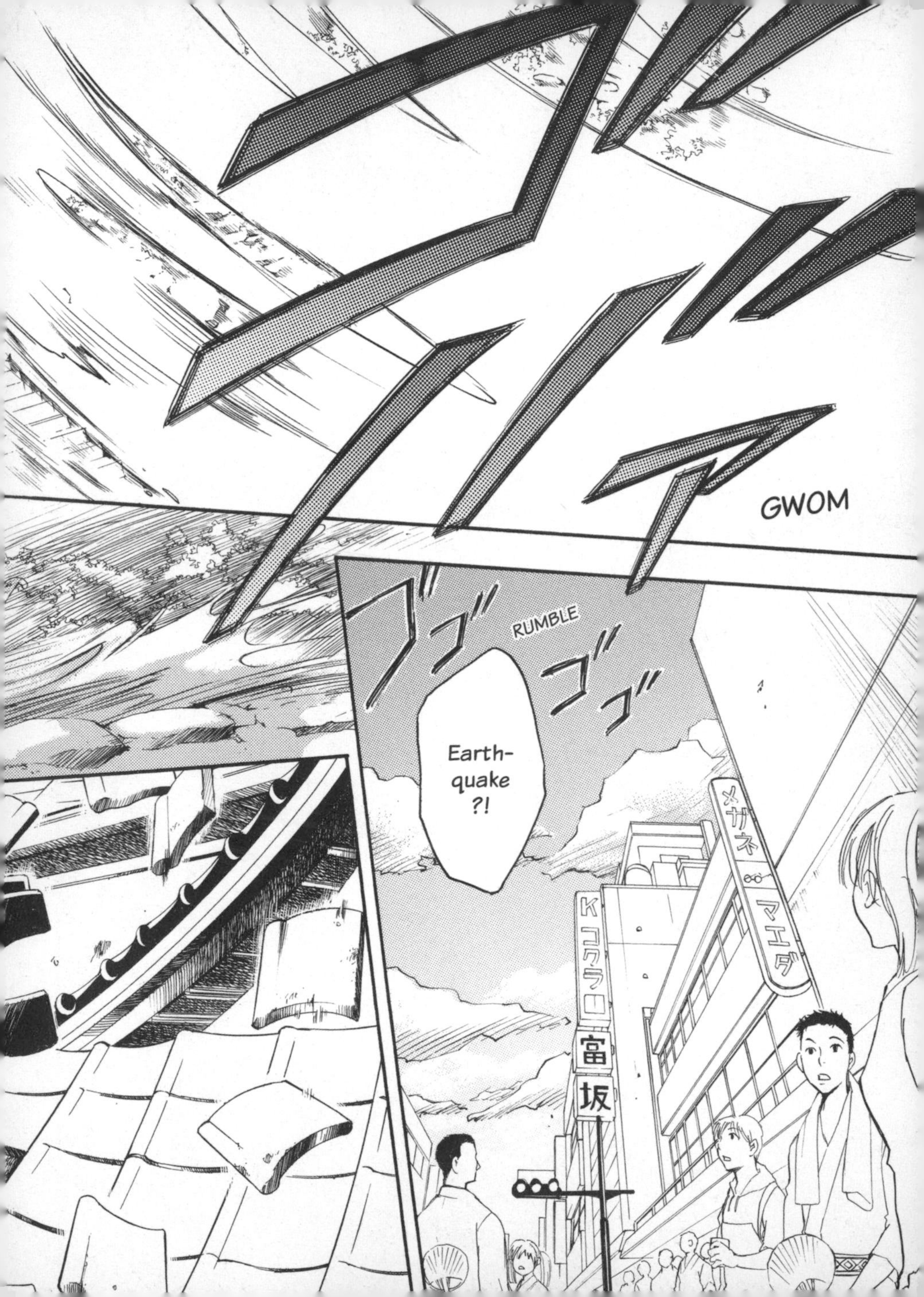
GWOM
RUMBLE
Earth-quake ?!
メガネ
マエダ
Kコクラ
富坂

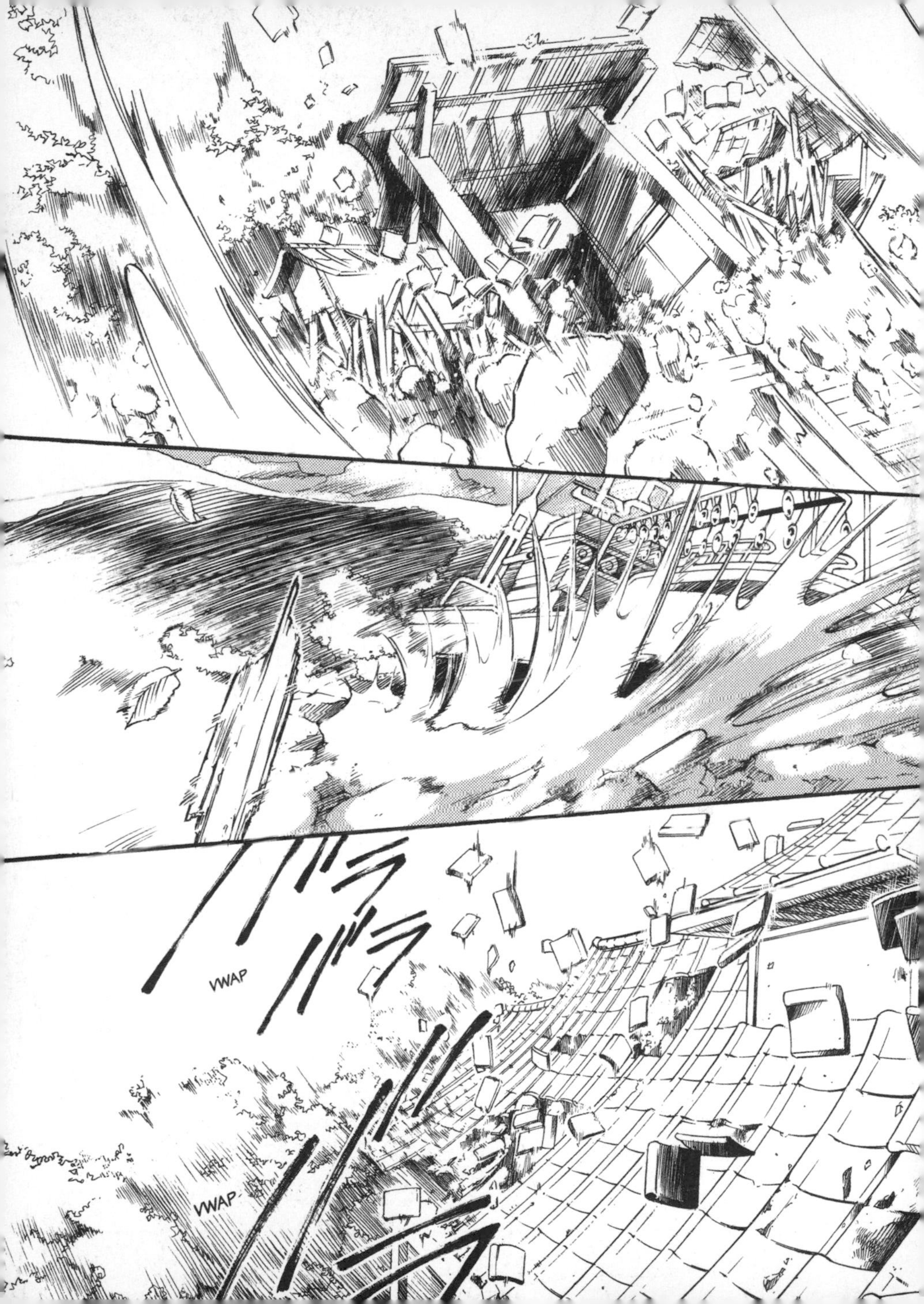

バラバラ
VWAP
VWAP

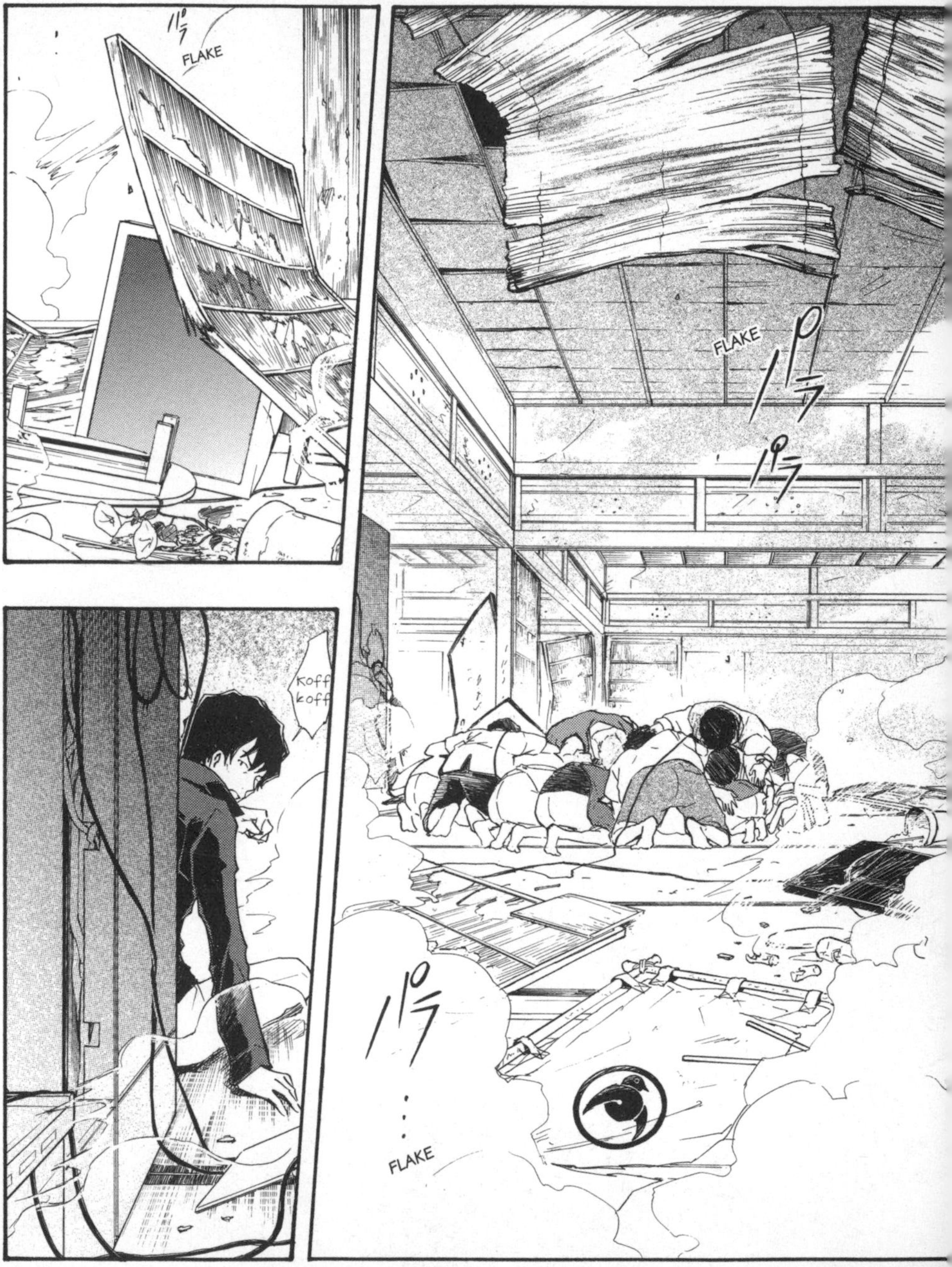
パ
FLAKE
パラ
パラ
パラ
...
FLAKE
パラ
FLAKE
koff
koff

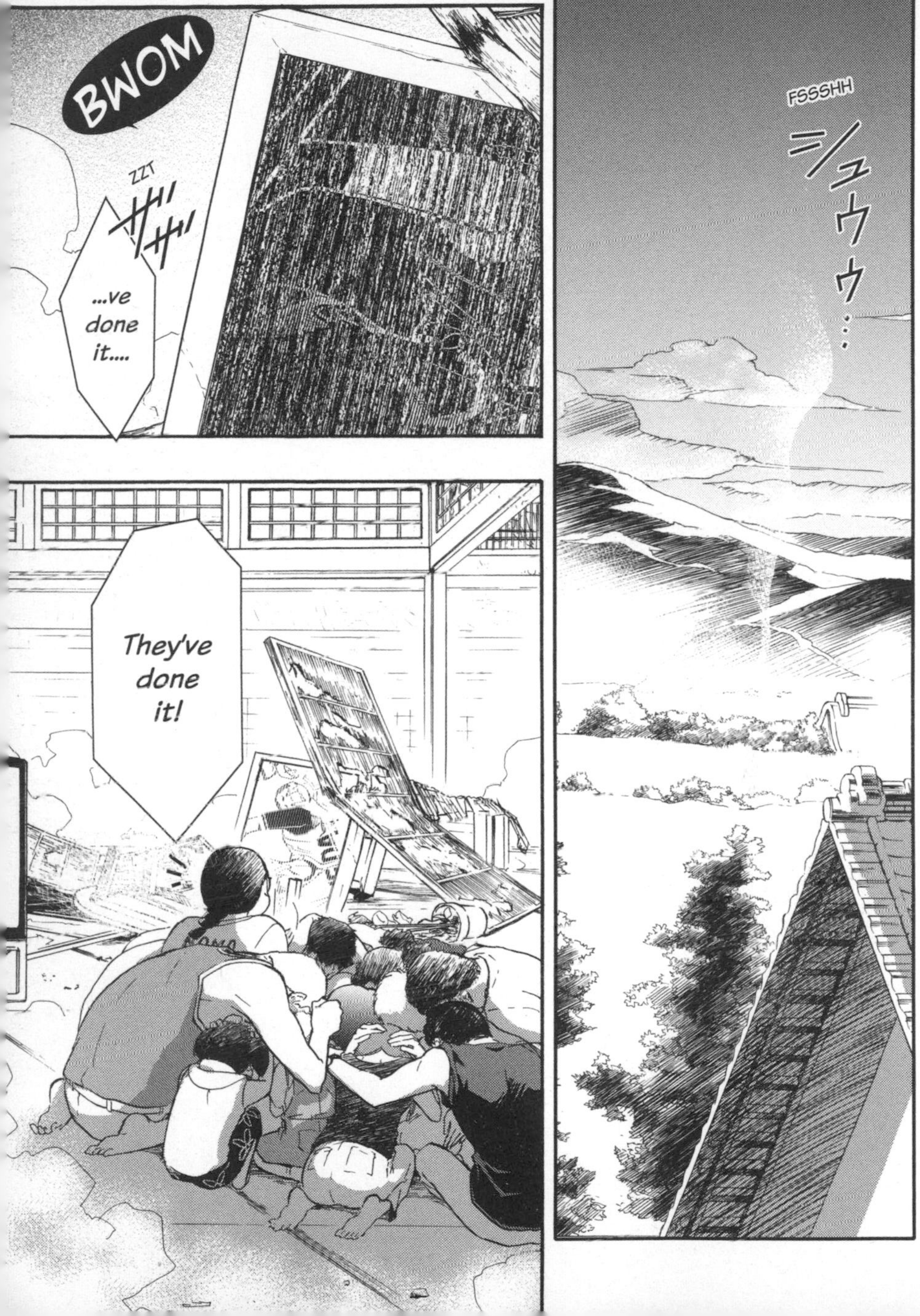
FSSSHH
シュウウウ…
BWOM
ZZT
ザザザザ
...ve done it....
They've done it!

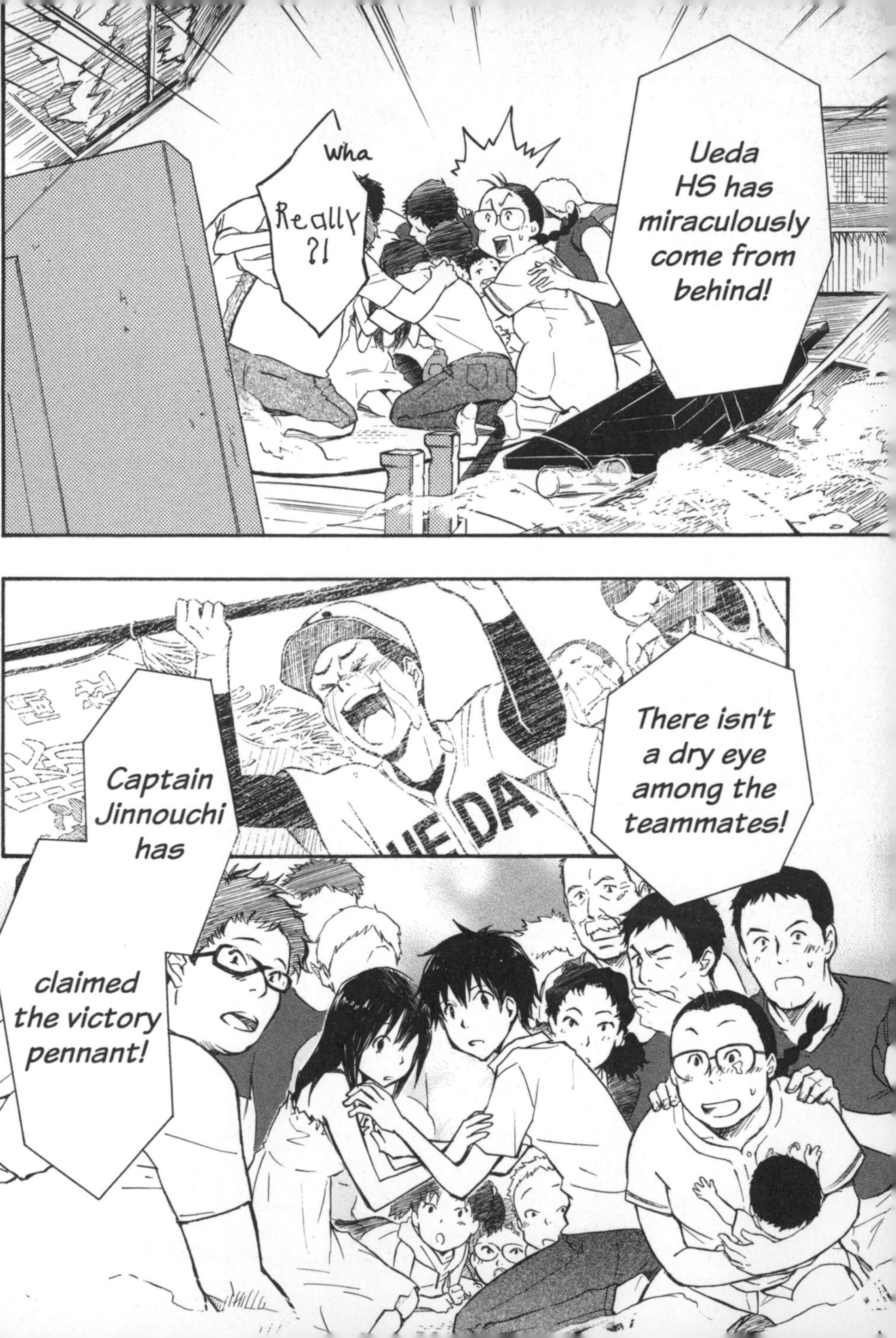
Ueda HS has miraculously come from behind!
Wha
Really ?!
There isn't a dry eye among the teammates!
Captain Jinnouchi has claimed the victory pennant!

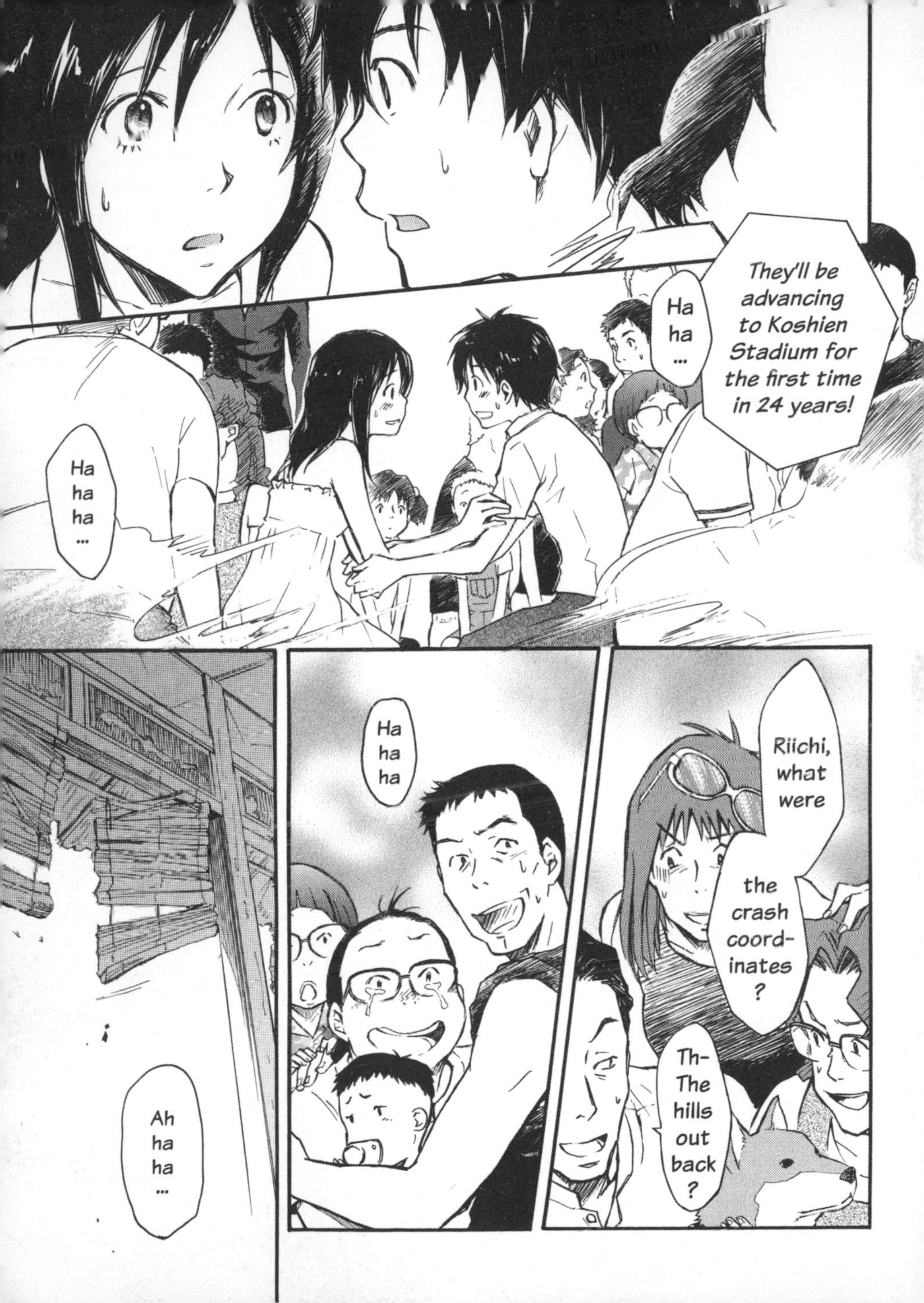
They'll be advancing to Koshien Stadium for the first time in 24 years!
Ha ha ...
Ha ha ha ...
Riichi, what were the crash coordinates?
Th- The hills out back?
Ha ha ha
Ah ha ha ...

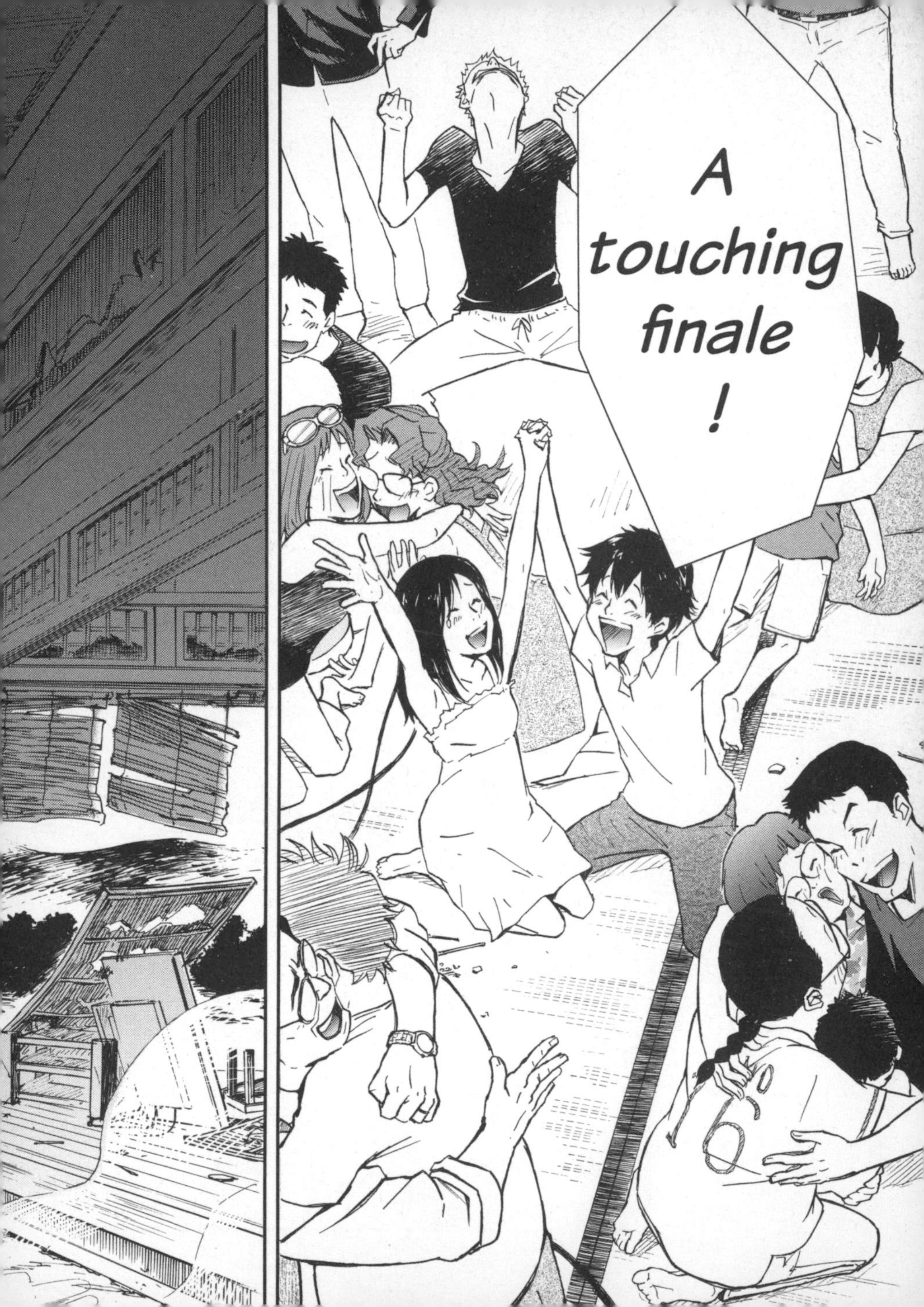
A touching finale !

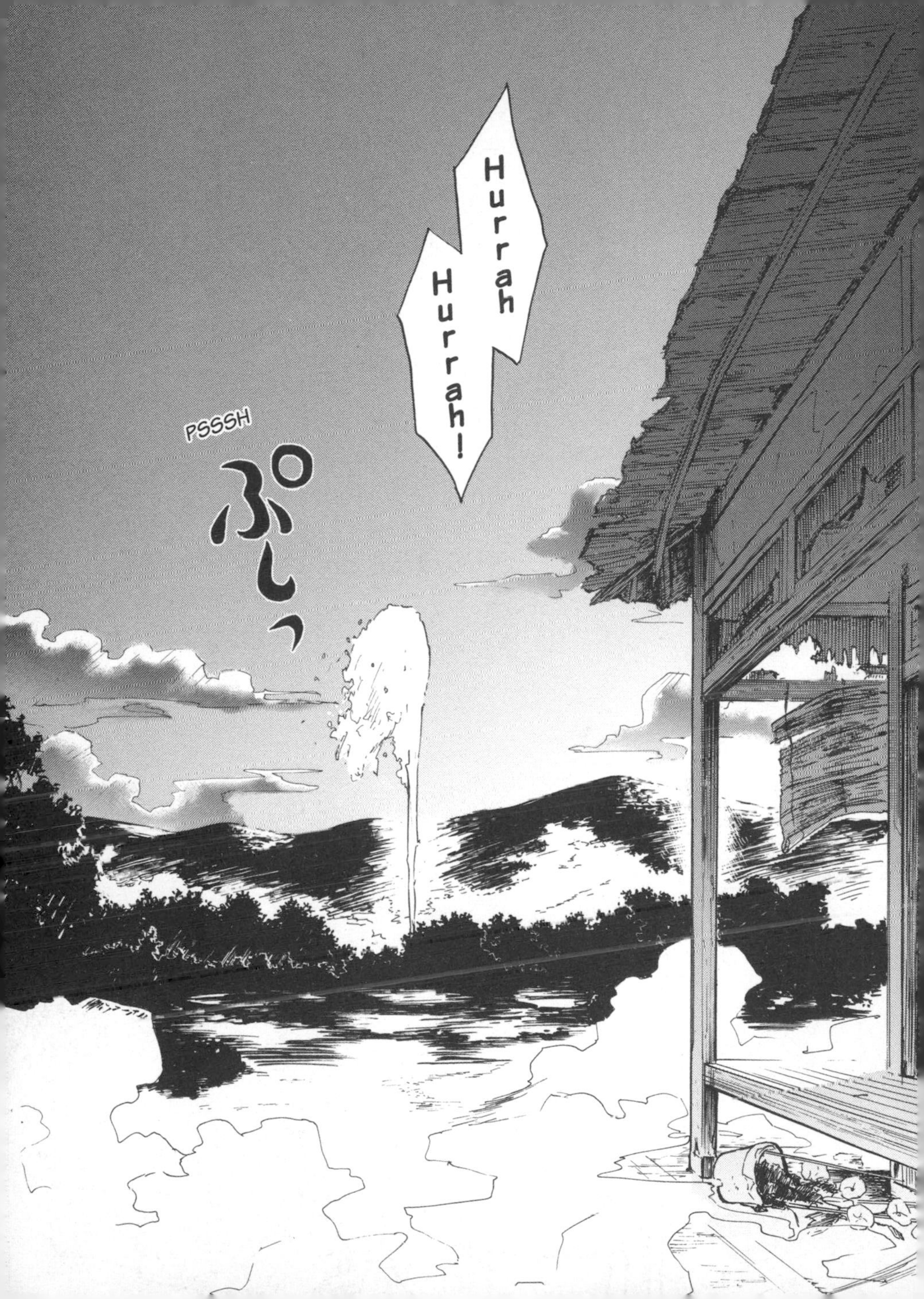
Hurrah Hurrah!
PSSSH
ぷしっ

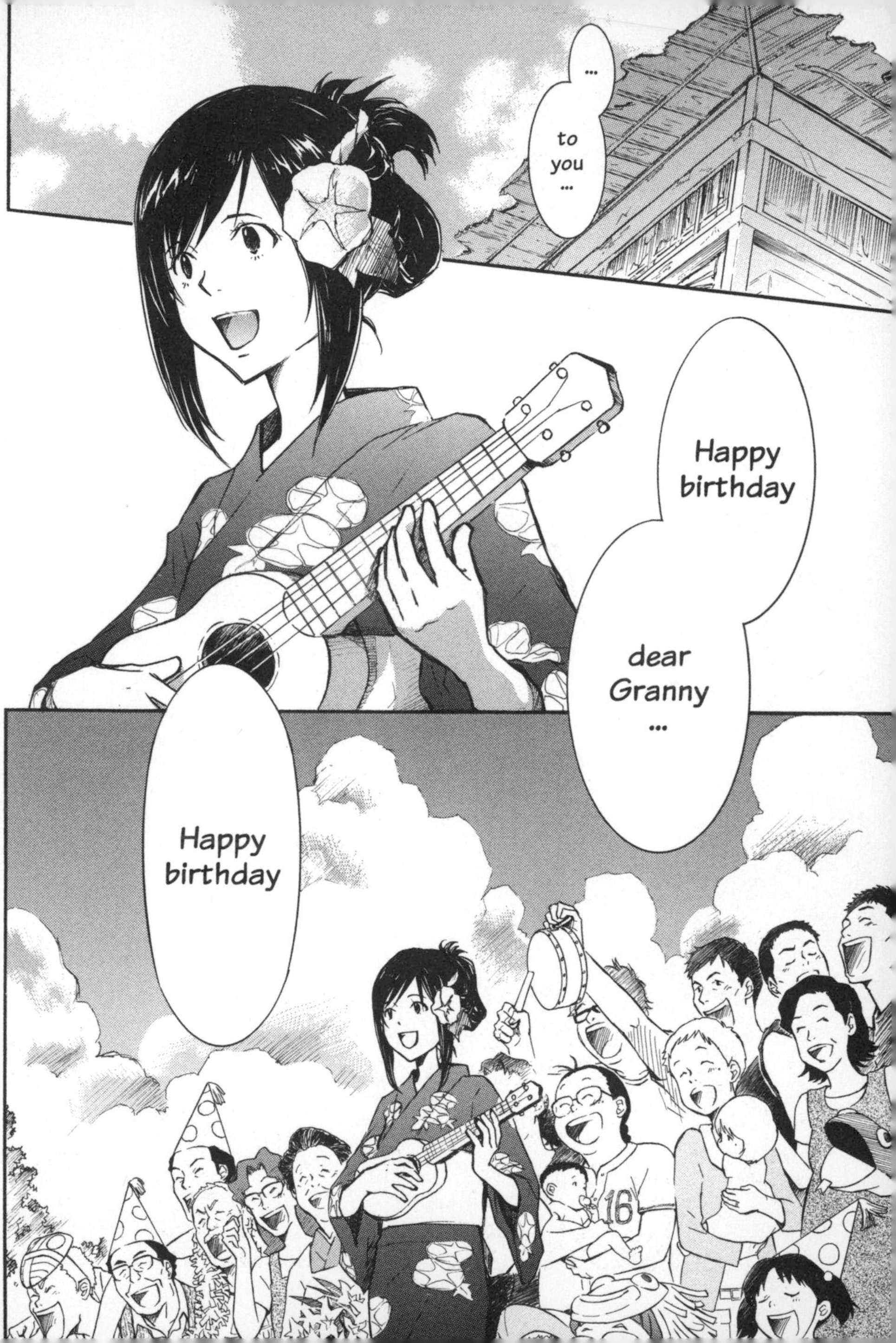
... to you ...
Happy birthday
dear Granny ...
Happy birthday

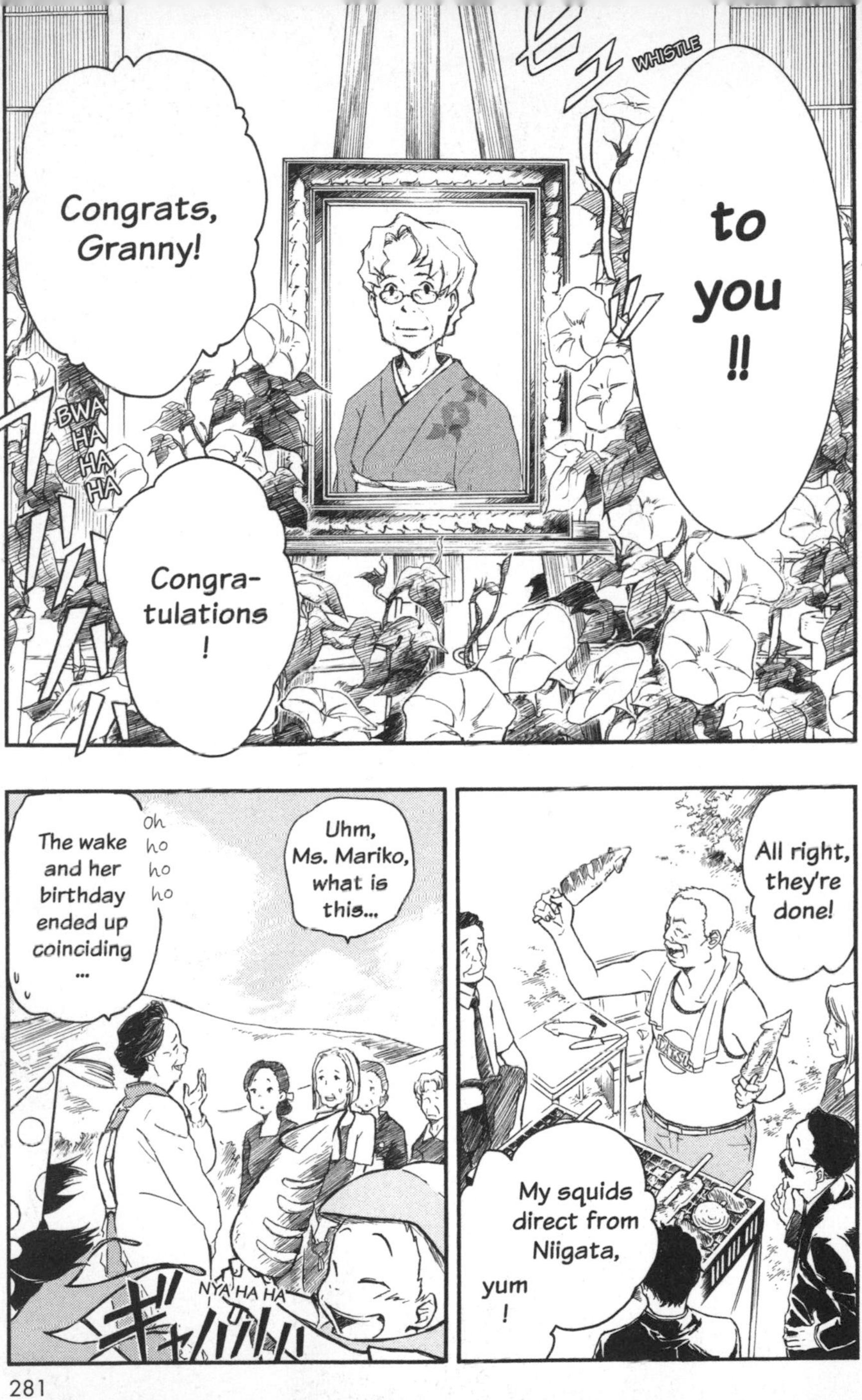
WHISTLE
to you !!
Congrats, Granny!
BWA HA HA HA
Congratulations !
All right, they're done!
My squids direct from Niigata, yum !
Uhm, Ms. Mariko, what is this...
oh ho ho ho
The wake and her birthday ended up coinciding ...
NYA HA HA

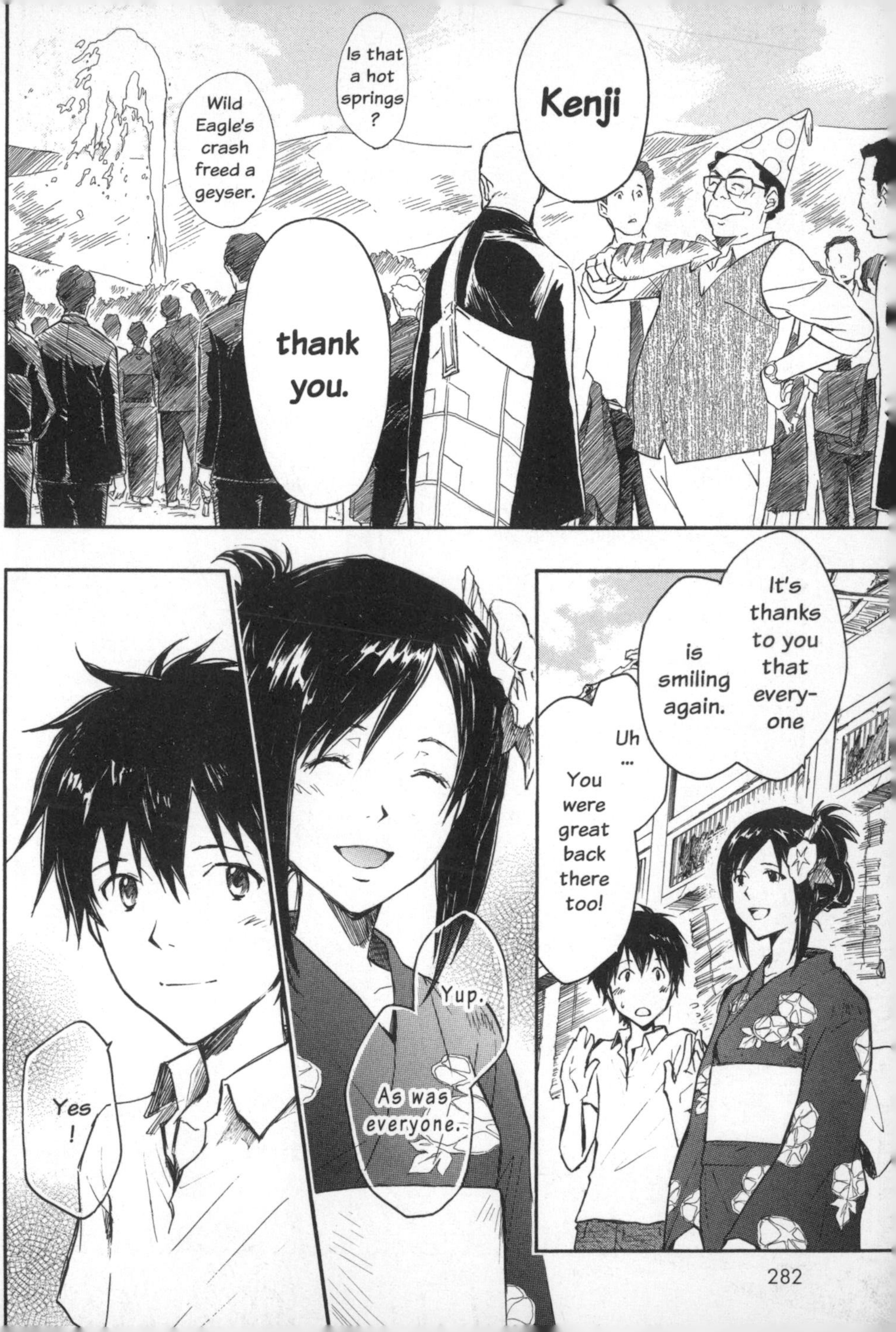
Kenji
Is that a hot springs?
Wild Eagle's crash freed a geyser.
thank you.
It's thanks to you that every-one
is smiling again.
Uh ...
You were great back there too!
Yup.
As was everyone.
Yes!

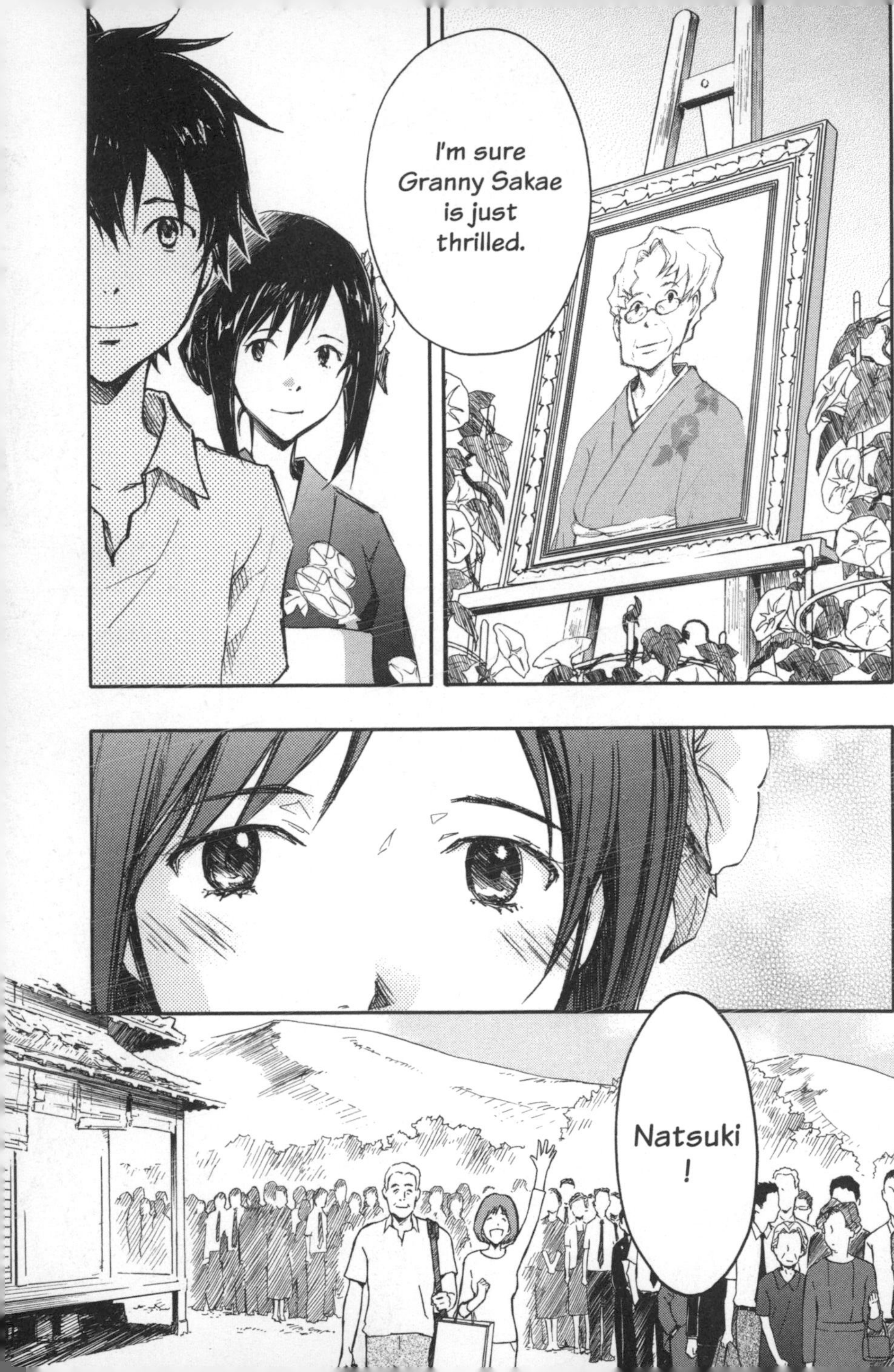
I'm sure Granny Sakae is just thrilled.
Natsuki!

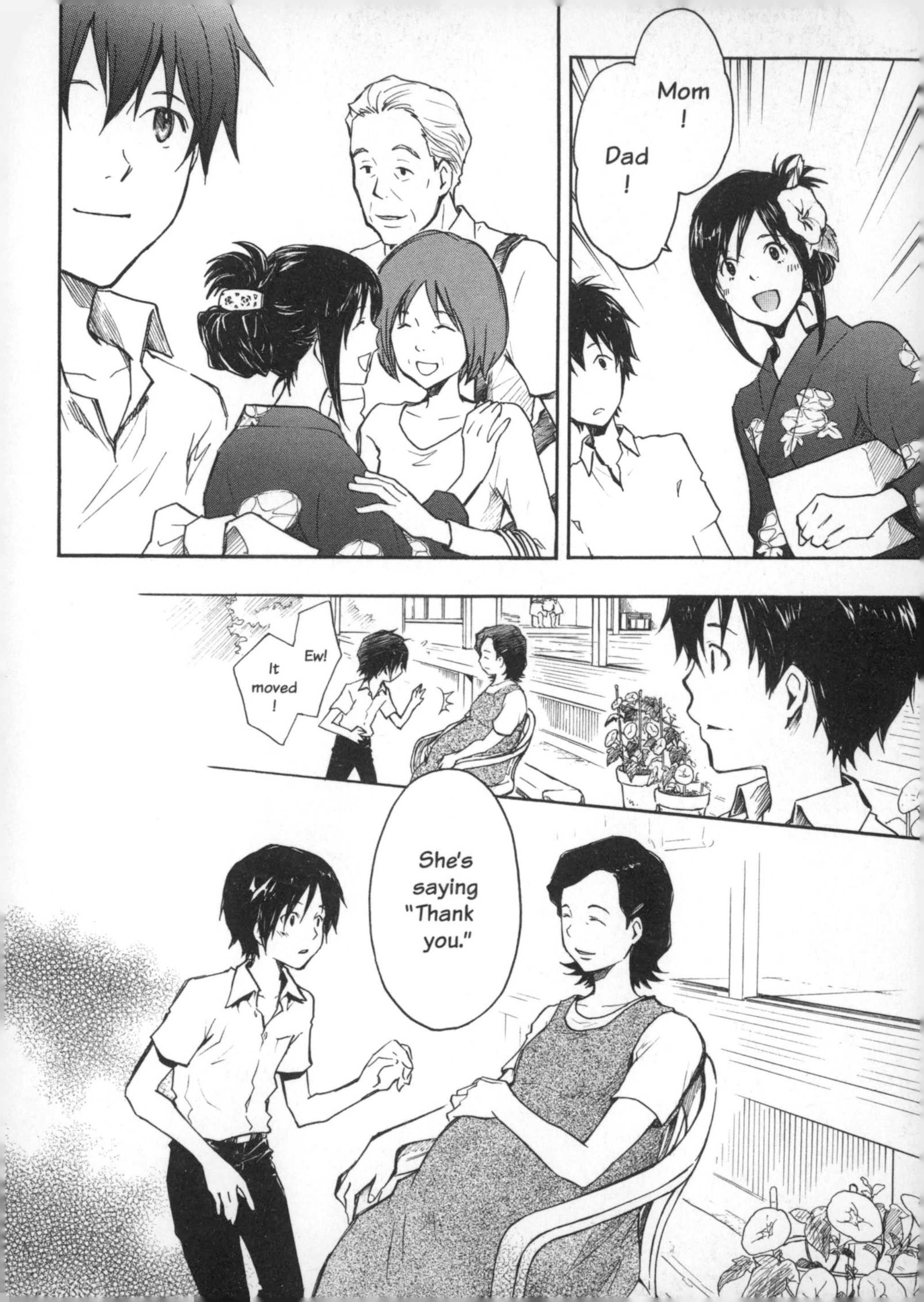
Mom! Dad!
Ew! It moved!
She's saying "Thank you."

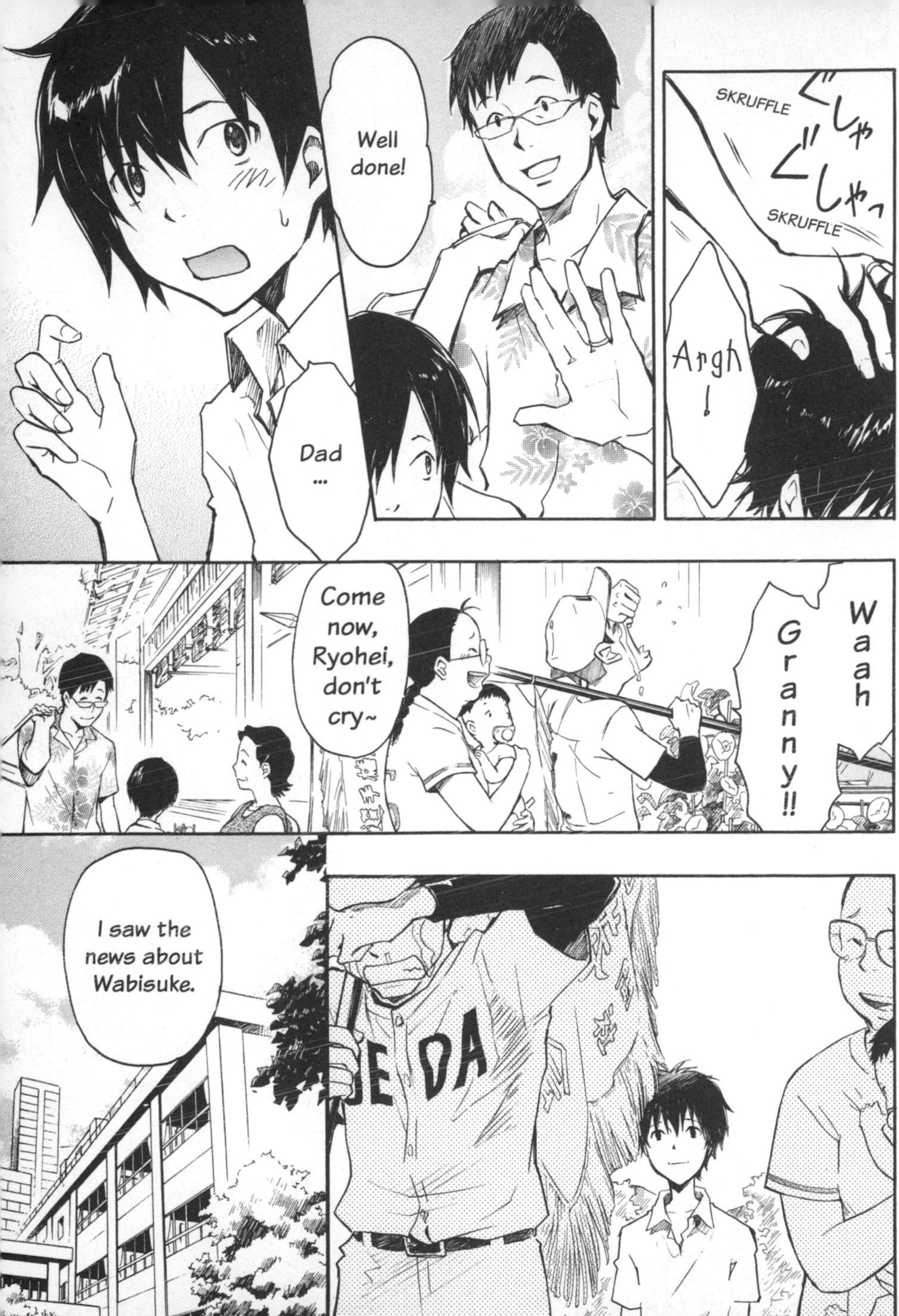
SKRUFFLE
ぐしゃ
ぐしゃっ
SKRUFFLE
Argh!
Well done!
Dad...
Waah Granny!!
Come now, Ryohei, don't cry~
I saw the news about Wabisuke.

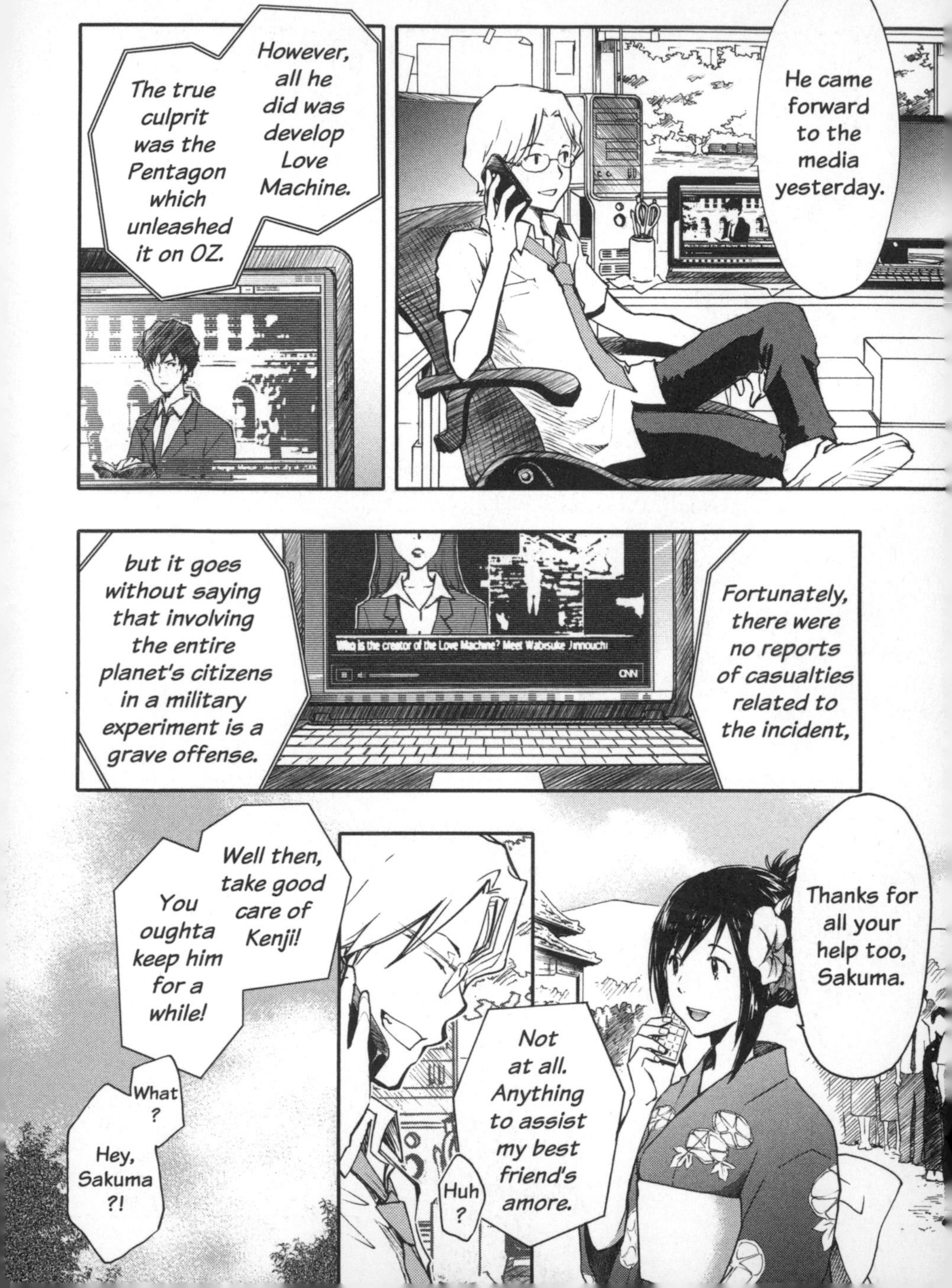
He came forward to the media yesterday.
However, all he did was develop Love Machine.
The true culprit was the Pentagon which unleashed it on OZ.
Fortunately, there were no reports of casualties related to the incident,
Who is the creator of the Love Machine? Meet Wabisuke Jinnouchi
CNN
but it goes without saying that involving the entire planet's citizens in a military experiment is a grave offense.
Thanks for all your help too, Sakuma.
Not at all. Anything to assist my best friend's amore.
Huh?
Well then, take good care of Kenji!
You oughta keep him for a while!
What?
Hey, Sakuma?!

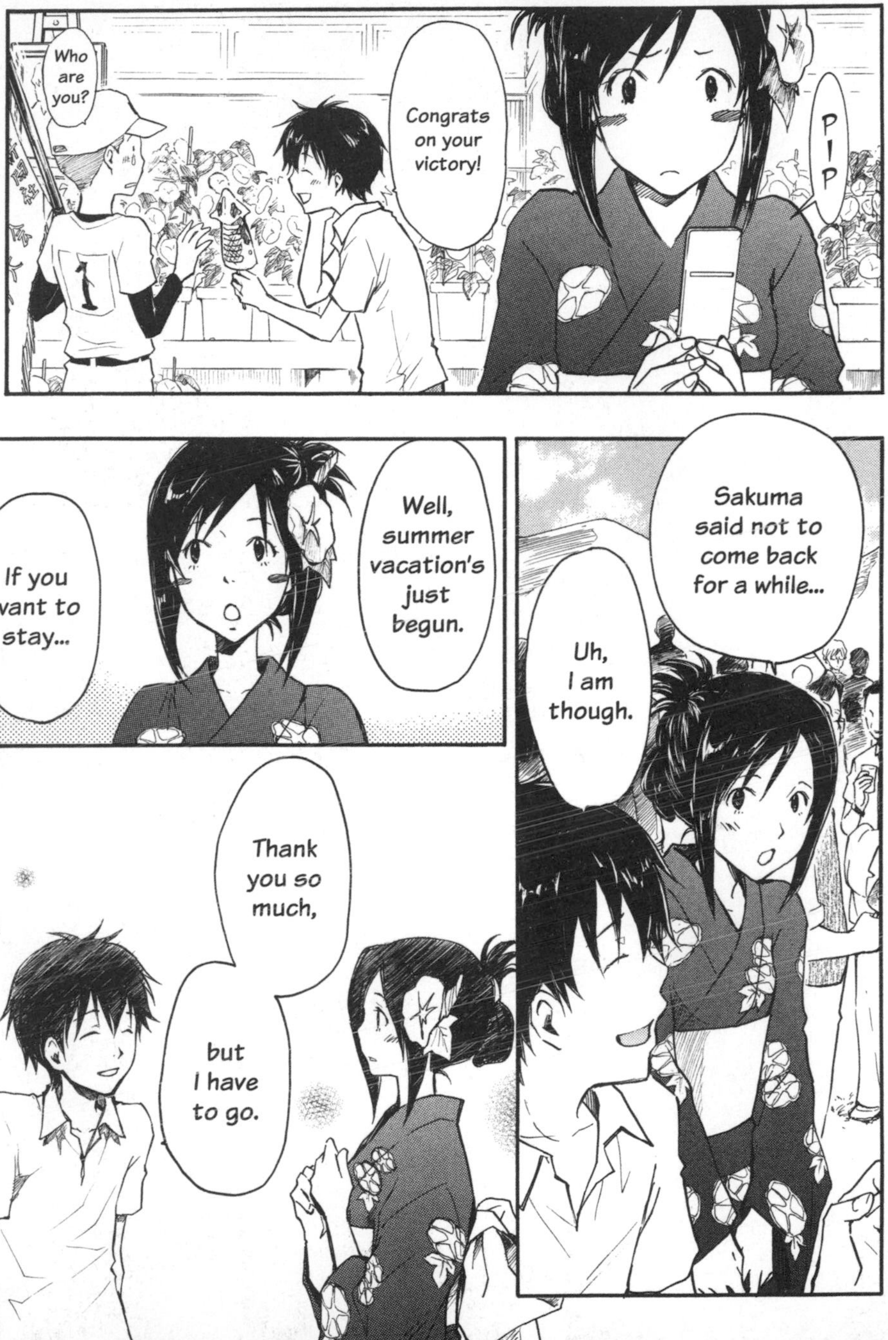
PIP
Congrats on your victory!
Who are you?
Sakuma said not to come back for a while...
Uh, I am though.
Well, summer vacation's just begun.
If you want to stay...
Thank you so much,
but I have to go.

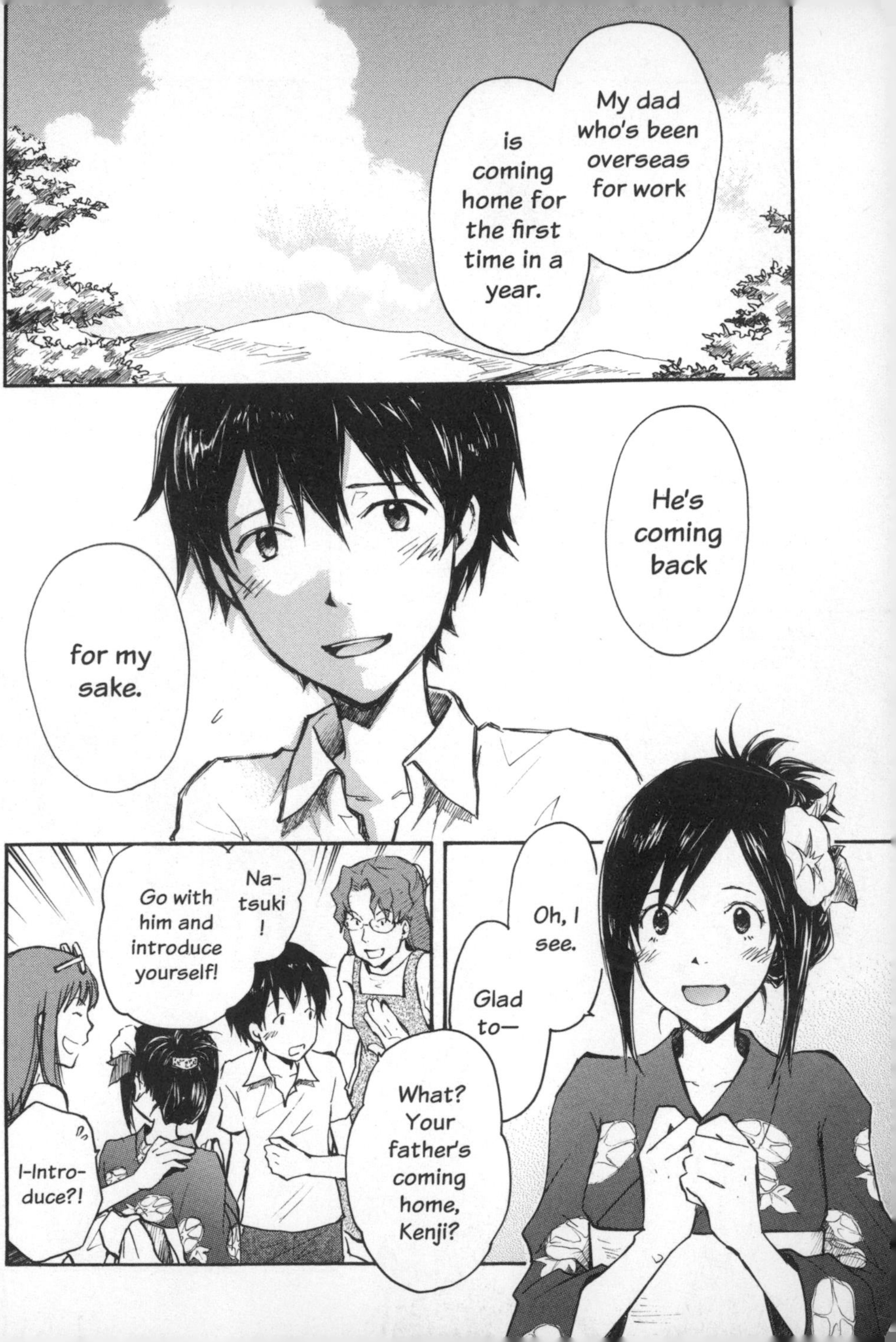
My dad who's been overseas for work
is coming home for the first time in a year.
He's coming back
for my sake.
Oh, I see.
Glad to—
Na-tsuki!
Go with him and introduce yourself!
What? Your father's coming home, Kenji?
I-Intro-duce?!

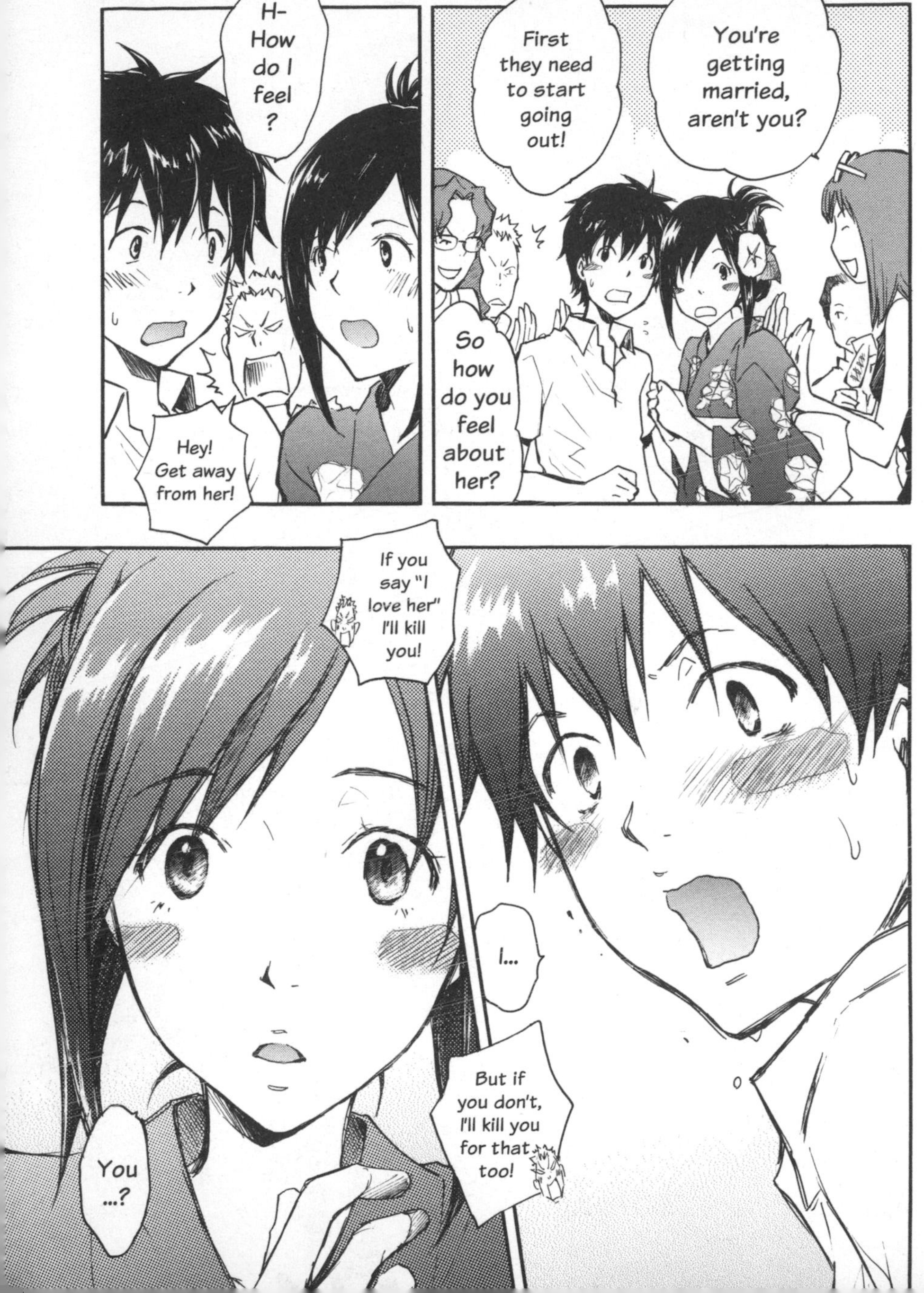
You're getting married, aren't you?
First they need to start going out!
So how do you feel about her?
H- How do I feel?
Hey! Get away from her!
I...
If you say "I love her" I'll kill you!
But if you don't, I'll kill you for that too!
You ...?

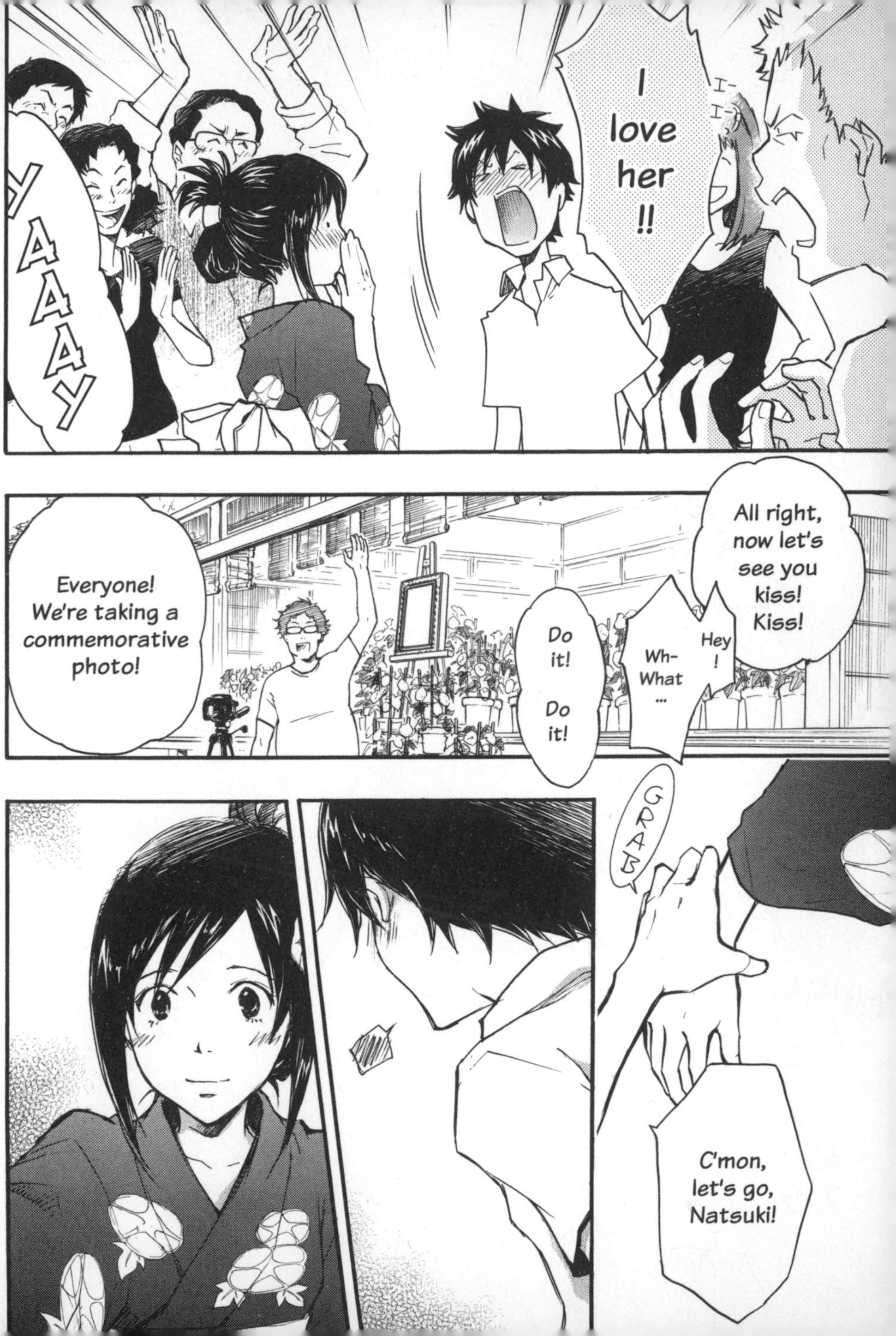
I- I-
I love her !!
YAAAY
All right, now let's see you kiss! Kiss!
Hey!
Wh- What...
Do it! Do it!
Everyone! We're taking a commemorative photo!
GRAB
C'mon, let's go, Natsuki!

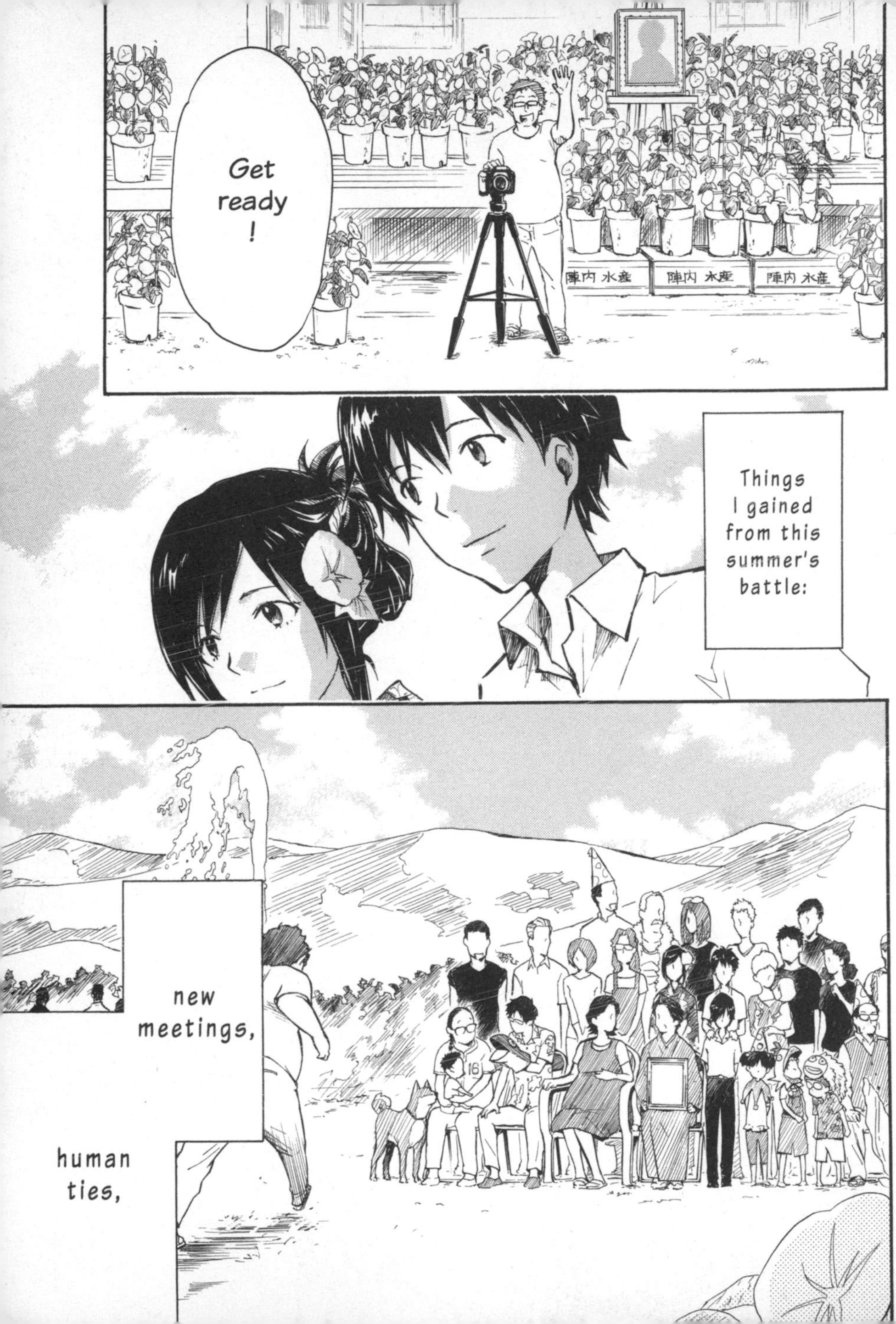
Get ready!
陣内 水産
陣内 水産
陣内 水産
Things I gained from this summer's battle:
new meetings,
human ties,

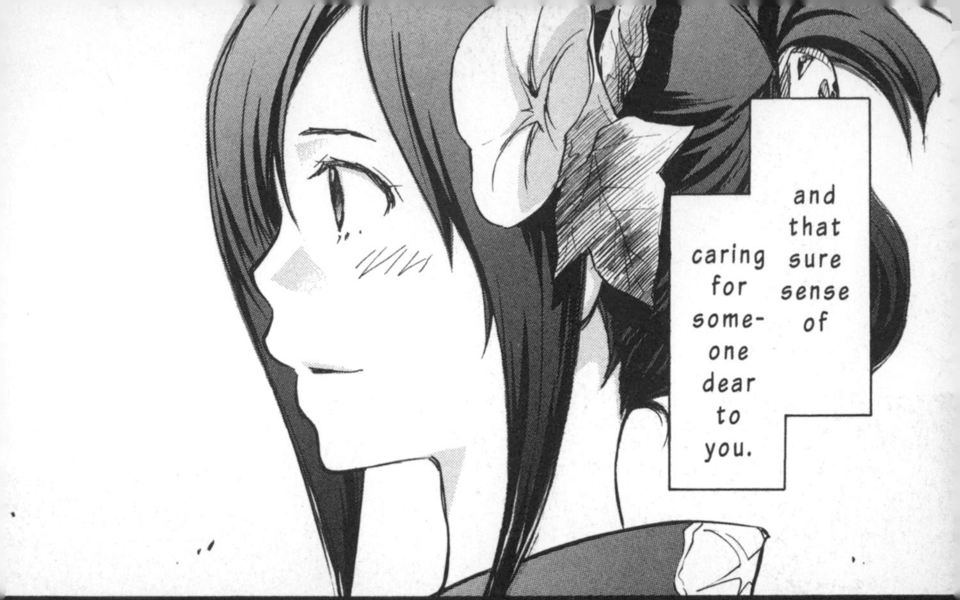
and that sure sense of caring for some-one dear to you.

Original Story: Mamoru Hosoda

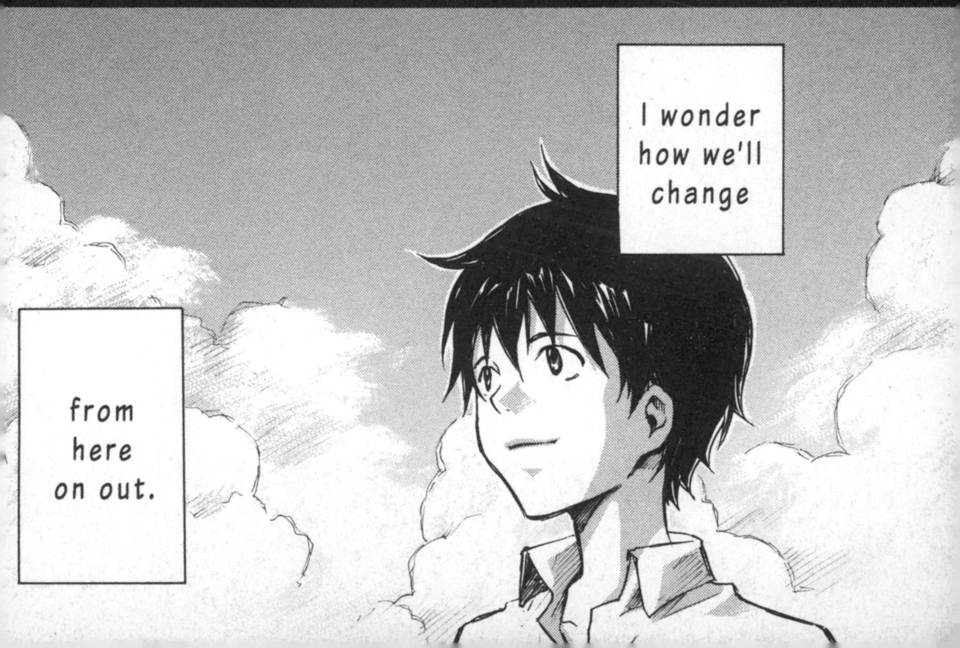
I wonder how we'll change
from here on out.

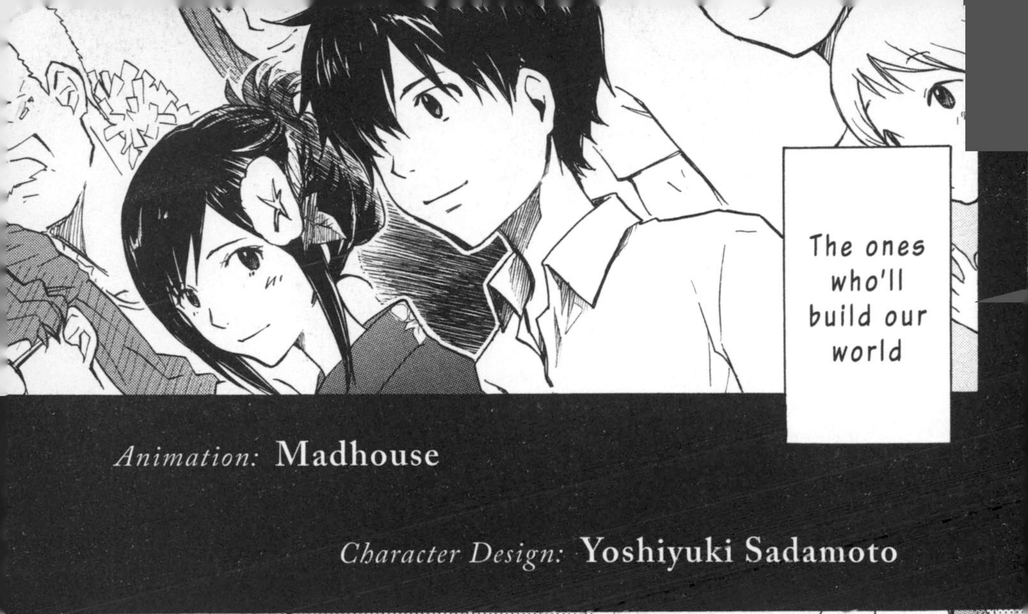
The ones who'll build our world

Animation: Madhouse

Character Design: Yoshiyuki Sadamoto

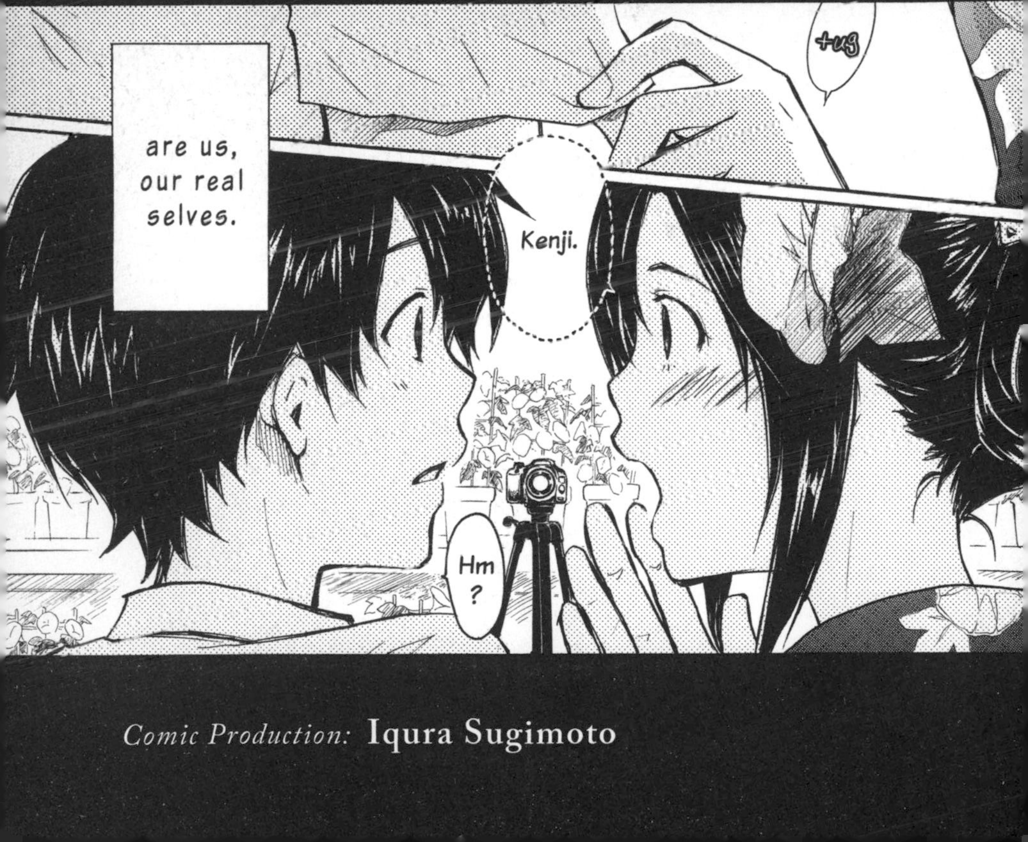
tug
are us, our real selves.
Kenji.
Hm?

Comic Production: Iqura Sugimoto

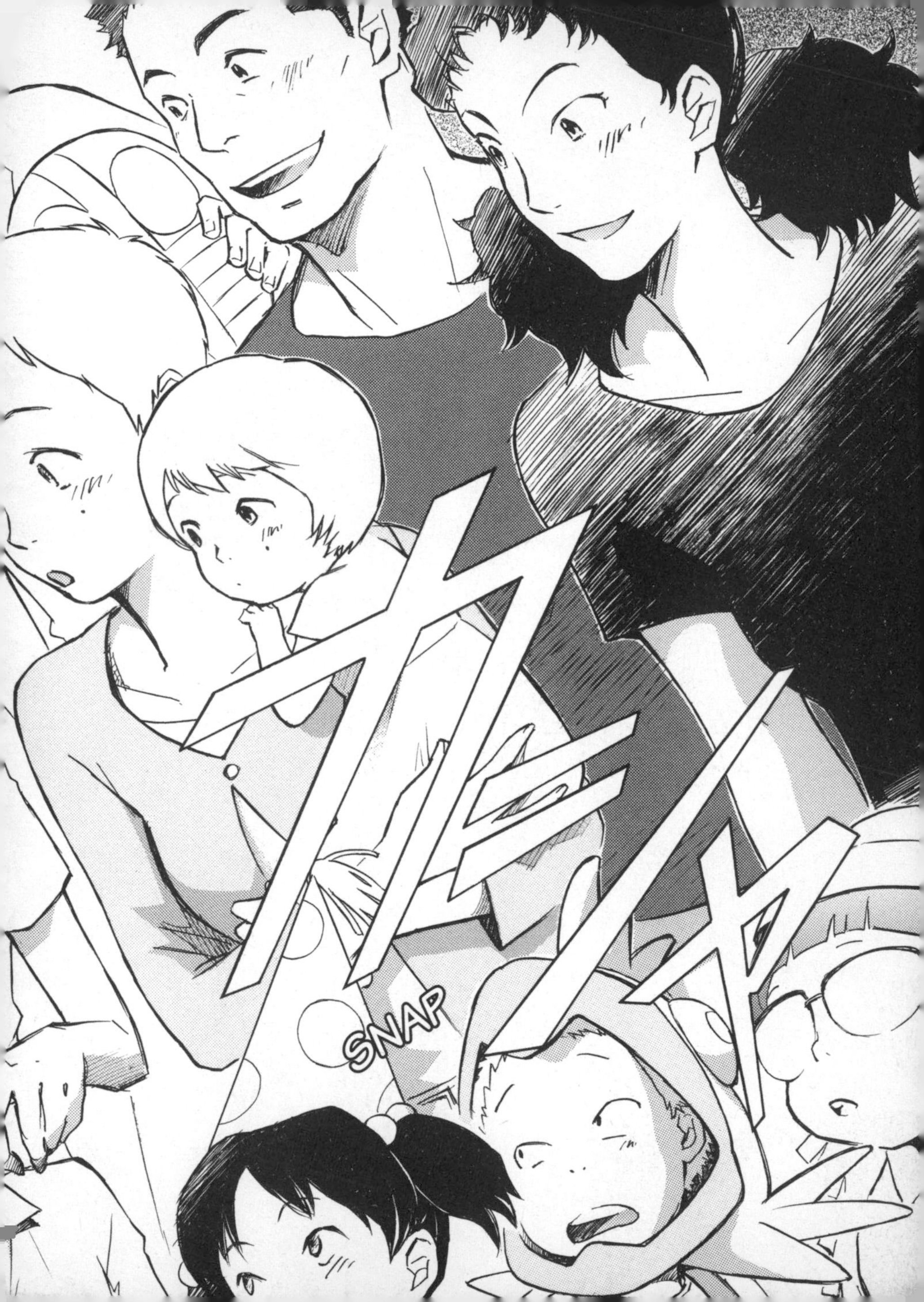
SNAP

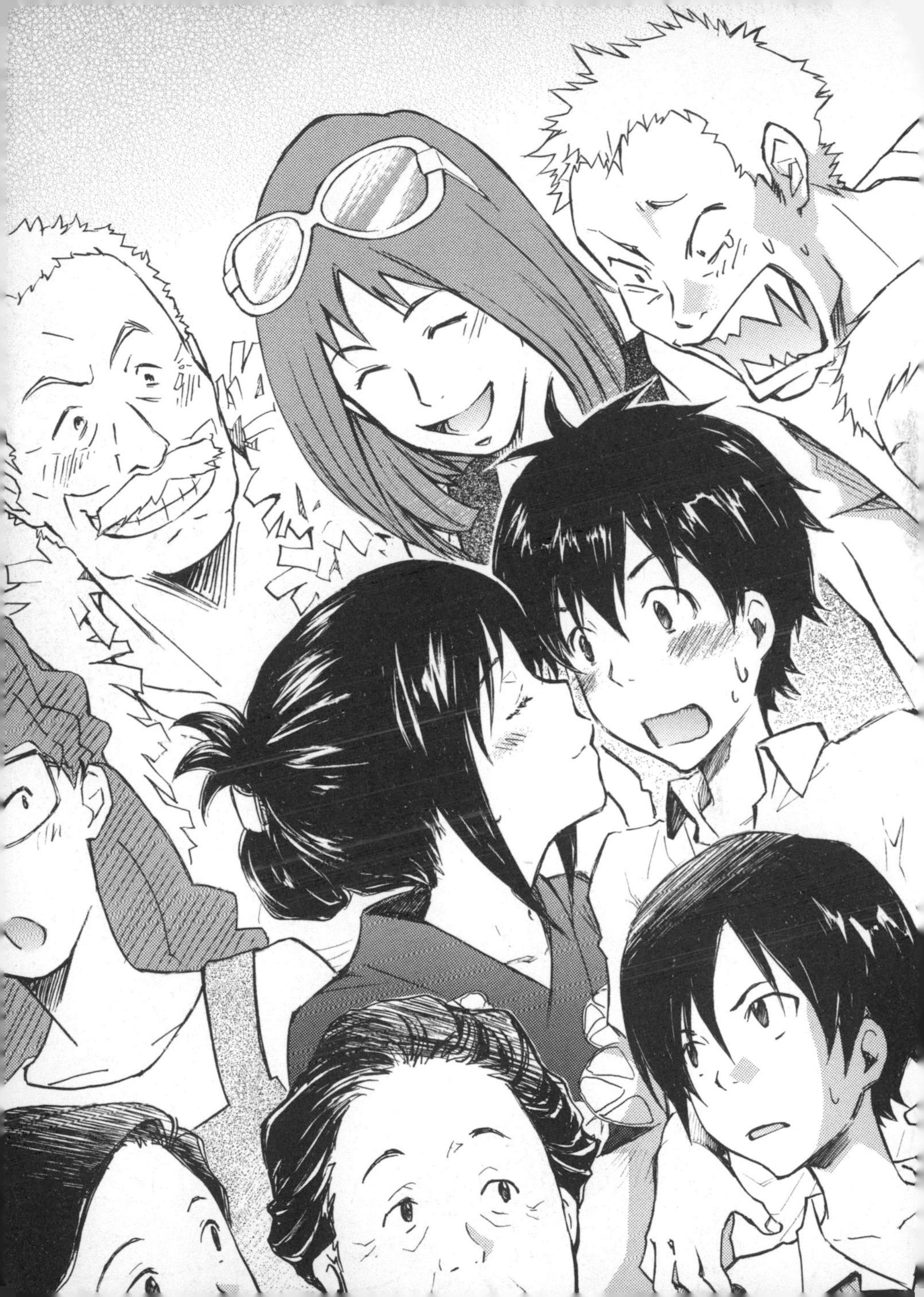

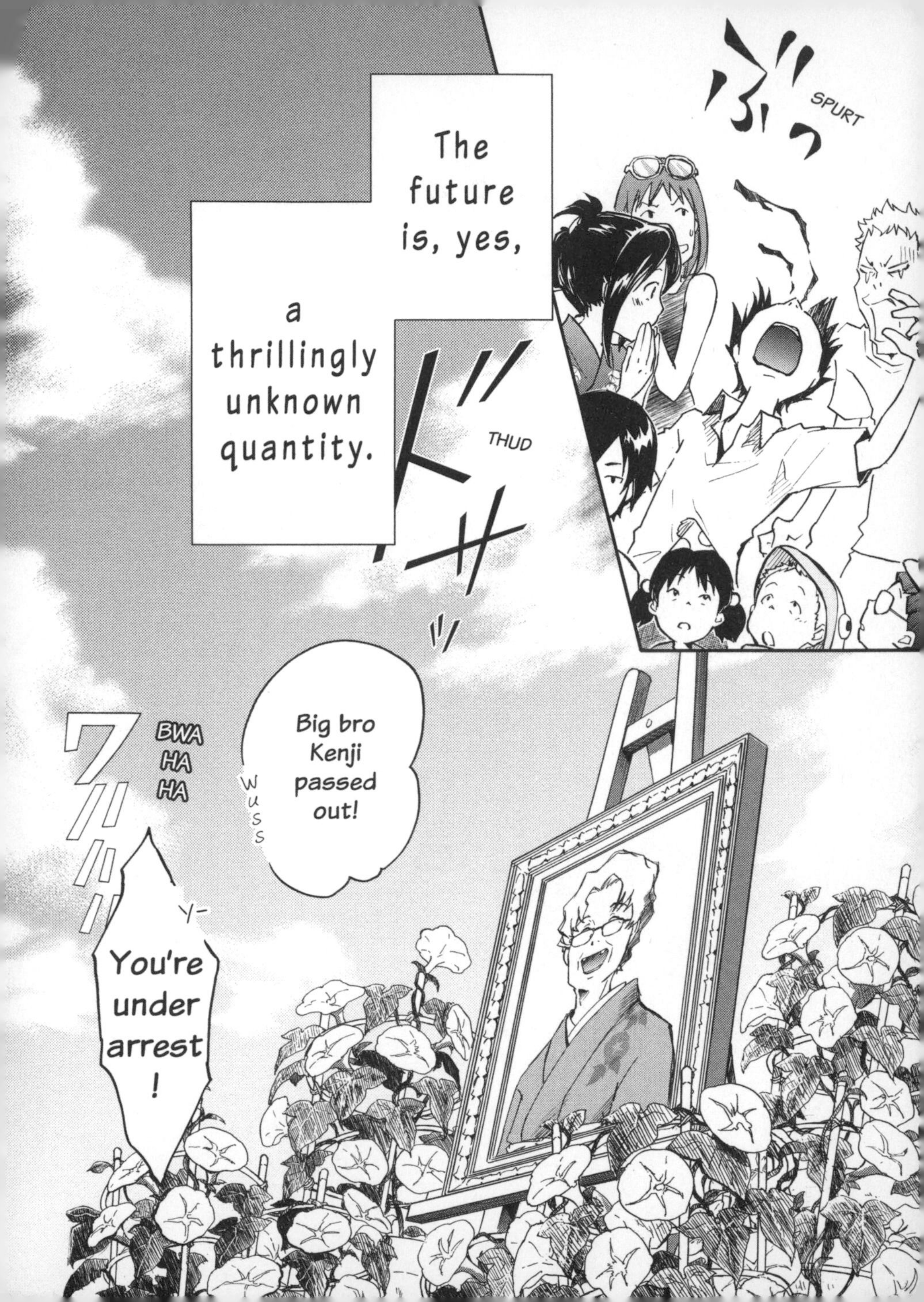
SPURT
The future is, yes,
a thrillingly unknown quantity.
THUD
Big bro Kenji passed out!
WUSS
BWA HA HA
You're under arrest!

SUMMER WARS

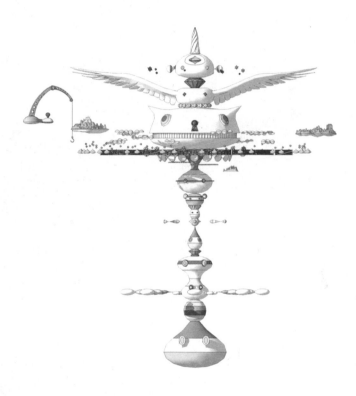

...HAPPY ENDINGS!

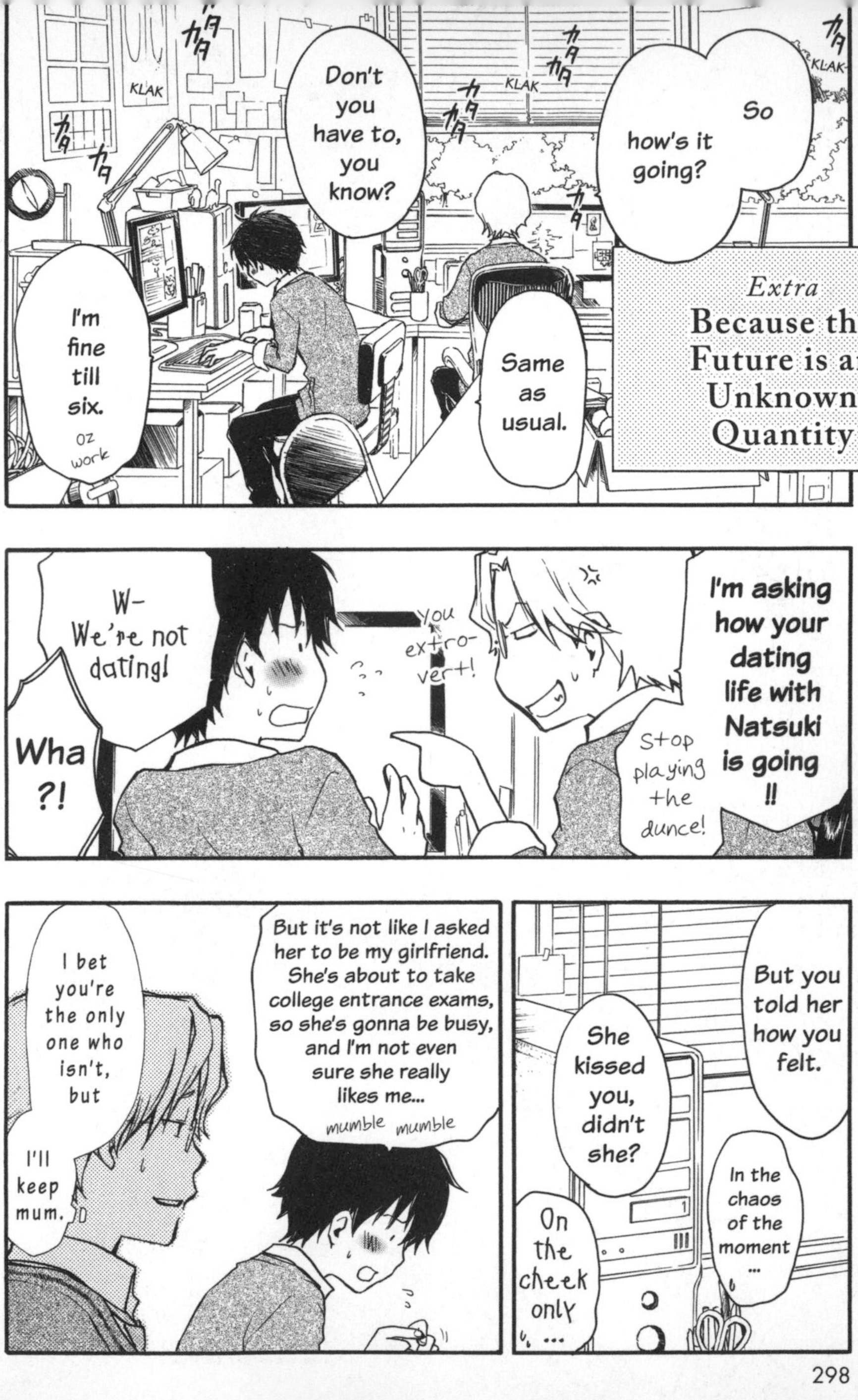
カタ
KLAK
So how's it going?
Extra
Because the Future is an Unknown Quantity
Don't you have to, you know?
Same as usual.
I'm fine till six.
oz work
I'm asking how your dating life with Natsuki is going!!
Stop playing the dunce!
you extro-vert!
W- We're not dating!
Wha?!
But you told her how you felt.
She kissed you, didn't she?
In the chaos of the moment ...
On the cheek only ...
But it's not like I asked her to be my girlfriend. She's about to take college entrance exams, so she's gonna be busy, and I'm not even sure she really likes me...
mumble mumble
I bet you're the only one who isn't, but
I'll keep mum.

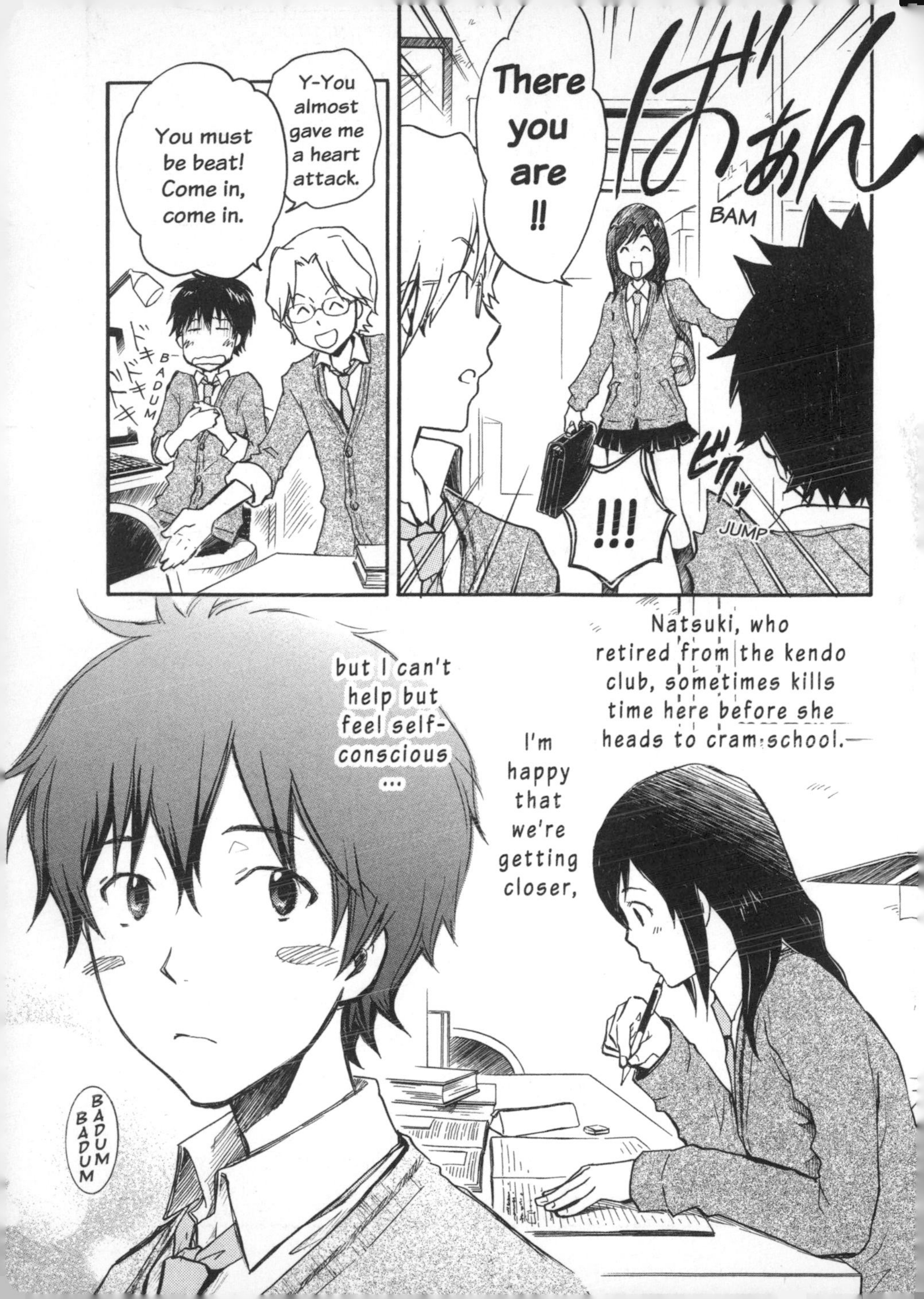
There you are !!
ばぁん
BAM
ビクッ
JUMP
!!!
Y-You almost gave me a heart attack.
You must be beat! Come in, come in.
BADUM
Natsuki, who retired from the kendo club, sometimes kills time here before she heads to cram school.
I'm happy that we're getting closer,
but I can't help but feel self-conscious ...
BADUM BADUM

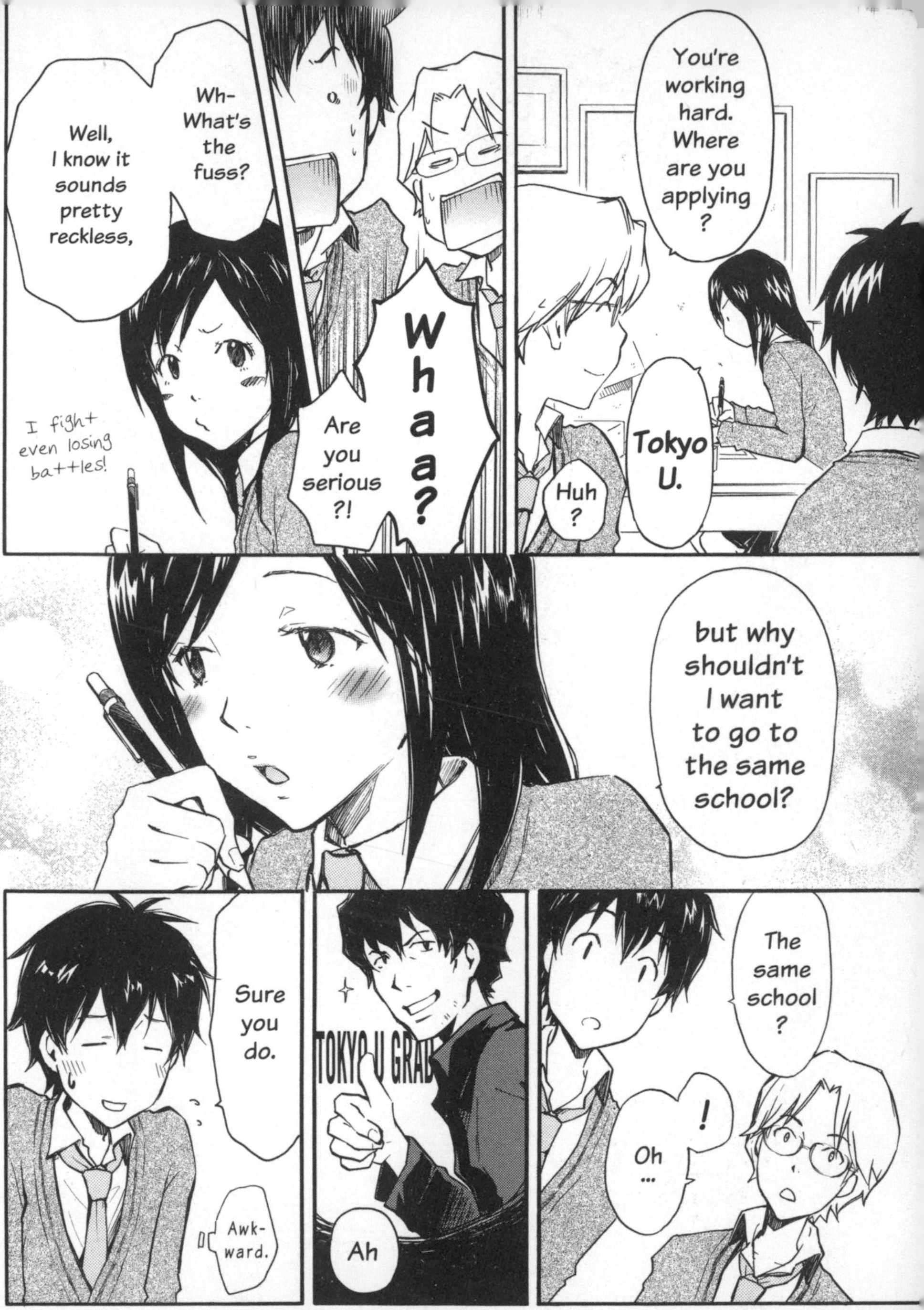
You're working hard. Where are you applying?
Tokyo U.
Huh?
Whaa?
Are you serious?!
Wh- What's the fuss?
Well, I know it sounds pretty reckless,
I fight even losing battles!
but why shouldn't I want to go to the same school?
The same school?
!
Oh...
TOKYO U GRAD
Ah
Sure you do.
Awk-ward.

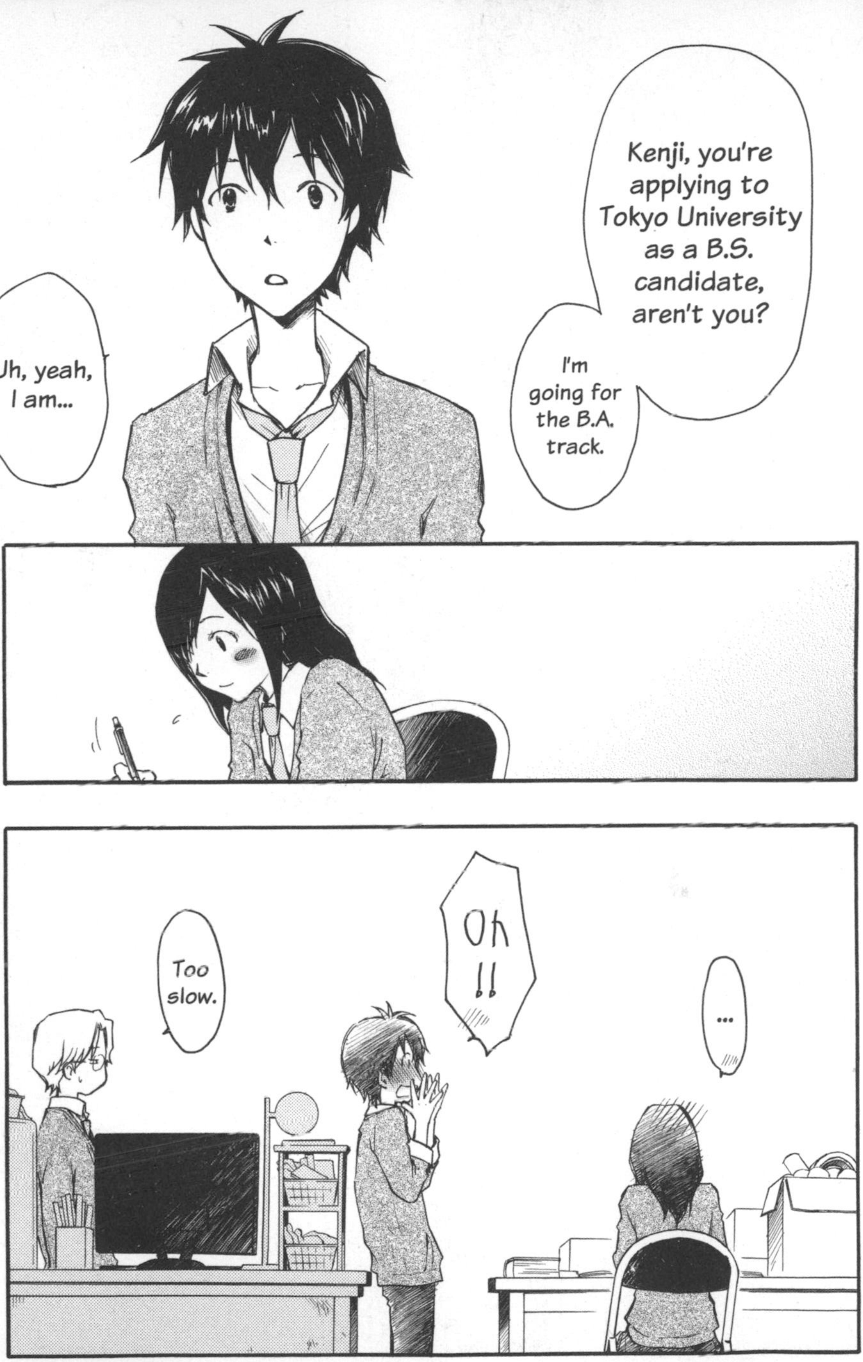
Kenji, you're applying to Tokyo University as a B.S. candidate, aren't you?
I'm going for the B.A. track.
Uh, yeah, I am...
...
Oh!!
Too slow.
END

SUMMER WARS
PART 2

Production: Grace Lu
Anthony Quintessenza

Edited by KADOKAWA SHOTEN
First published in Japan in 2009 by KADOKAWA CORPORATION, Tokyo.
English translation rights arranged with KADOKAWA CORPORATION, Tokyo through TUTTLE-MORI AGENCY, INC., Tokyo.
English language version produced by Vertical, Inc.

Translation provided by Vertical, Inc., 2013
Published by Vertical, Inc., New York

Originally published in Japanese as *Samaa Wouzu 2, 3* by KADOKAWA SHOTEN, 2010
Samaa Wouzu first serialized in *Young Ace*, 2009-2010

This is a work of fiction.

ISBN: 978-1-939130-16-7

Manufactured in Canada

First Edition

Second Printing

Vertical, Inc.
451 Park Avenue South
7th Floor
New York, NY 10016
www.vertical-inc.com